PERSPECTIVES ON WRITING
Series Editor, Susan H. McLeod

PERSPECTIVES ON WRITING
Series Editor, Susan H. McLeod

The Perspectives on Writing series addresses writing studies in a broad sense. Consistent with the wide ranging approaches characteristic of teaching and scholarship in writing across the curriculum, the series presents works that take divergent perspectives on working as a writer, teaching writing, administering writing programs, and studying writing in its various forms.

The WAC Clearinghouse and Parlor Press are collaborating so that these books will be widely available through free digital distribution and low-cost print editions. The publishers and the Series editor are teachers and researchers of writing, committed to the principle that knowledge should freely circulate. We see the opportunities that new technologies have for further democratizing knowledge. And we see that to share the power of writing is to share the means for all to articulate their needs, interest, and learning into the great experiment of literacy.

Recent Books in the Series

Charles Bazerman, *A Rhetoric of Literate Action: Literate Action Volume 1* (2013)
Charles Bazerman, *A Theory of Literate Action: Literate Action Volume 2* (2013)
Katherine V. Wills and Rich Rice (Eds.), *ePortfolio Performance Support Systems: Constructing, Presenting, and Assessing Portfolios* (2013)
Mike Duncan and Star Medzerian Vanguri (Eds.), *The Centrality of Style* (2013)
Chris Thaiss, Gerd Bräuer, Paula Carlino , Lisa Ganobcsik-Williams, and Aparna Sinha (Eds.), *Writing Programs Worldwide: Profiles of Academic Writing in Many Places* (2012)
Andy Kirkpatrick and Zhichang Xu, *Chinese Rhetoric and Writing: An Introduction for Language Teachers* (2012)
Doreen Starke-Meyerring, Anthony Paré, Natasha Artemeva, Miriam Horne, and Larissa Yousoubova (Eds.), *Writing in Knowledge Societies* (2011)
Martine Courant Rife, Shaun Slattery, and Dànielle Nicole DeVoss (Eds.), *Copy(write): Intellectual Property in the Writing Classroom* (2011)

WAC AND SECOND LANGUAGE WRITERS: RESEARCH TOWARDS LINGUISTICALLY AND CULTURALLY INCLUSIVE PROGRAMS AND PRACTICES

Edited by Terry Myers Zawacki and Michelle Cox

The WAC Clearinghouse
wac.colostate.edu
Fort Collins, Colorado

Parlor Press
www.parlorpress.com
Anderson, South Carolina

The WAC Clearinghouse, Fort Collins, Colorado 80523-1052
Parlor Press, 3015 Brackenberry Drive, Anderson, South Carolina 29621

© 2014 by Terry Myers Zawacki and Michelle Cox. This work is licensed under a Creative Commons Attribution-Noncommercial-No Derivative Works 3.0 United States License.
Printed in the United States of America on acid-free paper.

Library of Congress Cataloging-in-Publication Data

WAC and Second language writers : research towards linguistically and culturally inclusive programs and practices / Edited by Terry Myers Zawacki and Michelle Cox.
    pages cm. -- (Perspectives on writing)
  Includes bibliographical references.
   ISBN 978-1-60235-503-3 (pbk. : alk. paper) -- ISBN 978-1-60235-504-0 (hardcover : alk. paper) -- ISBN 978-1-60235-505-7 (adobe ebook) -- ISBN 978-1-60235-506-4 (epub)
   1. English language--Rhetoric--Study and teaching--Foreign speakers. 2. Report writing--Study and teaching (Higher) 3. Second language acquisition--Study and teaching (Higher) 4. Interdisciplinary approach in education. 5. Writing centers--Administration. I. Zawacki, Terry Myers, editor of compilation. II. Cox, Michelle, 1971- editor of compilation.
  PE1128.A2W123 2014
  418.0071--dc23
                                            2014015318

Copyeditor: Don Donahue. Designer: Mike Palmquist
Series Editor: Susan H. McLeod

The WAC Clearinghouse supports teachers of writing across the disciplines. Hosted by Colorado State University, it brings together scholarly journals and book series as well as resources for teachers who use writing in their courses. This book is available in digital format for free download at http://wac.colostate.edu.

Parlor Press, LLC is an independent publisher of scholarly and trade titles in print and multimedia formats. This book is available in paperback, cloth, and Adobe eBook formats from Parlor Press at http://www.parlorpress.com. For submission information or to find out about Parlor Press publications, write to Parlor Press, 3015 Brackenberry Drive, Anderson, South Carolina 29621, or e-mail editor@parlorpress.com.

CONTENTS

A Note to Readers *3*
    Michelle Cox and Terry Myers Zawacki

Foreword: Multilinguality Across the Curriculum *5*
    Jonathan Hall

Introduction *15*
    Michelle Cox and Terry Myers Zawacki

SECTION I. LEARNING FROM/WITH L2 STUDENTS: STUDENT STRENGTHS, COPING STRATEGIES, AND EXPERIENCES AS THEY WRITE ACROSS THE CURRICULUM. . . . 41

Chapter 1. Adaptive Transfer, Writing Across the Curriculum, and Second Language Writing: Implications for Research and Teaching . . *43*
    Michael-John DePalma and Jeffrey M. Ringer

Chapter 2. Developing Resources for Success: A Case Study of a Multilingual Graduate Writer *69*
    Talinn Phillips

Chapter 3. "Hey, Did You Get That?": L2 Student Reading Across the Curriculum *93*
    Carole Center and Michelle Niestepski

Chapter 4. Bridging the Gap between ESL Composition Programs and Disciplinary Writing: The Teaching and Learning of Summarization Skill *113*
    Qian Du

Chapter 5. On Class, Race, and Dynamics of Privilege: Supporting Generation 1.5 Writers Across the Curriculum *129*
    Kathryn Nielsen

Chapter 6. Writing Intensively: An Examination of the Performance of L2 Writers Across the Curriculum at an Urban Community College . *151*
    Linda Hirsch

Section II. Faculty Concerns and Expectations for L2 Writers *181*

Chapter 7. Negotiating "Errors" in L2 Writing: Faculty Dispositions and Language Difference *183*
   Terry Myers Zawacki and Anna Sophia Habib

Chapter 8. "I don't know if that was the right thing to do": Cross-Disciplinary/Cross-Institutional Faculty Respond to L2 Writing *211*
   Lindsey Ives, Elizabeth Leahy, Anni Leming, Tom Pierce, and Michael Schwartz

Chapter 9. Let's See Where Your Chinese Students Come From: A Qualitative Descriptive Study of Writing in the Disciplines in China ... *233*
   Wu Dan

Chapter 10. English is Not a Spectator Sport: Privileged Second Language Learners and the For-Profit ESOL Classroom *257*
   Marino Fernandes

Chapter 11. Making Stance Explicit for Second Language Writers in the Disciplines: What Faculty Need to Know about the Language of Stance-taking *269*
   Zak Lancaster

Chapter 12. In Response to Today's "Felt Need": WAC, Faculty Development, and Second Language Writers *299*
   Michelle Cox

Section III. WAC Practices and Pedagogies Transformed *327*

Chapter 13. Developing Writing-Intensive Courses for a Globalized Curriculum through WAC-TESOL Collaborations *329*
   Megan Siczek and Shawna Shapiro

Chapter 14. Graduate Writing Workshops: Crossing Languages and Disciplines *347*
   Elaine Fredericksen and Kate Mangelsdorf

Chapter 15. Teaching Writing in a Globally Networked Learning Environment (GNLE): Diverse Students at a Distance *369*
   Jennifer Lynn Craig

Chapter 16. Campus Internationalization: A Center-based Model for ESL-ready Programs *387*
   Karyn E. Mallett and Ghania Zgheib

Chapter 17. Reconstructing Teacher Roles through a Transnational Lens: Learning with/in the American University of Beirut *415*
   Amy Zenger, Joan Mullin, and Carol Peterson Haviland

Chapter 18. Writing Histories: Lingua Franca English in a Swedish Graduate Program *439*
   Thomas Lavelle and Alan Shima

Afterword: Writing Globally, Right Here, Right Now *465*
   Chris Thaiss

Notes on Editors and Contributors *477*

> # WAC AND SECOND LANGUAGE WRITERS: RESEARCH TOWARDS LINGUISTICALLY AND CULTURALLY INCLUSIVE PROGRAMS AND PRACTICES

A NOTE TO READERS

Michelle Cox
Dartmouth College

Terry Myers Zawacki
George Mason University

We hope you find this collection as compelling and thought-provoking as we have during our process of reading, thinking with, and editing these chapters. Before you begin reading, we'd like to note two points.

First, you may notice that we've listed Terry's name as first editor of the collection and Michelle's name as first author of the introduction, and we want to explain this choice. Throughout this project and our previous project, editing a special issue of *Across the Disciplines*, "WAC and Second Language Writing: Cross-field Research, Theory, and Program Development" (2011, December), our collaboration has been rich, productive, and even joyful. We have discovered that we make wonderful partners, matched in our work ethics and complementary in our strengths. In order to equally share credit for our collaborative work on both publications, in the *ATD* issue, we listed Michelle as first editor of the collection and Terry as first author of the introduction. With this project, we did the reverse.

Second, terminology related to the students highlighted in this collection is a complicated matter. In our introduction, we've chosen to use the designator "L2." While we understand that this term is problematic, in that English may be the third, fourth, etc., language of the students we're referring to, we have chosen to use this designation to connect the work in this collection to the wider scholarship of second language writing studies (for a further rationale for using this designation, see Matsuda, 2012). As editors, however, we did not ask our authors to use the term L2. Some used multilingual learner (MLL), some used non-native English speaker (NNES), and some used English language learner (ELL). Each term has its advantages and drawbacks, and each suggests disciplinary affiliations and/or implies a certain political stance. We invite our readers to engage in the conversation about terminology that is represented in this collection as well as in the wider scholarship of second language writing and composition-rhetoric/WAC.

REFERENCE

Matsuda, P. K. (2012). Teaching composition in the multilingual world: Second language writing in composition studies. In K. Ritter & P. K. Matsuda (Eds.), *Exploring Composition Studies: Sites, Issues, and Perspectives* (pp. 36-51). Logan, UT: Utah State University Press.

FOREWORD: MULTILINGUALITY ACROSS THE CURRICULUM

Jonathan Hall
York College, City University of New York

Writing Across the Curriculum (WAC) research was rather a latecomer to the project of investigating the impact of linguistic diversity among our students on our pedagogy, outcomes, and procedures. At the risk of grossly oversimplifying, one might almost say that research on second language (L2) writing issues followed something of a developmental curve, with the earliest work emerging from K-12 studies on bilingual education and Generation 1.5, then spreading to basic writing and the first-year composition level. The relation between WAC and multilingual issues was forcefully raised in the 1990s to early 2000s by scholars such as Paul Kei Matsuda, Ann Johns, and Ilona Leki. In recent years, WAC has been making a concerted effort to explore its own patch of L2 ground. Most recently, a special issue of *Across the Disciplines* (hereafter *ATD*) addressed the theme of "WAC and Second Language Writing: Cross-field Research, Theory, and Program Development." The call for that issue advocated a heightened attention to the presence of L2 writers in WAC and Writing in the Disciplines (WID) courses and called for "research that would contribute to the growing understanding of the complexities of writing across languages, cultures, and disciplines." Contributors to the issue applied a variety of theoretical perspectives, research methodologies, and institutional contexts to questions raised on multilingual writers and WAC/WID. Subsequently, a panel at the 2012 IWAC conference brought together several contributors for a live exchange on topics raised in the issue and directions for future research and WAC/WID practice.

The panel, like the *ATD* issue itself, advanced the argument that the concerns of multilingual writers are not in any way peripheral to or unusual in the way that our profession will evolve, but rather are rapidly assuming a central position in discussions of the future of WAC. The present volume, with the same editors as the special issue, continues that argument, applying it to the specific audiences and administrative functions of a twenty-first century WAC program. In this preface, I draw examples from that *ATD* issue and the present collection to identify and discuss three axes in WAC/WID research and practice on L1/L2 issues, polarities that may be in tension, but are not incommensurable:

local and global, student experience and faculty expectations, and traditional WAC pedagogy for all students and differentiated instruction for multilingual learners. These are, in many ways, the same conflicts and uncertainties that have been inherent in the WAC/WID project from the very beginning, yet all of them take on new meaning and new dimensions in the age of the multilingual majority.

LOCAL AND GLOBAL

Historically WAC has been both an international movement and an intensely local phenomenon. No two WAC programs are exactly the same, though, and there has always been a tension between, on the one hand, an almost evangelical fervor, a feeling of WAC as a universal and transformational pedagogy, and, on the other, an insistence on the local—this campus, this faculty, this student population, this course, this writer, this paper. But in today's interconnected world, the relation between the global and the local takes on added complexity as well as urgency.

The very names of the institutions from which Amy Zenger, Joan Mullin, and Carol Peterson Haviland (this volume) and Lynn Ronesi (*ATD* special issue) file their reports pose the global/local issue in all its contradictory complexity: the American University of Beirut (AUB) and the American University of Sharjah (AUS). The latter, with a faculty largely imported from abroad (not all from the US) and a student body representing 82 different nationalities, is a good example of an English as an International Language (EIL) context: an institution where English is the medium of academic instruction but not the dominant local language. As Ronesi details her efforts to adapt a US-style writing fellows model to the needs of local students and faculty, she delineates the need to re-think even well-known and successful models in new contexts. Even more fundamentally, as Zenger, Mullin, and Haviland suggest in their description of AUB, such projects raise the question of what exactly we might we mean by "English" in this context. How, for example, are the various "Englishes" present on a particular campus related to other languages that students might use both outside and inside the classroom? To what degree does the emphasis on "English" —especially within an "American" university with US accreditation but outside of the US —carry with it an inherent US/Western cultural imperialism in its very structure, and to what extent are students able to strip out these cultural associations, regarding English as a pragmatic, straightforward language to be used in business and other transnational transactions? Can they, as some of them desire, simply speak English without having English unconsciously speak them as well?

Martha Patton's contribution to the *ATD* special issue focuses on what the editors call "globalism at home": international students in a US context. These students come to the US with some literacy in their L1, but often not much familiarity with US academic procedures and little experience with writing in English. Patton's article is particularly timely given the current trend, both at cash-strapped public institutions still reeling from large cuts in state funding and at financially struggling private colleges, of importing full-paying international students to boost enrollments. But these students cannot ethically be educated on the cheap: they often require support services of various kinds, as Patton details while arguing for the value of conducting a systematic needs analysis at one's own institution.

On English as an International Language campuses, the need to accommodate WAC practices to local culture is easily evident, while in domestic US cases, the imperative for adjusting to local conditions is likely to be more subtle, but nonetheless urgent. Most campuses are now aware that examinations of linguistic diversity need to go beyond international students to consider the complex language backgrounds of US-resident multilingual students. The particular conglomeration of students (immigrants, "Generation 1.5," "heritage learners," etc.) in particular classrooms, with their various multilingualities and multicompetencies, requires our attention. In the US context, what are the cultural consequences of the decline of the subtractive model of language acquisition, i.e. the expectation that a student's second language will eventually replace the first (Hall, 2009, pp. 36-37)? How will students who maintain multicompetence in a variety of languages which they use for particular purposes, which they mix and match casually and skillfully in their everyday lives, bring a different sensibility to their academic studies? How will they read differently and write differently, between multiple languages and across diverse cultures, moving among and synthesizing genres and ideas in ways that we cannot predict in advance, but will have to respond to day after day in the present moment of the classroom?

The relation between the "global" and the "local" becomes yet more complex when interactions between instructor and student—or between student and academic support staff—take place neither on a US campus nor on a campus in another country but rather on a little bit of both and quite a lot in the vast nowhere/everywhere of cyberspace. In the particular Globally Networked Learning Environment (GNLE) described by Jennifer Craig in this volume, students work toward a master's degree in engineering at MIT in a program which includes 1) a one semester residency on the US campus, 2) continued coursework over synchronous video connecting MIT faculty with students residing in Singapore, 3) a research internship in Singapore, and 4) academic support provided online by staff in the US during the thesis-writing process. Who is "at home" and who is in the "international" position in such a scenario?

The comprehensive description by Dana Ferris and Chris Thaiss in the *ATD* special issue of the various forms that L2 work takes on the University of California at Davis campus emphasizes the complexity of the changes required, showing how serious attention to these issues goes well beyond the occasional faculty development workshop to impact nearly everything that we do on campus, from placement to first-year composition, to writing intensive courses, to curriculum within particular majors, to assessment, to writing centers and other academic support services. If we are truly to situate ourselves both critically and consciously in a global context and at the same time attend to the intensely local characteristics of a unique campus population, and of the various needs of the individuals within that population, a consciousness of linguistic diversity has to be a factor in all of WAC's administrative and pedagogical decisions; it must be explicitly included, because otherwise we may easily fall back on our unspoken assumptions of monolingualism.

STUDENT EXPERIENCE AND FACULTY EXPECTATIONS

Students and faculty, though they intersect in the same physical space on campus, often seem to be speaking different languages. Once this was a metaphor, but nowadays it is often literal. Faculty may find themselves not fully understanding, especially on an experiential basis, either the challenges faced or the resources brought to the table by their multilingual students, while students, both L2 and L1, often regard faculty expectations as a guessing game, a process of figuring out what the idiosyncratic instructor wants, rather than as an example of discipline-specific rhetorical expectations.

Faculty expectations for student writing are often complex and conflicted. The studies by Ives, Leahy, Leming, Pierce, & Schwartz, and Zawacki and Habib in this volume discuss this faculty ambivalence, finding that faculty "want to be fair and ethical in working with linguistically diverse students, but don't know how to do so while still sticking to the commonly held standards for writing in their disciplines and institutions" (Ives et al.) Peggy Lindsey and Deborah Crusan (*ATD*) show how assessments of student writing may be affected by knowledge that faculty have about students' nationality and language background, but that this effect may be in either direction, dependent, in part, on the method of assessment. Thus issues of L2 literacy become entangled with broader debates about how best to assess student writing, not only at the college level but also K-12. Would it be fairer, as Lindsey and Crusan ask, to assess writing based on a reading of a student paper in which the instructor is unaware of the identity of the student, and therefore unaware of the students' language background, nationality, and other factors that might impact their writing? Many writing instructors want to know more rather than less about their student writers, integrating literacy narratives and language background information into their pedagogy and their assessment of student writing. Or should we, as some suggest, adopt a distinction between "content" and "writing," exactly the sort of dubious dichotomy that much of composition research has laboriously debunked? The faculty in the Ives et al. study sometimes characterized their assessment procedures as a no-win situation: feeling guilty if they applied the same standards to monolingual and multilingual students—and also feeling guilty if they did not do so. There are no easy answers to these assessment questions, which are made more urgent by the frequent demands, often coming from outside the classroom, for a universal standard of writing proficiency, which all too often becomes defined reductively. How can we insist on complexity, critical thinking, and subtle attention to the nuances of language while also opening ourselves up to new insights that may arise from translingual processes in student writing? How can we find ways for students to access what they know—and what they are able to do in terms of writing skills—in their other languages, and apply these knowledges and abilities to the new rhetorical situations they encounter in their writing tasks in US academic contexts?

While we have become more aware of the multilinguality of our students, we have tended to overlook the equally complex—and potentially relevant—multilinguality of some of our faculty. Anne Ellen Geller's survey (*ATD*) focused on respondents who were teaching writing courses across the disciplines, and who also identified themselves as multilingual. If multilingual students are often invisible, multilingual faculty may be even more so, as they have adapted, in order to survive in US academia, to a norm of English-only in their professional publications and communications, and, often, as well, in their interactions with students, even those with whom they may share a non-English language. Yet, as Geller suggests, such faculty potentially constitute an under-utilized resource as we seek to re-invent WAC/WID in the era of global Englishes and translingual practices. But these faculty sometimes need encouragement to step forward and bring their expertise to the WAC/WID classroom, to participate in a program which they might otherwise perceive as dominated by unarticulated monolingualist assumptions. In addition, multilingual faculty are potentially a vital resource as we research the relationship between the process of entering a discourse community—often described as analogous to learning a new language (what Matsuda and Jablonski call "the L2 metaphor") —and the process of learning to write in a completely new language code. These faculty have done both, and often have complex insights to share about both processes and the relation between them, but we will only learn about these insights if we actively seek these faculty out and ask them.

TRADITIONAL WAC PEDAGOGY FOR ALL STUDENTS AND DIFFERENTIATED INSTRUCTION FOR MULTILINGUAL LEARNERS

Thus far, WAC/WID approaches to L2 issues have focused primarily—and appropriately—on changing faculty attitudes about multilinguality, and here I think we have been somewhat successful. The next step, though, is more difficult: persuading faculty to experiment with alternate pedagogical practices. In order to do this we need to be able to answer, with a high degree of specificity, the perenial question: "What can I do differently in class on Tuesday morning?" L2 students, like their L1 peers, need rigorous training and practice in academic writing, but some of our core WAC practices, such as in-class spontaneous freewriting, may prove particularly difficult, and even potentially counter-productive, for students who usually produce English text slowly and only as part of a complex translingual process which involves their L1 as well. Vivian Zamel (1995) suggests that ESL students need:

> multiple opportunities to use language and write-to-learn, course work which draws on and values what students already know, classroom exchanges and assignments that promote the acquisition of unfamiliar language, concepts, and approaches to inquiry, evaluation that allows students to demonstrate genuine understanding—is good pedagogy for everyone. (pp. 518-519)

From the point of view of WAC administrators, Zamel's view sounds like good news, for it is essentially an affirmation of the basic principles of WAC pedagogy. The suggestion is that we are doing the right things, as we advocate for better implementation of these principles in courses across the disciplines, but we just need to make sure that faculty apply them in an even-handed way to L1/L2 students. An opposing view, one first posed by Ilona Leki in reference to first-year composition, and extended to WAC/WID by Michelle Cox in the *ATD* issue, asks:

> Is it possible that WAC administrators and scholars, like our colleagues in L2 writing studies and first year composition,

place the same overemphasis on writing? Have we paid more attention to the potential benefits of integrating writing into curricula than the possible costs to some students? (n.p.)

In other words, is Zamel right that WAC is part of the pedagogical solution for L1/L2? Or is Leki right that our insistence on writing to learn may inadvertently be part of the problem? One midpoint between these positions would be to find ways of incorporating theoretical insights, research methodologies, and pedagogical techniques from other disciplines into our WAC/WID classroom practices. Zak Lancaster's article (*ATD*) provides an illustration of both the potential benefits and the particular difficulties of this approach. Drawing on the concept of stance from Systemic Functional Linguistics (SFL), Lancaster analyzes student writing from a particular course, and suggests potential pedagogical interventions. The course instructor found these techniques useful, but he clearly would never have come across the SFL-based analysis on his own; the breakthrough was only possible after a rather labor-intensive study of a sample of student papers on the part of Lancaster. Thus Lancaster's project highlights both the potential gains of a situated interdisciplinary approach—which examines the texts and practices of a particular pedagogical context using research-based tools—and also the difficulties inherent in exporting the hard-won findings of such a time-invested study in ways that ensure they will actually be used to help students in an upper-level disciplinary writing classroom. How can we present our findings to faculty in a way that is both useful and nonthreatening, and that is likely to filter through to the students? Michelle Cox's contribution to this volume addresses this question of professional development head on, describing specific workshop strategies for moving faculty gradually from a difference-as-deficit model to an interim difference-accommodation procedure and ultimately toward a difference-as-resource consciousness which even advanced theoretical work in the area is only now in the process of fully articulating.

Sound WAC pedagogy remains an indispensable prerequisite to the type of targeted differentiated instruction that a linguistically diverse student body demands. But we also need to incorporate new methods, models, and technologies which potentially offer previously unavailable means of implementing strategies tailored to L2 students while also serving the needs of L1 student writers. We are still in the relatively early stages of developing WAC-based multilingual-friendly instructional techniques that are suitable for a mixed population of students with a wide variety of linguistic backgrounds in the same classroom. Given the extensive variety of instructional situations that fall under the umbrella of WAC/WID, we will require a broad palette of approaches, some developed through painstaking situated studies in individual courses and classrooms, others incorporating more general principles of course and assignment design developed through interdisciplinary cooperation. Traversing this pedagogical frontier is one of the most important challenges that we face as WAC instructors, administrators, and researchers.

THE FUTURE

The future of WAC/WID in pedagogy, administration, and research will be determined by how well we negotiate the polarities represented by these axes. It would be easy to do more of the same in administration, without using local assessments to drive adaptations to the needs of specific populations, cultures, and conditions. It would be easy to repeat our traditional faculty development workshops on teaching effectively with writing in the discipline without adapting them for our new student populations, and without exploring ways of reaching these students directly using both emerging technology and new adaptations of traditional resources such as writing centers. WAC/WID can only maintain its viability as a twenty-first century pedagogical movement and academic discipline if it recognizes the ways that linguistic diversity is transforming our institutions. Multilinguality across the curriculum is not a matter of adapting multilingual students to a monolingual English norm, but rather of helping faculty adapt to the reality that multilingual students are not going to check their other languages at the door; rather, the academy has to open up the door and listen to what is being said in the hallway, and bring that conversation inside, where it can be continued. We need to find ways, in other words, for students to use their other languages in academic contexts—doing archival research in their home language(s), for example, as happens in the program Thomas Lavelle and Alan Shima describe in this volume, or providing linguistic or cultural commentary on assigned readings that are in English translation.

Our classroom practice, our pedagogical theory, and our research all need to change and develop in order to meet the challenges of the new mainstream. By building our pedagogy on a solid research base which combines global awareness with local specificity, we can adjust our college writing pedagogy in order to reach multilingual learners and help them to succeed at the highest academic levels. That is: Think globally. Research locally. Teach consciously.

The articles in this volume are a good place to continue that process and that journey.

REFERENCES

Cox, M. (2011). WAC: Closing doors or opening doors for second language writers? *Across the Disciplines, 8*(4). Retrieved from http://wac.colostate.edu/atd/ell/cox.cfm

Ferris, D., & Thaiss, C. (2011). Writing at UC Davis: Addressing the needs of second language writers. *Across the Disciplines, 8*(4). Retrieved from http://wac.colostate.edu/atd/ell/ferris-thaiss.cfm

Geller, A. E. (2011). Teaching and learning with multilingual faculty. *Across the Disciplines, 8*(4). Retrieved from http://wac.colostate.edu/atd/ell/geller.cfm

Hall J., Lancaster, Z., Lindsey, P., & Ronesi, L. (2012, June). *Multilingual writers and the future of WAC.* Panel presented at the International Writing Across the Curriculum Conference, Savannah Georgia.

Hall, J. (2009). WAC/WID in the next America: Re-thinking professional identity in the age of the multilingual majority. *The WAC Journal, 20*, 33-47.

Hall, J., & Navarro, N. (2011). Lessons for WAC/WID from language learning research: Multicompetence, register acquisition, and the college writing student. *Across the Disciplines, 8*(4). Retrieved from http://wac.colostate.edu/atd/ell/hall-navarro.cfm

Horner, B., Lu, M., Trimbur, J. & Royster, J. (2011). Language difference in writing: Toward a translingual approach. *College English, 73*(3), 299-317.

Johns, A. M. (2001). ESL students and WAC programs: Varied populations and diverse needs. In S. H. McLeod, E. Miraglia, M. Soven, & C. Thaiss (Eds.), *WAC for the new millennium: Strategies for continuing writing-across-the-curriculum* programs (pp. 141-164). Urbana, IL: NCTE.

Lancaster, Z. (2011). Interpersonal stance in L1 and L2 students' argumentative writing in economics. *Across the Disciplines, 8*(4). Retrieved from http://wac.colostate.edu/atd/ell/lancaster.cfm

Leki, I. (2003). A challenge to second language writing professionals: Is writing overrated? In B. Kroll (Ed.), *Exploring the dynamics of second language writing* (pp. 315-332). Cambridge, England: Cambridge University Press.

Leki, I., & Carson, J. G. (1994). Students' perceptions of EAP writing instruction and writing needs across the disciplines. *TESOL Quarterly, 28*(1), 81-101.

Lindsey, P., & Crusan, D. (2011). How faculty attitudes and expectations toward student nationality affect writing assessment. *Across the Disciplines, 8*(4). Retrieved from http://wac.colostate.edu/atd/ell/lindsey-crusan.cfm

Matsuda, P. K., & Jablonksi, J. (2000). Beyond the L2 metaphor: Towards a mutually transformative model of ESL/WAC collaboration. *Academic. Writing, 1*. Retrieved from http://wac.colostate.edu/aw/articles/matsuda_jablonski2000.htm

Patton, M. D. (2011). Mapping the gaps in services for L2 Writers. *Across the Disciplines, 8*(4). Retrieved from http://wac.colostate.edu/atd/ell/patton.cfm

Ronesi, L. (2011). "Striking while the iron is hot." A writing fellows program supporting lower-division courses at an American university in the UAE. *Across the Disciplines, 8*(4). Retrieved from http://wac.colostate.edu/atd/ell/ronesi.cfm

Zamel, V. (1995). Strangers in academia: The experiences of faculty and ESL students across the curriculum. *College Composition and Communication, 46*(4), 506-521.

Zawacki, T. M., & Cox, M. (2011). Introduction to WAC and second language writing. *Across the Disciplines, 8*(4). Retrieved from http://wac.colostate.edu/atd/ell/zawacki-cox.cfm

INTRODUCTION

Michelle Cox
Dartmouth College

Terry Myers Zawacki
George Mason University

> ESL students can become very fluent writers of English, but they may never become indistinguishable from a native speaker, and it is unclear why they should. A current movement among ESL writing teachers is to argue that, beyond a certain level of proficiency in English writing, it is not the students' texts that need to change; rather it is the native-speaking readers and evaluators (particularly in educational institutions) that need to learn to read more broadly, with a more cosmopolitan, less parochial eye. The infusion of life brought by these ESL students' different perspectives on the world can only benefit a pluralistic society which is courageous enough truly to embrace its definition of itself.
>
> —Ilona Leki, *Understanding ESL Writers: A Guide for Teachers* (pp. 132-133)

Ilona Leki made the observation that begins our introduction in 1992.[1] While much attention has been paid by composition and second language (L2) writing scholars in the intervening years to the "movement" to read the writing of our English second language (L2)[2] students with a "less parochial eye," we still see significant gaps in the WAC/WID literature on how L2 students experience writing in the disciplines, how teachers across the curriculum read the writing of their L2 students, and what constitutes an effective and linguistically and culturally inclusive pedagogy. With our co-edited special issue of *Across the Disciplines*—"Writing across the Curriculum and Second Language Writers: Cross-Field Research, Theory, and Program Development"—we brought attention to these gaps and the need for WAC theory and research that addresses the realities of what Jonathan Hall (2009) has called "the multilingual majority" at our institutions. In this collection, we extend that conversation, by including chapters that investigate more widely and deeply the experiences of L2 writers across the undergraduate and graduate curriculum, faculty expectations for these students, and courses and programs that have been developed to support both students and faculty.

While the chapters we've brought together here are primarily oriented towards research, our goal in assembling the collection was also to provide a wealth of pedagogical, curricular, and programmatic practices, a goal realized in each of the chapters. We've also been interested in presenting a range of perspectives and institutional locations and so the chapters here offer perspectives from students and faculty at large public universities, community colleges, smaller liberal arts colleges, a for-profit English language school, and locations outside of the US, including China, Sweden, Lebanon, and, virtually, Singapore. And, because L2 writing at the graduate level is increasingly becoming a focus for WAC programmatic efforts, we've included a number of chapters addressing this exciting and relatively new area of research and practice. Finally, the extensive lists of references provided at the end of each of the chapters offer an abundance of resources for further research and practice.

The overarching goal that drives this collection is this: that WAC theory, research, and practice must be expanded to include and "embrace," to echo Leki, the differing perspectives, educational experiences, and written voices of second language writers. As we noted at the outset, this is not a new argument, and, for that reason, we think it's important to review the second language writing (SLW) scholarship that has elaborated on this valuing-difference stance, a stance also endorsed by the authors in this collection. Organizing the eighteen chapters that make up the book into three discrete sections was no easy task, given that the themes and foci, not surprisingly, often overlapped in the authors' discussion of their research findings and the resulting programs and practices. To highlight these overlapping themes and findings, we took the liberty as editors—with the authors' consent—of embedding connections among these as relevant in each of the chapters.

Before turning to our review of the SLW literature and a description of our sections and chapters, we want to lay out three guiding principles that are integral to the work we do as WAC/WID professionals but that also, we believe, need to be interrogated and expanded in light of the diverse linguistic, educational, and cultural backgrounds of the L2 writers who are more and more the majority at our institutions. Derived from the WAC/WID literature, three key principles we see underlying WAC/WID work are:

- Writing is a powerful mode of learning and communication, with writers' and teachers' goals for the writing calling for varied writing processes and teaching approaches.

- Writing is situated, with structural, rhetorical, epistemological, and discoursal features varying according to the context of the writing (discipline, profession, activity system). These differences need to be taught and respected (i.e. writing across the curriculum is not writing-as-an-English-major across the curriculum).
- By promoting a paradigm shift in how writing is valued, understood, and taught, WAC programs can have transformative and widespread effects on pedagogy and wider campus cultures around teaching and learning.

When we consider these principles with an awareness of our students' multilinguality, we ask, as many L2 writing practitioners have asked, whether the same writing-to-learn approaches are equally beneficial to students who use English as a first language (L1) and L2 students. How might the writing and revision processes of L1 and L2 students differ and how can these differences be supported pedagogically? How might learned and culturally different rhetorical approaches be reflected in the academic writing L2 students produce? How do we WAC professionals and WID practitioners need to adjust our practices to make them more accessible to and inclusive of L2 writers? What language acquisition theories and research do we need to emphasize in our faculty development work? What information do faculty, even those versed in WAC practices, need to be given to help them understand their L2 writers and work with their writing more effectively? Regarding the latter, for example, Terry and Michelle have both worked with well-meaning faculty who focus predominantly on editing when giving feedback to L2 students, something they do not do when responding to the same kinds of writing activities by L1 students. We suggest, then, that each of the principles we've set out above need to be expanded to include the following awarenesses and practices (which is by no means an exhaustive list and which also reiterates principles articulated in the *CCCC Statement on Second Language Writing and Writers* [2009] and much of the SLW literature):

- Differences in Englishes should be respected. These Englishes include interlanguage (the language a language learner develops while learning a language), World Englishes, dialects of English, and the varieties of English students develop through code-meshing.
- Writing programs, courses, assignments, activities, and assessments should be constructed in such a way that linguistically and culturally diverse students have the potential to be as successful as L1 students and that allow them to draw on their cross-cultural and cross-linguistic resources.
- By promoting a difference-as-resource academic writing culture rather than programs and pedagogical practices aimed at assimilating L2 stu-

dents to Western culture and standard written English (SWE) norms, WAC programs can have a transformative and widespread effect on the ways faculty teach with writing across the disciplines and respond to the writing of all multilingual writers, whether students or colleagues.

As we noted, these principles are not original to us, but, in fact, have a long history in SLW scholarship, to which we now turn with our review of the literature organized according to the bulleted list above.

DIFFERENCES IN ENGLISHES SHOULD BE RESPECTED

In SLW scholarship, it has long been recognized that L2 writing differs in salient ways from L1 writing (for a succinct review of literature that examines these differences, see Silva, 1993). Second language acquisition is a long process, and, as the writer acquires the second language, their writing will reflect their "interlanguage" (Selinker, 1977) —a continuum that reflects the writer's developing understanding of the language as s/he "moves successfully toward closer and closer approximations of the target language" (Silva, Leki, & Carson, 1997, p. 405). How close these approximations ultimately become depends on a number of factors, but very few adult learners of second languages—researchers estimate only 5%—will develop a proficiency in the language that matches that of a native speaker, though "many if not most will attain the ability to communicate relative to their needs" (Silva, Leki, & Carson, 1997, p. 413).

As Leki suggests in our opening quote, SLW scholars have questioned the goal of L2 students writing like native speakers of the language. In 1979, Del Hymes proposed the goal of "communicative competence" for English Language Teaching (ELT), a pedagogical theory that focused on communication in the target language appropriate for a particular use and rhetorical situation. While this theory shifted the emphasis away from perfection in form to effectiveness of the language used for communicating within a particular situation, it was critiqued for leading to pedagogies focused too narrowly on particular tasks and on the rules and conventions for communicating within particular domains. Bronwyn Norton Peirce (1989), for example, critiqued communicative competence pedagogies for seeking to assimilate students to the norms in particular arenas (such as academic writing) without giving them the means to query those norms, and for limiting students to narrow arenas of writing without giving them the means to write in other arenas (such as civic writing). He acknowledges, however, that those who teach from a communicative competence stance do so with students' best interests in mind. To illustrate this stance, he quotes Braj Kachru (1986) who writes: "Knowing English is like possessing the fabled Aladdin's lamp, which permits one to open, as it were, the linguistic gates of international business, technology, science, and travel. In short, English provides linguistic power" (as quoted in Peirce, 1989, p. 402). But, he argues, English can be seen as a "Trojan horse" because, quoting David Cooke (1988), it is a language of "cultural intrusion ... [I]n a very real way, English is the property of elites, expressing the interests of the dominant classes" (as quoted in Peirce, 1989, p. 402). In light of Kachru and Cooke's positions, Peirce elaborates on the moral dilemma that faces English language teachers: "Are we contributing to the demise of certain languages or linguistic communities? Does the teaching of ESL or EFL (English as a Foreign Language) serve to entrench the power of an elite, privileged group of people who may have little interest in the welfare of the majority of the people in the country? Do teachers of ESL sometimes participate in [this] process?" (1989, p. 402).

It is this recognition of English language teaching as political, as endorsing a particular stance toward English and a particular variety of English, that has led to critical approaches to ELT. Echoing Cooke and Peirce, A. Suresh Canagarajah (1993) states that, "In practicing academic writing, students are acquiring not only a skill, certain cognitive processes, or communicative competence, but also the set of preferred values, discourses, and knowledge content of the academic community" (p. 303) and that, for L2 writers, the attempt to join the academic community may have detrimental consequences:

> Apart from the identity crisis or rootlessness this encounter will create, the community allegiances of students will also be affected as they face the danger of being ostracized by either their native or the academic community. That is, if they insist on membership in their native community (and maintain the identities and values associated with it) they will be judged unfit for the academic community, or vice versa. Even if they gain membership in the academic community, at whatever psychological or social costs, the chances are that they will be provided only negative subject positions by its discourse, such as being cognitively deficient, deviant, or even pathological. (p. 303)

Canagarajah (1993) argues for ELT pedagogies that "enable students to employ their local knowledge and counter-discourses to resist ideological domination, forge positive subject positions, and engage in emancipatory interests" (p. 303), goals he further elaborates in his later publications (Canagarajah, 1999; 2002; 2004; 2006a; 2006b).

SLW scholars have also questioned the focus on Standard Written English (SWE), a variety of English rooted in the US in Anglo-American English, arguing that this focus devalues the many other varieties of Englishes that L2 students use. These Englishes include varieties that have developed in other nations, such as Nepali English (Daniloff-Merrill, 2010), and Englishes created by L2 writers as they "code-mesh" (Canagarajah, 2011), drawing from their many linguistic, cultural, and rhetorical resources. SLW scholars have also argued that teachers should pay attention to the needs and goals of the students for learning English. For instance, Tony Silva, Ilona Leki, and Joan Carson (1997) argue that we should

> acknowledge that those who are learning to write in a second language in an institutional setting may be doing so only to satisfy the requirements of the institutional setting and may never again need to write, or perhaps even to read, a single word in their second language in the rest of their lifetimes, particularly if these learners return to their native countries. (p. 413)

Placing an emphasis on the formalities of academic American English for the writing of these students, they say, may lead to an "inappropriate negative evaluation of those who do not become particularly proficient" (p. 413).

It's important to note that this insistence on SWE has also been challenged on many fronts in the literature from composition studies: from process movement advocates (see, for example, Ken Macrorie's attack on "Engfish" in *Uptaught*, 1970), from arguments around valuing black English vernacular (see, for example, Geneva Smitherman's *Talkin and Testifyin: The Language of Black America*, 1977), from "alternate discourse" perspectives (see, for example, Pat Bizzell, Chris Schroeder, and Helen Fox's collection *Alt Dis: Alternative Discourses in the Academy*, 2002), and from "translingual" writing perspectives (see Horner, Lu, Royster, & Trimbur, 2011; Horner, NeCamp, & Donahue, 2011).

Indeed, in 1974, a position statement from the Conference of College Composition and Communication, *Students' Right to Their Own Language*, asserted that dialectic variations in student writing should be respected and honored. Mina Shaughnessy (1979) helped composition scholars and teachers see differences in the writing of basic writers as windows into the mind of the writer, by showing the logic behind what would typically be seen only as errors. And, most recently, Bruce Horner, Min-Zhan Lu, Jackie Royster, and John Trimbur (2011) have argued that "difference in language" should not be seen as "a barrier to overcome or as a problem to manage, but as a resource for producing meaning in writing, speaking, reading, and listening" (p. 303-304). These views are in concert with the stance toward L2 writing that we propose WAC endorse.

LINGUISTICALLY AND CULTURALLY INCLUSIVE WRITING PROGRAMS, COURSES, ASSIGNMENTS, ACTIVITIES, AND ASSESSMENTS

Related to the second bullet point in our list of expanded WAC/L2 principles, we turn now to another strand of research in SLW that has focused on the writing experiences of L2 students as they write in courses and contexts across the curriculum. Michelle Cox's (2011) review of this longitudinal research revealed that second language writers often struggle due to writing assignments that "assume deep cultural and historical knowledge of the US" (para. 9), the lack of scaffolding of assignments, the lack of time for completing the heavy reading and writing required by a project, and evaluation methods that focus too heavily on standard written English. There's also an abundance of SLW literature on developing linguistically and culturally inclusive assignments and writing curricula, noting especially the contributions made by Dana Ferris on teaching L2 writing (2004, 2009) and, in WAC contexts, Leki's pedagogical recommendations in her extensive body of work on L2 writers across disciplines. Also related to WAC contexts, Joy Reid and Barbara Kroll (1995) analyze eleven assignment descriptions from across the curriculum for accessibility and equity to L2 students, and then make recommendations for creating assignments that are more conducive for L2 student success. In their scholarship, SLW practitioners also address other faculty who work with L2 students, including composition instructors (such examples include work already cited, particularly Leki, 1992; Silva, Leki, & Carson, 1995) and WAC program administrators (see Cox, 2011; Hall, 2009; Johns, 2001; Matsuda & Jablonski, 2000; Zamel, 1995; Zamel & Spack, 2004).

Assessments of L2 writing have also been given a great deal of attention in the SLW literature considering the range of potentially detrimental effects of these assessments on L2 writers. Research in this area has focused on how L2 writers are evaluated in relation to their L1 peers (Lindsey & Crusan, 2011; Rubin & William-James, 1997; Song & Caruso, 1996), what features of L2 writing are particularly "irritating" to faculty (Santos, 1988; Vann, Meyer, & Lorenz, 1984), and how the background of the evaluator affects his/her evaluation of L2 writers (Weigle, Boldt, & Valsecchi, 2003). Another research area focuses on the ideological aspects of evaluation. Robert E. Land, Jr. and Catherine Whitley (1989), for example, argue that to evaluate an L2 student's essay according to the norms of SWE and Western rhetorical patterns not only disempowers the student, but ignores the realities of an increasingly pluralistic US culture and language and the rise of World Englishes. Other SLW scholars have argued that, given the additional cognitive load of reading and writing in a second language and the inevitability of what we may see as written accent in L2 writing (Leki, 1992, p. 129), it should be fair to assess L2 students differently in comparison to their L1 peers, by extending deadlines, adjusting page-length requirements, and not being as particular about SWE.

TRANSFORMATIVE EFFECT OF MULTILINGUAL AND MULTICULTURAL STUDENTS ON INSTITUTIONS OF HIGHER EDUCATION

Our assertion—that multilingual multicultural students have the potential to transform academic writing and teaching practices across institutions—can also be traced to L2 writing professionals who have often placed advocacy for L2 writers at the center of their work by partnering with students in their efforts to negotiate with "institutions that refuse to accommodate diversity" (Leki, 2002, p. 59). Why is it that the student is seen as needing to change, but not the institution? they ask. Sarah Benesch (1994), who is credited with bringing critical pedagogy to ELT, questioned why it is seen as "unrealistic to expect the university to adopt itself to the cultures, world views, and languages of nonnative-speaking students" and "realistic" for L2 students to adopt the cultures, world views, and language variety of the university (p. 711). To combat this tendency, L2 writing teachers have proposed pedagogies that invite L2 students to investigate relationships among language, power, and privilege (for one particularly innovative example, see Zamel, 2002), so that, as Vivian Zamel (2002) explains, the institutions themselves "can foster the language and critical thinking of students" and recognize "the ways in which these students, with their multicultures and their multivoices, can contribute to and transform the very institutions they inhabit and thereby enrich the lives of all of us who work there" (p. 339).

As will be clear in this collection, we and all of the authors who've contributed chapters are greatly indebted to this work and transformative vision as we carry on these vital WAC/L2 writing conversations and collaborations.

§

The eighteen chapters in this collection are organized into three sections, each corresponding to the three WAC/L2 writing-inclusive principles we described earlier, the first related to students as writers, the second to the contexts in which students write and faculty teach, and the third to the programmatic practices that have the potential to transform writing and teaching practices across the curriculum: Section I. "Learning from/with L2 Students: Student Strengths, Coping Strategies, and Experiences as They Write Across the Curriculum"; Section II. "Faculty Concerns and Expectations for Multilingual Writers"; and Section III. "WAC Programs and Practices Transformed." Along with the foreword by Jonathan Hall, the book closes with an afterword by Christopher Thaiss.

SECTION I: LEARNING FROM/WITH L2 STUDENTS: STUDENT STRENGTHS, COPING STRATEGIES, AND EXPERIENCES AS THEY WRITE ACROSS THE CURRICULUM

Each of the chapters in Section I features research that focuses on the resources multilingual writers bring to US undergraduate and graduate classrooms: their strengths as writers and rhetoricians, the ways in which they adapt writing knowledge for new writing situations, and the coping strategies they develop as they traverse and negotiate the US college and university curriculum. Framing this section is Michael-John DePalma and Jeffrey Ringer's investigation of how multilingual writers negotiate the various rhetorical situations in which they find themselves and how they transfer, apply, adapt or reshape the writing knowledge they've learned in one context for other different contexts. In "Adaptive Transfer, Writing Across the Curriculum, and Second Language Writing: Implications for Research and Teaching," the authors provide an extensive review of the research on transfer and then go on to show how instructors can support L2 students' agency as writers by valuing the ways they may be reshaping and transforming prior writing knowledge for their own linguistic and cultural purposes. Regarding the latter, their chapter offers a provocative rereading of Leki's central argument in her landmark study, "Coping Strategies of ESL Students in Writing Tasks Across the Curriculum" (1995), an article that is also referenced by other authors in this section. Addressing WAC researchers who wish to investigate the kinds and processes of adaptive transfer, DePalma and Ringer provide lists of questions that can be asked of students to discover the adaptive strategies they use in WID contexts. Such research and the adaptive transfer framework, they suggest, will help WAC professionals and WID teachers complicate their expectations for the writing knowledge students should have transferred from prior courses.

The next three chapters all show how students are adapting lessons learned in other courses, as well as creating new strategies that are self-taught. In "Resources for Success: A Case Study of a Multilingual Graduate Writer," Talinn Phillips presents a longitudinal case study of a multilingual graduate student to showcase the remarkable initiative he took to manage writing tasks successfully in his courses. Chozin, the student she follows, is, in many ways, an example of the kind of adaptative transfer Depalma and Ringer want readers and teachers to recognize. As with DePalma and Ringer, Phillips uses Leki's (1995) taxonomy of coping strategies as a pivotal point for her discussion, but she deepens Leki's categories by showing how Chozin benefitted by both positive and negative experiences around writing. What is particularly moving about this chapter, we think, is that Chozin is not a student that Phillips, who was his writing tutor, or his advisor expected to succeed given that he had "one of the lowest proficiency levels [she]'d encountered in over five years of tutoring [the] campus's multilingual graduate students" (p. 73). Due to the strategies this student developed, however, not only did he graduate successfully from the program, but he did so on time and with an outstanding thesis prize in hand.

The next chapter, Carole Center and Michelle Niestepski's "'Hey, Did You Get That?': L2 Student Reading Across the Curriculum," focuses on the strategies undergraduate L2 students develop to manage their heavy reading load, many of which are strikingly similar, as the authors note, to the coping strategies Leki (1995) reported. In an appendix, the authors provide a valuable inventory of reading practices useful as a guide for understanding the degree to which students write informally while reading, such as taking notes and marking and annotating passages they don't understand. Their chapter also gives us reasons to be optimistic as it shows faculty across disciplines being sensitive to their students' different cultural and linguistic backgrounds by allowing them to draw on their own cultural locations and experiences and making other accommodations to help them learn the material.

Qian Du's "Bridging the Gap between ESL Composition Programs and Disciplinary Writing: The Teaching and Learning of Summarization Skill" continues the focus on the reading-writing connection and the ability of L2 students to adapt their reading methods to learn the material, this time with research on one particular writing-to-read strategy: summary writing. In this chapter, Du describes the benefits, challenges, and complexity of summary writing, according to the literature and for the students she studied. For L2 students in particular, as she shows, summary writing (in response to test questions, in reporting on their reading and research, and so on) is a particularly complex process, requiring an understanding of different levels of information in a wide range of texts (e.g. oral lectures or multimedia productions in addition to print), along with the ability to represent the original text accurately and concisely. As such, the process of summary writing is a valuable learning tool; yet, as she argues, a summary is not a context-free genre and so must be taught by teachers in disciplines providing guidelines and support for the task.

With Kathryn Nielsen's chapter "On Class, Race, and the Dynamics of Privilege: Supporting Generation 1.5 Writers Across the Curriculum," we turn to a different kind of adaptation among a specific population of L2 writers—resident immigrant students, often termed generation 1.5 students. Although many of these students may face some of the same language and writing challenges as international students, they are also acutely aware of their linguistically and culturally in-between status and how this status might affect the way they are treated by their teachers and peers, as Nielsen's chapter shows. Nielsen argues that there are still large L2 writing areas that are not being sufficiently addressed, specifically how the variables of race, class, and gender, combined with culture and language, may affect the way the student writer is respected by peers and evaluated by teachers. With her research on the perceptions of five underserved generation 1.5 students from the Dominican Republic enrolled in a predominately white liberal arts college in the northeast, Nielsen begins to address the areas of class and race as important variables in how some L2 students experience writing and writing-intensive (WI) classrooms. She shows how they have adapted to a classroom and campus climate that they perceive as less than supportive when it came to peer review, group work and collaborative assignments, teachers' evaluation practices, and, overall, the classroom dynamic.

The final chapter of this section, Linda Hirsh's "Writing Intensively: An Examination of the Performance of L2 Writers Across the Curriculum at an Urban Community College," compares the success rates of L2 students enrolled in WI sections (sections L2 students were previously blocked from taking) and non-WI sections of the same course, examining the impact of WI courses on L2 students and the pedagogical practices that help them succeed. While Hirsch is looking at a community college context, the questions she's asking about the fairness of enrolling students in demanding WI courses are relevant at all levels, as are her surprising findings that L2 students in WI sections that provided language-support and scaffolded writing instruction passed the course at a higher rate than did ESL students enrolled in non-WI sections of the same course. Her chapter, which analyzes the strategies, techniques, and assignments that seemed to facilitate student learning, brings together many of the themes discussed in this section by speaking to both the coping strategies that students initiate and the faculty's responsibility for creating environments in which L2 students can succeed.

SECTION II: FACULTY CONCERNS AND EXPECTATIONS FOR MULTILINGUAL WRITERS

With Section II, we shift the focus from students to faculty with chapters exploring faculty perceptions of and reactions to L2 writing, their openness to professional development related to L2 writing, and approaches to WAC faculty development. In "Negotiating 'Errors' in L2 Writing: Faculty Dispositions and Language Difference," Terry Myers Zawacki and Anna Habib investigate faculty reactions to perceived error in L2 student writing, particularly "*how* they described the errors and *why* they seemed to be 'disturbed' by particular kinds of errors." While Zawacki and Habib agree with the translingual approach that values difference in writing, they wanted to see how theory met practice, particularly the practices of faculty across the curriculum. Their analysis reveals many of the complexities in the interaction between faculty and L2 writing, including concerns about students' comprehension of the material and the fairness of assessing the work of L2 students by a different standard than that for L1 students. As Zawacki and Habib report, however, they also found that the faculty who seemed least willing to negotiate meaning in L2 writing were also often the faculty who were most willing to spend time working with L2 writers on their writing. Further, they show that, while some faculty exhibited little tolerance for written accents, the majority expressed uncertainty about how to respond to and evaluate the writing in ways that would be most beneficial to the L2 student.

The chapter "'I Don't Know if That Was the Right Thing to Do': Faculty Respond to Multilingual Writers in the Disciplines," collectively researched and authored by graduate students at the University of New Mexico—Lindsey Ives, Elizabeth Leahy, Anni Leming, Tom Pierce, and Michael Schwartz—also takes up questions around faculty perceptions of L2 writing and writers. While Zawacki and Habib's investigation occurred at a research university with a large international student population in the mid-Atlantic region, Ives et al.'s research is based in a state university and neighboring community college in the southwest, an area that is historically bilingual. Like the faculty in Zawacki and Habib's study, however, the faculty that participated in Ives et al.'s study expressed conflicted feelings in relation to L2 writing. When presented with two sample pieces of student writing—one by an L2 student that exhibited some depth of thought but many surface-level errors and one constructed by the research team that was error-free but lacked depth—faculty unanimously rated the passage written by the research team more highly, indicating that surface errors prevented faculty from appreciating content. However, during interviews, faculty revealed that they expect that writing from L2 students will be accented and assess accordingly and are open to and interested in faculty development related to L2 writing.

Set in a university in China, the next chapter, Wu Dan's "Let's See Where Your Chinese Students Come From: A Qualitative Descriptive Study of Writing in the Disciplines in China," shows faculty across the curriculum voicing concerns about the quality of student writing and their own preparation for teaching with writing that are strikingly similar to those heard in the previous chapters in this section. Unlike so many disciplinary faculty in the US, however, these faculty do not say that students should have learned to write in someone else's course or earlier on in their student careers. As Wu Dan explains, China has had a turbulent higher education history with little time or attention given to teaching and learning processes and no tradition of general education; at the same time, however, as she points out, there has always been a deep regard for good writing in Chinese, giving her cause to be optimistic about the WAC concepts and practices she's introducing to her Chinese colleagues. While the broader purpose of Wu Dan's study was to examine the perceptions of Chinese faculty of the role of writing in learning and students' competence as writers in the disciplines at their Chinese institutions, she is also deeply committed to helping US faculty understand the educational and writing backgrounds of the increasingly large numbers of Chinese students who are coming to study at our institutions.

In "English Is Not a Spectator Sport: Privileged Second Language Learners and the For-Profit ESOL Classroom," Marino Fernandes introduces another, very different, educational context for teaching writing to L2 writers. His article describes the curriculum and typical student body of for-profit ESOL programs, which many international students attend in order to boost their TOEFL scores and English language fluency before either applying to or entering US colleges and universities. While the for-profit curriculum is tightly regimented and focused on rote language learning, as Fernandes describes it, he has found ways to deepen the learning experience of the students in his writing classes by adapting WAC pedagogies, particularly critical reading and writing approaches and process pedagogies, to fit the cultural and educational backgrounds of his students. As an immigrant English-language learner himself, Fernandes learned firsthand the difference between merely knowing how to speak in English and using English to achieve one's own educational dreams and aspirations. Now, as a master's student in language and linguistics, he is passionate about the need for even those students whom Vandrick (2002) calls "the global elite," who tend to be the majority population at for-profit language schools, to be engaged and critical participants in their English language learning. Writing is a means of acquiring agency, he argues, not just an exercise in learning a language. That this is the case for Fernandes is exemplified by his being a recipient of a 2012 CCCC Scholars of the Dream award. By happy circumstance, we had both gone to hear the panel on which Fernandes was presenting, and, after his presentation, we turned to each other to say that we should invite him to submit his paper to us for a chapter in our collection. This chapter, we are pleased to note, is an adaptation of the paper he delivered at the conference, his first publication.

In the remaining two chapters in this section, we shift from a focus on faculty concerns about student writing to approaches faculty can use to address these concerns. In "Making Stance Explicit for Second Language Writers in the Disciplines: What Faculty Need to Know about the Language of Stance-Taking," Zak Lancaster focuses on one rhetorical move that, when not done effectively, is often perceived as error—stance taking. L2 writers, in particular, he shows, are often judged as having problems with "thinking, understanding, or even effort" when they are unsuccessful in appropriating the stances and voices expected by their teachers. His analysis of the linguistic intricacies of appropriate stance-taking draws our attention to the importance for faculty to be more aware of their discipline-embedded but largely implicit expectations for the stances student writers should take when they express a position, make claims, present evidence, or use their "own" voice. While his is one of the longest chapters in the collection, we think it is also one of the most important in terms of bringing a systemic functional linguistics perspective to our work with faculty. Faculty make judgments all the time about which students are "good" writers at the sentence level and which are not, and yet most lack a nuanced vocabulary to explain how they arrive at this evaluation. Lancaster shows us at the sentence and phrase level what makes some writers sound like they are in control of the language and others sound unsure or unsophisticated. Although most faculty may not have the time or inclination to do the kind of close linguistic analysis Lancaster demonstrates, we think there is enormous value for our readers in understanding how to talk with faculty about the ways writers position themselves linguistically in their texts, and, by the stance-taking styles they choose, also position readers in certain ways.

While Lancaster focuses on a particular aspect of L2 writing and area of faculty development, Michelle Cox's chapter, "In Response to Today's 'Felt Need': WAC, Faculty Development, and Second Language Writers," which concludes this section, offers a wealth of suggestions for faculty development related to varied aspects of student writing, including writing processes, writing to learn activities, writing assignment design, peer review, and responding to and assessing L2 student writing. Cox argues that, while many faculty will initially take a "difference-as-deficit" stance in relation to student writing—a stance we see evidence of in Zawacki and Habib and Ives et al.'s chapters—WAC programs can, through faculty development, move faculty toward a "difference-accommodated" stance, and, ultimately, to what Canagarajah (2002) calls a "difference-as-resource" stance. One of the main stumbling blocks to offering faculty development on L2 writing, however, is that WAC program directors often don't feel equipped to do so. To address this concern, Cox describes approaches to collaborating with others on campus who advocate for L2 writers and where to gather information about these writers. She provides evidence from a wide range of SLW research for the effectiveness for L2 writers of the WAC pedagogies she recommends, such as those described in Hirsch's chapter, while also describing how these can be altered to accommodate L2 students by drawing explicitly on the linguistic and cultural resources they bring to the classroom. We intend for this chapter to provide a useful starting point for WAC program directors interested in transforming a campus to become more linguistically and culturally inclusive.

Section III: WAC Practices and Pedagogies Transformed

The chapters in this final section all demonstrate the kinds of transformations to classrooms and programs that are possible when attention is paid to creating inclusive and supportive L2 writing and learning environments.

The two chapters that open the section focus on academic writing courses the authors developed to support L2 undergraduate and graduate writers as writers in and across disciplines. Megan Siczek and Shawna Shapiro's "Developing Writing-Intensive Courses for a Globalized Curriculum through WAC-TESOL Collaborations" describes a model for a writing-intensive course designed by TESOL specialists. The authors describe two variations of the course, one taught at George Washington University in Washington, D.C. and open only to L2 students and the other taught at Middlebury College in Vermont and offered to both L1 and L2 students. They discuss the benefits and drawbacks of each model, describe the types of writing projects and readings assigned in each, and draw from course evaluations to share student perspectives of the benefits of the courses. But more than that, they also describe the obstacles that have prevented TESOL practitioners from making valuable L2-informed contributions to WAC programs and pedagogies. As they argue, the "persistent disciplinary segregation between WAC and TESOL" means that institutions whose missions increasingly focus on internationalizing their campuses are overlooking the expertise that TESOL faculty bring to conversations about cultivating global competence in their students. When TESOL and WAC program administrators and faculty collaborate, as they show, the resulting actions, such as the globally oriented courses they describe, can be educationally meaningful to all involved, perhaps most importantly to the students. Because they make such a powerful argument for putting into practice the institutional "buzzword" of "inclusiveness" when it comes to an institution's globalizing efforts, we've put their chapter first in this section to provide a frame for the other chapters, which illustrate, in varied ways, the transformative potential of innovative, collaborative courses and program curricula designed to support student writers across disciplines and institutional contexts.

While Sizcek and Shapiro focus on an undergraduate classroom, with the next chapter we turn to graduate student writing. As the chapter "Graduate Writing Workshops: Crossing Languages and Disciplines" by Elaine Fredericksen and Kate Mangelsdorf suggests, designing courses that support graduate-level writing is notoriously challenging, given the specialized nature of graduate study, the fact that graduate students who take such courses are at different points in their careers, and that such courses are often not credit-bearing, so attendance and commitment to the course can be issues. In their chapter, the authors offer a model for such a course that resolves some of these problems—a cross-disciplinary, linguistically mixed (English L1, L2, and bilingual) graduate writing workshop designed and taught by English department faculty at the University of Texas at El Paso (UTEP). What is notable about this course, in addition to the mixed population it serves, is its flexibility. In the first two weeks of the course, students develop a contract that determines their writing assignments and goals for the workshop, an approach to course design that highlights student agency; the course instructors also collaborate with the students' other teachers to offer instruction at the point of need. The authors report survey results from 26 graduate students who have taken the course on their perceptions of the effectiveness of the structural and pedagogical choices the authors made in designing and teaching the course.

Jennifer Craig's "Teaching Writing in a Globally Networked Learning Environment (GNLE): Diverse Students at a Distance" offers another model of graduate student writing support, but one that differs in salient ways from the one developed at UTEP. Unlike UTEP's course, the course Craig developed at MIT was not mixed L1/L2/bilingual, but was created only for international students; was not multidisciplinary, but was offered only to students enrolled in the Master of Engineering program created in collaboration with universities in Singapore; and was held not on campus but in a virtual learning space, a globally networked learning environment (GNLE) that used synchronous and asynchronous technologies to interact with students. Language and writing are central to GNLEs, as Craig points out, because the environment itself requires high levels of written interaction among the participants. The expectations for that interaction on the part of the students and her assumptions about how writing and talk about writing would take place in that environment are the focus of her chapter. As she explains, her analysis was first motivated by the students' reticence during course meetings and conferences, a reticence that she had previously been able to counter in her face-to-face interactions with students through the use of WAC pedagogical approaches. Drawing on her own critical self-reflection and on a student survey that explored student backgrounds and which aspects of the course were effective for their learning, she uncovered the assumptions she had brought to the course, how her goals and her students' were sometimes at odds, and how the many "distances" created by the technology affected not only writing instruction but also the classroom dynamic. Craig's chapter has important implications for graduate student writing support as well as for teaching in a GNLE, a model that is increasingly being used by institutions to offer courses to students in classroom locations around the world.

The last three chapters of this section broaden the focus from the classroom to the program level to provide models of cross-disciplinary, cross-cultural programs whose development and design is informed by research and practice from linguistics, L2 writing, and WAC/WID and which are coordinated and/or taught by administrators and faculty from all of these areas to enact a "difference-as-resource" approach to L2 writers and writing.

In "Campus Internationalization: A Center-Based Model for ESL-Ready Programs," Karyn Mallet and Ghania Zgheib describe a language supported, cross-disciplinary program—ACCESS—that transcends the "persistent disciplinary segregation" between TESOL and composition/WAC studies that Siczek and Shapiro critique. Developed collaboratively by WAC, composition, and ESL/applied linguistics faculty, ACCESS offers heavily recruited international students who've been provisionally admitted to the university the opportunity to enroll in a team-taught (by composition and ESL faculty) first-year writing course and introductory content courses, all of which include intensive language support and tutoring for students and faculty development for participating instructors. Drawing on survey and interview data, Mallett and Zgheib demonstrate that the program has benefitted both faculty and students involved, with students expressing satisfaction with the collaboration among writing and disciplinary teachers and faculty reporting an increased awareness of and sensitivity to the challenges faced by L2 writers, which, many said, carried over to the other courses they also regularly teach. More than just developing awareness and sensitivity, however, all of the participating faculty said they modified their course curriculum and pedagogical approaches throughout the semester to fit the needs of their L2 students. Because the participating faculty had numerous opportunities to talk together, through required workshops and planning meetings, they also shared their expectations for student writers with one another, and, in the process, these too were modified, a benefit that students also reported in focus groups and interviews. While not all institutions with globalization missions will be able, or even willing, to allocate significant resources to set up programs like ACCESS, Mallett and Zgheib's chapter provides a valuable model of an "ESL-ready" program with components that can be adapted to fit local contexts and available funding.

In the final two chapters, the context shifts from writing programs in the US to programs in two different international contexts. In "Reconstructing Teacher Roles through a Transnational Lens: Learning with/in the American University of Beirut," Amy Zenger, Joan Mullin, and Carol Peterson Haviland discuss the challenges of designing a writing program that positively recognizes students' cultural and linguistic differences. In a setting where administrators and many faculty have conservative understandings of acceptable academic writing in English, the authors explain how they worked against this "status-quo gatekeeping" by actively engaging with institutional language policies in the revision of an academic writing course for graduate students and the curriculum of the undergraduate general education program. The authors begin their chapter by describing the complex language histories and identities the students bring to AUB, which typically include speaking and writing experiences in two or more languages and Arabic dialects. While the students come with rich language backgrounds, the traditional pedagogies employed in the academic writing course seemed to define them as linguistically "deficient" by focusing on what the students lacked as writers in English. To better understand the students' strengths, the authors surveyed students about their language backgrounds and how they *feel* when they write in English and their other languages in their disciplines, among other questions. (The full survey is included in an appendix to their chapter.) The survey data, along with the translingual theories and practices they endorse, informed the authors' reconceptualization of the academic writing course and their approach to infusing more writing into the general education curriculum, an approach that relies on the varied language expertise of faculty across the disciplines. The authors' end goal for this WID-based pedagogical approach, as they write, is for faculty and administrators "to construct knowledge about writers collaboratively, to conceive of multilingualism as an asset, and to think transnationally."

With the final chapter, Thomas Lavelle and Alan Shima's "Writing Histories: Lingua Franca English in a Swedish Graduate Program," we provide an example of a program that has managed to embody a translingual ideal in the ways faculty collaborate across cultures and disciplines to read their students' theses with an appreciation for their scholarly contributions and a "let it pass" approach to surface errors. This readerly mindset can be at least partly ascribed to the writing support offered to students and the faculty development and assessment activities Lavelle and Shima provide as "semi-embedded" academic writing instructors. The interdisciplinary Roads to Democracy history program the authors describe is offered through a collaboration among Uppsala University in Sweden, Coimbra University in Portugal, and Siegen University in Germany. The fully international program, as they explain, enrolls students from over twenty different countries (though none from Sweden) and shares some common on-line courses while requiring students to take at least fifteen credits from two of the partner institutions although each institution grants its own degree. Understandably, then, given this enormous linguistic diversity, instruction at all three institutions occurs in lingua franca English in "contact situations" where writers employ and readers expect "flexible codes, semantic negotiations, and tolerance for temporary unintelligibility." How writing instruction occurs in the program offered at Uppsala and how participating faculty negotiate their expectations for the required thesis are the focus of their chapter, which draws on data collected from their multi-method case study of the Roads program. We have chosen to close this final section with this chapter, as it illustrates a program that has, to use Lavelle and Shima's words, "successfully created a context where multilingualism is an asset, not a deficit"—a goal shared by so many authors in this collection.

§

As we close, we want to recognize the challenges inherent in transforming writing courses, curricula, and programs to become linguistically and culturally inclusive. Even modest changes to the pedagogy of a single course require time and energy on behalf of a faculty member, difficult to find in this period of increasing faculty workloads without corresponding increases in compensation. Changes at the curricular and programmatic level require strong administrative support and the time and energy of writing program administrators, all of which are in short supply in the face of cutbacks in funding, increasing course caps, and shortage of tenured positions for both Composition Studies and TESOL professionals. The comprehensive ACCESS program for international students at George Mason University, as described by Karyn Mallet and Ghania Zgheib, for example, requires enormous support from many levels of administration and faculty. However, given the multilingualism and multiculturalism of today's students, we believe that the vision of linguistically and culturally inclusive writing courses, curricula and programs is a worthy goal, no matter how incremental the steps are that can be taken in any one classroom, college, or university at any given time.

Research into the ways in which L2 writers negotiate academic writing on US campuses, into US faculty expectations for and experiences with L2 writers across the curriculum, into approaches for faculty development in creating linguistically and culturally inclusive pedagogy, into the effects of particular approaches to structuring writing programs, and into the ways in which WAC pedagogies and practices get translated into online teaching environments and in writing programs abroad, such as presented in this collection, help pave the way for making this goal a reality for more students at more institutions of higher education. In closing, we return to the words from Ilona Leki with which we started: "The infusion of life brought by these ESL students' different perspectives on the world can only benefit a pluralistic society which is courageous enough truly to embrace its definition of itself" (1992, p. 133). We believe that WAC is, indeed, courageous enough to be transformed by the multilingualism and multiculturalism of our students.

FUTURE RESEARCH

Finally, we want to recommend some avenues for future research based on the topics and concerns explored by the chapters in this collection as well as by larger conversations occurring in composition studies, WAC, and L2 writing around the implications for our fields of increasing populations of US resident L2 writers (what we've called "globalism at home" [Zawacki & Cox, 2011]); increasing numbers of international L2 students on US campuses; and increased globalization of US institutions of higher education through partnerships with institutions abroad and the establishment of branch campuses outside of the US. We've organized these according to the section themes.

SECTION I RELATED TO L2 STUDENTS' EXPERIENCES:

- How do L2 students write across the curriculum in different institutional contexts?
- How do the dynamics of race, ethnicity, nationality, gender, and class affect L2 students and their writing development?
- How do L2 students use aspects of "multicompetence" to read and write about texts, to complete assignments, and to do research. What resources

do they draw on? What strategies are they using? How can we help them "activate multicompetence" (Hall & Navarro, 2011, n.p.)?
- How and what writing and rhetorical knowledge are L2 students transferring from other sites, contexts, and educational experiences? How are they adapting this knowledge? How might they be using this knowledge to resist US conventions of writing and rhetoric? (See, for example, Chris Tardy, 2009, and much of Mark James' work on transfer and L2 students.)

Section II related to faculty perceptions and teaching practices around L2 writing:

- How do the presence and contributions of L2 students affect campus and classroom climate? With increased populations of L2 students, do faculty reexamine their focus on SWE and Western rhetorical norms or tighten their grip on them?
- How are faculty reading, responding to, and assessing L2 students' texts in diverse locations within and outside of the US?
- What are faculty expectations for L2 students at the graduate level, within and outside of the US? And, related to this, what are expectations for L2 writing in professional contexts, within and outside of academia?
- How do the response and assessment practices of L1 and L2 faculty differ, if they do? In comparison with L1 faculty, are L2 faculty more sympathetic to the challenges that L2 students face or do they push them harder? From what perspective—lingua franca English or SWE or other—do L2 faculty tend to read?
- What kinds of faculty development work related to L2 writing are needed? What models and approaches have proven to be effective?

Section III related to a focus on courses, curriculum, and programs:

- What "ESL-ready" courses and programs are being developed at institutions in and outside of the US? Are there models of pedagogies and programs that embrace lingua franca English as the norm (rather than, for example, SWE) and that draw on L2 writers' resources and strengths?
- What writing pedagogies have L2 students experienced before entering US undergraduate and graduate programs and at US secondary schools, English language institutes, for-profit English language schools, and secondary education outside of the US?

AND, FINALLY, IN THINKING ABOUT THE IMPLICATIONS OF THE COLLECTION AS A WHOLE:

- What research has been/is being carried out on WID and English L2 outside of the US? (The newly inaugurated series *International Exchanges on the Study of Writing*, published by the WAC Clearinghouse and Parlor Press, is inviting book-length manuscripts that address worldwide perspectives on writing, writers, teaching with writing, and scholarly writing practices, specifically those that draw on scholarship across national and disciplinary borders to challenge parochial understandings of all of the above.)
- What research has been/is being carried out on tutoring writing in the disciplines at English-medium institutions outside of the US?

What collaborations between writing scholars are occurring/should be occurring and on what topics and across what disciplinary and national borders? (On the WAC Clearinghouse, see, for example, Bazerman et al.'s *International Advances in Writing Research: Cultures, Places, Measures* (2012) with chapters selected from the more than 500 presentations at the Writing Research Across Borders II Conference in 2011. Also see *Writing Programs Worldwide: Profiles of Academic Writing in Many Places* (2012) with chapters emerging from the WAC/WID International Mapping Project.)

NOTES

1. Throughout this project and our previous project, the special issue of *Across the Disciplines*, our collaboration has been rich, productive, and even joyful. We have discovered that we make wonderful partners, matched in our work ethics and complementary in our strengths. In order to equally share credit for our collaborative work, in the *ATD* issue, we decided to list Michelle as first editor of the collection and Terry as first author of the introduction. With this project, we did the reverse, and listed Terry as first editor of the collection and Michelle as first author of the introduction.
2. We realize that the designator "English as a Second Language" is problematic, in that English may be the third, fourth, etc, language of the students we're referring to. We have chosen to use this designation, however, to connect the work in this collection to the wider scholarship of second language writing studies. For a further rationale for using this designation, see Matsuda, 2012.

REFERENCES

Bazerman, C., Dean, C., Early, J., Lunsford, K., Null, S., Rogers, P., & Stansell, A. (Eds.). (2012). *International advances in writing research: Cultures, places, measures*. Fort Collins, CO: WAC Clearinghouse and Parlor Press. Retrieved from http://wac.colostate.edu/books/wrab2011/

Benesch, S. (1994). ESL, ideology, and the politics of pragmatics. *TESOL Quarterly, 27*, 705-716.

Bizzell, P., Schroeder, C. & Fox, H. (Eds.). (2002). *Alt Dis: Alternative discourses in the academy*. Portsmouth, NH: Boynton/Cook.

Canagarajah, A. S. (1993). Comments on Ann Raimes' "Out of the woods: Emerging traditions in the teaching of writing." *TESOL Quarterly, 27*, 300-306.

Canagarajah, A. S. (1999). *Resisting linguistic imperialism in English teaching*. Oxford, UK: Oxford University Press.

Canagarajah, A. S. (2002). *Critical academic writing and multilingual students*. Ann Arbor: University of Michigan Press.

Canagarajah, A. S. (2004). Language rights and postmodern conditions, *Journal of Language, Identity, and Education, 3*(2), pp. 140-145.

Canagarajah, A. S. (2006a). Toward a writing pedagogy of shuttling between languages: Learning from multilingual writers, *College English, 68*(6), 589-604.

Canagarajah, A. S. (2006b). The place of World Englishes in composition: Pluralization continued, *College Composition and Communication, 57*(4), 586-619.

Canagarajah, A. S. (2011). Codemeshing in academic writing: Identifying teachable strategies of translanguaging, *The Modern Language Journal, 95*, 401-417.

Conference of College Composition and Communication. (1974). *Students' right to their own language*. Retrieved from http://www.ncte.org/library/NCTEFiles/Groups/CCCC/NewSRTOL.pdf

Conference on College Composition and Communication. (2009). *CCCC Statement on Second Language Writing and Writers*. Retrieved from http://www.ncte.org/cccc/resources/positions/secondlangwriting

Cox, M. (2011). WAC: Closing doors or opening doors for second language writers? *Across the Disciplines, 8*(4). Retrieved from http://wac.colostate.edu/atd/ell/cox.cfm

Ferris, D. (2004). *Teaching ESL composition: Purpose, process, and practice*. New York: Routledge.

Ferris, D. (2009). *Teaching college writing to diverse student populations*. Ann Arbor, MI: University of Michigan Press/ELT.

Hall, J. (2009). WAC/WID in the next America: Redefining professional identity in the age of the multilingual majority. *The WAC Journal, 20*, 33-49. Retrieved from http://wac.colostate.edu/journal/vol20/hall.pdf

Hall, J., & Navarro, N. (2011). Lessons for WAC/WID from language learning research: Multicompetence, register acquisition, and the college writing student. *Across the Disciplines, 8*(4). Retrieved from http://wac.colostate.edu/atd/ell/hall-navarro.cfm

Horner, B., Lu, M.-Z., Royster, J., & Trumbur, J. (2011). Language difference in writing: Toward a translingual approach. *College English, 73,* 303-321.

Horner, B., NeCamp, S., & Donahue, T. (2011). Toward a multilingual composition scholarship: From English Only to a translingual norm. *College Composition and Communication, 63*(2), 269-300.

Hymes, D. (1979). On communicative competence. In C. Brumfit & K. Johnson (Eds.), *The Communicative Approach to Language Teaching (pp. 183-191).* Oxford: Oxford University Press.

James, M. (2010). An investigation of learning transfer in English-for-general-academic-purposes writing instruction. *Journal of Second Language Writing, 19*(4), 183-206.

James, M. (2008). Learning transfer in second language writing education: The impact of task similarity/difference. *Written Communication, 25,* 76-103.

Johns, A. M. (2001). ESL students and WAC programs: Varied populations and diverse needs. In S. H. McLeod, E. Miraglia, M. Soven, & C. Thaiss (Eds.), *WAC for the new millennium: Strategies for continuing writing-across-the-curriculum programs* (pp. 141-164). Urbana, IL: NCTE.

Land, R., & Whitley, C. (1989). Evaluating second-language essays in regular composition classes: Toward a pluralistic U. S. rhetoric. In D. Johnson & D. Roen (Eds.), *Richness in writing: Empowering ESL students* (pp. 284-293). New York: Longman.

Leki, I. (1992). *Understanding ESL writers: A Guide for teachers.* Portsmouth, NH: Boynton/Cook.

Leki, I. (1995). Coping strategies of ESL students in writing tasks across the curriculum. *TESOL Quarterly, 29*(2), 235-260.

Leki, I. (2002). Not the end of history. In L. Blanton & B. Kroll (Eds.), *ESL Composition Tales: Reflections on Teaching* (pp. 49-62). Ann Arbor, MI: University of Michigan Press.

Lindsey, P. & Crusan, D. (2011). How faculty attitudes and expectations toward student nationality affect writing assessment. *Across the Disciplines, 8*(4). Retrieved from http://wac.colostate.edu/atd/ell/lindsey-crusan.cfm

Macrorie, K. (1970). *Uptaught.* Rochelle Park, NJ: Hayden.

Matsuda, P. K. (2012). Teaching composition in the multilingual world: Second language writing in composition studies. In K. Ritter & P. K. Matsuda (Eds.), *Exploring composition studies: Sites, issues, and perspectives* (pp. 36-51). Logan, UT: Utah State University Press.

Matsuda, P. K., & Jablonksi, J. (2000). Beyond the L2 metaphor: Towards a mutually transformative model of ESL/WAC collaboration. *Academic. Writing, 1.* Retrieved from http://wac.colostate.edu/aw/articles/matsuda_jablonski2000.pdf

Peirce, B. N. (1989). Toward a pedagogy of possibility in the teaching of English internationally: People's English in South Africa, *TESOL Quarterly, 23*(3), 401-420.

Reid, J. & Kroll, B. (1995). Designing and assessing effective classroom writing assignments for NES and ESL students, *Journal of Second Language Writing, 4*(1), 17-41.

Rubin, D. L. & William-James, M. (1997). The impact of writer nationality on mainstream teachers' judgments of composition quality, *Journal of Second Language Writing, 6*(2), 139-153.

Santos, T. (1988). Professors' reactions to the academic writing of non-native speaking students, *TESOL Quarterly, 22*(1), 69-90.

Selinker, L. (1977). Interlanguage. *International Review of Applied Linguistics, 10,* 209-231.

Shaughnessy, M. (1979). *Errors and expectations: A guide for the teacher of basic writing.* New York: Oxford.

Silva, T. (1993). Toward an understanding of the distinct nature of L2 writing: The ESL research and its implications. *TESOL Quarterly, 27*(4), 657-677.

Silva, T., Leki, I., & Carson, J. (1997). Broadening the perspective of mainstream composition studies: Some thoughts from the disciplinary margins, *Written Communication, 14*(3), 398-428.

Smitherman, G. (1977). *Talkin and testifyin: The language of black America.* Boston: Houghton Mifflin.

Song, B., & Caruso, I. (1996). Do English and ESL faculty differ in evaluating the essays of native English-speaking and ESL students? *Journal of Second Language Writing, 5*(2), 163-182.

Tardy, C. (2009). *Building genre knowledge: Writing L2.* West Lafayette, IN: Parlor Press.

Thaiss, C., Bräuer, G., Carlino, P., Ganobcsik-Williams, L., & Sinha, A. (Eds.). (2012). *Writing programs worldwide: Profiles of academic writing in many places.* Fort Collins, CO: WAC Clearinghouse and Parlor Press. Retrieved from http://wac.colostate.edu/books/wpww/

Vann, R. J., Meyer, D. E., & Lorenz, F. O. (1984). Error gravity: A study of faculty opinion of ESL errors. *TESOL Quarterly, 18*(3), 427-440.

Weigle, S. C., Boldt, H., & Valsecchi, M. I. (2003). Effects of task and rater background on the evaluation of ESL writing: A pilot study. *TESOL Quarterly, 37*(2), 345-354.

Zamel, V. (1995). Strangers in academia: The experiences of faculty and ESL students across the curriculum. *College Composition and Communication, 46*(4), 506-521.

Zamel, V. (2002). From the margins to the center. In V. Zamel & R. Spack (Eds.), *Enriching ESOL pedagogy: Readings and activities for engagement, reflection, and inquiry* (pp. 331-340). Mahwah, NJ: Lawrence Erlbaum.

Zamel, V., & Spack, R. (Eds.). (2004). *Crossing the curriculum: Multilingual learners in college classrooms.* Mahwah, NJ: Lawrence Erlbaum.

Zawacki, T. M., & Cox, M. (2011). Introduction to WAC and second language writing, *Across the Disciplines, 8*(4). Retrieved from http://wac.colostate.edu/atd/ell/zawacki-cox.cfm

SECTION I

LEARNING FROM/WITH L2 STUDENTS: STUDENT STRENGTHS, COPING STRATEGIES, AND EXPERIENCES AS THEY WRITE ACROSS THE CURRICULUM

CHAPTER 1

ADAPTIVE TRANSFER, WRITING ACROSS THE CURRICULUM, AND SECOND LANGUAGE WRITING: IMPLICATIONS FOR RESEARCH AND TEACHING

Michael-John DePalma
Baylor University

Jeffrey M. Ringer
University of Tennessee, Knoxville

This chapter discusses how the framework of adaptive transfer might encourage more culturally and linguistically inclusive Writing Across the Curriculum (WAC) theory and practice regarding multilingual writers. Drawing upon the shared insights on learning transfer in educational psychology, education, and human resource development, we define adaptive transfer as the conscious or intuitive process of applying or reshaping learned writing knowledge in new and potentially unfamiliar writing situations. In tracing the implications of this framework for WAC research and teaching, this chapter aims to provide WAC scholars a means to better understand the complex ways in which multilingual writers learn to write across contexts.

> We need to ask ourselves: how can WAC/WID programs more effectively encourage *Multilingual Learning Across the Curriculum*? How can we find opportunities [...] to allow students to *use* those multilingual skills in an academic context?
>
> —Jonathan Hall, "WAC/WID in the Next America"

> [T]ransfer is often difficult to find because we tend to think about it from a perspective that blinds us to its presence. Prevailing theories and methods of measuring transfer work well for studying full blown expertise, but they represent too blunt an instrument for smaller changes in learning that lead to the development of expertise.
>
> —John D. Bradford and Daniel L. Schwartz, "Rethinking Transfer"

In our 2011 *Journal of Second Language Writing* article, "Toward a Theory of Adaptive Transfer: Expanding Disciplinary Discussions of 'Transfer' in Second-Language Writing and Composition Studies," we argued that discussions of transfer in second language (L2) writing studies and composition studies have focused primarily on the *reuse* of past learning and thus have not adequately accounted for the adaptation of learned writing knowledge in unfamiliar situations. Our goal in that article was to expand disciplinary discussions of transfer in L2 writing and composition studies by theorizing adaptive transfer, a construct forged from collective insights on transfer of learning in the fields of educational psychology, education, and human resource development. In an effort to extend that work, this chapter discusses how the framework of adaptive transfer might encourage more culturally and linguistically inclusive research and teaching practices related to multilingual writers across the curriculum. In tracing the implications of this framework for Writing Across the Curriculum (WAC) theory and practice, this chapter aims to provide WAC scholars a means to better understand the complex ways in which multilingual writers learn to write across contexts. It does so in response to an exigency that Jonathan Hall (2009) articulates: "The new reality to which we must adjust in US higher education is that *multilingual learners are part of the mainstream*" (p. 37). As such, it is incumbent upon WAC specialists to account for how multilingual writers negotiate the various rhetorical situations in which they find themselves.

Following from the 2009 *CCCC Statement on Second Language Writing and Writers,* which calls WAC specialists to account for multilingual writers in research initiatives and teaching practices, we focus our discussion on the following questions:

Research: In what ways might adaptive transfer inform research on multilingual writers across the curriculum?

Teaching with Writing in the Disciplines (WID): How might adaptive transfer inform L2 writing instruction across the curriculum?

In what follows, we first discuss research on transfer in WAC and L2 writing scholarship and highlight the narrowly conceptualized notions of transfer that have informed these disciplinary discussions. We then provide an overview of adaptive transfer, explaining how it is distinct from traditional transfer. Finally, we discuss the implications of adaptive transfer for WAC research and teaching with WID, particularly in relation to multilingual writers.

ADAPTIVE TRANSFER DEFINED

For more than two decades, research on transfer of learning has been an area of critical concern for scholars in WAC (Carroll, 2002; Dively & Nelms, 2007; McCarthy, 1987; Russell, 1995, 2001; Walvoord & McCarthy, 1990), composition (Bergmann & Zepernick, 2007; Brent, 2012; Dias, Freedman, Medway, & Paré, 1999; Downs & Wardle, 2007; Haswell et al., 1999; Petraglia, 1995; Russell, 1995; Smit, 2004; Voss, 1989; Wardle, 2007, 2009), and L2 writing (Currie, 1999; James, 2006a, 2006b, 2009; Johns, 1997; Leki, 1995; Leki & Carson, 1997; Snow, 1993; Spack, 1997). Attention to transfer among WAC scholars has occurred primarily in the context of debates surrounding the efficacy of first-year writing (FYW) courses. In examining whether or not general writing skills instruction (GWSI) courses sufficiently prepare students to write in subsequent disciplinary and professional contexts, compositionists have aimed to determine the kinds of knowledge and skills that transfer when students transition from one writing context to another. Among L2 writing specialists, discussions of transfer have also been important, especially to research on contrastive rhetoric (CR) and English for academic purposes (EAP). For scholars working in CR, transfer of learning is a key area of interest, because CR researchers have aimed to identify rhetorical patterns that are unique to each language and culture in order that they might offer multilingual learners strategies for facilitating the transfer of rhetorical knowledge from a first language (L1) to a second language (L2) (Connor, 1996; Grabe & Kaplan, 1989; Hinds, 1983a, 1983b, 1990; Kang, 2005; Kaplan, 1966, 1988; Kobayashi, 1984; Kubota, 1998; Oi, 1984; Simpson, 2000). In the case of EAP research, questions about learning transfer have been a primary concern because they relate in significant ways to arguments concerning the extent to which EAP courses prepare multilingual writers for coursework in their disciplines (Belcher, 1995; Belcher & Braine, 1995; Currie, 1999; James, 2006a, 2008, 2009; Johns, 1995, 1997; Leki, 1995, 2007; Leki & Carson, 1997; Riazi, 1997; Snow, 1993; Spack, 1988, 1997; Swales, 1990).

In surveying how transfer has been discussed in WAC, composition, and L2 writing scholarship, we contend that scholars have focused primarily on the *reuse* of past learning and thus have not adequately accounted for the adaptation of learned writing knowledge in unfamiliar situations (see DePalma & Ringer, 2011 for a full critique of traditional notions of transfer). As we explain in our 2011 article, definitions of transfer have implied that transfer does not occur unless skills learned in one context are consistently applied in other settings. Such emphasis on application limits transfer to the *reuse* of writing skills and prevents researchers from acknowledging what *does* happen when students encounter novel rhetorical situations. Narrow conceptualizations of transfer also ignore the agency of writers; assume the initial and target writing contexts are stable; reduce readers to decoders; deflect attention away from the moves students make to reshape and reform learned writing skills to fit new tasks; and neglect other important forms of transfer, such as lateral, vertical, near, far, literal, or figural transfer (see Haskell, 1998 and Royer, Mestre, & Dufresne, 2005 for discussions of various types of transfer).

As an alternative to traditional notions of transfer, we thus offer the construct of adaptive transfer. Drawing on the shared insights about learning transfer in educational psychology, education, and human resource development (Beech, 1999; Bradford & Schwartz, 1999; Broudy, 1977; Dyson, 1999; Greeno, Smith, & Moore, 1993; Haskell, 1998; Lave, 1988; Lave & Wenger, 1991; Royer, 1979; Royer, Mestre, & Dufresne, 2005; Wenger, 1998), we define adaptive transfer as a writer's conscious or intuitive process of applying or reshaping learned writing knowledge in order to negotiate new and potentially unfamiliar writing situations (DePalma and Ringer, 2011, p. 141). Specifically, adaptive transfer is *dynamic*, because it is premised on the notion that writing practices learned in one context may be reused or reshaped in another, thus allowing space for change and fluidity (Lobato, 2003; Matsuda, 1997; Parks, 2001). Processes of adaptive transfer are also *idiosyncratic* in that they are particular to individual learners and influenced by factors such as language repertoire, race, class, gender, educational history, social setting, genre knowledge, and so forth (Lobato, 2003). Adaptive transfer is also *cross-contextual*, occurring when learners recognize a resemblance between a familiar writing situation in which a skill was learned and an unfamiliar writing situation in which rhetorical production is required (Lobato, 2003; Pierce, Duncan, Gholson, Ray, & Kamhi, 1993, p. 67). Likewise, adaptive transfer is *rhetorical*, meaning that it takes place when a writer understands that the context, audience, and purpose of a text influence what is suitable; furthermore, adaptive transfer makes space for the possibility that differences in students' texts are "matters of design" (Lu, 2004, p. 26) or the result of a "strategic and creative choice by the author to attain his or her rhetorical objectives" (Canagarajah,

2006b, p. 591). Related to this, adaptive transfer is *multilingual* in that it views all language and varieties of language as fluid and in process, and it recognizes the agency of writers to draw from among a variety of discourses and languages in order to influence contexts of writing (Canagarajah, 2006a; Horner & Lu, 2007; Horner & Trimbur, 2002; Lu, 2006; Matsuda, 2002). Finally, adaptive transfer is *transformative*. It recognizes that writers shape and are shaped by rhetorical practice, and, as such, it allows for the possibility that newcomers working with a genre might act as a brokers who introduce new ways of seeing, doing, or knowing into writing practice (Beech, 1999; Wenger, 1998).

Given these characteristics, we argue that adaptive transfer offers WAC specialists a theoretical construct that will help reveal the complex ways in which multilingual writers learn to write across disciplines. It does so by emphasizing the agency of individual writers—"the processes by which learners form personal relations of similarities across situations, whether or not those connections are correct or normative" (Lobato, 2003, p. 20). Adaptive transfer thus provides a terministic screen that names what *does* happen when students traverse rhetorical contexts.

One empirical study that illustrates adaptive transfer is Susan Parks' (2001) "Moving from School to the Workplace." In her study of eleven francophone nurses transitioning from their respective French-speaking universities in Quebec, Canada to an English-speaking hospital in Montreal, Canada, Parks (2001) describes the ways these nurses adapted their prior writing knowledge to fit a new context. The locus of adaptive transfer in Parks' (2001) study is a genre known as care plans. As university students, the nurses viewed care plans as simply a school-based genre that would be of little use in the workplace. As these nurses shifted from an academic to a workplace setting, however, they started to see the significance of the genre to their professional work and "began to perceive differences between the way they had done care plans while at university and those which they had begun to do on the units" (p. 415). One of the key differences the nurses recognized between the genre knowledge they acquired in school and the writing of care plans in a hospital setting was the level of detail required and the structure of the care plans.

In their university coursework, the nurses had been taught to construct a detailed three-part care plan, outlining a patient's diagnosis, cause of illness, and symptoms. When writing the care plans, they were also instructed to steer away from the language of medical diagnosis. Through their interactions with colleagues and the genre of the care plan in a hospital setting, however, they recognized that the care plan did not often take the detailed three-part structure that they had been taught to use in school, and they realized that the language of medical diagnosis was encouraged in the writing of care plans in their professional context. Recognizing these crucial differences led to the simplification of their care plans—a reshaping which might at first glance appear to indicate linguistic incompetence or a lack of genre knowledge. As Parks (2001) explains, however, "the francophone nurses were simplifying the way they wrote care plans, not because they lacked language *per se*, but in response to the influence of peers" (pp. 417-418). In other words, the nurses were adapting a school-based genre to their socio-rhetorical situation; their use of "more simplified rhetorical structures emerged as a result of intersubjective functioning" (p. 417). Moreover, Parks (2001) explains that the ways the individual nurses engaged with this genre were influenced by their perceptions of the genre and the motives or purposes they associated with it—dispositions which were informed by their beliefs and personal histories (p. 408). In sum, the reshaping of the nurses' prior writing knowledge was not only a response to the demands of their new context, but was also adapted on the basis of their socio-rhetorical situation and each nurse's perceptions of and interactions with the genre. They adapted what they knew to fit a new context.

Another study that highlights adaptive transfer comes from A. Suresh Canagarajah (2006b). In his discussion of a Tamil scholar's construction of his introduction for three different research articles—one in his native language for a Sri Lankan publication, one in English for a Sri Lankan publication, and one in English for a European publication—Canagarajah (2006b) details how K. Sivatamby imports rhetorical patterns from his native culture into his academic writing for a Western audience. Sivatamby is, in our terms, adapting a rhetorical form related to his Tamil background for Western academics. In the process, he creates a "multivocal discourse that merges the strengths of [Sri Lankan] scholarly discourse with the dominant conventions of mainstream academic discourse" (Canagarajah, 2006b, p. 598). In the paper written for a Western academic audience, for instance, Sivatamby adopts the same narrative structure he uses in the papers written for the Sri Lankan audience. He does so, though, by couching his narrative analysis in rhetorical moves that would be familiar to Western readers, namely a statement of academic significance, explicit identification of the problem he is addressing, and a forecasting statement regarding his argument. In short, Sivatamby invents what Canagarajah (2006b) calls a "hybrid text," one wherein he adapts writing knowledge from one cultural, linguistic context to fit another. In so doing, Canagarajah (2006b) argues, Sivatamby illustrates the mutability of rhetorical forms and contexts, which corresponds to adaptive transfer's transformative nature, what we often refer to in this chapter as "reshaping."

We recognize that Sivatamby is a scholar and not a student in WAC courses. (For an example of a multilingual graduate student "reshaping" writing as he writes across a multidisciplinary MA program, see Phillips in this collection.) And yet Canagarajah (2006b) uses this example to argue for the need to recognize that multilingual students' native languages and cultures should be treated as resources instead of as problems. Adaptive transfer similarly recognizes multilingual students' diverse backgrounds as resources, though it does not assume every instance of reshaping will be intentional or appropriate. What it does do is provide a set of terms for understanding the complexity of learning to write across contexts, complexity that Canagarajah (2006b) and Parks (2001) illustrate. Specifically, their examples call attention to the dynamic nature of writing knowledge, rhetorical contexts, and genres of writing; highlight the idiosyncratic ways individuals perceive and interact with genres; emphasize the shift from one context to another; and acknowledge the rhetorical manner in which individuals envision how to reshape what they know to fit a new context. Though not about multilingual writers, Lobato's (2003) study of high school algebra students and Brent's (2012) case studies of undergraduates in writing co-ops also provide useful examples of the kinds of reshaping that the framework of adaptive transfer allows writing specialists to identify.

IMPLICATIONS OF ADAPTIVE TRANSFER FOR WAC RESEARCH AND TEACHING

In this section, we explore adaptive transfer's implications for WAC programs, paying particular attention to how it can help such programs adopt culturally inclusive practices regarding multilingual writers. We suggest how adaptive transfer can help reframe questions about multilingual writers across the curriculum by informing WAC research and teaching with WID.

Research

We see adaptive transfer as a lens through which WAC research can be problematized and extended, particularly in regard to how multilingual writers navigate diverse writing demands across the curriculum. Adaptive transfer invites WAC scholars to reframe the questions they ask when researching multilingual writers in WAC programs and to adopt multilayered methodological approaches similar to the ones employed by Parks (2001) and Lobato (2003). Specifically, the framework of adaptive transfer significantly shapes the kinds of questions WAC scholars ask about how multilingual and native English speaking (NES) students learn to write across the disciplines. To demonstrate this, we discuss at length a study that has bearing on WAC, ESL, and transfer: Ilona Leki's (1995)

"Coping Strategies of ESL students in Writing Tasks across the Curriculum." We then discuss two methods that can help researchers identify and understand the diverse ways in which NES and multilingual students navigate unfamiliar writing situations—focus groups and classroom-based reflective writing.

Lamenting the fact that little research existed about ESL experiences in writing courses across the curriculum, Leki's (1995) purpose in her study was "to develop insights into the academic literacy experiences across the curriculum" of multilingual writers. Specifically, she sought to learn "about how ESL students acquire forms and attitudes specific to various disciplinary discourses [and] how their experiences in disciplinary courses shape their understandings of appropriate and inappropriate discourse within those disciplines" (p. 237). Leki (1995) interviewed five ESL students, three graduate students and two undergraduates, whose majors included business, political science, speech, and education. Two of the students were from China and one each was from Taiwan, France, and Finland. Leki (1995) interviewed each student on a weekly basis, observed several classes, analyzed the students' writings, and interviewed their instructors. Based on the data gathered, Leki (1995) identified recurring themes and developed ten categories as a coding scheme. Of the ten coping strategies Leki (1995) identified, two speak directly to questions of transfer: "Relying on past writing experiences" and "Using current or past ESL writing training" (p. 240). (Chapters by Center and Niestepski and Phillips in this collection also draw from Leki's schema to describe the variety of coping strategies their L2 student informants employed to respond to the reading and writing demands of their courses.)

Leki's (1995) overall summary of her findings points toward a key aspect of adaptive transfer: "Although different students in this study used strategies to varying degrees, they all also displayed the flexibility necessary to shift among strategies as needed" (p. 241). While clearly aimed at flexibility in terms of shifting from one strategy to another, this statement nonetheless points toward several of the key characteristics of adaptive transfer, namely that it is idiosyncratic, rhetorical, and cross-contextual. As Leki (1995) shows, such flexibility results from each student's individual background and particular rhetorical situation.

One student Leki (1995) discusses is particularly relevant to adaptive transfer. Julie, an undergraduate business major from France, is described by Leki (1995) as "probably the most successful" student of the five (p. 242). Much of the reason why she was so successful centered on the fact that she "came equipped with a clear, conscious approach to her work" that involved "strategies ... for using past writing experiences" (Leki, 1995, p. 242). Julie had been carefully trained in the French rhetorical style and said that if she felt disorganized, she could always fall back on the three-part framing strategy for writing essays, namely thesis/antithesis/synthesis—look at a topic and develop a position, a counter position, and a synthesizing position. Though Leki (1995) admits that "the rigidity of the structure hemmed [Julie] in and constrained the expansive style she preferred" (p. 242), she does not discuss how Julie might (not) have adapted this strategy in later assignments. She does note, however, that in a later assignment, Julie resisted her teacher's guidelines and abandoned the organizational structure that had served her so well. As Leki (1995) puts it, Julie "rewr[ote] the terms of the assignment to suit what she thought she could do best" (p. 242).

Leki's discussion of Julie offers helpful ways to understand the differences between the kinds of questions traditional transfer would prompt versus the questions that adaptive transfer would raise. Encountering Julie, traditional transfer theorists might have asked questions like the following:

- What discursive features of the tripartite French rhetorical style, if any, did Julie transfer to her history term paper?
- If she transferred none, then what about the new rhetorical situation caused Julie to abandon the thesis/antithesis/synthesis structure?
- Is there a relationship between Julie's decision to resist her professor's assignment and her (in)ability to transfer knowledge from prior writing experiences? If so, what is that relationship?

While such questions could lead to productive insights regarding transfer, they could also limit researchers in terms of identifying a fuller range of the complexity associated with students learning to write across disciplines, genres, and contexts.

Questions derived from the framework of adaptive transfer, on the other hand, would allow researchers to account for a broader range of phenomena:

- How might Julie's background as a native speaker of French allow her to negotiate the novel rhetorical demands of writing the term paper for her history course?
- In what ways might Julie have transformed or adapted the tripartite French rhetorical structure to help her write her history paper? In other words, how might the theory of adaptive transfer reveal ways in which Julie didn't fully abandon that structure but rather reshaped and repurposed key elements of it?
- How might Julie's resistance toward her professor's assignment reflect what Canagarajah (2006b) has called "a strategic and creative choice by the author to attain his or her rhetorical objectives" (p. 591)?
- In resisting her professor's assignment and potentially adapting the tripartite French rhetorical structure, how might Julie have functioned as a

broker (Wenger, 1998) and thus introduced new ways of seeing, doing, and knowing to her academic community of practice?

Our purpose here is not to critique Leki (1995) but rather to show how adaptive transfer could help WAC scholars identify the complex, idiosyncratic ways in which multilingual writers such as Julie might be reshaping prior writing knowledge to fit new contexts. Adaptive transfer offers a lens, in other words, that can help WAC researchers acknowledge the complexity associated with multilingual writers writing across the curriculum. As Russell (2001) notes in his review essay of naturalistic studies in WAC/WID, "qualitative studies point faculty and program directors beyond the research for universal or autonomous approaches toward much more messy—and human—factors" (p. 261). Adaptive transfer, we contend, offers researcher a way to "see" this messiness more fully than traditional notions of transfer allow.

While Leki's (1995) intention was not to explore transfer or adaptive transfer, her study does provide insight into how WAC scholars might go about researching how multilingual writers learn to write across the curriculum. It also points to the benefit of designing multilayered methodologies that employ textual analysis, interviews, observations, rhetorical analysis, and genre analysis to explore adaptive transfer (see also Canagarajah, 2006b; Lobato, 2003; Parks, 2001). Recent WAC research that reflects this emphasis on multifaceted methodologies could also provide WAC scholars with a fuller understanding of how multilingual and native English speakers learn to write across disciplines, genres, and contexts. One example is Stitt-Bergh and Hilgers's (2009) recent discussion of WAC assessment at the University of Hawai'i at Manoa (UHM)—an example that is particularly relevant to our discussion given that Hawai'i recognizes Hawaiian as an official language.

In their article, Stitt-Bergh and Hilgers (2009) name a variety of methods that, if reconceived through the lens of adaptive transfer, could help expand WAC scholarship in productive ways. Some of the methods they name, such as interviews and text analysis, parallel those that Leki (1995) employed. But they also name several additional methodologies that could be useful, including ethnography, focus groups, and surveys. Given their interactional nature, focus groups might be ideally suited to helping WAC researchers identify instances of adaptive transfer, whether with alumni or current students. Focus groups might be particularly useful to help WAC researchers understand how recent graduates reshape prior writing knowledge learned in academic contexts to professional ones. Specifically, focus groups comprised of recent graduates could provide insight into how students transitioned from course to course in university writing contexts and from academic writing contexts to professional writing contexts. As Stitt-Bergh and Hilgers (2009) put it, focus groups could offer insight into "[a]lumni perceptions of workplace writing tasks and their level of preparedness to undertake those writing tasks" (Stitt-Bergh & Hilgers, 2009). Because participants in a focus group might be able to name instances of adaptive transfer more easily when they hear others do so, this approach could be particularly effective for multilingual writers. That said, focus group participants would need to be selected carefully. Participants, whether native English speakers or multilingual students, would need to have an awareness of and language for talking about how they negotiate the demands of shifting from one context to another. Our assumption is that advanced students or recent graduates would have a better-developed awareness and language than less experienced students.

To once again demonstrate how the theory of adaptive transfer could inform such research, we provide sample questions that researchers might ask in such focus groups. From the vantage of traditional transfer, such questions might include the following:

- Think about the writing you learned to do in college. How has it (not) prepared you to do the writing you're now doing in your profession?
- Think about your background as a native speaker of _____. How did that background help or hinder your writing in different classes in college? How has it helped or hindered your workplace writing?
- Reflect back on the different classes you took that included significant writing. How did the writing that you learned to do in earlier classes (not) prepare you to do the writing you did in later classes?

Again, while such questions would certainly provide valuable data, questions reframed using the theory of adaptive transfer could lead to even richer insights:

- Think back on the different classes you took that included significant writing. Describe your process of working through new or unfamiliar writing tasks.
- Think about the writing you do in the workplace. Describe your process of working through new or unfamiliar writing tasks.
- Think about the writing you learned to do in college. In what ways have you had to reshape what you learned in school to fit what you need to do at work?
- Reflect back on the different classes you took that included significant writing. How did your background as a native speaker of _____ help you complete that writing?
- Think of moments when you were told you had made an error or done something wrong. In any of these moments, did you feel like what you did was really a different way of writing that you felt was valuable, useful, and/or original?

Using focus groups as means of studying instances of adaptive transfer has the potential to highlight the diverse linguistic resources of alumni, particularly in terms of the rhetorical patterns multilingual writers might draw on to negotiate unfamiliar writing contexts. Put otherwise, by using the lens of adaptive transfer to analyze the ways multilingual and NES alumni discuss their processes of reshaping in a focus group setting, WAC researchers could learn much about the ways writers adapt writing knowledge learned in one context to suit their rhetorical purposes in another. To get at these adaptations in analyzing focus group transcripts, WAC research might ask the following questions:

- In describing their processes of carrying out writing tasks, what kinds of linguistic resources, rhetorical knowledge, and writing experience do focus group participants discuss?
- How did the focus group participants reuse or reshape prior writing knowledge to suit new contexts?
- In what ways have focus group participants' backgrounds as multilingual writers enabled them to negotiate the novel rhetorical demands of writing in their university coursework and in their places of work?
- Are there cases in which the use of alternative discourses were "matters of design" (Lu, 2004, p. 26) or the result of a "strategic and creative choice by the author to attain his or her rhetorical objectives" (Canagarajah, 2006b, p. 591)?
- What do such cases suggest about the malleability of genres, discourses, or contexts of writing?

Finally, adaptive transfer could also inform classroom-based research. Reflective writing assignments are common in WAC and could be revised to help faculty account for students' processes of adaptive transfer; such writing could also provide datasets that WAC researchers could analyze with the aim of understanding the ways students adapt to new writing tasks. Thaiss and Zawacki (2006), for example, offer a range of practices that faculty across the disciplines might employ, one of which includes, "Give students opportunities for reflecting on their own growth as writers and rhetors, in the academy and as related to the workplaces they will enter" (p. 152). Central to our concerns, such assignments could help students, instructors, and WAC researchers identify how and when adaptive transfer might be occurring. Thaiss and Zawacki (2006) recognize that students are not "tabula rasa[s]" but rather "have a history as writers" that could "either help them in future situations or limit their understanding or performance" (p. 152-3). Many of the reflective assignments they suggest (e.g., literacy narratives, journals, blogs, or eportfolios) could help faculty and WAC researchers understand how students might be drawing on their "history as writers"—and on their multilingual backgrounds—to navigate novel rhetorical tasks.

One particular assignment invites students to "analyze current rhetorical tasks in the context of relevant challenges" associated with prior writing experiences (Thaiss & Zawacki, 2006, p. 153). From the vantage of adaptive transfer, such assignments could also invite multilingual students to analyze current rhetorical tasks in light of a number of other factors, including their linguistic backgrounds and the resemblances they perceive between one writing context and another (Lobato, 2003). Specifically, such assignments could prompt students to identify and describe the rhetorical patterns or linguistic features of their native languages or dialects and then consider how they might use or reshape those patterns to help them complete a current writing task. Teachers might use questions like the following to help their students frame a reflective writing assignment:

- How does this writing task compare with those you have encountered in the past?
- What previous writing experiences might help you fulfill this task?
- How might you need to adapt what you did previously to fit the current rhetorical situation?
- How might the way you talk, think, and write in your native language(s) help you fulfill this task?
- How might your approach to this task differ from the approach of native English speakers?

For WAC researchers, such writing could point to evidence of when and how students reshape or reuse prior writing knowledge in new contexts. To help them analyze these texts, researchers might use questions like the following:

- What resemblances across rhetorical contexts do students perceive? What do these resemblances suggest about the potential malleability and fluidity of genres, discourses, or rhetorical forms?
- What types of prior writing experiences do students identify as potentially helping them fulfill the current task? What do their comments regarding their idiosyncratic processes of adaptation tell us about the nature of adaptive transfer in general? What do their comments suggest about learning to write?
- How do multilingual students perceive their linguistic backgrounds as shaping how they approach current tasks? What do such perceptions tell researchers about the fluidity of languages and contexts of writing?

What evidence, if any, suggests that students are intentionally altering discourses as the result of a "strategic and creative choice by the author to attain his or her rhetorical objectives" (Canagarajah, 2006b, p. 591)?

Overall, the purposes of such measures would be to expand WAC researchers' conceptions of what happens when students write across contexts by identifying the diverse ways in which NES and multilingual students navigate unfamiliar writing situations. It would do so by highlighting the complexity of learning to write, particularly in terms of how individuals reuse or reshape prior rhetorical and linguistic knowledge in new contexts. Understanding how these reshapings occur may help WAC researchers and administrators develop programs that take advantage of multilingual and NES students' diverse resources. As a result, the insights gained from such research would likely have significant implications for faculty who teach with writing in the disciplines.

TEACHING WITH WRITING IN THE DISCIPLINES

Along with helping WAC researchers understand how students navigate novel writing situations, adaptive transfer also has significant implications for the pedagogical practices that WAC professionals promote as they guide faculty to teach with WID. More specifically, WAC specialists might offer the lens of adaptive transfer as means by which to reinvigorate how faculty teaching with WID view language and language change; student writers and texts; contexts of writing; and the aims of writing instruction. In using the lens of adaptive transfer to reshape how faculty understand the nature of learning to write and the aims of teaching with WID, WAC specialists will have an opportunity to address faculty expectations regarding the transfer of writing knowledge. They will also be able to influence the kinds of assignments and evaluation methods that faculty employ in their courses.

The aims of learning to write across the curriculum are often premised on traditional notions of transfer, as is evident in Condon's (2001) articulation of the responsibilities of WAC faculty:

> Teachers—WAC faculty in particular—need to know what they can reasonably expect students to be able to do with and in writing, and they need to match those expectations with the level of expectations that are implicit in the teachers' own course objectives, objectives which, in turn, are determined by their location within the curriculum. Teachers need to know how to build more effective assignments—knowledge that involves both information about the writing students will do after taking a particular course (in careers or in subsequent courses) and information about the writing students have done to that point in the university's curriculum. (p. 31)

Though he does not mention transfer specifically, Condon (2001) is alluding to the possibility that students will be able to apply what they learned in prior courses when they encounter writing tasks in later courses or careers. As such, the implicit view of learning to write is that it occurs with a degree of predictability in terms of what students will learn, how they will learn it, and their ability to transfer such learning. While we certainly agree that it is important for faculty across the disciplines to understand where their course fits into the wider curriculum, we also contend that premising such discussions on traditional notions of transfer will likely result in unrealistic expectations: faculty will expect students to carry over generic, disciplinary, or rhetorical knowledge and will grow frustrated when this does not occur—a frustration that so often motivates criticisms leveled at first-year writing courses from faculty across the disciplines who complain that students "don't know how to write."

In drawing upon the framework of adaptive transfer to guide faculty teaching with WID, however, WAC professionals can promote a different picture of learning to write. Specifically, WAC specialists could use adaptive transfer to complicate faculty expectations regarding what students have learned prior to entering their courses and what they will do with that knowledge following those courses. Regarding multilingual students in particular, WAC professionals could offer adaptive transfer as a means by which to help faculty teaching with WID envision students not as passive recipients of writing knowledge, but as individuals with unique educational and linguistic backgrounds who may appropriate and transform prior or new writing knowledge for their own purposes (Canagarajah 2006b). This is not to say that every multilingual student will consciously reshape prior writing knowledge for his/her own ends, but it does provide space for this possibility. Likewise, WAC specialists might encourage faculty teaching with WID to consider the kinds of intuitive reshaping that may occur as students shift between writing contexts. In short, adaptive transfer might be productively used by WAC specialists to reinvigorate how faculty teaching with WID view language change, student texts, contexts of writing, and the purpose of writing instruction.

LANGUAGE

Adaptive transfer highlights the ways in which languages and language varieties are "always in process, located in and subject to ongoing and varying material practice" (Horner & Trimbur, 2002, p. 596). In recent years, specialists in second language (L2) writing have demonstrated the dynamic nature of language and the multiplicity of language uses (Canagarajah, 2002; Canagarajah, 2006a; Canagarajah, 2006b; Lu, 2004; Lu, 2006; Matsuda, 1997; Matsuda,

2002). These discussions have not only called attention to the need to alter views about language, but have also indicated the extent to which assumptions about writing and writing instruction must change if we are to adequately prepare NES and multilingual writers for the varied tasks they face as students and professionals. To this point, Horner and Trimbur (2002) argue, "If we grant that definitions of academic discourse and competence in it are arbitrary, then the notion of leading students through a fixed developmental sequence of stages to mastery of that language has to be rethought" (p. 620). Recognizing "the heterogeneity and fluctuating nature of writing" necessitates rethinking "how [instructors] design both individual writing courses and curricular programs" (Horner & Trimbur, 2002, p. 620). The framework of adaptive transfer helps to foreground the view that all language is invariably in flux. As such, adaptive transfer has the potential to help faculty across the curriculum rethink the ways that writing is taught in both L1 and L2 writing contexts. The lens of adaptive transfer, that is, might encourage faculty teaching with WID to adopt the kinds of culturally and linguistically inclusive approaches to writing instruction that L2 specialists have called for. These include the utilization of a "code meshing" strategy that will allow multilingual writers to blend standard written English (SWE) with other language varieties (Canagarajah, 2006a, 2006b); the adoption of pedagogical strategies for doing "Living-English Work" (Lu, 2006; p. 605); and the inclusion of pluralized forms of academic writing that have been brought to the fore by various scholars (Schroeder, Fox, & Bizzell, 2002; Thaiss & Zawacki, 2006).

STUDENT TEXTS

By encouraging progressive views of language use through the framework of adaptive transfer, WAC specialists can also help faculty teaching with WID consider how native English speakers and multilingual students might reshape writing skills they've learned in prior contexts to fit new ones. Working from an adaptive transfer perspective, that is, faculty teaching with WID might be less apt to claim that transfer did not occur when students' texts disrupt their expectations. Instead, faculty might ask how students have attempted to adapt writing skills learned in other settings to their current rhetorical situation. Further, if students defy a disciplinary convention, faculty might be more likely to ask students why they made the rhetorical choices they did instead of dismissing those choices as signs of error. The view of language encouraged by the framework of adaptive transfer, in other words, might help broaden faculty perceptions of student texts. Rather than approaching student writing with preconceived notions about what student texts should look like, adaptive transfer encourages faculty to recognize when students attempt to reshape prior knowledge to suit both the demands of the rhetorical situation and students' own objectives.

Such a reconception of student writers and texts could certainly inform teachers' processes of evaluation. For example, faculty working from the perspective of adaptive transfer might ask student writers to complete the kind of reflective writing we discussed earlier. Asking students to "analyze current rhetorical tasks in the context of relevant challenges of the writer's past" (Thaiss & Zawacki, 2006, p. 153) could lead to productive insights for faculty regarding students' writing knowledge, processes, histories, and challenges. By prompting students as Thaiss and Zawacki (2006) suggest, faculty teaching with WID are apt to learn valuable information about the assumptions guiding each writer's rhetorical and linguistic choices. For example, if Leki's (1995) student Julie had been provided an opportunity to reflect on the rhetorical choices she was making while composing her history paper, her teacher may have gained important insights into Julie's reasons for "rewriting the terms of the assignment to suit what she thought she could do best" (Leki, 1995, p. 243). Such information would have been valuable in evaluating Julie's written work because it would have highlighted her rhetorical processes of adaptive transfer. Specifically, it would have underscored that Julie's resistance resulted from a "strategic and creative choice [...] to attain [...] her rhetorical objectives" (Canagarajah, 2006b, p. 591). Such reflective writing could play an even more significant role for students who similarly rewrite assignments but do not fare as well as Julie. In such cases, faculty teaching with WID who know *why* students chose to write an assignment differently would be able to take such motives into account when evaluating written work.

Using this kind of reflective writing as part of teachers' processes of evaluating student texts might also allow faculty teaching with WID to see how factors such as race, class, gender, socioeconomic status, educational history, genre knowledge, and language repertoire shape how individuals encounter new writing situations (DePalma & Ringer, 2011; Zamel & Spack, 2006). Finally, such reflective writing will likely encourage faculty to more readily account for the highly diverse ways in which students will learn to write in new genres, disciplines, and contexts.

Contexts of Writing

Along with informing how faculty teaching with WID interact with students' texts, adaptive transfer might also encourage faculty to embrace a dynamic theory of writing, which has implications for both native English speakers and multilingual writers. In the dynamic model of multilingual writing that Matsuda (1997) proposes, both the writer's and the reader's backgrounds are included in the context of writing. Matsuda (1997) defines this space as "the dynamic environment that surrounds the meeting of the writer and the reader through the text in a particular writing situation" (p. 248). Because adaptive transfer stems from a dynamic view of writing that views contexts for writing as shared, negotiated, and constantly in flux, adaptive transfer has the potential to alter faculty members' views of and attitudes toward NES and multilingual writers across the curriculum. Rather than viewing students solely as novice writers with little to contribute to the discourse communities they are seeking to enter, adaptive transfer encourages faculty to see students as agents who possess a range of valuable language resources and knowledge that might shape their writing in productive ways. Students are thus reconceived of as potential contributors to an ever-changing rhetorical context rather than as repositories of genre knowledge and conventions. They are, in other words, *transformers* rather than *transferers* of writing knowledge and writing contexts (Brent, 2012). When thinking in terms of adaptive transfer, that is, faculty would be more likely to ask how students' texts might influence contexts of writing.

AIMS OF WRITING INSTRUCTION

In addition to influencing the ways faculty across the curriculum approach student texts and view student writers, adaptive transfer also has significant implications for how faculty teaching with WID understand the aims of writing instruction. Rather than seeing the goal of writing instruction as teaching students to master discourses of power, adaptive transfer foregrounds a pedagogy that allows students to question writing conventions at the same time that they are being taught to practice them. Because of this, adaptive transfer might encourage faculty to adopt an alternative discourses approach, such as that noted by Thaiss and Zawacki (2006). Whereas traditional pedagogies assume that all students desire to learn dominant discourses, an alternative discourses approach that informs adaptive transfer might help faculty acknowledge that students have different reasons for learning to write, one of which may include the desire to change contexts of writing. Thaiss and Zawacki (2006), for instance, note that the faculty they interviewed recognized "the dynamism of disciplines," such that "a teacher preparing students for academic writing would be hard pressed to label any discursive practice always unacceptable" (p. 137). Thus, rather than *only* using the expectations of the instructor's academic discourse community as a basis for determining instructional aims, adaptive transfer might urge faculty to also view students' strategic design to create new discourses as a legitimate goal of writing instruction in the disciplines.

While we would be remiss to argue that multilingual students' various reshapings are always conscious and strategic, we would be equally remiss to argue that they never are (Canagarajah, 2006b). In some cases, the decision to depart from disciplinary conventions is purposeful, and the framework of adaptive transfer helps us to recognize this kind of intentional reshaping. When considering adaptive transfer as a guide in structuring curricular goals, faculty members' ideas about how to encourage students to reshape and reform learned writing skills to fit new tasks are liable to shift. Instead of setting the reuse of disciplinary conventions as the primary goal of instruction, the framework of adaptive transfer might prompt faculty members to adopt a multilingual approach that takes full advantage of students' diverse rhetorical and linguistic resources.

CONCLUSION

Adaptive transfer has significant implications for multilingual and NES writers across the curriculum and for the WAC programs that support them. It thus serves as a framework that can help WAC scholars and faculty adjust their practices in ways that effectively serve the growing population of multilingual learners in US higher education. As we continue to realize the "New America" in which we live—an America, as Hall (2009) writes, wherein multilingualism is now more common than monolingualism—it is imperative that WAC scholars account for the complex ways in which all students learn to write across the curriculum. In doing so, it is our hope that WAC scholars and faculty will be able to recognize multilingual writers' rhetorical and linguistic backgrounds as resources and not liabilities (Canagarajah, 2006b). We hope that the framework of adaptive transfer will help achieve such ends, so that WAC researchers and faculty across the disciplines can ethically and effectively help students learn to write—and value students' multilingual, idiosyncratic ways of writing and knowing as part of that enterprise.

REFERENCES

Beach, K. (1999). Consequential transitions: A sociocultural expedition beyond transfer in education. In A. Iran-Nejad & P. D. Pearson (Eds.), *Review of research in education, 24* (pp. 101-139). Washington, DC: American Educational Research Association.

Belcher, D. (1995). Writing critically across the curriculum. In D. Belcher & G. Braine (Eds.), *Academic writing in a second language: Essays on research and pedagogy* (pp. 135-154). Norwood, NJ: Ablex.

Belcher, D. & Braine, G. (1995). *Academic writing in a second language: Essays on research and pedagogy*. Norwood, NJ: Ablex.

Bergmann, L. S. & Zepernick, J. (2007). Disciplinarity and transfer: Students' perceptions of learning to write. *WPA: Writing Program Administration, 31*(1/2), 124-49.

Bloch, J., Condon, W., Hickey, D., McLeary, L., Matsuda, P. K., Rilling, S., and Palmquist, M. (2001). Connecting WAC and ESL? *Academic. Writing, 2*. Retrieved from http://wac.colostate.edu/aw/forums/

Bradford, J. D. & Schwartz, D. L. (1999). Rethinking transfer: A simple proposal with multiple implications. In A. Iran-Nejad & P. D. Pearson (Eds.), *Review of research in education, 24* (pp. 61-100). Washington, DC: American Educational Research Association.

Brent, D. (2012). Crossing boundaries: Co-op students relearning to write. *College Composition and Communication, 63*(4), 558-592.

Broudy, H.S. (1977). Types of knowledge and purposes of education. In R. C. Anderson, R. J. Spiro, & W. E. Montague (Eds.), *Schooling and the acquisition of knowledge* (pp. 1-17). Hillsdale, NJ: Erlbaum.

Canagarajah, A. S. (2002). *Critical academic writing and multilingual students*. Ann Arbor, MI: University of Michigan Press.

Canagarajah, A. S. (2006a). The place of world Englishes in composition: Pluralization continued. *College Composition and Communication, 57*, 586-619.

Canagarajah, A. S. (2006b). Toward a writing pedagogy of shuttling between languages: learning from multilingual writers. *College English, 68*, 589-604.

Carroll, L. A. (2002). *Rehearsing new roles: How college students develop as writers*. Carbondale: Southern Illinois University Press.

Condon, W. (2001). Accommodating complexity: WAC program evaluation in the age of accountability. In S. H. McLeod, E. Miraglia, M. Soven, & C. Thaiss (Eds.), *WAC for the new millennium: Strategies for continuing writing-across-the-curriculum programs* (pp. 28-51). Urbana, IL: NCTE.

Conference on College Composition and Communication. (2009). *Statement on second language writing and writers*. Retrieved from http://www.ncte.org/cccc/resources/positions/secondlangwriting

Connor, U. (1996). *Contrastive rhetoric: Cross-cultural aspects of second-language writing*. New York: Cambridge University Press.

Currie, P. (1999). Transferable skills: Promoting student research. *English for Specific Purposes, 18*(1), 329-345.

DePalma, M.-J. & Ringer, J. M. (2011). Toward a theory of adaptive transfer: Expanding disciplinary discussions of "transfer" in second-language writing and composition studies. *Journal of Second Language Writing, 20*(2), 134-47.

Dias, P., Freedman, A., Medway, P., and Paré, A. (1999). *Worlds apart: Acting and writing in academic and workplace contexts.* Mahwah, NJ: Lawrence Erlbaum.

Dively, R. L. & Nelms, G. (2007). Perceived roadblocks to transferring knowledge from first-year composition to writing-intensive major courses: A pilot study. *Writing Program Administration, 31*(1/2), 214-240.

Downs, D. & Wardle, E. (2007). Teaching about writing, righting misconceptions: (Re)envisioning "first-year composition" as "introduction to writing studies." *College Composition and Communication, 58(4)*, 552-84.

Dyson, A. H. (1999). Transforming transfer: Unruly children, contrary texts, and the persistence of pedagogical order. In A. Iran-Nejad & P. D. Pearson (Eds.), *Review of research in education, 24* (pp. 141-171). Washington, DC: American Educational Research Association.

Grabe, W. & Kaplan, R. B. (1989). Writing in a second language: Contrastive rhetoric. In D. M. Johnson & D. H. Rohen (Eds.), *Richness in writing: Empowering ESL students* (pp. 263-83). White Plains, NY: Longman.

Greeno, J. G., Smith, D. R., & Moore, J. L. (1993). Transfer of situated learning. In D. K. Detterman and R. J. Sternberg (Eds.), *Transfer on trial: Intelligence, cognition, and instruction* (pp. 99-167). Norwood, NJ: Ablex Publishing Corporation.

Hall, J. (2009). WAC/WID in the next America: Redefining professional identity in the age of the multilingual majority. *The WAC Journal, 20*. Retrieved from http://wac.colostate.edu/journal/vol20/hall.pdf

Haskell, R. E. (1998). *Reengineering corporate training: Intellectual capital and transfer of learning.* Westport, CT: Quorum Books.

Haswell, R. H., Briggs, T. L., Fay, J. A., Gillen, N. K., Harrill, R., Shupala, A. M., Trevino, S. S. (1999). Context and rhetorical reading strategies: Haas and Flower (1988) revisited. *Written Communication, 16*, 3-28.

Hinds, J. (1983a). Contrastive rhetoric: Japanese and English. *Text, 3*(2), 183-95.

Hinds, J. (1983b). Linguistics in written discourse in particular languages: Contrastive studies: English and Japanese. In R. B. Kaplan (Ed.), *Annual review of applied linguistics III* (pp. 78-84). Rowley, MA: Newbury House.

Hinds, J. (1990). Inductive, deductive, quasi-inductive: Expository writing in Japanese, Korean, Chinese, and Thai. In U. Connor & A. M. Johns (Eds.),

Coherence in writing: Research and pedagogical perspectives (pp. 87-110). Alexandria, VA: TESOL.

Horner, B. & Lu, M. (2007). *Resisting monolingualism in "English": Reading and writing the politics of language*. Paper presented at the University of New Hampshire, Durham, NH.

Horner, B. & Trimbur, J. (2002). English only and US college composition. *College Composition and Communication, 53*, 594-630.

James, M. A. (2006a). Teaching for transfer in ELT. *ELT Journal, 60*(2), 151-159.

James, M. A. (2006b). Transfer of learning from a university content-based EAP course. *TESOL Quarterly, 40*, 783-806.

James, M. A. (2009). "Far" transfer of learning outcomes from an ESL writing course: Can the gap be bridged? *Journal of Second Language Writing, 18*, 69-84.

Johns, A. M. (1995). Teaching classroom and authentic genres: Initiating students into academic cultures and discourses. In D. Belcher & G. Braine (Eds.), *Academic writing in a second language: Essays on research and pedagogy* (pp. 277-91). Norwood, NJ: Ablex.

Johns, A. M. (1997). *Text, role, and context: Developing academic literacies.* New York: Cambridge University Press.

Kang, J. Y. (2005). Written narratives as an index of L2 competence in Korean EFL learners. *Journal of Second Language Writing, 14*, 259-79.

Kaplan, R. B. (1966). Cultural thought patterns in intercultural education. *Language Learning, 16*, 1-20.

Kaplan, R.B. (1988). Contrastive rhetoric and second language learning: Notes towards a theory of contrastive rhetoric. In A. C. Purves (Ed.), *Writing across languages and cultures* (pp. 275-304). Newbury Park, CA: Sage Publications.

Kobayashi, H. (1984). Rhetorical patterns in English and Japanese. *Dissertation Abstracts International, 45*(S), 2425A.

Kubota, R. (1998). An investigation of L1-L2 transfer in writing among Japanese university students: Implications for contrastive rhetoric. *Journal of Second Language Writing, 7*, 69-100.

Lave, J. (1988). *Cognition in practice: Mind, mathematics, and culture in everyday life.* Cambridge, UK: Cambridge University Press.

Lave, J. & Wenger, E. (1991). *Situated learning: Legitimate peripheral participation.* Cambridge: Cambridge University Press.

Leki, I. (1995). Coping strategies of ESL students in writing tasks across the curriculum. *TESOL Quarterly, 29*(2), 235-260.

Leki, I. (2007). *Undergraduates in a second language: Challenges and complexities of academic literacy development.* New York: Lawrence Erlbaum Associates.

Leki, I., & Carson, J. G. (1997). "Completely different worlds": EAP and the writing experiences of ESL students in university courses. *TESOL Quarterly, 31*(1), 39-69.

Lobato, J. (2003). How design experiments can inform a rethinking of transfer and vice versa. *Educational Researcher, 32*(1), 17-20.

Lu, M. (2004). An essay on the work of composition: Composing English against the order of fast capitalism. *College Composition and Communication, 56*, 16-50.

Lu, M. (2006). Living English work. *College English, 68*, 605-18.

MacDonald, S. P. & Cooper, C. R. (1992). Contributions of academic and dialogic journals to writing about literature. In Herrington, A. & Moran, C. (Eds.), *Writing, teaching, and learning in the disciplines.* (pp. 137-155). New York: Modern Language Association.

Matsuda, P. K. (1997). Contrastive rhetoric in context: A dynamic model of L2 writing. In T. Silva & P. K. Matsuda (Eds.), *Landmark essays on second language writing* (pp. 241-255). Mahwah, NJ: Erlbaum.

Matsuda, P. K. (2002). Alternative discourses: a synthesis. In C. Schroeder, H. Fox, and P. Bizzell (Eds.), *ALT/DIS: Alternative discourses and the academy* (pp. 191-96). Portsmouth, NH: Boynton/Cook.

McCarthy, L. P. (1987). A stranger in strange lands: a college student writing across the curriculum. *Research in the Teaching of English, 21*(3), 233-65.

McLeod, S. H. & Miraglia, E. (2001). Writing across the curriculum in a time of change. In McLeod, S. H., Miraglia, E., Soven, M., and Thaiss, C. (Eds.), *WAC for the new millennium: Strategies for continuing writing-across-the-curriculum programs* (pp. 1-27). Urbana: NCTE.

Oi, K. (1984). Cross-cultural differences in rhetorical patterning: A study of Japanese and English. *Dissertation Abstracts International, 4, 5*(8), 251 IA.

Parks, S. (2001). Moving from school to the workplace: Disciplinary innovation, border crossings, and the reshaping of a written genre. *Applied Linguistics, 22*, 405-438.

Petraglia, J. (1995). *Reconceiving writing, rethinking writing instruction.* Mahwah, NJ: Erlbaum.

Pierce, K. A., Duncan, M. K., Gholson, B., Ray, G. E., & Kamhi, A. G. (1993). Cognitive load, schema acquisition, and procedural adaptation in nonisomorhpic analogical transfer. *Journal of Educational Psychology, 85*, 66-74.

Prior, P. A. (1998). *Writing/disciplinarity: A sociohistoric account of literate activity in the academy.* Mahwah, NJ: Erlbaum.

Riazi, A. (1997). Acquiring disciplinary literacy: A social-cognitive analysis of text production and learning among Iranian graduate students of education. *Journal of Second Language Writing, 6*, 105-37.

Royer, J. M. (1979). Theories of the transfer of learning. *Educational Psychologist, 14*, 53-69.

Royer, J. M., Mestre, J. P., & Dufresne, R. J. (2005). Framing the transfer problem. In J. P. Mestre (Ed.), *Transfer of learning from a modern multidisciplinary perspective* (pp. vii-xxvi). Greenwich, CT: Information Age Publishing.

Russell, D. (1995). Activity theory and its implications for writing instruction. In J. Petraglia (Ed.), *Reconceiving writing, rethinking writing instruction* (pp. 51-77). Mahwah, NJ: Erlbaum.

Russell, D. (2001). Where do the naturalistic studies of WAC/WID point? A research review. In S. H. McLeod, E. Miraglia, M. Soven, & C. Thaiss (Eds.), *WAC for the new millennium: Strategies for continuing writing-across-the-curriculum programs* (pp. 259-98). Urbana: NCTE.

Schroeder, C. L., Fox, H., & Bizzell, P. (2002). *ALT DIS: Alternative discourses and the academy*. Portsmouth, NH: Boynton/Cook.

Simpson, J. M. (2000). Topical structure analysis of academic paragraphs in English and Spanish. *Journal of Second Language Writing, 9* (3), 239-309.

Smit, D. W. (2004). *The end of composition studies*. Carbondale: Southern Illinois University Press.

Snow, M. A. (1993). Discipline-based foreign language teaching: Implications from ESL/EFL. In M. Krueger & F. Ryan (Eds.), *Language and content: Discipline- and content-based approaches to language study*. Lexington, MA.: D.C. Heath & Co.

Spack, R. (1988). Initiating ESL students into the academic discourse community: How far should we go? *TESOL Quarterly, 22*, 29-51.

Spack, R. (1997). The acquisition of academic literacy in a second language: A longitudinal case study. *Written Communication, 14*(1), 3-62.

Stitt-Bergh, M. & Hilgers, T. (2009, December 3). Program assessment: Processes, propagation, and culture change. [Special issue of Writing Across the Curriculum and Assessment] *Across the Disciplines, 6*. Retrieved from http://wac.colostate.edu/atd/assessment/stittbergh_hilgers.cfm

Swales, J. (1990). *Genre analysis: English in academic and research settings*. Cambridge: Cambridge University Press.

Thaiss, C., & Zawacki, T. M. (2006). *Engaged writers and dynamic disciplines: Research on the academic writing life*. Portsmouth, NH: Boynton/Cook Heinemann.

Thomas, F. L. (2009, December 3). Developing a culture of writing at Virginia State University: A new writing emphasis. [Special issue of Writing Across the Curriculum and Assessment] *Across the Disciplines, 6*. Retrieved from http://wac.colostate.edu/atd/assessment/thomas.cfm

Voss, J. F. (1989). On the composition of experts and novices. In E. Maimon, B. Nodine, & F. W. O'Connor (Eds.), *Thinking, reasoning, and writing* (pp. 69-84). New York: Longman.

Walvoord, B. E. & McCarthy, L. P. (1990). *Thinking and writing in college: a naturalistic study of students in four disciplines.* Urbana: NCTE.

Wardle, E. (2007). Understanding "transfer" from FYC: Preliminary results of a longitudinal study. *Writing Program Administration, 31*(1/2), 65-85.

Wardle, E. (2009). "Mutt genres" and the goal of FYW: Can we help students write the genres of the university? *College Composition and Communication, 60*(4), 765-89.

Wenger, E. (1998). *Communities of practice: Learning, meaning, and identity.* New York: Cambridge University Press.

Zamel, V. & Spack, R. (Eds). (2004). *Crossing the curriculum: Multilingual learners in college classrooms.* Mahwah, NJ: Lawrence Erlbaum.

CHAPTER 2
DEVELOPING RESOURCES FOR SUCCESS: A CASE STUDY OF A MULTILINGUAL GRADUATE WRITER

Talinn Phillips
Ohio University

> *This is the story of Chozin, a graduate multilingual writer who was an unlikely success story. I followed Chozin through two years in a writing-intensive, interdisciplinary graduate program; here I describe the numerous strategies he developed to overcome writing failures and a low level of English proficiency and then consider how his experience might benefit other writers. Chozin's story deepens our understanding of the strategies multilingual graduate writers use to navigate their programs of study.*

Chozin (Koh-ZEEN) was a bright, engaging Indonesian graduate student who participated in my research project on how international multilingual graduate writers learn to write for their fields. Initially a very poor writer in English, Chozin managed to overcome the low expectations of his advisor (and this researcher) to become a highly successful graduate student in his interdisciplinary program and a much-improved writer. Chozin was a very unlikely success story; thus his experience highlights the resourcefulness that multilingual writers may bring to their writing development. Chozin's particular resourcefulness also deepens our understanding of the strategies multilingual learners use when they encounter writing assignments in the US academy. Chozin's story reminds us too of the value of having a support network and of receiving feedback as we write. Finally, his story provides a compelling example of what it means for a multilingual graduate student to write across multiple, largely unfamiliar, disciplines and of the value of WAC to international students who may not be well prepared for the demands of writing in graduate school.

I begin by describing the larger study that Chozin was part of and then introduce readers to Chozin and his primary professor, Dr. G. before moving to a discussion of some of the key strategies that Chozin developed in order to succeed—strategies for receiving useful feedback, for collaborating successfully on group projects, for managing the data collection process for his papers, and for improving his overall literacy. I conclude by considering the implications of Chozin's experience.

INTERNATIONAL GRADUATE STUDENTS' DEVELOPMENT AS WRITERS

Chozin's eventual success was largely the result of his own diligence and resourcefulness; he was quick to develop successful strategies to overcome his writing challenges and developed a number of these strategies throughout his graduate career. Chozin's case study adds to a growing body of research on international graduate students, including well-known studies by Casanave and Leki. Research by Casanave (2002) and a research collection by Casanave and Li (2008) examine international graduate students' development as writers in great detail. Casanave and Li's (2008) edited collection, for example, provides an unusual yet useful way of understanding how graduate students learn to write. Structured as a series of personal narratives, many by non-native speakers of English, on the graduate writing life, most of the chapters focus on writers encountering new writing challenges and subsequently developing a better understanding of themselves and/or of writing in their disciplines. In *Writing Games*, Casanave (2002) includes a chapter on the academic enculturation of five graduate MATESOL (master's degree in TESOL) students, some of whom were native-English speakers and others non-native English speakers. Casanave's aim is "to look closely at students' experiences with and attitudes toward writing and to discover any changes over time in how the students viewed themselves and their field" (p. 93). Casanave employs the metaphor of "writing games" as she focuses on the writers' shifting identities and on how the MATESOL program functions as a community of practice. Explaining her choice of "game" to describe such a serious topic, Casanave writes that the notion of writing games

> seems to depict people's sense that academic writing consists of rule- and strategy-based practices, done in interaction with others for some kind of personal and professional gain, and that it is learned through repeated practice rather than just from a guidebook of how to play. (p. 3)

As I'll show, Chozin learned to play the "writing game," not only through repeated writing experiences but also through the strategy-based practices he developed. (Also see DePalma & Ringer [this volume] for an examination of how L2 writers can and do become effective agents of their own learning as they develop strategies to cope with unfamiliar writing demands and expectations through the process of adaptive transfer). Chozin's story provides an example of how one graduate student adapted his practices to carry out—and sometimes resist—the writing tasks assigned across his courses.

Leki's (1995) study "Coping Strategies of ESL Students in Writing Tasks Across the Curriculum" was the first to attempt to research and catalogue the strategies that multilingual writers employed when they encountered writing assignments. Leki followed five students (three graduates and two undergraduates) through a semester of courses and catalogued their strategic moves, grouping them as follows: clarifying strategies, focusing strategies, relying on past writing experiences, taking advantage of first language/culture, using current experience or feedback, looking for models, using current or past ESL writing training, accommodating teachers' demands, resisting teachers' demands and managing competing demands (1995, p. 240). As I will discuss, Leki's categories provide a good context for analyzing Chozin's resourcefulness at the same time that his experiences also problematize some of Leki's (to be fair, preliminary) categories and suggest new or broader ones. For example, whereas Leki's participants relied on past successful writing experiences for positive transfer to other writing tasks, one of Chozin's most effective strategies was to learn from failure, i.e. to take negative writing experiences and craft a plan to avoid the same outcome in the future.

RESEARCH METHODOLOGY

While in this chapter I'm focusing on Chozin, he was one of five participants in my two-year, IRB-approved study on how incoming international multilingual graduate students learn to write for their fields and the resources they use to support their writing development. Though Chozin is only one writer, Newkirk (1992) argues that although qualitative approaches like the case study have no internal mechanism for generalization (such as a large, representative sample size), these approaches instead allow readers to perform the act of generalization; readers determine whether the case study looks like their own students or classrooms and therefore whether it should inform, alter, or trigger an overhaul of their own theories and pedagogies. Further, Newkirk argues that "the case study gains generalizability through particularity—

through the density of detail, the selection of incidents, the narrative skill of the researcher" (1992, p. 130). The case study thus functions as a heuristic, offering possible explanations and possible solutions to its readers. The reader is then prompted to engage in the analytical act of assessing which features of the case study might best be generalized to his/her own situation and which are irrelevant, perhaps because of differences in contexts. I thus offer Chozin's story and suggest potential implications, but leave readers to make their own determinations.

Chozin and other participants were recruited through campus flyers and email messages to various international student organizations. I sought and chose participants who were beginning their programs and who had not previously attended an English-medium institution other than to take English-language classes; therefore, these writers would be new to graduate school and new to taking disciplinary courses in English. I also attempted to recruit participants who were linguistically and disciplinarily diverse, though with limited success. Two participants were Chinese, one was Sudanese, and two were Indonesian, one of whom was Chozin. Both Chozin and the other Indonesian participant were in the Southeast Asian Studies program. The remaining students were in linguistics, environmental studies, and communication studies.

I followed these five writers through the first year of their programs and continued to follow Chozin and another participant for a second year until they completed their master's degrees. I recorded audio interviews with them at least twice a month, collected copies of the syllabi for their courses and their drafts and final papers with teacher responses, and interviewed the instructors who made themselves available after the term had ended. For Chozin, I analyzed six seminar papers, two conference papers, three drafts of his thesis, four short projects for blogs and local newspapers, and nearly two dozen focus/response papers and other short assignments. He provided me with papers from his anthropology, political science, biological sciences, geography, and graduate writing classes.

I also read writing center observation reports if and when the students worked with writing tutors. Participating in writing tutoring was not a requirement for participation in the study, however. Although I was interested in how participants used the writing center, I was far more interested in the resources that they chose for themselves so that I could see the full range of resources they chose to employ as they developed as writers and scholars.

After the data collection was complete, the interviews were transcribed, read repeatedly and analyzed to understand the resources the writers used to support their writing development. I coded the data for both institutional resources like the writing center and graduate writing classes as well as personal resources such as developing a network of proofreaders. Bishop (1999), among others, argues that the validity of qualitative results is strengthened through data triangulation, investigator triangulation, and methodological triangulation, or in other words, by collecting multiple types of data from multiple sources and by multiple means. This study used three groups of "investigators," these being myself, the writing center staff, and the student writers' teachers, as well as multiple types of data. However, I was the only person who coded the data.

I chose to focus on Chozin in this chapter because he was enrolled in an interdisciplinary master's program in Southeast Asian Studies, and thus was being asked to write in anthropology, sociology, marine biology, political science, and geography courses, many of which were writing intensive. I look primarily at the first year of his program as that is when most of his writing for his courses occurred, thus when he was receiving the most feedback. Chozin completed his thesis quite quickly and with little problem by the middle of his second year.

I also focus on Chozin because he was such an unlikely success story. At the beginning of my study his English was very weak. He had one of the lowest proficiency levels I'd encountered in over five years of tutoring our campus's multilingual graduate students.[1] Moreover, I knew some of his fall quarter professors, and I knew how much writing they required of their students. Having tutored a number of students in the Southeast Asian Studies program, my initial assessment was that Chozin wouldn't be able to complete it. I was very happy to be proven wrong when he graduated on time, having presented at international conferences and having been awarded his department's outstanding thesis prize.

INTRODUCING CHOZIN

Chozin's undergraduate degree was from a Bahasa-medium institution in Indonesia where he had studied marine biology. He had just arrived at our university from coordinating tsunami relief work near Aceh, Indonesia, and had contacted me via email after learning about my study during international student orientation and from the international student association. We arranged an initial meeting so that Chozin could learn more about the requirements of the study and so that I could assess his suitability as a participant. After Chozin had formally enrolled in the study, we began meeting every week or two. From the beginning, Chozin was friendly and easy to talk with. He was quite willing to share his own struggles and as his language proficiency grew, so did his willingness to talk. In our early interviews, I would struggle to understand him, and we would spend a fair amount of time negotiating meaning and clarifying what he had to say. By the end of the study, he required very little prompting from me in order to talk for long stretches about his writing and research. Chozin seemed to develop a reflective habit of mind over the course of his graduate career, and as that habit of reflection developed, he became more and more willing to share what he was learning about himself as a writer.

In our initial interview, Chozin reported that he had struggled through his undergraduate work, that he had not graduated on time, and that he had often been behind on his work. He was now entering a master's program "centered on interdisciplinary curricula that combine the traditional foundations in the social sciences and humanities, components within the natural sciences, and the professions" (Center for International Studies, para. 1). In this program, students take a standard core of courses which are themselves interdisciplinary (educational research, geography, anthropology), and they then have wide latitude to specialize in a particular aspect of Southeast Asian culture; Chozin chose to specialize in maritime studies.

Given Chozin's undergraduate struggles, he was now entering a challenging master's program that would require him to take courses in multiple disciplines, to engage in regular field research and intensive writing, and to do all of this in a second language, without having had prior writing instruction in English, Javanese, or Bahasa. In their examination of the roles of writing in international academic contexts, Russell and Foster (2002) note that the "ubiquitous tradition [of first-year composition] in the United States—perhaps the only common denominator in what is otherwise a sprawling and diverse higher education system—strikes many teachers in other nations as strange" (p. 7). Russell and Foster remind us that Chozin's lack of writing instruction before entering the US academy is more likely to be the rule than the exception among multilingual writers, making their task of succeeding in the academy—and doing so at the graduate level—even more difficult.[2]

Chozin readily acknowledged that he struggled with writing. His other English language skills were weak as well, and these weaknesses were highlighted by the nature of research in his program. Over the course of his first year, Chozin's assorted writing projects required him to interview farmers at the local farmers' market, Caucasian American-born Muslims, a Southeast Asian, a person who had given him a gift, university food service personnel, and Indonesian blast fishers. Each of these interviews constituted the primary source for different writing projects and formed the bulk of the content for his respective papers. The necessity of conducting all these interviews to complete so many different papers made his language difficulties all the more obvious. It also meant that he struggled with the entire writing process, not just with composing, but also with comprehending the input needed to produce even a rough draft.

When I first asked Chozin to describe his writing ability, he identified organization and length of composing time as his primary difficulties: "I have problem with writing to arrange the uh, paragraph. Uh, yeah. It's maybe for my friend, when we have assignment two page, she already just need one hours but for me, need four hours to do that."[3] Chozin's experience is consistent with research in second language studies that has shown that multilingual writers need more time to compose (Silva, 1993, pp. 661-662). In addition to struggling to understand the language input of his interviewees, Chozin did indeed have problems with organization, as my own assessment of his work confirmed, along with development and with integrating secondary sources. Chozin did make marked improvement in composing fluency and in writing style over the course of his program. He was less successful at improving his organization, development, and source use and, in fact, never gave any indication that he recognized these problems. Rather, he focused on increasing his fluency and building his vocabulary and on developing strategies to manage other problems that he encountered during his program. I will return to Chozin and the strategies he developed to succeed below; first, however, it is important to introduce another research informant, Chozin's recruiter, teacher, and advisor, Dr. G.

INTRODUCING DR. G.

Chozin's story would be incomplete without including Dr. G., a faculty member in his program. Dr. G. was interested in writing studies and had become a convert to writing-to-learn theory through a series of WAC workshops. The WAC program at this institution was fairly new and was growing quickly at that time. John Bean's (2001) *Engaging Ideas,* particularly his extensive use of writing-to-learn activities, had been a focal point in the WAC program's faculty development seminars.

Chozin took one course with Dr. G. each quarter of his first year, and each of those courses utilized writing-to-learn activities extensively, typically in the form of weekly "focus papers." These were 1-2 page response papers that sometimes became dialogue journals as described by Carter and Gradin (2001). The papers did not have specific prompts; instead the topics were student-driven based on their reaction to the readings. In some cases the papers were simply submitted as response papers. At other times students would be asked to trade papers during class and engage in written dialogue about the ideas in the paper. The papers were treated as informal writing projects, with comments focused on students' ideas and grades based on engagement.

Dr. G. therefore provided me with vital insight into Chozin's development as a student and a writer. As Chozin's advisor, he was also a key player in that development since Chozin's thesis was an extension of Dr. G.'s research. Chozin had actually been directly recruited by Dr. G. while Dr. G. was doing field research in Indonesia. Dr. G.'s insight was also important because he was the only one of Chozin's professors who agreed to be interviewed.[4] Chozin was clearly fond of Dr. G. and respected him. He had formed this relationship before even arriving at the university, and he continued to cultivate it throughout his program and beyond. I return now to the strategies Chozin developed as he made his way through his master's program.

DEVELOPING STRATEGIES TO SUCCEED

During his first year Chozin developed a number of strategies to manage the writing process and to improve his writing. Throughout this section I contextualize Chozin's strategic moves within the categories described by Leki (1995). Chozin never mentioned engaging in some of the strategies Leki identifies and he complicates others, as I discuss below. Chozin also developed several other strategies not mentioned by Leki's participants, as I noted earlier, including seeking feedback, developing a personalized course, and managing the data collection process. I begin by discussing Chozin's strategy for seeking feedback.

A Network of Editors

Chozin sought feedback throughout his program from teachers, professional editors, and from a carefully developed network of peers that I term his "editor-friends." Initially these friends were other Indonesians, but after his first quarter Chozin began seeking out native-English-speaking (NES) students in his courses and asking them for help. He preferred to work with NES students who were also studying Bahasa, thus enabling him to "trade" writing tutoring for language tutoring. Being able to provide help in return seemed to make Chozin feel better about asking for assistance and thus allowed him to develop a more equitable relationship with his editor-friends.

It was obvious from our conversations that these editor-friends provided Chozin with a measure of moral support, but I found no evidence that they helped him engage in the kind of substantive revision that, based on my own assessment, his papers needed. When I compared first drafts, edited drafts, and final drafts, only sentence-level changes and corrections were evident yet there were often significant problems with development and organization. In some cases I could not identify a purpose and, in several others, basic requirements of a genre were missing (e.g. a conclusion), a problem two of his teachers noted in their final paper comments. It is possible that Chozin was unable or unwilling to enact more substantive revision based on conversations with his editor-friends, but their written comments were focused almost exclusively on sentence-level issues, not on development, organization, genre, or other global issues. To Chozin, though, these corrections were apparently adequate, even though professors continued to lower his grades because of his writing. He often identified NES students in his classes who were also studying Javanese and asked them to read his writing. Chozin identified these students and then sought to "trade" writing tutoring for language tutoring.

Finally, although I (and, one might argue, Chozin's professors) found the feedback provided by Chozin's editor-friends to be lacking, Chozin *was* proactively seeking writing support. From his first quarter of graduate school, Chozin developed the valuable habit of seeking out feedback on his work. During his program he also transitioned to working with more professionalized "editor-friends." Chozin began working regularly with his graduate writing teacher in spring quarter of his first year, which proved much more successful, as I discuss below. He also began working with a semi-professional editor in the community who had been recommended by a professor. It's difficult to imagine that Chozin received no benefit from so much editing and so many conversations about his writing, even if we can also imagine how he could have benefited more from a reader who challenged him to improve his organization, develop his ideas, and use secondary sources more effectively.

Developing a Personalized Course

Chozin developed a number of new strategies in winter quarter, beginning by enrolling in a graduate writing course to "accommodate his professor," a strategy described in Leki's (1995) taxonomy. During fall quarter, Dr. G. deemed Chozin's writing so poor that he told Chozin to enroll in a graduate writing class for winter quarter. In my meeting with Dr. G., he had noted that Chozin had significant problems with organization and described his English skills as "among the worst" he had ever seen in the program. He described Chozin as being "in that category that I kind of dread because they know enough English to pass the test,[5] but not enough to write a clear paper by himself."

Chozin took Dr. G.'s advice this time, enrolling in the second of a sequence of three cross-disciplinary graduate writing courses that were designed for international multilingual writers and which were taught by faculty from the TESOL program. The courses were Introduction to Graduate Writing,

Advanced Graduate Writing, and Thesis/Dissertation Writing. Although the courses were designed as a sequence, there were no prerequisites; therefore, students could take any course at any point. During the winter quarter, Chozin took the middle course, Advanced Graduate Writing. In this course students completed a variety of summaries and critiques that were sometimes based on texts he was reading in his disciplinary classes.

Chozin seemed to benefit minimally from this course, however. He received little positive feedback from his teacher, and the feedback he did receive seemed overly critical.[6] She identified problems like "lang. is non-idiomatic" and "sentence structure" but rarely offered Chozin alternative language. Her final comments on his first paper, a critique of two articles, identified problems but did not seem to offer any particularly constructive comments towards revision or future writing projects. She wrote:

> You are clearly confused in this assignment. 1) The outline is wrong. 2) Discussion of comparison/contrast between the articles is too short. 3) There is no evaluation/response part that conveys your opinion (or position) in response to the articles summarized.

Throughout the quarter her comments suggested that he did not understand the assignments he was given. He never mentioned any specific benefits from the class and also seemed slightly frustrated that the course did not include "grammar instruction," something that he believed he needed. Chozin was most enthusiastic about the class when discussing the individual conferences he'd had with his teacher. After one conference, Chozin said, "She give me comments and she give me, like, tips or strategies how to write it, how to compose the paragraph, how to arrange the whole writing with some paragraphs. She give me a lot of lessons." When Chozin took the graduate writing course a second time, as I describe in the next paragraph, his teacher worked with him to create a more individualized experience.

In the spring term Chozin attempted to sign up for the third writing class, Thesis/Dissertation Writing, so that he could work on his thesis proposal; however the course was full. Instead, he registered for Advanced Graduate Writing again, but this time with a different teacher. At the teacher's suggestion, he worked with her to develop what was essentially a personalized syllabus so that he could still benefit from repeating the class.[7] The spring course primarily consisted of one-on-one tutoring with the instructor as Chozin wrote his thesis proposal. (This iteration of the course is similar to the graduate writing seminar described by Fredericksen & Mangelsdorf [this volume], which requires students to create individual learning contracts based on writing tasks assigned in other coursework.) He was able to develop a positive relationship with this new teacher and found this course much more beneficial. In a sense, Chozin added his graduate writing teacher to his network of editor-friends. She provided frequent proofreading and feedback as Chozin wrote his thesis proposal during spring quarter. Yet again, Chozin had taken a writing struggle and developed a strategy to succeed.

FINDING THE RIGHT COLLABORATORS FOR GROUP PROJECTS

One of the greatest challenges Chozin faced during his program was devising a strategy for completing group projects. On the surface, Chozin had been quite successful in his first quarter and had earned strong grades. But it turned out that Chozin had—involuntarily—played a *very* minimal role in writing a group paper that comprised a large portion of the grade in his geography class. Chozin's group experience in this class was a major site of frustration for him. I quote extensively from our conversation here so that readers can see Chozin's own description of the group project and then compare it to his description of a group project in a later course.[8] When asked about the outcome of his geography paper, Chozin reported:

> C: In the geography class, actually, I have paper, but it's not individual paper. We make, like, report for my project for people in my group, and actually, I didn't—I didn't write much because all my group know that I'm not English speaking, so they write. I do the reading, I do some research with them, and they write a lot of the report .... So the report is not mine, actually; it's not my writing. [It's] my friends' [members of the group] writing.
>
> Talinn (T): So did you feel ... like, did it bother you at all that everybody else did the writing for that project?
>
> C: Uh, actually, just once doing the writing. I mean, I send just my conclusion—my report and then give it to another and she write it for to be combined and edited ....
>
> T: Were you happy with how you did with that class?
>
> C: In the group? In the group I feel like I didn't enjoy in the

group. In the class I enjoy, but in the group I didn't enjoy because, uh, because everybody is, um, native speaker but I am in the group. I am limited in my language and everybody talking ... I am just quiet in my group. And I just waiting. One day they give me "You—you do this one" and I do in my home and then give it to him. But the group—they make a decision about my work. Yeah. They do more work than me, actually, but actually, I need to do more but I cannot do that because I have limited language to communicate with them. And also the study, the report area, is Cincinnati. I don't know about the area at all, so I just follow my group. They decided everything [because I didn't know anything about the Cincinnati area].

T: So would you have rather done something—written your own paper?

C: Yeah, yeah. Because if I had my own paper I can, I mean, I can express my—my opinion in my paper and then I also can, uh, get advice from other people. I can consult my paper to others, but in the group—in the group I have problem with my speaking, my expression. And maybe, yeah, because I'm not native speaking, so some of my group think that you are not expert in this area so they do everything. They help me a lot so that I can't do everything. Because they do everything in the group, so I don't feel involved.

T: So did they do everything because they didn't think you could do the work, or because you didn't think you could do the work?

C [forcefully]: I can work.

T: So maybe they didn't really give you a chance to do the work?

C: Yeah.

T: They just kind of decided, "We'll give him something that's easy"?

C: Yeah, because when they have meeting, I have to contact it. When they have meeting, I want to come.

T: So they weren't contacting you about the meetings?

C: Yeah the one. Once they had announcement the meeting and then they never send me email again, so I always contact them, "When we meeting?" and "When can I do the meeting? And what can I do? What my role in this group?"

T: Wow.

C: Yeah I just follow their order.

Many of us have watched or been part of groups where one student was clearly taking advantage of the rest of the group, but Chozin's group seems, at some point in the project, to have chosen to exclude one of its members. As the only multilingual writer and the only person who knew nothing about the city of Cincinnati, Chozin was at a double disadvantage before this project ever started and, presumably, his group thought he had nothing to contribute to their success. Although they probably knew relatively little about environmental hazards, they were "authorities," to some degree, on Cincinnati—at least when compared with Chozin. He had no other source of authority to counterbalance whatever knowledge they had of Cincinnati and their belief that his poor English skills were a liability. Thus, instead of including him in the project, they chose to exclude him.

This kind of exclusion is certainly not unheard of among multilingual writers. Leki (2001) reports on the negative "collaborative" experiences of Ling and Yang. Ling's group was dominated by two other members and thus Ling "was not allowed to bring in her particular expertise; nor was she able to benefit from the expertise of the [native-English-speaking] group members" (p. 55). Yang had a much better personal relationship with her group members, but her weak oral skills in English still meant that she "was also constructed as something of a burden or a problem to be fixed" (p. 55). Yang, who seemed to be reduced to the role of holding up posters and introducing group members, says "'My job just—a lot of job is done by my classmate—easy .... . The other conversation job was done by my classmates .... But I do best I can'" (Leki, 2001, p. 55). Cox (2010) reports a similar case with Min. Though not described as being actively excluded by her peers, those peers do not seek out Min's obvious expertise either. Further, Cox reports that while other students saw themselves as learning from each other, Min "did not seem to be part of this network" (p. 86).

Whereas Yang, in Leki's (2001) study, seems to blame herself for her weak speaking skills, and Min, in Cox's (2010) study, seems unaware of (or at least unconcerned with) her exclusion, Chozin was both conscious of his exclusion and upset with his group members as a result. When winter quarter began, Chozin discovered that he was again required to participate in a group paper. Not surprisingly, he was concerned that he might be excluded from another group; however, when I checked in with him several weeks into the quarter, he gave me a glowing report of his successful strategy. I turn again to an excerpt from the interview to let Chozin explain in his own words.

> Chozin [excitedly]: Very different from group last term—was bad experience. I learning from this experience so this term I tried to make new strategy—trying to make it better. [My partner] become my best friend, I think, and she understands me .... When we become closer we can, like, make joking each other. That's a good thing with learning English so it means that I can catch up some expression in English. She's an undergraduate, not a graduate because there were only two graduate students in the class. I was the only international student in class, so I'm the only one who has problems with language. My writing, my language, but I'm trying to get better. I try to speak. I don't care whether they understand my language or not. When the teacher asked us to work in pairs to do research, my research was at the farmers market. I think, "If I don't initiate the research topic, I won't have a group because no one will ask me." So my strategy was, "I have idea so I have to speak to some of my classmates, and anyone who wants to follow my topic, then he or she will be my partner."

> I initiate I will do the Farmers Market because I know some people there and I have some data already. One of my friends wants to join me. It was good experience because we worked, like, equally. Even if I have limit with my language—with my writing—but she understand me and so she always give me chance to work. I work like my idea, like, I decide which one I have to interview and then she follow me. And after I writing, she read it and she edit it so it's like, we

work equally. We always go together to interview. Before interview I always write my question and give it to her. If I have problem with my language when I ask question, she will understand my objective, what I want to say; she can explain. It's very helpful.

I was impressed when Chozin told me about this project. He really seemed to have taken responsibility for his own learning and had shown great resourcefulness. In contrast to Leki's informant Yang, who sadly reported, "Just hate myself, I can't get good English" (2001, p. 57), Chozin says, "I don't care whether they [my group members] understand my language or not"; he is determined to press ahead with his learning. When he entered the class, he recognized that there could easily be a repeat of last term's problems if he weren't proactive. In a class where there was only one other graduate student and no other multilingual writers, Chozin knew he was positioned to be excluded from another group project. But he also recognized that his past research could work to his advantage if he developed a topic quickly and presented potential partners with a fully formed idea, thereby saving them the bother of coming up with one on their own. Chozin successfully thought of a topic for the paper—one that he had already studied during fall. His prior experience gave him added marketability to potential partners.

Choosing the topic—one that he was familiar with and interested in—also gave Chozin a level of control and authority that was never possible in his other group when they were asked to write about the culturally-bound topic of environmental hazards in Cincinnati, Ohio—an area completely unfamiliar to Chozin. However, in winter quarter, Chozin was able to barter his initiative in choosing a topic and his prior research on the farmers' market when finding a partner. He was then able to use that authority to balance his lack of authority as an English speaker. This created a much more equitable dynamic in Chozin's group and a better learning environment for him. Developing strategies to find the right collaborators was a highly effective move on Chozin's part. Not only did he feel better about himself after participating in the second group, but this time he actually got some practice with writing, a feature missing from his earlier experience.

Here, Chozin seems to be complicating the categories Leki (1995) developed—or perhaps introducing a new one. She reports that her participants "rel[ied] on past writing experiences" and "us[ed] current experience or feedback to adjust strategies" (p. 248). For example, she writes that her participant Tula "had done a great deal of essay exam writing in Finland and so felt relatively unconcerned about the demands of essay writing here" (p. 248). Tula had been successful in the past and used that experience as a roadmap for current writing projects. Likewise, Leki writes that her participants used current feedback on early assignments to shape their future work. I would argue that Chozin is doing something a bit different when he strategizes to write a successful group paper: He is learning from failure. While Leki implies that Tula relied on past successful writing experiences, Chozin wasn't able to do that. Instead, he took a moment of failure, analyzed the decisions that led to it, and mapped out a plan to avoid that same failure again.

Managing Data Collection

During winter quarter Chozin also developed a new strategy for managing the data collection process. Not only did Chozin's weak English skills mean that some of his classmates didn't trust him, but they also meant that he struggled in interview situations. He recognized that his English was sometimes difficult to understand, so he developed additional strategies to bridge the gap.

> Chozin: When I went to interview I always ask my American friends to accompany. So because the problem is, when I interview by myself, sometimes—sometimes I'm asking that something that he already answered. Because I interview Ed and he was talking a lot, a lot, and talking much, and—a lot of information. And I hearing, hearing and then when he finish the talking, I asking [the same] questions again. But [the interview failed because I [already] asking [him that] thing. If [I] interview students, it's easy for me to understand because they're speaking, maybe, formally [at the university], but people on the street are using slang or maybe something they understand. Also I have strategy to always bring my recorder.

Once again, Chozin had learned from failure. He had actually devised a number of strategies to help him bridge from his current listening and speaking abilities to the point of writing a successful paper built on primary sources. He drafted his interview questions beforehand and asked a native-English speaker to check them to ensure clarity. He then interviewed his participants in tandem with a native-English speaker so that his partner could clarify, either for Chozin or for the interviewee. Finally, he recorded all of the interviews to further improve his comprehension. In order to do all this, Chozin had to demonstrate a remarkable amount of planning and coordination—and all this was just to gather the primary sources for his papers.

TAKING A HOLISTIC APPROACH TO LITERACY

Throughout the first year of his program, Chozin had been working to improve his writing by tackling specific problems. He sought feedback on most papers, he accommodated his professor by taking graduate writing classes and worked to make those courses useful for him, and he learned from failure by developing strategies to manage group writing projects as well as writing projects that required him to engage in oral interviews for source material. Though I had observed Chozin developing these strategies to address specific challenges, in the spring of his first year it became clear that Chozin was also taking a broader, holistic approach to improve his writing. He had been developing several tactics to improve his vocabulary, fluency, and style and had begun engaging in a number of additional literacy tasks in English like journaling, online chatting, and extra-curricular reading. Reporting on his progress, Chozin said:

> Yeah, I feel I start to get my writing style I think, because when I writing I feel like "Oh, I have to use this word. I have to exchange this sentence with this sentence." So I think I've increased my capability with writing because I feel my style now. Before that I never feel it, just write, write, and write .... I used to write poems, so when I write, like, essay I'm not feel good in essay. Because when I read, like, three or four paragraph I feel tired, exhausted even though I still have many ideas—even in Indonesian, so I tend to write poems to express my mind. But I cannot do this in English because I cannot write poetry in English. I just use words to represent the ideas so I try more to write easy in English by writing my diary in English. I try to send email to my friend in Indonesia in English. I try to doing chat [rooms] in English. I think it useful for me to improve my writing and in English.

Chozin then continued to list his tactics to improve:

> And I took graduate writing class, and I read more because, yeah, I know—I know—I believe as more I read, as more I get new words, so it will enrich my words to use in writing and so I read more. I read more magazine, more books, and yeah, it's also very helpful.

By this point in his first year, Chozin seemed to be demonstrating recognition that all of his discreet literacy activities were interrelated and mutually supportive. He didn't view his personal writing or even his writing in Javanese and Bahasa as separate from his academic writing in English, and he didn't view vocabulary development as divorced from his speaking fluency. Instead, he recognized that all of his language experiences—in Javanese, Bahasa, and English—and all of their component parts—reading, writing, speaking, listening—were vitally connected to one another. He understood that to improve one part affects all of the others, improving the whole. In consequence, this final strategy might be termed "taking a holistic approach" or "understanding the relationships between the parts and the whole." (In all of these respects, Chozin might be said to be demonstrating the kind of adaptive transfer—and agency—that DePalma & Ringer [this volume] describe.)

REALIZING THE INVESTMENT

At the end of his first year Chozin's writing remained quite weak in many ways, but it was improving noticeably and he was increasingly proactive in addressing those weaknesses. His writing had actually appeared to get worse instead of better during winter quarter. He had continued to rely on friends to provide him with editing, but his winter paper load was high and his editor-friends were very busy, so they were less able to help him. As a result, Chozin paired high levels of sentence-level errors with a lack of understanding of basic academic genres; he continued to leave out sections that his professors expected him to include like conclusions, evaluations, and responses. He received writing feedback that was almost exclusively negative and his grades suffered. It appeared as though he were stagnating or even sliding backwards. Chozin seemed to be in the middle of a "u-shaped learning curve," a common feature of writing development in which the cognitive overload of learning so much new material results in temporary setbacks in areas that writers seemed to have already mastered (Feldman & Benjamin, 2004; Perrault, 2011). Feldman and Benjamin (2004) argue that these "essential backward movements ... prepare the way for positive advances" (p. 98).

This backward action to pave the way forward is exactly what Chozin seemed to be experiencing in winter quarter. He had been busy developing strategies that would bring significant rewards during the rest of his program and the tremendous number of writing-to-learn assignments Dr. G. asked him to complete had begun to pay off. It wasn't obvious at the time, but Chozin was beginning to make large strides in fluency and composing speed. At the end of his first year, he described the impact of his strategies and the last six months of intensive writing in various courses.

> This is my last focus paper and, yeah, once a week, two pages is not hard anymore. It's like before that it's hard for me to write it, but now it's—I don't have any problem to write two pages every week. I get—I get used to write it.

A few weeks earlier he had been caught off-guard by the due date of a focus paper assignment. He surprised himself by successfully writing the paper in the hour before class began. And by the end of Chozin's two-year program, he had successfully defended both his thesis proposal and his thesis ahead of most of his classmates.

The case of Chozin therefore stands in contrast to some of the more recent research on multilingual writers and WAC, which has suggested that multilingual writers may receive little benefit or even be harmed by WAC pedagogies that encourage the intensive use of writing in courses, particularly if that writing does not have some relevancy to the writer's future field (Leki, 2003b) or if that writing occurs in the form of high-stakes assessment (Cox, 2011). In Cox's (2011) recent review article, she argues that "literature emerging from second language writing studies ... reveals WAC as a program that can close doors for L2 students" if teachers are encouraged to assign more writing without also being offered professional development to help them work effectively with multilingual writers (para. 1). Leki (2003a) goes so far as to ask, "Is writing overrated?" (p. 315). In critiquing Sternglass's study on the benefits of writing for students, Leki writes, "My L2 students found their writing requirements occasionally satisfying and sometimes frustrating, but most often they regarded writing assignments as necessary evils they would have preferred to avoid" (p. 317).

In remarkable contrast, Chozin neither complained about nor reported feeling disadvantaged by the heavy writing requirements in his courses. On the contrary, those assignments provided Chozin with a vivid indicator of how much his writing fluency had increased.

CONCLUSION

After examining Chozin's thesis and other writing projects from late in his master's program, I still placed him in the bottom half to one-third of graduate writers I had worked with as a tutor. Yet he managed to be highly successful as a graduate student and much of that success was signified by some kind of writing achievement. As I mentioned earlier, his conference papers were solicited for journals, he received grants to support his research, and his thesis won the department's award and was later published. At the end of Chozin's first year, Dr. G. said, "I think he's done really well. He's not fluent, but he's come a long way. As far as his academic work, he's doing fine."

Ultimately, I concluded that Chozin's success did not really hinge on his writing ability. It seemed much more connected to his resourcefulness, leadership, and to his knowledge of his field. Further, Chozin also drew upon his lived experience as a Southeast Asian, doing so explicitly in several classes and again in his thesis; he was no doubt a stronger student as a result. Particularly when compared to a monolingual Caucasian American who entered graduate school immediately after completing an undergraduate degree, Chozin had some marked advantages in his program.

Yet his lived experience was certainly not the only resource that Chozin brought to his graduate work. Interviews gave repeated indications that Chozin's research area was of great interest to his colleagues. It was also clear that Chozin was a leader in his class and had deep knowledge of his field. The best conclusion I could reach when trying to reconcile the mismatch between his writing ability and achievements was that people valued Chozin's other abilities and his research so highly that they were willing to overlook Chozin's writing challenges.

Chozin brought valuable experience to his graduate program and those experiences encouraged his success, but he then also developed many new resources to solve writing problems. He thus offers an example of a successful multilingual student who developed as both a professional and as a writer. The strategies that he developed were all quite personal, yet most have broad applicability. Using Chozin's choices as examples, teachers of multilingual writers might recommend that their students map out concrete plans for how they will manage an interview, or consider how they can position themselves as valued members of a group project. As teachers, we might even explicitly build such moments of planning into our courses in order to encourage a deeper learning experience.

Further, Chozin's strategy of learning from failure offers discouraged writers a means of productive response. Chozin struggled with writing throughout his graduate career. Instead of simply being discouraged or defined by his failures, however, he seemed to focus on the path that led to the problems he experienced and tried to identify ways that he could shift that path the next time.

Chozin's experience also highlights the importance, at least for some writers, of feedback and human connection through the sometimes difficult process of composing. Chozin deeply wanted to be in relationship with others and to talk about his writing. In consequence, he carefully cultivated relationships with his classmates, with his teachers, with other Indonesian students, and even with me. Chozin's story reiterates the value of creating multiple feedback opportunities for our students. Although Chozin was clearly quite motivated to seek feedback, Dr. G. was deeply tied to many of the feedback experiences Chozin had.

Finally, Chozin offers other students a rich example of a writer who seemed to understand that all of his languages and literacies were parts of the same whole and that the time spent engaging in each literacy act had positive implications in a range of other contexts. Instead of compartmentalizing his English academic literacy away from the other aspects of his life and from his home language, Chozin recognized that his personal and professional literacies were intertwined and worked to improve both. Chozin was an unlikely success story and that makes what he accomplished all the more impressive and potentially encouraging to other struggling multilingual writers. His case study offers us yet another model for considering the complex, integrated process by which second language graduate students acquire the competence to write successfully in their chosen fields.

NOTES

1. My work with graduate students as a writing tutor was one of my motivations for the project, but I was not a tutor during the study. During the second year of the study I was the interim Writing Center Coordinator but I did not tutor or respond to the writers' papers. I did provide moral support and at times offered very general advice as a peer, such as recommending a meeting with a professor or a session with a writing tutor.
2. See Zawacki et al. (2007) for additional stories of non-native-speakers' (lack of) writing instruction in their home languages and the challenges they faced in understanding American academic genres.
3. These were direct quotes from oral interviews and therefore are full of the pause fillers, false starts, and repetitions that are part of oral speech. Reporting oral speech verbatim often makes the speaker sound inarticulate at best, but I wanted to preserve Chozin's real speech at this point in his language learning and felt that editing out the "ums" and "uhs" would create an inaccurate representation. Preserving his actual speech also makes his gains in vocabulary and fluency all the more evident as his story progresses.
4. Chozin's other professors did not explicitly decline to be interviewed; they simply did not respond to repeated email requests to discuss Chozin's work.

5. Dr. G. is referring to meeting the qualifications for admission, not to any particular assessment tool.
6. Chozin's teacher did not respond to requests for an interview.
7. Because Chozin's second teacher also did not respond to requests for an interview, it was unclear whether Chozin was unique in being offered this "personalized course" or whether this was common practice. However, I do know from other students that the third writing class focuses exclusively on drafting and revising a thesis/dissertation; significant portions of class time are devoted to writing and conferencing with the teacher. Chozin's report of his modified "advanced course" seemed comparable to reports of the content in the Thesis/Dissertation course.
8. Readers may note several moments in this excerpt where I seem to ask Chozin very leading questions. During this conversation I was following Chozin's tone and nonverbal cues in addition to his speech; both suggested that there was a more serious problem than the spoken language of the transcript reveals. Specifically, I had the impression that Chozin was quite upset by what had happened in the group and yet that he was also trying to avoid disparaging other group members. Instead of trying to infer what had happened in the group, I chose to ask Chozin clarifying questions and give him the opportunity to correct my understanding of events. Instead, Chozin's words, tone, and nonverbal cues confirmed my preliminary understanding of what had happened.

REFERENCES

Bean, J. C. (2001). *Engaging ideas: The professor's guide to integrating writing, critical thinking, and active learning in the classroom.* San Francisco, CA: Jossey Bass.

Bishop, W. (1999). *Ethnographic writing research: Writing it down, writing it up, reading it.* Portsmouth, NH: Heinemann.

Carter, D., & Gradin, S. (2001). *Writing as reflective action: A reader.* New York: Addison Wesley Longman.

Casanave, C. P. (2002). *Writing games: Multicultural case studies of academic literacy practices in higher education.* Mahwah, NJ: Lawrence Erlbaum.

Casanave, C. P. & Li, X., (Eds). (2008). *Learning the literacy practices of graduate school: Insiders' reflections on academic enculturation* (pp. 14-31). Ann Arbor, MI: University of Michigan Press.

Center for International Studies, Ohio University. (n.d.). *Master of arts.* Retrieved from http://www.internationalstudies.ohio.edu/academic-programs/grad/index.html

Cox, M. (2010). Identity, second language writers, and the learning of workplace writing. In M. Cox, J. Jordan, C. Ortmeier-Hooper, & G. G. Schwartz (Eds.), *Reinventing identities in second language writing* (pp. 75-95). Urbana, IL: NCTE.

Cox, M. (2012). WAC: Closing doors or opening doors for second language writers? *Across the Disciplines,* 8(4). Retrieved from wac.colostate.edu/atd/ell/cox.cfm

Feldman, D. H., & Benjamin, A. C. (2004). Going backward to go forward: The critical role of regressive movement in cognitive development. *Journal of Cognition and Development, 5*(1), 97-102.

Leki, I. (1995). Coping strategies of ESL students in writing tasks across the curriculum. *TESOL Quarterly, 29*(2), 235-60.

Leki, I. (2001). A narrow thinking system. *TESOL Quarterly, 35*(1), 39-67.

Leki, I. (2003a). A challenge to second language writing professionals: Is writing overrated? In B. Kroll (Ed.), *Exploring the dynamics of second language writing* (pp. 315-331). New York: Cambridge University Press.

Leki, I. (2003b). Living through college literacy: Nursing in a second language. *Written Communication, 20*(1), 81-98.

Newkirk, T. (1992). The narrative roots of the case study. In G. Kirsch & P. A. Sullivan (Eds.), *Methods and methodology in composition research* (pp. 130-52). Carbondale, IL: Southern Illinois University Press.

Perrault, S. T. (2011). Cognition and error in student writing. *Journal on Excellence in College Teaching, 22*(3), 47-73.

Russell, D. R., & Foster, D. (2002). Rearticulating articulation. In D. Foster & D. R. Russell (Eds.), *Writing and learning in cross-national perspective: Transitions from secondary to higher education* (pp. 1-47). Mahwah, NJ: NCTE/Erlbaum.

Silva, T. (1993). Toward an understanding of the distinct nature of L2 writing: The ESL research and its implications. *TESOL Quarterly, 27*(4), 657-77.

Zawacki, T. M., Hajabbasi, E., Habib, A., Antram, A., & Das, A. (2007). *Writing process, readers' expectations, and grammar anxiety. Valuing written accents: Non-native students talk about identity, academic writing, and meeting teachers' expectations* (2nd ed.). Diversity Research Group. Fairfax, VA: George Mason University.

CHAPTER 3

"HEY, DID YOU GET THAT?": L2 STUDENT READING ACROSS THE CURRICULUM

Carole Center and Michelle Niestepski
Lasell College

This chapter reports on a qualitative research study investigating reading demands in college courses during the first and second year for seven second language students. The study focuses on the expectations for student reading in courses across the curriculum and the strategies that these students developed for responding to those expectations. Our findings suggest that second language students learn to prioritize assignments; approach their instructors for clarification, help, and/or modifications with assignments; and limit the number of courses with high reading and writing demands that they enroll in each semester. Instructors in all disciplines can help all students become stronger readers by assigning reading for which students are held accountable, by providing a context and guidelines for reading, and by making use of writing-to-read activities.

This study investigates the experiences first and second year second language (L2) college students have with reading across the curriculum. As our small, private, four-year college plans for an increase in the international student population, we, as composition specialists, sought to learn more about L2 students' abilities and needs as academic readers and writers. Agreeing with Horning (2007) in her *Across the Disciplines* article, "Reading Across the Curriculum as the Key to Student Success," that "reading and writing must go hand-in-hand" (para. 6), we interviewed seven L2 students to try to understand the strengths, weaknesses, and strategic moves that these students bring to their reading assignments. Hedgcock & Ferris's (2009) claim that "it has been well established in L1 and L2 research that, although successful readers may not necessarily be effective writers, it is virtually impossible to find successful writers who are not also good readers" (p. 215), confirms our consistent observation as teachers of both L1 and L2 students that less able readers are less able writers, and, conversely, the best writers in our classes also read with facility and insight. Like many college instructors, we are concerned that so many of our students, both L1 and L2, lack the ability and/or willingness to read assigned texts closely and critically. Whether prompted by inability or unwillingness, their failure to read assigned texts in-depth limits their access to writing proficiency. This concern has led us to focus on reading across the curriculum, exploring the expectations for reading in courses in other disciplines. We believe that to understand the challenges that reading assignments present for many students, we need to understand the contexts and purposes for reading in all their classes (Hedgcock & Ferris, 2009, p. 50). In focusing on the subgroup of L2 students, we have collected information from student interviews, syllabi, students' reading diaries and writing samples, and inventories of student reading strategies to form a picture of the texts, contexts, and purposes for which they read in all their classes.

We came to focus specifically on L2 students' reading after investigating the frequently-voiced alarm that today's college students in general are less able readers. As Horning (2007) puts it, if one "asks teachers about the problems students have with reading ..., they will invariably say that students can't read and don't read" and that contemporary students are unable "to read complex texts with full understanding" (para. 10). Similarly, a survey by Sanoff (2006), reported in *The Chronicle of Higher Education*, found that only one-tenth of the college faculty surveyed thought that entering students were well-prepared for reading assignments. In addition to these reports of students' deficits in reading ability, Jolliffe and Harl (2008), in a study of student reading at the University of Arkansas, reported detailed evidence of students' unwillingness to read for their courses, finding that "many of the participants rushed through their required reading simply to get it done" (p. 612), which was not surprising as the students reported that the assigned reading was "uninspiring, dull, and painfully required" (p. 611). As incoming students' preparation for the demands of assigned reading decreases, college teachers across the disciplines are forced to pay more attention to the ways that we can help students to read and write about complex, college-level texts.

If reading is such a burden for so many L1 students, how, we wondered, do L2 students cope with the greater burden that the demands for reading in their courses across the curriculum place on them and what can their teachers do to help? As Hedgcock and Ferris (2009) note, "all L2 students struggle with academic reading" due to the more sophisticated and often specialized vocabulary in academic texts and the greater amount of reading expected (p. 55) as well as the differences in the writing system and its linguistic and textual structures that these readers may encounter in the L2 (p. 106). The focal student,

Yuko, in Spack's 2004 case study provides poignant testimony of this struggle: "I used to open some reading and the printed words used to scare me" (p. 31).

With considerable variation between categories of L2 students and among individuals within these categories, many L2 students lack the advantage of years of oral language exposure, which allow L1 learners to come to reading with extensive vocabulary and knowledge of the way words and sentences are put together (Hedgcock & Ferris, 2009, p. 50). These issues tend to manifest differently for international and immigrant students, with international students typically having the advantage of being experienced L1 readers with a foundation of grammar and vocabulary instruction in the L2, but experiencing disadvantages when it comes to genre knowledge and cultural background. Immigrant students, on the other hand, may not be experienced readers in their L1 or their L2, depending on their educational and immigration circumstances, but will usually have more knowledge of text genres and more cultural familiarity (Hedgcock & Ferris, 2009, pp. 51-55). As Hedgcock and Ferris (2009) comment, it is rarely possible for an L2 language learner, who is an international student or a recent immigrant, to put in the years of study or exposure to the L2 that would give the learner the equivalent preparation for reading in the new language that a L1 reader acquires (p. 59). Reid (2006) points out that many international students are, in her terms, "eye readers" who have studied L2 vocabulary and linguistic rules, often extensively, but who may be weaker listeners and speakers than they are readers (p. 79). Nevertheless, international L2 readers often lack confidence in their reading. Reid (2006) characterizes immigrant L2 students as "ear learners," who, having taken in American culture for a number of years, are often fluent speakers and listeners, but whose reading skills may be weaker than they acknowledge or than teachers anticipate (p. 77).

In addition to these potential issues of competence, L2 students may experience a "confidence gap," which predisposes them to reading behaviors, such as word-by-word translation, that interfere with their L2 reading (Hedgcock & Ferris, 2009, p. 61). We saw this confidence gap in action when one of our international participants, a second year student, initially refused to be interviewed because she felt that her English language skills were not up to having the conversation. In an email to us she explained, "I actually do not have confidence to help the research (because of my English skills), so I am not be able to help it. I am sorry" (personal communication, November 7, 2010). As Spack reports in her case study, L2 students may find that an increase in confidence is the most beneficial outcome of persisting with academic reading in the L2 because, as Yuko concludes, it "is not the improvement in the vocabulary (or background knowledge)" as much as the "confidence/boldness not to be bothered by what I didn't understand" that leads to her academic success (as quoted in Spack, 2004, p. 43). Often such boldness will be seen when students are able to move from word-based reading, in which they may read word-for-word, read too slowly, translate, and/or overuse the dictionary (Hedgcock & Ferris, 2009, p. 219), to a more fluent reading in which they are able to read for the gist of a text without understanding every word (Auerbach & Paxton, 1997, p. 244; Leki, 1993, p. 9). Until they are ready to take this step, L2 readers remain, as Paxton eloquently describes, "prisoners of the unknown words" (Auerbach & Paxton, 1997, p. 253). Both reading competence and confidence can be boosted by instruction and practice in a combination of intensive and extensive reading. When reading intensively, readers use before, during, and after reading strategies to engage closely with a text. Extensive reading—general, self-selected reading for information and pleasure—can compensate to some extent for L2 readers' lack of exposure to the patterns of language in the L2 (Hedgcock & Ferris, 2009, p. 214).

All writers benefit from reading as they accrue tacit knowledge of the genres and conventions of written language and are exposed to ideas and data that spur their thinking. In the considerable body of research into the reading-writing connection for L2 students— Hedgcock and Ferris (2009) cite fourteen articles that review research on reading-writing interaction (p. 215)—the strong correlation between reading proficiency and writing ability found in studies of L1 students, while sometimes evident, is not as consistent as in L2 research (Ferris & Hedgcock, 1998, p. 31). Ferris and Hedgcock (1998) suggest that "we cannot assume reading-writing relationships to be as clear or predictable for ESL students as they might be for their NES counterparts" due to some L2 students' underdeveloped knowledge of the L2 and of the writing skills measured in empirical studies (p. 31). While L2 students may have more variation between their reading and writing skills, i.e. one cannot assume that a good reader will necessarily be a good writer and vice versa (Flahive & Bailey, 1993, p. 133; Grabe, 2004, p. 30), nevertheless, scholars agree that for L2 students as for L1 students, reading and writing are mutually reinforcing activities because "reading facilitates the development of writing skills" just as writing experiences help to improve reading (Ferris & Hedgcock, 1998, p. 43). As composition specialists, our interest in students' attitudes and approaches to their assigned reading stems from this reading/writing connection.

PARTICIPANTS

Our research site is a small college, which, like many US colleges, is actively recruiting international students. We sought our research participants from

English 101 for ESL students, a credit-bearing, first-year writing class for L2 students, recruiting four first-year students, all of whom happened to be either immigrant students or, in the case of a student from Guam, a multilingual US citizen. To balance the number of immigrant and international students, we then recruited three international students: two sophomores who had completed the first-year writing courses during their freshmen year and a sophomore transfer student new to the college (see Table 3.1). The students volunteered to participate and received a small stipend.

We met with six of the seven students twice for thirty-minute recorded interviews. The exception was Martin, whose first interview could not be scheduled until almost the end of the semester; consequently, we did not interview him a second time. The first interviews focused on the reading demands students faced in their courses across the curriculum and their ways of meeting those demands; the second, follow-up interview focused mainly on the writing assignment the students selected for our examination. As detailed in Table 3.1,

Table 3.1 Student Demographics

	Pseudo-nym	Gender	L1	Major	Native Country	High School
First-Year Students	Maria	female	Spanish	Legal Studies	Dominican Republic	2 years in US
	Chase	male	Vietnamese	Accounting	Vietnam	middle school/ high school in US
	Felix	male	Portuguese	Fashion Design	Brazil	high school in US
	Martin	male	Chamorro English	Athletic Training	Guam	Guam
Second-Year Students	Teddy (transfer)	male	Vietnamese	Accounting	Vietnam	1 year ESL school and 2 years international school in Vietnam
	Aya	female	Japanese	Psychology	Japan	International school in Hong Kong and high school in Japan
	Rina	female	Japanese	Hospitality	Japan	Japan

gender and first- and second-year standing were quite evenly distributed among our participants with a good mix of ethnicities, languages, and majors. While all of the second-year students were international students and all of the immigrant students were first-year students, we found little difference in the attitudes and strategies that students brought to their reading assignment between students in either of the two groups: international/immigrant or first-year/second year. Students across both groupings used strategies for accommodating and managing teachers' demands around reading that are strikingly similar to the strategic moves that Ilona Leki found in her study of L2 students dealing with writing assignments, "Coping Strategies of ESL Students in Writing Tasks Across the Curriculum" (1995). And while we assumed the sophomores would have more reading demands because they were taking more 200-level courses, in fact, the majority (5/6) of courses with the highest reading demands were 100-level courses.

The students' test scores indicated weaknesses in English proficiency with low TOEFL scores or low critical reading and writing test scores on the SAT despite the fact that all of the immigrant students had attended at least some years of high school in the US and the international students had studied English for several years. In addition, each of the international students had had some additional classes in English before entering our college; these experiences ranged from an English language school in the US to community college classes. Coming from Guam, Martin had all of his schooling in English. Some of the immigrant students had a year of ESL instruction in high school and/or special language tutoring in a public school. However, as Hedgcock and Ferris (2009) note "[e]ven L2 readers mostly or entirely educated in English-speaking environments typically have read relatively less than their native-speaking counterparts ... [as they] face the added challenges of a later start in learning English and living in a non- or limited English-speaking home" (p. 219). The international students reported that little of their English instruction involved reading.

The courses the students were taking during the fall semester 2010 are shown in Table 3.2.

READING DEMANDS

As we expected, our interviewees told us that their reading and writing assignments in college were more demanding than those they had faced in high school, whether in their native country or in the US. However, they made it clear that the reading demands varied considerably from course to course, with humanities courses, social science courses, and one of the first-year seminar courses presenting the most demand for reading. Most students reported that in one or more of their courses, no reading of a textbook or other whole text was required. For example, Rina volunteered, "We really don't read" for all three of her 200-level courses and added, "I actually bought the book for this class but we never used that" for two of her three courses. When we examined syllabi for the classes in which the students were enrolled, we found reading assignments listed in most. In a few cases, the course schedule in the syllabi listed topics without a reference to a particular reading, so it was difficult to determine whether those topics were merely covered in class or if they corresponded to reading assignments. All of the syllabi listed at least one required textbook. In the specific cases where students told us that there was no reading assigned during the semester, the syllabi did list weekly reading assignments. Therefore,

Table 3.2 Majors and Courses

	Pseudonym	L1	Major	Courses
First-Year Students	Maria	Spanish	Legal Studies	5 courses: ENG 101 for ESL Students, Legal Studies 101, Math 104, Political Science 101, and First-Year Seminar
	Chase	Vietnamese	Accounting	5 courses: ENG 101 for ESL Students, Economics 101, Math 104, Business 101, First-Year Seminar
	Felix	Portuguese	Fashion Design	5 courses: ENG 101 for ESL Students, Art 101, Fashion Design 103 and 105, First-Year Seminar
	Martin	Chamorro English	Athletic Training	5 courses: ENG 101 for ESL Students, Athletic Training 101 and 103, Math 203, First-Year Seminar
Second-Year Students	Teddy (transfer)	Vietnamese	Accounting	5 courses: English 104, Academic Reading and Writing (an elective), Math 205, Math 208, Sociology 101, First-Year Seminar
	Aya	Japanese	Psychology	4 courses: Human Services 101, Sociology 101, Psychology 221, History 104
	Rina	Japanese	Hospitality	4 courses: Business 206, Business 220, Communications 206, History 104

we are not sure whether the students meant that, while reading was assigned, they felt that they did not actually have to do the assigned reading in order to do well in the course or whether the assignments in the syllabi were not actually enforced. For example, Aya and Rina both reported that there was no textbook assigned for some of their courses (in sociology, human services, and business), but the syllabi show an assigned textbook and chapter assignments to be completed each week.

What was clear from the interviews is that often professors would lecture about the material in the textbook and/or make their Power Point notes available on the course website, and, in some cases, students found that there was therefore no reason to do the reading even if it was assigned. Reading the teacher's notes is, of course, still reading, but such reading does not make the same demands as reading a book. One textbook even came with an instructional DVD, obviating the need for Martin to rely on his reading skills alone. However, it was not always the case that lectures or online Power Points meant that the students did not do the reading, as Aya reported that she always did the reading for her 200-level psychology course and then depended on the lectures to explain things she did not understand when reading on her own, having found that both were necessary to fully understand the material. Similarly, Felix read the textbook for his fashion design course, Clothing Construction, because he found that it reinforced what the teacher conveyed in class. The students did report a number of assignments that required shorter readings, such as the assignment in Economics 101 to locate an article from the *Wall Street Journal* or another business-oriented newspaper or magazine online and then write about it or report on it to the class. Such reading, according to Chase, is "easy." The fact that reading is not necessary in all courses is consistent with reports that typical L1 students can do well in their courses and receive good grades without doing much of their assigned reading. Jolliffe & Harl (2008), for example, report that "[p]rofessors admit that students can actually pass exams if they come to lectures and take (or buy) good notes, whether or not they have read the assigned material" (p. 600).

Of the thirty-three courses in which the seven students were enrolled, they identified six as posing high reading demands: Felix's first-year seminar, an introductory history course that Aya and Rina took together, Teddy's introductory sociology course, Maria's introductory legal studies course, and Rina's psychology course, the only 200-level course so identified. The difficulties these courses posed included the amount of required reading, the unfamiliar content of the reading, and the lack of the cultural background that would have provided scaffolding for the readings. These difficulties in unfamiliar language and content are consistent with the challenges that reading assignments pose for L2 students described in the literature. In addition, the interviews revealed that issues outside of the linguistic demands of reading in the L2 can also make reading difficult. These additional difficulties include limitations on students' time for reading and writing posed by the requirements of other kinds of assigned work, student activities, and team sports; the difficulty of performing critical thinking tasks; and the challenge of sustaining the concentration required for reading when the subject is not among one's interests.

In the history course, Aya and Rina experienced the kind of difficulties that the literature describes as typical for international students, finding that the amount of reading, the vocabulary, and their lack of background knowledge all presented challenges. Aya said that her history and psychology courses presented the most difficulty, partly because she isn't interested in history, but more so because the vocabulary is difficult: "I kind of understand but for some few sentences the wordings are difficult that I sometimes get stuck with it." Rina reported that she needed considerable translation to understand the words in the history textbook. For both the textbook and an additional book, *My Battle of Algiers* (Morgan, 2005), Rina and Aya noted their lack of background knowledge. For example, Aya said that she had no context in which to understand topics such as the Mughal Empire or Islam and world trade. Although Rina and Aya felt at a disadvantage in comparison to the L1 students, their instructor commented that the L1 students did not know much, if anything, about these subjects either.

Maria reported that the reading load and the technical language in her legal studies reading assignments presented difficulty, particularly at the beginning of the semester. The reading was longer and more complex than any she had encountered before. According to the department chair, most students in this class find the terminology difficult and benefit from creating a glossary. Maria probably experienced no more difficulty than the native speakers in her class. In fact, research in second language writing has found that faculty consider L2 students more adept than L1 students at learning the vocabulary in a discipline that is new to them, which may be attributed to the L2 students' experience in acquiring new vocabulary while learning new languages (Leki, 2006, p. 143). It is clear that Maria, according to her self-report, spends more time studying than most U. S. college students do, as she reports spending five hours a night, seven days a week while the National Survey of Student Engagement found the majority of college students spend fewer than sixteen hours per seven-day week (Jolliffe & Harl, 2008, p. 601).

The first-year seminar courses, which all the first year students and Teddy, the transfer student, were taking, are theme-based courses designed to engage students in a specific area of interest while providing support for making a smooth transition to the college community. The courses vary widely in terms of their reading demands. Felix's first-year-seminar was the most demanding, as his instructor required students to read four novels and write three analytic papers, a requirement that he found he could not meet partly because, as he candidly reported, he could only spend about forty-five minutes a day reading one of the assigned novels before he became too bored to continue. Although he knew this was not enough time to keep up with his reading assignments, he found it impossible to continue reading past that point.

While Teddy had little difficulty with vocabulary in reading his sociology textbook, he found it difficult to read and understand the case studies that were also weekly reading. While lack of shared cultural background made it hard for Teddy to grasp the nuances in the American situations the case studies described, his bigger difficulty was in thinking critically in the ways the writing assignments required. When asked to apply the general sociological concepts he had read about in the textbook to the case studies, Teddy felt that his lack of experience in critical thinking made this quite challenging:

> Maybe it's because I wasn't born here that I don't have that skill [critical thinking] that everyone has. Everybody in my class doing so well but not for me ... I understand the concept, I understand what is value, what is norm, what is sanction, what is bureaucracy, and everything, but when they ask me to apply it to one of the story [case studies], I cannot do it, I cannot get the inside like everybody else.

Teddy made clear in subsequent interviews that during his schooling in Vietnam, students were expected to memorize, not to express ideas or apply concepts. In this, he is like some of the student informants in Zawacki and Habib's 2010 study, such as Sri, who reported that in India, "You learn it by memory and put it back on the page word for word ... Your own expression was not really accepted, unlike here where there's a lot of emphasis on your thoughts and expression" (p. 61).

MEETING THE DEMANDS: READING STRATEGIES

To explore the students' use of the reading strategies that the literature describes as typical practices of experienced readers, we asked each of the six students to complete an inventory listing multiple strategies based on a reading inventory developed by Auerbach and Paxton (1997). In Table 3.3, we list the strategies employed before, during, and after the reading that three or more students reported using regularly.

Even though only four of the participants reported using a dictionary when they came across unknown words, during the interviews all of the students said they look up unknown words to varying degrees. Rina, who had little focus on reading in her English studies in a Japanese high school and never reads for pleasure in her L1 or L2, and Teddy, who had considerable experience reading in English both in his community college and on his own, represent opposite ends of the continuum between hesitant, word-for-word reading and more confident, fluent reading. While Rina remains heavily dependent on translation and electronic translators, Teddy reported that he used to use a translator but

Table 3.3 Student Reading Strategies

Before you start reading, what (if anything) do you typically do?	Responses (out of 6)
Glance at the whole text first, checking length or other text features	4
Skim the whole article	4
Read the title and think about what might be coming	4
While you are reading, what goes on in your mind? What are you doing?	
Taking notes, marking the text	5
Asking questions	4
Writing	4
Skimming or skipping parts	3
Going back and forth between parts	3
Making predictions	3
What do you do when you come to unknown words or passages you don't understand?	
Guess	4
Use the dictionary	4
Re-read	3
Mark the word/passage and come back to it	3
After you finish reading, what do you do?	
Go back and re-read specific parts	4
Re-read the article	3
Stop and turn immediately to the assignment	3
Go back and re-read specific parts	4

found it "expensive and very annoying" to spend so much time looking up words. He made the transition from word-based to meaning-based reading in his international high school. Teddy has developed a higher tolerance for not understanding every word and more facility in guessing meaning from context: "There's a lot of words I'm not sure about but based from my experience, I just read the whole thing and I just guess. That usually does help, and it saves me a lot of time ... Reading without a dictionary, I can enjoy the content of a story; reading with a dictionary, it just makes the reading really boring." Rina, in contrast, translates continually, even translating some of the words in the history syllabus she showed us; she worries that "sometimes I check every time the same word," meaning that she isn't adding the words that she translates to her vocabulary.

Overall, the results indicate that these L2 students make use of many of the strategies emphasized in intensive approaches to reading. What is equally interesting are the practices that the students did not report making use of. For example, only one student said that while reading he thought of something from his own experience or thought about other articles/courses. The students we interviewed seemed to focus solely on understanding the text and were not able to use experiences outside of the text to help them understand it.

MEETING THE DEMANDS: COPING STRATEGIES

In her study of L2 students dealing with writing assignments, "Coping Strategies of ESL Students in Writing Tasks Across the Curriculum," Leki (1995) found that students employed a number of strategic moves to deal with the writing tasks assigned. The students in this study used similar strategic moves in response to the reading demands they faced. Like Leki's participants, they took advantage of their first language and culture, approached their professors and, in some cases, peers, for clarification and help, managed competing demands by choosing the number of courses and the type of courses they enrolled in each semester with reading and writing demands in mind, managed their work load by setting limits on their investment in particular courses or assignments, and regulated their cognitive load by strategically using reading to reinforce what they had heard in class. (A number of these moves are similar to those employed by Chozin, the graduate student who is the subject of Phillips' case study [this volume]; he too learned to take the initiative in managing his learning and writing environment in order to complete his assignments successfully.)

Some of the students' strategies for managing their reading tasks involved taking advantage of their first language by doing "outside research" in the

L1 in order to understand texts and lectures. Most often this took the form of looking up background information on the Internet about the topic. For example, Aya reports that in her history class, "on the syllabus it says like the title of what she's going to talk about today, so I like go on the Internet and look up kind of like an overview or background information in Japanese and kinda get the idea and I go to the class." Both Aya and Rina talked about looking online for information in Japanese about the Battle of Algiers in order to help them understand *My Battle of Algiers* (Morgan, 2005). Similarly, Chase found his economics instructor's notes hard to understand, so he would read material on Google until he was able to understand the concepts and complete his homework. Rina reported that at the beginning of the semester she had her mother send her Japanese books on business to help with her business courses.

Teddy was the most assertive of the students we interviewed in asking for adaptations of assignments so that he could take advantage of this first culture. He negotiated adaptations in his introductory sociology class by asking the instructor to let him use his knowledge of his own background, Vietnamese culture, rather than examples from US culture, an accommodation that the professor allowed for a group presentation and an exam. For the exam, instead of writing about a subculture in the US (which he did not clearly grasp), his instructor allowed him to write about a subculture in Vietnam. By allowing him to examine the subculture in Vietnam, his instructor was able to gauge how well he understood the sociological theories he was learning without penalizing him for his lack of understanding of American subcultures. (Like Chozin with his writing assignments, as described by Phillips [this volume], Aya, Rina, Chase, and Teddy show L2 students drawing on knowledge from their L1 to complete reading and writing-about-reading assignments. As DePalma and Ringer argue [this volume], when we consider what writing knowledge L2 students might be transferring across cultural, linguistic, and academic contexts, many of which are unfamiliar to them, we need to recognize how they are reusing, and in many cases, reshaping concepts and information from their L1.)

Another approach students used when struggling with the readings was to ask someone, typically a classmate or the instructor, for help. Students indicated that often times they did not feel comfortable asking the instructor questions about the text during class, but would instead wait until after class to talk with the instructor or they would email him or her. Martin indicated that if he still didn't understand after rereading, "I'll like ask another Athletic Training major, 'Hey, did you get that?' and if they don't know, we'll just look it up and kind of discuss." Chase also reported working with his classmates to complete the homework problems that were assigned in his economics class.

Aya and Rina managed the high reading demands that they expected to find in their history course by taking the course together and by limiting their course load to four 3-credit courses instead of the usual five that semester. (We recently learned that Chase and Teddy are currently following the same strategy of taking their history course together.) In our follow-up interviews with five of the seven participants during the 2011-2012 academic year, most readily acknowledged that, when they plan their schedules each semester, they seek a balance between courses with high demands for reading and writing and courses with less demands. For Teddy and Chase, for example, math-based courses are much less onerous, so they balance reading/writing-intensive courses with those that are more math-based. Teddy averred that he could handle a 50-50 balance while Chase said that he preferred a 70-30 balance in favor of math-based courses. The content of the reading makes a significant difference, however, as reading in the student's major, such as Rina's reading about restaurant and hotel management, was seen as much more manageable than reading in a discipline outside the major. Similarly, Felix finds his fashion textbooks useful and readable and does not sell them back to the bookstore, keeping them to use for future reference.

In Leki's study (1995), students made conscious choices to limit their investment in particular assignments, courses, and in academic work overall, choosing, for example, not to reread because it took too much time away from other assignments or to participate in college activities, socialize or travel rather than to study in order "to get a more well-rounded educational experience" (p. 251). Similarly, in our study, some students prioritized the hands-on work assigned in classes, such as Felix's fashion design courses, and their student activities over completing their reading assignments. For example, Felix was part of the Student Government Association and Martin, as a soccer player, had daily practices and frequent games during the season. Interestingly, they are the two students who were most forthright about the choices they made to limit the amount of time they devoted to reading in areas outside their career-oriented majors because the reading became too boring to tolerate. As Felix reported, "If it was a book about like about fashion design or like a designer or something else that I'm like into it, I would just totally, I would just like spend my entire night not sleeping and just reading the book, but [the assigned reading in his first-year seminar] is just boring," so "when I'm reading, I start thinking about something else and my head just goes like, it doesn't stick with the book." Martin similarly reported that after awhile "I can't keep reading, I'm gonna get off track and then I'm not going to be paying attention."

The participants in Leki's study (1995) had a number of strategies to prepare for and follow up class lectures, including reading ahead in order to preview what the instructor would say in class and not taking notes in order to concentrate in class, strategies Leki terms "regulating cognitive load" (p. 252). Aya used strikingly similar stratagies. Following the design of the course in the syllabus, she prepared for the topic to be discussed by reading in her L1 on the Internet, providing her own scaffolding for the upcoming lecture, then focused on listening in class, and finally read the textbook after the lecture to reinforce and clarify what she heard. The follow-up interview revealed that Aya is continuing to regulate her cognitive load in her upper-level psychology courses. She reads the textbook chapter before class, listens in class, and then prints out the Power Point slides that are posted on the course website and goes over these after class to reinforce her learning. In one psychology class, she can't predict what the professor's lecture will cover from the syllabus, so she listens during class first, then reads the Power Point slides, then reads the textbook chapter. Teddy follows a similar routine of reading the textbook before class to provide scaffolding for the lectures. He reported that he depends heavily on the textbook for his learning, particularly when the professor is not an effective lecturer. Teddy observed that "I don't want to put myself in the situation that I rely on the professor too much ... so I develop a style of studying rely mostly on the book."

CONCLUSIONS AND RECOMMENDATIONS

The interviews revealed that, in most cases, these L2 students coped well with the demands for reading in their courses. Only one student mentioned resorting to *Spark Notes* when the reading was too time-consuming. In addition to the students' self-reports, the writing samples students brought to their second interviews, all graded as A's or B's, showed evidence of at least rudimentary skills in selecting and integrating information from readings into the writing. The students were aided by their own strategies and the help of instructors, who spoke to students after class, during office hours, and on email to answer questions about the readings; modified assignments to allow students to use their own cultural experiences; made accommodations for students who needed to translate during exams; and used visual modalities to convey information to students. Students consistently mentioned how helpful it is if instructors are available to meet with students after class and during office hours. From the students' comments, it is very clear that they usually do not feel comfortable asking questions in class and are at times quite self-conscious. In cases where the students were not able to meet face to face with their instructors after class, they found it helpful to be able to email the instructor. During Maria's second interview, she explained that only one of her instructors knew she was not born in the United States and that she did not want to be treated differently from the other students as it was already hard to be in college. However, she too discussed how helpful it was to be able to email an instructor for clarification on one of her assignments.

In general, an opportunity for a visual component is helpful for L2 students. Both Aya and Rina talked about an assignment from history class in which they were asked to respond to a review of a book. Instead of a written review, students were given the link to a YouTube video interview of the person reviewing the book. They found it helpful to be able to watch the video repeatedly.

Based on what we learned from our study and from second language reading pedagogy, there are several additional practices that could aid students and promote reading across the curriculum that did not appear to be widely used, such as providing a context for assigned readings in advance and making greater use of writing-to-read activities. Several students discussed how helpful it would be if instructors would provide a context for the readings beforehand. For example, Aya and Rina struggled with reading *My Battle of Algiers* because they had no context for it. Felix struggled with the dialect in Zora Neale Hurston's *Their Eyes Were Watching God* (1937/2006) and stated, "For me, it wasn't English. It was Greek." If instructors are able to give students an overview of what the reading material will be about, the time period or key persons involved, or ways to decipher the dialect, this might go a long way in helping students to understand the reading. In addition, instructors across the disciplines should help students to become aware of how they read, so that they begin to recognize the practices that inhibit the development of fluency. Instructors can then "encourage students to read first for overall meaning without trying to understand every single word" (Spack, 1993, p. 189).

While many of the students used notetaking, glossing, and annotating when they read, they did not mention using other writing-to-read strategies either on their own time or in their classes. Hirvela (2004) discusses three writing-to-read strategies that help students to understand the material they are reading: summary, synthesis, and response papers. Hirvela (2004) draws on previous studies that have found "more complex writing tasks involving some degree of composing (e.g., analytic and response-based essays) have a greater impact on students' learning than do less demanding activities such as notetaking and answering study questions" (p. 84). While study questions may guide students to important places in a text, when students are asked to write a summary, they are forced to decide what information in the text is of the most importance. According to Hirvela (2004), "In situations where we have reasons to expect our students to encounter difficulties while reading, adding a writing component such as summarizing might be the best reading gift we can give them" (p.

91). This is confirmed by a L2 student, Karimatu, interviewed in Zawacki, Hajabbasi, Habib, Antram & Das's study (2007), who said, when asked what she would tell students coming to the United States, "Get used to the habit of reading, and, if you can read it, take a piece of paper .... when you read, write. Just write a part from what they learn. Let's say you read two pages, and you ask yourself what you read. Sometimes you read and your mind is somewhere else you don't understand. Summarize it in your own words, just to get in the habit of doing it" (p. 18). (Qian Du [this volume] describes the benefits of summary writing for L2 students. While a particularly complex process for these students, as she explains, because it requires an understanding of different levels of information in the text along with the ability to represent the original text accurately and concisely, summary writing is a valuable learning and writing tool for the reasons raised in this chapter.)

Another written component is synthesizing, which allows students to move beyond summarizing one text to summarizing and describing the relationship among multiple texts. Given that when our interviewees described their reading strategies, only one student mentioned thinking about another text, synthesis assignments might be a useful technique for instructors to use to help students see the connections among texts. A third type of writing-to-read activity is the response assignment, which can take a variety of forms ranging from pre-reading writing in which students are asked to write about the topic of the text to post-reading writing in which students describe their reactions to the texts. Many instructors assign journals in which students respond to the texts. Like the summaries, response assignments can give instructors insight into the challenges students are facing with the texts assigned and can easily be incorporated into classes from all disciplines.

Yet, other than in the writing courses, we found no evidence that instructors assigned summaries, syntheses, or response assignments so that students were able to write in response to readings. Perhaps the use of writing-to-read assignments is one of the reasons that the students taking writing courses reported that they read the assigned readings from their composition readers easily.

Ultimately, instructors in all disciplines can help all students become stronger readers by assigning reading for which students are held accountable, so that they continuously practice reading. As noted previously, L2 students may benefit even more than L1 students do from extensive reading practice because frequent reading can build tacit knowledge of the L2 and prompt more fluent reading. Additionally, instructors across the disciplines can design writing activities and assignments that invite students to go beyond comprehension and the accumulation of information to analyze, synthesize, and evaluate what they read. As Carson (1993) notes, "Language is always used to do something; it is not meaningful in and of itself" (p. 99). Reading is meaningful when students think about the content of their reading and do something with it, composing their thoughts in response to the language on the page or screen.

REFERENCES

Auerbach, E. R. & Paxton, D. (1997). It's not the English thing: Bringing reading research into the ESL classroom. *TESOL Quarterly, 31*(2), 237-261.

Carson, J. (1993). Reading for writing: Cognitive perspectives. In J. Carson & I. Leki (Eds.), *Reading in the composition classroom: Second language perspectives* (pp. 85-104). Boston, MA: Heinle and Heinle Publishers.

Ferris, D. & Hedgcock, J. (1998). *Teaching ESL composition*. Mahwah, NJ: Lawrence Erlbaum Associates.

Flahive, D. & Bailey, N. (1993). Exploring reading/writing relationships in adult second language learners. In J. Carson & I. Leki (Eds.), *Reading in the composition classroom: Second language perspectives* (pp. 128-140). Boston, MA: Heinle and Heinle Publishers.

Grabe, W. (2004). Reading-writing relations: Theoretical perspectives and instructional practices. In D. Belcher & A. Hirvela (Eds.), *Linking literacies: Perspectives on L2 reading-writing connections* (pp. 15-39). Ann Arbor, MI: University of Michigan Press.

Hedgcock, J. & Ferris, D. (2009). *Teaching readers of English*. New York: Routledge.

Hirvela, A. (2004). *Connecting reading and writing in second language writing instruction*. Ann Arbor, MI: University of Michigan Press.

Horning, A. (2007). Reading across the curriculum as the key to student success. *Across the Disciplines, 4*. Retrieved from http://wac.colostate.edu/atd/articles/horning2007.cfm

Hurston, Z.N. (2006). *Their eyes were watching God*. New York: HarperCollins. (Original work published 1937).

Jolliffe, D. & Harl, A. (2008). Studying the "reading transition" from high school to college: What are our students reading and why? *College English, 70*(6), 599-617.

Leki, I. (1993). Reciprocal themes in ESL reading and writing. In Leki & Carson (Eds.), *Reading in the composition classroom: Second language perspectives* (pp. 9-32). Boston, MA: Heinle and Heinle Publishers.

Leki, I. (1995). Coping strategies of ESL students in writing tasks across the curriculum. *TESOL Quarterly, 29*(2), 235-260.

Leki, I. (2006). Negotiating socioacademic relations: English learners' reception by and reaction to college faculty. *Journal of English for Academic Purposes, 5*, 136-152.

Morgan, T. (2005). *My battle of Algiers*. New York: Harper Collins.

Reid, J. (2006). Eye learners and ear learners: Identifying the language needs of international students and US resident writers. In P. K. Matsuda, M. Cox, J. Jordan, & C. Ortmeier-Hooper (Eds.), *Second-language writing in the composition classroom* (pp. 76-88). Boston, MA: Bedford/St. Martin's.

Sanoff, A. (2006, March 10). A perception gap over students' preparation. *Chronicle of Higher Education*. Retrieved from http://chronicle.com/article/A-Perception-Gap-Over/31426/

Spack, R. (1993). Student meets text, text meets students: Finding a way into academic discourse. In J. Carson & I. Leki (Eds.), *Reading in the composition classroom: Second language perspectives* (pp. 183-196). Boston, MA: Heinle and Heinle Publishers.

Spack, R. (2004). The acquisition of academic literacy in a second language: A longitudinal case study, updated. In V. Zamel & R. Spack (Eds.), *Crossing the curriculum: Multilingual learners in college classrooms* (pp. 19-45). Mahway, NJ: Lawrence Erlbaum Associates.

Zawacki, T. M. & Habib, A. (2010). "Will our stories help teachers understand?": Multilingual students talk about identity, voice, and expectations across academic communities. In M. Cox, J. Jordan, C. Ortmeier-Hooper, & G. G. Schwartz (Eds.), *Reinventing identities in second language writing* (pp. 54-74). Urbana, IL: NCTE.

Zawacki, T. M., Hajabbasi, E., Habib, A., Antram, A., & Das, A. (2007). *Valuing written accents: Non-native students talk about identity, academic writing, and meeting teachers' expectations*. Retrieved from http://writtenaccents.gmu.edu/monograph/valuing-written-accents-second-edition.pdf

CHAPTER 4

BRIDGING THE GAP BETWEEN ESL COMPOSITION PROGRAMS AND DISCIPLINARY WRITING: THE TEACHING AND LEARNING OF SUMMARIZATION SKILL

Qian Du
Ohio University

Summary writing has long been perceived as a core academic literacy skill necessary for students studying in American universities to achieve academic success, yet limited research has been conducted with regards to the actual summary writing tasks that L2 writers encounter across the curriculum. To fill in this gap, this qualitative study examined the summary writing experiences and practices of a group of international undergraduate students as they navigate across different disciplinary courses. The major findings of the study will be discussed in this chapter, and pedagogical implications outlined.

In Anglophone universities, reading-based writing tasks are commonly assigned (Bridgeman & Carlson, 1984; Hale et al., 1996), and students are often expected to effectively work with source texts in various assignments, such as reading responses, critical reviews, and research papers. Of the major source-based assignments, summary writing has long been perceived as a core academic literacy skill necessary for students studying in American universities to achieve academic success. Because of this, ESL writing programs, which are designed to socialize second language writers into the target academic community, often incorporate summary writing as an important component of the curriculum. ESL students enrolled in such courses are provided with ample opportunities to practice summarization skill based on the readings selected by the writing teachers. Despite this central focus on the teaching of summarization, however, ESL writing courses often do not seem to take into consideration L2 writers' actual uses of summarization in disciplinary courses. In ESL writing courses, the readings chosen for summary writing are usually unrelated to students' academic backgrounds, and the criteria used for the evaluation of summaries are largely a result of the writing teachers' own understanding of the genre. In other words, summary writing is often taught as a "context-free" skill in ESL writing programs.

Recent research on second language writing has started to explore the relationship between ESL writing programs and L2 writers' literacy experiences in their chosen disciplines (e.g. Leki, 2007). Nevertheless, few studies have examined the discrepancies in the teaching and learning of specific academic writing skills. To fill in the gap, this study examines summary writing experiences of a group of international undergraduate students in various disciplinary courses. By documenting the focal participants' summarization practices across the curriculum, this qualitative study seeks to unveil the connections (or disconnections) between ESL composition programs and content classes in terms of summary writing, hoping to shed light on how summarization could be more effectively taught in second language writing courses. In this chapter, I will review key literature on summary writing to contextualize the study, and then introduce the research design, including the setting, the participants, and methods for data collection and analysis. Next, I will present major findings in relation to international undergraduate students' summary writing experiences across the disciplines, and outline pedagogical implications accordingly.

REVIEW OF THE RESEARCH

The importance of summary writing in higher education has been emphasized by a number of second language writing researchers (Kirkland & Saunders, 1991; Yang & Shi, 2003). As is generally agreed by university writing instructors, summary writing constitutes as "a gateway skill" (Frey, Fisher & Hernandez, 2003, p. 48) for undergraduate as well as graduate students to complete various types of source-based writing assignments in university settings. Also, summarization skill itself functions as an effective learning strategy for students to synthesize information from source texts and improve reading comprehension (Davis & Hult, 1997; Friend, 2001; Rinehart, Stahl & Erickson, 1986; and also see Center & Niestepski's chapter [this volume], in which the L2 students they interviewed talk about using summary writing to help them read and learn course material.) Conceptualizing summarization as an important literacy skill in English academic writing, writing researchers have examined novice writers' summary writing practices from different perspectives. The complexities of this particular reading-based writing task have drawn focused attention from researchers. In order to produce quality summaries, students need to interact with the source texts recursively, constantly reflecting on the reading materials and making decisions regarding the level of importance of information (Kim, 2001; Rinehart & Thomas, 1993). In other words, writers need to develop an accurate comprehension of the source texts and distinguish between the main substance and trivial details to produce a good summary. In addition, students are also expected to explain key points of the source texts in concise language, which is particularly challenging for second language learners with developing English proficiency. As Hill (1991) explains, "[t]he process of learning to write summaries is a long one, accomplished in stages as text-related variables interact with the developing writer" (p. 539).

Acknowledging the complexities of summarization, second language writing researchers have investigated major difficulties and challenges that novice academic writers encounter while working on such tasks. Johns and Mayes (1990), for instance, examined the processes of summarization by comparing the summaries produced by writers with high and low English proficiency. Their findings showed that although students with a lower level of English proficiency were more likely to rely on the original wording of the source text, both groups of writers struggled with generating main ideas in a condensed manner based on the text. Another study by Johns (1985) also demonstrated that although less proficient English writers were more inclined to focus on sentence-level information and infrequently combined idea units at a macro level, both novice and more experienced college writers distorted the ideas of the source text to a certain level and included personal comments in their summaries, the practices of which were inconsistent with the general expectations of academic summaries.

Kim (2001) explored Korean university students' summary writing practices in English. According to Kim, the participants most frequently utilized deletion as a strategy to generate a condensed version of the source text, and the EFL learners found it challenging to generalize and re-organize information to present main ideas. Also looking into summary writing processes, Yang and Shi (2003) investigated how six first-year MBA students (three Chinese ESL learners and three native English speakers) approached a disciplinary summary task that involved the reading and critical examination of a company case. Their findings suggested that the participants employed a wide range of composing strategies while working on the task, and students' previous learning experiences influenced their summarization performances. According to Yang and Shi (2003), among the six participants, those who had background knowledge in the content area and previous experience writing about topics within the discipline were in general more confident of and skilled in completing the task, whereas those who were relatively new to the field found the summarization task to be difficult. As graduate students have already chosen an area of study to pursue and are commonly expected to demonstrate their competence of providing meaningful discussions about disciplinary specific topics, content knowledge thus becomes an important variable that determines the level of success of disciplinary summarization.

Another challenge that novice academic writers often experience while completing summarization tasks involves using their own words to explain the meaning in written form. Keck (2006), for example, explored students' paraphrasing practices for summary writing. By comparing the paraphrasing behaviors of native-English speaking students and ESL writers, Keck (2006) showed that ESL writers relied on the original wording of the source texts more than their American counterparts, highlighting the role that language proficiency plays in influencing writers' summary writing abilities. Also looking into the relationship between language competence and summary writing, Baba (2009) examined one particular aspect of lexical proficiency and how it affected L2 writers' summarizing abilities. According to Baba (2009), the participants' competence of defining words and manipulating synonyms played a critical role in determining the quality of their summaries. Comparing original source texts and students' summaries, Basham and Rounds (1984) found out that writers seemed to have difficulties maintaining the original tones of the authors through appropriate manipulation of verb tenses, adverbs and modal verbs. Also exploring wording and meaning changes, Hood (2008) analyzed the processes of summarization based on brief notes taken along the source text. The researcher showed how the seemingly straightforward process is in fact a complex one, where writers needed to attend to subtle meaning implications of changed wordings while using their own words to express meanings.

These studies have all demonstrated multifaceted factors that may influence the quality of the final write-up of a summary. As Kirkland and Saunders (1991) aptly point out in their article, both internal constraints (e.g. language proficiency of the writers, knowledge about the content of the readings, cognitive and metacognitive skills to distinguish between important and trivial information and to control the processes of summary writing) and external constraints (e.g. the types of materials being summarized, the nature of the assignments, time limit, the target audience of the summaries) affect how the writers approach various summarization assignments. Moreover, these internal and external constraints "are all interactive" (Kirkland & Saunders, 1991, p. 114), which further complicates summary writing processes.

Considering the challenges that college students experience while working on summarization tasks, writing researchers have also examined potential teaching strategies that can help learners to develop an adequate ability of summary writing. Day (1986) contended that when dealing with challenging tasks such as summarization, writers would benefit from explicit instruction of specific writing strategies integrated with self-regulatory skills that help to monitor their own performances (e.g. checking and paying attention). Friend (2001) conducted a study to examine how explicit instruction on reading strategies may help novice writers to develop the ability of differentiating between main ideas and details in source texts. The participants of the study included three groups of college writers: one group was taught the strategy of argument repetition, a second group learned the strategy of generalization, and a third group (the control group) was asked to rely on their personal reactions to the texts while identifying main ideas. The results suggested that both experimental groups outperformed the control group in terms of the ability to distinguish between different levels of information. Based on the findings, Friend (2001) pointed out that explicit instruction on generalizing information of source texts is crucial in helping novice academic writers to develop the ability of going beyond the exact wording and understand the gist. Also advocating for explicit instruction, Casazza (1993) emphasizes the importance of directly showing students how to interact with texts and engage in meaning construction when summarizing. Cox, Bobrowski, and Maher (2003) also support explicit instruction on summary writing by sharing their experiences about how to teach business majors to critically evaluate source texts and identify key claims and ideas.

Kirkland and Saunders (1991) maintain that when teaching summarization, teachers may need to first attend to the instruction of essential study skills such as note taking in order to help learners to keep track of the different levels of information presented in the texts. Ko (2009) investigated the effectiveness of a module used to teach summary writing. The quantitative and qualitative findings showed that the Korean university students who participated in the study improved in terms of their ability to distinguish between different levels of information, and developed a more positive attitude towards their own ability of summary writing and the importance of learning to summarize effectively. Radmacher and Latosi-Sawin (1995) explained that engaging students in meaningful comparisons of summaries of different qualities would help learners to develop a clearer understanding of the criteria often used to evaluate summaries. The authors also advocated for the use of disciplinary reading materials as source texts for summarization tasks in order to expose students to authentic writing contexts that they are likely to encounter in different courses.

Although the extant literature has generated insights about the challenges that novice academic writers (ESL students in particular) encounter when working on summarization tasks and how writing courses could help learners to develop the ability to summarize, many of the studies are based on specially designed summary tasks in writing programs, with insufficient attention directed to the actual types of summarization assignments that students are expected to complete in disciplinary courses. To fill in the gap, the study reported here examined the summarization practices of a group of ESL undergraduate students studying in various disciplines at a US university.

METHODS

To shed light on ESL undergraduate writers' summarization experiences across disciplinary courses, this qualitative-oriented study tracked six focal participants pursuing undergraduate degrees at a comprehensive mid-western US university. The following research questions guided data collection and analysis.
- In what types of summarization tasks did the ESL writers engage in different disciplinary courses, including their major courses, general education courses, and elective courses? What expectations are commonly associated with such tasks?
- What are the participants' perceptions of the usefulness of summarization skill across the disciplines?
- What are the major connections and disconnections between what is taught in the ESL writing program and disciplinary expectations regarding summarization?

The study took place in a mid-western US university, which features a large international student population from Asian countries, China and South Korea in particular. The university offers a three-course sequence of ESL writing program that aims to help these international students develop an adequate understanding of academic writing so that they can successfully handle writing tasks commonly assigned in disciplinary courses. All incoming international undergraduates are required to take a placement test at the beginning of their studies and are then placed into one of the three courses according to their writing proficiency reflected by the test. Although there are a number of students who need to take the lowest-level course, the majority of international undergraduates are able to skip it because of their quality performance in the placement test and directly start with the latter two courses in the sequence. Both of these courses focus on source-based writing, with summary writing constituting a major component of the curricula, although in the most advanced course, summarization is often taught in relation to research paper writing.

The participants for this study were all students who took one or two required ESL composition courses with me in the past year. I first distributed a short survey that elicited information from a large number of students regarding whether they had experiences with summary writing in their disciplinary courses and invited those who had such experiences to participate in the study. Altogether, six core participants—Yvonne, Lee, Carla, Leslie, Gloria, Cherry (all pseudonyms)—completed the whole project with me. Lee was originally from Korea, whereas the rest of the participants were from China. Of the participating students, Yvonne and Lee were studying accounting, Carla was a finance major, Leslie was double majoring in mathematics and economics, and Gloria and Cherry were both studying in the architecture program. All the participants were international students who were relatively unfamiliar with English academic writing in general and summarization in particular before taking the ESL composition course. After recruiting the participants, I conducted semi-structured interviews with them, seeking information about the types of summarization assignments they were required to complete in various disciplinary courses and asking the participants to explain in detail the purposes and nature of the summarization tasks.

I also collected relevant documents, such as course syllabi where requirements about different writing tasks were explained as well as students' summarization products. In addition, I examined the course syllabi of the ESL writing courses regarding the teaching of summary writing, aiming to identify connections and disconnections between what participants did in the writing program and in different content courses. For data analysis, I adopted the commonly used "thematic analysis" (Glesne, 2006, p. 147), and continuously created and refined codes and categories based on my research questions.

FINDINGS

In this section, I briefly report major findings based on my analysis, focusing on three trends regarding summarization practices in disciplinary courses, namely, the incorporation of summarization as a prerequisite skill for source-based writing assignments, the diverse formats of source texts in different courses, and the extensive use of summarization as a tool for learning.

SUMMARIZATION AS A PREREQUISITE SKILL FOR SOURCE-BASED WRITING ASSIGNMENTS

As reported by the participants, summarization constitutes a threshold skill that they are expected to master in order to complete such larger writing tasks as article critiques, reading responses, and analysis papers commonly assigned in general education courses. As one participant, Leslie, said in the interview: "You just have to know how to summarize, because it's the beginning of almost every writing assignment." Leslie had abundant experiences with summary writing in a variety of courses that she took across the curriculum. In the introduction to design course that she took as an elective, for example, she was asked to read extensively on chosen topics according to the syllabus, and respond to the readings. In one week, she was asked to look for information about several designers, choose one to introduce his/her life and work, and then discuss how the person influences her thinking about design. The following guidelines were provided in the syllabus outlining the expectations of the assignment:

> ... choose one of those three designers and write an in-depth essay about their life, work, contributions, etc. Also include your own thoughts about their life, work, contributions, etc. Length is at your discretion, but remember you are in college now.

As the requirements show, this particular assignment features a mixture of summary writing and the expression of one's own ideas based on source information. In order to discuss how a particular designer's life and work impacted her, Leslie needed to know about the person first and introduce him/her. In the theater course that she took to fulfill the general education requirement, she was also required to explain her reactions, but this time based on show performances that she was expected to watch. To contextualize her own thoughts, she would always present a short summary paragraph in the beginning that briefly described the content of the performances, even though the theater teacher did not provide explicit requirements regarding the necessity of a summary paragraph. According to Leslie, even though the teacher did not specify this, she believed that a short summary of the performances at the beginning of the response paper was indispensable, since it would help readers who were not familiar with the performances to understand her later discussions.

Leslie's experiences with summary writing across the curriculum were quite representative of those of other participants who took different courses than she did (e.g. biology, food science and technology, history, economics, women's studies, architecture —many of which serve to fulfill the general education requirement). In these courses, students were frequently asked to read about certain topics in relation to the content of the courses, and discuss their ideas and perspectives accordingly. Due to the different focuses of the courses, these assignments often took on different forms. In her biology class, for example, Yvonne was asked to evaluate *New York Times* articles that introduced current developments in biological research and related controversies. In one assignment, she read an article about whether pregnant women in labor should follow a restricted diet, and then expressed her understanding of this issue from a Chinese perspective. (See Hirsch [this volume] for examples of writing projects in WID courses that include summary writing.)

Despite the various formats of the assignments, the essential task is quite similar, that is, to express one's informed opinions about certain topics based on source texts. Because of the central role reading plays in most of the disciplinary courses, summarization, which entails adequate reading comprehension, has become a tacit need for source-based assignments, although very few instructors directly explained this to the participants of the study. Although the ability to understand the given source texts seems to be assumed across the disciplines, L2 learners, who are quite unfamiliar with the content of the materials and are still developing their English language proficiency, often struggle with reading comprehension when being asked to complete summarization tasks. As the participants explained, they tended to spend a long time reading the assigned texts in order to make sure that their comprehension was accurate. (For a longer discussion of the challenges L2 students face when completing readings assigned in undergraduate US courses as well as strategies they develop to negotiate these challenges, see Center & Niestepski [this volume]). Sometimes, even after they tried to read the materials multiple times, they still felt uncertain about what the texts were discussing. As a result, the participants had to rely on guessing to some extent while working on their summaries, which inevitably influences the accuracy of the final write-ups.

When asked whether what they had learned in the ESL writing courses about summary writing was helpful for them to complete disciplinary writing tasks, the participants agreed that the content covered in the writing courses enabled them to understand the genre of summary in English, which was relatively unfamiliar to them. Leslie and Gloria, for example, were completely new to the concept of summarization before they took the ESL writing courses. As both of them explained in the interviews, they had never been asked to complete a summary task in their native Chinese language and had no previous knowledge about how to write a good summary. In this sense, the ESL writing courses provided basic information about summarization that functioned as building blocks for the L2 writers to deal with various disciplinary summarization tasks. Despite the general satisfaction with the content covered in the ESL writing courses, all participants also explained that they would have liked the writing classes to focus more on how to generate key ideas from long texts instead of the writing conventions associated with summary writing (e.g. the use of topic sentences and reporting verbs). As the participants described in the interviews, when evaluating the summary assignments, the disciplinary course instructors usually emphasized the accuracy of the information and often did not pay too much attention to their language style in which the summaries were written (See Zawacki & Habib and Ives, Leahy, Leming, Pierce, & Schwartz [this volume] for further discussion of faculty expectations for L2 writers).

DIVERSE FORMATS OF SOURCE TEXTS

The important role of summarization in disciplinary courses is probably not news to writing instructors; yet what is quite unexpected is the wide range of source texts that students are expected to work with across the curriculum. Although students are always expected to submit their summaries in written form, the source texts assigned for the summary tasks are not necessarily printed articles or books. Instead, students are often asked to summarize a variety of sources, including guest lectures, movies, video clips, paintings, and architectural models. One of the participants, Gloria, who majored in architecture, was asked to summarize guest lectures given by invited architects as well as her major learning from the talks. In such situations, what she needed to do was to listen to the lectures carefully, identify important points covered by the guest speakers, note them down in succinct manners, and write them up after the lectures. According to Gloria, such tasks were challenging in that she had to attend to both listening and note taking at the same time. As she explained in the interview, although she had studied in the United States for quite some time, she still encountered trouble listening to native-speaking professors and lecturers, and often had to spend extra time in her head to decode and digest the information from lectures. Often times, new vocabulary, discipline-specific terminologies, and cultural jokes that frequently appeared in the guest lectures caused her additional difficulties to understand the information. Consequently, she found it hard to keep up with the fast speed and unfamiliar content of the lectures. Also, since each of the lectures lasted for an hour, Gloria found it extremely demanding to keep track of the gist and distinguish between different levels of information. As she vividly described, "The lectures are long, and my mind begins exploding, and I just cannot tell which is the gist, which is the detail." (See Center & Niestepski [this volume] for ways in which L2 students use reading to better understand course lectures.)

Because of these major challenges, Gloria had to make the best use of what she was capable of doing when working on the summarization tasks: she only selected points that she was relatively confident of to include in the final write-up. As Adamson (1990) points out, note taking is a cognitively and linguistically challenging task for most ESL students, since learners need to comprehend the information obtained from lectures, differentiate between the gist and details, identify certain logic that guides the presentation of the information and then concisely write down the most important points. ESL students, whose English proficiency is still developing, will naturally confront major difficulties in trying to understand the terminology-heavy lectures as well as finding the most effective language to note down important information. As Adamson (1990) aptly explains, faced with the challenges of note taking, ESL learners often "had to make a trade off between understanding what the teacher was saying and taking notes" (p. 71), which inevitably led to partial comprehension of the lectures.

Leslie also had the experience of working with multimedia source texts in her elective dance and design classes. In her dance class, she was asked to watch short video clips that demonstrated key movements of certain styles of dancing, and describe them in a written summary. As Leslie explained, the content of the video was not particularly challenging, since the information presented in a visual manner was straightforward enough for her to understand. Also, since the key movements demonstrated by the dancers were quite obvious, she did not experience much trouble identifying the major movements that characterize a particular dance style. Yet, she still found the task quite demanding in that it was difficult for her to transform the visual information that she obtained from the video clips into written English. As she said in the interview, "I can easily describe all the movements in speaking, but when you ask me to write them down, everything is different." According to Leslie, she always had trouble finding vivid words and phrases to describe the artistic dancing movements that she saw in the video clips. Although she got full grades for all the reports, Leslie believed that her summaries were inadequate in capturing the stylistic dancing gestures. As an ESL writer who had taken several academic writing courses, Leslie was still not confident of her ability to complete such summarization tasks.

For second language learners who are developing their English language proficiency, the summarization task itself is already challenging enough; yet, what these writers are expected to do in various disciplinary courses is often more demanding. Although these participants were fairly satisfied with what they had learned in the ESL writing program about summarization, they all discussed how the information introduced in the writing courses is, as Gloria puts it, "a little bookish," and does not transfer easily as they tackle disciplinary summarization tasks based on a wide range of multimedia source texts. With the increasing use of multimedia sources in disciplinary courses, the traditional text-based summarization strategies commonly taught in ESL composition courses, such as underlining key points, paraphrasing topic sentences, selecting and omitting words from source texts, seem rather insufficient in helping L2 writers to achieve success in summarization tasks across the curriculum.

EXTENSIVE USE OF SUMMARIZATION AS A LEARNING TOOL

Apart from relying on summarization skill to complete various source-based writing assignments, the participants also used it extensively in their studies as an effective way to organize information. Although the students were majoring in different disciplines, they all had to read widely on diverse topics in most courses. Yvonne, for example, was asked to read six books throughout a quarter for her general education women's studies class. Lee, who was an accounting major, often had to read thick textbooks in her major accounting courses. Cherry, an architecture major, was expected to read theoretical articles that explained the rationales behind the design of certain buildings. For them, summarization became an indispensable tool to keep track of all the information obtained from the heavy readings. According to the participants, they were expected to differentiate between the main ideas and less important details in most of the courses that they took. Although the professors might not explicitly ask them to summarize the texts, quizzes were regularly used to assess whether the students had read the required materials and understood the most important points presented in them. Because of this implicit expectation, the participants consciously employed summarization as a study aid to help themselves distinguish between different levels of information. Lee, for example, would take notes while reading her thick textbooks. After reading a page or so, she would write down in her notebook what she considered as key points. To save time, she chose not to compose paragraphs of summaries; rather, she used bullet points to list the most important concepts introduced in the books. As she explained in the interview, "In this way, I get to remember the knowledge better, and I don't have to go back to the whole book when I need to look up something." According to her, the summary notes were particularly helpful for exam preparation, since she normally did not have sufficient time to go through the thick textbooks again towards the end of a quarter when assignments and tests started to pile up.

Similarly, another participant, Carla, also actively used summarization in her reading to take notes; yet, unlike Lee, Carla chose to write her notes down on the margins of the texts. When she was preparing for the discussion sessions of her human resources class, she wrote brief notes (both in English and her native Chinese language) on the margins of the articles that she was assigned to read. She also printed out discussion questions that were provided by the instructors and wrote down her short responses based on her summary notes. For example, when answering the question "What policies could the firm or the nation implement if they wanted women to lessen their specialization in home production?" she jotted down several points ("provide same or more wages than men; regulate their working time") based on her reading notes. As Carla said in the interview, "I can understand the academic articles more clearly if I use my own words to express the information. If I don't do this, I feel that I don't really get what the authors want to say." As the cases of the participants demonstrate, the skill of summarization permeates their undergraduate studies because of the large amount of reading in which they are expected to engage. Even though course instructors may not require them to summarize all the texts, the participants still did so in their own ways in order to grasp the most important points discussed in the texts. Gloria vividly explained her understanding of the role that summarization plays in her disciplinary courses, "We always do summarizing in various cases, but sometimes we do not even realize that."

DISCUSSION AND CONCLUSION

Based on the findings generated by this qualitative study, it is not unreasonable to conclude that summarization skill does play an essential role in L2 undergraduate students' academic literacy experiences across the disciplines. Since most courses require students to work with source texts, summarization is indispensable for learners to distinguish between the gist and less important details. As the study has shown, summarization functioned as a prerequisite skill for these ESL students to complete source-based assignments, such as article critiques and reading responses. In a variety of courses, students were also expected to work with non-traditional multimedia source texts and express their ideas and perspectives accordingly. In addition, due to the large amount of reading in which they were required to engage, the participants also used summarization as a learning strategy that helped them to organize information obtained from reading materials.

In ESL writing courses, summary writing is often taught as a separate and well defined genre: students are asked to read an article and produce a coherent paragraph of summary. Because it is considered primarily a writing task, ESL composition courses tend to focus more on the final product of the summaries, highlighting the importance for writers to adopt an expected academic style in their write-ups. In disciplinary courses, however, the emphasis of summarization is placed on comprehension, and learners are expected to display an accurate understanding of source texts. Accordingly, disciplinary course instructors often do not pay much attention to the style in which the summaries were written. Such a discrepancy in the emphasis of summarization in writing and disciplinary courses may serve to explain why ESL students who have learned about summary writing in composition courses still experience difficulties while summarizing disciplinary texts. Although general knowledge covered in writing courses helps L2 writers, who are often unfamiliar with summarization conventions in English (Moore, 1997), to develop some understanding of the task, it seems inadequate for the learners to deal with the often more complex expectations in disciplinary courses regarding summarization.

In order to best help ESL writers to cope with the diverse summarization tasks in disciplinary courses, writing programs need to re-conceptualize summarization as an essential literacy skill apart from teaching it as an important genre. Considering the challenges that L2 writers encounter while reading source texts, ESL writing courses need to place more emphasis on how to interact with texts effectively. To prepare L2 learners for the large amount of reading on various topics expected in disciplinary courses, L2 writing courses also need to take into consideration the range of topics while choosing source texts for summarization tasks. In addition, instead of using reading materials (e.g. stories, newspaper articles) as the only type of source texts, writing courses could incorporate multimedia sources and assist L2 writers to work with them. For example, ESL writing courses could introduce note taking as a particular type of summarization (Kirkland & Saunders, 1991), and help familiarize learners with the situations where they are expected to shuttle between different skills, such as listening and writing, or reading and writing. In addition, writing instructors may need to spend more time teaching embedded summarization to better prepare students for larger source-based assignments that require them to express their opinions based on the summaries.

As for instructors across the disciplines, it is important to develop the awareness that ESL writers, who are still developing their language proficiency in English and who are generally unfamiliar with disciplinary expectations in the Anglophone academic context, often encounter major challenges and difficulties as they work on summarization tasks. Instead of assuming that L2 learners have already developed sufficient reading skills to comprehend source texts and a linguistic repertoire to explain the main points and substance of the material, disciplinary instructors need to provide more specific guidance as they assign summarization tasks. For example, course instructors could provide brief reading guides that outline the general organization of the reading materials to help L2 learners cope with the large amount of reading filled with disciplinary terminologies and background knowledge. Also, worksheets that contain key disciplinary vocabulary would also be beneficial for L2 writers to complete the write-up of the summaries. (These recommendations for instructor support and guidance are similar to those given by Center & Niestepski [this volume] in their chapter on L2 students' strategies for coping with the heavy reading demands of their courses.) Although the focus of most disciplinary courses is not on writing, explicit instruction about how to approach major writing tasks is still needed to facilitate novice academic writers, L2 learners in particular, to cope with varied disciplinary expectations across the curriculum.

REFERENCES

Adamson, H. D. (1990). ESL students' use of academic skills in content courses. *English for Specific Purposes, 9*, 67-87.

Baba, K. (2009). Aspects of lexical proficiency in writing summaries in a foreign language. *Journal of Second Language Writing, 18*, 191-208.

Basham, C., & Rounds, P. (1984). A discourse analysis approach to summary writing. *TESOL Quarterly, 18*, 527.

Bridgeman, B., & Carlson, S. (1984). Survey of academic writing tasks. *Written Communication, 1*(2), 247-280.

Casazza, M. (1993). Using a model of direct instruction to teach summary writing in a college reading class. *Journal of Reading, 37*(3), 202-208.

Cox, P., Bobrowski, P., & Maher, L. (2003). Teaching first-year business students to summarize: Abstract writing assignment. *Business Communication Quarterly, 66*(4), 36-54.

Davis, M., & Hult, R. (1997). Effects of writing summaries as a generative learning activity during note taking. *Teaching of Psychology, 24*(1), 47-49.

Day, J. (1986). Teaching summarization skills: Influences of student ability level and strategy difficulty. *Cognition and Instruction, 3*(3), 193-210.

Frey, N., Fisher, D., & Hernandez, T. (2003). "What's the gist?" Summary writing for struggling adolescent writers. *Voices from the Middle, 11*(2), 43-49.

Friend, R. (2001). Effects of strategy instruction on summary writing of college students. *Contemporary Educational Psychology, 26*, 3-24.

Glesne, C. (2006). *Becoming qualitative researchers* (3rd ed.). Boston, MA: Pearson Education.

Hale, G., Taylor, C., Bridgeman, B., Carson, J., Kroll, B., & Kantor, R. (1996). *A study of writing tasks assigned in academic degree programs*. Princeton, NJ: Educational Testing Service.

Hill, M. (1991). Writing summaries promotes thinking and learning across the curriculum-but why are they so difficult to write? *Journal of Reading, 34*(7), 536-539.

Hood, S. (2008). Summary writing in academic contexts: Implicating meaning in processes of change. *Linguistics and Education, 19*, 351-365.

Johns, A. (1985). Summary protocols of "underprepared" and "adept" university students: Replications and distortions of the original. *Language Learning, 35*(4), 495-511.

Johns, A. M., & Mayes, P. (1990). An analysis of summary protocols of university ESL students. *Applied Linguistics, 11*, 253-271.

Keck, C. (2006). The use of paraphrase in summary writing: A comparison of L1 and L2 writers. *Journal of Second Language Writing, 15*(4), 261-278.

Kim, S. (2001). Characteristics of EFL readers' summary writing: A study with Korean university students. *Foreign Language Annals, 34*(6), 569-581.

Kirkland, M. R., & Saunders, M. A. (1991). Maximizing students' performance in summary writing: Managing cognitive load. *TESOL Quarterly, 25*, 105-121.

Ko, M. (2009). Summary writing instruction and student learning outcomes. *English Teaching, 64*(2), 125-149.

Leki, I. (2007). *Undergraduates in a second language: Challenges and complexities of academic literacy development.* New York: Laurence Erlbaum Associates.

Moore, T. (1997). From text to note: Cultural variation in summarisation practices. *Prospect, 12*, 54-63.

Radmacher, S. A., & Latosi-Sawin, E. (1995). Summary writing: A tool to improve student comprehension and writing in psychology. *Teaching of Psychology, 22*(2), 113-115.

Rinehart, S. D., Stahl, S. A., & Erickson, L. G. (1986). Some effects of summarization training on reading and studying. *Reading Research Quarterly, 21*(4), 422-438.

Rinehart, S. D., & Thomas, K. E. (1993). Summarization ability and text recall by novice studiers. *Reading Research and Instruction, 32*(4), 24-32.

Yang, L., & Shi, L. (2003). Exploring six MBA students' summary writing by introspection. *Journal of English for Academic Purposes, 2*, 165-192.

CHAPTER 5

ON CLASS, RACE, AND DYNAMICS OF PRIVILEGE: SUPPORTING GENERATION 1.5 WRITERS ACROSS THE CURRICULUM

Kathryn Nielsen
Merrimack College

The purpose of this qualitative study was to better understand generation 1.5 student perceptions of WAC and writing faculty, their interactions with white, native English speaking peers in the classroom, and to hear ideas from them about ways to create more inclusive writing practices and environments across the disciplines. The study found that despite being valued for their diversity of thought and experience, these multilingual students experienced discrimination both inside and outside the classroom. It is argued in this essay that in order to create and maintain inclusive classrooms, instructors must also take into consideration attitudes pertaining to the socioeconomic, racial, and linguistic climate of their institution.

Diversity must be couched within a context of institutional engagement, be driven by transformational leadership, be valued by the faculty community, and be experienced by all students as a core component of their educational experience.

—James A. Anderson, *Driving Change through Diversity and Globalization: Transformative Leadership in the Academy*

Only thirty years ago, it would have been nearly impossible to locate scholarship on multilingual, multicultural students' literacy and learning experiences, yet the field has grown exponentially in the last decade and a half. This surge of academic inquiry acknowledges that we are living in times where technology and global migration patterns are changing the identities of neighborhoods, universities and workplaces. In higher education, teachers are working to meet the needs of differing student populations in composition and writing-in-the-disciplines classrooms with varying pedagogical approaches and degrees of institutional support. For small colleges whose demographic makeup has been predominantly white, monolingual, and monocultural, these demographic changes present both opportunities and challenges.

Such is the case at my home institution, a small liberal arts college in the northeastern US, where the goals and objectives of an equity program evolved from serving French-speaking Canadian hockey players to identifying, admitting, and supporting talented bilingual students from the greater surrounding community who are facing educational and financial difficulties.

Recognizing the needs of a neighboring immigrant city struggling to provide services for its growing Latino immigrant population, my institution created a pathway for local generation 1.5 students to gain admission and scholarships to the school. The admission of resident, immigrant multilingual, multicultural newcomers resulted in increased need for support services across institutional contexts, as well as highlighted the need for faculty development around writing and teaching. In an effort to help us better understand the writing needs of generation 1.5 students across the curriculum and to better support the faculty who teach them, my research invokes the voices of five multilingual, multicultural students from the Dominican Republic. The perceptions discussed in this study represent the participants' initiation into living, learning, and writing as a minority subculture within a predominantly white, affluent, monolingual campus culture. This IRB-approved, action research study was designed to explore multilingual writing experiences across the disciplines for the purposes of assisting composition and WAC faculty in the context of my institution. Pointedly, the results are not designed to be prescriptive; rather, they are intended to help frame some of the issues that must be addressed in order to achieve well-adapted, inclusive writing environments.

GENERATION 1.5 AT THE INTERSECTION OF CLASS AND RACE

The term generation 1.5 has come to represent a diverse range of multilingual, immigrant learners who were born and educated outside the United States and who enter the US educational system while in the process of learning English. Because generation 1.5 students arrive with vastly different educational, political, social and economic histories, it becomes imperative that researchers and instructors broaden and deepen their understanding of their students' academic realities (Roberge, 2009). Generation 1.5 learners in higher education may be traditionally-aged students between the ages of 18 and 22 or they may draw from non-traditionally aged demographics. Generation 1.5 students are highly differentiated in socioeconomic as well as documentation status (citizen, resident—documented or undocumented, and refugee). While it is difficult to secure accurate numbers for undocumented immigrant populations, the sending countries have typically been Mexico, El Salvador, and Guatemala (Louie, 2009). It is worth noting that contemporary immigration populations draw from all socio-economic levels from unskilled to highly skilled labor; however, there is a correlation between socioeconomic status and country of origin, specifically:

> Immigrants from "low SES [socioeconomic status]" tend to be from the sending nations of the Dominican Republic, El Salvador, Guatemala, Honduras, Haiti, Laos, and Cambodia. At the other end of the immigrant spectrum are "high SES groups" from many Asian, African, European, and South American nations. (Louie, 2009, p. 38)

According to a report by the Migration Policy Institute (2004), 82% of the immigrant Dominican population resides in the Northeast where this study was conducted; correspondingly, Dominican generation 1.5 students comprise a majority of enrollment in area colleges' equity programs. The resulting factors of low socioeconomic status such as underfunded schools, poverty, and crime, as well as family and employment responsibilities can affect student success and retention rates; as such, SES becomes an important consideration for WAC educators and researchers trying to reconceptualize writing pedagogies for immigrant learners in higher education

Inquiry into understanding cultural and linguistic minority students' experience with college and the subject of inclusion in higher education, in particular, continues to proliferate across disciplinary boundaries (Hale, 2004; Sheared, Johnson-Bailey, Colin, Peterson, Brookfield & Associates, 2010; ; Sheared & Sissel, 2001; Watson et al., 2002). Watsonet al. (2002) contend that the work of educating multilingual, multicultural minorities while expanding White student and faculty cultural awareness and competence remains a challenging one. However, in the fields of second language writing and WAC, research on class, race, relations of power, and other equity issues remains scant. In a study on the dynamic nature of identity formation among L2 writers in a secondary context, Ortmeier-Hooper (2010) reveals how class and peer dynamics influence the complex and difficult moves multilingual students make in order to gain acceptance among peers and in group settings. Researching the social class identity of three privileged second language writers whom the author labels as "the new global elite," Vandrick (2010) examines how privilege appears to mediate the effects of the deficit model, an attitude "so commonly applied (consciously or unconsciously) to second language writers" (p. 258). (See Fernandes' argument [this volume] for the need to rethink the curricula of for-profit language schools who serve this population.) Kubota (2003) corroborates the observation that the categories of race, class, and gender are commonly overlooked in the field of second language writing, especially as they apply to issues concerning positionality. In her article, Kubota highlights the need for new, interdisciplinary approaches to race, class, and gender in second language writing that move beyond locating rhetorical and linguistic differences associated with second language writers and toward understanding the politics behind inequality in specific contexts. In this regard, Roberge (2009) recognizes that multilingual, immigrant students who arrive and live in the US with lower socioeconomic status and whose "histories, experiences, and individual needs don't match traditional institutional profiles" (p. 4) may face additional challenges in terms of adaptation, identity formation, and marginalization. This recognition resonates well with this study.

As diversification trends continue to evolve across campuses nationwide, researchers are beginning to openly discuss the politics behind the scholarly and institutional silence on race and diversity that affects multilingual and multicultural writers. Pointedly, Anson (2012) asserts that WAC scholars have remained notably silent on issues concerning racial and ethnic diversity, particularly as they apply to assessment practices. In a comprehensive literature review focused on race and ethnicity, Anson broadens his claim to state that WAC scholars either "skirt issues of race or ignore them entirely" (p. 18). But it is precisely there, in the assumptions, forces, and barriers that underlie the silence surrounding class, race, ethnicity, and linguistic inequality that the conversation must begin. It is my sense that Hall (2009) is speaking to the issue of inequality when he challenges WAC/WID faculty who often self-identify as institutional change agents to work toward developing "differentiated instruction methods so that *both* monolingual, English speakers and multilingual learners simultaneously have a rich and satisfying classroom experience *in the same writing classroom*" (emphasis in the original, p. 42). We must explore local diversification trends, Hall asserts, as we begin to "rethink everything that we do to meet the new realities that we face on our campuses and in our classrooms" (2009, p. 42).

Anson (2012) speaks plainly about the thorniness and unease of the work ahead, as the journey involves addressing issues that commonly induce discomfort and illustrate our under preparedness, especially in predominantly white, monolingual writing classrooms and campus environments. This study describes the early stages of one faculty member's attempt to answer Hall's call to action. By beginning a dialogue with immigrant multilingual writers on a campus where their demographic status places them as a decided socioeconomic and racial minority, I hope to better understand student perceptions of WAC and writing faculty, their interactions with white, native English speaking peers in the classroom, and to hear ideas from them about ways to create more inclusive writing practices and environments across the disciplines.

My research examines participant responses to a central question: How do generation 1.5 students describe their writing experiences in the context of a predominantly white, monolingual college? During the interview process, which I'll describe shortly, the five Dominican participants were asked to describe their experiences as writers in the Introduction to College Writing (CW) course and writing-intensive (WI) courses, with attention being paid to working with faculty and working with their peers. Other open-ended questions included: With regard to improving your writing skills, what helped or hindered you in your CW and WI courses? What did you find the most rewarding? What did you find the most challenging? Given the lack of faculty development and diversity training at the research institution, I was particularly interested in hearing how these generation 1.5 students were faring.

METHODS

Setting

The institution where this research occurred is situated on the grounds of two affluent, predominantly white, suburban communities in the Northeast; the institution also borders an urban city that has been the home of immigrants since the twentieth century and continues to be so today with 30.6% of the population being foreign-born and where 28.2% of the population are naturalized citizens.1 Further, the city is the "street" site for the majority of the community projects that the college sponsors. Demographic statistics highlight several marked differences among these neighboring cities. According to recent census data for the immigrant city, the Hispanic or Latino population is 59.7% of its overall population and 34.3% of all households living below the poverty line. Compare these statistics to the college's city census data where the population is 93.7% white and 2.1% of the overall population live below the poverty line. The college comprises mainly self-selected students who resonate with the mission to "Enlighten minds, Engage Hearts, and Empower Lives." The demographics of the student population also reflect those who can manage the high cost of a small private college. Diversity data from 2010 show the largest percentage of full-time students identified as "white non-Hispanic" (81%); followed by "Race/ethnicity unknown" (12%); "Hispanic" (3%); "Asian/Pacific Islander" (1.7%); "black non-Hispanic" (1.3%), and "American Indian/Alaskan Natives" (.1%). (See Cox [this volume] on the importance of understanding local demographic contexts and student populations when planning WAC faculty development and outreach around second-language writing across the disciplines.)

Participants

Utilizing Roberge's (2009) of generation 1.5 students as those who "immigrate as young children and have life experiences that span two or more countries, cultures, and language" (p. 4), I contacted the Academic Counselor for International and Intercultural Students in order to generate as comprehensive list of candidates as possible for the study. In this project, a homogeneous sampling was chosen in order to describe a particular subgroup of learners and instructors in depth (Patton, 2002). In consultation with the academic counselor, 39 students were identified based on Roberge's definition and subsequently invited to participate in this study. Sixteen students responded with interest; however, only seven met the criteria I'd set for the study, which included enrollment in the equity program, arrival time to the US, and completion of both Introduction to College Writing and a Writing Intensive (WI) course in the disciplines, which all students must take as an institutional requirement. Introduction to College Writing (CW) is typically taken in a student's first or second semester of freshman year; and a writing course in the disciplines with a writing intensive (WI) designation, can be taken at any point prior to graduation.[2] The seven students who met these qualifications were invited to participate in the study; five accepted the invitation.

The five participants in this study are traditionally aged, male and female, generation 1.5 students between the ages of 19 and 22 who emigrated from the Dominican Republic to the US between the seventh and eighth grades. In middle school, they were placed in an immersion program that included bilingual classrooms, as well as in ESL courses focused on English language development. It is relevant to note that the institution's equity program partners primarily with one neighboring high school; as such, the participants are drawn from the same secondary institution, which has a predominantly Hispanic, immigrant student population. Specifically, participants attended a public high school where the student population was 88.2% Hispanic (largely Dominican and Puerto Rican), and resided in a city showing a median household income of $25,983. Their success in high school was recognized by their acceptance to an equity scholarship program at my institution where the city median household income is $116,723. As Hispanics, they would represent 3% of the college's student population. All participants were enrolled as full-time, matriculated students who were taking four, four-credit courses each semester. All five participants worked part-time jobs.

Instruments

Using standardized, open-ended questions, I conducted two in-depth, taped and transcribed interviews with each of the participants.
- *Interview One: Focused Life History.* (Centered on the participant's background including immigration history, culture, prior education, family, and language acquisition. Students filled out and submitted their responses to a questionnaire to me ahead of the first interview. See Appendix A.)
- *Interview Two: The Details of Lived Experience.* (Follow-up centered on present experiences in first-year writing and writing across the disciplines.)

During the interviews I noted that the participants seemed to struggle to arrive at specific suggestions for improvements faculty could make in their teaching and classroom management. I suspected that either the participants needed more time to form a response and/or they were reluctant to share with me, a white primarily monolingual faculty member. As a result, I wrote individually to the students via email and revisited the question: "What could writing and writing intensive instructors do to improve your experience as a multilingual writer and student?" Four of the five students responded. I read through the transcriptions and written responses during the first stage of the analysis process to get a holistic sense of the participants' responses. As I moved closely through the data, I noted emerging themes in the margins that related to the central research question and reflected on these in my research journal. For a second analytic, I utilized a general accounting scheme for codes that were not content specific, but instead pointed to categories for which codes could be inductively developed (Miles & Huberman, 1994). The remainder of the coding process during data analysis followed Creswell's (2008) six-step process where codes changed, decayed, were eliminated, and reduced. Following that format, two main themes emerged in their responses.

The first theme I discuss in this chapter focuses on participants' perceptions of how they are viewed by faculty at the research institution. The second theme presents participants' perceptions of working with white, native English speakers (NES) in the writing classroom. Findings for these two themes include participants feeling valued for their diversity of thought and experience in the classroom by their writing and writing intensive instructors; the pedagogical practices that signaled inclusive attitudes from their instructors and which served to better support their writing and learning, and, conversely, discriminatory behaviors and practices from instructors and peers that served to distance them from their writing and campus learning experiences.

PARTICIPANT PERCEPTIONS OF FACULTY ATTITUDES

Based on a two-year study of generation 1.5 writing experiences, Goen-Salter, Porter, and vanDommelen (2009) concluded that it is critical for writing instructors to inquire about students' educational backgrounds and literacy and language experiences, as well to provide opportunities for students to comfortably describe them. While their study focused primarily on ESL and first year composition courses, this conclusion is just as relevant to WAC instructors as can be seen in the student responses to my question about how students felt faculty perceived their cultural and linguistic backgrounds. All five participants in my study expressed feeling as though they brought a different perspective to CW and WI courses across the disciplines that was recognized and appreciated by faculty. The students stated that, when choosing topics to research, offering peer feedback, and participating in classroom activities, they brought diverse interests and perspectives to the experience that were valued by the faculty. One participant said, "I think the teacher likes reading my papers because they are different from white students, because most of the time I write about my culture." Another offered, "I feel like my life experiences have been different than the typical [culturally and linguistically dominant] student. I feel like instructors saw the potential in me and my ideas, what I was bringing to the table." She continued with the following example:

> I have been doing research about immigration because that is what I know the most about from my personal experience and from my research on the topic, often times I am able to offer/add an insightful idea about the subject. Continuously, I lead towards topics that interest me and that I am in most interaction with daily. My classmates are not exposed to the things I am exposed to as a bilingual, minority student here; therefore, we do not write about the same things.

(See Hirsch [this volume] for a discussion of designing writing assignments that allow L2 students to draw on cultural knowledge and make connections to daily life, and see Phillips [this volume] for a description of a graduate student who found similar success by drawing on experience and knowledge from his home culture.) Another described her passion for writing, her love of reading, and how hard she is willing to work as real strengths that her teachers recognized. All five participants said that it was their grammar that caused them the most difficulty with writing, not their ideas.

I asked the participants if their CW and WI instructors inquired about their literacy history in class, during their individual conferences, or in a survey; all five responded no, but each of them assumed that their professors knew that they were not native English speakers owing to their accents and/or ethnicity. One participant stated:

> My instructor did not know my literacy history. She might have noticed because of my grammatical errors. I think that she might have noticed that I wasn't black because one of my papers was about the DR and stuff. My writing might be accented. I believe it is. My writing is different from other [student] writings that I have read. I don't know. I have an accent in speaking. I would have to say I write with an accent because I write like I talk.

Another participant said, "If it weren't for my accent, I think I'd be okay." Another smiled before alluding to her WI professor's knowing that she was not a member of the dominant student population: "I mean when I speak I don't sound like a white girl's [speech]. I don't sound like Paris Hilton, for example!" The same student added, "At first I was not comfortable doing presentations because I was self-conscious of my accent." Another participant discussed how an incident that occurred out of the classroom affected her sense of confidence in the classroom:

> I had a bad experience but that started out of class, you know. It was on Facebook and everywhere. They said that I couldn't speak English. It's the accent, you know, [it] makes it hard to be confident in class and to share your words. I was in shock at our first orientation. Everyone was just staring at you when you speak like they understood nothing. The white kids are more confident in class.

While no interview question discussed "writing with an accent" or specified the words "accent," "ethnicity," or "race," three of the five students perceived one or more of the latter as identifying markers of being a linguistic, cultural minority in the WI classroom.

When discussing their writing experiences, all five participants indicated that CW and WI faculty were willing to make accommodations for them, such as giving them opportunities for additional individualized meetings and modifying assignments in order to address their specific writing needs. (In this volume, Zawacki & Habib also share findings that indicate that faculty are often willing to make accommodations for L2 students, and Hirsch demonstrates that the scaffolding inherent in writing-intensive pedagogy can also work to provide similar support.) Pointedly, all participants cited one-to-one contact time with their instructors as critical to their success. Individual conferencing has been established as a core pedagogical approach to meeting the needs of linguistically diverse writers, although it can place considerable demands on the instructor (Reynolds, Bae, & Wilson, 2009). In addition to benefiting the writing process in general, Watson et al. (2002) cite that for minority students on predominantly white campuses, faculty/student relationships remain "one of the most effective predictors of student outcomes" (p. 79). During the interviews, the students reported that both their CW and WI instructors made time or were willing to meet with them individually to discuss their writing, which they valued; all participants agreed that conferencing with faculty helped them to understand the assignments better and to improve their writing. One participant explained that her WI instructor "worked with me one-on-one for every paper I wrote. She worked with me directly, so I got a lot better in that class, and I learned how to write better." Another participant described one way that his (WI) math instructor worked to individualize a reflective writing assignment:

> I had to write two papers for my math class. So bad. She gave us theories. It was abstract math. We had to think of problem solving math, not normal number problems and we would write and it was really long, really extensive and I thought, "I can't do this." So the professor said if you draw me a picture of what the writing was, I'll give you that grade. I drew the picture, and she liked it. She was showing people the picture. It wasn't a research paper; it was a reflective paper, like a page. Writing the paper wasn't that bad. Putting it together was the problem. I gave her what the reading was about in the drawing—the main theories. I think she framed it and put it in

the math center. She told me she was going to do that.

While it's unclear whether this accommodation fit into the WI course objectives or the purpose of the writing assignment in particular, the modification did serve to reduce this student's anxiety. During the interview, the participant's response and demeanor demonstrated a felt connection to his learning experience. This connection instilled a sense of confidence that he had not only met the assignment goals, but that his work was valued and respected by his instructor.

In terms of working with faculty, all respondents cited not fully understanding the assessment practices of their instructors, which they felt was an added challenge to them as cultural and linguistic minorities. (See Zawacki & Habib [this volume] for faculty perspectives on evaluating and grading L2 students' writing.) Participants differed in how they described these assessment practices. Despite meeting with their professors and despite expressing feeling that their writing was improving, all participants shared frustration at seldom earning a higher grade than a B on most assignments. One student offered that in her CW course she could "never get an A on a paper. I'd have to rewrite it a lot. I always talked to the instructor about what I could do, and she saw my effort—but never an A." Another participant said that some faculty would help her; however, there was one instructor who "didn't get it." She recalled an incident that occurred in her WI psychology course when, after turning in her paper, she was called to meet with the instructor. The instructor informed her that the writing that she turned in was "too good." The participant interpreted this to mean that the instructor was calling her a cheater, although plagiarism was not specifically mentioned in their meeting. She went on to explain that she had worked extensively on the paper over the course of the semester; in fact, the paper was an extension of a shorter paper that she had started in another course and was a topic that she'd been interested in pursuing in-depth. She explained that this professor had only seen one other piece of her writing at the beginning of the semester—a brief reflection paper. As a result, the participant concluded that she had been judged inappropriately, especially in light of the professor's limited knowledge of her writing.

WORKING WITH CULTURALLY AND LINGUISTICALLY DOMINANT PEERS

In questioning participants about experiences involving group, collaborative, and peer review writing activities in their CW and WI courses, participants were asked about their perceptions and levels of comfort in working with linguistically and culturally dominant English L1 peers. In the majority of responses, participants referred to their CW course where peer review occurred regularly throughout the semester. While peer review may or may not be pedagogically central to WI courses, the participant's experiences offer insights for WI faculty who choose to assign collaborative activities or use peer review. Participants regularly measured their language skills in relation to their white, English L1 peers and viewed the classroom as a competitive environment. For example, one participant mentioned competition explicitly:

> I want to compete with the other students in the class. Not so much for the teacher, I mean I know what the teachers like, but I would like to be much better than my classmate than for my teacher to like it. I think it's definitely because of the second language. I mean because I write in a second language it makes me like want to be better. I have to try harder to be better. It has to do with me having to struggle in high school to learn English. I want to do extremely better. It's nice to get a great grade. I need to know that I did well, or as well as the other students. Or better would be good. It's just me trying to prove myself. I didn't have that when I was in high school. It only started when I came here.

Another participant concurred, "You're competing to gain approval. You feel you have to stand out." One participant reported that her lived experience as a bilingual minority directly informed the topics she commonly researched, which placed her "in a position of advantage." She added, "and that reduces my reader's critical point of view when reading my work." (See also Phillips [this volume] for a graduate student's perspective on how writing about knowledge gained from living in multiple nations and cultures gave him an advantage when seeking peers for a group project.)

Two participants expressed feeling comfortable during peer review even when they were the only multilingual writer in the class. One specifically preferred working with dominant students:

> I prefer to work with a native English speaker [during peer review]. I had that class [CW] with my roommate, and he had no grammatical errors ever. Nothing like me. So I don't think he would mind [working with a non-native writer]. I can offer the native students ideas. But that wasn't done at

the time. Only grammar. But we would talk about our papers all the time in the beginning.

The same participant expressed feeling discouraged, however, when seeing how many grammatical errors were present in his writing in comparison to other students' writing:

> My college writing was really, I mean sometimes I felt kinda weird because my writings had a lot of grammatical errors. Other people writing was like perfect. We had to put an X on sentences that had grammatical errors, and the paper that I got back were full of Xs. Others was almost perfect or with one X. I would definitely know how to fix the X, but it was discouraging.

One participant expressed frustration with working with a white, NES, student whose lack of response to the content of her writing left her feeling confused and distanced:

> I remember one time I was reading this guy's paper, and we were talking about the same thing ... something about an event in your life ... something that changed you. I was writing about my grandmother dying, and how I was watching my mother cry. It was a true story. And he was writing about when his grandfather died and how his father was going through that pain. So we were writing about the same thing, but we read our papers, and there was nothing there, and I got no feedback from him. No reaction, really dry. Maybe we needed more time, but for me it was one of those or maybe it could be something we worked together and feed each other ideas, but no response. I said, Oh, we're basically writing about the same thing, and he didn't say anything. I was taken off guard. I didn't know what to think of it, so I like pulled back.

In their responses, participants recalled tacitly comparing their writing to that of their NES peers during peer review. During one peer review session when a dominant student did not offer any response to one participant's writing, the participant indicated feeling that the dominant student was likely judging her: "[Maybe] he thought my paper wasn't as good. He was thinking, how can this girl be in this writing course with me? There is no comparison level. I don't know. I couldn't say anything because I don't know what he was thinking."

One participant reported on collaborative experiences with majority students that left him feeling marginalized:

> I had to deal with some students that were afraid that I could bring their grades down or that I would not be able to carry my load during a group presentation or lab projects. Sometimes students will ask me to take the easiest part or give me the least amount of time to present, which I was always against. I believe that every student in the group should have the same amount of responsibility and the same amount of time to present regardless of their abilities. How can you change this?

(Phillips [this volume] reports on a graduate student's similar experiences of being marginalized by English L1 group members when they worked on a collaborative project. See Cox [this volume] for advice for faculty on structuring peer review that avoids some of the problems described by the L2 students here.)

All participants made connections between their classroom experiences with writing and the attitudes of majority students inside and outside the classroom.

> They have told me that the numbers have gone up for diversity. I feel okay being in class as a minority. It's not that bad. I've heard a lot of stories about people treating other people bad because of their ethnicity in the classroom. Not by the teacher, but by other students. Um, I think it's more the attitude of the students. One of my friends was speaking Spanish in my writing class to another person and another person said, "Shut up. Don't talk Spanish in front of me because it's disrespectful." It was before the class started. It wasn't during class time. It was about disrespect to the other student. It's an attitude thing.

The participant shook his head while telling this story. I asked him if the stories of other multilingual students affected him in working with white, NES students. He posited:

> I would say that some of the stories affect me, but I try to not have any feelings like that during classroom. I know they

feel more comfortable with their group. Like if I'm here and there's a white girl here and a white guy here that she would prefer to talk to him in class discussion because they're more comfortable. That happens in the classroom. Everywhere.

One participant offered the following example of an interaction with majority students outside the classroom that affected her sense of self-worth and negatively affected her learning:

> One day last semester I was having lunch with an administrator and other students who were part of a leadership training. One student asked the VP what were they going to do with the academic levels of the incoming students. The student went on saying that when sitting in class some of these classmates asked questions that makes him think, "How can this kid be in class with me?" Apparently, he feels some of his classmates are not smart enough to be in class with him. Certainly me and other multilingual students felt uncomfortable with his comment, and he later apologized. The point is that this comment affected me because I feel uncomfortable when my fellow classmates think less of me for having less knowledge or being less smart than they are. It discourages me to express an opinion, and it could lead to lower self-esteem and self-doubt. The multilingual student knows a lot about other different things that his fellow [dominant] classmates do not know about.

The feelings of continuously being judged by and against the cultural and linguistic majority and needing to perform better than the NES students were not uncommon experiences for the students in this study. One participant stated that she felt WI faculty were also likely comparing their writing to that of their NES peers. She offered the following;

> The professor knew I knew the material, it's just the way I was writing it down didn't sound like the person next to me. Um, so that happened in that class and again this semester in another course where I had to write papers.

All participants emphasized the need for faculty to do more to raise the cultural awareness of the linguistic and cultural majority students on campus within the context of the classroom. Additionally, and across all interviews, students placed an enormous value on open discussions of one's culture. One participant articulated, "I think informing, educating others about the issues we encounter as minorities through discussion and lectures by experts on the topic would help." One respondent acknowledged that some WI faculty are working to raise student awareness of cultural differences by introducing inter/cross cultural topics into their coursework:

> It depends on the type of professor you have. In (WI) psychology my professor was from the Middle East, and he put in a lot of cultural things. He said that culture has an effect on psychology, and he would bring videos from other cultures and that had a big impact on class and the topics students could consider writing about.

Another participant felt that majority and minority students needed more opportunities to interact with one another on campus. She surmised that increasing interactions would help to engage students more fully in the classroom by reducing apprehension, increasing participation, and would serve to draw upon the strengths of all students:

> I believe that if students were given the opportunity to develop an open mind through interaction with the different ethnic groups on campus, students in general will have a chance of speaking up, of not shying away from all the opportunities presented to them, and of understanding the differences each and every one of us as students bring into a classroom. If students do not learn to accept, listen, and appreciate what the classmate is sharing, chances are that by the end of the day, a student will not learn to appreciate where each of us come from and thus will never understand that a classroom is not only composed of an instructor's teachings, but of the knowledge every individual brings forth in a shared community ... a diversified classroom.

IMPLICATIONS

While the findings from this study reflect a relatively small sample of students, they provide needed insight into the experiences of resident, multilingual writers who are navigating predominantly White, monolingual, socioeconomically privileged classrooms and campuses. I was surprised yet heartened to hear that the students overwhelmingly felt their instructors valued the diversity of thought and experience they brought in the classroom, especially in light of the fact that the instructors did not formally inquire about their cultural and linguistic backgrounds. However, the findings also suggest that these multilingual students experience discrimination, particularly in relation to their written accent, from peers and instructors, in relation to peer review and group work, assessment practices, and in the social dynamics of the classroom. Sue (2010) calls these "microaggressions," which he defines as "the brief and commonplace daily verbal, behavioral, and environmental indignities, whether intentional or unintentional, that communicate hostile, derogatory, or negative racial, gender, sexual-orientation, and religious slights and insults to the target person or group" (p. 5). These microaggressions (to which I would add "class") can have damaging consequences. The findings that center on discriminatory attitudes and behaviors in this study are particularly and more holistically troublesome when one considers that the institution partners with the neighboring immigrant city (where the generation 1.5 students draw from) for the dual purposes of providing community service and assistance and transformative learning opportunities for its undergraduate students. Ultimately, the participants in this study reported feeling, at times, alienated and distanced from the majority demographic based on perceived attitudes about difference, attitudes which could potentially affect their writing development considering that participants reported pulling back or being marginalized during peer and group writing activities. And the consequences are not limited to writing development; they also work to deny educational opportunities not only for the immigrant, multilingual writers in the classroom, but also for the white, monolingual majority.

Discovering the best practices for working with multilingual and multicultural writing students in a globalized educational context cannot focus solely on the multilingual students themselves. It must also include increasing the cultural and linguistic awareness of white faculty, students, and administrators and developing inclusive pedagogical practices. The five generation 1.5 student voices in this study support this argument. Sociocultural theorists posit that, increasingly, students "see themselves as the 'portfolio' of their experiences and achievements, gained through experience inside, and more and more importantly, outside of school" (Gee, 2001, p. 120). The student participants' responses support this connection between the campus climate around diversity and their in-class writing experiences. Correspondingly, WAC/WID professionals can benefit from understanding the impact of a hostile

campus climate on multilingual, multicultural students as they work to create and maintain welcoming, inclusive, and safe writing classrooms across the disciplines. The generation 1.5 student responses in this study suggest potential places to begin:
1. Ask about student literacy histories in writing and writing-intensive classrooms.
2. Develop ways to individualize course curricula, assignments, and pedagogical practices based on these histories.
3. Frame peer review practices to include discussions of accented voice (both oral and written), appropriation,[3] and the cultures of silence.[4]
4. Imbed one-to-one conferencing time into the syllabus or semester planning in order to individually talk about current writing experiences.
5. Develop assessment practices that acknowledge cultural and linguistic diversity.
6. Commit to understanding the cultural, linguistic, and socioeconomic climate on campus as well as increasing personal cultural awareness, especially as it applies to one's own institutional context.

At my institution, we are in the beginning stages of designing a series of ongoing faculty workshops and brown-bag lunches for the purpose of addressing these very issues.

According to Watson et al. (2002), existing research on linguistic and cultural minority students' experiences on predominantly white campuses exposes the tenuous nature of the relationships that minority students share with their non-minority faculty and fellow students. The causes of strained interactions and relationships are varied but appear to center on "a lack of critical mass of minority students, harassment based on ethnic [and/or linguistic] identification, curricula that imply assimilation as the only measure of success, low expectations from professors, social events and hangouts that are off limits, and negative attitudes from labeling and placement" (p. 70). Additionally, Louie (2009) points out low SES students may also face dominant majority concerns that "immigration will alter our language (witness the English-only movement) and debates about whether immigrants serve as a benefit to or drain on the nation's economy" (p. 38). The responses provided by the generation 1.5 participants in this study are consistent with many of the concerns articulated in the literature cited above and point to the need for critical, transformative, and emancipatory research that addresses how issues of class and race affect multilingual writers.

Writing is fundamentally a social act, and because we ask students to work collaboratively in our classrooms and to meet our expectations for their writing, it is imperative that we consider the implications of class, race, and language in these requests with a grounded knowledge of the local institutional setting and the students' experiences. Secondary research such as that I've presented here can also help us understand better our multilingual, multicultural students. Hall posits that the future of WAC "is indissolubly tied to the ways in which higher education will have to, willingly or unwillingly evolve in the wake of globalization in response to the increasing linguistic diversity of our student population" (p. 34). It is my belief that the success of *all* our students will depend on our commitment to addressing issues of equality and fairness in both our classrooms and campus environments.

NOTES

1. References to demographic and institutional data have been reported without citation in order to maintain anonymity for the institution and study participants.
2. My institution does not have a formal WAC program; instead, a well-funded writing center and writing fellows program provide support for faculty and student writers. Once students are admitted to the college, there are no language placement exams; correspondingly, CW is the sole credit-bearing, first-year writing course option—there are no basic, ESL, blended or linked course options offered. All CW and WI courses have enrollment caps of 15.
3. References to demographic and institutional data have been reported without citation in order to maintain anonymity for the institution and study participants.
4. Paulo Freire (1972) referred to cultures of silence as places where voices of oppressed groups were marginalized. He sought pedagogies that served to transform environments where such marginalization persisted.
5. Adapted from pp. 238-240 of Goen-Salter, Porter, and vanDommelen (2009).

REFERENCES

Anderson, J. A. (2008). *Driving change through diversity and globalization: Transformative leadership in the academy.* Sterling, VA: Stylus.

Anson, C. (2012). Black holes: Writing across the curriculum, assessment, and the gravitational invisibility of race. In A. B. Inoue & M. Poe (Eds.), *Race and writing assessment* (pp. 15-28). New York: Peter Lang.

Creswell, J. W. (2008). *Educational research.* Upper Saddle River, NJ: Pearson.

Freire, P. (1972). *Cultural action for freedom.* Harmondsworth, UK: Penguin.

Gee, J. P. (2001). Identity as an analytic lens for research in education. *Review of Research in Education, 25,* 99-119.

Goen-Salter, S., Porter, P., & vanDommelen, D. (2009). Working with generation 1.5 pedagogical principles and practices. In M. Roberge, M. Siegal, & L. Harklau (Eds.), *Generation 1.5 in college composition: Teaching academic writing to US-educated learners of ESL* (pp. 235-259). New York: Routledge.

Hale, F. W. (2004). *What makes racial diversity work in higher education.* Sterling, VA: Stylus.

Hall, J. (2009). WAC/WID in the next America: Re-thinking professional identity in the age of the multilingual majority. *WAC Journal, 20,* 33-47.

Kubota, R. (2003). New approaches to gender, class, and race in second language writing. *Journal of Second Language Writing, 12,* 31-47.

Louie, V. (2009). The education of the 1.5 generation from an international migration framework: Demographics, diversity, and difference. In M. Roberge, M. Siegal, & L. Harklau (Eds.), *Generation 1.5 in college composition: Teaching academic writing to US-educated learners in ESL* (pp. 35-49). New York: Routledge.

Migration Policy Institute. (2004). *The Dominican population in the United States: Growth and distribution.* Retrieved from http://www.migrationpolicy.org/pubs/MPI_Report_Dominican_Pop_US.pdf

Miles, M. B. & Huberman, A. M. (1994). *Qualitative data analysis* (2nd ed.). Thousand Oaks, CA: Sage.

Ortmeier-Hooper, C. (2010). The shifting nature of identity: Social identity, L2 writers, and high school. In M. Cox, J. Jordan, C. Ortmeier-Hooper, & G. G. Schwartz (Eds.), *Reinventing identities in second language writing* (pp. 5-28). Urbana, IL: NCTE.

Patton, M. Q. (2002). *Qualitative research and evaluation methods* (3rd ed.). Thousand Oaks, CA: Sage.

Reynolds, D., Bae, K-H, & Wilson, J. (2009). *Generation 1.5 in college composition: Teaching academic writing to US-educated learners in ESL.* New York: Routledge.

Roberge, M. (2009). A teacher's perspective on generation 1.5. In M. Roberge, M. Siegal, & L. Harklau (Eds.), *Generation 1.5 in college composition: Teaching academic writing to US-educated learners in ESL* (pp. 3 -24). New York: Routledge.

Sheared, V., Johnson-Bailey, J., Colin, III, S., Peterson, E., & Brookfield, S.D. (2010). *The handbook of race and adult education.* San Francisco: Jossey-Bass.

Sheared, V., & Sissel, P.A. (2001). *Making space: Merging theory and practice in adult education.* Westport, CT: Bergin and Garvey.

Sue, D. W. (2010). *Microaggressions in everyday life.* Hoboken, N.J.: Wiley & Sons.

Vandrick, S. (2010). Social class privilege among ESOL writing students. In M. Cox, J. Jordan, C. Ortmeier-Hooper, & G. G. Schwartz (Eds.), *Reinventing identities in second language writing* (pp. 257-272). Urbana, IL: NCTE.

Watson, L. W., Wright, D., Terrell, M., et al. (2002). *How Minority Students Experience College: Implications for Policy and Practice.* Sterling, VA: Stylus Publishers.

APPENDIX: STUDENT SURVEY QUESTIONS[5]

Your Student Information
   Name:
   Email:
   Phone Number:
   Class level: Freshman Sophomore Junior Senior Other:
   What is your major?
   How many credit hours are you taking this semester?
   Are you a Massachusetts resident or an out of state student?
   Are you working this semester? If so, how many hours per week?
   Where were you born?
   When did you arrive to the US?
   When did you start school in the US?

Your Family Information
   What language(s) does your father speak? Mother?
   What language(s) does your father write? Mother?
   What is the highest level of education your father received? Mother?
   What langue does your family use at home? At work?
   Do they use more than one language at home? At work?
   Do you have brothers and sisters? What are their ages?
   Where do they live and with whom?
   What languages do you use with your brothers and sisters?
   Do you/your parents or relatives visit your home country? How often?
   How often do you/they call your relatives in your home country?
   How often do your relatives come to visit you in the US?
   How long do they stay here?

Your College Reading and Writing Experiences
   What writing or English courses have you taken at this school?
   Who were your instructors?

What writing or English courses have you taken at other schools over the past few years?
What Writing Intensive course did you take?
Who was your instructor?
Have you worked with a writing fellow before? If so, in what class?
Have you worked with a tutor in the Writing Center?
How often would you say you visit the Writing Center?

Your Language Background
How long have you been speaking English?
How long have you been reading English?
How long have you been writing English?
What language(s) do you speak in addition to English?
Do you read and write in another language? If so, which one(s)?
What language would you consider your "home" language(s)?
What's your strongest language for listening and speaking? (Check one)
English _____ My other language(s)_____Both (all) are strong_____
What's your strongest language for reading and writing? (Check one)
English_____ My other language(s)_____Both (all) are strong_____
Do you read for pleasure? If so, what and in what language(s)? For example, books, magazines, newspapers, other media?
Do you write for pleasure? If so what do you write and in what language(s)? For example, poetry, music, journals, social media (Facebook, MySpace, blogging) short stories, letters etc.

CHAPTER 6

WRITING INTENSIVELY: AN EXAMINATION OF THE PERFORMANCE OF L2 WRITERS ACROSS THE CURRICULUM AT AN URBAN COMMUNITY COLLEGE

Linda Hirsch
Hostos Community College, CUNY

Using both qualitative and quantitative measures, a WAC Coordinator examines the academic performance of ESL students in Writing Intensive (WI) classes at an urban community college. Drawing on comparisons of pass/fail rates and grades of ESL students in WI sections and non-WI sections of the same course, Hirsch reveals higher pass rates and greater retention for ESL students in WI sections. To contextualize and amplify the quantitative findings, Hirsch analyzes two WI syllabi from WI sections available to ESL learners to identify the pedagogical practices which may have contributed to student success. She concludes that ESL students can benefit from and succeed in WI classes that provide pedagogical supports including scaffolded writing assignments, informal writing-to-learn activities which recognize connections between reading and writing, models for writing, instructor feedback, opportunities for revision, practice in oral language development, and faculty open to addressing their needs.

I study, and I think I got the intelligence what is with this, but it's too much. And without help ... I can read, but I need three days. I need some few days to understand this work and compare with my dictionary. —Astrubal, ESL student enrolled in Introduction to Business (Hirsch, 1986, 1988)

I have to read [Dewey's chapter] twice because when I read first time I don't understand. I'm lost ... My questions is I'm not sure

> if [Dewey] believe in science or he just believe in philosophy ... Because I'm not sure ....
>
> —Neha, ESL student enrolled in Introduction to Philosophy WI (Fishman & McCarthy, 2001).

Though decades apart, the voices of the English-as-a-Second Language (ESL)[1] students above reverberate, reminding us of the seemingly intractable hurdles they must overcome on their quest to academic success. This quest is only intensifying with increasing numbers of students entering our campuses with native languages other than English. The impetus to mainstream ESL students into English-language content courses has quickened over the last decade with more and more of these students finding themselves sitting alongside native speakers of English (NES) in college classes. Today ESL students will not only be enrolled in a college-level content course taught in English, but they may also be taking writing-intensive (WI) courses as part of a Writing Across the Curriculum (WAC) program. Since their start in the 1970s, WAC programs have proliferated with substantial growth over the past twenty years. Thaiss and Porter (2010) report that since the previous nationwide survey of WAC/WID undertaken in 1987, the presence of such programs in the US has increased by one-third. But how much do we know about their effects and effectiveness on the academic performance of second-language (L2) learners? In her comprehensive review of the literature on ESL students in WAC programs and WAC scholarship, Cox (2010) notes that few studies exist on the experiences of L2 writers in courses designated as WI and that WAC research, until quite recently, has not addressed the issue of supporting these students in WAC programs. Research on the impact of WAC programs on community college students is even more limited (Gardner, 2010), perhaps owing to the smaller presence of WAC programs on community college campuses as compared to other higher education institutions (Thaiss & Porter, 2010).

With many campuses implementing such programs along with their concomitant requirements of more complex and genre-specific writing, the demand for academic language proficiencies has become even greater. A number of second language and WAC researchers (Leki, 1995; Zamel, 1995; and Zawacki & Habib, 2010) have provided us over the years with voices of ESL students as they describe the tensions inherent in their attempts to negotiate the differing linguistic demands of courses across the curriculum. Their narratives reveal that ESL students in WAC programs have more than writing to worry about. The transition from an ESL class to academic classes in English is a huge leap in the complexity of material to be comprehended and the corresponding linguistic and cognitive proficiencies required. The multi-competencies needed to succeed in academic courses are broad and take time to acquire (Collier, 1995, and also see chapters by Center & Niestepski and Phillips [this volume] on the coping strategies L2 students employ to meet the reading and writing demands and expectations of their teachers across the disciplines). This chapter presents research undertaken at one urban community college to add to our understanding of the impact and academic effects of WAC programs on ESL students enrolled in WI classes across the curriculum as well as to identify those pedagogical practices which might explain these outcomes.

The ESL student struggle to succeed academically is readily apparent in the City of University of New York (CUNY), the nation's largest public university system, whose mission is to provide access to quality higher education for the full range of the city's inhabitants, regardless of income, gender, or ethnicity. The university serves more than 480,000 students at 23 colleges and institutions in New York City, including 11 senior colleges, seven community colleges, the Macauley Honors College, the Graduate center, and Graduate Schools of Journalism, Law, Professional Studies and Public Health. The CUNY system is also the nation's most diverse with a student population that is over 41% foreign born. It is against this backdrop of an urban, multi-campus, diverse student body that CUNY sought to strengthen its students' writing proficiencies. Recognizing the vital role that writing plays both in a college education and in future academic and professional success, the CUNY Board of Trustees passed a resolution in 1999 establishing a CUNY-wide Writing Across the Curriculum (WAC) Initiative, which mandated that writing instruction be a university-wide responsibility and that writing proficiency become "a focus of the entire undergraduate curriculum" (http://policy.cuny.edu/board_meetng_minutes/1999/01-25/pdf/#Navigation_Location). Each CUNY campus has developed its own WAC Initiative responsive to its own particular needs though most share pedagogical underpinnings derived from a broad range of WAC theorists and compositionists2 (Hirsch & Paoli, 2012). To bring this ambitious university-wide plan to fruition, the initiative is linked to a CUNY Writing Fellows Program which places CUNY doctoral students from a variety of disciplines on each member campus to assist in project implementation.

Of the approximately 230,000 CUNY undergraduates enrolled in fall 2011, 44% spoke a native language other than English. While lower levels of ESL instruction still exist at some of the CUNY community colleges, the ESL designation has virtually disappeared at the CUNY senior colleges. Yet the students have not. As it completes its first decade of its mandated university-wide WAC initiative, the City University continues to address the pedagogical needs of students whose placement tests indicate they are ESL or developmental students or whose language proficiency issues are not fully resolved upon admission or transfer to the four-year college. Often still lacking college-level proficiency in reading and writing, these students may not fare as well as their more prepared peers as they enter the college mainstream.

With many CUNY ESL students barred from admission to the senior colleges until they are able to pass CUNY-mandated proficiency exams in writing, reading and math, the university's seven community colleges have become the institutions responsible for welcoming these students into higher education and helping them become "college-ready." Hostos Community College, established in 1968 to serve the needs of NYC's impoverished South Bronx community, is an urban, bilingual college of 6000 students located just blocks away from Yankee Stadium. Fifty-five percent of Hostos' first-year students require developmental composition and 43% require developmental reading courses. The majority of these students plan on transferring to a four-year institution and will need more advanced literacy skills to make this transition. The Hostos WAC Initiative, renamed WAC/RAC (Reading Across the Curriculum) in 2005 to reflect the reciprocal relationship between reading and writing, is committed to serving the language and writing needs of all its students including ESL students, speakers of Black Vernacular English (BVE), and Generation 1.5 English-language learners. To that end, the WAC/RAC Initiative provides opportunities for writing and reading at all levels of a student's academic experience both generally throughout the curriculum and in specially designed WI classes. These courses require both informal writing and 10-12 pages of formal writing along with required faculty professional development. (See www.hostos.cuny.edu/wac for a description of WI criteria and policies.) At Hostos, WIs are certified by section based on faculty presentation of a WI syllabus designed for the course they teach. Thus in courses with multiple sections, only some sections may be designated WI. Though WI requirements vary among CUNY campuses, in many institutions, including most of CUNY's 11 senior colleges, WIs are viewed as capstone or higher-level courses. Yet developmental students and ESL students seem most in need of early exposure to increased writing and reading, including in WI courses which can support their evolving literacies.

Hostos requires that students complete two WI courses prior to graduation and permits students at the end of the ESL sequence (ESL 091/092) and developmental levels (ENG 091/092) to enroll in one WI course prior to passing CUNY exams for admission into Freshman Composition. But student gaps in reading and writing proficiencies provide a formidable challenge to a WAC program and raise a number of issues regarding its implementation. Can WAC principles and pedagogies help these students to succeed in college-level course work? Is it an unfair burden to second-language students to enroll them in more demanding WI sections when non-WI sections of the same course are often available? And is it unreasonable to expect faculty who teach WI courses to also address the more complex reading and writing difficulties these students bring to class?

With course pre- and co-requisites set by departments, and with more departments raising the pre- and co-requisite English-levels for WI courses to a minimum first-year composition level (ENG 110), it seemed the time had come to look closely at the performance of ESL and developmental students in those WI sections which did permit them to enroll along with students at higher levels of English proficiency (HEP). If faculty perceptions that ESL and developmental students could not succeed in these courses were borne out, then perhaps it was unwise to allow them to take WI classes. While the Hostos WAC/RAC Initiative has assessed its program every year since its inception, in spring 2011, with the help of graduate student research assistant Carole K. Meagher, my WAC Co-Coordinator, Andrea Fabrizio, and I began a study to determine if ESL and developmental students could and should compete with HEP students in these sections. We examined student success by combining the performance of ESL and developmental students in WI sections and comparing their success in terms of grades and pass/fail rates to HEP students in WI and non-WI sections of the same courses. Our findings revealed that, overall, ESL, developmental, and HEP students in WI sections passed at a higher rate than they did in non-WI sections and did so with no statistically significant differences according to student composition levels. In fall 2011 and spring 2012 we expanded this work by de-aggregating our data from spring 2011 to isolate the performance of ESL students from developmental students and also examining ESL student performance in WI courses in fall 2011.

This chapter addresses the academic implications of offering WI courses to linguistically underprepared students by drawing on the qualitative and quantitative studies undertaken both in academic year (AY) 2011 and spring 2012 on the effects of WAC and WI courses in the mainstreaming of ESL students. Qualitative data is drawn from student responses to a survey instrument administered to all students enrolled in WI courses that measures student satisfaction with WI courses and self-reported writing improvement. Quantitative data reflecting AY 2011 focuses on two key components of academic success: grades and retention. For the study reported here, these include, 1) examining the pass/fail rates of ESL students in WIs and non-WIs; 2) comparing the grades of ESL students in WI sections to the grades of ESL students in the same courses which are non-WI; and 3) comparing ESL student grades to the grades of students at other levels of English in the same WI sections.

The chapter is divided in two sections. Part I begins with an analysis of the qualitative and quantitative data outlined above and its implications for second-language learners in WAC programs. In order to amplify and provide a basis for understanding the significance of the quantitative data gathered in AY 2011and to identify those WAC strategies which might have led to these statistical findings, Part II analyzes two WI syllabi from AY 2011 courses—CHE 210 (General Chemistry) and HLT 110 (Introduction to Community Health), both of which have English-language pre/co-requisites making them available to ESL and developmental students as well as HEP students. The syllabi reviewed here have been selected specifically because the faculty who designed them are committed to serving the needs of ESL students and ESL students have had success in passing these sections. What do these WI sections look like, and how do they address the needs of L2 students? In what ways, if any, might they differ from those WI sections that do not permit L2 students to enroll?

Through these pluralistic measures we have sought to determine the effects of mainstreaming ESL students into WI sections as well as to gain an increased understanding of how WAC can best support their emerging literacies. The trends that emerged regarding student success and the suggestions that conclude the chapter may provide new perspectives on ways in which WAC programs and scholars can indeed open rather than close their doors to ESL students (Cox, 2011).

PART I: ASSESSING THE PERFORMANCE OF L2 STUDENTS IN WI SECTIONS

Addressing the needs of ESL students has been a Hostos priority since its founding as CUNY's first college with a bilingual mission. Our attempts to understand how to best serve this population have informed our work since the college's inception. In order to better appreciate the principles that underlie our current WAC program, it is instructive to look back on some of the research which led to the evolution of today's program design. In 1984 Hostos undertook one of the first studies to determine if WAC principles and practices, especially talking and writing-to-learn, were applicable to ESL students through an investigation of the academic performance of ESL students across disciplines (Hirsch, 1986, 1988). Using both qualitative and quantitative measures, the study compared the success of those engaged in principles of "language across the curriculum" through a specially designed tutorial model which included writing-to-learn and the use of talk as a learning tool to a control group of ESL students not partaking in similar practices and receiving no additional support. The tutorial model also employed cognitive strategies such as activating prior knowledge and making personal connections between new and known material to aid in comprehension of course material. The tutoring-model was discontinued due to lack of funding, but the knowledge we gained regarding ESL students across the curriculum formed the basis for much of our present-day CUNY-funded WAC Initiative.

While the earlier study demonstrated the statistically significant academic gains made by participants engaged in WAC practices and the primacy of talk in the learning process for ESL students, it also documented the difficulties confronted by ESL students in mainstream classes (Hirsch, 1996). Over time ESL educators have become even more familiar with and attuned to the cognitive, linguistic, sociocultural and affective hurdles confronted by these students across the curriculum. In addition to the challenges presented by course readings and vocabulary, note taking, oral communication, and complex discipline-specific writing assignments, ESL students also face the demands of twenty-first century literacies, including blogs, discussion boards, social networks, and wikis, which require navigating the rules and voices of all these differing discourses. (In her chapter [this volume], Du describes the challenge of summarizing information from digital and multimedia "texts," along with oral texts such as course lectures, for the purpose of providing evidence of one kind or another in response to writing assignments they're given.) Drawing on our earlier research on the effectiveness of talk and writing for ESL students, we designed our current WAC/RAC Initiative to address the many writing challenges confronted by our linguistically diverse population and to assist faculty in designing curriculum to support their academic success.

As noted previously, the Hostos WAC/RAC Initiative seeks to broaden student experience with writing and reading generally throughout the curriculum and in WI sections specifically. Supporting its view that ESL and developmental students can only benefit from early exposure to more complex reading and writing tasks, it permits students to enroll in one WI prior to passing CUNY exams in reading and writing. It is important to determine empirically if ESL students are provided with the support they need and if they actually can and do succeed in WI courses. The next section describes both qualitative and quantitative measures undertaken to ascertain the effect of WI classes on the academic performance of second language (L2) learners. While the focus is on L2 learners, their success is compared with developmental students and students at higher-levels of English-language proficiency enrolled in WI sections. Proficiency levels are determined by student performance on CUNY-mandated exams: The CAT-W writing test and the ACT Reading test. Students are placed into ESL, Developmental English or Freshman Composition based on exam scores set by CUNY. The same exams are also used to exit ESL and developmental reading and writing courses. Students must pass these exams in order to enroll in Freshman Comp (ENG 110), a gateway to many other academic courses and programs.

ASSESSING THE WI EXPERIENCE: QUALITATIVE RESULTS

Each semester, students in WI classes are surveyed to determine their satisfaction with these sections and their perceived improvements in the learning of content and writing. For example, they are asked to *Strongly Agree, Agree, Disagree* or *Strongly Disagree* with statements such as, "*This course helped me understand course topics and concepts*" as well as assess the course's helpfulness in improving their writing. There is also space for student comments. Table 6.1 breaks down student responses for spring 2011 by English-language levels. "Basic Skills" refers to students who are either ESL or developmental; "Freshman Comp" refers to those students taking Freshman Composition 1 (ENG 110); and "Post-ENG" refers to students who have finished Freshman Composition 1 and are either taking the second semester of freshman year comp, Comp 2; no English course, or higher-level English courses, such as an English Department

Table 6.1: Students who responded "Strongly Agree" or "Agree" by composition level

WI Class Improved:	All Students		Basic Skills		Freshman Comp		Post-ENG	
	n	%	n	%	n	%	n	%
Overall writing	494	87.1	25	83.3	49	86.0	324	89.0
Paraphrasing and quoting	506	89.7	28	93.3	47	85.5	330	91.2
Grammar	516	90.8	28	93.3	50	89.3	336	92.1
Organization	518	92.0	28	93.3	52	91.2	335	93.3
Clarity of main idea	530	93.6	29	96.7	55	98.2	343	94.5
Incorporation of details	528	94.1	28	93.3	50	92.6	347	96.1
Understanding of the topic	540	95.1	29	96.7	54	94.7	350	96.2

elective. "Basic Skills" students are in WI sections which permit their enrollment alongside students at higher English-language proficiency levels. While HEP students may enroll in all WI courses, ESL and developmental students may only enroll in those with pre- or co-requisites at the ESL/ENG 091/092 levels.

In terms of student satisfaction, there appears to be little difference in responses by composition course level. Approximately 83% of "Basic Skills" students report improvements in overall writing as compared to 86% in "Freshman Comp" and 89% who are "Post-ENG." Indeed, in many categories, the "Basic Skills" respondents report greater improvements than the "Freshman Comp" students with the "Post-ENG" group often reporting the highest levels of satisfaction.

While analysis of the questionnaires does not separate developmental and ESL students, students do note their current English courses on the survey instrument. A sampling of ESL student comments indicates the perceived benefits of the WI course in which they were enrolled along with an indication of the kinds of language difficulties students bring to these classes:

> It made my writing to get better. The professor allways [sic] was there to help me or explain the work. (EDU 116 Child Development)

> I had a great experience with this course. That is because I learned all with it. With this course I got a more concentrate in reordering and reading . ... (LIN 100 Introduction to Linguistics)

> I had taking [sic] 2 writing [sic] intensive classes already. This one had being the best ever. The professor is very professional and she could help any student to learn and improve their writing [sic]. (GERO 103 Introduction to Gerontology)

> This course helped me a lot because it has given me an idea how to do a lab report, citation, and researching skills. (CHE 210 General Chemistry 1)

The in-depth analysis of CHE 210 in Part II will demonstrate how the syllabus was designed to further the various skills acknowledged by the student in the last quote. The syllabi for the other WI sections referred to above share many of the same characteristics that might account for student satisfaction and success in these WI courses.

ASSESSING THE WI EXPERIENCE: QUANTITATIVE RESULTS

The survey instrument described above yields important information regarding student satisfaction with WI courses. It is also designed to elicit information as to the amount and kinds of writing that occur in the courses including opportunities for revision, affording some insight as to what actually takes place in the classroom regarding the implementation of WAC/RAC practices. Yet useful as this information is, it is not sufficient to allow for a comprehensive assessment of our program's success. With so little quantitative data on the performance of students in WAC programs in general, it seemed vital to try and gain an understanding of how ESL students perform in these WI sections. As stated earlier, it would not be prudent to encourage them to enroll in classes where their grades would suffer if alternatives (non-WI sections) were available, and students would no doubt avoid these classes if possible. Table 6.2 compares the pass rates of ESL students in WI and non-WI sections of the same courses:

In analyzing these data, we were immediately struck by the small numbers of ESL students enrolled in WI sections, reflecting their disinclination to enroll in these sections even when they are available to them. Yet the figures also indicate that ESL students in WI sections had a higher pass rate than their peers in non-WI sections of the same courses: 86% vs. 75% as well as lower rates of course withdrawal: 7% vs. 16%.

Table 6.2: ESL Pass/Fall rates in WI vs. non-WI sections

			Number	Percent
WWI	Pass		24	86
	Fail		2	7
	W		2	7
	Total		28	100
Non-WI	Pass		43	75
	Fail		5	9
	W		9	16
	Total		57	100

While it is impossible to know precisely the role and extent of writing in non-WI sections, our experiences in collaborating with faculty to transform non-WI sections into WIs provide a window into the pedagogical practices in non-WI sections. Prior to eligibility for WI certification, these courses often rely on multiple choice or short answer exams. Writing assignments in non-WI sections most commonly consist of an end-of-semester 10-12 page term paper which faculty frequently (and justifiably) complain is plagiarized. There is little or no drafting or revision of the paper, and students are often referred to the library for workshops on conducting research with little follow-up to see how well they have grasped research practices. By contrast, WI syllabi reflect more frequent opportunities for both formal and informal writing with a term paper usually assigned as one of at least three other revised writing assignments. From a student perspective, WI classes are more demanding and more difficult, so it is encouraging to observe that ESL 091/092 students in WI courses received a higher percentage of passing grades than ESL students in non-WI sections of the same courses, as shown in Table 6.3, indicating that they are not putting themselves at risk in taking these WIs, and they may actually be receiving tangible benefits.

Table 6.3: ESL student grades in courses by WI and non-WI enrollment for AY 2011

Grade Group	WI		Non-WI	
	Number	Percent	Number	Percent
A	4	14.3	7	12.2
A-	2	7.1	4	7.0
B	2	7.1	9	15.8
B+	2	7.1	6	10.5
B-	3	10.7	8	14.0
C+	2	7.1	2	3.5
C	6	21.4	4	7.0
D	2	7.2	2	3.5
F	2	7.2	5	8.8
INC	1	3.6	1	1.7
W/WU	2	7.2	9	16
Total	28	100	57	100

This determination of higher pass rates lends support to the benefit of engaging ESL students in WAC/RAC principles and practices. Yet how well students do in these classes is also important. Recognizing the importance of a student's GPA, we further examined the actual grades ESL students receive in their WI classes as compared with those of ESL students in non-WI sections of the same courses.

Grade distributions, as shown in Table 6.3, reflect some of the difficulties faced and successes earned by students in WI vs. non-WI sections. For example, students who enrolled in WI sections received a somewhat higher percentage of A's: 22% vs. 19% for those in non-WIs. But students in WIs received fewer grades in the B range: 25% vs. 40% for those in non-WIs. ESL students in WI sections also received a greater percentage of C grades. The average grade for the two groups was a B- for those in non-WIs compared to a C+ for those in WIs, a negligible difference. Yet, as noted previously, their percentage of failing grades and withdrawals (W) was less than those of students in non-WI classes.

Many faculty have expressed fears that ESL students will fail in WI classes, but these concerns are not supported by Tables 6.2 and 6.3. While no firm conclusions can be drawn from such small sample sizes, the trend indicates that ESL students enrolled in WI sections can succeed. But the pass/fail grade analyses reveal a more significant outcome and predictor of student success. The figures suggest a greater retention rate for ESL students in WI sections. ESL students are persisting in these classes, passing them, and not dropping out. While the coursework of WIs may be more intense and difficult for a population still acquiring language proficiencies, it may also be more interesting. It would seem there are supports in place that enable L2 learners to persist and succeed, supports which are absent in non-WI sections of the same course and in WI sections with higher English-language pre/co-requisites. These very supports—the pedagogical practices embedded in WIs accessible to ESL students which might account for their success—will be examined in the review of syllabi in Part II.

While the pass/fail rates and grade comparisons of ESL students in WI sections compared to those in non-WI sections suggests student success in WIs, we also wanted to know how mainstreamed ESL students fared in comparison to their fellow students of varying English-language proficiency levels in the same WI class.

Table 6.4 outlines how ESL students performed in comparison to developmental students and students enrolled in either Freshman Comp I or 2 (ENG110/111) taking the same WI section. ESL students were enrolled in WI sections of courses in Biology, Business, Chemistry, Community Health, Education, Latin American & Caribbean Studies, Linguistics, Office Technology, and Physics. Data has not been broken-down by discipline though this is something that merits future research for all of our WI sections.

We note that the number of developmental students (ENG 091/092) reported here is too small on which to base any observations. While an additional 18 developmental students were enrolled in other WI sections, these sections did not enroll any ESL students for comparison purposes. There were also students enrolled in the WI sections examined above who had already

Table 6.4: Comparing grades of ESL students/developmental students/HEP students within WI classes AY 2011

Spring 2011: ESL 091/092 Students by WI Course Grade						
WI Grade Group	ESL091/092 ESL		ENG091/092 Developmental		ENG110/111 HEP – Fresh Comp	
	Number	Percent	Number	Percent	Number	Percent
A	2	25	1	50	10	29
B	4	50	1	50	10	29
C	1	13	0	0	8	24
D	0	0	0	0	2	6
F	1	13	0	0	4	12
W	0	0	0	0	0	0
Total	8	100	2	100	34	100

Fall 2011: ESL 091/092 Students by WI Course Grade						
WI Grade Group	ESL091/092 ESL		ENG091/092 Developmental		ENG110/111 HEP – Fresh Comp	
	Number	Percent	Number	Percent	Number	Percent
A	4	20	1	20	17	25
B	3	15	3	60	19	28
C	7	35	1	20	13	19
D	2	10	0	0	3	4
F	1	5	0	0	7	10
INC	1	5	0	0	1	1
W	2	10	0	0	9	13
Total	20	100	5	100	69	100

completed Freshman Comp, but since Freshman Comp is the level upon which WI enrollment is often based, we have focused on the grades of this group in our comparison to the ESL and ENG 091/092 students and not those students who have already completed all English requirements.

It is not surprising that the Freshman Comp group performed well. As Table 6.4 indicates, they had a higher percentage of A grades (54% vs. 45%) than ESL students. Their percentage of B grades was a bit lower—57% vs. 65%—though ESL students had a greater percentage of C grades—48% vs. 43%. HEP students also withdrew (13% vs. 10%) and failed (22% vs. 18%) at slightly higher rates than ESL students.

In addition to an analysis of student grades in WI and non-WI content courses, our examination of the performance of ESL students revealed some unanticipated information with significant implications for our WAC work. Those students taking a WI course concurrently with their ESL course had a greater pass rate in the ESL class, and thus moved onto Freshman Composition more quickly than ESL students who were not taking a WI. Forty-one percent of ESL students not taking a WI passed their ESL class compared to 52% of those enrolled in a WI. While reiterating our earlier precaution about small sample sizes, the data suggest that, if engagement with WAC principles and practices in WI courses can improve student success in ESL classes enabling them to move onto to more advanced levels of English and college-level courses, then more WI classes should be made available to them—classes that contain the supportive pedagogies discussed in the syllabi below.

PART II: ESL STUDENTS WRITERS IN THE SCIENCES AND SOCIAL SCIENCES

As we observed in our initial study published in 1986, multiple measures can provide multiple perspectives with each insight building on and enhancing the other. The comparison of grades and pass/fail rates provides a picture of how student learning is evaluated in the college setting. Grades provide students with a powerful signal as to what constitutes "successful" learning. The grade comparisons discussed earlier offer an aspect of how students learn, but grades do not tell us how these results were obtained. In what ways might a WI section available to ESL students support their success in meeting course demands? What strategies, techniques, and/or assignments are embedded within the course that facilitate student learning and account for their success and satisfaction? Below is an examination of two representative WI syllabi selected from among the WIs which are available to advanced ESL and developmental students that are designed to help them access and respond to discipline-specific texts and concepts through both reading and writing. The strategies employed here provide a good roadmap for supporting ESL students in mainstreamed WI courses.

WRITING INTENSIVELY IN THE SCIENCES: CHE 210 GENERAL CHEMISTRY

With faculty in the natural and physical sciences often resistant to incorporating WAC principles and practices, it was a welcome surprise to find faculty in these areas receptive not only to creating WI syllabi, but also to making them accessible to L2 and developmental learners. The excerpts below, from a WI syllabus for CHE 210, General Chemistry I created by Professors Nelson Nunez-Rodriguez and Yoel Rodriguez in collaboration with CUNY graduate student Writing Fellow Kate Wilson, point to the ways in which courses in the STEM fields can utilize WAC strategies to improve the learning and literacy needs of students representing a wide-range of language proficiencies. Rather than relying on a lecture-mode delivery of material, a pedagogy of limited success for L2 learners because of its reliance on student ability to comprehend concepts orally and synthesize and paraphrase material quickly in order to take effective notes (see Du [this volume] for more on the challenges ESL students face when attempting to learn from lectures), this class makes frequent use of a wide variety of informal writing assignments meant to help students improve their conceptual understanding of course material. At the same time, it provides an introduction to writing in the disciplines (WID) while helping students bridge the use of discipline-specific language with that of language for a broader audience.

Writing in CHE 210

In this description, assignments and assignment passages have been copied from the professor's syllabus, followed by a discussion of the pedagogical benefits.

> **Informal writing**
> Most of the informal writing will happen in the lecture component of this course through the Blackboard Discussion Board. A smaller part of the informal writing will be done in the laboratory.
>
> **Informal writing in lecture**
> Each week students will have the opportunity to choose from

three prompt options posted by faculty on the Discussion Board. Two of these prompts remain the same throughout the semester with only the necessary thematic adjustments.

Students are expected to respond to at least 12 Discussion Board exercises throughout the semester (Blackboard tallies student participation.)

By being allowed to choose three prompts posted on the class discussion board, students are actively engaged in the learning process and, crucially for L2 learners, given the opportunity to use language to make meaning not only for themselves, but also for an audience of teacher and peers. The instructions for the Blackboard prompts highlight this further:

Blackboard prompt
Based on what you learn in Chapter "Atoms, Molecules, and Ions" (please note that the title will change weekly), craft your own exam question. You must justify why you consider this question should appear in the exam. For this, I suggest that you explain what skills are tested in the question you are crafting. For example: Is your question asking fellow students to remember valuable information? Is it asking to analyze information, or maybe apply knowledge, etc.? Any kind of question is accepted (multiple choice, true or false, short filling, short essay, etc.). In addition to crafting your own question you can also engage in dialogue with other students based on what they submit. You can give your opinion to support a previous posted question and/or you can add a comment to somebody else's opinion showing your support, agreement or disagreement with another student's comment regarding a question or the tested skill.

The assignment above requires that students create their own exam questions and comment on each other's questions. This opportunity to articulate material in their own words with their own language resources is vital for L2 learners (Hirsch, 1986). The assignment also allows students to make decisions as to what is important or "test-worthy," thus demonstrating how much they have understood of the class material and if their perceptions of what's important match those of the professors.

Connect the content of Chapter "Chemical formulas,
Reactions, Equations, Stoichiometry" (please note that the
title will change weekly) to your daily life. Have in mind that
I am not asking for your opinion; I want you to think of an
example of how the material we covered about "Chemical
formulas, Reactions, Equations, Stoichiometry" relates to
your daily life.

Unable to rely on pre-coded experience with chemistry, students must be helped to forge a link between new and existing material. Earlier research at Hostos established the importance for learners of finding personal significance or establishing a personal connection to the new subject matter (Hirsch, 1986). Bransford (1999) defines the learner's task as activating previous knowledge and bringing it into contact with new material, seeking the familiar in the unfamiliar and vice versa. The assignment above asks students to make this personal connection by relating the chapter's content to their daily lives. This device to aid cognition and retention will reappear throughout the syllabus.

Summary of articles
An online scientific article for the lay public will be chosen
(for example, from the science section of The New York
Times or other scientific online publications) and posted
on Blackboard for students to read. Summarize the three
main points of the article adding a personal comment on the
article, for instance, whether you find the article informative,
if it is clear, if you agree with the argument presented, etc.

Peer-reviewing a lab report
Each student will have the opportunity to review in written
form the draft of the formal laboratory report of another
student. This will be done in class. (More about this activity
in the "formal writing" section of this syllabus.) The professor
will give feedback on the Discussion Board postings in class
and, whenever possible, the professor will start the class by
talking briefly about students' input on Blackboard.

This low-stakes assignment to summarize articles allows students to synthesize the science material in their own words. The addition of a "personal comment" again allows them to make a personal connection to the material bridging the new and the known. The lab report requires an initial non-graded draft providing an opportunity for students to "try-on" this WID format, and, through peer review, places students in the role of teacher/expert giving them more control of their learning and letting them make active use of their own language resources.

Informal writing in the laboratory

In order to prepare for a laboratory session, students will be asked to read the "Procedure" section and "translate" the essential information into a flowchart. Aside from preparing the student for the experiment to come, this assignment will train the student in how to synthesize information. The flowcharts should be presented at the beginning of each lab session and will count as participation but will not be graded.

Sample of the assignment

Read the "Procedure" section of your Lab manual. When you finish reading make a flowchart that synthesizes the information offered in the narrative. Keep in mind that your flowchart should function as a "recipe" for the experiment you are about to do. The instructor will discuss the flowchart mechanics and will model one on the board for the first two labs to help you produce your own for the following labs. Example:

Experiment: Use of aqueous (aq) chlorine (Cl_2(aq)) to identify iodide salts.

Directions: In a small test tube, dissolve a small amount (about the size of a pea) of sodium iodide, NaI, in 1 mL of distilled water; add 5 drops of bleach. Note the color, then add several drops of mineral oil, shake, and allow to separate, which takes about 20 sec. Note that the mineral oil is the top layer. Record your observations on the report sheet.

The language of the textbook and lab manual may be difficult for many of the students due not only to the discipline-specific vocabulary but also because of the "every day" and idiomatic vocabulary that might be unfamiliar to L2 and developmental students. By asking students to "translate" the *Procedure* section of the lab manual from written form to a flow chart, students are able to synthesize, re-conceptualize and re-visualize the material, in essence making the text visible and providing them with another means to access difficult text.

Formal writing
There will be nine lab reports in the course. Six of these reports will be reviewed and commented on by the professor in order to reinforce students' familiarity with the lab report format. Students are not required to submit a revised/rewritten version. Three lab reports will require revision and one of them will serve as the basis for an essay.

In week 3 of the semester, students submit a draft of their first lab report for feedback and revision ensuring that they become familiar with lab report format early on in the semester. One of the lab reports will later become the basis for a larger writing project, described below:

Consumer Information Pamphlet: "Chemicals in Everyday Life"
This assignment starts in week 7 of the semester and

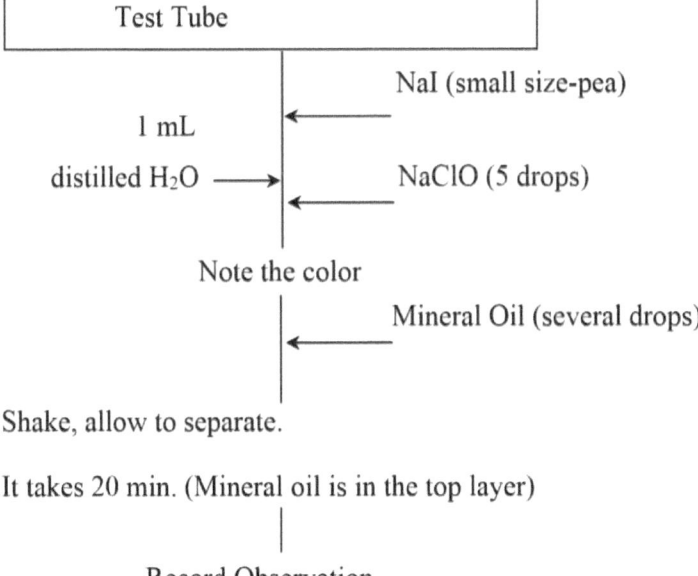

Figure 6.1 Flowchart

continues until the end of the semester. You will use your lab on "Chemicals in Everyday Life" as the basis for a larger writing project: a "Consumer Information Pamphlet" about one chemical component frequently used in daily products. Write with a hypothetical audience in mind. Your written product should resemble a Consumer Information Pamphlet very much like those that accompany most medications.

The goal of this assignment is to help you become familiar with common chemicals, their properties and relations with other chemicals.

As evidenced above, the formal writing components of this class are scaffolded and guide students through a variety of connected tasks. The lab reports provide an introduction to writing in the disciplines. Support is provided through professor feedback and opportunities for revision. As described above, one lab report will become the basis for a new writing task, a "Consumer Information Pamphlet." In order to write this pamphlet for a new, non-academic audience, students will have to be thoroughly familiar with the material and be able to present it in a way that mimics the voice and tone of these information booklets. The instructor delineates the steps students will follow as they expand the lab report and eventually reconfigure its information in a new genre. Steps include: 1) a lab report on "Chemicals in Everyday Life" which receives instructor feedback; 2) field research conducted in students' homes to identify the chemical components of kitchen and bath products; 3) an informal reflective writing assignment regarding the chemical products found in the home; 4) formal research that begins with Wikipedia for general information and continues with articles from a scientific peer-reviewed database; and 5) incorporation of information gathered through observation and research into a first draft of a Consumer Information Pamphlet. Students are instructed as to specific content and to write for a "lay audience." Significantly, the instructor provides an example of the type of writing associated with this genre. Feedback will be provided leading to submission of the revised pamphlet on the last day of class.

This carefully scaffolded assignment offers students feedback and support and makes visible the processes they must undergo to successfully complete the tasks. Students are actively engaged in the process moving from a representational flowchart, to a written lab report, and then through research, reflection and revision, to a transformation of the material studied into a new genre. All along the way, from informal through formal assignments, students are permitted and encouraged to make use of their own language resources to gain multiple perspectives on the material. By semester's end, they will reinforce their conceptual comprehension of this material by engaging in a "Peer Reviewed Lab Report" in which they critique each other's work and make suggestions for revision. A reliance on the textbook (written on a more advanced reading level) and lecture would not provide L2 students with the support they need to access and make sense of this material. Instead students are able to make connections among the concepts introduced, find a personal connection to the material, and become comfortable using the new language of a discipline while furthering their comprehension of course material.

Other ESL researchers have observed the success of these kinds of strategies. Leki (1995), for example, notes how ESL students seek out models of writing to help them with academic writing tasks, but their efforts are often thwarted by selecting inappropriate examples. In contrast, the CHE 210 professors provide students with models for writing an information pamphlet offering some familiarity with the kind of discourse required. Fishman and McCarthy (2001) observe the importance of peer interaction and talk for ESL students as a means of making sense of the material. As described earlier, the Hostos WAC/RAC Initiative draws on a learning model that employs principles of "language across the curriculum." In CHE 210, students have frequent opportunities to meet with peers and discuss the material. Talk, then, is central to the learning process and, while theorists have applied these findings to native English speakers (Martin, D'Arcy, Newton, & Parker, 1976), they are all the more relevant to ESL students who are often unable to articulate what they have learned in writing before they have had a an opportunity to orally "try on" the language of the discipline. The WI syllabus for CHE 210 also employs principles of active learning (Bruner, 1966, 1969; Fishman & McCarthy, 2001; Torbe & Medway, 1981) in which students are actively engaged in the learning process. For example, in CHE 210 students write their own exam questions, becoming both teachers and learners as they focus on questions posed by themselves and their classmates. The social science syllabus examined next echoes a number of these same strategies.

WRITING INTENSIVELY IN THE SOCIAL SCIENCES: "INTRODUCTION TO COMMUNITY HEALTH"

A review of the syllabus for "Introduction to Community Health," designed by Professor Iris Mercado in collaboration with CUNY Writing Fellow Dave Pier reveals ways in which it too is designed to accommodate the language needs of L2 and developmental students. There are a number of informal assignments such as describing the resources provided by the Department of Health Website; responding to student-selected newspaper or magazine articles related to public and community health, including writing brief summaries; and an analysis of an article on epidemiology supported by instructor prepared study-guide questions. There are two formal writing assignments that require writing for different audiences and purposes as well as student use of oral language skills. While both formal assignments are carefully scaffolded, here I describe in detail only the first one, a " Community Need Assessment and Health Promotion Programming," which is completed in the following four steps: 1) *My Community Health Survey* for which students are referred to a government website to answer questions regarding the health profile of their community; 2) *My Neighborhood Mapping* which requires students to assess the needs and resources of one city block of their neighborhood and write a two-page assessment of the health needs and resources of that block along with a detailed map; 3) *Community Interview* for which students select a specific health problem in their community and a target population and then identify persons that match the health profile and interview them, following specific instructions. This interview results in a two-page report; and 4) *Letter of Intent for a Health Promotion Program Grant Proposal* in which students write a four-page letter for a grant proposal application.

This scaffolded assignment clearly supports student learning not only through the series of steps provided but also through the additional support provided for completing each of the steps. For example, the survey in step 1 helps students gather the data they need. It assumes they are unfamiliar with designing survey instruments, and so provides a template for them to follow. They are also given specific questions to answer regarding their community based on their visit to the government website including demographics and their effects on health services. And, using these data, they are asked to discuss and present to the class the potential interventions for the issues they identified along with their community overview. To accomplish step 2, they are offered specific guidelines to determine possible neighborhood health or safety problems. The professor specifies how many causes and resources they need to use, instructs them to "explore two blocks" if necessary, and prompts them to "Remember to look up and down, as well as from side to side." They attach the map they sketched when they have finished the walk and write a two-page assessment of the block. Each of the remaining steps also provide guidelines; for example, the interview requires students to describe prevention measures for the health problem they selected and then interview a family member or friend about this problem, resulting in a two-page report that includes a summary and suggestions for further research. The grant proposal letter requires students to apply to a mock foundation for funding of a project related to public health. A template and model is provided to assist students in writing this proposal.

As in the chemistry WI class, students are provided with meaningful opportunities for writing throughout the community health WI, both to increase their comprehension of the discipline and to experience writing specific to the professional health care field. Both courses encourage students to produce graphic representations of the material being learned—the chemistry flow chart and the neighborhood map—a strategy that provides ESL students with another avenue for processing information and expressing what they know (Fu, 2007). For L2 learners specifically, the variety of both informal and formal writing assignments, the guided procedures and steps to follow, the oral interview encouraging active language use, the detailed scaffolding, and the strategies for responding to written texts all enable ESL students to utilize multiple resources as they try on the language of a discipline.

This examination of the WI syllabi for General Chemistry and Community Health demonstrates how WI classes can accommodate the needs of L2 learners and developmental students. Each provides multiple pathways for students to access new and difficult content material including formal and informal assignments, scaffolding, models of writing, frequent feedback throughout the process and opportunities for revision. These sections do not assume student familiarity with modes of writing and recognize that students do not always bring sufficient background knowledge to these tasks. In addition to strengthening student writing proficiencies, the assignments also provide practice in oral language development and allow students to use their oral language strengths rather than rely solely on writing as a means of participating in the class and obtaining information. This may be a particular benefit for generation 1.5 students who have attended US high schools or have lived in the US for a number of years and have developed oral language proficiency (Reid, 2006). It is interesting to note that the professors who created these ESL-accessible WI sections for General Chemistry and Community Health are themselves non-native speakers of English which may explain their sensitivity to the needs of L2 learners as well as their willingness to accept them into their classes.

The WI courses examined above also acknowledge the connections between reading and writing and provide students support in reading and responding to written texts through strategies such as paraphrasing, summarizing and reacting. This integration of reading and writing avoids what Leki (2001) has termed "reading for no real reason" (p. 176) or the isolated teaching of reading skills devoid of meaningful content. "Real reading," Leki argues, should not be deferred until ESL students are deemed adequately prepared, but that "plunging into the struggle with meaning" is in itself a means of preparation (p. 181) (For further discussions of the connections among writing and reading for ESL students, see Center & Niestepski and Du [this volume]). The connections between reading and writing and the interconnections between texts frame much of our WAC work for all students but may have particular significance of L2 learners across disciplines. As part of our Hostos Reading Across the Curriculum (RAC) component, students are encouraged to write before, during and/or after reading, although a cross-section of our WI courses reveal these practices occur in varying amounts. Hirvela (2004) underscores the value of "writing to read" and "reading to write" and observes that writing about text helps students engage it more directly. "The physical act of writing creates a kind of contact point with the text and brings perceptions and impressions half-formed during reading out of the shadows and into the light of emerging understanding" (p. 75) lending support to the use of "writing to read" in the college classroom and its value in enabling L2 students to further their acquisition of academic literacy. Hirvela highlights especially the benefits of summarizing, synthesizing and responding to written texts, writing activities which help students focus on the important features of a text, draw comparisons between texts and reflect on their learning all the while revealing areas of disconnection between the reader and text (see Du [this volume] for an examination of the role of summary writing as a writing-to-read strategy for ESL students). It is therefore particularly reassuring to see these strategies implemented in the syllabi presented here and may account for the success of ESL learners in these classes.

INSIDE THE WI FOR STUDENTS WITH HIGHER ENGLISH-LANGUAGE PROFICIENCY

All of the WI classes that are open to ESL and developmental learners utilize many of the strategies described above and most include assignments that are scaffolded. While all WI sections require informal and formal writing and opportunities for revision, those that are **not** available to ESL students and developmental learners do not always provide the support seen in CHE 210 or HLT 110. In many WI courses, for example, the assignments are not scaffolded. Frequently students are merely instructed to write a research paper with little guidance compared to the strategies for discourse negotiation provided in the sample syllabi reviewed here. An assignment for the WI course HIS 4665: US History from Reconstruction to the Present, for example, instructs students as follows:

> Using the documentary films we saw in class, primary

documents and the textbook, write a paper that compares the two cases [Sacco-Vanzetti and Scottsboro] and the historical circumstances under which they took place. Your paper must explain:

What are the cases about? Who did they involve? When and where did they take place? What were the charges against the defendants?

What are the main differences and/or similarities between the cases? (emphasis should be on the meaning of the cases, not on petty details such as the different dates, different charges or different penalties)

What is their overall significance? For example, what do they tell us about American society and politics in the 1920s and 1930s? What do they suggest about American attitudes toward class, race and immigration?

What were the implications or impact of these cases on American society?

What are the lessons we can draw from these two cases?

Be sure to include a full bibliography. Below are some reading suggestions.

Although students are provided with questions to consider, it is assumed that they are prepared to undertake the steps necessary to write a research paper and that they know how to conduct research, summarize and write compare/contrast essays. While they are required to submit a draft, there is not much scaffolding built into the assignment. Even students with higher English-language proficiencies may struggle with this assignment, and it is obviously not as "user-friendly" as the two previous WI syllabi which outline steps to follow and include frequent feedback throughout the writing processes.

Other sample WI assignments for HEP students had their own impediments to ESL student success. Many were too broad, a common flaw in writing assignments (Reid & Kroll, 2006) allowing for too few pages to accomplish broadly conceived tasks that often also required advanced research and reading skills. Some offered little assistance in selecting or developing topics. Others failed to provide an audience and purpose, unlike the CHE 210 Consumer Information Pamphlet or the HLT 110 Letter of Intent, leaving students directionless as to how to frame information. But what all WI classes for HEP students lacked was an instructor willing to address ESL language issues even when their syllabi did contain many of the strategies which can lead to ESL success.

CONCLUSION AND IMPLICATIONS

The research conducted at Hostos Community College in AY 2011 on the role of WAC pedagogies in furthering ESL students' development in writing and improving conceptual comprehension of course material provides demonstrable benefits regarding their involvement in WAC programs and in WIs carefully designed to address their needs. Though small numbers of ESL 091/092 students enrolled in the specially designed WI sections, their pass rates were higher than ESL students in non-WI sections of the same course, they did not withdraw, and of great significance, they had improved pass rates in the ESL class, the gateway class to freshman composition and a host of additional college programs. As noted earlier, however, the surprisingly small numbers of L2 learners (and developmental students) in available WI sections in 2011 seems to indicate that most preferred to take non-WI sections presumably fearing the greater linguistic demands of a WI section. Their reasons for avoiding WI sections merit further study especially in light of the outcomes presented here. It is possible that those who enrolled in WI sections were stronger and/or more confident students, which could also explain their pass rates and good grades.

The WAC pedagogical principles employed in the WI classes described here are vital to all students, not just ESL students or developmental learners. Though over 80% of students in Hostos WI classes are at the freshman composition level or beyond, many of these students continue to struggle with meeting the demands of writing in the disciplines. For example, a HEP history student enrolled in Freshman Comp 1 still grapples with English-language proficiency as evident in his written comments on the WI survey: "Great expereince [sic] as the feedback and overall teaching method made my writing; and comprehension improve since start [sic] of the semester." It is not surprising that language problems persist since so many of our students begin at the developmental or ESL levels. The spring 2011 analysis of students in WI classes indicated that 20% of the HEP students enrolled in Freshman Comp 1 or 2, and 15% of those who had completed all English requirements had taken at least one ESL course in their histories at Hostos. Other HEP students attend part-time or take breaks over the course of their study resulting in regression of language proficiency. A HEP nursing student observed, "This writing-intensive class ... helped me to revisit my writing skills since I never took another English course since 2008," reminding us that all students, even proficient ones, risk skills degradation if they don't have opportunities to practice and reinforce their written proficiencies (Roberts, 2008).

Our review of WI syllabi presumed that writing assignments were written out for students, a presumption WAC programs need to challenge. In many instances, assignments in classes which were not designated as WI were sketchily written (if at all) and often augmented by oral in-class amplification as to instructor expectations. Writing Fellows working with students reported that once out of class and pondering the assignments, students could no longer recall the orally added information or weren't sure if they understood it, a problem for many students, and especially L2 learners. Making sure students receive written prompts is a WAC program priority and often the first step in faculty professional development.

The WI syllabi reviewed here have English-language pre/co-requisites that make them available to advanced ESL students and developmental learners, but more than available, they are accessible. Assignments are comprehensible, scaffolded and reflect course objectives. They have well-designed prompts, clear instructions and vocabulary and syntax appropriate to the task. They provide opportunities for revision and instructor feedback. They also make frequent use of a variety of informal "writing-to-learn" assignments drawing on the relationship between reading and writing and permitting students to engage material orally before writing.

We are all writers. We write letters, poems, emails, memos, reports, text messages, tweets and much more. Writing is an integral part of who we are and how we express ourselves. For students for whom English is not a first language, learning to write clearly and concisely is a tremendous challenge. But what our data show is that it is not overcoming the challenge that is the important part; it's accepting the challenge in the first place. The fact that ESL students are choosing to stay in WI classes with their greater demands on writing proficiencies and are passing these classes at a higher rate than their non-WI counterparts indicates that participating in well-designed WI classes that utilize the academic supports described in this chapter may be in and of itself an academic benefit. The research reported here is only a beginning and more is needed. As educators, we must keep the doors to education and opportunity wide open, providing our students with the means to succeed. Perhaps the WAC/RAC studies discussed here will encourage WAC programs to help ESL students find their place across the curriculum.

NOTES

1. In this chapter I am using the terms English-as-a-Second Language (ESL) and L2 (second language) learner to refer to students who are learning English in addition to their native language. While they are all English language learners (ELLs), the students studied here are enrolled in ESL programs, and that is how they are identified in the college.
2. While each CUNY campus has developed its own WAC program responsive to its needs, most share a common set of WAC principles and practices such as the connections between writing and critical thinking, the value of "writing-to-learn" and exploratory writing in the classroom, writing as a process including revision, the importance of crafting assignments which are developmentally appropriate and reflect course objectives and the need for appropriate assessment of students' written work. Many use John Bean's *Engaging Ideas* as a primary faculty development text.

REFERENCES

Bransford, J. (1979). *Human cognition: Learning, understanding and remembering*. New York: Wadsworth.

Bruner, J. (1966a). *On knowing: Essays for the left hand*. Cambridge, MA: Belknap Press.

Bruner, J. (1966b). *Toward a theory of instruction*. Cambridge, MA: Belknap Press.

City University of New York. (1999). *Board of Trustees minutes of proceedings, January 25, 1999*. Retrieved from http://policy.cuny.edu/board_meeting_minutes/1999/01-25/pdf/#Navigation_Location

Collier, V.P. (1995). Acquiring a second language for school. *Directions in Language and Education, 1*(4).

Cox, M. (2011). WAC: Closing doors or opening doors for second language writers? *Across the Disciplines, 8* (4). Retrieved from http://wac.colostate.edu/atd/ell/cox.cfm

Fishman, S. M. & McCarthy, L. (2001). An ESL writer and her discipline-based professor: Making progress even when goals do not match. *Written Communication, 18*(2), 180-228.

Fu, D. (2007). Teaching writing to English language learners. In T. Newkirk & R. Kent (Eds.), *Teaching the neglected "R": Rethinking writing instruction in secondary classrooms* (pp. 225-243). New York: Heinnemann.

Gardner, C. (2010). Special issue: WAC at community colleges. *Across the Disciplines, 7.* Retrieved from http://wac.colostate.edu/atd/community_colleges/

Hirsch, L. (1986). *The use of expressive function talk and writing as learning tools with adult ESL students across the curriculum* (Doctoral dissertation). New York University, New York City). Dissertation Abstracts International, 47-08, 2927A.

Hirsch, L. (19988). Language across the curriculum: A model for ESL students in content courses. In S. Benesch (Ed.), *Ending Remediation: Linking ESL and content in education* (pp. 67-89). Washington, D.C., TESOL.

Hirsch, L. (1996). Mainstreaming ESL students: A counterintuitive perspective. *College ESL, 6*(2) 12-26.

Hirsch, L. & Paoli, D. (2012). The City University of New York: The implementation and impact of WAC/WID in a multi-campus urban university. In C.Thaiss, G. Braeuer, P. Carlino, L. Ganobcsik-Williams & A. Sinha, (Eds.), *Writing programs worldwide: Profiles of academic writing in many places* (pp. 439-454). Fort Collins, CO: WAC Clearinghouse and Parlor Press. Retrieved from http://wac.colostate.edu/books/wpww/

Hirvela, A. (2004). *Connecting reading and writing.* Ann Arbor, MI: University of Michigan Press.

Hostos Community College. (n.d.). *Writing Across the Curriculum at Hostos Community College.* http://commons.hostos.cuny.edu/wac/

Leki, I. (1995). Coping strategies of ESL students in writing tasks across the curriculum. *TESOL Quarterly* 29(2), 235-60.

Leki, I. (2001). Reciprocal themes in ESL reading and writing. In T. Silva & P. K. Matsuda (Eds.), *Landmark essays on ESL writing* (pp. 173-190). Mahwah, NJ: Lawrence Erlbaum Associates.

Martin, N., D'Arcy, P., Newton, B., & Parker, R. (1976). *Writing and learning across the curriculum.* London: Wardlock Educational.

Reid, J. (2006). "Eye" learners and "ear" learners: Identifying the language needs of international student and US resident writers. In P. K. Matsuda, M. Cox, J. Jordan, & C. Ortmeir-Hooper (Eds.), *Second-language writing in the composition classroom* (pp. 76-88). New York: Bedford/St. Martin's.

Reid, J. & Kroll, B. (2006). Designing and assessing effective classroom writing assignments for NES and ESL students. In P. K. Matsuda, M. Cox, J.Jordan, & C. Ortmeier-Hooper (Eds.), *Second-language writing in the composition classroom* (pp. 260-283). New York: Bedford/St.Martin's.

Roberts, L. (2008). An analysis of the National TYCA Research Initiative Survey Section IV: Writing across the curriculum and writing centers in two-year college English programs. *Teaching English in the Two-Year College, 36*(2), 138-153.

Thaiss, C. & Porter, T. (2010). The state of WAC/WID in 2010: Methods and results of the US survey of the international WAC/WID mapping project. *College Composition and Communication, 61*(3), 534-570.

Torbe, M. & Medway, P. (1981). *The climate for learning.* London: Wardlock Educational.

Zamel, V. (1995). Strangers in academia: The experiences of faculty and ESL students across the curriculum. *College Composition and Communication, 46*(4), 506-521.

Zawacki, T. M. & Habib, A. (210). "Will our stories help teachers understand?" Multilingual students talk about identity, academic writing, and expectations across academic communities. In M. Cox, J. Jordan, C. Ortmeier-Hooper, & G. G. Schwartz (Eds.), *Reinventing Identities in second language writing* (pp. 54-74). Urbana, IL: NCTE.

SECTION II
FACULTY CONCERNS AND EXPECTATIONS FOR L2 WRITERS

CHAPTER 7
NEGOTIATING "ERRORS" IN L2 WRITING: FACULTY DISPOSITIONS AND LANGUAGE DIFFERENCE

Terry Myers Zawacki and Anna Sophia Habib
George Mason University

This chapter reports on a study of faculty dispositions towards language difference, including the ways they talk about second language writers and the errors—actual and perceived—that they identify as well as how willing, or not, they seem to be to engage in negotiations around these errors. The authors describe the theory and research that motivated and informed their study, their interview methods, and their findings, which are organized by two primary concerns expressed by the faculty informants: whether the students comprehend the material they are writing about and whether L2 students are being fairly and adequately prepared for other courses and the workplaces they will enter if errors are not addressed.

My strength in Spanish is [my] personal style of how to write, and that's something that people like, and my grammar and vocabulary in Spanish are really good. In English, I would like to have more vocabulary. When I don't know a word, I just try to describe what I meant with [other words], so that makes my sentences longer or hard to read. Not good.

—Diana, international student from Columbia

At some point, you are going to have to take a position on second language writing errors. You can't give them special consideration, but you can consider alternative ways to grade that are fair. I do take points off for the writing in a paper, but, in ESL cases, for example, I tend to look for persistent errors, [which] I'll take as just one case of a grammatical error. There's some room I think to work with that.

—Anthropology professor

A translingual approach proclaims that writers can, do, and must negotiate standardized rules in light of the contexts of specific instances of writing. Against the common argument that students must learn "the standards" to meet demands by the dominant, a translingual approach recognizes that, to survive and thrive as active writers, students must understand how such demands are contingent and negotiable.

—Horner, Lu, Royster, & Trimbur, 2011 (p. 305)

"Not good," Diana says about her efforts to compensate for not yet having found the right words to write in the academic style—correct, concise, appropriate vocabulary—she believes her US teachers expect, a style different from what her Spanish readers seemed to enjoy. This perception of her own limitations—a deficiency as she sees it—as a novice academic writer navigating a new linguistic terrain is echoed by so many international and/or multilingual students in study after study on English second language (L2) writers in postsecondary institutions.[1] Yet, despite this sense of their own perceived shortcomings, we see these L2 students, like Diana, as actively negotiating reader expectations for writing in a home language and writing in English in a new academic context.

For many faculty, there is "some room to work with that," as the anthropology professor we quoted above suggests. Both he and Diana are attempting to reconcile the "errors" that emerge in the translingual written product: she by writing longer sentences; he by minimizing points off for persistent errors rather than penalizing a student for repetition of the same error. While Diana, like many L2 writers, recognizes that her lack of vocabulary is causing sentence and syntax errors, many faculty may also be recognizing that linguistic struggle, just as the anthropology professor does, by "taking a position on second-language errors" that includes finding alternative ways to think about fair grading practices for L2 writers. For both teacher and student, however, error is the focus of their observations about L2 writing, just as it is for so many of the faculty and the L2 students we've encountered in our work as WAC and writing center directors and in the interviews we conducted for the research we're reporting on here.

Admittedly we purposely selected these quotes on error to highlight what we see as the most frequent and anxiety/frustration-producing point of contact for faculty and students when it comes to second language writing at the postsecondary level. While we endorse a translingual approach that sees "the standards" as "contingent and negotiable" (Horner, Lu, Royster, & Trimbur, 2011), we also appreciate the dilemma faculty face in deciding what constitutes an error and when and in what contexts it should be "counted" in evaluating an L2 student's communicative competence. Horner, Lu, Royster, and Trimbur (2011) believe that we—teachers and students—can take up a translingual approach by "changing the kind of attention we pay to our language practices, questioning the assumptions underlying our learned dispositions toward difference in language, and engaging in critical inquiry on alternative dispositions to take toward such differences in our reading and writing" (p. 313). In this chapter, we're interested in what those faculty dispositions are towards language difference, what kind of attention they pay to students' language practices, and how willing—or not—they seem to be to engage in negotiations around perceived and actual error[2] in L2 student writing.

We begin by describing our initial motivation for undertaking this research, including an interest in the translingual theories and World Englishes research that we'd been reading and that provide an underpinning for our work. Next we describe our interview methods and how we coded the transcripts, noting that "error" emerged as a recurring theme in the faculty interviews. To present our findings on faculty dispositions towards error, we've organized the data according to what errors seemed to be most disturbing to faculty in our interviews, echoing Leki's (2007) description of the anxiety many L2 students feel about writing for faculty already "disturbed" by their errors (p. 248)[3]. We categorize our findings according to two primary concerns expressed by our informants: Do the students understand the material and expectations for writing in the course and the major? And, following from that concern, are they, the faculty, adequately preparing students for their other courses and for the workplace if the students are not able to meet their expectations for the writing? For many, this latter concern was also bound up with a strong sense of fairness, i.e. the need to be fair to the L2 student, whatever form that took in grading the writing, as well as to be fair to the other students in giving equal grades for equal work. Interestingly, but not surprisingly, as we'll explain, several teachers mentioned reflective writing as a genre through which L2 writers experienced the most success. We conclude with implications of this research for faculty and writing program administrators to consider when deciding how to best serve their multilingual students.

OUR STUDY: MOTIVATIONS AND UNDERPINNING THEORY AND RESEARCH

In previous articles on this research, we've reported on the experiences of multilingual students with academic writing across the curriculum and the attitudes expressed by cross-disciplinary faculty about reading and evaluating the writing of these students. We undertook our initial investigation of second-language student writers several years ago, motivated by a desire to more deeply understand the students' concerns so that we could convey these in faculty development and tutor training workshops. While neither of us has a background in linguistics or TESL, we were becoming more interested in the intersections between second-language writing and WAC/Writing Center scholarship. At that time, Terry was directing the writing center, along with WAC, and Anna[4] was the associate director,[5] so we asked four graduate and undergraduate tutors, three of whom were multilingual themselves, to assist with our study. We called our first report on the student research *Valuing Written Accents* (Zawacki, Habib, Hajabbasi, Antram, & Das, 2007*)*,[6] echoing Tonka, a student from Bulgaria, who was insistent about wanting her writing to reflect who she is and where she comes from. Even as she defined "good writing" as "grammar-responsible," "well-structured," and "good flow," characteristics she'd no doubt learned from her US teachers, she finished her list with this observation: "When you ultimately succeed in writing is when you have your own accent." In our conclusion to the monograph, we expressed the hope that our research would help teachers value the diverse written accents they encountered in their students' papers and to see their L2 students as language resources rather than as writing challenges.

As a follow up to the student research, we began interviewing faculty across the disciplines to hear their perspectives on L2 student writing in general and to share the students' concerns, an action research project we'll say more about shortly. At the same time, we were also following arguments in the literature about the "English Only" bias implicit in writing instruction (Horner & Trimbur, 2002; Matsuda, 2006) and the need for a new translingual paradigm that sees "difference in language" not as error but rather as evidence of a writer negotiating meaning across fluid and heterogeneous linguistic boundaries (Canagarajah, 2002, 2006, 2007, 2009; Horner et al., 2011).[7] This reframing of "error" fit well with our appeal to faculty to value students' written accents, as did a translingual approach that encourages teachers to ask "not whether the language is standard but what the writers are doing with language and why" and to read "with patience, respect for perceived differences within and across languages, and an attitude of deliberative inquiry" (Horner et al., 2011, pp.

304-305). In our interviews with faculty, we were interested in comparing what they said about the "standards" and their expectations for "good" writing, in general and in their disciplines, to the perceptions of good writing and teacher expectations expressed by our multilingual student informants. But we were also interested in the genres the faculty informants regularly assign; their sense of the challenges, if any, that L2 students face with the assignments; and the advice and assistance they might give to help students improve as writers.

As we conducted the interviews, we noted that faculty kept coming back to their concerns about the errors they saw in their "ESL" students' writing and their inability to diagnose the cause of the errors or even explain how to fix them. While most acknowledged that they couldn't be sure if a student was ESL, they explained that the kinds of errors they saw in the papers and/or the student's identity and accent generally led them to believe this was the case. The issue of "error" thus emerged as a common theme throughout the interviews, leading us to become interested in looking closely at the language the faculty used to talk about L2 error and how open they seemed to an interpretation of error as translingual code-meshing or, to use Canagarajah's (2006) formulation, "the learner's active negotiation and exploration of choices and possibilities" (p. 593).

Theoretically, we were interested in the wider contexts in which negotiations around language difference occur. If error, in Canagarajah's terms, can, depending on the context, be seen as a "refusal to negotiate,"[8] we wondered what the grounds for refusal might be when it comes to L2 students' academic writing, along with who has a stake in the negotiations. We mapped out the stakeholders present at the scene of writing, placing the L2 student writer and the instructor at the center with each bringing his/her own individual, cultural, and school writing lessons-learned to the rhetorical encounter. At the same time, both the student writer and instructor are also influenced by and/or accountable to the stakeholders in the background, actual or perceived, representing "the standards"—other faculty and administrators, institutional policies, accrediting bodies, and interested publics, including those driving mandates for writing assessment. The negotiations, in other words, are never just between the student and the instructor but include a whole host of interested others who populate the contact zone where error is negotiated, with the student writer, whether English L1 or L2, having the least power but the highest stake in the negotiations.[9]

The classroom is a "powerful site of policy negotiation," Canagarajah (2006) argues in his much-cited "The Place of World Englishes in Composition: Pluralization Continued." In this space, "standard" English policies are reconstructed from the "ground up" through the "pedagogies practiced and texts produced" (p. 587). If we can see our way to allowing students to use vernacular English or World Englishes, he argues, their and our academic texts will be enriched. Yet, he also admits that he himself has been so "disciplined" into using standard English in his own academic writing that he has trouble extending his "pluralizing" argument into deeper structures of grammar and syntax (pp. 612-613) where error is most often read. There *is* such a thing as "error," Horner, Lu, Royster, and Trimbur (2011) agree, "[All] writers make mistakes, and all writers are usually eager to remove mistakes from their writing" (p. 310). Like Canagarajah, however, the authors urge teachers to "reserve" the "possibility of error … as an interpretation of last resort" (2006, p. 304) and to be more humble about what constitutes a mistake (and about what constitutes correctness) in writing, rather than assume that whatever fails to meet their expectations, even in matters of spelling, punctuation, and syntax, must be an error (p. 310).

Given our own position on valuing students' written accents, we find these translingual arguments theoretically persuasive, as we've said. Theoretical is the operative word here, however. To enact theory, in our pedagogy and writing program administration, we needed to first understand teachers' attitudes towards L2 errors and the kinds of errors they described as most troublesome or problematic or "disturbing." Without that understanding, it would be difficult, not to mention presumptuous, to suggest that they consider other possible interpretations of the mistakes they reported students making. We were not as much interested, then, in looking at *what* errors they found most "disturbing," but rather *how* they described the errors and *why* they seemed to be "disturbed" by particular kinds of errors. Based on what we were seeing as we analyzed the faculty interview transcripts, we also wanted to consider other possible causes, apart from the translingual explanations we've just described, for the errors they said they noticed, including the difficulty L2 students face in learning to write not only in English as an additional language but also in the unfamiliar genres and discourses of a discipline.

The complexity of learning to write in a discipline has been well documented in both the L1 and L2 literature; to write like an insider, in addition to knowing the subject matter, students need to acquire knowledge of the genres, discourse conventions, and rhetorical contexts typical of the discipline, along with effective composing and research processes (see models of discourse/genre knowledge in Bean, 2001; Beaufort, 2007; Tardy, 2009). Whether they are English monolingual or multilingual, students are bound to make missteps and mistakes in the process of acquiring these skills and knowledges. With experience and opportunities for practice in courses across the curriculum, student writers will become more fluent in the target genres and also learn appropriate voices and styles for the writing tasks. It is the accumulation of general writing process knowledge along with local knowledge of the genres and conventions of the discipline that leads to fluency, Carter (1990) explains in "The Idea of Expertise: An Exploration of Cognitive and Social Dimensions of Writing." For second language writers, however, the acquisition of expertise departs in significant ways from Carter's formulation, with writing processes much more constrained and difficult for L2 writers as they search for the correct and/or appropriate language with which to express what they know[10] (see, for example, Silva's (1993) "Toward an Understanding of the Distinct Nature of L2 Writing: The ESL Research and Its Implications"). With sufficient writing practice across the curriculum and time to acquire the necessary language skills and genre and writing knowledge, however, L2 students will likewise develop fluency and accuracy even though their writing may still be marked by some language differences. (See, for instance, Phillips' [this volume] discussion of the successes of a multilingual graduate student in an interdisciplinary master's program despite enduring language proficiency concerns).

In considering the intersections of language knowledge, writing expertise, and genre knowledge in his review article, "A Biliteracy Agenda for Genre Research," Gentil (2011) adds "strategic competence" to Tardy's (2009) integrated model of the components of L2 genre knowledge, which itself closely resembles other L1 models (Bean, 2001; Beaufort, 2007). As Gentil explains, "strategic competence" involves being able to evaluate the task or communicative situation and the correctness or appropriateness of the response, deciding how to respond and "what elements from language knowledge and background knowledge are required," and "retrieving and organizing the appropriate elements" to carry out the task (2011, p. 12). In short, he says, "What distinguishes so called skilled and less-skilled writers is precisely this ability to assess the writing situation, set goals in responding to it, harness language and conceptual resources, and monitor their uses while composing" (2011, p. 13).

A daunting task for most students, as we noted above, and even more daunting for L2 writers for whom, as Leki (2007) found, writing was often a process fraught with anxiety and fear that their "language deficiencies" would be exposed to teacher audiences "already disturbed by them" (p. 248). In *Undergraduates in a Second Language,* Leki (2007) notes that one of the "most neglected" areas in the L2 research has to do with L2 students' interactions with faculty, faculty attitudes towards these students, and the students' perceptions of faculty attitudes and expectations.[11] Similar to the faculty we interviewed, her faculty informants generally expressed admiration for the L2 students' motivation to study in another language with some being willing to accommodate the student learners and others not (pp. 270-274). As we looked at our faculty interview transcripts, however, we could see that the language a number of them used in talking about student error—which included such phrases as "zero tolerance for error," "a 'take no prisoners' approach," "blast students on errors," "no broken English," and "no scatter shot writing, just one bullet at the target"—seemed to belie their good intentions and also made us think again about the aptness of the "contact zone" metaphor. While this kind of language suggests that errors are non-negotiable—and will certainly inspire fear in their students, whether English L1 or L2—we'll note that some of the faculty using these expressions were among the most generous with their time and attention to struggling L2 writers.

OUR METHODS

For all of the reasons we've described above, in interviewing faculty across disciplines we wanted to understand their experiences with L2 writers, their perceptions of the writing challenges faced by these students, the kinds of language differences in students' written work that they found most troublesome or problematic, the kinds of errors they were willing to overlook in a paper, and the strategies they used, if any, to help these students succeed (see interview questions in Appendix A). We conducted hour-long semi-structured interviews with eighteen full-time faculty from sixteen different disciplines. In choosing faculty to interview, we focused, for the most part, on those teaching required writing-intensive (WI) courses in majors enrolling the largest numbers of international students, according to 2011-2012 George Mason *Factbook*: engineering/computer science/IT, business (with largest numbers in accounting and finance), economics, nursing and social work, and biology. We interviewed four faculty from engineering (electrical, civil, systems, bioengineering); three from business (marketing and management); two from sociology, and one from each of the following: math, geology, psychology, economics, nursing, social work, anthropology, art and visual technology, and English. Five of our informants are English L2 writers themselves.

One limitation of our research, as we noted earlier, is that our faculty informants didn't know how many of the student writers they were describing in their interviews were, in fact, second-language (or third, fourth, etc) writers of English. While most assumed that the students with the most pronounced language difficulties were L2 writers, they sometimes told us when they had other ways of knowing the backgrounds of the students they were describing. They didn't, however, always share with us these other identifying markers or the racial or ethnic backgrounds of their students, so we don't know how those identities may have contributed to their attitudes on error or why certain errors may have disturbed them. Some said that many of their struggling writers were likely immigrant students given their idiomatic speech or writing, and many also pointed out that some of the most error-filled writing was often produced by their English L1 students. While faculty may not necessarily know whether the students they are working with are L2 or immigrant students with second-language needs, we do know that many of our institution's students are multilingual and that they are often being sent to the university writing center to "fix their errors" because faculty either do not know how to help them or do not have the time to work with them individually.[12]

With the exception of one joint interview with three faculty members from business where the paper had been provided in advance for all of us to look at, we did not read or have access to students' papers to see what kinds of errors the teachers pointed out nor the feedback they gave to students about those errors. While these limitations meant that we weren't able to do any first-hand error analysis or an analysis of the teacher's written feedback, we were, as we said, chiefly interested in their perceptions of L2 students' errors and the language they used in talking about those errors and about the L2 student writers themselves. The business teacher who sent us the paper in advance, for example, wanted us "to see for ourselves" the kinds of "frustrating" language errors she was "dealing with." (In our discussion of our findings, we include a passage from the interview related to this paper.) Regarding these limitations, L2 writing scholars have recognized the complexity of defining error in student writing. Leki, Cumming, and Silva (2008), for example, find in their synthesis of research on L2 error that "error" is difficult "to define precisely, identify reliably, and relate directly to writing or language development" because more fluent writers produce different types of errors while "the perceived severity of errors varies by aspects of language or texts as well as the situations or interests of people assessing them" (p. 84). Ferris (2004) critiques studies on teacher response to error, finding that the researchers frequently fail to operationalize what they are calling "error" or use ambiguous or vague definitions.

All of the interviews were transcribed by the student research assistants who also participated with us in coding and analyzing the transcripts. While our coding yielded a range of L2 writing themes around which we could organize a research report, for this chapter we're going to focus on passages where they seemed to be negotiating with language difference—or refusing to negotiate—as they talked with us about the "errors" they noticed in the writing of their L2 students. We also noted the language they used in talking about the L2 writers/writing and whether their dispositions toward error seemed to be related to disciplinary contexts and/or to their own individual preferences and/or writing and language backgrounds, a theme identified by Thaiss and Zawacki (2006) in their faculty interviews.

While one goal of this research is to contribute faculty and L2 student perspectives to the scholarly conversation on translingual approaches to writing and teaching with writing in US postsecondary institutions, our research, only part of which is included here, also aims to help faculty appreciate the wealth of linguistic diversity our students bring with them, a point which is sometimes easy to forget when we're in the throes of grading papers. As one of our faculty interviewees recalled,

> A student from Vietnam came to my office to rework something in her paper, and she burst into tears and said another teacher had written on a paper that she was linguistically deficient. And I said "How many languages do you speak?" and she said "Vietnamese and French." And I said, "And you've only been here six months and you already know so much English!" You are just the opposite of linguistically deficient.

Still, we can't ignore the fact that this linguistic diversity, albeit enriching, raises important questions for faculty about how best to evaluate L2 students' writing and what is "fair" in relationship to the other students and to the L2 students themselves. By sharing our research with faculty, we hope to stimulate conversations among them about what constitutes "good" writing as it mirrors the conventions and genres of their disciplines and fits with the professional goals of their students, the workplaces they want to enter, and the variety of Englishes people are using there. In the process, we may all learn to hear and value the written accents our L2 students bring to our classrooms.

OUR FINDINGS

CONTENT-KNOWLEDGE AND COMPREHENSION: DOES THE STUDENT UNDERSTAND?

For many faculty, as we could see in the interviews, decisions about whether to ignore errors, correct them, take off points, or fail the paper became much more complicated when the errors involved lexical choices that raised worrisome questions about comprehension. These also tended to be the kinds of errors that were most frustrating for the faculty we interviewed as well as, for some, non-negotiable. Our interview with the three business faculty who'd sent us the student's paper in advance illustrates not only the frustration the faculty felt about the mistakes but also their sense that the student "was missing the boat entirely," as one complained.

For this assignment, the students were asked to develop a "job recruitment strategy," to incorporate a "sufficient overview of the job, including *essential* duties, *skills*, knowledge, etc. and "evidence-value added *research.*" We've italicized the words "essential," "skills," and "research" since it appears the student may have been echoing these words from the assignment without having a clear sense of what they might mean in the context of a recruitment strategy she was describing.

> **Speaker 1**: In the second paragraph, this is where I said, "What are they talking about? This student chose to recruit for a job as a singer in a restaurant, so the first sentence of the second paragraph says, "One of the research essential skills is an audition."
>
> **Speaker 2:** She's definitely a second language writer, and she's not using the right terms "research" or "essential" or "skills."
>
> **Speaker 3:** What she wants to say is that we would make candidates audition.
>
> **Speaker 2:** Or one of the essentials is … I know what she wants to say but she's not using the right word. She wants to say part of the research in finding a good singer is to have an audition, you know if you think of research in that way … which we don't.
>
> **Speaker 1:** No, the term research is not even close to being right. [Nor is] describing skills as an audition. The audition is the way to measure skills. I was so frustrated [by this paper] because I could see the ideas throughout were not completely bad [but] they are not doing their job if they can't explain this to me.
>
> **Speaker 2:** This is a perfect example [of a paper that] conveys a lack of understanding of what they think the audition is in regards to human resource management. It's like I'm just

> throwing words out there, but I don't really understand what I'm saying.

Clearly, these teachers feel the student understands the material, even if imperfectly—"I know what she's trying to say, but she's not using the right words"—but were unwilling to negotiate with his/her wrong word choices. Rather, as speaker 2 says, "It's like [the student] is just throwing words out there" but doesn't understand what s/he is saying. And yet speaker 1 admits that she could "see the ideas throughout were not completely bad" and both speaker 2 and 3 are able to rephrase the student's sentences ("what she wants to say," "she wants to say"). The problem, then, seems to be that, while the student may generally understand what is being asked, s/he is expected to be able "to do the job" by using the "right" words. Here we see an opportune learning moment for the student and a place for negotiation for the faculty (after all, they *are* negotiating the lexical errors in the passage above) if they are willing to spend time talking with the student about the expected vocabulary and why the "right words" matter to them and to others in the field.[13]

What struck us about this discussion, however, is not only how obviously concerned the faculty informants were about their student's misuse of the course vocabulary, but also their own lack of a vocabulary to talk about the writing at the sentence and word-choice level—at least as they analyzed the passage with us—which, in turn, made them dismiss the writing as unacceptable. It seemed to us, as we discussed the passage later, that, while the word choice errors they pointed out might well be rooted in the student's difficulty in accessing the content, it's also likely that the error is rooted in the student's lack of discourse knowledge, that is, how to go about writing what seems to be the hybrid genre of a "job recruitment strategy." Even English L1 undergraduate students might be challenged by this assignment, given that it calls for a "social action" (Miller, 1984) that seems quite specific to a particular course with even the name sounding like a teacher's idiosyncratic phrasing rather than a writing task that is an accepted "way of doing" (Carter, 2007) in the management major. If the business faculty had a way of thinking about the cause(s) of the word choice errors, they may have been more patient with the student and better able to help him/her find the appropriate terminology to use. (See Lancaster [this volume] for another possible explanation related to stance-taking as the cause of the error and the teachers' reaction.)

As students become more experienced with the genres and conventions of their majors, their fluency and accuracy can be expected to improve. How long it takes them to improve, however, often depends on how frequently they are asked to write and whether they are writing in the same or quite similar genres or in widely variant, even idiosyncratic, genres, e.g. a "job recruitment strategy" from course to course in the major. We know, for example, that students writing in "template forms," as our psychology informant called the lab report, achieve accuracy and fluency more quickly than those writing in varied forms to varied audiences (see Leki, 2007; Tardy, 2009; also Thaiss & Zawacki, 2006). The psychology professor we interviewed said that she finds all of her students "share the same challenges" with the format of the scientific report, and once the L2 students learn the format, they generally do as well as the English L1 students in presenting the content. If the conventionalized forms of the lab report are easier to learn than, say, the socially negotiated genres students might encounter in business, the scientific audiences for empirical research are also generally easier to imagine than those diverse potential audiences for, say, a management report or a marketing strategy. While English L1 students may also find it hard to acquire the right voice and style to write for business professionals, L2 writers have the added challenge of finding not only the right words to use but also the culturally appropriate ways to address US business people in writing while also figuring out what the teacher thinks is appropriate.

While at the surface, students' wrong word choices might be overlooked as part of a language acquisition process and not necessarily a lack of comprehension, what the business faculty's discussion suggests is that it's not always possible to differentiate between the two. If the teacher evaluating the paper can't be sure if the student is getting the content and understanding the writing expectations, s/he also can't be sure that the course objectives are being met and is therefore at a loss for how to move forward with the grading. A second language professor from bioengineering, a Brazilian with a doctoral degree from a German institution who told us that she expects her students, no matter what their first language is, to produce error-free writing, explained the problem this way:

> I'm sort of upset by the grammatical mistakes, but, if I can't understand half of [what is written] I feel like I'm losing so much. I have to trust the writer completely understands and ... it's like watching TV, but half of the pixels are gone. So, if on this screen half the pixels are gone, you could see the image, but it's not clear. You could make some other image. [So] I cannot understand their study unless the channel is transparent.

As an example of the problem, she pointed to a sentence from a student report she had shown us: "'Since the concentration of NA which is sodium increases it causes the brain to polarized'." "At that point," she said, "I don't even know if it's right or wrong, you know, because I can't understand it." In this case, it seems to us that the student writer has acquired the disciplinary lexicon, what Johns (2001) calls the "bricks" but is struggling with the "mortar"—the syntax and even the punctuation—that would hold the sentence together. With some work on her part, the teacher might see that the sentence could be corrected to read as follows: "Since the concentration of NA, which is sodium, increases, it causes the brain to become polarized." Whether the point itself is correct, we can't say; however, she would be able to comprehend what the student is attempting to say once the correct syntax and punctuation are inserted.

Another L2 faculty informant from geology told us about her process of learning to write "correctly" for graduate school in the US. While she was able to learn the scientific vocabulary and genres relatively quickly, she realized that she was still using the constructions of a typical Italian sentence. "I go back and review that," she said, "and now, when I read it with an English mindset, it sometimes doesn't make sense even to myself." When she submitted the first draft of her dissertation, her committee told her it sounded like she was telling a story and that it was not scientific writing. And yet, she said, "No one ever told me we don't understand what you're talking about." Instead, the comments were on the style of the writing, and these helped her to negotiate her way through to more standard sentence structures, syntax and word choices.

While errors that disturb the sense of a sentence or the whole piece of writing aren't easy to negotiate and certainly demand time and patience from the reader, the geology and bioengineering professors, like a number of the faculty we interviewed, are willing to spend extra time with the L2 student writers to help them succeed. In reflecting on why she's so tough on errors, especially in the writing of her L2 students, the bioengineering professor said, "I frequently ask myself why is this bothering me so much? Is it because it's also my mistake? This could be." Although her own L2 writing experiences may be informing her expectations for correctness, she also seemed to feel a strong sense of obligation to her multilingual students, meeting with them outside of class on their papers, helping them to read course texts, and giving them the books she herself read to acquire fluency, e.g. *Great Expectations,* and asking them to summarize chapters and meet with her to discuss them. (We can't resist pointing out the appropriateness of this title, if not the novel itself, for the aspirations of most L2 writers.)

With her, as with a number of our other informants, the goal was to push the students to higher levels of accuracy, so that they would be better prepared for their other classes and/or the workplace. The greatest challenge for L2 students, the psychology professor told us, is not at the idea level, once they learn the expected format, but rather at the sentence and word choice level. So "it's not correctness per se," she explained, "but those sorts of unwritten rules about the words that are appropriate to convey a particular point. Maybe other words would work, but they aren't conventional, and readers will have to stop and say 'What do you mean?' rather than flowing through the logic." Yet, she added,

> Personally, you know, I think that those mistakes are part of what makes the world so interesting. I don't see those as flaws. However, I worry for the students that that will prohibit them from succeeding in the [major] and the field. So there is a standard way of communicating and should they not learn and apply that standard then they'll have a harder time succeeding. And so ultimately that's sort of my concern for them.

ACADEMIC AND WORKPLACE WRITING EXPECTATIONS: WHAT IS FAIR?

Concern about what would happen for their L2 students when they wrote in other courses in the major or entered the workplace was repeated by a number of the faculty we talked with.[14] While many of the students' lexical and discourse errors could potentially be negotiated, the faculty questioned what might be an acceptable level of error, if any, in their discipline as well as what was in the best interest of their L2 students. We know from much of the L2 research on response to student writing (see Ferris, 2003, for example) and from our own interviews with L2 students that most students do want error correction to help them acquire academic language proficiency.[15] For both the students and the faculty, then, there is a strong sense that L2 students need to acquire communicative and strategic competence (Ferris, 2003; Gentil, 2011) to succeed in the university and in their chosen fields. While we have been arguing, based on our research, that determinations of "competence" are often dependent on the context and readers' dispositions, the data we report in this section indicate that these faculty felt that it would be remiss and unfair of them to expect less of their L2 students than they do of their English L1 students.

Careful, error-free writing is *the* key to success in systems engineering, according to the professor we interviewed. For a requirements engineer, the hardest part of the job, she said, "is finding out what everyone is doing and getting the problem down accurately and correctly [so that] the user is happy. The easy part is the quantitative stuff." Clear communication is critical, so, when she grades the papers, she applies the same standards to everyone, although she, like the bioengineering professor, spends a great deal of time working with all of her students to help them meet the standards she sets. In grading papers, she told us, she makes it a practice not to even look at the name of the writer until she has given the grade because "No one's going to give them a break when they're working because they're from wherever. You just get left behind, so why not get told that now when you're a student rather than get hit in the face with it when you get out there working." For much the same reason, faculty and administrators in the School of Management expect all students to be able to produce writing in standard English with few mistakes, based not only on workplace expectations but also on the accreditation requirements for the field. They are firmly supported by the dean who speaks and writes Spanish as his first language.

While questions about "fairness" emerged as a real concern for our faculty informants (as it did for the faculty interviewed by Ives, Leahy, Leming, Pierce, & Schwartz [this volume]), what's interesting is that the way they talked about fairness didn't seem to revolve around being equitable in their grading, but rather about doing all they can to best prepare their students for future success. Although negotiating meaning may be their preferred approach, they feel pressure, as we said, to help their students meet standards for writing academic English. If the stakes are perceived to be high for L2 writers as students, there are also real stakes around correct usage in the fields some of the students will enter. A faculty member from social work, for example, explained that, although there may be "minimal mistakes," if students

> are going into health care, they have to make sure that what they are writing is exactly what they are meaning to say; any case records that they do and any communication has to reflect exactly what they mean. So people aren't reading between the lines for those kinds of things.

She also described, however, what we would consider a translingual approach to negotiating meaning around the misuse of terms tied to cultural differences. "I try not to be too hard on students," she said, "if they're using words that we wouldn't necessarily use here, but the usage is based on their culture." As an example, she mentioned the word "abuse," which, she said, is sometimes "overused relative to what we mean by it here and what it means in other countries where it can be perceived differently based on how children are disciplined in other countries or how elderly people are treated in the US." For that reason, she spends time in class talking about culturally different perceptions of key social work issues, while cautioning *all* of her students to take great care in the choosing the terms they use to describe the social conditions they're writing about given the diverse populations they will be working with if they remain in the US.

The math professor we interviewed provided a different kind of insight on the reasons correct word choice is important in his field. "English allows for a degree of vagueness, which is generally bad in communicating mathematical ideas," he told us. In math, correct article usage is crucial, he said, even though, as we noted to him, most language specialists would generally recommend not spending too much time on this relatively minor grammatical feature. As he pointed out, however,

> Math is a precise discipline, so if we say that there is "a" solution, we know that there may be another solution, but if we say "the" solution, that means there cannot be another solution. So in this case knowing the articles is very important and this goes back to how they translate their thinking to English.

For the faculty we've described in this section, there is a strong sense of the stakes involved in students being able to produce writing that is mostly free of lexical errors and reflects an understanding of the importance of correct usage in the fields and workplaces they plan to enter. While they do penalize students for making errors, most are also willing to help students by conferencing with them on their writing or by requiring them to go to the writing center. In contrast, a civil engineering professor, also multilingual, told us that he takes off only a small percentage for poor writing even though he cares about and expects standard written English. In describing his reasons, he explained,

> I want to talk about engineering not writing. [As much as writing is important,] there's not much bang for the buck to work with undergraduate writing. They can learn on the job. They need a certain level of intellect to survive the rigors of engineering. An engineering major who can't write still has the job. The English major doesn't.

For this professor, then, being fair to his students means preparing them to be engineers, not writers. Worrying about errors in their writing takes attention away from worrying about their ability to succeed as engineers.[16]

READERLY DISPOSITIONS AND REFLECTIVE WRITING

In our interviews, several faculty mentioned assigning reflective writing tasks, and it was interesting to hear how the reflection genre itself seemed to evoke a different readerly disposition towards error on the part of the faculty we talked to, generally because they saw the stakes involved as being very different for students. As the management teacher explained, "It's not really like right and wrong; it's more like a self-discovery process." As she described it, the goal of the "non-academic" reflective paper she assigns is "to give students practice thinking through a challenge or problem for which there is no easy answer, [one that] is inherently meaningful to them ... and that might help them think through an issue they're confronting right now or might confront in the future." All of the students, including the L2 writers, generally do very well on this assignment, she noted, partly because

> they definitely feel that the reigns are looser. I don't go in there with any expectations. And it's not such a technical piece, although some students are very technical, it can be very personal. I tell them I want to hear your voice come through if possible in this paper. I don't want it to be so formal.

As we see it, the "looser reigns" seem to free up the space for the faculty member to stop worrying about perceived external pressures and expectations, and to focus on *how* the students are learning the material and on their processes for writing about that learning. Teachers read with a different disposition, in other words. The social work professor told us, for example, that reflective writing is a regular part of social work assignments and noted that students are even better at reflection than at their other writing, while also adding "or at least [reflective writing] is easier for me to assess because I don't worry about the grammar and sentence structure as much. And I think because of that too, they're more free to just write what they're thinking." She continued, however, that, while reflection is easier for students to write and for her to grade, "it may be harder for ESL students in terms of language translation." We're particularly interested in that observation given that much of the second-language writing research indicates that drafting and free writing may be painstaking for L2 students who are also struggling with word choice and phrasing in English.

And yet, just as with English L1 writers, reflection on learning and writing plays an important role in L2 students' language and writing development. In discussing the components of specific-purpose language ability, Gentil (2011) explains that learners need not only the ability to choose appropriate responses for a task, but they must also be able to reflect on and evaluate their choices (p. 13). Tardy's (2009) model of genre knowledge includes "process knowledge," which involves not only the ability to use appropriate processes but also an awareness of one's own and others' composing processes for written genres. Still, the concept of reflection may feel foreign to many L2 students who may be uncomfortable and even resistant to writing about themselves as learners, writers, or as individuals with a literacy history to bring to their learning and writing. For many, just as with English L1 students, reflective writing can also appear to be a "waste of time," as Leki (2007) notes was the case for some of the L2 undergraduates she studied (p. 247) and as we found in some of our L2 student interviews, suggesting, we think, that the students also understand the stakes to be lower. They reason that if the work isn't going to be graded, then why expend the effort? As with any writing assignment teachers give, students need an explanation of the learning goals for the task and even, perhaps, an opportunity to reflect on the value of reflection. Both the faculty and student informants in our research, for example, commented on how the interview itself had led them to reflect on themselves as teachers and writers in ways they hadn't before.

CONCLUSION

We opened our chapter with Diana's self-perceived deficiencies, her "not good" feeling about her writing in English. This feeling is understandable when multilingualism itself is perceived as a deficiency rather than a strength. We must actively resist this perception by helping faculty learn how to read with patience, respect for language difference, and a deliberative attitude (Horner et al., 2011) that seeks to understand the causes for perceived error and is open to the possibility of negotiation. As Shaughnessy reminds us, "English has been robustly inventing itself for centuries—stretching and reshaping and enriching itself with every language and dialect it has encountered," so this "battle" *is* "worth waging" (1979, p. 13). Our goal in this translingual encounter should be to move students from feeling "not good" to a place described by Ayesha, a Pakistani student at the end of her undergraduate studies:

> When you are given a topic, the more you read about it, and the more research you do about it, the more it broadens your vision. And I really enjoy that everything is so new to me ....

> I get so excited. I'm like, okay, I am going to learn something new today .... And it feels so light when I have done my research properly and then I write something down. And I just feel so good.

As we think about faculty expectations for their students' writing and their attitudes towards errors, as well as students' expectations and attitudes, we're reminded of Shaughnessy's (1979) words: "In a better world, it is true, readers might be more generous with their energies, pausing to divine the meaning of a writer or mentally to edit efforts, but it would be foolhardy to bank on that kind of persistence except perhaps in English teachers or good friends" (p. 12). While we found many of the faculty we interviewed to be generous with their energies in helping L2 writers succeed and more than a few willing to try to divine the students' meaning, we could also see that, for many, their expectation of standard written English is driven by a strong sense of the stakes involved, whether perceived or real, e.g. accrediting agencies, state mandates, future job performance. When required to evaluate the students' comprehension of the course content, our informants, like so many teachers, feel pulled in two directions—wanting to respect the multilingual expression because they recognize the challenge of writing about difficult material in a language still being acquired, while simultaneously wanting to ensure that they are best preparing their students for the perceived less-forgiving expectations of readers in other contexts. Further, for many teachers, the possibility of negotiating with lexical and domain-specific errors may not be practical if they don't also have some understanding of the causes for the errors. When a teacher has to evaluate a piece of writing and is faced with errors that could originate from a wide range of possible causes, the diagnosis of the error becomes less important than a consideration of how to give a grade that is fair to the student, fair to the system of grading devised for all of the students in the class, and fair to stakeholders in the courses and fields the students will be entering.

As we see it, then, there is not so much a "refusal to negotiate" with translingual writing on the part of faculty, at least those we talked to, but rather that their willingness, or not, to negotiate derives from a complex mix of motives, including their learning and writing goals for students, their sense of what's fair to L2 students along with the other students, and their understandings—and misunderstandings—of L2 error. WAC practitioners thus emerge as stakeholders who can facilitate the process of negotiation through informed faculty development, focusing on inclusive practices for teaching with writing, including recognizing the strengths L2 students demonstrate in their writing and fairly evaluating the students' communicative and strategic competencies. (See Lancaster [this volume] for an examination of stancetaking in L2 writing—one element of writing that faculty often mistake as error—and approaches for working with faculty to recognize it. See Cox [this volume] for a range of strategies that can be used in faculty development workshops, on websites, and in newsletters.)

There should, of course, be institutional incentives for faculty who are "generous with their energies" and willing to engage in inclusive pedagogies. Haifeng from China, a student in public policy, noted that what helped him learn to write according to the "American" conventions of his field was "getting feedback on his writing and suddenly [understanding] that all my sentences could be expressed in a better way." The professor who gave him this feedback was

> very responsible and just [did] all the things he thinks can benefit [his students.] Besides grammar and writing mistakes and [highlighting] awkward English, he definitely [gave] us suggestions on topics. Before we start to write the paper, the professor tells us how to write an academic paper with the introduction, background, the methodology. He already showed us how to do this from scratch.

The approach Haifeng's professor takes with his multilingual students is time-consuming, but necessary if we want to be fair to all of the students who enroll at our institutions. Here too WAC programs can serve an important role not only as resources for faculty who strive to support multilingual writers but also by working at the institutional level providing research, data and evidence that allows universities to rethink resource distribution that supports multilingual students. In addition to the kinds of funding often allotted to international initiatives, i.e. funding for travel and classroom technologies, institutions must reconsider how faculty are rewarded for engaging in inclusive pedagogies that successfully retain and teach the international populations being targeted. Faculty workloads might accommodate particular curricular and pedagogical work; curriculum may be reconsidered in light of multilingual support and the affordances such changes also bring to L1 students negotiating an international future. In each case, the rewards will be tailored to the local context, but that can only be realized if research, such as that engaged in here, and as represented in other chapters in this collection, becomes part of the institutional culture.

NOTES

1. In our interviews with second language writers, for example, in addition to Diana, a student from Pakistan, Ayesha, lamented, "I do have ideas, and I do want to put something down, but I am really short of words." Another, Sri, who writes in Telugu and Hindi, told us, "It all comes down to vocabulary; it's not your thought because everyone who does even a bit of schooling has some thought in his or her chosen field ... but you have to know which words to use to express your thoughts."
2. Not all errors are "invented" by readers, Bitchener and Ferris (2012) point out; rather, linguists take a "theoretically and empirically grounded view of error," seeing errors in writing as "lexical, morphological, or syntactic deviations from the intuitions of a literate adult native speaker of the language." Such errors may be caused by "interlanguage" interference as well as L2 acquisition stages of development (p. 42). Ferris and Roberts (2001) used the following error categories as codes in their research on actual errors teachers marked: verb errors, noun ending errors, article errors, wrong word choice or word form, and sentence structure, including sentence boundary errors, word order, omitted words or phrases, unnecessary words or phrases, and other non-idiomatic structures (pp. 161-84).
3. In their review of research of second language writing in English, Leki, Cumming, and Silva (2008) show that, while faculty responses to L2 writing vary according to a range of factors, e.g. age, gender, content area, the errors that cause distraction, disrupt meaning, or seem "the most 'foreign'" are apt to elicit the most "irritation" or "cranky responses" (p. 30).
4. Anna's interest in this research also stems from her personal experience as a multilingual writer and speaker herself from the post-colonial, multilingual context of post-war Lebanon. After her family fled Beirut, she grew up as a refugee in Cyprus where she attended a Lebanese school that followed the French Lycee system and where English and Greek were taught as third and fourth languages. Her personal experience as a code-mesher/switcher informed her contributions to our linguistically inclusive research team.
5. During the course of our research, Anna became the interim writing center director when Terry stepped down to devote full attention to directing WAC.
6. The full title of our short monograph is *Valuing Written Accents: Non-native Students Talk about Identity, Academic Writing, and Meeting Teachers' Expectations*. The research was published under the auspices of the Office of University Life and the Diversity Research Group. University Life subsequently funded the creation of a website to present this research; it can be found at **writtenaccents.gmu.edu**.

7. In "Towards a Multilingual Composition Scholarship: From English Only to a Translingual Norm," Horner, NeCamp, and Donahue (2011) explain how a translingual model is different from both monolingual and traditional multilingual models. A multilingual model, they argue, sees languages as "static" and "discrete," with "fluency" determined by the user "achieving an 'appropriate' target," and with "bilingual" users "imagined as two monolinguals in one person." In contrast, a translingual model opens up these language "confines" to see languages as "fluctuating" and "in constant revision"; fluency as the ability to code-switch, borrow, and blend; and "bilingual" as "a unique and shifting blend of practical knowledge and language use." In this model, "mutual intelligibility" is the goal, not appropriate usage in one language or another (p. 287).

8. The view of error as a "refusal to negotiate" comes up in much of Canagarajah's work on Lingua Franca English (LFE), mainly in his research on the professional writing of South Asian English writers/speakers. In "Lingua Franca English, Multilingual Communities, and Language Acquisition" (2007), for example, Canagarajah writes, "Breakdown in LFE communication is possible only in rare cases of refusal to negotiate meanings—which is itself a form of communication as it conveys the participant's desire to cut off the conversation" (p. 929).

9. Here we're echoing Canagarajah, who takes up Pratt's idea of the contact zone in much of his work on English Lingua Franca, recognizing the power differences and unequal roles of those involved in negotiations around "native 'norms'" and sociolinguistic change. See, for example, "The Place of World Englishes in Composition: Pluralization Continued" (Canagarajah, 2006).

10. There is abundant L2 research (and debate) on cognitive, social, and academic processes involved in the acquisition of fluency and accuracy and most effective approaches to teaching both. See, for example, Casanave's (2007) chapter "Paths to Improvement" in *Controversies in Second Language Writing*, Ferris's *Treatment of Error in Second Language Student Writing (2002)* and *Response to Student Writers: Implications for Second Language Students (2003)*.

11. She addresses that gap in the research in "Negotiating Socioacademic Relations: English Learners' Reception by and Reaction to College Faculty" (2006) in which she looks at the kinds of accommodations, if any, faculty made for L2 students, their comments about L2 students, and the L2 students' comments on their experiences with faculty.

12. Writing center usage data consistently indicate that almost half of all students making appointments come from first-language backgrounds other than English and that 60% of all users were referred to the writing center by a teacher.

13. The business teachers, in fact, talked about how they try to help multilingual students negotiate unfamiliar terms on essay exams by giving them permission

to ask about idiomatic usage that is not specific to course concepts, e.g. "harness energy," a word that one L2 student asked them to explain. At the same time, the college has a "zero-tolerance" policy on errors, and, in the assessment rubric they use for their accreditation, they spell out the numbers and kinds of errors that are grounds for failure, which, as Terry has found in working with them, is enormously problematic for a number of reasons, including their own failure to agree on how serious certain errors really are or even to identify accurately the errors they see or don't see, as the case may be.

14. While we would like to argue that teachers' concerns about what other imagined readers and rhetorical contexts will require should be put aside to focus on their own priorities and expectations for student writers, the responses of many of our "take no prisoners" informants indicates that their concerns are not unwarranted.

15. In her breakdown of academic language proficiency, Ferris (2009) includes, among other proficiencies, *sociolinguistic* proficiency, i.e. an understanding of register and the ability to carry out both social and academic tasks, and *discourse* proficiency, i.e. how to introduce, conclude, and organize texts; how to present and balance ideas in texts (p. 27).

16. His comment brings to mind Leki's critique in "Is Writing Overrated?" of compositionists' assumptions about the role of writing in learning and the arguments we make for requiring writing-intensive courses in the disciplines.

REFERENCES

Bean, J. C. (2001). *Engaging ideas: The professor's guide to integrating writing, critical thinking, and active learning in the classroom.* San Francisco, CA: Jossey Bass.

Beaufort, Anne. (2007). *College writing and beyond: A new framework for university writing instruction.* Logan, UT: Utah State University Press.

Bitchener, J. & Ferris, D. R. (2012) *Written Corrective Feedback in Second Language Acquisition and Writing.* NY: Routledge.

Canagarajah, A. S. (2002). Multilingual writers and the academic community: Towards a critical relationship. *Journal of English for Academic Purposes, 1,* 29-44.

Canagarajah, A. S. (2006). The place of World Englishes in composition: Pluralization continued. *College Composition and Communication, 57*(4), 586-619.

Canagarajah, A. S. (2007). Lingua franca English, multilingual communities, and language acquisition. *The Modern Language Journal, 91,* 923-939.

Canagarajah, A. S. (2009). Multilingual strategies of negotiating English: From conversation to writing. *Journal of Advanced Composition, 29*(1-2), 17-48.

Carter, M. (1990). The idea of expertise: An exploration of cognitive and social dimensions of writing. *College Composition and Communication, 41*(3), 265-286.

Casanave, C. (2007). *Controversies in second language writing: Dilemmas and decisions in research and instruction.* Ann Arbor, MI: University of Michigan Press.

Ferris, D. R. (2003). *Response to student writing: Implications for second language students.* New York: Routledge.

Ferris, D. R. (2004). The "grammar correction" debate in L2 writing: Where are we, and where do we go from here? (and what do we do in the meantime ...?). *Journal of Second Language Writing, 13,* 49-62.

Ferris, D. R. (2009). *Teaching college writing to diverse student populations.* Ann Arbor, MI: University of Michigan Press.

Ferris, D. R. & Roberts, B. (2001). Error feedback in L2 writing classes: How explicit does it need to be? *Journal of Second Language Writing 10*(3):161-84

Gentil. G. (2011). A biliteracy agenda for genre research. *Journal of Second Language Writing, 20,* 6-23.

George Mason University Factbook 2011-2012. Office of Institutional Research and Reporting. irr.gmu.edu/factbooks/1112/Factbook1112_Intro.pd

Horner, B. & Trimbur, J. (2002). English only and US college composition. *College Composition and Communication, 53*(4), 594-630.

Horner, B., Lu, M-Z, Royster, J. J., & Trimbur, J. (2011). Language difference in writing: Toward a translingual approach. *College English, 73*(3), 303-321.

Horner, B., NeCamp, S. & Donahue, C. (2011) Toward a multilingual composition scholarship: From English only to a translingual norm. *College Composition and Communication, 63*(2), 269-300.

Johns, A. M. (2001). ESL students and WAC programs: Varied populations and diverse needs. In S. H. McLeod, E. Miraglia, M. Soven, & C. Thaiss (Eds.), *WAC for the new millennium: Strategies for continuing writing-across-the-curriculum programs* (pp. 141-164). Urbana, IL: NCTE.

Leki, I. (2003). A challenge to second language writing professionals: Is writing overrated? In B. Kroll (Ed.), Exploring the dynamics of second language writing (pp. 315-332). Cambridge, UK: Cambridge University Press.

Leki, I. (2006). Negotiating socioacademic relations: English learners' reception by and reaction to college faculty. *Journal of English for Academic Purposes 5,* 136-152.

Leki, I. (2007). *Undergraduates in a second language: Challenges and complexities of academic literacy development.* New York: Routledge.

Leki, I., Cumming, A., & Silva, T. (2008). *A synthesis of research on second language writing in English.* New York: Routledge.

Matsuda, P. K. (2006). The myth of linguistic homogeneity in US college composition. *College English, 68*(6), 637-651.

Miller, C. (1984). Genre as social action. *Quarterly Journal of Speech, 70*, 151-167.

Shaughnessy, M. (1979). *Errors and expectations: A guide for the teacher of basic writing.* New York: Oxford University Press.

Silva, T. (1993) Toward an understanding of the distinct nature of L2 writing: The ESL research and its implications. *TESOL Quarterly, 27*(4), 657-677.

Tardy, C. (2009*). Building genre knowledge: Writing L2.* West Lafayette, IN: Parlor Press.

Tardy, C. (2011). Enacting and transforming local language policies. *College Composition and Communication*, 62(4), 634-661.

Thaiss, C. & Zawacki, T. M. (2006). *Engaged writers and dynamic disciplines: Research on the academic writing life.* Portsmouth, NH: Heinemann.

Zawacki, T., Habib, A., Hajabbasi, E., Antram, A., & Das, A. (2007). *Valuing written accent:. International voices in the US academy.* Retrieved from http://writtenaccents.gmu.edu

APPENDIX A: INVITATION TO FACULTY PARTICIPANTS AND INTERVIEW QUESTIONS

Terry Zawacki, director of George Mason University's Writing Across the Curriculum (WAC) Program, Anna Habib, English and CISA faculty member, and other WAC/writing center co-researchers, have been conducting HSRB-approved research on the experiences of faculty when working with second-language writers in courses across the disciplines. This research is intended to add faculty perspectives to an earlier research study, also HSRB-approved, on the experiences of international and immigrant students with writing in the academic disciplines both in the US and in their countries of origin. Our research findings will serve as a resource for both second-language writers and for professionals interested in how best to teach or tutor these writers.

Following is a list of the questions that will be used to guide our semi-structured interviews:

Questions on disciplinary genres and the performance of L2 writers:

- What courses do you usually teach? Approximately, what percentage of your students are L2 writers as far as you can tell?
- What kinds of writing are most typical of your discipline? Do you expect undergraduates to be able to write in these typical ways?
- What genres of writing do you typically assign? What assignments do you typically give undergraduates? Do these differ depending upon the level of the course?
- What are your expectations for this writing in terms of general academic and more specific disciplinary standards? In your discipline, what things are valued in writing?
- What advice do you/would you give undergraduates about writing in your discipline?
- Do you require students to write in e-spaces? If so, how do you see L2 students performing as writers in these spaces?
- Do you assign collaborative projects? If so, what, are your goals for writers? If you assign collaborative projects, what, if anything, have you noticed about L2 students' participation in these projects?
- What characterizes good and poor writing for students in your discipline?
- What are your principal concerns when grading the writing of non-native students?
- What similarities and/or differences, if any, do you see in the areas that need improvement in the writing of L1 and L2 students?
- In your experience, are there areas where L2 writers tend to have significantly more difficulty than L1 writers? Do you find that L2 students do better on some genres than on others? If yes, which of those areas are most significant to student learning or meeting your classroom objectives?
- How is credit given to sources in your discipline? What difficulties, if any, do you see L2 students having with citation and documentation?

Questions on faculty practices for teaching with writing:

- When giving feedback on student's papers do you tend to focus more on the global (i.e. thesis, conclusion, organization) or local (i.e. grammar) concerns in a paper? Is there a specific reason you focus on one over the other?
- How much error and what kinds of errors are too much error in your view?
- How do you respond to sentence level errors in the writing of your L2 students?

- What, if any, kinds of adjustments have you made in your instruction and materials to address the needs of a diverse classroom?
- What advice would you/do you give to L2 students who are trying to learn to write in the major and/or your courses?

QUESTIONS ON FACULTY READING AND WRITING EXPERIENCES:

- What is your native language? Can you read and write in that language?
- Do you speak, read, and/or write in a language (s) in addition to your native language? What language (s)?
- If yes, do you recall how you learned to write in English?

CHAPTER 8

"I DON'T KNOW IF THAT WAS THE RIGHT THING TO DO": CROSS-DISCIPLINARY/CROSS-INSTITUTIONAL FACULTY RESPOND TO L2 WRITING

Lindsey Ives
University of New Mexico

Elizabeth Leahy
University of Arizona

Anni Leming
Central New Mexico Community College

Tom Pierce
Central New Mexico Community College

Michael Schwartz
St. Cloud State University

This chapter investigates faculty expectations for student writing, specifically L2 writers of English, across disciplines at a flagship university and an urban community college in the southwest. Drawing from a faculty survey and follow-up interviews with faculty from various disciplines, the authors argue that study participants tend to hold multilingual writers to a monolingual standard, but that they are conflicted and/or ambivalent about this practice. The survey and interview data show, first, that markers of nonnative speaker status or any features that depart from Standard American Academic English often discourage and even preclude engagement with higher order concerns like ideas and argument. Second, the data show that study participants want native-like prose but do not necessarily expect it, despite what

> they may claim. Third, the data suggest that many faculty across disciplines are open to discussions about language variety and working with multilingual writers.

Matsuda (2006) observes that composition instructors often operate with the assumption that all students who enroll in their classes are "native speakers of a privileged variety of English" (p. 638), and that they come to class having previously acquired Standard American Academic English (SAAE). Within the framework of WAC, we extend Matsuda's "myth of linguistic homogeneity" by investigating the experiences and expectations of faculty in the disciplines at a local university and community college. In short, do these faculty assume and demand a native speaker standard for their multilingual writers? Not only have we seen some anecdotal evidence that this might be the case, but scholarship in second language writing also suggests that such expectations are likely. For instance, Ferris (2008) points out that

> While we language professionals may rest in our enlightened awareness that language acquisition takes time, and that progress and not perfection should be our objective, the realities and expectations of the world outside of our classrooms often pressure us to reach that unattainable goal. (p. 92)

Although our study was guided by many questions, this chapter focuses on two of these: What do faculty across disciplines and college contexts expect from L2 student writing and how do these expectations shape the ways that they respond to their multilingual students' writing?

Hall (2009) argues that embracing the needs of multilingual writers requires WAC to transform itself so that these needs are acknowledged and addressed within the scope of the goals and mission of WAC programs. Cox (2011) concurs, stating that "... WAC has increased emphasis on writing across undergraduate programs without creating mechanisms that help second language (L2) students succeed as writers and without creating faculty development programs that offer training in working with L2 writers" (n.p.). Our study responds in part to these calls for more articulation between second language writing and WAC research, seeking to understand the ways in which WAC and second language writing can complement each other in their collective efforts to better serve the needs of faculty in the disciplines and multilingual writers in those disciplines.

To investigate our study questions, we surveyed and conducted follow-up interviews with tenured and tenure-track faculty, adjunct instructors, and graduate teaching assistants across disciplines at two different institutions. The themes that emerged from the data are somewhat contradictory, as we'll explain. While some responses to the survey and follow-up interviews indicate that faculty across disciplines expect unmarked SAAE from multilingual and monolingual writers alike, other statements in the survey and interviews, often from the same participants, indicate that this is not actually the case. Instructors across disciplines do in fact expect language diversity to be reflected in their students' writing but don't know how to address this diversity, resulting in continued insistence on writing that meets a monolingual ideal, however this is interpreted. Our data further indicate, however, that many faculty, like those who participated in our study, *are* open to discussing new ways of addressing language diversity in the classroom.

METHODS

For all of us, the driving force behind this project was to become more informed about the communicative situations that our students will face in the future so that we, as teachers, can talk more knowledgeably with them in pre-college writing courses and first-year composition (FYC) about what they need to know to prepare to communicate effectively with a variety of academic audiences. When this study began, we were all graduate students—Anni and Michael in educational linguistics, Lindsey, Elizabeth, and Tom in rhetoric and writing—who wanted to collaborate on this project because of a shared interest in second language writing and WAC. At the time, Lindsey, Elizabeth, and Michael were teaching at the university and Tom and Anni were teaching at the community college less than a mile away, which is why we chose these two locations as our research sites.

Further, as even our small group of researchers indicates, there is much overlap between our university and the neighboring community college. Many graduate students in English, linguistics, and other disciplines support themselves by teaching pre-college writing and FYC at the community college, or by teaching some courses at the university and some at the community college. Community college instructors in English and across the disciplines are often alumni of graduate programs at the university and were trained to teach there. Some university undergraduates choose, for financial reasons, to take approved summer courses at the community college instead of the university. Further, freshmen who have been admitted to the university but whose ACT scores are not high enough to place them into college-level composition must first take pre-college writing courses that are provided through the community college and staffed by community college instructors, but that are taught on the university campus. While taking these community college writing courses (which they don't necessarily know are community college courses), these students are simultaneously enrolled in university courses in biology, psychology, and other disciplines. That the two institutions have so much overlap contributed to our decision to include both in our study.

In addition, the two institutions where our study was conducted can be seen as a microcosm of the growing multilingual population of the United States. As Hall (2009) observes, multilingual learners are now part of the mainstream (p. 37), and this is certainly true for our institutions. Although language data are not collected by the two institutions that are our study sites, they are located in New Mexico, which is identified as a Minority-Majority state with many cultures and languages represented. The most predominant language after English is Spanish and its many varieties. Many Native American languages are also spoken throughout the state, including Navajo, Keres, Tiwa, Towa, Tewa, and Zuni. Additionally, many resident-immigrant languages are included in the mix, such as Vietnamese, Tagalog, Mandarin, and Korean to name just a few. Finally, both of the study institutions have large international student populations, representing over 90 different countries. Given this diversity, it is safe to assume that Hall's (2009) "Next America" is very much already present in the institutions where our study was conducted.

We want to note here that, while neither of the institutions we studied has a formalized WAC program, we are currently making efforts at the university to build a program informed by the Writing Across Communities (WACommunities) philosophy. According to Kells (2007), a leader in this movement, "A Writing Across Communities approach to WAC foregrounds the dimensions of cultural and sociolinguistic diversity in university-wide writing instruction" (p. 90), so WAC programs following this model are necessarily informed and infused by scholarship in second-language writing.

The first phase of our research was a faculty survey distributed through surveymonkey.com. The survey asked respondents to report on several different facets of writing in their classes, such as assignments, instructions, the use of rubrics, and assessment. Additionally respondents were asked to rate two paragraphs on the same topic—issues concerning poverty—that were written as conclusions to an essay. The first paragraph, Passage 1, was written by a multilingual writer from Hong Kong enrolled in an intermediate writing course at an intensive English program in the United States. The second paragraph, Passage 2, was a control paragraph, written by the research team to control for subject matter, content, organization, and surface-level features.

> **Passage 1 Non-native speaker of English**
> In conclusion, poverty indeed creates some negative consequences for society, includes illiteracy, unemployment,crime rate, lack of science and technology, we know there is still some problems need to resolve. Due to this negative consequences, we supposed to pay more attention about third world countries; instead of ignoring the problem, we can make some decision to reduce the negative consequences and make these countries better.
>
> **Passage 2 Control passage**
> In conclusion, illiteracy, unemployment, crime rate, and lack of science and technology are negative effects of poverty. These problems can be resolved. We should do something to improve poor countries.

Survey respondents were asked to rate each passage on three categories: content, organization, and mechanics. The rating options for each category were "exemplary," "above average," "average," and "substandard." In addition to rating the passages, respondents were given the opportunity to provide qualitative comments following each passage. While all the members of the research team expected Passage 1 to be generally rated as "substandard" in the "mechanics" category, the research team thought that the ideas expressed in Passage 1 were more complex than those in Passage 2, in which sentences were shortened and edited. We also agreed, independently, that the organization of the control passage, Passage 2, conformed more closely to the expectations of SAAE, but thought that it transitioned less effectively from one idea to the next than did Passage 1.

A total of 104 faculty responded to the survey, with 72 coming from the university and 31 coming from the community college (see Appendix A). When asked about their language background, 96 of the respondents identified as native speakers of English, while eight identified as nonnative speakers. Aside from English, the respondents identified their native languages as Serbian, Spanish, Tewa, Cherokee, Tagalog, Chinese, and Dutch.

Survey respondents were invited to provide contact information if they were interested in participating in an hour-long follow-up interview. We contacted those who provided their information and interviewed them in a location of their choice. Roughly 11% of survey respondents participated in follow-up interviews. The qualitative data we present here, however, include only eight of the 12 interview participants since four interviews have yet to be transcribed at the time of this writing (see Appendix B). The interview questions aimed at giving us a more detailed picture of the participants' understanding of the role of writing in their field, the relationship of that understanding to the writing they assign, and how they respond to their students' writing. We also directly asked "What are your expectations for multilingual writers?" since we were especially interested in helping multilingual writers enter the discourse communities that our participants represent. We expected that our participants would have had some experience with multilingual students and that they would be able to discuss those experiences. The interviews were recorded and transcribed. We worked collaboratively to analyze the data, engaging in the process of discourse analysis as conceptualized by Gee (1999) and Cameron (2001), by which we sought to understand the construction of faculty roles and expectations of student writing in the local community college and university. Further, we allowed themes to emerge via open and axial coding processes (Creswell, 1998).

While our team had previously heard anecdotal evidence that some instructors at the university impose a rigorous monolingual standard for their multilingual students, we did not assume that this would be the case with our interviewees. Initially, however, some of us on the research team believed we would find differences between the university and community college faculty regarding expectations for their students in terms of academic writing, while others on the research team anticipated relative uniformity between the faculty groups. For example, Tom, Anni, and Michael's experiences at the community college and the university led them toward an expectation that community college faculty might be more likely to focus on sentence-level errors, while faculty at the university might be more concerned about the content of ideas expressed. While the data did not confirm this initial expectation, in our discussion of our findings in this chapter, we are not going to make comparisons between expectations for student writing at the community college and the university, even though we think the comparative analysis is important. While there were significant differences between community college and university participants on some of the survey questions, we found no a significant difference in the passage ratings, which are the focus of this chapter, between these two demographics. In addition, delays with the community college Internal Review Board shortened the amount of time that we had to conduct interviews at the community college, so, as of this writing, we lacked enough interviews from the community college to draw any conclusions about them in comparison to the university interviews. Of the interviews that we have so far conducted with community college instructors, however, there is enough overlap in the categories with which this article is concerned to discuss them together.

In this chapter, we draw upon survey and interview data to argue, first, that markers of nonnative speaker status or any features that depart from SAAE discourage and even preclude faculty engagement with higher order concerns like ideas and argument. Second, we argue that the faculty who participated in our study want native-like prose but do not in fact expect it, despite what they may claim. Third, we suggest that some of the interview responses indicate that the faculty participants would be open to discussions about language variety and working with multilingual writers.

OUR FINDINGS

FEATURES SIGNALING ENGLISH L2 STATUS NEGATIVELY AFFECT AVERALL PERCEPTION OF THE WRITING AND THE WRITER

The results, illustrated in Figures 8.1 through 8.3, show content for Passage 1 being rated as "substandard" by 44% of respondents as opposed to only 18% for Passage 2. They show organization for Passage 1 being rated "substandard" by 55% of respondents and for Passage 2 only 20%. Finally, they show, as we expected, mechanics rated as "substandard" by 92% of respondents for Passage 1, and only 9% for Passage 2. The fact that Passage 1 was rated as "substandard" in all three categories at a much higher rate than Passage 2, which tended to be rated as "average," indicates that features signaling non-native speaker status tend to negatively affect instructors' perceptions of student writing overall. Survey participants were given the option of explaining their passage ratings, and their explanations also support this interpretation, as do our interviews.

Many of the respondents who rated Passage 1 as "substandard" overall explained that the mechanical issues in this passage preclude comprehension. An instructor in anthropology noted in the comment section for Passage 1 that "This appears to be an ESL student's work, and if so, I would take that into consideration in grading. However, it is so garbled as to be nearly incoherent." An instructor in biology in the comment section agreed, saying "If the mechanics are below average, I find it difficult to read the passage and make sense out of it. If something is poorly written, the reader will get bogged down and it doesn't matter how it is organized or what the content is."

Both of these instructors indicate that, indeed, features signaling non-native speaker status make it difficult, if not impossible, for them to respond to

Ives *et al.*

aspects of the student's writing beyond grammar and mechanics. While the first instructor suggests that she takes language background into account in grading for sentence-level issues, and, while she would like to respond to the content and organization, she suggests that the passage departs so far from SAAE that she cannot even do so. (This response aligns with the evaluations of L2 writing that Zawacki and Habib [this volume] report from their faculty interviews regarding concerns about their L2 students' comprehension of the material.) The second instructor equates "poor writing" with "below average mechanics," seemingly reducing the meaning of writing to sentence-level concerns, placing other elements like content and organization outside of the category "writing." While the commentary on Passage 2 is also negative, it is important to note that the respondents, seeing native-like usage, are more willing to address higher order concerns in the student's writing.

A few respondents directly compared Passage 2 favorably to Passage 1. An instructor in biology said that Passage 2 "is better, but it doesn't flow very well." An instructor in anthropology views Passage 2 as "Concise and with acceptable grammar and spelling." Most of the comments about Passage 2 focus on the passage's content and what it lacks. An instructor in biology advised that the student "specify 'improve WHAT in poor countries' and how ..." An instructor in communication and journalism saw Passage 2 as characterized by:

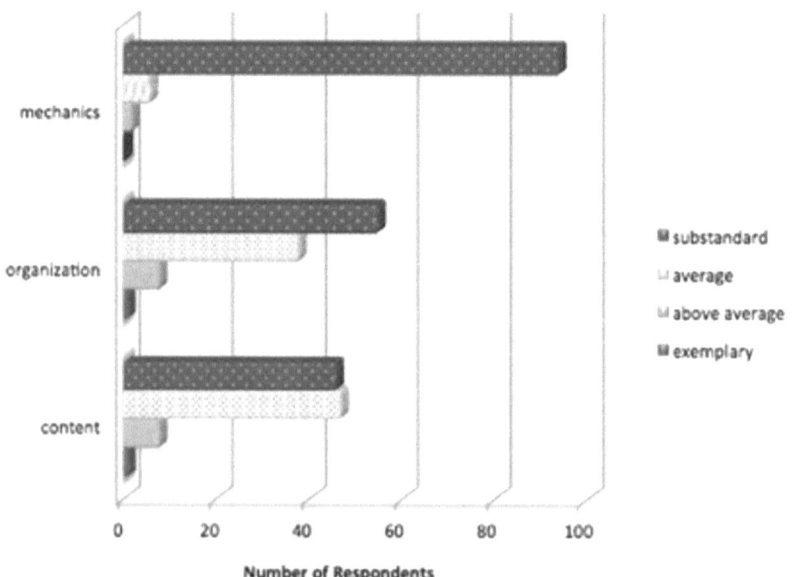

Figure 8.1 Passage 1: Non-native Speaker

Substandard content, a low level of critical thought. Short and glib. No passion. The student is not struggling or highly engaged with the topic. They are writing to turn in a requirement. Clarity in organization. The brevity of course makes it easy to follow the flow of their ideas. This student is good at organizing their ideas, but not making an effort further than organization.

An instructor in education explained that she would "object to the use of 'poor' in this passage because 'poor' is frequently not within the power of a country to change but is the place where that country is assigned by its neighbors and world powers." Engagement with the student's thoughts and encouragement to think more critically about the topic are evident in the comments about the second passage. While such comments would also be valuable to the writer of Passage 1, respondents offered almost none of such feedback to that passage, focusing instead on grammar and mechanics.

The questions about and implications of this division of commentary on the two passages are too multiple and complex to address in detail here, but it is worth considering some of the more obvious ones, i.e.: Does adherence to SAAE facilitate instructor comprehension and therefore permit more

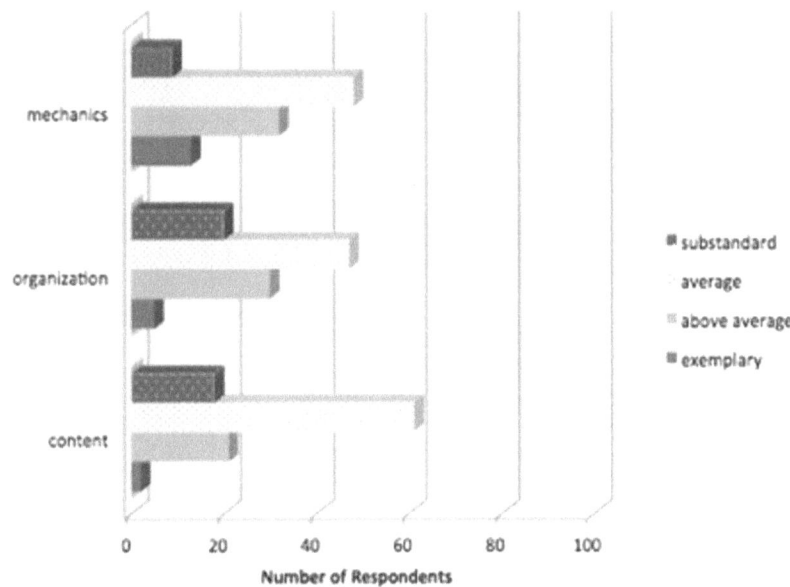

Figure 8.2 Passage 2: Control

discipline-specific critical questioning? Does the lack of instructor comments about higher-order concerns for a paper that does not follow SAAE conventions hinder the student's cognitive development in that particular content area? Does the instructor focus on sentence-level features rather than higher-order questioning negatively influence a student, who may otherwise have a high level of interest in the subject and whose perspective may provide useful and creative insight?

In a follow-up interview with an instructor in sustainability studies, she told us that she marks all of her student papers for grammatical issues. "I mark up their papers thoroughly every time. I give comments and suggestions in terms of content and also in terms of grammar because sometimes I have a hard time grading their work if I can't get past all of the grammatical issues, so I try to work with them to the extent that I can." This response indicates that, while she is committed to helping her students to write successfully in her discipline, departures from SAAE at the sentence level make it difficult for her to engage with other aspects of student writing, a position that echoes many of the respondents' comments for Passage 1, the non-native speaker passage. Her response suggests, then, that writing that does not adhere to the conventions of SAAE invites sentence-level commentary rather than higher order commentary, even when an instructor is committed to focusing on the content of the students'

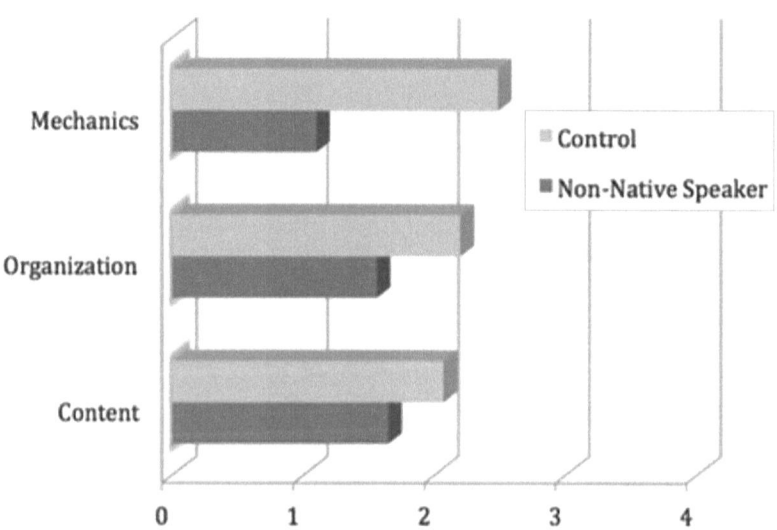

Mean Score: 1=substandard, 2= average, 3= above average, 4= exemplary

Figure 8.3: Average Scores for Each Passage

writing rather than being distracted by errors, as another interview participant from linguistics explained. When asked what kinds of writing her students do, the linguistics instructor talked at length about a final paper, explaining that she tries "to weight it more heavily on content and not be distracted by the illiteracy evident" in many of them. While this instructor expressed a commitment to focusing on the content of her students' writing regardless of whether their sentences conform to the standards SAAE, she said she does find departures from SAAE distracting and tries to communicate that to her students:

> When they give me these answers on the tests I do correct the grammar on them. At the bottom of their test I will write "Boy you really need to work on that comma splice problem if you're going to continue in academic study." [...] You know if I can correct their grammar I will do it! [...] Agreement errors I also comment on, you know. Especially for nonnative speakers that's a toughy.

We also want to note that, while this instructor may appear to be understanding of and attentive to the relationship between language background and student writing, she equates sentence-level issues with illiteracy, which suggests to us that she has little tolerance for other varieties of English that do not meet the standard.

The linguistics instructor's use of the word "illiteracy" to describe errors in students' writing calls attention to another theme that emerged from the interviews: that readers often make judgments about a writer's level of literacy based on errors they see or perceive in the writing. That sentence-level errors influence the decision-making process for gatekeepers, such as, for example, potential employers and those who weigh admission to an institution and/or program, is a well-documented fact (a fear also expressed by faculty interviewed by Zawacki and Habib [this volume]). In a follow-up interview with an instructor in physical therapy, he explained that only about 10% of all applicants are accepted into the physical therapy program and that few of those admitted are multilingual students. When asked why, he said, "I don't think we have that issue as much. I think it's people that come in and English is their first language. I think because our applicant pool is so rigorous, and we have the luxury of taking the very high level people. The test scores and the people who, you know, English is their second language don't obviously score as well up front ... They have a tougher time getting in."

His comments can be understood in multiple ways. One interpretation might be that the winnowing process for admission, because of the sheer number of applicants, is warranted, even necessary for no other reason but efficiency. Another may be that physical therapy is such a technical profession that "highly sophisticated" English is a requisite for successfully completing the program. Yet another interpretation of the admissions practices that the instructor described, considering his exclusion of multilingual writers from the pool of "high level people," may be that he has conflated intelligence and cognitive ability with language skill, as Zamel (1995) has observed often happens. We also considered whether the highly selective process could be attributed to the profession requiring the ability to communicate health issues or life threatening emergencies expertly, accurately, and efficiently. If this is the case, then we wondered why, given our location, being multilingual and having the ability to communicate effectively in, say, Spanish, Navajo, or Keres is not as valuable, if not more so, than speaking and writing only in English?

A similar gatekeeper position was reiterated in a follow-up interview with a faculty member in communication and journalism, who recounted a story about how an undergraduate from Bulgaria had asked her to write a letter of recommendation for her as she was planning to apply to the graduate program in communication and journalism. The instructor's response to the international student, as she told us, was, "… you know what, I can't because you need to take some intensive English courses that I'm not qualified to provide for you." The instructor acknowledged that it was difficult for her to say this to the Bulgarian student, but she also felt as if would be doing the student a disservice if she did write a letter of recommendation for her. Here again surface-level features are serving as a mechanism for preventing some L2 students from pursuing their academic and career goals.

Faculty Want Native-like Prose but They Do Not Really Expect It

Our results indicate that the faculty we surveyed and interviewed want all of their students to produce unmarked SAAE prose, but they do not really expect it even though they might claim to. They do, in fact, expect language diversity to be reflected in their students' writing; at the same time they don't know how to address that diversity, which seems to lead to their continued insistence upon writing that conforms to a monolingual standard.

These contradictory views are evident in the survey passage ratings. Three of the survey respondents remarked in the comments section of the survey that Passage 1, the passage from the L2 writer, is average for students at their institution, whether the community college or university. An instructor in communication and journalism lamented, "Unfortunately if you are looking for 'average' this reflects a lot of the writing that I receive. But it is substandard to what I expect and require." An instructor in psychology wrote, "I personally think this is awful overall, but it is about average for a [student at this institution]. The grammar is particularly sub-standard however." Finally, an instructor in communication and journalism reiterated the statements above, going on, however, to qualify his/her assessment by stating that it is beyond the purview of his/her responsibility to address surface level features, but that he/she feels that this is something that must be done. Another instructor, quoted below, focused her initial comments on the students' critical thinking skills and content knowledge and then addressed the passage's surface level issues. That the instructor first acknowledged the student's ability to critically analyze and comment on the issue of poverty is worth noting.

> The student shows evidence of average content: critical thought on cause and effect and lists categories in their domain knowledge that I assume are summaries of content in their paper .... The organization is above average, in that the student attempts to create lists, associate cause and effect, and includes a call to action directed at the reader. Although the student is not accomplished in grammar, he/she makes an above average attempt to organize his/her thoughts. Mechanics, of course, are atrocious. But that's the type of student we have at our [institution]. It is not my role to teach grammar and sentence structure, but I do make strong levels of editing in the abstract and conclusion to show the student how to introduce and summarize their thoughts using the standards to which I hope they aspire. We work on a little bit of their writing together, the most important part, in mandatory one-on-one office meetings, but only one meeting per student is required. They can come back for seconds, and a few do return.

For this instructor, unlike the majority of survey respondents, sentence-level departures from SAAE do not preclude focus on content or organization. Although s/he is dissatisfied with the student's work at the sentence level, s/he expressed understanding that levels of conformity to the prescribed standards of SAAE will vary in linguistically diverse classrooms. S/he also seems somewhat confident about working with linguistically diverse groups of students, but this is not the case with many of her colleagues across disciplines. (The faculty's recognition that the most important work on student writing happens during conferencing is affirmed by Chozin, the international graduate student featured in Phillips [this volume]).

The quality of writing, particularly at the sentence level, was quite obviously at the forefront of many of the survey responses. And while the respondents appeared to be highly critical of the quality of student writing they see in their classes, the survey and follow-up interviews also show that faculty seem to be conflicted about how to handle the variations to SAAE that they encounter on a regular basis. During the follow up interviews, faculty participants were asked if they had ever encountered papers that might reflect language issues. An instructor from sustainability studies replied,

> You know, I haven't taken the time to pursue those sorts of things necessarily. Up until this point, I haven't given it special consideration. I try to grade people fairly and the same across the board, and I have rubrics. I don't think that's necessarily the right thing to do. However, when there are students that are having difficulties, I tell them to come to me.

Yet this same instructor, in a statement we quoted earlier, also said that she holds all of her students to the same set of expectations as outlined in her rubric. Still she struggles with this expectation, recognizing that holding multilingual writers to the same standard in terms of SAAE as she does her native English writers may not always be as fair and equitable as it seems. (This issue of fairness also came up in many of the interviews Zawacki and Habib [this volume] conducted.)

An instructor from communication and journalism, when asked in an interview about her expectations for multilingual writers, responded, "My expectations for multilingual writers are the same as my expectations for native speakers." Having said that, however, she immediately went on to say:

> However, I am willing to work with them on a one-on-one basis. I am encountering this in the graduate realm, where um, I strongly disagree with admission of students to this type of program who are not highly fluent in English because it's taught in English. I had a transfer student from Bulgaria and a visiting student from Spain, and the Bulgarian student was pretty fluent but the transfer student from Spain had a horrible time ...

This statement indicates that this instructor, like the others we've quoted, does not actually expect all of her students to have the native-like fluency in English necessary to consistently produce unmarked SAAE in their writing. She wants to be able to expect this, however, and thinks the placement of students who cannot produce native-like SAAE into courses like hers is an injustice to them. Further describing her experience with multilingual students, she said:

> And you know we have a problem. I have three Asian students who I'm working with now in a seminar. So I'm trying to help them with their writing. 'Cause once you admit them I think you have a responsibility, and not everybody feels that way .... And it's not really the students' fault. They're being told if you want to go to the United States [passing the TOEFL] is what you have to do and this is how you do it. But then they get here and have trouble because they don't understand our system.

The insistence on native-like SAAE even among an increasingly diverse student population expressed by the faculty and instructors quoted above supports Matsuda's (2006) point that "implicit in most teachers' definitions of 'writing well' is the ability to produce English that is unmarked in the eyes of teachers who are custodians of privileged varieties of English" (p. 640). However, as much as our study participants might want linguistic homogeneity, they are acutely aware that this is not the situation in their classes. In fact, the majority of the interview participants seemed genuinely concerned with the success of all of their students, regardless of language background, even as they seem to be at a loss as to how to work most effectively with non-native speakers of English. This finding leads us to several implications.

FACULTY ARE OPEN TO CONVERSATIONS ABOUT LANGUAGE VARIETY IN THE CLASSROOM

The faculty who participated in our study, with a few notable exceptions, seemed to be open to thinking more systematically about language diversity in their classrooms and to having conversations, such as WAC promotes, about how to work more effectively with multilingual writers. The need for such conversations is most clearly indicated by the self-doubt two of the instructors we quoted earlier expressed about working with multilingual students. One, for example, concluded her remarks about a student whose organization and ideas were good but whose grammar "was atrocious," by saying, "I held him to the same standard, and I don't know if that was the right thing to do." This was the second time within just a few sentences that she had indicated doubt as to whether holding multilingual students to a monolingual standard is the best practice. Another questioned herself by saying, "I pass everybody. I'm responsible for some of the problem, right?" indicating, presumably, that she too is at fault for passing students who do not write in native-like SAAE by the time the class is finished, thus allowing them to enter still other classes for which they're not prepared to meet existing expectations.

The doubt that both of these instructors express indicates that they want to be fair and ethical in working with linguistically diverse students but may not know how to do so while still sticking to the commonly held standards for writing in their disciplines and institutions. The first question that comes to mind, and perhaps the first question that we might raise with stakeholders across disciplines, is whether and why writing standards have to be the same as they were in a monolingual, idealized, and largely fictional past. As Horner and Trimbur (2002) argue, standards and norms for academic writing have shifted throughout the history of American higher education and should not remain static now:

> While Bartholomae was being ironic in suggesting that students needed to "invent" the university in their writing, there is a real sense in which students, like all the rest of us writers, do participate in re-inventing—not simply reproducing but potentially altering—university language in each act of writing ... If we reject the reification of academic language and competence in it, we cannot use instances of students' language to deny them academic citizenship. (pp. 620-621)

Cross-disciplinary, and even cross-institutional, conversations focusing on the development of language standards that reflect our institutions' unique regional location as well as the values of our individual disciplines would be a productive response to the self-doubt that both of the instructors we quoted express. (It is interesting to note that the students enrolled in a mixed L1/L2/bilingual graduate writing workshop, described in Fredericksen & Mangelsdorf [this volume], were open to working across languages and cultures, which the authors attributed to the university's location near the Texas/Mexican border).

A primary concern to address in these conversations should be how to grade L2 students work in a way that is fair to all students. Several of our interview participants explained how they negotiate this concern in their linguistically diverse classes. One instructor said, for example,

> Some of them are just not ready to be in the class, but they're in there and you've got to work with that. And you give them a grade that reflects where they were when they came in and how much improvement they've made, rather than an absolute grading scale.

This instructor's explanation can lead to questions about what makes students prepared or unprepared to be in a class. And is the grade reflecting improvement applied to all aspects of all assignments, or just selected aspects of selected assignments? And would a grade that reflects improvement be appropriate for all students in a given class?

In these conversations, faculty can also be asked to talk about whether and why adherence to SAAE standards is important in grading. An instructor in history, for example, said in his follow-up interview that, in his class,

> They, you know, really have to show that they know the subject material. And they have to show that they have some kind of argument .... Organization to me is very crucial, but I see it as tied in with argument .... You can't fail a paper for spelling and grammar and mechanics alone.

Here the instructor is asserting his view on which aspects of SAAE are important to him and which are less so. Organization, presumably organization fitting the typical Western pattern in academic writing of stating a thesis at the beginning and relating each paragraph directly back to that thesis, is important to the instructor because he sees this structure as integral to making a convincing argument. However, that his students' grammar and mechanics conform strictly to the standards of SAAE is less important to him. Questions for further conversation in response to this point could include, for example: What constitutes strong organization in a history paper? Why is this type of organization necessary for a student to present a convincing argument? Is it possible to make a convincing argument following organizational patterns from other rhetorical traditions? When, if ever, should a paper be failed for grammar and mechanics alone?

Even seemingly fair and reasonable grading approaches to departures from SAAE standards in student writing can be problematic, as we could see in our interview responses. An approach described by an instructor in math and science, for example, seemed to embrace linguistic diversity:

> When I would grade anything that was written, I would look for the content. As long as the student ... as long as I could see that the student understood, then that would be good enough for me. The writing has to be good enough that I can discern that. If the writing is so poor that I can't .... then I can't read the student's mind.

While this instructor's practice may fit with a translingual approach, our study suggests that it's also potentially problematic, since the faculty responses to Passage 1 in our survey indicate that what is and is not considered understandable can vary greatly from one reader to the next. Questions for further conversation, then, might be: What departures from SAAE inhibit understanding for you? (See Zawacki & Habib [this volume] for faculty responses to this same question.) And where does the burden of communication lie?

In this context, we find Lippi-Green's (2004) argument useful:

> When native speakers of USA English are confronted by an accent that is foreign to them or with a variety of English they dislike, they must first decide whether or not they are going to accept their responsibility in the act of communication. What can be demonstrated again and again is this: members of the dominant language groups feel perfectly empowered to reject their portion of the burden and demand that a person with an accent (that is, an accent that differs from their own accent) carry a disproportionate amount of the responsibility in the communicative act. (p. 298)

While Lippi-Green is referring here to oral communication, we argue that the question of communicative burden can and should, in fact, be applied to written communication, especially when a student is communicating in writing to a teacher. After all, it is the instructor's job to help students become more knowledgeable about their subject. As part of that responsibility, instructors should expect that it will be necessary for them to help students to communicate more effectively to audiences within their field, instead of expecting that students will be able to communicate seamlessly with them upon entering the class. Such assistance also entails helping students to learn the content and ways of knowing, doing, and writing in the discipline. And it may also entail helping students to determine which sentence-level features require the most attention when writing in that discipline.

The question of who should bear the communicative burden can also carry over into discussions that instructors have with their students. It could be particularly beneficial for monolingual native speakers of English to begin taking on the burden of understanding and communicating with L2 speakers/writers because, as Canagarajah (2006) points out:

> There are online journals, discussion circles, and websites that anyone in the world can go to for information. But without a willingness to negotiate Englishes, we get little from these resources. Scholars studying transnational interactions in English show the creative strategies multilingual speakers use to negotiate their differences and effectively accomplish their purposes, often with no deference to native speaker norms .... ME/ monolingual speakers come off as relatively lacking in these negotiation skills in comparison with WE speakers ... with dire implications for their ability to succeed in such transactions. (pp. 590-591)

Monolingual speakers who cannot or refuse to understand varieties of English that depart from the norms to which they are accustomed are at a distinct disadvantage when it comes to communicating in linguistically diverse settings, even when English is the language of communication. Therefore, shifting standards to allow for language variety in American classrooms and clearly communicating that the burden of communications falls equally on all parties, not primarily on L2 English writers (and those whose writing does not, for whatever reason, conform strictly to the standards of SAAE), has potential benefits for all students regardless of language background.

CONCLUSION

Our findings—that instructors acknowledge their role in helping multilingual students, but don't know how, that they recognize their role as gatekeepers, and that they struggle with knowing the right thing to do in responses to student writing—reiterate the need expressed in this volume and in the special WAC/L2 writing issue of *Across the Disciplines* to conduct faculty development around WAC and second language writing. (See Cox [this volume] for strategies for faculty development related to L2 writing). In our scholarship, we should continue to investigate multilingual students' experiences as writers in their disciplines along with their goals for their own writing, a project that our research team is currently undertaking.

Finally, returning to our overarching concern in this chapter and Matsuda's and Hall's observations of the need to reconceptualize university and college classrooms as being multilingual and to embrace the rhetorical traditions that our multilingual students bring to the classroom, our study indicates a desire by faculty in the disciplines to understand this shifting demographic, but they still feel conflicted. Our data show that faculty are keenly aware of their "gatekeeper" status. They want their students to succeed and view the ability to communicate effectively, along with discipline-specific knowledge, as integrally linked to success. This is where WAC, WACommunities initiatives, and Second Language Writing scholars can and should intervene through departmental and college level discussions, workshops, and colloquia, helping to redefine with faculty in the disciplines what it means to communicate effectively. In a global environment where L2 speakers of English outnumber L1 speakers of English by nearly two to one (Saville-Troike, 2006), it is incumbent on all of us to re-imagine the role of SAAE in the American academic tradition.

REFERENCES

Cameron, D. (2001). *Working with spoken discourse*. Thousand Oaks, CA: Sage Publications.

Canagarajah, A. S. (2006). The place of world Englishes in composition: Pluralization continued. *College Composition and Communication, 57*(4), 586-619.

Cox, M. (2011). WAC: Closing doors or opening doors for second language writers? *Across the Disciplines, 8*(4). Retrieved from http://wac.colostate.edu/atd/ell/cox.cfm

Creswell, J. W. (1998). *Qualitative inquiry and research design: Choosing among five traditions*. Thousand Oaks, CA: Sage Publications.

Ferris, D. (2008). Myth 5: Students must learn to correct all their writing errors. In J. Reid (Ed.), *Writing myths: Applying second language research to classroom teaching* (pp. 90-114). Ann Arbor, MI: The University of Michigan Press.

Gee, J. P. (1999). *An introduction to discourse analysis: Theory and method* (2nd ed.). New York: Routledge, Taylor & Francis Group.

Hall, J. (2009). WAC/WID in the next America: Redefining professional identity in the age of multilingual majority. *The WAC Journal, 20*, 33-49.
Horner, B. & Trimbur, J. (2002). English only and US college composition. *College Composition and Communication, 53*(4), 594-630.
Kells, M. H. (2007). Writing across communities: Deliberation and the discursive possibilities of WAC. *Reflections, 11*(1), 87-108.
Lippi-Green, R. (2004). Language ideology and language prejudice. In Finegan, E. & Rickford, J. R. (Eds.) *Language in the USA: Themes for the twenty-first century* (pp. 289-304). Cambridge, UK: Cambridge University Press.
Matsuda, P. K. (2006). The myth of linguistic homogeneity in US college composition. *College English, 68*(6), 637- 651.
Rose, M. (1985). The language of exclusion: Writing instruction at the university. *College English, 47*(4), 341-359.
Saville-Troike, M. (2006). *Introducing second language acquisition*. Cambridge, UK: Cambridge University Press.
Swales, J. M. (1990). *Genre analysis: English in academic research settings*. Cambridge, UK: Cambridge University Press.
Zamel, V. (1995). Strangers in academia: The experiences of faculty and ESL students across the curriculum. *College Composition and Communication, 46(4)*, 506-521.

APPENDIX A

SURVEY DEMOGRAPHICS

A total of 104 respondents completed the survey, with 72 coming from the university and 31 coming from the community college. One respondent did not identify an institution. Twenty-two departments are represented in the survey. The majority of our respondents, 62, identified as female, while 41 participants identified as male and one as transgender. When asked about language background, 96 of the respondents identified as native speakers of English, while eight identified as nonnative speakers. Aside from English, the respondents identified their native languages as Serbian, Spanish, Tewa, Cherokee, Tagalog, Chinese, and Dutch.

The following table shows that a little over half of our respondents, 56, identified as graduate assistants, teaching assistants, or part- time instructors, while fewer than half, 40, identified as faculty (lecturer or professor), and eight participants identified as other. The significant representation of graduate instructors aligns with Hall's (2009) "Next America" theme, as these respondents are the faculty of the future, and their attitudes point toward the writing expectations that future generations of college and university students will face.

Please identify your position at your institution (n = 104)

Answer Options	Response Percent	Response Count
Graduate Assistant/ Teaching Assistant	23.1%	24
Part-time Instructor/ Adjunct	30.8%	32
Lecturer	5.8%	6
Assistant Professor	7/7%	8
Associate Professor	11.5%	12
Full Professor	13.5%	14
Other	7.7%	8
Answered Question		104
Skipped Question		0

APPENDIX B

Interview Participants

Pseudonym	Discipline	Native Language
Dr. Carter	Law	English
Dr. Anderson	Physical Therapy	English
Mr. Thompson	History	English
Dr. Jacobs	Math	English
Dr. Russelman	Sustainability	English
Ms. Mason	Anthropology/Linguistics	English
Dr. Smith	Communication	English
Dr. Bremmel	Math	English

CHAPTER 9

LET'S SEE WHERE YOUR CHINESE STUDENTS COME FROM: A QUALITATIVE DESCRIPTIVE STUDY OF WRITING IN THE DISCIPLINES IN CHINA

Wu Dan
Xi'an International Studies University (XISU),
Xi'an, Shaanxi Province, China

Written by a scholar in China who received her PhD in writing in the US, this chapter reports on a study examining faculty perceptions of the role of writing in learning and students' competence as writers and speakers in the disciplines at their Chinese institutions. Wu introduces the role of writing in China's higher education system with implications for those who work with Chinese students, and she argues that WAC should be introduced into China to promote better faculty teaching and student learning. Wu first provides a review of Chinese higher education system with indigenous and imported historical heritages from Confucianism, a Soviet higher education structure, and the US higher education system. She then reports on the status of writing in the disciplines in China based on interviews with ten faculty members from six disciplines in four Chinese universities. Interview results indicate that faculty believe that students' writing in the disciplines in both Chinese and English is not satisfactory and that they are interested in the potential for WAC to improve teaching and student learning and writing. Suggestions to faculty in both Chinese and US universities are provided to help them understand and assist their Chinese student writers.

According to *Open Doors Report 2012* (Institute of International Education, 2012), China is the leading sender of students to US higher education, with a majority of them being graduate students who completed their undergraduate study in China. Various studies have been conducted to examine Chinese students as second language (L2) writers in the US, and these studies have provided suggestions to US professors and higher educational institutions to enhance Chinese students' learning on different levels and in different disciplines. The challenges for their academic study in the US have been reported to come from students' lack of English proficiency (Berman & Cheng, 2001; Huang, 2005), their academic learning anxiety (Upton, 1989), and their perceptions of learning cultures (Feng, 1991; Huang & Brown, 2009), among other issues.

However, limited research has been done to study what current English writing is like and especially how it is taught, or learned, in the disciplines in Chinese higher education system, which has been feeding US higher education institutions at all levels from first-time students to post-doctorate researchers. And no previous research has been done on linking the needs of writers in Chinese higher education to Writing Across the Curriculum (WAC). Once these Chinese students begin writing in their courses at US institutions, they may get comments like "awkward English" on their papers but still do not know why they get these "awkward" comments nor how to improve. The help they can receive from their professors or even writing center tutors is most of the time limited as there is a lack of understanding of how English writing has been used, taught, and practiced in China. Trying to help Chinese students in the US without an understanding of where they come from in terms of English writing costs more than wasted time or energy, but also precious learning opportunities for these students.

This study provides a snapshot of writing in the disciplines in China based on interviews with ten faculty members from four Chinese universities and six disciplines. The purpose of the study was to examine faculty perceptions of the functions of writing and other communication competencies at their institutions. One goal of the study was to introduce the role of writing in China's higher education system, and the implications of that role, to those who work with Chinese students. Although some of the interview questions asked about other communication competencies, the focus of this chapter is on how these faculty members perceive the functions of writing in the curriculum and their expectations for students' writing. Students in Chinese higher education still need more guidance and engagement in writing as faculty regard writing as products rather than processes and perceive student writing quality in both Chinese and English as unsatisfactory. This unsatisfactory status will remain until Chinese higher education system accepts and adopts educational reforms like WAC to help improve students' writing and learning.

However, the Chinese higher education system, as higher education systems in other countries, is complicated and comes with indigenous and imported historical heritages from Confucianism, a Soviet higher education structure, and the US higher education system. Therefore, it is necessary to provide an introduction to this system before analyzing how faculty perceive and utilize writing in their disciplines.

CHINESE HIGHER EDUCATION SYSTEM

Currently, the higher education system in China is the largest higher education system in the world, surpassing the US in 2003 (Knight, 2006) as a result of its six-fold increase in enrollment between 1997 and 2007. This system consists of two thousand years of Chinese traditional education and more than a hundred years of Western higher education influences (Min, 2004).

Traditional Chinese higher education institutions were officially established in the Han Dynasty (135 BCE). These institutions were set up to prepare the elite class to work as government officials. Later, in order to recruit students from the lower classes to address the lack of a qualified workforce for the government (Lee, 2000), an imperial exam system was established and continued to be used for about two thousand years. These exams were based on the Four Books and Five Classics in the School of Confucius, and they were the only avenue available for lower-class Chinese to gain access to the upper class (Kirby, 2008). As the only evaluation tool was the students' writing on these classic books, it was not surprise that Chinese people developed and retained not only their worship for Confucianism, but also an appreciation for good writing, which influenced China and many neighboring countries and cultures (Altbach, 1998). This possibility of social mobility also created the emphasis on education in Chinese families, which formed the underpinning needs among Chinese people for better access to higher education in hope for better jobs and higher social status. These needs helped in the decision-making process of the very recent large scale enrollment expansion from 1998 to 2008 that not only increased access to higher education but also posed issues for an education system that was designed for "elite education" but now faces "mass education." Therefore, this indigenous tradition, even though it was interrupted several times, has functioned as one of the forces for enrollment expansion, and the appreciation for good writing still has its influences among Chinese people, which sets up a solid but less obvious foundation for introducing WAC pedagogies into China.

In the second half of the nineteenth century, universities modeled after Western ones were established by the government and missionaries and through other efforts. These new Western-style universities, together with the indigenous Confucian traditions, laid the foundation for modern Chinese higher education, forming an indispensable part of its tradition. Although the Western-style universities were replaced by the Soviet model in the 1950s, these "traditions and memories of excellence remained, and they have helped to fuel more recent efforts" (Kirby, 2008, p. 140).

In the Soviet model, higher education faculty and students were assigned to specialized institutions, each focusing on one area, creating a planned workforce to serve the planned economy (Mok, 2005). As the universities in this period served the needs of their respective ministries, the Ministry of Education was not the only one administering higher education. Other ministries, such as the Ministry of the Coal Industry or the Ministry of the Machine Building Industry, had their affiliated universities, setting their own enrollment plans and assigning jobs to their graduates. Not only the enrollment but also the curriculum, including course syllabi and textbooks, were determined by the respective government units or agencies in charge throughout the country (Mok, 2005). This structure made it difficult for different disciplines to exchange pedagogical insights or share concerns. The Soviet model represented not only a separation of the disciplines but also a centralization of knowledge and a uniformity of thought (Hayhoe, 1989). Its far-reaching impact included departmentalization, segmentation, overspecialization, and the separation of teaching and research between the teaching institutions and research units (Min, 2004). As a result, there was no exchange between domestic and international researchers (other than the Soviet scholars) or between teachers and researchers; this lack of research and communication made it impossible for WAC concepts or practices to be brought up in China during that time.

The reform era begun in 1979 marked the beginning of improved, although still limited, freedom (Zarrow, 2008). The Chinese higher education system attempted to recover from the Cultural Revolution; however, resources and attention were primarily focused on economic reform in the industrial sector (Shirk, 1993) until after the 1997 Asian Economic Crisis. This crisis spurred the government to increase domestic consumption, and family educational expenses were added to the agenda (Xi, 1999). At the same time, the government had to address market pressures for a highly educated workforce as the economy was being transformed from labor-intensive to knowledge-based (State Department, 1999). This change resulted in the expansion reform, a strategy employed by the government to address the needs of the labor market and the need to stimulate domestic consumption for the "soft landing" of the economy needed to maintain the double digit growth in the GDP (Bai, 2006). Therefore, higher education, especially enrollment, attracted much attention.

As a result of this attention, the total number of students increased from 3.2 million to 18.8 million from 1997 to 2007 (not including the institutions of higher education for adults), while the number of faculty increased only from 0.4 million to 1.17 million. This difference resulted in a change in the student-faculty ratio from 8:1 to 16:1. Although this 16:1 student-faculty ratio may not seem problematic, this number does not reflect the reality. First, because of the separation of research and teaching units (Hayhoe, 1989), researchers also take faculty positions in the institutions but do not teach, so the faculty data do not reflect the actual number of teaching faculty. In addition, as more Chinese higher educational institutions strive to become research institutions, more faculty members prefer not to teach undergraduate courses. Secondly, many full-time faculty members in regular higher education institutions teach courses in institutions for adults as the two are frequently affiliated (Yi & Li, 2004), meaning these faculty member have an extra teaching load on top of what the official statistics show. Third, the lack of qualified faculty remains a problem. For example, a 2005 survey of 23 Shanghai higher education institutions conducted by the Shanghai Institute of Educational Evaluation (Postiglione, 2005) found that only 39% of all professors teaching undergraduate courses held master's degrees, and only 17% held doctoral degrees. Therefore, this 16:1 student-faculty ratio poses more challenges than the number indicates on the surface.

Although Chinese young people are now given more opportunities to receive a higher education, the speed and the scale of this expansion have posed problems for the Chinese higher education system, and university professors in various disciplines have begun to look into the effects of this enrollment increase, finding, for example, that the increased enrollment and the slow reform of higher education concepts have made the mathematics education in colleges less effective than before (Tang, 2007). In addition, English professors have begun changing the training models, revising the national curriculum, and updating textbooks to address the consequences of the "increased numbers of students, a shortage of language teachers, the lack of teaching resources and inadequate language training in larger classes" (Chang, 2006, p. 519). Various researchers have also focused on the quality of teacher training (Jiang, 2005).

The Chinese higher educational system has also been greatly influenced by its political culture, especially in terms of English education. English is the dominant language in international organizations, trade, and business. As a result of the recent reforms in the Chinese educational system in the late 1980s, English is required for almost all Chinese students from their third year in primary school or first year in middle school, equivalent to the seventh grade in the US, through college. Students going on to graduate schools in China have to take English exams for both master's and PhD programs. If they want to study abroad, most need to take the TOEFL, EILTS, and/or GRE in order to study in English-speaking countries. The emphasis now put on English in the Chinese education system is further supported by the fact that students have to pass a test of their English skills to move to the next educational level. The combination of the indigenous Confucius emphasis on writing and the recent prevalent emphasis on English education has contributed to the current teaching and learning of English writing in the disciplines, which hasn't been revealed much to the world.

As this historical overview suggests, the Chinese higher education system incorporates traditions from both indigenous Confucianism and Western modern education. However, given its turbulent history, Chinese higher education first had to recover in the 1980s after the Cultural Revolution. Then in the 1990s, the system was put in the position of having to meet the economic needs of producing a well-educated workforce. Thus, the focus of attention in Chinese higher education has been on survival until the tension between access and quality was drastically intensified by the recent fast, large-scale growth (Hayhoe, 2000; Jiang, 2005; Li, Morgan & Ding, 2008; Lin, 2006; Min, 2004; Mok, 2005; Postiglione, 2005). This focus on survival and recovery has meant that the Chinese higher education system has centered on rebuilding the institutions and restoring the social status of teaching and learning that were destroyed during the ten years of the Cultural Revolution. Therefore, institutions have not paid much attention to research on the effectiveness of teaching and learning. Therefore, although students are writing in English in various disciplines, China did not develop its own version of WAC or "import" a WAC model from other countries to guide the development of writing instruction in English. However, recent reforms and their resulting impact on Chinese higher education have redirected attention to the quality of teaching and learning, and this change in focus shows promise for introducing WAC into China.

Still, there has been limited research attention to students' writing in both English and Chinese in the disciplines, as the teaching and learning of writing have remained as a training process in the foreign language courses they take in college. This study was designed with the goal of probing the feasibility of introducing WAC theory and practice into China, although the broader purpose was to gather faculty members' perspectives on the goals for higher education, the learning outcomes for college students, the students' written and oral communication abilities, and their expectations on these aspects of communication modalities. During the interviews, WAC was introduced to the interviewees, and the faculty participants were asked whether similar programs were feasible in Chinese higher education, what they saw as the possible obstacles, and what were their own concerns.

METHODOLOGY

Ten face-to-face faculty interviews were conducted in China in 2009. All interviewees were contacted as a result of a personal relationship network. Two of the interviewees were suggested by earlier interviewees, reflecting snowball sampling. These interviews varied in length from 22 to 48 minutes, with the average being 35 minutes. After the interviews were completed, they were transcribed by a college student in China. To ensure their accuracy, a second Chinese college student reviewed the transcriptions. These students highlighted any unfamiliar words and phrases, most of which were English terms used by the Chinese interviewees, marking the recording time to allow me, the principal investigator, to verify the words and spelling. The transcription of the ten interviews in the faculty group contains 64,705 Chinese characters (47 single-spaced pages, 11 point font size). The standard conversion ratio for Chinese characters to English words is 2:1, meaning the transcriptions of the Chinese interviews result in approximately 130,000 English words.

The ten faculty interviewees ranged in age from 26 to 58, with the average age being 37. They are from four universities and six disciplines, including business administration, computer science, English, journalism, law, and medicine. Five of these faculty members are female and five male, four having doctorates and six master's degrees. Similar to the US, there is a faculty track in Chinese higher education, but the difference is that the Chinese faculty track includes lecturers, and there is no such rank as assistant professor. Therefore, this track has the ranks of lecturer, associate professor, and full professor. All of those interviewed were on the faculty track, with seven of them being lecturers, two associate professors, and one full professor. Their average teaching experience in higher education ranged from one to 18 years, with the average being seven. Six had overseas higher education experiences: one completed his MBA at a British university in Malaysia, one had a master's degree from Australia, and the other four had conducted research at overseas universities.

The interview questions were divided into two sections. The first section focused on demographic information, and asked about interviewee's affiliation, age, gender, highest degree, rank of professorship and administrative role (if available), teaching experiences and major courses, and overseas study or research experience. The second section focused on writing instruction and included questions about faculty members' opinions on the quality of students' writing in both Chinese and English, their motivations in assigning writing tasks, their perceptions of the importance of writing in learning, their willingness to participate in programs like WAC or programs that have WAC components, and reasons for possible difficulties and challenges in doing so. All interviews were done in Chinese, and the questions were translated from English to Chinese as the study was designed in English and implemented in Chinese. The findings in the analysis of this study were coded according to the interviewees' answers to the questions. If more than 50% of the interviewees agreed on one answer, then that answer became a finding. Then the eleven findings were grouped into the following four themes, with findings on similar topics being put together under one theme.

Theme One: While faculty are integrating writing into their courses, they believe that the quality of Chinese students' writing in both Chinese and English is not satisfactory.

Theme Two: While the faculty found the writing unsatisfactory, they believe the students' Chinese and English speaking and presentation competencies are satisfactory for the university, if not the workplace.

Theme Three: Communication is important and has been integrated into the curriculum for assessment and preparation for future jobs.

Theme Four: Faculty are willing to participate in WAC programs, but workload is the biggest disincentive.

Implications of these findings are discussed at the end of each thematic section. At the end of this chapter, implications for introducing WAC into Chinese universities are also discussed. The findings may help readers understand that Chinese international students who are going to study in the US have a very different orientation to writing in the disciplines. However, as WAC takes hold in China, the students who come to the US to study should be more confident in, and adapt more easily to, their academic writing.

THEMES AND RESULTS

The data analysis of the ten interviews resulted in the following four central themes. These four central themes can be used to understand Chinese college students' writing quality and faculty's expectations. Each theme is followed by findings from questions that are related to that theme and then by a discussion of the implications of that theme for WAC in China.

THEME ONE: WHILE FACULTY ARE INTEGRATING WRITING INTO THEIR COURSES, THEY BELIEVE THAT THE QUALITY OF CHINESE STUDENTS' WRITING IN BOTH CHINESE AND ENGLISH IS NOT SATISFACTORY.

Finding 1: Communication practices and skills are important for student learning.

The first finding under Theme One emerged from the responses to two closely related questions on the relationship between student communication competencies and their learning and job performance after graduation. The two questions were: *Do you have a desire to integrate communication components into your course?* and *To what degree do you think integrating communication into your courses will enhance your students' learning of the subject?* All of these interviewees answered that they had already integrated communication components into their courses and agreed that this integration enhanced the learning of their students. These responses indicate that these faculty members agree on the importance of teaching communication skills in universities. However, one of them mentioned that although many faculty members are integrating communication components, some of these were just end-of-semester papers or oral presentations with very limited guidance because, with huge numbers of students and heavy teaching loads, professors cannot spend too much time with specific training regarding writing, speaking and other communication modalities in class. Although some interviewees said that they integrated writing and speaking into their course because they hope this could make students more active learners, they also said that these kinds of assignments are not as effective because students do not get comments back for their end-of-semester papers or oral presentations. However, they believed it is important to have these components in the courses, and some writing is always better than nothing.

Finding 2: The quality of Chinese writing is thought to be unsatisfactory.

Among the 10 faculty, 80% said they read students' Chinese writing, and only one, a journalism professor, said she was satisfied with its quality. Forty percent said the writing they read was not good, and 30% indicated that it varied according to students' attitudes, their disciplines, or their experiences as student leaders. According to a computer science professor, the quality of an individual student's work may vary from writing task to writing task depending on his/her attitude. If the writing task tends to be an interesting topic to the student, s/he might spend more time and work on it, which can be clearly shown in the final draft submitted to the professor. According to a journalism professor, students in the humanities write better than those in science and engineering. She also said that student organization leaders also write better than the rest. This professor believed the reason was that student organization leaders got more chances to use and practice writing. She also explained that, most of the time, those students who apply to work as leaders and those who choose to major in humanities tend to be stronger writers in high school and would not worry about being challenged too much in the related tasks in the organizations or the majors.

Finding 3: The quality of the English writing is thought to be unsatisfactory.

Seventy percent of the faculty members said that they read English writing from students. Among them, 71% did not think the quality was satisfactory. The one professor who said that students' English writing was adequate was an English professor teaching English majors, the faculty member adding that her students were able to produce grammatically correct essays but had problems such as using Chinese styles in English writing or choosing inappropriate words to express the meaning. This comment supports Li's (2003) research on the influence of Chinese writing styles on students' English writing. When asked what were the problems in students' English writing, faculty interviewees did not really focus on the grammatical mistakes the students made, but talked more about expressing theideas by using proper words and expressions so that their sentences can "make sense." This echoes the "awkward English" comment mentioned at the beginning of this chapter that Chinese students see written on their papers in the US (as well as those reported by Zawacki & Habib and Ives et al. [this volume] from faculty teaching at the US institutions that were the sites of their investigations into attitudes about and expectations for their L2 student writers). However, most of the professors said that they did not have enough time or proper methods to help students' English writing. Some of them even said that their own English writing needs to be helped for publishing internationally.

Finding 4: Strengthening communication skills should be a critical focus in Chinese higher education.

All of the interviewees agreed that strengthening writing and other communication skills should be a critical focus area in higher education. The responses generating this finding also relate to Finding 1 reflecting the impact of communication on student learning and job performance. When asked why they thought communication skills should be a critical focus, many said that these are basic competencies in all disciplines and will determine students' chances at key intersections in their lives. An English professor pointed out that these competencies "will benefit students for their whole life and would never expire." Knowledge and skills are represented through communication competencies in all disciplines. A mass media professor said that the lack of these skills are like "a short board" or even a "bottleneck" for students, affecting both the "input" and "output" of knowledge and training. Communication skills determine students' chances at key intersections in their life. A medical professor said that every key intersection students experience in their lives after college, including job hunting, promotions, and personal relationships, requires them to present themselves to others. Therefore, when we prepare student for their future, we should help strengthen their writing and other communication skills. Apparently, though, working on communication skills has not been a critical focus in Chinese higher education, as curricular goals are not set by faculty but rather from the top down, so it was interesting that all faculty interviewed in this study agreed on this point.

As shown by the four findings described above, we could say that Chinese professors do have high expectations for their students' writing in both Chinese and English and are disappointed by the writing they get from their students. They also realize that writing is important, but they could not provide much guidance due to the time constraints and the lack of proper preparations provided to faculty themselves on writing and teaching writing. Although all college students should have passed their English test and Chinese test in the college entrance examination, that test result cannot tell us much about their writing. Therefore, faculty's answers have pointed out the urgent need to help students write and help faculty teach how to write. This urgent need might appear to be familiar to those who know the history of development of WAC in the United States. It was faculty's realization of these needs that helped start grassroots WAC programs and initiatives in American higher education institutions in the 1970s. Now we have this realization in China, and this could serve as the starting point for introducing WAC into China.

For now, however, the perceived poor quality of students' Chinese and English writing does pose problems when they go abroad to study. This does not mean that their grammar or vocabulary are not good enough, but this touches the communication functions of English, which makes it difficult for them to follow others' ideas and express their own. When taking tests like the GRE or TOEFL, these Chinese students can achieve high scores, but they are able to score high because they spend a lot time and energy in test preparations. They are able to pass the writing components in these tests, but their writing skills are only trained to cope with the tests but not "real world" needs in academia. Therefore, once they get into US universities, their professors might find the gap between the language test scores and the writing and speaking quality of the students.

THEME TWO: WHILE THE FACULTY FOUND THE WRITING UNSATISFACTORY, THEY BELIEVE THE STUDENTS' CHINESE AND ENGLISH SPEAKING AND PRESENTATION COMPETENCIES ARE SATISFACTORY FOR THE UNIVERSITY IF NOT THE WORKPLACE.

Finding 5: The overall speaking competency was thought to be satisfactory.

The faculty group was the most positive when asked to comment on students' speaking competency, with 100% of them indicating that it was satisfactory, although some provided additional comments. One faculty member said that the students' speaking abilities were generally better than their writing. Two faculty members said that students had the potential to do a better job if they received proper training in both speaking skills and critical thinking so that they could "make a breakthrough on both personal and social limitations." The two professors who said that their students speaking competency was excellent taught communication studies. Fifty percent of the interviewees pointed out that they wanted their students to be articulate when speaking, and 40% said that students should be proactive, taking advantage of every opportunity in class to practice so that they could get immediate feedback from the professor and their peers.

Finding 6: Presentation competencies were thought to be satisfactory in universities but not in the workplace.

When asked their expectations for presentations, 50% of the interviewees commented that they should be clear, to the point and within the time allowed, and that the tools used for presentations should "serve the purpose of the presentation well." Sixty percent of the interviewees were satisfied with students' presentation competencies, especially when they used software like PowerPoint to do presentations. Two professors even commented that students were sometimes better than the faculty themselves and could offer technical help. The two communication studies professors from one of the top two universities in China said that their students' performances when giving presentations sometimes exceeded their expectations and predictions. This was not mentioned by faculty from other universities or disciplines. However those who said that their students' speaking was excellent said this is because their students are mostly journalism majors who have received better and more training in speaking than students in other disciplines. Furthermore, because they teach in one of the top two universities in China, the students are selected with higher standards.

Although speaking and oral presentations are two communication competencies that are not the focus of this chapter, this second central finding explains that students' speaking and presentations are better rated than their writing by faculty. When professors in the US try to understand how well their Chinese students can speak and present, they probably need to speak to the students themselves to find out if the quality fits their demands, as test scores, once again, cannot tell much about the students' competencies.

It was also interesting that many faculty members, when asked about presentations, refered to PowerPoint presentations immediately. They did not mention any other forms of presentations, such as prepared or unprepared speeches, or poster presentations. They almost equate presentations to PowerPoint presentations. However, the styles used and preferred in Chinese classroom PowerPoint presentations are quite different from those in the US. The presentations slides tend to be more flashy, more colorful, and use more animations and art words in order to show the technical knowledge of the students in using the software. Although this is just a personal observation that has not been supported by data yet, the fact that only 30% of the faculty mentioned that the tools used for presentations should "serve the purpose of the presentation well" might have echoed this observation. Therefore, this satisfactory status for students' presentation skills in China might not translate into the same evaluation in the US.

THEME THREE: COMMUNICATION IS IMPORTANT AND HAS BEEN INTEGRATED INTO THE CURRICULUM FOR ASSESSMENT AND PREPARATION FOR FUTURE JOBS.

Finding 7: International and intercultural communication is considered important for college students.

When asked whether it's important for college students to have some knowledge and skills in international/intercultural communication in today's global economy, only one faculty member said that it depended on the discipline the students were in or the kinds of jobs they wanted in the future; however, 80% of the faculty also said they had already integrated international and intercultural communication into their courses. The primary major approaches used included bilingual courses, exchange study programs, invited speakers, and specialized courses for English and communication majors. Bilingual courses are courses taught in both Chinese and English, which demand faculty to be prepared for teaching certain courses in their disciplines in English, as all courses were previously only taught in Chinese. Therefore, students taking these bilingual courses also need to complete assignments in English, including writing.

However, the respondents indicated that these approaches were not effective. Bilingual courses, the most frequently mentioned method, had not been as effective as expected because 1) they involved no actual communication situations and tasks, and 2) many faculty members were not prepared to teach in English. One faculty member said that the academic exchanges students could be exposed to were far more "tolerant" than workplace communication tasks. In the academic exchanges, there was no punishment for making mistakes, and sometimes errors were not even pointed out to the students by faculty or foreign experts. This situation is quite different from workplace intercultural and international communication expectations, especially in the discipline of business management. Errors in workplace might result in a huge loss to the company and cannot really be tolerated so easily. Therefore, these simulated tasks and visiting international scholars cannot give students a real "sense" of what is required. Actually, the students cannot know the proper ways to handle communication tasks, if they are not corrected in simulated tasks in class or by kind-hearted foreign experts.

Finding 8: Communication modalities have been integrated into university courses.

All of the faculty members interviewed assigned writing in the courses they taught, with 20% of them assigning only English writing assignments and 30% only Chinese; 50% of the faculty members in management, computer science, law, and medicine indicated they had integrated multiple communication modalities into their courses, asking students to complete tasks by writing, speaking, presenting, and using digital educational technologies in both Chinese and English. These responses indicate a faculty buy-in and a realization of the importance of integrating these components, supporting the introduction of WAC into China. However, as indicated in Finding 7, the integration of communication tasks into courses did not always lead to satisfactory results, suggesting it is time to review the how and why of this integration process. The quantity of integrated courses does not guarantee the quality of this integration.

Professional research and support should be provided so that this faculty buy-in does not lose momentum and become an obstacle for introducing WAC programs.

Finding 9: The two major motivations for engaging students in writing are assessment and preparation for study in the disciplines or work in related fields.

Seventy percent of the interviewees clearly stated that one of the motivations for engaging students in writing was assessment of students' learning of the course contents. The assessment mentioned by these faculty members refers to using writing tasks for grades assigned in their courses, with most of the tasks being term papers. Students' writing in these tasks directly influences their final grade for the courses, making these high-stakes writing tasks. Fifty percent of the interviewees also mentioned the importance of the writing tasks they assign to their students' future study in their disciplines or the workplace. The computer science professor said that all the documents she required students to write in the course, such as PRD (Product Requirements Documents), DD (Design Documents), and TD (Test Documents), were similar to the types of documents her students would be required to write in the workplace as computer science engineers. Two business professors gave similar reasons for assigning writing, saying that in their field of study there often were no right or wrong answers, so the writing the students did could reveal their entire thinking process on a topic, something that could never be seen in standardized tests that have only multiple choice questions. As the higher education system in China has been more discipline-specific and there are limited number of requirements for general education courses, students do get trained to write in the disciplines if they are given writing assignments or writing tasks. However, there is no top-down requirement on how much and how often students should write, so this kind of training really depends on how much faculty members would like to try to explore by themselves. With the big class sizes and teaching loads since enrollment expansion, it does take some courage to assign writing tasks to the students. The importance of writing and other communication competencies has been stated by the faculty members interviewed in this study. However, none of the faculty interviewees mentioned "writing to learn," a key concept in WAC in the US. They only focus on grading students' writing or the documents their students are to encounter in future. Therefore, if WAC is to be introduced into China, it is important to let faculty understand "writing-to-learn" pedagogy so they do not think that writing tasks are only for "learning to write." By doing so, students may also learn to understand writing as process, not only product.

THEME FOUR: FACULTY ARE WILLING TO PARTICIPATE IN WAC PROGRAMS, BUT WORKLOAD IS THE BIGGEST DISINCENTIVE.

Finding 10: Faculty members are willing to participate in WAC programs.

"What is your level of desire to participate in such an initiative to integrate writing, communication, and digital technologies for learning into your courses?" was the last question asked of all interviewees, and all of them expressed great interest in participating in WAC. When WAC was introduced to them in the interviews, the name "WAC" was not emphasized at all as the concept does not mean much to Chinese professors. The concept of WAC was explained to them as helping faculty and students learn to write and write to learn so that students not only practice writing but also learn more and better in courses with well-designed writing components. After stating their interest, almost everyone added a "but" and explained the conditions they would want to be met before committing themselves into programs like WAC.

Rewards from both a sense of accomplishment and compensation are important to these faculty. One faculty member was very straightforward, saying that the reward system had to recognize the faculty effort involved in participating in the workshops and incorporating WAC pedagogies; in addition, it was also a prerequisite that the pedagogies had to be worth the effort and time commitment, and, as a result, student learning had to be enhanced. If attending workshops becomes an added obligation, they probably would not choose to participate. Regular meetings appear to be a burden. As a result, some suggested online webinars or podcasts so that faculty can participate whenever and wherever they want to. Further, the quality of the workshops has to be guaranteed. One professor pointed out that the workshop facilitators had to have a good understanding of the disciplines and be able to provide concrete suggestions for courses, or it becomes a waste of time. Although faculty development is provided through the university, most of it is related to teaching technologies rather than methodology. There is also a tendency that older professors do not appear to be interested in workshops designed for faculty development as they think these are for younger professors or novice teachers.

Finding 11: Workload is the biggest disincentive for faculty assigning students writing tasks.

While 30% of the faculty denied there was any disincentive for assigning writing tasks, 57% of the remaining faculty stated that workload was one. They said that they already have a heavy workload due to the enrollment expansion which caused student-faculty ratio to increase from 8:1 to 16:1, and they have found through experience that it takes much more time to grade writing assignments than standardized tests. Why would they want to increase their own burden? Therefore, this workload issue should be considered as a challenge for initiating WAC in China. However, some professors did not think this was a good enough reason for not assigning writing. A law professor, whose average teaching load per week is 12-14 hours, said, "It is much easier for me if I do not assign writing assignments to my students, but our goal should not be to make things easy for ourselves but to make sure students can learn things in our courses." Other interviewees said their students might complain about more work caused by writing assignments, which might cause some bad students evaluations at the end of the semester. Some worried they might experience failures in trying to realize learning outcomes through writing. Some pointed out that they would be considered to be "showing off their teaching" by their peers, so there is peer pressure from other professors who do not use much writing in their courses.

From this last central point, we can know that faculty do have an interest in helping students learn by learning themselves how to design and use writing components in their courses, but they would not want to devote extra energy or time if they will not be rewarded or if their already heavy workloads are made even worse.

IMPLICATIONS

From the four central themes and eleven findings described above, we know that Chinese college students or graduates need to improve their writing in both Chinese and English. Most Chinese college graduates have experience dealing with written assignments in both Chinese and English, although the guidance they receive is not sufficient or to the point. Therefore, there are certain implications for higher education professionals who work with Chinese students on writing, speaking or other communication modalities in China or the US or in any other country.

The quality of students' Chinese writing is not considered very satisfactory by the faculty interviewed, even by Chinese standards. As pointed out by Chinese professors, this is the general status with exceptions of limited types of students and majors. Therefore, high expectations cannot be met. As research has shown that first language literacy facilitates second language literacy (Durgunoglu, 1998; Lanauze and Snow, 1989), students' unsatisfactory Chinese writing can be said to lead somewhat to their unsatisfactory English writing. It is then easier to understand why some Chinese students' papers were marked "awkward English" by their professors after they enter graduate schools in English-speaking countries.

The poor quality of writing does not mean that there is a corresponding poor quality in other Chinese or English language skills since, when it comes to their student writing, faculty members interviewed admitted that they cannot spare too much time reading or commenting on students' writing due to the workload and also lack of recognition in the reward system. Some of them did not even have the confidence to help students with their English writing. If provided time and faculty patience, Chinese students can improve their writing as they learn to use their grammar and vocabulary by following the norms in their disciplines.

Students are also more used to writing tasks as assessment rather than as learning processes. They have been evaluated in the Chinese higher education system by using writing, so they have actually been treating their writing assignments as products rather than processes. Therefore, they might find it quite difficult to understand or to handle comments they may get in courses at institutions in other countries, as they have previously only known numbers as grades.

This dissatisfactory status of writing instruction in China has been and will remain with Chinese students for a while because the effects of college expansion are still pervasive. Although faculty rated the importance of different modalities of communication, they do not have the time, energy or support needed to make these improvements as they have been busy dealing with student numbers. It is hoped this can gradually improve as expansion has slowed down since 2008.

In order to help with the current quality problems in Chinese higher education, it is feasible that WAC could be effectively introduced. Faculty interest in WAC concepts and programs is quite obvious from the results of this study. We could even say that WID is already practiced in the disciplines, but we would need more research to describe the practice. However, this faculty interest in WAC could easily be turned into faculty resistance if no theoretical and pedagogical support is provided to the faculty members who have been integrating or want to integrate communication components into their courses. The workload is also a big challenge for WAC or similar programs as the problematic student-faculty ratio will probably stay longer than we want. While WAC could be feasible in Chinese universities, the results of this study further point out the opportunities and potential challenges. Chinese higher education system has one of two indispensable components for starting WAC programs—faculty interest. And with proper connection, it is reasonable to believe that the second indispensable component—support of the high-level administrators—can also be obtained.

Hopefully, understanding the history and the current issues in Chinese higher education can also help understanding Chinese college students so that proper assistance can be provided to support their academic success, in both Chinese universities and universities abroad (for another study on the educational backgrounds on international students in the US, see Fernandes [this volume], who examines the curriculum at for-profit English language programs, which many international students attend before entering US colleges and universities). What the 10 faculty members from different disciplines have shared in the interviews cannot provide a whole picture of the status of writing or communication practice in Chinese higher education, but at least this study peeks into this area and attempts to initiate the conversation. Future research might focus on the links between WAC and the existing writing centers or writing programs in Chinese higher education institutions. Longitudinal qualitative studies can be conducted on those students who were helped in writing centers or took courses with WAC components to see how well these might help them if they go to the US to study.

WAC can be introduced into Chinese universities, but it will take quite some time and efforts before we can translate this US-originated idea into a Chinese one. This introduction of WAC into China has the potential to contribute to the overall development of students' writing, which will help both domestic students and those students who go to study in the US face fewer challenges and obstacles in coping with the writing tasks in their courses. Hopefully, they will also become more confident and adapt with less difficulty to writing to learn and learning to write pedagogies, whether in a US or Chinese higher education institution.

REFERENCES

Altbach, P. G. (1998). *Comparative higher education: Knowledge, the university, and development.* Westport, CT: Ablex Publishing.

Bai, L. (2006). Graduate unemployment: Dilemmas and challenges in China's move to mass higher education. *The China Quarterly, 185*(1), 128-144.

Berman, R. & Cheng, L. (2001). English academic language skills: Perceived difficulties by undergraduate and graduate students and their academic achievement. *Canadian Journal of Applied Linguistics, 4*(1), 25-40.

Chang, J. (2006). Globalization and English in Chinese higher education. *World Englishes, 25*(3), 513-525.

Durgunoglu, A. Y. (1998). Acquiring literacy in English and Spanish in the United States. In A.Y. Durgunoglu & L. Verhoeven (Eds.). *Literacy development in a multilingual context: Crosscultural perspectives* (pp. 135-146). Mahwah, NJ: Lawrence Erlbaum Associates.

Feng, J. H. (1991). The adaptation of students from the People's Republic of China to an American academic culture. (ERIC Document Reproduction Service No. ED 329 833).

Hayhoe, R. (1989). *China's university and the open door.* Armonk, NY: M.E. Sharpe.

Hayhoe, R. (2000). Redeeming modernity. *Comparative Education Review, 44*(4), 423-439.

Huang, J. (2005). Challenges of academic listening in English: Reports by Chinese students. *College Student Journal, 39*(3), 553-569.

Huang, J., & Brown, K. (2009). Cultural factors affecting Chinese ESL students' academic learning. *Education, 129*(4), 643-653.

Institute of International Education. (2013). Open doors 2012 fast facts. *Open Doors Report on International Educational Exchange.* Retrieved from http://www.iie.org/Research-and-Publications/Open-Doors/Data/Fast-Facts

Jiang, W. (2005). Creating a quality higher education teacher base and measures for undertaking reforms. *Chinese Education and Society, 38*(6), 7-16.

Kirby, W. (2008). On Chinese, European & American universities. *Dædalus,* (Summer), 139-146.

Knight, J. (2006). *Higher education crossing borders: A guide to the implications of the General Agreement on Trade in Services (GATS) for cross-border education.* Retrieved from http://unesdoc.unesco.org/images/0014/001473/147363e.pdf

Lanauze, M., & Snow, C. E. (1989). The relation between first- and second-language skills: Evidence from Puerto Rican elementary school children in bilingual programs. *Linguistics and Education, 1,* 323-340.

Lee, T. H. C. (2000). *Education in traditional China: A history.* Leiden, NL; New York; and Koln, DE: E. J. Brill.

Li, F., Morgan, W. J., and Ding, X. (2008). The expansion of higher education, employment and over-education in China. *International Journal of Educational Development, 28,* 687-697.

Li, X. (2003). Track (dis)connecting: Chinese high school and university writing in a time of change. In D. Foster &, D. R. Russell (Eds.), *Writing and learning in cross-national perspective: Transitions from secondary to higher education* (pp. 49-87). Mahwah, NJ: Lawrence Erlbaum Associates.

Lin, A. (2006). Quality of higher education and evaluation of colleges and universities. *Higher Education of Sciences, 4,* 339-350.

Min, W. (2004). The legacy of the past and the context of the future. In P. Altbach, & T. Umakoshi (Eds.), *Asian universities: Historical perspectives and contemporary challenges* (pp. 53-84). Baltimore, MD: The John Hopkins University Press.

Mok, K. (2005). Globalization and educational restructuring: University merging and changing governance in China. *Higher Education, 50,* 57-88.

Postiglione, G. (2005). Higher education in China: Perils and promises for a new century. *Harvard China Review, 1,* 138-143.

Shirk, S. (1993). *The political logic of economic reform in China.* Berkeley, CA: University of California Press.

State Department. (1999, June). *Resolution on the further development of educational reform and quality education working meeting on 13 June 1999.*

Tang, J. (2007). The popularization of China's higher education and its influence on university mathematics education. *Educational Studies in Mathematics, 66*(1), 77-82.

Upton, T. A. (1989). Chinese students, American universities, and cultural confrontation. *MinneTESOL Journal, 7,* 9-28.

Xi, M. (1999). Market confronts education reform. *Beijing Review, 42*(44), 21-34.

Yi, C., & Li, C. (2004). The five key points in the quality control of Chinese adult higher education. *Journal of Adult Education College of Hubei University, 22*(5), 239-254.

Zarrow. P. (2008). Social and political developments: The making of the twentieth-century Chinese state. In K. Louie (Ed.), *The Cambridge companion to modern Chinese culture* (pp. 20-45). Cambridge, UK: Cambridge University Press.

APPENDIX

Interview Questions

Demographic Section

1. Institution 学校名称
2. Age 年龄
3. Gender 性别
4. Highest Degree Earned 最高学历
5. Rank of Professorship 职称
6. Administrative Role 行政职务

7. Years of Teaching in Higher Education 高校执教时间____年
8. Major Teaching Areas and Courses 主要教学专业及课程
9. Overseas Study or Working Experiences (time, type of study/work, purpose, countries) 海外学习或工作经验（时间，学习工作类型，目的，哪些国家）

Information Section
10. What are your primary course goals for teaching the subject (science, engineering, economics, business management…)? 请谈谈您在本专业教授课程的目标
11. Have you recently read any students' writings in Chinese? If yes, how would you assess the quality of your students' Chinese writing? 您近来是否读过学生写的中文的东西？如果读过，您认为学生中文写作质量如何？
12. Have you recently read any students' writings in English? If yes, how would you assess the quality of your students' English writing? 您近来是否读过学生写的英文的东西？如果读过，您认为学生英文写作质量如何？
13. What are your major motivations for having your students engage in writing assignments? 您给学生布置写作作业的主要动机是什么？
14. What are your major disincentives for having your students engage in writing assignments? 有哪些因素会妨碍您给学生布置写作形式的作业？
15. Comment on your students' communication competencies in speaking. Do you have expectations for these? If yes, what are they? 请评价学生的口头沟通交流能力。您对此能力有一定的期望吗？如果是，那么有哪些期望？
16. Comment on your students' communication competencies on presenting. Do you have expectations for these? If yes, what are they? 请评价学生做演示的沟通交流能力。您对此能力有一定的期望吗？如果是，那么有哪些期望?
17. Comment on your students' competencies on using digital technologies. Do you have expectations for these? If yes, what are they? 请评价学生使用数码技术的能力。您对此能力有一定的期望吗？如果是，那么有哪些期望？
18. What do you see as the major overall objectives for higher education? 在您看来，高等教育的主要目标是什么？
19. Do you think that strengthening writing, other communication skills such as speaking and presenting, and the use of technologies should be a critical focus area for educators in higher education? Why or why not? 您认为加

强学生的写作及其它沟通能力，例如口头表达，做演示及使用数码技术，是否应当引起高等教育工作者的重视和相当的关注？为什么？为什么不？

20. Do you have a desire to integrate communication components into your course? 您觉得您想在所教授的课程中加入加强学生沟通能力的内容么？
21. To what degree do you think integrating communication into your courses will enhance your students' learning of the subject? 您认为在课程中加入沟通能力的培养是否能够提高学生对该科目的学习？能够起到多大的作用？
22. Is it important for college students to have some knowledge and skill in international/intercultural communication in today's global economy? If yes, how could it be integrated into your course? 在当今全球经济条件下，国际交流和跨文化交流的知识和能力对于高校学生来讲重要吗？如果重要的话，您认为在您所教授的课程中能够如何融入这些知识和能力？
23. Please talk about the effects of the Five-Year-Circle Evaluation on your teaching. To what degree do you think integrating communication into your courses may help you on preparations for the evaluation? 请谈谈高校评估对您教学工作的作用和影响。您认为在您的课程中加入沟通能力的成分对您准备评估检查会有帮助么？有什么样的帮助？
24. To what extent would a campus-wide writing and communication initiative contribute to the overall objectives for higher education? 如果在全校范围内开展写作和沟通交流的项目帮助老师在课程中融入写作和其他沟通能力的培养，这是否有助于实现高等教育的主要目标？会有何种程度的贡献？
25. Is a campus-wide, holistic, writing and/or communication initiative the best way to enhance student communication skills? 您觉得一个全校范围的写作和沟通交流的倡议项目是不是提高学生沟通交流能力的最好的办法？
26. What other ways would you suggest? 您有其他的建议吗？
27. What is your level of desire to participate in such an initiative to integrate writing, communication, and digital technologies for learning into your courses? 如果有机会的话，在您所在的学校开展一个项目帮助老师把写作，沟通交流能力的培养和数码技术的应用融入各个课程，您有多大的兴趣参加？

CHAPTER 10

ENGLISH IS NOT A SPECTATOR SPORT: PRIVILEGED SECOND LANGUAGE LEARNERS AND THE FOR-PROFIT ESOL CLASSROOM

Marino Fernandes
University of New Hampshire

This chapter argues that students of the global elite who attend for-profit language schools may have power, but they do not have access to classroom writing experiences that lead them to develop a feeling of agency and control over language. Curricula at for-profit language schools are focused on imparting academic language skills with an eye to improving things like SAT and TOEFL scores. In contrast, second language learners in college writing classrooms are asked to position themselves in relation to the world they are writing in and out of, thus experiencing a classroom that admits of real consequences. At the same time that this kind of classroom experience creates vulnerability, it also helps to generate agency. I suggest that a redesigned curriculum may be one way to help students understand that agency is a crucial element of power.

On February 11, 1994, my brother and sisters and I arrived in this country for the first time. My mother and father, already in the US, met us at John F. Kennedy Inernational Airport. I was fourteen years old. My parents asked me, the best English speaker in the family, to find out where we might find a taxi or a shuttle to drive us to Boston, but every time I opened my mouth to say "Where can I find a taxi?" I got the stock response: "I can't hear you." I asked louder, but, still, they couldn't hear me. When I told my parents that no one could hear me they asked me if I was sure I was saying it right. This was my first of many experiences with the disconnect between learning a language in the safe confines of a classroom and using a language to communicate in the world.

I have spent over two thirds of my life learning a new language. Born in Portugal, I moved to my father's home country of Cape Verde as a boy, where I needed to quickly learn Kriolu. Then, at fourteen, my family moved to the United States where I learned English. I was the oldest of four children, and, as often happens, I quickly became the translator of language and culture and custom to my entire family.

There is little doubt that these experiences have led me to develop a great interest in the study of languages and the complexity of learning them; further, they have greatly affected how I approach the teaching of English in the ESOL classroom. Having come to teach ESOL as a second-language learner myself, my charge in my classroom was colored by the idea that English was something that unlocked doors for me and my family, and I was finally going to be able to pass that on to my students. As I began to focus more on the teaching of writing at my school—a for-profit school that contracts out space from a major university in the Northeast but is not connected to or governed by the university—I began to notice that my own experiences learning English were quite different from the population I was working with: economically elite, second- or other-language learners from all over the world for whom learning English seems to be more of a trophy than an act of survival as it was for me.

Teaching these "trophy" students is most often happening in a for-profit setting. The traditional writing curricula used in this setting, I will argue, does not and cannot support a richer context for learning English because, instead of engaging students in their learning and writing in English, it engenders a spectator attitude. This chapter—based on a "Scholars of the Dream" presentation I gave at the 2012 convention of the Conference on College Composition and Communication—examines the "global elite" language learner and looks into the curricula at a private, for-profit ESOL school. I argue for a curriculum infused with elements that draw from the process approaches English L1 (first language) composition classroom, despite the critique of such classrooms by Horowitz (1990), Matsuda (1997) and Silva (1993) as effective learning experiences for the English L2 (second language) learner.

FOR-PROFIT LANGUAGE SCHOOLS AND THE PRIVILEGED L2 LEARNER

Many composition classrooms ask that students position themselves in relation to the world they are writing in and out of. The fact that they are asked to define and position themselves in a way that admits of real consequences creates vulnerability, but also can generate a feeling of agency and control over language. Second language learners in these settings also have access to this kind of writing experience. Language learning in this setting is, therefore, high stakes; not having dominion over a language denies second language learners (as it denies *any* student) very real and tangible opportunities and experiences.

On the other hand, curricula at for-profit language schools are focused on imparting academic language skills with an eye to improving things like SAT and TOEFL scores. The writing curriculum for students in these programs has correctness and standard formulaic production of writing as its goals. And most students attending these programs desire little else by way of writing instruction, as I have seen and as Vandrick (2010) describes in her essay "Social Class Privilege among ESOL Writing Student," in which she looks at the way membership in a privileged social class shapes the identity of some second language learners, those that she calls "students of the new global elite." She examines the ways that these students behave differently than other second language learners and how that behavior affects, in turn, the behavior of instructors who teach them. For-profit language schools are almost exclusively attended by the students Vandrick describes. While the global elite students enrolled in these programs report that English writing proficiency gives them access to better jobs, academic opportunities, increased (geographical) mobility, these same students have also remarked to me that failing to achieve proficiency is not dangerous in any way because they have their own lives back in their respective countries. The cloak of privilege that Vandrick talks about is clear in how these students see the role of ESOL writing in their lives. During a class discussion in an advanced integrated skills class at my for-profit school, for example, one student said, "It is good for me if I can write well, but I can live in my country without it."

To better understand the subset of students I am talking about, I will tell you a little about the school's curriculum. It is important to note here that, though this curriculum is not the same for every for-profit school out there, it is true of my institution that operates at an international level and occupies a significant portion of the market worldwide. The classes at the particular for-profit school where I teach ran in cycles of ten weeks per proficiency level with students coming in and out after passing a multiple choice level test. Any particular class could have a student in her tenth week with that teacher and three students in their second and third weeks. Following the curriculum, these classes tended to shape in one-week arcs at best. Though it is prescribed in the curriculum, students don't have to stay for ten weeks, but they do have to get A's for eight weeks straight in order to be allowed to take the level test early. Once students find out about this option almost everyone asks to take the level test early. Students often say that they need their certificate of graduation to indicate that they passed the highest level possible. An A in the class means scoring a

90% on a 30-question grammar test, a 30-question listening and speaking test, and a 30-question reading and writing test which asks general comprehension questions that make use of the grammar points and vocabulary of the week. There is no weekly writing assignment given at this particular school. Most important is that teachers keep strict records of student attendance to make sure they are in compliance with federal visa regulations.

Classes meet for three hours a day, five days a week for ten weeks per level. Each day the instructor is expected to cover four areas: listening, speaking, reading, and writing. Many teachers' manuals that we used at the school suggested that the students spend a few minutes discussing something related to a topic, read the text in class, and, finally, answer 10 or 15 comprehension questions, either alone or in groups. Students also work out of skills books that introduces them to one grammatical principle for the week and one aspect of writing that will ultimately contribute to the formation of a five-paragraph essay.

The students at my school tended to manipulate the structure of the curriculum in a way that fit their goals. Some students raced through the curriculum in order to attend classes at one of the area universities or to be able to return home and report that they had reached a certain level. Other students, on a kind of language-learning holiday, prolonged their stay in a particular level if they liked the teacher or their classmates. One student from France whose parents had sent him to the program as a finishing touch before going into the family business stayed in my class for 28 weeks. This student had no reason to speed through the curriculum—or even to finish it. Simply *attending* fulfilled his and his family's expectations. Despite my respect and good feelings for this student, this, in my mind, struck me as an instance of low-risk spectating, even though nothing in his performance was in conflict with the existing curriculum, which largely follows what many TESOL scholars suggest *should* happen in the ESOL classroom.

In *Critical Academic Writing,* TESOL scholar Canagarajah (2002) helps us understand the disparity between the ESOL writing instruction and instructors and L1 Composition while seemingly critiquing both:

> It is true that ESOL writing teachers sometimes conceive of their task as a pragmatic one of teaching value-free grammatical features or form-related aspects of essays to their students. Rhetorical and ideological issues are considered irrelevant to the students' practical needs of learning another language for utilitarian purposes in educational and professional life. While L1 [English as first language] Comp

> teachers have found it fashionable to indulge in theoretically and politically sophisticated discourse on writing, ESOL teachers have confined themselves to clinically circumscribed classroom-based empirical research on their students' linguistic and cognitive development. (p. 25)

While Canagarajah is talking here about the state of the TESOL discipline, the same tendencies are reflected in implementation at the classroom level. The ESOL students' in-class time is managed toward the "practical needs of learning another language," whereas in L1 composition classrooms students more often engage in discussions around higher order concerns in the text or about the text.

Despite the limitations of TESOL goals for L2 learners in a writing classroom, composition studies does not immediately suggest a clear alternative. I am not unaware that there are critics of English L1 composition classrooms for L2 learners. Tony Silva (1993) cautions us that L1 and L2 writing and writers are very different from one another and that L2 writers would be at a disadvantage if one treated their writing process as one would L1. Silva's findings show that while L1 and L2 writers had basically the same composing process, the L2 writing was more constrained, less fluent and less effective. He goes on to say that L2 writers planned less, had more trouble setting goals and organizing materials, and reviewed, reread, and reflected on their work less than their L1 counterparts. Thus, Silva and other scholars caution against assuming the value of L1 composition instruction for the L2 learner.

OFFERING A DEEPER LEARNING AND WRITING EXPERIENCE

But the problem of the for-profit classroom remains and requires new thinking about TESOL instructional goals and those of the L1 composition classroom when it comes to international students. In her argument, Vandrick (2010) notes the dearth of research on the role of social class in second language learning and, in particular, the role of privileged social class. This absence of research is only compounded for the for-profit classroom—the site (sometimes the *only* site) where many of these students experience the second language writing classroom.

Students of the global elite often have economic power but no rhetorical agency; a redesigned curriculum is one way they may find their way to that agency. I want to argue that the unique limbo created by privilege that elite second language writers find themselves in would benefit from an infusion of process elements most often valued in L1 composition classrooms. Contrastive rhetoric scholars like Kaplan (1966) made us aware of a variety of rhetorical organizations different writing cultures use. Since many L2 writers are writing from different cultural and rhetorical understandings, it stands to reason that, without some instruction and time for practice, they wouldn't be able to write using the rhetorical conventions that are expected in the American composition classroom. Students are often surprised that writing done in some US classrooms places the responsibility on the writer, and not so heavily on the reader. "You mean you want us to write so that the reader doesn't have to do any work?" one student asked in my composition course.

A redesigned curriculum would pay attention to the nuances of contrastive rhetoric and value different processes and rhetorical approaches so that students can be aware of these differences and, at the same time, understand what processes and rhetorical styles are valued by US readers. A redesigned curriculum would put this kind of work at the forefront of the students' experience. To address the pragmatic concerns that Horowitz (1990) and Silva (1993) have for these students, I argue that assignments that engage in rhetorical analysis of US forms of argumentation, for example, in comparison to their own writing culture's forms of argumentation are vital, and not simply to help them do well in an American composition classroom. Rather, it is important for instructors who teach these students to understand that this kind of assignment is not simply academic: it asks students to be more thoughtful about their own lives and decisions. An awareness of rhetorical differences, including the shapes of written arguments, is right next door to an awareness of those same kinds of differences outside of the classroom.

If these students do choose to stay for college in the US, the for-profit ESOL classroom can prepare ESOL students by exposing them to American styles of argumentation, but, if they don't, and they typically won't (although this is changing very quickly), what the composition classroom has to offer to students who are not going to stay here are opportunities to make critical arguments, to engage in critical reading in English, which is often presented in a structure that they are not familiar with, and to engage in an analysis of self (for example, in the personal essay) in relation to these arguments.

Students also need to be given time to engage substantially in their reading by talking and writing about the texts. Some teachers' manuals in for-profit ESOL schools often suggest that students take 45 minutes to read a text in class and then answer a set of 10 or 15 comprehension questions about the reading. An activity like this can take the better part of an hour in a class of beginning-advanced or advanced students. That hour is then *not* spent talking about choices the writer made and the reasons he or she made them, nor does it allow for time to talk about the *issues* addressed in the text. If you are spending a full hour on reading in a class, you aren't spending that time in the writing and thinking and discussion exercises that will allow students to make use of the language they are there to learn in the first place; that is, language and writing that enables them to communicate important ideas that matter to an audience.

In the hope for more substantial engagement with reading, I borrowed from the first year composition classroom. I copied readings and gave students questions to answer as they read the text at home. Students came to class with short written "reader's notes" that we could use as a basis for our in-class conversation. This isn't some crazy, new-fangled assignment, I know, but it is a vastly different assignment than is typically required in my for-profit school. In addition to not having to spend that class time reading, the students had prolonged exposure to the text, which then made it possible for us to have in-class discussions and analyses of the higher-order aspects of the texts as they intersected with their lives. Though most students complained about this work at the beginning of their time in my classroom, many came to actually appreciate the experience. One student in my advanced integrated skills class told me at the end of her time there that she felt that the writing allowed her to "really talk about something that was happening in my life or in the community at that time," and she felt like her ideas and her thinking mattered because they were out there—being talked about in class, validated or disagreed with. In this and the other assignments I'll describe next, ideas were being made real in (our piece of) the world through the students' use of written language. Many students said that this was a way they could really use the language they were learning to talk about real things, not the kinds of broad, empty topics the textbooks we were using had them read about: internet and cell phone addiction or "the media."

Another notable difference between the kind of reading and writing the textbooks typically asked for and the reading and writing I asked students to do in my classes was that I asked, really required, students to engage with the argument and ideas of a reading *personally*. I wanted to know what they thought and what experiences in their lives influenced how they read and understood the text. One assignment asked that students write about a feature of their home culture that they thought would not survive if they were to move to the US permanently, and examine *why* that feature would not survive. This prompt also asked them to use their native status in their culture to examine what about that feature was particularly symbolic of their culture. To provide a fuller response, students had to answer questions such as *What is particularly Korean [for example] about this behavior?, What are the cultural values reflected in and through this behavior?"*, and *Why would these behaviors/attitudes/values not survive in American society?*

This was a very difficult assignment in the beginning for the students because what they had been taught to write were "compare and contrast" essays, which meant that their essays were little more than lists of behaviors people have in each country. "In my country, we kiss cheeks and here people shake hands" and so on. Working in the process model allowed us to refine and give weight to the theses of their papers. Students had to spend some time thinking about how their home countries had shaped them and, by putting their culture in conflict with American culture, many of them came to identify some causes of confusion or culture shock. Their writing moved beyond just a list of characteristics, and, instead, attempted to get at what it meant to them to be Korean or Saudi or Chinese. For many, this was a positive experience that validated their sense of their own national identity; for others, it was a moment for them to seriously consider what it meant to be a representative of their culture living in the US (even if for only a short time).

Another assignment I gave required students to research the platforms of the possible candidates for the 2012 US presidential election with respect to their own countries' interests and to persuade voters to vote for one candidate over all of the others. After many trips to the library, one student became visibly angry with all of the possible candidates: "As a Chinese, this was difficult for me to write, because no one had any good words for us." The title of her essay ended up being "Of the Two Evils, Choose the Lesser." This student was pointing at the fact that none of the platforms she had examined depicted China in a very positive light. Suddenly, in this moment, the rosy lens with which she saw her experience in the US disappeared because of her new understanding of how she must have been viewed as a Chinese National by the US citizens and students around her. (For more examples of writing assignments that ask L2 students to think and write critically about international issues, see Siczek & Shapiro's [this volume] description of a course model focused on world Englishes.)

A for-profit ESOL writing class would benefit from exercises in topic generation, brainstorming, organization of ideas, prioritization, revisions (all things Silva's study suggests these students could use some work on), along with discussions of the rhetorical patterns each of the students adopts in his or her writing and assignments calling for a personal investment in learning to write in English. (Hirsch's [this volume] analysis of effective writing curricula for L2 students also finds that this type of scaffolding leads to L2 student success). These process-focused activities are beginning to show up in some for-profit curricula, but, as Terry Santos (1992) points out, just because they show up there doesn't mean that these activities actually make their way into the classroom. One major reason for this is that instructors at for-profit schools aren't paid for the many hours it takes to read essays. Many of my colleagues also admitted that they didn't feel confident in their training to teach writing with a focus on the process approach.

The American composition classroom has been understood for over thirty years as a place where process and product are emphasized, but that is not the case in the for-profit second language classroom. Though a call for process in the for-profit classroom might seem less than revolutionary, the results of such an infusion could be. I am calling for genuine engagement in the experience of process. This is not a complete revamping of the for-profit ESOL curriculum but a suggestion that the for-profit ESOL classroom would benefit from an infusion of pedagogical tools from the composition classroom. The strategies and kinds of assignments I mention above are not original or particularly innovative. Of greater importance here is the that these strategies and assignments ask students to engage in the process of writing, reading, and thinking rather than simply produce brief, uniform products and short essay responses.

ENGAGED WRITING FOR AGENCY

Writing, when there is not much at stake, becomes an exercise in low-risk spectating —just another ride the student can take while on his/her language journey. Social privilege along with the current curriculum design at for-profit schools affords students who are able to take a year leave to perfect their English a certain distance between themselves and the material they are being asked to engage with at a personal level. They are spectators and not participants. The kinds of writing and methods of teaching writing I describe here demand an active engagement that requires visiting and revisiting the ideas and the writer's relationship to them.

Considering the assignments that I've described, it can't come as any surprise when I say that another thing that the for-profit ESOL classroom could take from the field of rhetoric and composition is a good dose of critical pedagogy. Vandrick (1995) made this same recommendation in an early article on this ESOL elite population, "Privileged ESL University Students." Critical pedagogy is inspired by the teaching and scholarship of Paulo Freire and asks teachers and students alike to consider their relationship to power in and out of the classroom. Critical pedagogy is often understood as a way to empower the otherwise disenfranchised. ESOL students, especially those we see in public schools, are often members of those disenfranchised groups that critical pedagogy aims to empower and usually the group of students we most often identify with the label "ESL."

But I would suggest that it is equally important to engage students on the other end of the power divide in critical pedagogy classrooms. David Nuremberg (2011) discusses Freire's (1974) influence in his own teaching at a "high-powered, affluent, suburban public high school." Referencing Freire, Nuremburg argues that

> it is impossible to humanly exist without assuming the right and the duty to opt, to decide, to struggle, to be political and therefore the teacher has some responsibility and duty to help students become aware of and empowered by their own ability to make these choices. Teaching inevitably involves calling students' attention to social issues as matters of ethical choice and not merely as the result of societal determinism. Therefore, Freire says, teachers should work to help students make concrete connections between what they have read and what is happening in the world, country, or the local community. (p. 34)

Despite the fact that for some of my students' power can sometimes feel "socially determined," they cannot be said to have agency if their actions are not accompanied by reflection and a more complete articulation of their reasons for acting. What has become clear to me is that while these students have power, they do not necessarily have agency because they don't know in what ways they are powerful. They don't know that the consequence of being a member of this global elite is that they could come to make decisions that could affect large numbers of individuals in the world.

Having power but no agency is just as crippling as having no power at all. Even those who are socially and economically privileged can't go through doors they don't know exist. These students still need for someone to show them how to pass through those doors. Given the potential power that the students at these schools are likely to inherit or come to exert in the world, more attention should be given to how private for-profit ESOL curricula are designed and taught.

REFERENCES

Canagarajah, A. S. (2002). *Critical academic writing*. Ann Arbor, MI: The University of Michigan Press.

Freire, P. (1974, 1998). *Pedagogy of freedom: Ethics, democracy and civic courage.* Lanham, MD: Lanham, Rowman & Littlefield.

Horowitz, D. (1990). Fiction and nonfiction in the ESL/EFL classroom: Does the difference make a difference?. In T. Silva & P. K. Matsuda (Eds.), *Landmark Essays on ESL Writing.* Mahwah, NJ: Lawrence Erlbaum.

Kaplan, R. (1966). Cultural thought patterns in intercultural education. *Language Learning, 16,* 1-20.

Matsuda, P. K. (1997). Contrastive rhetoric in context: A dynamic model of L2 writing. *Journal of Second Language Writing, 6,* 45-60.

Nuremberg, D. (2011). What does injustice have to do with me? A pedagogy of the privileged. *Harvard Educational Review, 81*(1), 50-63.

Santos, T. (1992). Ideology in composition: L1 and ESL. In T. Silva & P. K. Matsuda (Eds.), *Landmark Essays on ESL Writing.* Mahwah, NJ: Lawrence Erlbaum Associates.

Silva, T. (1993). Toward an understanding of the distinct nature of second language writing: The ESL research and its implications. *TESOL Quarterly, 27,* 657-677.

Vandrick, S. (1995). Privileged ESL university students. *TESOL Quarterly, 29*(2), 375-381.

Vandrick, S. (2010). Social class privilege among ESOL writing students. In M. Cox, J. Jordan, C. Ortmeier-Hooper, & G. Schwartz (Eds.), *Reinventing Identities in Second Language Writing* (pp. 257-272). Urbana, IL: NCTE.

CHAPTER 11

MAKING STANCE EXPLICIT FOR SECOND LANGUAGE WRITERS IN THE DISCIPLINES: WHAT FACULTY NEED TO KNOW ABOUT THE LANGUAGE OF STANCE-TAKING

Zak Lancaster
Wake Forest University

Expressing an authorial stance in contextually valued ways may be especially challenging for English as a Second Language (L2) writers (in addition, certainly, to many L1 writers), as the subtle ways that writers in the disciplines go about evaluating evidence and positioning the reader toward their views are largely tacit and therefore not often made explicit to students. In response to this problem, this chapter discusses ways that writing specialists can assist faculty in the disciplines to become explicitly aware of stance expressions in their students' writing. Drawing on analysis of student writing in two disciplinary contexts (political theory and economics) as well as interviews with the course instructors, I offer examples of stance features that appear to be valued in these two contexts even though they run below the instructors' fully conscious awareness. I then discuss ways that disciplinary faculty can be assisted to identify these features explicitly. The larger goal of this chapter is to argue for a way of reading students' disciplinary writing that is sensitive to the details of stance-taking and to the language-related problems that many students experience when writing in the disciplines.

Students in upper-level writing in the disciplines contexts are expected, often implicitly, to construct stances in their writing in ways that are recognized by readers as appropriate and authoritative—i.e., assertive, knowledgeable, critically distant, and aligned with a specific disciplinary culture. To meet these stance expectations, writers must use language in specialized ways, as revealed by linguistic analyses of specific disciplinary discourses (see, e.g., Charles, 2003; Hyland, 2004, 2005; Macken-Horarik & Morgan, 2011; Schleppegrell, 2004; Soliday, 2011). These specialized ways of using language, however, are not typically recognized as such by faculty in the disciplines, due largely to assumptions about the transparency of academic discourses (Turner, 1999). In particular, there is not often conscious awareness of the ways that disciplinary stances are accomplished through language, for example through wordings that subtly foreground valued epistemologies, construct a critical reader-in-the-text, or otherwise index the stance of a student who is engaged with the disciplinary discourse.

As brief illustration, consider the following two texts written by students in an advanced economics course.

> (1a) Using an ex post analysis of share prices and product prices, I was able to show that the Supreme Court decision had negligible effects on the industry, and therefore a better outcome could have been achieved. (Eric)

> (1b) Using my personal opinion to analyze the remedies used in this case, I determined the District Court was correct in allowing the merger to proceed. (Nancy)

These texts are from students' final essays in the course. One difference between them, as suggested by just these concluding sentences, is that Eric adopts a contrastive stance toward the reasoning of Supreme Court, while Nancy adopts a stance of agreement (*the District Court was correct*). Subtler differences can be found in the details of the language. Eric's text, for instance, thematizes (or linguistically foregrounds)[1] the analytic framework that he uses to reach his judgment (*Using ex post analysis of share prices and product prices*), while Nancy's text thematizes the subjective basis of her judgment (*Using my personal opinion to analyze the remedies used in this case*). Through these and other language resources, Eric's text conveys more critical distance and authority.

It is unlikely that many faculty think in such explicit terms about stance when evaluating student work. This lack of explicit attention may not cause problems for students who have learned "organically" how to construct valued stances in their writing, i.e., through trial and error and unconscious noticing of patterns in genre exemplars. It can present problems, however, for students who have difficulty meeting implicit stance expectations, due either to limited exposure to academic registers and genres or to a variety of linguistic, socio-cultural, and individual factors. To provide meaningful support for these students, it would be useful for faculty to be aware of the various linguistic means through which valued stances are realized in their discourse contexts. With such awareness, they could learn to read student work in new ways and provide feedback that takes into account the complexities involved in taking on a disciplinary stance.

Recent research shows that stance-related challenges may be especially acute for English as a Second Language (L2) writers (Chang, 2010; Feak, 2008; Hyland & Milton, 1997; Lancaster, 2011; Schleppegrell, 2004; Tardy, 2009). When L2 writers' styles of stance-taking are not explicit enough, inconsistent in evaluative position, not measured enough, too measured, or otherwise subtly off the mark, the students can be judged as having vague "language" or "grammar" problems and thus directed to the campus writing center, where writing specialists who are likely untrained in the disciplinary context may or may not be able to help (Feak, 2008). Students can also be judged in a very different way as having problems comprehending the subject matter (Lancaster, 2011). Specifically, faculty may interpret what are actually problems in linguistic expression of stance as problems with thinking, understanding, or even effort. (See Zawacki & Habib [this volume] for similar faculty explanations of L2 student error, many of which could be attributed to inappropriate stance-taking.) For instance, in some disciplinary genres, inconsistent use of "hedges" (e.g., *perhaps, research suggests, it appears/seems that*) may contribute toward the impression that the writer has not engaged in sufficiently cautious reasoning. In other disciplinary genres, foregrounding of personal opinion, as in Nancy's text, may be perceived as insufficient "analytic rigor." Evidence that stance does matter can be found in research that reveals connections between the types of stances students project and their grades or scores (Barton, 1993; Coffin, 2002; Lancaster, 2012; Soliday, 2004; Wu, 2007).

That adopting an effective stance in disciplinary writing comes with linguistic challenges presents a conundrum for writing instruction, one well known to writing scholars. The conundrum is that, while faculty in the disciplines best understand the close text-context interrelations in the disciplinary genres that they themselves have mastered and are asking their students to engage with, they typically feel ill-equipped, under-prepared, or under-motivated to deal with "language" in their classroom instruction. While linguistic issues in writing may fall under the expertise of writing specialists, discipline-specific ways of using language are best understood (at least potentially) by experts in the respective disciplines.

In response to this knotty and long-standing problem, I suggest ways in this chapter that writing specialists can work with faculty in the disciplines to become explicitly aware of stance expressions in student writing. My main suggestion is that, if faculty are to develop strategies for reading and commenting on their students' papers in ways that are sensitive to expression of stance, they need to be able to identify textual patterns in their students' writing that are more and less related to valued disciplinary stances. The capacity to identify patterns of stance in students' texts, furthermore, requires a meaningful metalanguage (or language about language), one that potentially can be used to assist students to recognize how valued stances are realized through language.

I begin by clarifying what I mean by "stance." I then offer examples of patterns in stance-taking that faculty could be assisted to identify. My examples are pulled from two distinct disciplinary contexts, an upper-level course on economic regulation and antitrust policy (henceforth Econ 432) and an upper-level course on twentieth century political theory (henceforth PolSci 409). In the larger research project from which my examples are taken, I used appraisal theory from systemic functional linguistics (Martin and White, 2005) to analyze argumentative essays written by consistently high- and low-performing students. I also interviewed the course instructors about their goals and values for student writing in order to interpret how patterns of stance were related to valued meanings in the contexts. I describe these methods more fully in Lancaster (2012). After discussing relevant patterns in example texts, I finally turn to specific strategies for assisting faculty to read student work in terms of stance-taking.

STANCE: WHAT IS IT AND WHY IS IT SO TRICKY?

Stance is a slippery concept that faculty across the disciplines, including writing faculty, have difficultly discussing with their students in clear terms. As Soliday (2011) points out, students are frequently advised to "take your own position" and offer judgments, but to avoid sounding "biased" (p. 39-40). Similarly, they are expected to show commitment to their arguments and even "passion" for their topics, but also to remain "objective" or critically distant. Other potentially contradictory messages that students may hear include: Use your own words, your own "voice," but don't be colloquial in your use of language; use "I" in your writing, but not too frequently; write assertively and with authority, but don't forget you're a student and lack expertise; engage with others' views and voices, but don't just summarize what others have said; display understanding of the target material, but don't just reel off facts; try new things, experiment with new ways of thinking and arguing, but be sure to write clearly and concisely. The cumulative effect of these apparently contradictory instructions can lead students to the (not unreasonable) conclusion that every instructor wants something different: Instructors have their own idiosyncratic tastes for what counts as an effective style of stance taking.

Stance has been hard for linguists to pin down, too, as suggested by the wide range of definitions that have been offered (see, e.g., Engelbretson, 2007; Hyland, 2005; Jaffe, 2009; Martin & White, 2005). Furthermore, in some traditions of applied linguistics, stance has been treated as nearly or completely synonymous with the construct of *voice*. Hyland (2011), for instance, equates the two constructs when he explains that "stance refers to the writer's textual 'voice' or community recognized personality" (p. 197).

In this chapter, I am using the term *stance* rather than *voice* because I examine how writers' interpersonal moves (like use of counterargument strategies) relate to issues of reader positioning. Expressing stance is both a writer-oriented and reader-oriented concept, a point that is reflected in Johnstone's (2009) definition of stance as "the methods, linguistic and other, by which interactants create and signal relationships with the propositions they utter and with the people they interact with" (p. 30-31). I am, in fact, equally comfortable referring to the linguistic construction of an "authoritative voice" as I am an "authoritative stance," but other textual qualities that I discuss below, like contrastiveness, have to do with the signaling of relationships with others' views and voices. Thus a "contrastive stance"—or adopting a stance of contrast towards others' views— makes more intuitive sense than a "contrastive voice." Likewise a dialogically expansive or contractive stance (as explained in White, 2003, and discussed below) makes more intuitive sense than a dialogically expansive or contractive voice.

Stance, then, refers to the ways that writers—as they go about analyzing and evaluating things, making assertions and recommendations, providing evidence and justifications and so forth—project an authorial presence in their texts, one that conveys attitudes and feelings and that interacts with the imagined readers by recognizing their views, identifying points of shared knowledge, conceding limitations, and otherwise positioning them as aligned with or resistant to the views being advanced in the text. According to this expansive definition, stance expressions are pervasive throughout disciplinary genres, including ones often thought of as objective and "faceless" like research articles and lab reports. (See the Appendix for examples of stance moves from various disciplinary contexts.)

As suggested by the discussion so far, expressing stance in academic writing requires more complex decision-making than whether or not to adopt a formal tone or use the active voice or the pronoun "I." It requires making decisions (usually tacitly) about such matters as when to tune up or down one's level of commitment to assertions; whether and how to comment on the significance of evidence; when and how to engage with alternative perspectives; how to construct a text that engages with the imagined reader; and many other interpersonal considerations that can vary widely according to genre and disciplinary context (Hyland, 2004; 2005). These subtle interpersonal moves can be highly challenging for both L1 and L2 student writers. They can also be difficult for experienced writers to think about consciously and to identify in discourse explicitly, as they tend to be so deeply embedded within their social knowledge of genre.

In terms of my own difficulties as a writing specialist, I can only go so far in conjecturing whether or not certain stance features, such as the ones I identified in Eric's and Nancy's texts above, are valued or not in their contexts, as I am not trained in economics or political theory. Eric's stance is both more "critical" (or contrastive) and critically distant than Nancy's. Through my analysis (in Lancaster, 2012), I showed that these and other qualities do correlate with students' grades in the courses. That is, the high-performers more consistently adopt stances marked by contrastiveness and critical distance, among other qualities. The difficulty for me lies in pinpointing why a particular pattern or type of wording might be valued, either with regard to the pedagogical purposes of the assignment or the epistemological values of the disciplinary culture—or a combination of the two. Is the stance that Nancy projects not as effective as the one that Eric projects? If so, is this because it is in agreement with the District Court's reasoning and thus is not "critical"? Or is it because her text foregrounds the subjective basis of her reasoning? I can, of course, speculate that foregrounding personal opinion is not the most effective way to go about recommending a course of action in the context of an economically-driven public policy analysis. But the person who is in the best position to comment on these meanings, and perhaps connect them to other important meanings in the context that I have not identified, is the course professor. This is why it would be ideal for him and other faculty in the disciplines to gain experience in identifying patterns of stance that are more and less valued in their own students' writing.

EXAMPLES OF LINGUISTIC PATTERNS THAT REQUIRE INSTRUCTIONAL ATTENTION

In this section I focus in more detail on types of language use that my research suggests warrant close attention, especially in disciplinary contexts that call for evidence-based arguments. I begin with the case of Econ 432. My analysis of high-and low-graded papers in this course revealed that the wordings in ***bold*** *italics* in the sentences below are instances of a larger pattern of language use that can present particular difficulties for L2 writers.

> (2a) Of the defendants involved in Utah Pie Company's case only one ***seems*** to have emerged as exceptionally successful. Continental, now known as Morton Frozen Foods Division, had a 13, 11, and 13th percentage share of the market in 1974, 1975 and 1976 respectively (see table 1).

> (2b) It ***appears*** that maximum price fixing does the greatest harm when set below a competitive level.

> (2c) The rise of Mrs. Smith's, fall of Utah Pie, and relative success of Continental in the resulting time frame ***suggest*** internal management, and not the Supreme Court, played the most significant role in market performance and conduct.

These highlighted wordings appear significantly more frequently in the high-performing students' writing in the course, and for this reason they may warrant instructional attention. Given that, how can they be discussed?

Often referred to in the applied linguistics literature as **hedges** (see Hyland, 2004; 2005), these devices are used to weaken authorial commitment to claims and signal openness to alternative views. In the specific sentences above, hedging is realized through appearance-based evidential verbs (*appears*, *seems*, and *suggest*), which highlight the evidence-based nature of the reasoning and represent the writers' judgments as "based on plausible reasoning rather than certain knowledge" (Hyland, 2005, p. 179). Hedging can also be realized through low-probability modal expressions (e.g., *could*, *might*, *may*, *perhaps*, *possibly*, *I think*)—in addition to a variety of other lexical and grammatical means for expressing a claim as a possibility rather than fact or pronouncement.

In the case of genres that require evidence-based argumentation, it is useful to distinguish between two sub-types of hedging: **evidentializing** (e.g., *the research suggests*; *based on these facts it appears/seems*) and **conjecturing** (e.g., *perhaps*; *it is likely/possible that*; *in my view*), which are terms that I borrow from Tang (2009). Both are instances of hedging, with the difference being that evidentializing expresses sustained consideration of evidence—a process that shifts focus somewhat away from the immediate subjective experience of the writer—while conjecturing expresses an internalized process grounded in the subjectivity of the authorial voice. My analysis of Econ 432 papers revealed that high-graded papers used more instances of evidentializing, while the lower-graded papers used more instances of personalized conjecturing (or "personalizing"), for example *it seems to me* and *in my view*. As I discuss below, this differential pattern does not hold for the case of PolSci 409 writing because this context calls for a different kind of evidence-based writing.

In Econ 432, the specific *pattern* of evidentializing that was revealed as especially valuable, because it works to construct an authoritative stance, involves three elements. These comprise an initial presentation of facts, which are either categorically asserted or strongly boosted, followed by a hedged judgment of the evidence, and finally a statement of recommendation. This sequencing strategy allows the writers to adopt a stance marked by cautious evaluation of evidence. Examples are provided below. (Key wordings are in ***bold italics***.)

(3a) From Ken's high-graded essay

Presentation of Evidence (boosted)	As ***shown*** in a recent survey of physician satisfaction by Harvard Medical School, physician autonomy and the ability to provide high-quality care, ***not*** income, are ***strongly*** associated with changes in job satisfaction.
Judgment (hedged)	Thus, it ***seems reasonable to assume*** that health care providers would take advantage of the greater bargaining power to improve the quality of care.
Recommendation (hedged)	Such measures ***might*** take the form of measures included in many state patient protection bills ...

(3b) From Luis's high-graded essay

Presentation of Evidence (boosted)	***Clearly***, Von's did ***not*** accomplish what it set out to achieve: ***countless*** subsequent antitrust cases have ***completely*** ignored the reasoning set forth by the Court.
Judgment (hedged)	***It would seem,*** then, the Von's decision was a failure. This statement leads to a natural question: if the Court got it wrong in Von's, what ***might*** the correct decision have been?
Recommendation (hedged)	For several reasons, the Supreme Court ***should*** have ...

In these excerpts, Ken and Luis are moving from analysis to recommendations. To accomplish this move in an authoritative manner, they ramp up persuasive effort through strategic use of hedging and boosting.

Boosters (see, e.g., Hyland, 2005; Perales-Escudero & Swales, 2011) are something of a counterpart to hedges in that they increase authorial commitment while closing down discursive space for other views. Analyzed as resources of high-force **graduation** in Martin and White (2005), boosters express the writer's involvement with the topic. They also draw attention to the importance of the ideas, persuading the reader to accept the proposition being put forth. Instances of boosting are seen in 3a and 3b in the stance expressions *strongly*, *clearly*, *countless*, and *completely*. Cooperating with these boosters is the verb *shown* and the explicit denials (*not*). Like boosters, these latter devices—endorsements and denials—work to shut down space for alternative views (White, 2003). Ken could have chosen less committed wordings like *as suggested* or *indicated in*, but instead he chose *as shown in*, which expresses a stronger endorsement of the survey results. He further closes down room for negotiation in this phase of discourse by directly denying a possible alternative view (*not income*). The result of these maneuvers is a highly committed stance. However, when offering his most general judgment, Ken reduces authorial commitment and opens up the discursive space by hedging (*seems reasonable to assume*). The wording here expresses a very different kind of stance than if Ken were to have written *It is therefore obvious/certain/clear that*. The use of hedging enables him to express a carefully reasoned stance, which may be rhetorically useful before proceeding to offer recommendations.

In general, the movement from boosting to hedging in Ken's and Luis's texts creates the impression of highly involved but cautious analysts. Such a stance is likely to be valued in academic genres calling for evidence-based recommendations. It is also likely to be one that is difficult to construct and sustain for many L2 writers (as well as many L1 writers), especially those who have not had prior training in working with academic registers.

Hedges are used somewhat differently by the high-performing writers in the political theory course (PolSci 409). This is an important point to make because the differences in use suggest that faculty must go further than simply telling their students that hedges are valuable; they also need to understand whether, where, and how hedges are used to create valued meanings in their contexts. In the PolSci 409 essay, which requires interpretation, explanation, elaboration, and critical juxtaposition of theoretical arguments, hedges are used less to convey cautious consideration of evidence and more to mitigate the force of critical challenges to others' arguments.

Offering challenges to texts by the likes of Michel Foucault, John Rawls, Nancy Fraser, and others assigned in the class is a delicate procedure, especially for student writers. Abruptly executed problematization moves can project a stance marked by brashness or under-appreciation of the assigned readings. When using the rhetorical strategy of **problematization**, which involves "showing that a prevailing assumption, idea, view, or situation needs reexamination, reconceptualization, or reevaluation of some kind" (Barton, 1993, p.

748), hedges are often useful to suggest a stance of openness and willingness to negotiate critical positions. This dialogically open stance can be seen in 4a and 4b.

> (4a) In this sense, the trial *somewhat* contradicts Foucault's theory of the modern exercise of power. In modernity (according to Foucault), power is diffused so much as to make it impossible to locate the source of power. In the trial, however, the source of power is clearly identifiable; therefore, the trial *seems* to be more in line with Foucault's pre-modern concept of justice and power. (Maria)

> (4b) Fraser prefers the transformation strategy, which would reconfigure the social structure by eliminating the groups as such. While this method *may* be more decisive in eliminating the injustice, it *appears* to have the drawback of not being in the immediate interests of any group, as they would stand to lose their identities. Therefore, while Fraser's matrix *may* help soften there distributive-recognition dilemma, it doesn't offer any *obvious* solutions to the problem of recognition in modern society. (Ethan)

Problematization is a highly valued argumentative practice in academia (Barton, 1993; Wu, 2006), and it may be implicitly expected across academic discourse contexts. Even if students are aware of the need to be "critical" in this way, however, many struggle to do so in genre-appropriate ways, for example by maintaining a carefully-reasoned or critically distant stance. In an interview, the professor of PolSci 409 praised one of the top essays in the class for being, in his words, both "critical" and "sympathetic" toward the main text under analysis. Both Maria's and Ethan's texts are examples of how hedging can be used to bring these two potentially contradictory stances together.

In contrast to these two writers, two of the self-identified L2 writers in PolSci 409, Victor and Ryan, had trouble with this stance of critical sympathy, but for different reasons. Victor's writing suggests that he was not aware of the implicit expectation to adopt a critical or contrastive stance when carrying out the assignment. His essay, in fact, was one of the few that did not use problematization strategies at all. Consider, as illustration, the different ways that Ethan (the high-performing writer of 4b above) and Victor respond to the same essay prompt in their introductory paragraphs. The prompt is reproduced here, and key stance differences in the students' writing are in ***bold italics***.

Prompt: Nancy Fraser argues that conventional "distributive" theories of justice cannot address contemporary problems related to the politics of "recognition." Explain and elaborate on Fraser's argument. Then consider how Rawls or Nussbaum would respond to Fraser's view.

(5a) from Ethan's introduction (high-graded) …

> … Fraser's proposal posits that "the remedy for cultural injustice … is some sort of cultural or symbolic change." She calls this cultural change "recognition." **Rawlsian theory, however, disputes Fraser's sharp division between socioeconomic and cultural injustice**. In fact, Rawls would respond to Fraser by saying that his theory fairly addresses cultural injustice, and her attempt to redress cultural injustice through recognition may actually lead to unjust outcomes.

(5b) from Victor's introduction (low-graded) …

> … Both Fraser and Nussbaum put forward ideas on how to eliminate social and economic inequalities and provide justice to people, although Fraser is more concerned with the means of bringing justice to people who need it, whereas Nussbaum looks at the ends by which we can evaluate if justice is provide or not. *Therefore, in my opinion their views complement each other* by providing suggestions on two aspects of the same problem: how to provide social and economic justice and the grounds on which we can judge if this goal is accomplished.

Ethan's text in 5a assumes a contrastive stance by positioning Rawls in a critical relationship with Fraser. Ethan maintains this stance throughout his essay by engaging in frequent problematization moves. Victor's stance, in contrast, is focused on complementarity. Throughout the course, in fact, his writing displays a desire to locate points of agreement among different thinkers' views (and possibly a reluctance to problematize). Partly for this reason, his writing elicits such feedback from the professor as "simple compare and contrast" and "you've done a good job summarizing, but you haven't developed an argument." Victor's stance of assumed agreement seems to have caused his difficulty in critically juxtaposing texts in specific ways.[2]

Victor's writing, then, suggests that he may not have been aware of the implicit expectation to place the texts under analysis in a critical relationship with one another. In contrast, another L2 writer in the course, Ryan,[3] had difficulty *executing* problematization moves in genre appropriate ways. In example 6, Ryan attempts to problematize an aspect of Foucault's argument as a way to transition into a discussion of Walzer. But he realizes this move in a way that reflects lack of critical distance. (Wordings that I discuss below are in **bold italics**.)

> (6) One thing that Foucault doesn't address, ***not saying that he should have because it isn't one of his ideas***, is whether the old form of public executions and the new form of punishment is an act of dirty hands or not. ***According to Walzer's argument I think*** the act of public executions would ***definitely*** be an unjustified act of dirty hands, but what about the new forms of punishment such as jail time? Giving someone jail time for a crime that they've committed seems to be completely necessary, but is there a better way of taking care of the problem? (Ryan)

As indicated in this excerpt, Ryan seems to be aware of the expectation to assume a critical stance and to negotiate positions with the reader. But his prose does not demonstrate control over that critical stance. It is at times difficult to tease apart material he is attributing to others from his own assertions, as seen in the second sentence (*According to Walzer's argument I think*). In addition, the imagined reader that Ryan projects in his text appears to be the course professor rather than a peer discussant. This is seen in the quick personal aside that qualifies the problematization of Foucault (*not saying that he should have because it isn't one of his ideas*), his personalizing move (*I think*), and conversational register (e.g., *one thing, definitely, but what about*). These features reflect a tenor marked by closeness and familiarity. Ryan could learn to mitigate the force of his problematization moves in a more critically distant way through the use of register-congruent hedges, such as those used above in examples 4a and 4b.

To sum up, there appear to be at least two different reasons why L2 writers experience difficulty constructing an authoritative stance in their writing. Students like Victor, may not see the educational stakes in adopting a critical stance or may even resist doing so. Then there are students like Ryan who may be aware of the value in adopting a certain kind of stance but do not command the discursive resources needed to project an authoritative stance in their texts.

There is research evidence that this second difficulty may be more common. Hyland and Milton (1997), for instance, found that the English L2 writers in their study tended to respond to the implicit expectation to project an authoritative stance in research report writing by repeatedly expressing their views in direct and highly committed forms (e.g., *it is certain that*; *this will definitely*)—which can result in a hasty or ill-considered stance—instead of by strategically modulating between doubt and certainty. Similar problems among L2 writers in controlling valued linguistic resources for expressing stance are reported in Schleppegrell (2004) and Wu (2007). In light of this research, simply advising students in abstract terms to adopt an authoritative (or critical, critically distant, measured, etc.) stance would be insufficient for assisting them to project these stances in their texts and to make choices about the types of stances they wish to convey. Many students need help in identifying the stance moves that are prototypical and valued in samples of the discourse they are being asked to write. They could be supported in this effort by faculty who are aware of the complexities involved in constructing interpersonal meanings in academic writing, ones that more often than not go unnamed and therefore unnoticed by students.

ARGUMENTS FOR AN EXPLICIT STANCE-FOCUSED METALANGUAGE

When pointing out valued stances and rhetorical strategies to students, should specific stance-related terms like *hedging, evidentializing, conjecturing, boosting*, and *problematizing* be used? Behind this question are at least three more pointed pedagogical questions:

Is it necessary or beneficial to draw students' attention to fine-grained levels of textual detail (or sentence-level strategies) when discussing stance in disciplinary writing?

Is a specific analytic terminology or metalanguage useful for faculty and students, or could it be burdensome or distracting?

How can faculty who are untrained in text analysis be assisted to read students' texts for fine-grained expressions of stance and to develop a vocabulary that connects micro-level textual choices to epistemological values in the discipline?

In terms of the first question, the research and examples discussed above suggest that L2 writers (in addition, certainly, to many L1 writers) need to be shown instances in texts—possibly their own texts—in which abstract rhetorical effects like an authoritative stance are achieved. They also need ample opportunity to reflect on the discursive resources that are available to them for realizing important stances in their writing. Class activities that can help achieve these aims include instructor-led discussions with students about what sorts of "critical" stances are valued in certain disciplinary genres; tasks that require students to rewrite excerpts from students' papers that they find problematic in terms of stance and reader-positioning; and tasks that require that students reflect explicitly on their own stance-taking strategies while writing, for example by inserting meta-reflective comments in the margins of their papers. See Lancaster (2011) for more detailed discussion of these activities.

In terms of whether or not to use a specific metalanguage with students, there is now good evidence that use of a meaning-based (rather than traditional grammar-based) metalanguage can assist students to gain conscious awareness of valued linguistic resources and patterns in the genres with which they are engaging. Such affordances have been documented by scholars working in the tradition of systemic functional linguistics (SFL), as well as in other traditions of applied linguistics. For example, the use of a meaning-based metalanguage has been shown to help learners to identify subtle patterns of evaluation in political opinion texts and thus improve their capacities for critical reading (Perales-Escudero, 2011). It has also been shown to help teachers of history identify language areas that create problems for their students in learning to read history discourse (Schleppegrell & de Oliveira, 2006). For both secondary- and tertiary-level student *writing*, direct instruction in use of metadiscoursal strategies has been shown to assist students to improve their writing. For instance, Cheng & Steffensen (1996) found through interviews and analysis of pre- and post-test writing samples that first year composition students improved both in their rhetorical awareness and use of metadiscoursal strategies in their writing, including reader engagement devices like *one may expect* and attitude markers like *surprisingly*. Focusing on the writing of twelfth grade Chilean students, Concha and Paratore (2011) likewise found through text analysis and think-aloud protocols that students who learned an explicit metalanguage for reflecting on issues of *local coherence* (LC)—which the authors define as "the relationship between adjacent propositions in text" (p. 37)—improved in their ability to think and talk about LC and to control language resources for constructing LC in their own writing.

Robust frameworks for talking about linguistic choices in rhetorical terms are offered by, among others, Graff and Birkenstein (2006), Hunston and Thompson (2000), Hyland (2005), Martin and Rose (2007), Martin and White (2005), Swales and Feak (2012), and Thompson (2001). Depending on the context, the linguistic concepts identified in these studies can be used in focused ways to raise instructors' conscious awareness of the ways language creates important meanings in their disciplinary discourses and their students' writing. For example, in the context of empirically-based research arguments, instructors can learn to identify how *evidentializing* (or hedging that is based in sustained consideration of evidence) can contribute to a more authoritative stance than *conjecturing* (or hedging that is grounded in the subjectivity of the authorial voice). (See the Appendix for further examples of both types of hedging.) In general, a meaningful metalanguage about the sentence-level details of stance is needed if faculty in the disciplines are to come to notice how language is working more and less effectively in their students' writing to project valued interpersonal meanings.

The third question above—how can faculty be assisted to read students' writing in terms of stance?—is knottier. Given the inevitable time constraints in a busy academic year and the lack of linguistic/rhetorical training among most faculty in the disciplines, one natural objection to this chapter's argument is that use of a specific metalanguage, while ideal, is unrealistic. It is unduly burdensome. A second objection is that patterns of language use can be identified more informally, without employing a specific metalanguage. I respond to the first objection below in detail. To the second one, I would suggest that many linguistic features of texts cannot be recognized, at least consciously and explicitly, without some kind of underlying concept. The accompanying terminology like *hedges* and *boosters* may appear "jargony" because the concept is unfamiliar, or, perhaps more accurately, because the concept is regarded as such a transparent part of the discourse that explicit identification appears unnecessary.

Continuing with this point just a bit, it is true that authors like Graff and Birkenstein (2006), whose textbook *They Say / I Say: The Moves That Matter in Academic Writing* has been used successfully with both L2 and L1 writers, use non-specialized terminology to identify "the moves that matter in academic writing." To refer to attributions, for instance, they use the descriptive phrases "introducing what 'they say'" (p. 163), "introducing 'standard views'" (p. 163), and "capturing authorial action" (p. 165). Below each strategy, they list wordings or templates associated with each function. The sorts of strategies they identify could be very useful for student-writers who are struggling with basic discoursal resources for reviewing others' arguments and taking a stance. However, by keeping the description of language at the very general level that they do, the authors do not discuss patterns of language that operate at more specific levels of discourse (often below writers' fully conscious awareness) and that create valued meanings in *particular discourse contexts*, such as the strategic uses of hedging in genres calling for evidence-based recommendations. The authors' use of what could be referred to as a "commonsense" metalanguage for describing academic moves, that is, may be more useful for first year writing courses and other general introductions to academic discourse and less useful for advanced disciplinary contexts, such as Econ 432 and PolSci 409, where a more specialized metalanguage may be needed to identify subtly valued disciplinary moves.

As an example of where a more specific metalanguage could be useful, consider the following examples from Graff and Birkenstein's textbook. The authors offer these examples when discussing the importance of "entertaining objections" (p. 78; 170) in academic writing.

> (7a) Yet some readers may challenge the view that ...
>
> (7b) Of course, many will probably disagree with the assertion that ...
>
> (Graff & Birkenstein, 2006, p. 170-171)

In light of hedging patterns discussed above, these examples are interesting because of the second layer of "entertaining" brought into play through the hedges *may* and *probably*. Unacknowledged by the authors, these hedges subtly entertain objections to the claims that there are objections. That is, *some readers **may** challenge the view, but they may not*. In projecting this second layer of "entertaining," these texts convey a more measured stance than if they were worded in a more committed manner, as in *Undoubtedly, many readers **will** challenge the view that ...* or *Of course, many will **most certainly** disagree with the assertion that ...* The decision to hedge rather than boost the assertion is important in terms of the resulting authorial stance. Also unacknowledged are the counter (*Yet*) and concede move (*Of course*). The authors do not explain how these resources, which could trigger important interpersonal meanings depending on the context, relate to entertaining objections.

By pointing out these more micro-level features, I do not mean to suggest that every stance resource needs to be identified every time discourse is examined, and for Graff and Birkenstein's aims in *They Say / I Say*, such detail may be unnecessary. However, research cited above shows that in more advanced academic writing contexts rhetorical moves like hedging, boosting, subtle countering, and conceding points are important strategies and ones with which many students struggle. Acknowledging how these meanings are expressed in text at the level of the sentence may therefore require a non-commonsense way of talking about texts. Finally, Graff and Birkenstein themselves cannot entirely avoid employing technical terms. As two instances, they refer to "embedding voice markers" (p. 70-71; 170) and "metacommentary" (p. 123-132; 176). These (or similar) terms are necessary, as I believe the authors would acknowledge, if they are to make the points about language that they need to make. In general, the degree of specialization in metalanguage is influenced by the type of meanings and the level of linguistic detail that require attention. It is also influenced, of course, by students' level of academic discourse knowledge. While Graff and Birkenstein's approach may be ideally suited for first-year university writers, working with upper-level students in specific disciplinary contexts may require more specialized terminology for making disciplinary stance moves explicit.

Returning to the first objection, how realistic is it to propose using any kind of specialized metalanguage in faculty development contexts focused on stance and reader positioning? Which linguistic concepts should be addressed and how? Above, I focused on hedging, boosting, and related concepts because these areas proved important after detailed discourse analysis of upper-level student writing. How can faculty in other contexts learn to identify meaningful patterns of language use in their own students' writing? A positive effect of this kind of analysis would be that faculty come to recognize the complexity of the writing they are asking their students to take on and to better understand the nature of the difficulties that weaker student writers experience. This kind of recognition could potentially lead to more nuanced grading and commenting practices, as well as to strategies for making stance expectations explicit when designing writing assignments.

To be sure, learning to track micro-level stance moves in disciplinary discourses is a tall order. Nevertheless, while faculty in the disciplines may not be trained in discourse analysis, they do have the clear advantage of being trained in the disciplinary discourse itself. Valued uses of language are thus an *implicit* part of their overall communicative repertoire for making meaning in disciplinary genres. The task for faculty in the disciplines, therefore, is to learn to identify these valued uses of language explicitly. I make some suggestions for assisting them to do this in the next section.

SUGGESTIONS FOR WORKING WITH FACULTY IN THE DISCIPLINES

My suggestions for working with faculty in this section are focused on two types of metalanguage about stance, one more general and the other specific. I explain how these could be useful to writing specialists who aim to assist faculty in the disciplines to track meaningful patterns of stance in their disciplinary discourses and in their students' writing.

The first, more general metalanguage comprises concepts such as stance, reader-positioning, dialogic expansion and contraction, dialogic control, authoritativeness, contrastiveness, critical distance, and discoursal alignment. Concepts such as these (which are illustrated in the Appendix) are "general" because they have to do with rhetorical effects that are abstracted away from word/phrase, sentence, and text-level patterns. They have to do with abstract qualities of stance that are constructed through recurring configurations of language use. When examining student writing, writing specialists and disciplinary faculty could use general concepts like these to guide their process of identifying and interpreting more specific patterns of language use in student work.

In terms of *how* they could use these concepts, I would suggest that the metaphorical orientation of academic writing-as-conversation, which Graff and Birkenstein, among many others in composition studies, endorse, could serve as a useful overarching framework for facilitating workshop activities. As I discuss below, this metaphorical orientation could be more useful than other metaphors about writing, such as argument-as-war (Lakoff & Johnson, 1980), especially when the task at hand is to identify patterns of stance in students' texts. This is because it offers a lens through which to introduce related conceptual metaphors about stance. These may include *reader positioning* (or moves to bring the reader into alignment with the author's views), *dialogic control* (or use of language to establish a sense of control over various participants in the discourse) and *dialogic expansion* and *contraction* (or use of language to decrease and increase authorial commitment and thus involve and guide the reader through the argument). Through the use of these dialogically-oriented concepts, other more general stance concepts can be introduced in coherent ways.

For example, an *authoritative* stance can be discussed as a quality that is achieved not just through use of highly assertive language—through *boosters*, for example—but through rhetorical strategies that work to manage a dialogic exchange among various interactants in the discourse. Connected to this, reader-positioning can be introduced as a lens through which to examine how student writers use language to engage and interact with the reader when developing their arguments and thereby establish an authoritative stance. For example, workshop participants can practice identifying textual moves for offering concessions to the reader and then countering (e.g., *It is indeed the case that ...; but ...*), identifying points of shared knowledge (e.g., *Of course, it is widely understood among compositionists that ...*), correcting potential misunderstandings (e.g., *This is not to say that ...; but rather ...*), and other strategies that extend hands of solidarity to readers, especially readers who are not already aligned with the writer's views.

In general, the writing-as-conversation metaphor, while certainly not new to writing scholars, could be useful for anchoring discussions of stance with faculty from various disciplinary contexts. Importantly, it could also lead to the formation of new questions about student writing that motivate close examination of language use in student-produced texts, i.e., to the features of language that operate to realize the abstract concepts explained above.

The second type of metalanguage is more directly tied to text-level details. While less intuitive for instructors who have not been trained in discourse analysis, this metalanguage—e.g., hedging, boosting, evidentializing, conjecturing, problematizing, and other canonical discourse analytic concepts discussed in Barton and Stygall (2002), Hyland (2004), Swales and Feak (2012), and elsewhere—might be drawn on selectively as faculty begin to notice salient patterns of language use in their own students' writing. As discussed above, identifying linguistic patterns is facilitated through a metalanguage that gives a name to specific linguistic concepts, and whichever linguistic features are discussed must be determined by the discourse context.

Before suggesting specific examples of this way of talking about stance with faculty in the disciplines, I would like to suggest that the writing-as-conversation metaphor could supplement or re-orient (rather than entirely replace) participants' existing metalanguage about writing. This is so they can practice examining student texts through lenses that are both familiar and new. Terms that might be more familiar to describe qualities of student writing, such as evaluative descriptors like *well-structured, clear, critical, engaging, formal/informal,* and *awkward,* could in fact serve as starting places for infusing faculty development workshop activities with metaphors that place emphasis on meanings related to stance. Barton (2002), for instance, explains how her motivation to figure out what types of language use contributed to the impression of "awkwardness" in student writing led to her to the linguistic concept of *evidentiality* (defined, after Chafe (1986), as attitudes toward knowledge). She then used this linguistic concept to systematically analyze stance in student writing (in Barton, 1993).

I now turn to specific examples of how faculty in the disciplines might be encouraged to track patterns of stance in their students' writing. Starting with the case of PolSci 409, the professor's term to describe effective student writing is "control." This is a concept he spoke about enthusiastically in our interview and one that he reported to be using with students when discussing writing. Understandably, however, he had some difficulty identifying specific places in students' essays where control is accomplished, as well as places in Victor's and other low-performers' essays where control wanes. Refining the concept of "control" to *dialogic control* might usefully direct his attention to meaningful patterns in his students' writing for navigating between different theoretical viewpoints. The question, that is, could subtly shift from *how a sense of control is accomplished in the text* to *how the student writer establishes control over the dialogue between theorists.* This latter question is well-suited to the particular essay assignment because the assignment required students to juxtapose two or more theoretical arguments. It required that they orchestrate a critical discussion among theorists. This can be accomplished in ways that convey varying degrees of dialogic control.

With this subtle shift in emphasis from *control* to *dialogic control*, the workshop discussion could explore how high-performing students use language to control the dialogic exchange between different theoretical perspectives. Identifying patterns of language use related to dialogic control could lead, for instance, to an examination of problematization moves. This is because the high-performers in the course often used problematization as a structuring device. That is, in order to make the transition from one theorist to another, they would often identify gaps in reasoning that could only be resolved by turning to another theorist. For example, Ethan's problematizing of Fraser's argument in 4b (above) worked as rhetorical motivation for turning the discussion to Rawls. Moving the attention down to text-level features with a focus on problematization could then open up a discussion about ways to problematize in more and less measured ways, which might then lead to the observation that hedges are useful for constructing a stance that is both contrastive and measured or "aware" of other dialogic possibilities.

In Econ 432, the instructor's metalanguage about student writing, as revealed in our interview and his comments on students' essays, is guided largely by the conceptual metaphor of argument as war (Lakoff & Johnson, 1980). In our interview, he spoke about the need for students to build, in his words, "strong," "defensible," and "airtight" arguments. He identified counterargumentation as one strategy that students could use to better defend their positions. Making this argument-as-war metaphor explicit in faculty development workshop settings could be useful for opening up discussions with faculty in other disciplines about goals for student writing. Interestingly, this particular metaphor does correspond to the highly adversarial quality of the discourse on antitrust law and economics (McCloskey, 1985/1998), a quality which is realized in the high-graded Econ 432 essays partly through repeated counterargument moves. But the argument-as-war metaphor does not account for all of the instructor's explanations of valued features of student writing.

For example, the instructor praised Ken for insightfully "step[ping] outside of economics" to make his argument. This suggests a view of academic writing as participating in a disciplinary (or interdisciplinary) conversation. It suggests that writing is a matter of staying within or stepping outside of a particular disciplinary area and thus perhaps participating in a disciplinary culture. If, therefore, the conceptual metaphor for evaluating student writing were shifted from argument-as-war to argument-as-conversation, an interesting question becomes, how might counterargumentation be seen and talked about differently? This is a question that could be put to this Econ 432 instructor. Discussions might lead toward viewing counterargumentation less in terms of defending positions or sealing up holes in arguments and more in terms of increasing argumentative complexity by engaging with alternative views and voices in the discourse.

In a faculty development workshop setting, the Econ 432 instructor could be encouraged to consider how counterargumentation correlates with taking a step back or outside of the discourse. Stemming from this discussion, different uses of countering could be introduced to workshop participants. For example, deny/counter pairs (*it is not the case that ... rather ...*) and concede/counter pairs (*yes, it is true that, but ...*)—both highly assertive maneuvers—could be discussed as reader-oriented strategies for steering the reader through the discussion and thus controlling the conversation. In contrast, hedge/counter pairs (*it could be/ possibly/perhaps ... at the same time, though ...*) could then be discussed as moves for negotiating with others' views, for opening up the conversation and then pushing it forward. This type of explicit language-based discussion would preserve the instructor's focus on counterargumentation while also shifting the concept from one metaphorical system to another, from argument-as-war to argument-as-conversation. In other words, counterargumentation moves could be explained as a rhetorical strategy for guiding the readers through the argument.

In addition to using conceptual metaphors to facilitate interaction about patterns in student writing, it would also be possible to build activities that start with instructors' comments on students' essays (rather than with the essays themselves). Instructors could be encouraged to examine patterns in their own commenting practices, perhaps with a special focus on those pertaining to language use. What types of features in student writing elicited their comments? From there, discussions could focus on how students' use of language index particular kinds of stances.

For instance, the Econ 432 instructor's comments on students' papers suggest that he was sensitive to their level of commitment when putting forth critical evaluations. This was seen, for example, in his suggestion on one essay to "use a weaker word here than 'could'." His suggestion for alternate wording was "maybe 'might' or 'conceivably could'?" Pausing on a comment like this could open up space for reflecting on the question of where in students' writing they should try to adopt a committed stance and where they should strive for a more expansive or less committed one. The instructor's comment about using a "weaker word" could have left the student confused, and so this is an example of a good opportunity to comment on rhetorical strategies in the specific context. In particular, if the larger goal is for students to construct an assertive, committed, strong argument, what exactly is the purpose of backing off from full commitment when offering a critical evaluation? Why not, as it were, use the "stronger" word? Such a question ties in directly with the metaphor of writing-as-conversation because it suggests that authoritativeness has just as much to do with manipulating dialogic space in strategic ways, with opening up space for others' views and voices, as it does defending positions by sealing up holes in arguments.

Examples of useful workshops discussions/activities could go on. But in general, the suggestion I am making is that it is important to create opportunities for meaningful interaction among disciplinary faculty and writing researchers about language use in student writing, specifically language use related to stance. This interaction can be guided by a general metalanguage about stance and reader positioning, which could help to promote conscious noticing of patterns in language in student-generated texts. (Zawacki & Habib [this volume] suggest that having a language to talk about language would have been useful for the faculty they interviewed who expressed a willingness to help their L2 students improve their writing but also frustration with their inability to diagnose the causes of the problems or how to fix them.)

CONCLUDING THOUGHTS

The principal pedagogical implication that has emerged from my own and others' linguistics work on stance in student writing is greater awareness among faculty in the disciplines of valued and less valued patterns of stance in student writing. Sharing results of text analyses is one way to foster such awareness. Another way that may have greater potential for sustainability is through faculty development workshops that are designed to assist faculty to identify subtle patterns of interpersonal meanings in their students' writing and in their responses to students' wordings. Since this second option is especially challenging considering that most faculty in the disciplines do not have prior training in text analysis, it is important that the pedagogical stakes of attending closely to micro-level meaning-making in student writing be made apparent. For instance, writing specialists can assist faculty to identify how styles of stance-taking in their students' writing operate to position the instructor-reader in certain ways—for example, as aligned or not with a shared analytic framework or with a certain kind of epistemological and attitudinal orientation to disciplinary concepts.

With a keener eye to the ways specific linguistic patterns interrelate with learning goals and epistemological values, faculty in the disciplines can become more reflexive about how and why they respond to student writing in the ways that they do. They can also learn to discuss with their students in explicit ways what rhetorical moves are valued in the course writing and why. Armed with a rich metalanguage for making connections between texts and contexts, faculty could enable high-performing students like Ken, Luis, Ethan, Eric, and Maria to draw on their discursive expertise in strategic ways to respond effectively to less familiar writing contexts. For students like Victor and Ryan, who appear to be putting forth effort in their writing but not employing the necessary rhetorical and linguistic strategies needed to create valued stances, it is doubly important that faculty be explicit about their genre expectations and work with these students to closely read genre exemplars, to identify how patterns of language are working, and to learn to monitor and evaluate their own discursive choices.

NOTES

1. In systemic functional linguistics (SFL), the *theme* is the "point of departure" for the message of a text (Halliday, 1994, p. 94). The theme includes the grammatical subject of the sentence as well as any material that may precede the subject, for example circumstantial adjuncts (e.g., **From there** *Microsoft Excel and Matlab were used to analyze data.*), fronted dependent clauses (e.g., **If people were just as aware of the value in their endemic biodiversity**, *curbing the spread of exotic species would take an easier turn),* and other options.
2. There are, of course, other stance differences that can be identified in the two texts above. Ethan's stance is, for instance, more critically distant than Victor's. But for now I point out that Victor's stance of assumed agreement is one reason his essay also does not use hedging strategies. That is, he does not need to mitigate the force of his critiques because he does not develop critiques.
3. Ryan's native-language is Korean, and the professor's sense was that Ryan's writing is more representative of "1.5 Generation" writers than it is L2 writers because, while his control of syntax, local coherence and cohesion is advanced, the register he selects is often highly conversational. This conversational register can be seen in example 6. I grouped Ryan as an L2 writer in my study because he responded that English is not his native language in a pre-term course survey.

REFERENCES

Barton, E. L. (1993). Evidentials, argumentation, and epistemological stance. *College English, 55,* 745-769.

Barton, E. L. (2002). Inductive discourse analysis: Discovering rich features. In E. L. Barton & G. Stygall (Eds.), *Discourse studies in composition* (pp. 19-42). Cresskill, NJ: Hampton Press.

Barton, E. L. and Stygall, G. (Eds.) (2002). *Discourse studies in composition*. Cresskill, NJ: Hampton Press.

Chafe, W. (1986). Evidentiality in English conversation and academic writing. In W. Chafe & J. Nichols (Eds.), *Evidentiality: The linguistic coding of epistemology* (pp. 261-272). Norwood, NJ: Ablex.

Chafe, W. & Nichols, J. (Eds.) (1986). *Evidentiality: The linguistic coding of epistemology*. Norwood, NJ: Ablex.

Chang, P. (2010). *Taking an effective authorial stance in academic writing: Inductive learning for second language writers using a stance corpus* (Unpublished doctoral dissertation). University of Michigan, Ann Arbor. Deep Blue Dissertation and Theses database. Retrieved from http://hdl.handle.net/2027.42/77860

Charles, M. (2003). "This mystery": A corpus-based study of the use of nouns to construct stance in theses from two contrasting disciplines. *Journal of English for Academic Purposes, 2*, 313-326.

Cheng, X. & Steffensen, M. S. (1996). Metadiscourse: A technique for improving student writing. *Research in the Teaching of English, 30*(2), 149-181.

Coffin, C. (2002). The voices of history: Theorizing the interpersonal semantics of historical discourses. *Text, 22*(4), 503-528.

Concha, S., & Paratore, J. (2011). Local coherence in persuasive writing: An exploration of Chilean students' metalinguistic knowledge, writing process, and writing products. *Written Communication, 28*(1), 34-69.

Engelbretson, R. (Ed.). (2007). *Stancetaking in discourse*. Amsterdam: Benjamins.

Feak, C. B. (2008) Culture shock? Genre shock? Paper presented at the British association of lecturers in English for academic purposes. University of Reading, Whiteknights, UK.

Graff, G. & Birkenstein, C. (2006). *They say, I say: The moves that matter in academic writing*. New York: Norton.

Halliday, M. A. K. (1994). *An introduction to functional grammar* (2nd ed.). London: Arnold.

Hunston, S. & Thompson, G. (2000). *Evaluation in text: Authorial stance and the construction of discourse*. London: Oxford University Press.

Hyland, K. (2004). *Disciplinary discourses: Social interactions in academic writing*. Ann Arbor: University of Michigan Press.

Hyland, K. (2005). Stance and engagement: A model of interaction in academic discourse. *Discourse studies, 7*(2), 173-192.

Hyland, K. (2011). Disciplines and discourses: Social interactions in the construction of knowledge. In D. Starke-Meyerring, A. Paré, N. Artemeva, M. Horne, & L. Yousoubova (Eds.), *Writing in knowledge societies* (pp. 193-214). Fort Collins, Colorado: WAC Clearinghouse and Parlor Press. Retrieved from http://wac.colostate.edu/books/winks

Hyland, K. & Milton, J. (1997). Qualifications and certainty in L1 and L2 students' writing. *Journal of Second Language Writing, 6*(2), 183-205.

Jaffe, A. (Ed.). (2009). *Stance: Sociolinguistic perspectives*. New York/Oxford: Oxford University Press.

Johnstone, B. (2009). Stance, style, and the linguistic individual. In A. Jaffe (Ed.), *Stance: Sociolinguistic perspectives* (pp. 29-52). New York/Oxford: Oxford University Press.

Lakoff, G. & Johnson, M. (1980). *Metaphors we live by*. Chicago: Chicago University Press.

Lancaster, Z. (2011). Interpersonal stance in L1 and L2 students' argumentative writing in economics: Implications for faculty development in WAC/WID programs. *Across the Disciplines, 8*(4). Retrieved from http://wac.colostate.edu/atd/ell/lancaster.cfm

Lancaster, Z. (2012). *Stance and reader positioning in upper-level student writing in political theory and economics* (Unpublished doctoral dissertation). University of Michigan, Ann Arbor.

Macken-Horarik, M. & Morgan, W. (2011). Towards a metalanguage adequate to linguistic achievement in post-structuralism and English: Reflections on voicing in the writing of secondary students. *Linguistics and Education, 22*, 133-149.

Martin, J. R. & Rose, D. (2007). *Working with discourse: Meaning beyond the clause* (2nd ed.). London: Continuum.

Martin, J. R. & White, P. R. R. (2005). *The language of evaluation: Appraisal in English*. New York: Palgrave Macmillan.

McCloskey, D. N. (1998]). *The rhetoric of economics*. Madison, WI: University of Wisconsin Press. (Original work published 1985)

Perales-Escudero, M. D. (2011). *Teaching and learning critical reading with transnational texts at a Mexican university: An emergentist case study* (Unpublished doctoral dissertation). University of Michigan, Ann Arbor. Deep Blue Dissertation and Theses database. Retrieved from http://hdl.handle.net/2027.42/86301

Perales-Escudero, M. D. & Swales, J. M. (2011). Tracing convergence and divergence in pairs of Spanish and English research article abstracts: The case of *Ibérica*. *Ibérica, 21*, 49-70.

Schleppegrell, M. J. (2004). Technical writing in a second language: The role of grammatical metaphor. In L. J. Ravelli & R. A. Ellis (Eds.), *Analysing aca-*

demic writing: Contextualized frameworks (pp. 172-189). New York/London: Continuum.

Schleppegrell, M. J. & de Oliveira, L. C. (2006). An integrated language and content approach for history teachers. *Journal of English for Academic Purposes, 5*, 254-268.

Soliday, M. (2004). Reading student writing with Anthropologists: Stance and judgment in college writing. *College Composition and Communication, 56*(1), 72-93.

Soliday, M. (2011). *Everyday genres: Writing assignments across the disciplines.* Carbondale & Edwardsville, IL: Southern Illinois University Press.

Swales, J. M. & Feak, C. B. (2012). *Academic writing for graduate students* (3rd ed.). Ann Arbor, MI: University of Michigan Press.

Tang, R. (2009). A dialogic account of authority in academic writing. In M. Charles, D. Pecorari, & S. Hunston (Eds.), *Academic writing: At the interface of corpus and discourse* (pp. 170-190). New York/ London: Continuum.

Tardy, C. (2009). *Building Genre Knowledge.* West Lafayette, IN: Parlor Press.

Thompson, G. (2001). Interaction in academic writing: Learning to argue with the reader. *Applied Linguistics, 22*(1), 58-78.

Turner, J. (1999). Academic literacies and the discourse of transparency. In: C. Jones, J. Turner, & B. Street (Eds.) *Student writing in the University: Cultural and Epistemological Issues.* Amsterdam & Philadelphia: John Benjamins.

White, P. R. R. (2003). Beyond modality and hedging: A dialogic view of the language of intersubjective stance. *Text, 23*(2), 259-284.

Wu, S. M. (2006). Creating a contrastive rhetorical stance: Investigating the strategy of problematization in students' argumentation. *RELC Journal, 37*, 329-353.

Wu, S. M. (2007). The use of engagement resources in high- and low-rated undergraduate geography essays. *Journal of English for Academic Purposes, 6*, 254-271.

APPENDIX: EXPLANATION OF KEY TERMS AND CONCEPTS

Confusing "Teacher Talk" about Stance:

Be critical: offer judgments and critical evaluations
… *but don't be judgmental or biased*
Display excitement and commitment to your argument
… *but be objective*
… *and try not to use "I" or other self-mentions*
Use your own words, your own voice

... but don't be colloquial and address the wrong audience
Write assertively and with authority
... but be sure to allow for other viewpoints
... and don't forget you're not yet an expert
Engage with others' views and voices
... but don't just summarize what others have said
Be interesting, experiment with new argument strategies
... but be sure to write clearly and concisely

Stance: refers to the ways that writers—as they go about analyzing and evaluating things, making assertions and recommendations, providing evidence and justifications and so forth—project an authorial presence in their texts, one that conveys attitudes and feelings and that interacts with imagined readers by recognizing their views, identifying points of shared knowledge, conceding limitations, and otherwise positioning them as aligned with or resistant to the views being advanced in the text.

Reader-positioning: the reader-oriented side of stance. Reader-positioning is the use of stance strategies for engaging and interacting with the imagined reader, including marking concessions and counters, identifying points of shared knowledge, correcting potential misunderstandings, acknowledging points of contention, and other strategies designed to bring the reader into alignment with the writer's views.

EXAMPLES OF STANCE AND READER POSITIONING MOVES IN PUBLISHED ACADEMIC DISCOURSE

These example texts are discussed in Ken Hyland's (2005) article "Stance and Engagement: A Model of Interaction in Academic Discourse," *Discourse Studies*, 7(2), 173-192.

> *I argue* that their treatment is superficial because, ***despite appearances***, it relies solely on a sociological, as opposed to an ethical, orientation to develop a response. (Sociology)

> Chesterton was ***of course*** wrong to suppose that Islam denied "even souls to women." (Philosophy)

> This measurement is distinctly different from the ***more familiar*** NMR pulsed field gradient measurement of solvent

> self-diffusion. (Physics)

> Our results *suggest* that rapid freeze and thaw rates during artificial experiments in the laboratory *may* cause artifactual formation of embolism. Such experiments *may* not ... (Biology)

> ... two quantities are *rather important* and, for this reason, the way they were measured is re-explained here. (Mechanical engineering)

SOME KEY DISCURSIVE RESOURCES OF STANCE

Hedging: a stance-taking strategy used to reduce authorial commitment to the proposition being forwarded, for the purpose of expressing cautiousness and/or opening up discursive space for alternative views. Hedging is accomplished through low-probability modal expressions (*may, might, could*), appearance-based evidential verbs (*seems, appears, suggests*), low-certainty adverbs (*perhaps, possibly*) and other linguistic resources.

Evidentializing: a type of hedging that expresses sustained consideration of evidence. e.g.:

> In national terms, Pabst became the third largest brewer in 1961, three years after the acquisition, with 5.83% of the national beer market. These numbers *suggest* that the anticompetitive damage done to the beer market, no matter how it is defined geographically, must have been minimal.

Conjecturing: a type of hedging that expresses an internalized process grounded in the subjectivity of the authorial voice. e.g., "Regulation of prices **may** be left best to companies with more stable cost structures."

Boosting: a stance-taking strategy used to increase authorial commitment to the proposition being forwarded, for the purpose of drawing attention to the importance of the topic and tightening up discursive space. Boosting is accomplished through the expressions of certainty, as in *strongly, clearly, countless*, and *completely*.

Dialogic expansion: The use of various linguistic resources, including hedges, attributions, rhetorical questions, and others, for releasing the author from full commitment or responsibility for a proposition. e.g.

However, this case is ***not without*** concerns. There is the ***possibility*** for abuse ***if*** the producer sets different maximum prices for different retailers, allowing some to reap higher profits. There is also a ***possibility*** that for new retailers to enter the market they would have to charge higher prices initially, in which case a maximum price ***could*** deter competition. It ***appears***, then, that maximum price fixing does the greatest harm when set below a competitive level. In Case 4 it ***could potentially*** do harm to small retailers trying to enter the market, but does so for the benefit of consumers and the producer. ***Based purely on the models, it appears*** that, ***at the very least***, maximum prices deserve a Rule of Reason approach to evaluate their cost and benefits.

Dialogic contraction: The use of various linguistic resources, including boosters, denials, counters, and others, for increasing the author's commitment and closing down space for alternative views. e.g.

> If what Foucault says is true ... should we abandon the idea of a human reasoning, able to reflect over choices? ***My answer is no***. ***I do not deny*** that we all have notions of what is right and wrong behavior and many of these notions are without a doubt acquired through Socialization .... ***However*** we would ***hardly*** accept that every action is strictly a result of Socialization.

Problematization: A rhetorical strategy for "showing that a prevailing assumption, idea, view, or situation needs reexamination, reconceptualization, or reevaluation of some kind" (Barton, 1993, p. 748). Problematization is often used to prepare the ground for the author's research and argumentative contribution to an ongoing discourse.

SOME ABSTRACT STANCE QUALITIES VALUED IN ACADEMIC DISCOURSES

Critical distance: a quality of stance marked by interpersonal detachment toward the entities that are being analyzed and evaluated. This quality can be accomplished by some hedging devices. It can also be accomplished through the use of various "embedded" wordings, for example when writers use wordings to objectify their own mental processes. e.g.

> Young's concept of the "five faces of oppression" offers ***a***

perspective from which to view the various relationships in the novel as ones that are typical of societies imbued with systemic oppression. Young's definition of oppression is also useful *in examining* the different ways in which, and to what degree, different groups suffer from oppression in the novel.

Contrastiveness: a quality of stance marked contrast against others' views and voices. Frequent use of contrastive connectors (e.g., *however, nevertheless, but,* etc.) and denials (e.g., *it is not, never, failed,* etc.) index a contrastive stance, as do frequent problematization moves.

Dialogic control: a quality of stance marked by control over a conversation with the reader and other discourse participants. It can be achieved through strategic deployment of dialogical expansion and contraction for regulating the dialogic space. Problematization moves can help to construct a sense of dialogic control, as can more sentence-level features like deny/counter strategies (e.g., *I am not suggesting that ... but rather that ...*) and hedge/counter strategies (e.g., *There is a possibility that ... However ...*). Further resources can include strategic transition devices (or "roadmapping"), as well as elaboration strategies (e.g., *in other words, that is, what I mean is that*) and exemplification strategies (*for instance/example*).

Discoursal alignment: a quality of stance marked by assimilation of the language of the discourse with the writer's "own language." It is often accomplished by use of language that frames evaluations in terms of disciplinary constructs while also positively evaluating those constructs, conveying assimilation of the disciplinary discourse. e.g.

> The realities raised by Fraser offer *important complexities* to Young's political discourse. Young provides *a useful schematic* for understanding oppression both in Coetzee's Disgrace and contemporary society.

Authoritativeness: a very general quality of stance, one that is highly context-sensitive and construed through a configuration of various linguistic resources. In many academic discourses, a sense of authoritativeness may be related to such qualities as critical distance, contrastiveness, dialogic control, and discoursal alignment.

CHAPTER 12

IN RESPONSE TO TODAY'S "FELT NEED": WAC, FACULTY DEVELOPMENT, AND SECOND LANGUAGE WRITERS

Michelle Cox
Dartmouth College

With increased awareness of the presence of second language writers in courses and programs across the disciplines comes increased requests for faculty development focused on second language writing. Drawing from scholarship on second language writing pedagogy and theory, as well as the author's experience as an instructor of ESL writing and a WAC program director, this chapter presents approaches to working with faculty on issues related to L2 writers. After discussing alliances WAC program leaders can make with other groups on campus who work with L2 writers, this chapter presents a framework for thinking about the differences in L2 writing when compared to writing by native English speakers and approaches for working with faculty during consultations and workshops, with specific attention to shifting faculty perspectives on L2 writing from a difference-as-deficit stance (Canagarajah, 2002) to a difference-accommodated stance, and ultimately, a difference-as-resource stance (Canagarajah, 2002). Throughout the chapter, specific workshop activities and materials are shared.

My experience with teaching ESL students is that they have often not received adequate English instruction to complete the required essay texts and papers in my classes. I have been particularly dismayed when I find that they have already completed 2 ESL courses and have no knowledge of the parts of speech or the terminology that is used in correcting English grammar on papers. I am certainly not in a position to teach English in my classes. (The problem has been particularly acute with Chinese/S. E. Asian students.) These students may have adequate intelligence to do well in the courses, but their language skills result in low grades. (I cannot give a good grade to a student who can only generate one or two broken sentences during a ten-minute slide comparison.)

—Professor of art (as quoted in Zamel, 1995)

For the research paper for the English class they are in for getting your writing skill better, so they will be more patient. But for the computer science class, no. They expect you to know everything, to have good writing skills. If you do not that's not their problem, right? You should go back to the ELI [English Language Institute].

—Undergraduate student enrolled in writing-intensive course (quoted in Wolfe-Quintero & Segade, 1999)

Teachers in the disciplines who are told they do not need to know about grammar in order to use writing in their classes feel betrayed when faced with a non-native speaker's grammatical and syntactic tangles in a writing-to-learn assignment. Many WAC directors themselves feel at the edge of their competence in dealing with such situations.

—Susan McLeod & Eric Miraglia, 2001

The above passages illustrate a growing tension in Writing Across the Curriculum (WAC) program administration: faculty are becoming increasingly aware of (and perhaps frustrated by) the presence of second language (L2) students in their classrooms and reach out to WAC program leaders for direction, L2 students enrolled in writing-intensive courses want more writing support from their instructors across the curriculum, and WAC program directors are not always sure how to respond.[1] Though research that engages both WAC and L2 writing has proliferated, the question that remains central to WAC program administrators is the question of how to implement faculty development focused on L2 writing. We have seen a number of what I term "calls to action" (Cox, 2011) —calls by scholars, typically L2 writing scholars, for WAC campus leaders to pay more attention to L2 writers in our program administration, scholarship, and faculty development (Cox, 2011; Hall,

2009; Johns, 2001; Matsuda & Jablonski, 2000). The special issue of *Across the Disciplines*, "Writing across the Curriculum and Second Language Writers: Cross-Field Research, Theory, and Program Development" (2011), which I co-edited with Terry Myers Zawacki, begins to address questions of how to develop linguistically and culturally inclusive program administration, how to inform WAC research with L2 writing scholarship, and how to investigate the writing practices and experiences of L2 students as they write across the curriculum, as does this edited collection.

But questions around how to implement faculty development remain. How can WAC program directors help faculty who come to us with concerns and questions about working with L2 writers? What do we tell faculty about L2 writing pedagogy, culturally sensitive approaches to writing assignment design, and approaches for responding to and assessing L2 student writing? How do we convince faculty not only to infuse their pedagogy with writing, an already challenging task in some cases, but also to create linguistically and culturally inclusive classrooms? And how do we WAC professionals, who often feel "at the edge of [our] competence" in this area (McLeod & Miraglia, 2001), convince ourselves that we know enough about L2 writing to do so? In this chapter, I draw from research on L2 writing development and pedagogy, as well as my own experiences as a L2 writing scholar and a former WAC program director at Bridgewater State University,[2] to share approaches to working with faculty on issues related to L2 writers. While research and theory on working with L2 writers inform this chapter, I highlight practice—concrete activities, sources of information, and handout materials that WAC program directors and L2 writing specialists can use during faculty workshops and consultations.

ONE INSTITUTIONAL CONTEXT

Bridgewater State University (BSU) is a teaching-mission comprehensive master's state university with, as of fall 2011, 11,294 students (with 9,552 at the undergraduate level), 316 full-time faculty and approximately 900 adjunct faculty (BSU, 2011b). I launched BSU's WAC program in spring of 2007, a program that the provost asked me to initiate in response to a newly implemented core curriculum that required that students complete a series of writing-intensive courses. Like other regional universities and community colleges, BSU enrolls relatively few international visa students: between 2006 and 2011, there were between 97 and 120 of these students enrolled (BSU, 2011b). And also like most universities, BSU does not keep track of the number of US resident L2 students. However, the local region from which 95% of BSU students are drawn (BSU, 2011b) is rich in linguistic and cultural diversity, as it is home to many immigrant communities. School profile data from the cities and towns that surround BSU show that between 21.4% and 43.9% of the students use English as a second language with 52% of these students speaking Spanish as their first language (Massachusetts Department of Education, 2011). Given this diversity, from the start of BSU's WAC program, attention to L2 student writing was interwoven into WAC programming, faculty development workshops, and faculty consultations. Below, I describe how I found allies to partner with in this work.

NATURAL ALLIES

Those charged with starting a new WAC program are often cautioned by experienced WAC directors to first get a lay of the land: pay attention to who on campus is already invested in student writing, who in the past has already worked on WAC initiatives, and who is doing related work in faculty development. We know that it is critical to do this groundwork before initiating a new WAC program so that we don't step on toes, so that we build on work already done, and so that we create a network of allies, critical for collaboration. This step may be even more important for initiating faculty development related to second language writing. Unlike other areas of writing, WAC directors are often not the experts on campus when it comes to L2 students. Many campuses have an English Language Institute (ELI), an English as a Second Language (ESL) Program, ESL sections of first-year composition, an international student services office, a diversity center, and/or a center for international and global partnerships. At BSU, I worked with Second Language Services (an office that sets up conversation partners for international L2 students), the First Year Writing Program, the Office of Teaching and Learning, the Office of Institutional Research, the Office of Institutional Diversity, and the Office of Undergraduate Research when creating and implementing faculty development related to L2 writing and writers. These partners and allies helped me find information about L2 students at BSU, provided venues for faculty development on L2 writing, and collaborated with me to promote linguistically and culturally inclusive pedagogy. Many of these offices are natural allies for WAC, while some of the others, like the offices related to linguistic and cultural diversity, may not typically be thought of as WAC allies, and yet they too can be powerful partners in creating culturally and linguistically inclusive pedagogies.

An important first step for WAC directors interested in creating such programming is to reach out to those directing, staffing, and teaching within programs like these, for several reasons: (1) to learn from information gathered on international and/or multilingual students on your campus; (2) to learn about other faculty development efforts related to L2 students; and (3) to form partnerships for researching L2 writers on campus and offering faculty development. These stakeholders, who share a focus on or interest in multilingual and multicultural students, may be brought together as a working group or taskforce, or, if there isn't the means to organize a formal group, serve individually as potential collaborators whom the WAC director may call upon to co-lead a workshop or present on a particular topic during a workshop.

But what expertise do we, as WAC program directors, bring to this group? In addition to our knowledge of faculty development and the institutional landscape, the important piece we bring is our perspective on student writing. Many ELIs, ESL courses, and ESL sections of first-year composition (FYC) are led from an applied linguistics perspective and focus more on the structure of the English language—grammar, usage, syntax, vocabulary—and on other language skills—speaking, listening, and reading—than on writing (Matsuda, 1999; Zawacki & Cox, 2011). In fact, at first, conversations on ESL writing with this group may focus solely on grammar, with requests for the WAC director to enforce *grammar across the curriculum*, a perspective reflecting a structural view of language. As I will discuss further, however, the philosophies of many WAC programs—with their focus on writing as process, as a form of expression and communication, and as a mode of learning—are effective pedagogies for supporting L2 writers.

A FRAMEWORK FOR FACULTY DEVELOPMENT

In my experience as a WAC director, I have found it critical to first understand the assumptions that underlie faculty attitudes toward L2 writers before deciding on an approach for working with faculty. As reflected in the quote from the art professor used to open this chapter, faculty who come to us to discuss L2 student writers may first come out of frustration with the number of surface-level errors in the writing, with writing that appears disorganized, and with writing that seems uncritical. Canagarajah (2002), in *Critical Academic Writing and Multilingual Students*, has argued that these frustrations emerge from a tendency to see the writing of native English speaking (NES) students as setting the bar, so that differences in L2 writing are then seen as problematic, as indicative of "deficits" in L2 student writing. This "difference-as-deficit" stance is the perspective taken when L2 writers' "distance from the English language and Anglo-American culture has been treated as depriving them of many essential aptitudes required for successful academic literacy practices" (p. 217). Canagarajah argues that this perspective affects not only how L2 students' writing is viewed, but also how their thinking is viewed: "Some have gone further to stigmatize multilingual writers as illogical in thinking and incoherent in communication, by virtue of their deficient L1 and native culture" (p. 217). In fact, in her research on faculty attitudes on L2 writers, Zamel (1995) observed that faculty sometimes conflated what they termed "bad language" with "insufficient cognitive development" (p. 509), equating linguistic ability in a second language with intelligence. (Some of the faculty interviewed by Ives et al. [this volume] expressed this very concern.) Canagarajah (2002) suggests that, in place of this "limiting" stance, we move toward a "difference-as-resource" stance, in which we "respect and value the linguistic and cultural peculiarities our students may display, rather than suppressing them" (p. 218). In this stance, the focus shifts from deficits to strengths, emphasizing what L2 students *can* do with language rather than what they cannot.

While research that maps the linguistic strengths of L2 students is scant, there are a few points we can draw from the literature. In her study on L2 student-faculty interactions, Leki (2006) reported that faculty described L2 students as having stronger vocabulary acquisition skills than NES students, giving them an advantage when learning discipline-specific discourse (p. 143). Leki (2006) also reported that faculty in her study noted the "cultural sophistication" of L2 students, due their cross-cultural experiences (p. 143). Jordan (2008), in his study of the rhetorical competencies of L2 students, has described the ways in which they draw on their cross-cultural knowledge as well as rhetorical skills when working with NES students in peer review groups. Further, given the experiences L2 students have had writing across multiple cultures, educational systems, languages, and communities, it stands to reason that they have gained rhetorical flexibility, astuteness, and savvy (Cox & Ortmeier-Hooper, 2008).

During faculty development, my goal is to move faculty toward the difference-as-resource stance. However, the leap from difference-as-deficit to difference-as-resource is a large one, so I find it useful to consider a third, middle stance: difference-accommodated. In this stance, faculty understand that there will be syntactic, rhetorical, and cultural differences in L2 writing, but seek to accommodate L2 students in some way. While the difference-as-resource stance asks faculty to transform their pedagogy, the difference-accommodated stance asks them to make adjustments to their pedagogy, representing an important incremental step. Below, I describe how I move faculty from a difference-as-deficit approach toward a difference-accommodated approach, and, ultimately, a difference-as-resource approach.

MOVING FACULTY FROM A DIFFERENCE-AS-DEFICIT STANCE

The best approaches to addressing frustration with L2 writers, I find, are to create empathy for L2 students and share information about L2 writing development. One of the most valuable strategies for creating empathy is to put the faculty member in the L2 writer's shoes, using an activity first suggested by Leki (1992) in *Understanding ESL Writers*. So, for example, when I lead a workshop on L2 writing, I begin by asking participants to raise their hand if they ever studied a foreign language. Usually, all hands go up. I then give a freewriting prompt. (My most recent prompt, given to writing center tutors on the heels of a winter storm that cut off power to most of the area—in fact, the campus was running on generators when I arrived—was this: "Write about an experience or memory related to snow.") First, I ask participants to respond to the prompt in their second language and tell them they will have five minutes. I say everything I would usually say when giving students a freewriting prompt: Don't worry about grammar or word choice; I won't be collecting these; you won't be required to read this aloud; write without stopping; if you run out of things to say, write, "I can't think of what to say next" until something comes to you. After five minutes of freewriting, I ask them to respond to the same prompt in their first language. After another five minutes, I ask them to do one more freewrite: to reflect on the differences between the two experiences, focusing on how they felt during the two experiences, what they wrote about each time, and the length and level of depth of each piece. I then ask participants to report out, based on this reflection. Invariably, participants tell me that they felt much less stress writing in their first language, that even though I told them not to worry about grammar and word choice, they did worry about these issues when writing in their second language, that they could not write about what they wanted in their second language because they didn't have the vocabulary to express it, that their writing in their second language was far briefer than the writing they produced in their first language, that they felt embarrassed when they got stuck when writing in their second language, because they didn't even have the ability to write "I can't think of what to say next." This is a highly effective exercise, as the comments I've just listed are the same ones I hear from L2 students.

At BSU, I had an advantage over many WAC directors at other institutions in that I not only directed a WAC program, but I also taught sections of FYC designated for ESL writers. So, when the faculty describe their frustrations in trying to write in a second language, I tell them how their experiences mirror those experienced by students in my classes. Workshop leaders do not need to have direct experience with L2 students to make this move. Instead, they may follow this exercise with materials that present the voices of L2 students or information on L2 writing development and language acquisition, and then ask participants to reflect on how the information presented connects with their experience during this exercise.

The voices of L2 students shared during the workshop may come from a variety of sources: surveys conducted on your campus, quotes by L2 students captured in the literature, literacy narratives by L2 writers (published or from campus), or films (either publicly available or from campus). The allies I described above may be good resources for such materials. Below, I have provided samples from a workshop handout that I compiled from a language and literacy questionnaire given to an ESL section of FYC (see Appendix A for the full handout):

> I have never taken a class that focuses only on writing. In my ESL classes we did very short writing assignments. The longuest [sic] piece of writing I've written in English is one paragraph. In my ESL classes we read short paragraphs and answered basic questions. [...] It is easier for me to understand English when I hear it or read it. It is more difficult for me to speak and write because I have trouble choosing the correct words. —Mexican student, who took ESL courses at a college in California

> I haven't received any writing instruction in English. I studied reading for TOEFL Test, so the longest text I've read English is TOEFL text book. —Japanese student, who went to an English Language Institute in the US

> [In this course] I hope I achieve English obstacles in my life as much as I can.

> [In this course] I would like to learn writing as American. Sometimes I write dialy [sic] in English but I can't do well so I would like to practice.

These voices, describing the students' past experiences with writing in English and goals as writers, inform faculty about their own students, as well as create empathy. I have also created handouts from published material. The following are examples from a handout I created drawing on Zawacki and Habib's (2010) article on the experiences of L2 students writing across the curriculum (see Appendix B for the full handout):

> In America, when I write totally different style of paper, the professor say, "Where are you from? How did you get into this college? Your writing is behind the line, so you can't really catch up to the class." So, I don't know how to figure that out. —Yoon, student from S. Korea

> I would really love to learn nice words, because I do have ideas, and I do want to put something down, but I am short of words. —Ayesha, student from Pakistan

> When you ultimately succeed in writing is when you have your own accent. When I speak, my accent reflects who I am and where I come from. Well, I want my writing to reflect me in that way. —Tonka, student from Bulgaria

Studies by Zamel (1995), Zamel and Spack (2004), and Leki (1995, 1999, 2001, 2007), along with chapters in this collection, can also provide powerful voices of L2 students.

I have also made of use of videos and literacy narratives that are available publicly. A video I often turn to is *Writing Across Borders*, written and directed by Wayne Robertson and produced by the Oregon State University Center for Writing and Learning and Writing Intensive Curriculum programs, which features L2 undergraduate and graduate students as well as L2 writing scholars speaking to such issues as second language acquisition, culturally distinct patterns of organization, and cultural approaches to argument and critique, as well as information on how to respond and assess L2 writing. I have shown the entire 32-minute video during a workshop or sometimes just one of the 10-minute sections (each section is available on YouTube). Several literacy narratives are also available, through publications and YouTube. The following literacy narratives, for example, are all by first-year L2 students:

- Jun Yang's "Lost in the Puzzles" (2010), describes the student's challenges moving between Chinese, English, and "Chenglish," which she describes as the "language of birds" (published in Cox, Jordan, Ortmeier-Hooper, & Schwartz, *Reinventing Identities in Second Language Writing*)

- Jean Mervius' "I Am a Survivor" (2011), describes the student's experience surviving the 2010 earthquake in Haiti, and then negotiating immigration to the US, learning English, and becoming a college student.
- Wilson Castillo, "Losing Was Never an Option" (2011), describes the student's experience immigrating alone to the US from the Dominican Republic at age 11, without knowing English, to escape poverty and illiteracy.

These kinds of videos and literacy narratives help faculty understand the challenges of learning a second language from the perspectives of L2 students. Whether I use a handout or video material depicting voices of L2 students, I follow up on this material by asking participants to write about what surprises them, how these voices connect to their experiences working with L2 students, and what questions these passages raise for them about second language writing.

It is also important to share information from the literature about L2 writing development, as faculty need not only to have empathy for L2 writers, but also to understand that L2 writers are not a monolithic group but have a wide range of linguistic, educational, cultural, and literacy history backgrounds that have an impact on language acquisition, and that language acquisition itself is a long and complicated process. Further, some faculty will be more persuaded by data and research than by narratives and testimony by L2 students. To provide information about L2 writers and writing, I use a handout I created that highlights key differences between two broad categories of L2 students—international visa students and permanent resident students—and that also focuses on the complexity of learning and writing in a second language that cuts across these two L2 categories (see Appendix C for the handout). My goal with this handout is to show that second language acquisition is a long process and that native-like writing cannot, and should not, be the goal. In fact, it is unethical to demand native-like (or error-free) writing from L2 students. To do so is to require L2 students to do something that NES are not required to do: pay for copy-editing, as writing centers, rightly so, do not provide copy-editing services for students (a fact that some faculty may not know). I also want faculty to question the goal of asking L2 students to write in standard written English. I point out that, just as we expect L2 students to speak with an accent, we can expect them to write with an accent (a point also made in Leki, 1992, and Zawacki et al., 2007). I use the following example: if we were to go to a conference presentation given by a multilingual speaker, and if we were to comment that the presentation wasn't very good because the speaker spoke with an accent, we'd be seen as prejudiced. And yet, it's been seen as acceptable to make a similar kind of statement in relation to differences in writing that are related to written accent.

It is also important to share with faculty data on L2 students on campus, particularly the number of L2 students enrolled at the institution, the numbers of students enrolled in each program, and national origins and languages of these students. All institutions are required to maintain data on international visa students, and this information is typically available through the institutional research office. In fact, universities often include information about the number of countries and languages represented on its campus as part of their advertising campaigns to showcase the institution as multicultural and globalized. These data are also collected on the *Open Doors* website, which makes available profiles of different states as well. It is more difficult to come by data on residential L2 students, as admissions offices are prohibited from collecting data on student linguistic background or English language status, as this information may be used to discriminate against students from minority groups. However, for institutions that draw heavily from the local region, you may construct a picture of the residential L2 population of students on your campus by collecting data on local K-12 school systems through the Department of Education (DOE) website, since school districts do collect information on the number of English Language Learners (ELL), English Limited Proficiency (ELP) students, countries of origin, and home languages. It's also possible that an ESL office, the first year writing program, or the writing center on your campus collects language data on L2 students. Many of the available sources of data, however, are limited in the information they provide. For instance, with respect to information found on DOE's website, according to the terms used by the DOE, a student may move from ELP to ELL, but once tagged as ELL, the student will always be marked as ELL, even if that student exited the ESL programs while in elementary school. Further, this data will tell you little about the students' literacy experiences—their experiences with reading, writing, speaking, and listening in their different languages. For this type of information, you may need to construct a survey that asks students to report on various strengths and experiences with English. A powerful example of such a survey, developed by Angela Dadak at American University, is available at **http://wac.colostate.edu/atd/ell/cox.cfm**.

WORKING WITH FACULTY TO ACCOMMODATE DIFFERENCE

Once faculty learn more about L2 writers and feel empathy for these students, they are generally ready to make changes to their pedagogy to accommodate them, but their first reaction may be that they feel overwhelmed. They may tell you that they feel that they have to start over—that they feel that everything they knew about supporting student writers has to be thrown out the window. Not true. Research has shown that many of the same pedagogical approaches for writing in an L1 are effective for supporting writing in an L2. Second language students benefit from clear and detailed writing assignments (Hirsch, this volume; Reid & Kroll, 1995), from seeing samples of student writing from the same assignment (Hirsh, this volume; Leki, 1995), and from teacher-student conferences on their writing (Ewert, 2009; Phillips, this volume). It has proven beneficial for L2 students to receive feedback focused on expression and communication as well as structure, grammar, and usage (Goldstein, 2005; Hyland, 1998; Jacobs, Curtis, Braine, & Huang, 1998; Phillips, this volume; Reid, 1994; Truscott, 1999; Wolfe-Quintero & Sedage, 1999), participate in peer-review groups (Berg, 1999; Tsui & Ng, 2000; Zhu, 2001), and engage in writing-to-learn activities (Fishman & McCarthy, 2001; Phillips, this volume). However, there are adjustments that faculty can make to their pedagogy that will better support the L2 students in their courses, particularly in relation to giving feedback, peer review, writing-to-learn activities, writing assignment design, and evaluation of writing assignments.

FEEDBACK TO L2 STUDENT WRITING

The advice WAC specialists tend to give to faculty when working with any student – comment on both content issues and structural issues, focus on two or three "error trends" in a draft rather than comment on every error, and give both positive feedback and feedback oriented toward revision—also work to support second language students. I have noticed, though, that faculty often leave this advice behind when reading and responding to L2 student writing. Faculty unaccustomed to giving feedback to L2 writers tend to take either a hands-off approach, reading past all errors and responding only to content, or a heavy-handed approach, marking every syntactic, usage, and grammatical error (Matsuda & Cox, 2009). Neither approach is very helpful, as the first doesn't help a student improve as a writer, and the second can be overwhelming to the writer. Second language students, do, however, require feedback on English language issues, as they are still in the process of acquiring the language. Ferris, a leading scholar on error feedback in L2 writing, has demonstrated that most L2 students need only to have their errors pointed out to them, through circling or checkmarks in the margins, and then they can edit their own work (Ferris, 2002; Ferris & Roberts, 2001). Research has also shown that L2 students tend to assume that feedback on their writing is focused only on English language issues and not on discipline-specific issues and so tend to revise only at the surface level. For this reason, it's important that instructors distinguish between the two types of comments (Cox, 2010) and that they also indicate to students that they are, in fact, interested in and value what the students have to say.

PEER REVIEW

While the processes of giving and receiving peer feedback, as well as simply seeing peers' drafts-in-progress (Kietlinska, 2006), have all been shown to be effective for L2 writers, there are pedagogical approaches instructors can use to enhance the experience for L2 students, approaches that are useful to share during faculty development. Research has shown that international visa students tend to be unfamiliar with the process of peer review and tend to trust teacher feedback over peer feedback (Kietlinska, 2006; Nelson & Carson, 1998; Zhang, 1999) and also that, in peer review groups that include both NES and L2 students, the NES students tend not to trust comments from L2 students (as indicated in some of the student comments reported in Fredericksen & Mangelsdorf [this volume]) and L2 students have difficulty finding openings to offer oral comments (Zhu, 2001). It may be that the instructor also doubts the value of contributions by L2 students in the peer review process. However, L2 students have strengths in commenting on rhetorical moves in writing (Jordan, 2008) as well as grammatical issues. International students in particular, who learned English through grammar drills and translation (Reid, 1998), have training in the grammatical structure of English, unlike most NES students. Therefore, in order to maximize the benefits of peer review, it is important the instructor prepare students by explaining to the class the value of peer review, the role of peer review in the writing process, and the value of comments from L2 students (Berg, 1999).

Further, the instructor should let students know the extent to which they should comment on surface-level issues and how they should attend to these. In early drafts, students can be advised to pay attention to higher-order concerns (HOCs), such as idea development, focus, and overall organization, and only comment on grammatical issues that get in the way of comprehension. In later drafts, students can be advised to pay attention to lower-order concerns (LOCs), but to focus only the two or three types of errors that are most disruptive to the reading experience. Since L2 students do often need additional time to read and respond to drafts, it is helpful to require students to exchange drafts ahead of the workshop and/or to provide adequate time in class to respond to drafts (a strategy described by Fredericksen & Mangelsdorf [this volume]). It is also helpful if the instructor provides worksheets that include specific questions to focus the feedback, so that students can provide both written and oral commentary, an approach that draws on multiple language strengths.

WRITING-TO-LEARN ACTIVITIES

Writing-to-learn activities, such as freewriting, double-entry journals, and tickets-to-leave, all support L2 student learning (Hirsch [this volume]) as well as their facility in writing in English. It is important to remind faculty that writing produced by L2 students during these activities should be treated the same as writing by NES students: as a low-stakes activity meant more for the eyes of the student than for the instructor. I have seen well-intended instructors take a red pen to L2 students' low-stakes writing, feeling compelled to attend to English language issues. As it would for any student, this move raises the stakes of the assignment, which may impede learning. As these writing activities are meant to facilitate thinking, and not all L2 students can think fluently in their L2, L2 students can be encouraged to use their first language during writing-to-learn activities (Bean et al., 2003; Hirsh & DeLuca, 2003) as well as early in the drafting process (Murphy & Roca de Larios, 2010; Ting, 1996). Because it takes more time for cognitive processing in a second language, it is also a good idea to ask instructors to provide additional time for in-class writing-to-learn activities, or to assign writing-to-learn activities as homework, so that L2 students can work at their own pace.

WRITING ASSIGNMENT DESIGN

In addition to these pedagogical approaches, during faculty development workshops, we should encourage faculty to design writing assignments that are culturally inclusive. In her ethnographic research on undergraduate L2 writers in courses across the curriculum, Leki (1995) came across writing assignments that "required an implicit and sophisticated knowledge of everyday US culture that was far out of the reach of a student just arrived in the US" (p. 241). Instructors often assign projects that ask students to draw from US history and pop culture, in an effort to help them connect course content with what they already know. However, an assignment that does this kind of connection can turn what might be a personal reflection or reader response assignment for an English L1 student into a research assignment for an L2 student. We would not want to discourage instructors from giving these kinds of assignments, but instead to expand the options for the assignment, so that students are invited to draw on personal experience and knowledge based in the US or in another country. (See Hirsch [this volume] for examples of assignments that allow undergraduates to draw on knowledge from daily life) and see Phillips [this volume] for details on how a graduate student drew on knowledge related to his home country to be successful with course projects). To address assignment design during workshops, I hand faculty descriptions of three or four assignments and ask them to look at them through the lens of an L2 student. Which assignment is the most culturally and linguistically inclusive? How can the assignments be adjusted to become more inclusive? This activity invariably leads to rich conversations about multilingualism, multiculturalism, and assignment design.

EVALUATION OF WRITING ASSIGNMENTS

When I was a WAC program director, the question I heard most from faculty on my campus was, "How do I assess L2 students in a way that is fair to all students in my class?" (See Ives et al. and Zawacki & Habib [this volume] for faculty perspectives on fairness in evaluating L2 writing). First, faculty should be made aware that L2 students are doing something much more difficult than are English L1 students: they are learning and being evaluated on their learning in a second language. To make evaluation truly equitable, faculty would need to ask English L1 students to complete writing assignments in a second language. Second, we should point out to faculty that L2 writing, when compared to English L1 writing, will almost always appear to fall short. In his landmark article, "Toward an Understanding of the Distinct Nature of L2 Writing: The ESL Research and Its Implications," Silva (1993) reviews 72 research reports that compare English L1 and L2 student writing, to state that L2 writing has been shown to be "less fluent (fewer words), less accurate (more errors), and less effective (lower holistic scores)" (p. 200) and that L2 writing is "strategically, rhetorically, and linguistically different in important ways from L1 writing" (p. 201). It would be unfair to evaluate L2 writing using the same criteria for length, grammatical accuracy, and overall organization as would be used to evaluate English L1 students. However, for most faculty across the curriculum, length, number of surface errors, and organization aren't all that they are looking for when they give a writing assignment. They are also looking at the ways in which students meet the learning outcomes of an assignment, and in most courses across the curriculum, learning outcomes don't include writing for length, grammatical accuracy, or organization. My advice to faculty, then, is to create a rubric focused on learning outcomes. One part of the rubric may focus on "presentation," which may include length, editing, and citation format, but even here, I advise faculty to be flexible in terms of required length (asking for a range of page lengths, say five to seven pages), and to focus on readability, rather than error-free writing. In my rubrics, I include this statement: "The writer edited areas pointed out by readers, particularly areas that readers found confusing due to grammatical issues." L2 students can be expected to edit areas of their drafts pointed out by readers as being incomprehensible due to grammatical errors. I also encourage faculty to ask students to hand in, along with the final draft, the first draft, feedback from peers and/or the instructor, and a cover letter that explains what was revised and why, and that reflects on what the student would revise further had there been more time. Looking through this "mini-portfolio" will help the instructor better assess the progress the student has made as a writer through the project, how the writer revised and edited using reader feedback, and what the writer knows about writing that s/he can't quite enact at this time.

To address the issue of evaluating L2 writing during faculty workshops, I hand out an assignment description, a rubric (based on learning outcomes, with one area focused on presentation, as described above), and two or three samples of student writing. I select the samples so that one is practically error-free but has little depth or rhetorical sophistication and one is riddled with surface-level errors (but none that render the message incomprehensible) but displays depth of understanding and rhetorical savvy. I ask the participants to evaluate each essay, using the rubric, and then discuss their choices. Each time I've done this, faculty first talk about the error-free essay as being the strongest until someone points out that, according to the rubric, the error-laden essay is the strongest, leading to a rich discussion on what we prioritize in student writing.

The approaches I have described in this section can be seen as taking up Universal Instructional Design (UID) strategies—adjusting pedagogy so that it meets the needs of a broad spectrum of students, including L2 students, a framework that has proven useful in rethinking writing pedagogy for students with disabilities (Dolmage, 2008). Canagarajah (2002), as well as Horner and Trimbur (2002) and Horner, Lu, Royster and Trimbur (2011), has been challenging compositionists to go further than just accommodating difference, but to value difference, and to create writing pedagogy that builds on the strengths of multilingual and multicultural students, a challenge that faculty across the curriculum face as well. Similar to Canagarajah's call for faculty to assume a difference-as-resource stance, Horner, Lu, Royster and Trimbur (2011) propose that compositionists take up a "translingual approach [which] sees difference in language not as a barrier to overcome or as a problem to manage, but as a resource for producing meaning in writing, speaking, reading, and listening" (p. 303). These two approaches call on faculty to create curriculum that builds on the rhetorical, cultural, linguistic, and literacy resources of student writers. In the following section, I explore the complexity of designing linguistically and culturally inclusive pedagogy that draws on L2 students' strengths as learners and writers.

WORKING WITH FACULTY TO BUILD ON L2 STUDENTS' STRENGTHS

The field of composition-rhetoric is currently grappling with the question of how to create pedagogy using a difference-as-resource stance. Little has been published in this area, though two CCCC pre-conference workshops have focused on this question. In 2010, in "Building on Their Strengths: Advocating for L2 Writers through Teaching, Administrating, Mentoring," workshop participants focused on "the theoretical framework of 'difference-as-resource' (Canagarajah, 2002) as a heuristic for exploring how writing instructors and writing program administrators can create pedagogy and programming that builds on the rhetorical, cultural, linguistic, and literacy resources of second language writers" (Cox et al., 2010). In 2012, the question was brought to bear on WAC in a workshop titled, "Embracing the Richness of Multilingualism through WAC/WID: Re-envisioning Institutional Leadership, Advocacy, and Faculty Support." During both workshops, participants struggled to translate this rich area of theory into practice.

If we are working at the edge of our knowledge in this area in composition-rhetoric, how can we work with faculty across the curriculum to create linguistically and culturally inclusive pedagogy? In discussing how the "translingual approach" would be enacted in composition-rhetoric, Horner, Lu, Royster and Trimbur (2011) say this:

> In short, new work, in which many faculty cannot yet claim expertise, will be demanded of both faculty and their students. That is the challenge of embracing a translingual approach, and its promise: the necessity of working on writing collaboratively with our students, our current colleagues, and those who can become our colleagues amid the realities of a translingual nation and world. (p. 309)

Horner, Lu, Royster and Trimbur (2011) thus call on composition scholars to collaborate with colleagues and students to create linguistically and culturally inclusive pedagogy. I call on WAC leaders to take the same approach when working with faculty across the curriculum, an approach not dissimilar to one taken when the WAC movement was just getting off the ground. Russell (2006), in his introduction to *A History of Writing Across the Curriculum: Composing a Community*, describes the WAC movement as "an extraordinary example of grassroots change in education" (p. 3). When the movement began, as Russell tells us,

> [it] did not have an elaborated theory but rather a few powerful ideas, which might be summarized as "Writing to learn; learning to write." Nor did it have a single curricular agenda, but rather a wide range of possible models, to be adapted or rejected according to local institutional needs and personalities. (p. 5)

WAC leaders are accustomed to taking these "few powerful ideas" and "possible models" to faculty across the curriculum and trusting faculty to do the hard work of translating these ideas and curricular models into pedagogy that supports their disciplinary and classroom contexts. We WAC program leaders do not need to have all of the answers, only the questions, the seeds of pedagogical change, which faculty then take up and use to transform teaching and learning across the curriculum. An initial step WAC leaders might take is to gather like-minded faculty and begin the conversation by posing the following questions:

- How we can design writing curricula that invites students to draw on their multiple languages, cultures, literacy experiences, and areas of rhetorical knowledge as resources?
- How we can value students' "written accents" in our curricula?
- Where, in your discipline, does pedagogy that builds on the strengths of linguistically and culturally diverse students already exist? Where, in your discipline, does "written accent" or writing that draws on multiple languages already exist? How can these examples of pedagogies and texts be used to showcase multilingualism and multiculturalism as part of your field?

But what can we offer faculty as curricular models of linguistically and culturally inclusive pedagogy? I suggest that we ask faculty to pay attention to the ways in which L2 students in their courses reshape assignments. In "Coping Strategies of ESL Students in Writing Tasks Across the Curriculum," Leki

(1995) tells us that in order to succeed, L2 writers often "rewrit[e] the terms" of writing assignments, giving the example of Julie, a business major from France, who negotiates a history assignment on a novel's representation of US southern women in the 1950's—an assignment that assumes deep cultural and historical knowledge of the US—by adapting the assignment to instead focus on the novel's female character she could most connect to as an international student (p. 243). Rather than see these reshapings of assignments as "errors" or "misunderstandings," we may see them as clues to approaches to creating pedagogy that builds on L2 writers' strengths.

CONCLUSION

Russell tells us that the first WAC programs "began with faculty in various disciplines sitting down to talk about a felt need—poor writing (or thinking) among students" (p. 11). The model that WAC leaders turned to was the faculty workshop—a model that Russell describes as "egalitarian": "The faculty workshop was a place to share ideas and practices, not a place to learn from an expert, ordinarily" (p. 11). Today's "felt need" is the question of how to work with L2 writers, and faculty from across the curriculum are turning to WAC program leaders for guidance. Though WAC directors often are not experts in L2 writing studies, we do have expertise in bringing faculty together around the same table, sharing a "few powerful ideas" about student writing, learning from what is already happening in classrooms across the curriculum, and engaging faculty in collaborative inquiry into pedagogy. Fulwiler (2006) tells us that when asked why he and WAC colleague Art Young continue, even a decade into retirement, to help colleges and universities develop WAC programs, he answers, "because exploring good ideas with interested colleagues is the most exciting work we've learned to do" (p. 167). Linguistically and culturally inclusive writing pedagogy is currently theory that is waiting to be translated into practice, and that pedagogy can only be created in collaboration with faculty across the curriculum. This is, indeed, an exciting time to do WAC work.

NOTES

1. Many thanks to Kimberly Harrison, Christina Ortmeier-Hooper, and Terry Myers Zawacki, whose comments, suggestions, and insights greatly enriched this essay.

2. While writing this chapter, I left Bridgewater State University to become a Multilingual Specialist at Dartmouth College, where I develop writing support and oral presentation support for L2 international graduate students and teach writing courses in the Institute for Writing and Rhetoric.

REFERENCES

Bean, J., Cucchihara, M., Eddy, R., Elbow, P., Grego, R., Kutz, E., ... Matsuda, P. K. (2003). Should we invite students to write in home dialects or languages? Complicating the yes/no debate. *Composition Studies, 31*(1), 25-42.

Berg, C. E. (1999). The effects of trained peer response on ESL students' revision types and writing quality. *Journal of Second Language Writing, 8*(3): 215-241.

Bridgewater State University. (2011a). *Bridgewater State University Factbook 2010-2011*. Retrieved from http://www.bridgew.edu/depts/IR/Factbook2010-2011/BSU_FACT_BOOK_1011.pdf

Bridgewater State University. (2011b). *BSU at a glance: Fall 2011*. Retrieved from http://www.bridgew.edu/depts/IR/AAG_F11.pdf

Canagarajah, A. S. (2002). Understanding critical writing. Reprinted in P. K. Matsuda, M. Cox, J. Jordan, & C. Ortmeier-Hooper (Eds.) (2006), *Second Language Writing in the Composition Classroom: A Critical Sourcebook* (pp. 210-224). Boston, New York: Bedford/St. Martin's.

Castillo, W. (2011). *Losing was never an option*. Writer's Café, Bridgewater State University. Retrived from http://www.youtube.com/watch?v=6vn8hn2HdWo&feature=related

Cox, M. (2010). Identity, second language writers, and the learning of workplace writing. In M. Cox, J. Jordan, C. Ortmeier-Hooper, & G. G. Schwartz (Eds.), *Reinventing identities in second language writing* (pp. 75-95). Urbana, IL: NCTE.

Cox, M. (2011). "WAC: Closing doors or opening doors for second language writers?" In "Writing across the Curriculum and Second Language Writers: Cross-Field Research, Theory, and Program Development [Special Issue]." *Across the Disciplines, 8*(4). Retrieved from http://wac.colostate.edu/atd/ell/cox.cfm

Cox, M., Dadak, A., Nielsen-Dube, K., Canagarajah, A. S., Shuck, G., EricDepew, K., Miller-Cochran, S., & Matsuda, P. K. (2010, March). Building on their strengths: Advocating for L2 writers through teaching, administrating, collaborating. Workshop presented at the annual convention of the Conference on College Composition and Communication, Louisville, KY.

Cox, M. & Ortmeier-Hooper, C. (2008). Beyond the deficiency model: Second language writers as rhetorically savvy. Paper presented at the annual convention of the Conference on College Composition and Communication, San Francisco, CA.

Cox, M. & Zawacki, T. M. (Eds.). (2011, December). Writing across the Curriculum and Second Language Writers: Cross-Field Research, Theory, and Program Development [Special Issue]. *Across the Disciplines, 8*(4). Retrieved from http://wac.colostate.edu/atd/ell/index.cfm

Cummins, J. (1981). Age on arrival and immigrant second language learning in Canada. A reassessment. *Applied Linguistics, 2*, 132-149.

Dolmage, J. (2008). Mapping composition: Inviting disability in the front door. In C. Lewiecki-Wilson & B. J. Brueggemann (Eds.), *Disability and the Teaching of Writing: A critical sourcebook* (pp. 14-27). Boston: Bedford / St. Martin's.

Ewert, D. E. (2009). L2 writing conferences: Investigating teacher talk. *Journal of Second Language Writing, 18*(4), 251-269.

Ferris, D. (2002). *Treatment of error in second language student writing*. The Michigan Series on Teaching Multilingual Writers. Ann Arbor: University of Michigan Press.

Ferris, D., & Roberts, B. (2001). Error feedback in L2 writing classes. How explicit does it need to be? *Journal of Second Language Writing, 10*, 161-184.

Fishman, S. M. & McCarthy, L. (2001). An ESL writer and her discipline-based professor: Making progress even when goals do not match." *Written Communication, 18*(2), 180-228.

Fu, D. (1995). *My trouble is my English: Asian students and the American dream*. Portsmouth, NH: Heinemann.

Fulwiler, T. (2006). Writing across the Michigan Tech curriculum. In S. H. McLeod & M. I. Soven (Eds.), *A history of Writing Across the Curriculum: Composing a community* (pp. 168-199). West Lafayette, IN: Parlor Press.

Goldstein, L. (2005). *Teacher Written Commentary in Second Language Writing Classrooms*. The Michigan Series on Teaching Multilingual Writers. Ann Arbor: University of Michigan Press.

Hall, J. (2009). WAC/WID in the next America: Redefining professional identity in the age of the multilingual majority. *The WAC Journal, 20*, 33-49. Retrieved from http://wac.colostate.edu/journal/vol20/hall.pdf

Hirsh, L. & Deluca, C. (2003). WAC in an urban and bilingual setting: Writing-to-learn in English y en Espaňo. *Language and Learning Across the Disciplines, 6*(3). Retrieved from http://wac.colostate.edu/llad/v6n3/hirsch.pdf

Horner, B., Lu, M-Z., & Royster, J. J. (2011). Opinion: Language difference in writing: Toward a translingual approach, *College English, 73*(3), 303-321.

Horner, B. & Trimbur, J. (2002). English only and US college composition,. *College Composition and Communication, 53*(4), 594-630.

Hyland, F. (1998). The impact of teacher written feedback on individual writers. *Journal of Second Language Writing, 7*(3), 255-86.

Jacobs, G. M., Curtis, A., Braine, G., & Huang, S. Y. (1998). Feedback on student writing: Taking the middle path. *Journal of Second Language Writing, 7*(3), 307-17.

Johns, A. M. (2001). ESL students and WAC programs: Varied populations and diverse needs. In S. H. McLeod, E. Miraglia, M. I. Soven, & C. Thaiss (Eds.), *WAC for the new millennium: Strategies for continuing writing-across-the-curriculum programs* (pp. 141-164). Urbana, IL: NCTE.

Jordan, J. (2008). Rethinking competencies in linguistically diverse composition courses. Paper presented at the annual convention of the Conference on College Composition and Communication, San Francisco, CA.

Kietlinska, K. (2006). Revision and ESL students. In A. Horning & A. Becker (Eds.), *Revision: History, theory, and practice* (pp. 63-87). West Lafayette, IN: Parlor Press and WAC Clearinghouse. Retrieved from http://wac.colostate.edu/books/horning_revision/

Leki, I. (1992). *Understanding ESL writers*. Portsmouth, NH: Heinemann.

Leki, I. (1995). Coping strategies of ESL students in writing tasks across the curriculum. *TESOL Quarterly 29*(2), 235-260.

Leki, I. (1999). "Pretty much I screwed up": Ill-served needs of a permanent resident student. In L. Harklau, K. M. Losey, & M. Siegal (Eds.), *Generation 1.5 meets college composition: Issues in the teaching of writing to US-educated learners of ESL* (pp. 17-43). Mahwah, NJ: Erlbaum.

Leki, I. (2001). "A narrow system of thinking": Nonnative-English-speaking students in group projects across the curriculum. *TESOL Quarterly 35*(1), 39-67.

Leki, I. (2006). Negotiating socioacademic relations: English learners' reception by and reaction to college faculty. *Journal of English for Academic Purposes 5*(2), 136-152.

Leki, I. (2007). *Undergraduates in a second language: Challenges and complexities of academic literacy development*. Boston: Routledge.

Massachusetts Department of Education (2011). *School/District profiles*. Retrieved from http://profiles.doe.mass.edu

Matsuda, P. K. (1999). Composition studies and ESL writing: A disciplinary division of labor. *College Composition and Communication, 50*(4): 699-721.

Matsuda, P. K., & Cox, M. (2009). Reading an ESL writer's text. In S. Bruce & B. Rafoth (Eds.), *ESL writers: A guide for writing center tutors* (2nd ed.; pp. 42-50). Portsmouth, NH: Boynton/Cook Heinemann.

Matsuda, P. K. & Jablonksi, J. (2000). Beyond the L2 metaphor: Towards a mutually transformative model of ESL/WAC collaboration. *Academic. Writing, 1.* Retrieved from http://wac.colostate.edu/aw/articles/matsuda_jablonski2000.pdf. 20 May 2011

McLeod, S. & Miraglia, E. (2001). Writing across the curriculum in a time of change. In S. H. McLeod, E. Miraglia, M. I. Soven, & C. Thaiss (Eds.), *WAC for the new millennium: Strategies for continuing writing-across-the-curriculum programs* (pp. 1-27). Urbana, IL: NCTE.

Mervius, J. K. (2011). *"I Am a Survivor."* Writer's Café, Bridgewater State University. Retrieved from http://www.youtube.com/watch?v=6vn8hn2HdWo&feature=related

Murphy, L. & Roca de Larios, J. (2010). Searching for words: One strategic use of the mother tongue by advanced Spanish EFL writers. *Journal of Second Language Writing, 19*(2), 61-81.

Nelson, G. N., & Carson, J. G. (1998). ESL students' perceptions of effectiveness in peer response groups. *Journal of Second Language Writing, 7*(2), 113-131.

Ortmeier-Hooper, C. (2010). The shifting nature of identity: Social identity, L2 writers, and high school. In M. Cox, J. Jordan, C. Ortmeier-Hooper, and G. G. Schwartz (Eds.), *Reinventing identities in second language writing* (pp. 5-28). Urbana, IL: NCTE.

Reid, J. (1994). Responding to ESL students' texts: The myths of appropriation. *TESOL Quarterly, 28*(2), 273-292.

Reid, J. (1998). "Eye" learners and "ear" learners: Identifying the language needs of international student and US resident writers. In P. Byrd and J. M. Reid (Eds.), *Grammar in the composition classroom: Essays on teaching ESL for college-bound students* (pp. 3-17). New York: Heinle.

Reid, J., & Kroll, B. (1995). Designing and assessing effective classroom assignments for NES and ESL students. *Journal of Second Language Writing, 4*(1), 17-41.

Russell, D. R. (2006). Introduction: WAC's beginnings: Developing a community of change agents. In S. H. McLeod & M. I. Soven (Eds.) *A history of Writing Across the Curriculum: Composing a community* (pp. 3-15). West Lafayette, IN: Parlor Press.

Silva, T. (1993). Toward an understanding of the distinct nature of L2 writing: The ESL research and its implications. In T. Silva & P. K. Matsuda (2001) *Landmark Essays on ESL Writing* (pp. 191-208). Mahwah, NJ: Erlbaum.

Ting, Y. R. (1996). Looping forward: Drafting in my own language. *ELT Journal, 50*, 135-142.

Truscott, J. (1999). The case for "The case against grammar correction in L2 writing classes": A response to Ferris. *Journal of Second Language Writing, 8*(2), 111-22.

Tsui, A. B. M. & Ng, M. (2000). Do secondary L2 writers benefit from peer comments? *Journal of Second Language Writing, 9*(2): 147-170.

Valdés, G. (1992). Bilingual minorities and language issues in writing: Toward professionwide responses to a new challenge. *Written Communication 9*(1), 85-136.

Vandrick, S. (2010). Social class privilege among ESOL writing students. In M. Cox, J. Jordan, C. Ortmeier-Hooper & G. Schwartz (Eds.), *Reinventing Identities in Second Language Writing* (pp. 257-272). Urbana, IL: NCTE.

Wolfe-Quintero, K. & Segade, G. (1999). University support for second-language writers across the curriculum. In L. Harklau, K. M. Losey, & M. Siegal (Eds.), *Generation 1.5 meets college composition: Issues in the teaching of writing to US-educated learners of ESL* (pp. 191-209). Mahwah, NJ: Erlbaum.

Yang, J. (2010). Lost in the puzzles. In M. Cox, J. Jordan, C. Ortmeier-Hooper, and G. G. Schwartz (Eds.), *Reinventing identities in second language writing* (pp. 51-53). Urbana, IL: NCTE.

Zamel, V. (1995). Strangers in academia: The experiences of faculty and ESL students across the curriculum. *College Composition and Communication, 46*(4), 506-521.

Zamel, V. & Spack, R. (Eds). (2004). *Crossing the curriculum: Multilingual learners in college classrooms.* Mahwah, NJ: Lawrence Erlbaum.

Zawacki, T. M. & Cox, M. (2011, December). Introduction to WAC and second language writing. *Across the Disciplines, 8*(4). Retrieved from http://wac.colostate.edu/atd/ell/zawacki-cox.cfm

Zawacki, T. M., Hajabbasi, E., Habib, A., Antram, A., & Das, A. (2007). *Valuing Written Accent: Non-Native Students Talk about Identity, Academic Writing, and Meeting Teachers' Expectations.* Fairfax, VA: George Mason University. Retrieved from http://writtenaccents.gmu.edu/

Zawacki, T. M. & Habib, A. (2010). "Will our stories help teachers understand?" Expectations across academic communities. In M. Cox, J. Jordan, C. Ortmeier-Hooper, and G. G. Schwartz (Eds.), *Reinventing identities in second language writing* (pp. 54-74). Urbana, IL: NCTE.

Zhang, S. (1999). Thoughts on some recent evidence concerning the affective advantage of peer feedback. *Journal of Second Language Writing, 8*(3), 321-326.

Zhu, W. (2001). Interaction and feedback in mixed peer response groups. *Journal of Second Language Writing, 10*(4): 251-276.

APPENDIX A: VOICES OF BSU ESL STUDENTS, FROM AN ENGL 101 SURVEY

In response to, "Please describe the writing instruction in English you've received."

- I have never taken a class that focuses only on writing. In my ESL classes we did very short writing assignments. The longuest [sic] piece of writing I've written in English is one paragraph. In my ESL classes we read short paragraphs and answered basic questions. [...] It is easier for me to understand English when I hear it or read it. It is more difficult for me to speak and write because I have trouble choosing the correct words. — Mexican student, who took ESL courses at a college in California
- I haven't received any writing instruction in English. I studied reading for TOEFL Test, so the longest text I've read English is TOEFL text book. —Japanese student, who went to an English Language Institute in the US
- The writing basically has three parts: Introduction, body, and conclusion. Introduction has hook, background, thesis. Body has usually three paragraphs. Each paragraph's first sentence usually is the thesis of the paragraph. It's better has [sic] transition words for each of these three paragraphs. The last paragraph is conclusion. It is good for writer to repeat the thesis in another words. —Chinese student, attended an English Language Institute I attended high school in Cape Cod, 2 years.
- My longest piece written in English is 2-3 pages. —Cape Verdean student, immigrated to the US two years ago.

In response to, "Please describe the reading instruction in English you've received," and "What kinds of reading have you done?"

- First, read the first and last sentences of each paragraph. Second, read the questions and then go back to the paragraph to find out the answers. Skip the new words if you haven't seen before or you can according to the context, try to guess the meaning of the words that you don't know. I have red [sic] short novel, SAT reading, TOEFL reading, and newspaper. —Chinese student, attended an English Language Institute
- I'm reading "Art History." There are so many technical words so at first, I need to check these vocabrary [sic] and after that, I need to read two times. It takes a lot of time but understanding the content of textbook is the most important. —Japanese student, attended an English Language Institute

In response to, "What do you hope to learn in this course?"

- I hope I'll get more writing skill in draft that that [*sic*] I wrote before. In addition, I wanna [*sic*]express notion or an abstruct [*sic*] concept because I'm poor at those expression on the draft.
- I hope I can speak English fluently and can write easily.
- I want to improve my writing skills so I could write properly in other classes.
- I hope I achieve English obstacles in my life as much as I can.
- I would like to learn writing as American. Sometimes I write dialy [*sic*]in English but I can't do well so I would like to practice.

APPENDIX B: L2 STUDENT VOICES FROM ACROSS THE CURRICULUM

These voices are from Terry Myers Zawacki and Anna Habib's (2010) research on the experiences of linguistically and culturally diverse students across the curriculum at George Mason University.

> In America, when I write totally different style of paper, the professor say, "Where are you from? How did you get into this college? Your writing is behind the line, so you can't really catch up to the class." So, I don't know how to figure that out. —Yoon, student from S. Korea

> I had my initial friction between the cultures here when I was told over and over again "you know you have to cut down, clean up your paragraphs." I was very offended because I came with a lot of confidence behind me and suddenly I find that it is totally different. But it didn't take me long to catch up though. I realized any nice language I use is wasted; no one is going to look at it in that way. —Kanishka, student from Sri Lanka

> "My strength in Spanish," Diana said, "is my personal style of how to write, and that's something that people like. And my grammar and vocabulary in Spanish are really good. In English, definitely, I would like to have more vocabulary, so I can do that [same thing]."

I would really love to learn nice words, because I do have ideas, and I do want to put something down, but I am short of words. —Ayesha, student from Pakistan

When you ultimately succeed in writing is when you have your own accent. When I speak, my accent reflects who I am and where I come from. Well, I want my writing to reflect me in that way. —Tonka, student from Bulgaria

APPENDIX C: BASIC INFORMATION ABOUT L2 WRITERS AND WRITING

International students: These are visa-holding students studying in the US for a set amount of time, usually with plans to return to the home country afterward. In general, international L2 students:

- Have a wide range of experiences with English in home country; some students will have studied English since elementary school while others will have studied English for only a few years
- Undergraduates tend to be high-performing students from privileged backgrounds (Vandrick, 2010); graduate students tend to come from a wider range of socioeconomic backgrounds
- Tend to have learned English "through their eyes" (Reid, 1998), though grammar exercises, memorization of vocabulary, and translation
- Tend to have limited experiences with writing, speaking, and listening in their second language
- May have enrolled in an English Language Institute (ELI) prior to enrolling in college, which tend to teach formulaic approaches to writing (thesis-drive, five-paragraph essays)

Permanent resident students: These are students who moved to the US for a wide range of reasons, including seeking a US education, opportunities for work, and political unrest or war in their home country. In general, among permanet resident students:

- Some will have studied English in home country; others will have only learned English after arriving
- Some will have literacy in first language; others will have had their education disrupted by war and political unrest

- Some will live in ethnic enclaves, using their primary language in their homes and communities
- Many will have experience in US public schools, ranging from one or two years to longer enrollment
- Most tend to have learned English primarily "through their ears" (Reid, 1998), through American TV, pop culture, and socializing with peers
- Many will have had limited experience with writing, as high school ESL programs focus on oral communication over written, and ESL students tend to be placed in low tracks in high school, where the emphasis is on grammar and worksheets over extended writing (Fu, 1995; Ortmeier-Hooper, 2010)
- ESL permanent resident students jumped through many hoops to make it to college, so they tend to be driven, high-performing students who take advantage of resources available to them at the university

What is generally true about L2 college writers?

- It takes five to seven years of being immersed in the target language to become fluent in that language (Cummins, 1981)
- Fluency ≠ Native-like; L2 students will retain a "written accent" which may never disappear (Valdés, 1992)
- L2 college writers have written across multiple languages, educational systems, cultures, and rhetorics, building important rhetorical knowledge Section III WAC Practices and Pedagogies Transformed

SECTION III
WAC PRACTICES AND PEDAGOGIES TRANSFORMED

CHAPTER 13

DEVELOPING WRITING-INTENSIVE COURSES FOR A GLOBALIZED CURRICULUM THROUGH WAC-TESOL COLLABORATIONS

Megan Siczek
George Washington University

Shawna Shapiro
Middlebury College

This chapter makes the argument that WAC and TESOL should work together to create new curricular spaces for enacting an institution's commitment to diversity, inclusion, and global perspectives. Though internationalization is often touted as an institutional goal, universities tend to overlook the potential contributions of students—particularly second language writers—toward this goal. TESOL faculty are similarly excluded from conversations about how to cultivate global competence across the curriculum. The authors make the case for writing-intensive, globally-oriented courses that are developed through coordination between WAC and TESOL programs. The first section provides a framework for internationalization, articulating its relationship to diversity and inclusion. The second section describes the persistent disciplinary segregation between WAC and TESOL and explains why their collaboration provides a viable means of contributing to an inclusive and globally-relevant curriculum. The third section offers a WAC course model that unites internationalization goals with this collaborative potential.

INTERNATIONALIZATION: A MISSED OPPORTUNITY?

There is little doubt that "internationalization" has become a buzzword across most US college campuses. Most institutional mission statements include phrasing such as "global perspectives," "global citizenship," "cross-cultural understanding," and "engaging the world," implying that this ethos is indeed embedded in their philosophy and practice. The rationale for this movement toward a global orientation stems in part from a recognition of increasing global interdependence. We can look at this interconnectedness in humanistic terms, as indicated by the American Association of American Colleges and Universities (AACU)'s endorsement of global education "to prepare students for ... [a] shared future marked by justice, security, equality, human rights, and economic sustainability" (Stromquist, 2007, p. 82). We can also regard this impetus in highly practical terms, motivated by "a firm grasp of practical and competitive realities in the contemporary world" (Taylor, 2004, p. 153). The overarching goal of internationalization in higher education, then, is to prepare students to inhabit a shared world community.

Internationalized practices may take many forms, including branch campuses in other countries, joint degree programs with other institutions, study abroad programs, learning of foreign languages, globalized curricular content, and the enrollment of international students in US institutions (see, for example, Craig and Lavalle & Shima [this volume]). The assumption behind these practices is that they cultivate global competency, which Olson and Kroeger (2001) define as "substantive knowledge, perceptual understanding, and intercultural communication skills [needed] to effectively interact in our globally interdependent world" (p. 117). In essence, global competency involves developing skill sets—such as global analysis and intercultural communication— as well as mindsets for critical inquiry, global consciousness, and appreciation of diversity. Students must be given the opportunity to interrogate their own understandings of the world, to consider how and why others may perceive things differently, and to position themselves and their own experiences in the context of the "other." Ultimately, according to Mezirow, this can result in "transformative learning," whereby students change their "structures of habitual expectation to make possible a more inclusive, discriminating, and integrating perspective" and then begin to act according to this perspective (as cited in Van Gyn, Schuerholz-Lehr, Caws, & Preece, 2009, p. 29).

Unfortunately, many of the internationalization initiatives undertaken at US colleges and universities fall short in meeting this ideal of transformative, globally-competent education. Often, internationalization is interpreted to mean simply that US students should be encouraged to spend time abroad or that campuses should recruit more foreign-born students. This attitude allows internationalization to remain external to the classroom experience of many students and faculty. Jones and Killick (2007) have mined the literature in the field to identify some of the features of a truly internationalized curriculum: it should "demand culturally inclusive behavior ... engage critically with the global plurality of knowledge ... [develop] an awareness of [students'] own culture and perspectives ... recognize and appreciate different cultural perspectives on the same issue ... [and] apply critical thinking skills to problems with an international or intercultural dimension ..." (p. 112). However, much of the literature concedes that curricular responses to internationalization tend to be tacked on, rather than thoughtfully embedded across disciplinary spaces. Although there may be specific programs, departments, or individuals devoted to teaching about international perspectives, this orientation is generally not sustained throughout the curriculum. As a result, few students graduate with a solid grounding in global competency. Citing decades of research, Hunter, White, and Godbey (2006) have concluded that "few American college graduates are competent to function in different cultures, speak another language, or have any significant understanding of the world beyond US borders" (p. 272).

In order to be longstanding and transformative, internationalization must be an integrative *process*. It must be guided by a vision that is "ongoing, future oriented, multi-dimensional, interdisciplinary, leadership-driven" and "involves many stakeholders working to change the internal dynamics of an institution" (Ellingboe, 1998, as cited in Taylor, 2004, p. 150). Internationalization must not only be outward-looking, but also inward-looking. It requires that we acknowledge the diverse values and perspectives within our own institutions, and take into account who might be excluded or marginalized by our existing institutional practices. It also asks that we consider how institutional diversity might be tapped as a resource for cultivating global competency. In this way, internationalization is closely tied to another recent buzzword in higher education: *inclusion*. As Jones and Killick (2007) point out, a diverse student body is "the most obvious, and perhaps least utilized" mechanism for improving teaching and learning for global purposes (p. 113). Taking advantage of the potential contributions of our student body requires pedagogical practices that are inclusive of diverse backgrounds and viewpoints.

Rarely, however, do institutions recognize the link between internationalization and inclusion. All too often, the students who have the most to offer to a globally-oriented curriculum—particularly second language writers—are excluded from the mainstream, segregated into language support or remediation programs. As a result, many institutions ignore the diversity that exists within their walls, and instead operate "in isolation of the wider world," creating a space "where the student body, staff, curriculum context and supporting materials all reflect a single dominant culture" (Caruana, 2012, p. 34; also see Matsuda, 2006). Ironically, we may miss an opportunity to engage second language writers in globalizing our classrooms, despite the fact that they have crossed multiple cultural, linguistic, national, and epistemological boundaries to become members of our college communities. TESOL specialists—who also have a great deal to offer to an inclusive, internationalized curriculum, tend to be similarly segregated—often operating in isolation from more mainstream academic programs such as WAC.

Thus despite the rhetoric of internationalization, our schools are missing an opportunity to draw on the cultural and linguistic diversity that actually exists within our campuses, and to create a curriculum that is both inclusive and globally-oriented. In this chapter, we argue that WAC and TESOL can lead the way in developing courses that take advantage of what second language writers bring to institutions of higher education, and can thereby implement a more transformative and inclusive approach to internationalization. We articulate a rationale for collaboration between the two disciplines, and present a course model that provides rigorous writing instruction while at the same time recognizing and building on the global competencies of multilingual students. Such a course demonstrates the value of pedagogical and political alliances between WAC and TESOL.

WHY WAC AND TESOL?

Both of these disciplines have a great deal to contribute toward the aims of internationalization and global competency: they are both invested in promoting more inclusive, democratic institutional practice, and in supporting students who have traditionally been excluded from the curriculum (Matsuda & Jablonski, 2000). Both are concerned with issues of cultural and linguistic diversity as they relate to power and privilege. Moreover, both fields have in recent years become increasingly aware of the impact of globalization and internationalization on their work, as evidenced by trends in scholarship and pedagogy (see, for example, the CCCC Committee on Globalization established in March 2012). The two fields also complement each other in what they bring to a globally-oriented curriculum: TESOL offers a rich understanding of students as language users, and of the intersections between language, culture, identity, and power. WAC offers insights into literacy practices as they vary across disciplines and discourse communities, as well as strategies for how to embed literacy instruction throughout the academic curriculum. Together, the two disciplines offer a multi-dimensional framework for exploring language and literacy within a global context.

Before we discuss in greater detail the contributions that TESOL can make to WAC, it is important to consider what keeps them apart. One of the main reasons that these two fields rarely collaborate is disciplinary history. Although both fields draw a great deal on research methodology from the social sciences, they have historically been associated with different disciplines—TESOL with applied linguistics, and composition-rhetoric (which includes WAC) with English. As the two fields began to professionalize, they did so within separate institutional spaces, forming separate pedagogical alliances. This has resulted in what Paul Kei Matsuda (1999) calls a "disciplinary division of labor" in regard to the teaching of writing: "Language" is thought of as the domain of TESOL and "Writing" the domain of composition-rhetoric.

While the division of labor between WAC and TESOL is somewhat understandable given this disciplinary history, the persistence of that division has harmful effects. If language is conceived of as separate from writing, then the composition classroom is assumed to be a monolingual space, and the contributions of second language writers are likely to be overlooked (Matsuda, 2006). Language difference therefore comes to be thought of as deficiency, rather than a resource (Canagarajah, 2006). Multilingualism is then treated as "a problem to be solved, a disease to be cured" (Hall, 2009, p. 37). Another negative byproduct of disciplinary division of labor is curricular misalignment. Comparative case studies have found that the writing instruction in ESL courses is often approached from a "remedial" or "basic skills" perspective, and may diverge significantly from what is expected in first-year composition, writing-intensive courses, or other courses across the curriculum (Atkinson & Ramanathan, 1995; Braine, 1996; Harklau, 1994). This divergence is reflected in course policies as well: ESL coursework is often non-credit and may cost additional fees beyond regular tuition (Shapiro, 2012; Van Meter, 1990; also see TESOL, 2012). As a result, many students come to resent their ESL coursework, feeling that it is irrelevant to their academic goals and is more of a hindrance than a help (Leki, 2007; Roberge, Harklau, & Siegal, 2009; Shapiro, 2012).

Part of what prevents more equitable policies, as well as a more integrated curriculum, is the institutional alienation of TESOL professionals themselves. Research has found that many feel they are accorded "second class status" at their institutions, and that their work is considered "remedial" and/or "less academic" compared to that of other departments (Blumenthal, 2002, p. 48; Gray, Rolph, & Melamid, 1996, p. 77-78). This low status is instantiated in very tangible ways: ESL instructors tend to have lower pay, higher teaching loads, less job security, and fewer professional development opportunities compared with faculty in other disciplines (Blumenthal, 2002; Ignash, 1995; Williams, 1995; also see Shapiro, 2012). Given these dynamics, it is not surprising that faculty specializing in second language writing have little if any opportunity for cross-disciplinary collaboration.

Clearly, TESOL stands to benefit both pedagogically and politically from increased institutional integration and could be greatly aided in this aim through an alliance with WAC. This alliance might also help WAC to respond more proactively to the exigencies of internationalization and meet the needs of second language writers. As Jonathan Hall (2009) has pointed out, although WAC prides itself on promoting innovative pedagogical practices, it appears to have a blind spot of its own in failing to prepare for "the next America"—a "new psychic and pedagogical landscape" where multilingualism is the norm, rather than the exception (p. 34). "The future of WAC," Hall explains, "is indissolubly tied to the ways in which higher education will have to, willingly or unwillingly, evolve in the wake of globalization and in response to the increasing linguistic diversity of our student population" (p. 34). By turning to TESOL for insights on the implications of multilingualism and internationalization for its work, WAC can lead, rather than follow, in cultivating global competency and inclusive teaching across the curriculum. In sum, alliances between these two disciplines can help both of them to become further institutionally integrated.

We are not the first authors to discuss the possibilities for a reciprocal relationship between WAC and TESOL. Matsuda and Jablonski (2000) have called for a "mutually transformative" relationship between the disciplines, which they characterize as involving not only interdisciplinary borrowing but also collective action. The authors point out that such a relationship has political as well as pedagogical benefits: "By working together in the service of improving teaching and learning," they explain, "WAC and ESL could ... aid one another in securing increased institutional status" (p. 6). These and other scholars have enumerated a variety of possibilities for collaborative work between the disciplines. (A website put together by Michelle Cox has an excellent set of strategies and resources. See also Mallett and Zghreib [this volume] who offer a vivid illustration of how this kind of collaboration can result in a deeply thoughtful and carefully designed curriculum for international students.) However, there is a need for more articulation of models at the course level that draw on the expertise of both fields (Zawacki & Cox, 2011). The existing literature tends to focus on how the two can work together to support second language writers in other content areas, rather than on how they might themselves add to the curriculum through content-based, writing-intensive courses with a global orientation. As the landscape of higher education is being shaped by internationalization, there is tremendous opportunity for WAC and TESOL to make ground-level contributions, drawing on their collective expertise. Jonathan Hall (2009) has framed the opportunity that lies before us in this way: "We need to ask ourselves: how can WAC/WID programs more effectively encourage *Multilingual Learning Across the Curriculum*? (p. 37). In the section that follows, we present a course model that responds to this question.

A CURRICULAR RESPONSE: WRITING ABOUT GLOBAL ENGLISH

We have made the argument that the rhetoric of internationalization must be translated into inclusive opportunities to develop global competencies and global mindedness for students on our campuses. This entails leveraging the resource of student diversity and exploring avenues for coordination between TESOL and WAC programs. This particular model of coordination is a writing-intensive course about English as a global language designed and taught by a TESOL specialist, with support and input from WAC programs. The course content, global English, was selected because it crossed geographic and disciplinary boundaries, and also because it allowed for the inclusion of multiple/critical perspectives. We present this as an example of globally-relevant curricular content that can be academically purposed through WAC programs while at the same time being "international and relevant to the needs to all student groups" (Leask, 2001, p. 101). Variations of this course have been piloted at two institutions—George Washington University and Middlebury College. Although the two variations are quite similar, they differ in two respects—the mix of students (L2-only vs. mixed L1/L2) and their approach to writing instruction.

The course at George Washington University (GW) responds directly to the institution's mission statement, which highlights the core value of cultivating "a dynamic, student-focused community stimulated by cultural and intellectual diversity and built upon a foundation of integrity, creativity, and openness to the exploration of new ideas" (http://www.gwu.edu/~ire/info/mission.htm). This statement represents the potential for transcending the monolingual/monocultural classroom, as well as the institutional boundaries that can limit cross-disciplinary collaboration. In regard to international engagement, the university also aims to "promote the process of lifelong learning from both global and integrative perspectives" by "provid[ing] a stimulating intellectual environment for its diverse students and faculty." This emphasis brings to light the university's commitment to engage with diverse perspectives and global-mindedness in both teaching and learning.

While the writing program at GW endeavors to foster a "stimulating intellectual environment," the global perspectives and respect for diversity articulated in the university mission statement are not always evident in the course options it puts forward. First-year writing course options tend to be humanities-oriented and skewed toward American cultural themes. This can disadvantage second language writers who may lack the cultural knowledge base of their US counterparts as well as overlook the development of global competencies that are so necessary in our interconnected society. Among the writing-intensive

(WI) courses offered, global options can be similarly limited. At the time this course was designed, many of the WI courses available were in the humanities, particularly British and American literature, and the few social science options on the schedule had a focus on the American perspective, such as US diplomatic history and American politics and government. Courses with global content were most likely to be offered through departments of foreign languages or international affairs. Thus, second language writers at the university faced limited opportunities to take composition and writing-intensive courses that were inclusive of their diverse experiences and perspectives.

Though the TESOL and WI programs were part of separate departments in the institution, with TESOL instruction housed in the credit-bearing English for Academic Purposes (EAP) program and WI located in the University Writing Program (UWP), they were aligned in particular ways. Both programs focused on writing only, and the second language writers who took an EAP writing class went on to complete the full series of required courses in the University Writing Program. This literacy series included a rigorous first-year writing course and two WI courses that were grounded in the content of particular academic disciplines but had a significant writing component "designed to facilitate student involvement with particular bodies of knowledge, their methods of scholarship, and modes of communication" (http://www.gwu.edu/~uwp/wid/wid-about.html). At least one of the WI courses needed to be taken within a student's major, but the other course could be from another field of study. Because the writing courses were connected in this way, both the EAP program and the University Writing Program had a stake in the success of second language writers. In addition, the two programs shared a physical space, and this proximity created a collegial atmosphere and many opportunities for the sharing of experiences and ideas. This cross-pollination at GW led to the development of a social science WI course for international students called "English in a Global Context."

The rationale for this particular course was in part based on the challenges second language writers faced in WI courses at the university and the potential contribution of EAP's pedagogical approach, which tends to make explicit the practices, skills, and textual conventions associated with academic writing in English. The course was broadly described as an interdisciplinary examination of the global use of English, a subject matter that was particularly accessible to international students who had spent their lives operating in the arena of "global English." Course content included a study of the historical context that engendered the growth of English, a treatment of how English functions in global society, and an examination of cultural attitudes about the hegemonic power of English in the modern world. Course materials were drawn from a range of social science disciplines—including sociolinguistics, applied linguistics, anthropology, culture studies, and education—and represented the extent to which global English has become a subfield of increasing scholarly interest.

The objectives of this global English course linked content expectations with social science research and writing expectations. In keeping with the university's WI guidelines, students were expected to use critical reading strategies to analyze an interdisciplinary set of course materials; to develop research techniques relevant to the social sciences; to assess writing situations to compose for diverse purposes and audiences; and to produce 15-20 pages of finished text that demonstrated the conventions of social science writing including style, language use, and APA documentation format. The course objectives also emphasized scholarly collaboration and revision.

Specific assignments were designed to build on both the global theme and on the social science skill set and included four short papers that highlighted writing for diverse purposes and audiences (language profile, critical article review, policy memo, reflective writing), and two larger projects that focused on research—a survey analysis project and an annotated bibliography project. The survey analysis project was considered original social science research and required students to develop and administer a survey about English language use that considered practices and/or attitudes. The results of this survey were analyzed and presented in the form of a social science research article. Conducting original research and linking it to scholarly work in the field helped students realize the value of diverse experiences and develop their own voices as writers, completing projects with titles such as "Why English Cannot Dominate the World" and "Is an Initially Positive Experience with the English Language a Strong Factor in Motivating One to Learn the Language?" The other major assignment was an annotated bibliography on an independently conceived topic relevant to the course theme. For this project, students translated their own experiences and interests into an academic research focus, and topics included hybridized language use, English language educational practices, and the role of technology in the spread of English. This course, though initially designed via an experimental course designation, has been approved as a permanent WI offering.

Another variation on this course model has been implemented at Middlebury College, which, like George Washington University, sees internationalization as central to its mission: The college "strives ... to cultivate the intellectual, creative, physical, ethical, and social qualities essential for leadership in a rapidly changing global community" (**Middlebury College**). Middlebury seeks students who wish to "engage the world"—a phrase that is used frequently in its promotional materials. This emphasis on global understanding is reflected in the strong emphasis on foreign language study, international perspectives, and study abroad throughout the curriculum. It is also reflected in the strong representation from international students, who comprise 10% of the student body.

The writing-intensive World English course at Middlebury was designed to mesh with this commitment to internationalization, but also to meet a need for increased L2 writing support. As part of their undergraduate degree, all Middlebury students are required to take two College Writing (CW) courses, which are usually taught by faculty in the disciplines. Faculty in the Writing Program (WRPR) offer additional, supplementary courses for students who wish to receive more attention from a composition specialist. Many L2 writers had been encouraged by their faculty advisers to take a WRPR course but were reluctant to do so since those courses did not fulfill general education distributions or other graduation requirements and were not tied to their academic interests.

The World English course at Middlebury was designed to appeal more directly to L2 writers, by offering content that was more globally-oriented than that in other WRPR courses, and also met requirements for general education distributions. It was hoped that such a course would attract a mix of stronger and weaker writers, as well a range of cultural and linguistic backgrounds and academic interests. The course was open to L1 writers as well—in essence, responding the call put forth by Jonathan Hall (2009):"How can we develop differentiated instruction methods so that both monolingual English speakers and MLLs [multilingual language learners] simultaneously have a rich and satisfying classroom experience in the same writing classroom?" (p. 45). We hoped that a course with these attributes would be an ideal space for students who might be hesitant to select an "ESL" or "remedial" course.

The course we created, "The English Language in a Global Context," fulfills two general education requirements—one in social analysis and another in comparative cultures—and has been approved as an elective option for minors in Linguistics and Education Studies. The course is advertised to students in the syllabus as an interdisciplinary content course in English language/ sociolinguistics that helps students "develop a deeper understanding of the relationship between language and socio-political dynamics." It also fulfills the goals of the Writing Program, which include teaching "critical and creative thinking, conventions of academic discourse, and persuasive argumentation" (**Middlebury College**). As with other WRPR offerings, this course teaches writing via a process approach, offering multiple opportunities for feedback and revision. This particular WRPR course put greater emphasis, however, on critical reading, use of source texts, genre, and other disciplinary conventions.

Course material for this variation of the global English course included articles and essays from the social sciences, as well as supplementary material from the humanities, including poetry, prose, creative nonfiction, film, and other digital media. As with the GW model, the writing assignments for this course required research, analysis, and argumentation: For the first assignment, students researched and reported on a particular variety of English, drawing on course readings and outside sources, as necessary. Topics for this assignment included US-focused varieties, such as Boston English, Chicano English, or African American Vernacular, as well as Englishes in "outer" and "expanding" circle countries, such as Jamaica, Singapore, France, and China. Students presented their findings orally and in a written report. The second assignment was a position paper on a controversial question, such as one of the following: "How serious a problem is linguistic imperialism?" "Should the US (or another country) adopt English as its official language?" "What if anything should be done about language death, particularly if English is a contributing factor?" These assignments gave students the opportunity to practice expository and persuasive writing, as well as to improve their use of textual borrowing practices and academic register. The final project, entitled "World Englishes and Social Justice," took a more creative turn. Students wrote for a public audience in response to an issue or problem that had been raised throughout the semester, such as bilingual education, language loss, or linguistic prejudice. Student work for this project included autobiographical essays, editorial letters, informational pamphlets, public speeches, and works of fiction. For all three of these major assignments, students completed multiple revisions, receiving feedback from peers, peer tutors, and the instructor. They also reflected on what they had learned, in a Writer's Memo submitted with the final draft. (See http://shawnashapiro.com for more course materials).

The global English course model we have proposed and piloted in these two variations has been successful in a number of regards: It has drawn students from a diverse array of linguistic and cultural backgrounds, and has created the space for them to put their personal experience into dialogue with the course material. It has caused students to question their own assumptions about language, identity, and power, and to write in thoughtful and critical ways about complex concepts. Below, we discuss in greater detail how this course responds to our call for a more inclusive response to internationalization.

Cultivating Global Competency

This course model embodies the goals of internationalization by embedding curricular content that is global in nature. The spread and current use of the English language has been driven by global forces and is sometimes used as a symbol of our interconnected world. At the same time, this course speaks to both the humanist and the practical rationales for internationalization, as articulated earlier. A course on global English allows us to identify—and question—the structures of power that have enabled English to rise to its hegemonic position. Interrogating our own assumptions and asking questions about who "owns" English, as well as who may be advantaged or disadvantaged by its use in a global setting, can help students uncover global inequalities and perhaps envision the world as a community with a shared future. In terms of the global marketplace, this type of course offers a perspective on the language of global commerce and what it means to interact with those who speak the same language in very different contexts. Students in both variations of the course have commented on how it has expanded their global perspective. One student in the GW course said in the course evaluation that the most valuable aspect of the class was "to come to understand the vague term 'English as a Global Language' in a historical, sociological way." One of the Middlebury students wrote, "I loved this course, because it made me think about things I had never thought about before." Another Middlebury student said, "I learned to look at systems of power in the world more critically."

INCLUSIVENESS AND RELEVANCE FOR DIVERSE STUDENT POPULATIONS

Because this course model offers curricular material that is deeply global in nature, it can be inclusive of the experiences and needs of diverse student populations. The content of the course is relevant to students of any cultural and linguistic background but what truly distinguishes this course is that, by its very nature, it invites different perspectives and points of view. The classroom can become a shared space in which L1 and L2 students are co-creators of knowledge, with each drawing authority from his/her own experience and cultural background and interacting to make meaning of globally relevant concepts. Native speakers of English, who may have been socialized in monolingual, monocultural classrooms, are forced to look beyond their own understanding of the language, and to consider how it is perceived in other contexts (a benefit of linguistically diverse classes that was also noted by graduate students in Fredericksen & Mangelsdorf [this volume]). This awareness was reflected in the comments from students in the Middlebury course who said they appreciated the diversity of backgrounds represented in the course: "This course taught me to question my own culture," said one Middlebury student, "because I never thought that any English beside my own was correct." An L1 writer explained in a reflective assignment, "I have never had experience with losing my identity or culture because of language." For this reason, she wrote her final project about the cognitive benefits of being bilingual, in order to "help other people like me, who have not experienced that double identity, still appreciate and encourage bilingualism."

Second language writers in both variations of the course commented that the global content empowered them to share their personal experience more than they had in most of their other classes. One of the GW students said, "We can bring in our own learning experience to this class to make the class more diverse." This course is "very helpful for international students," explained another, "because they have more chances to express their opinions [and are] able to participate in class more vigorously." Making these sorts of connections helped L2 writers to understand themselves better. Similarly, one of the Middlebury students said the course "allowed me to tap in to my heritage and identity" (See Hirsch [this volume] and Phillips [this volume] for more evidence that curricula that invited L2 students to draw on their multicultural experiences as resources is beneficial to L2 writing development). Another wrote that the course helped him/her to "understand about the challenges I have been facing." When all students have an equal – though perhaps different— stake in the course content, we move away from the assimilationist assumptions that can disadvantage or silence students who are outside of the mainstream. In interacting with course content and peers, students are able to engage in reciprocal and transformative learning. This is where we can move from the skills of global competence into a deeper conception of global mindedness, one that is oriented toward diversity as a strength rather than a deficiency.

An additional benefit of the course derived from its approach to writing instruction which was responsive to students' needs as writers. According to Jonathan Hall (2009), the "hallmark of the EAP approach is a rigorous and detailed breakdown of common academic tasks into their components, which are examined independently and taught sequentially" (p. 44). The pedagogical expertise of the instructor as a TESOL specialist helped enable students to attend actively to the processes and practices of writing. One GW student remarked that "This class actually helps international students to develop their writing skills, while other WI classes just make students to write without teaching them how to." Another commented that the most valuable aspect of the class was being able to understand how to do social science research and writing, and another mentioned the benefit of the process-oriented approach and the high level of support offered in the class: "My writing only gets improved when I keep practicing and refining with comments from my instructor." (For examples of WI syllabi and curricula that effectively make use of WAC pedagogies to scaffold writing instruction for L2 students, see Hirsch [this volume]).

It integrates cross-disciplinary perspectives

Another benefit of the English in a global context course model is that it does not pretend to occupy a single discipline. Because the topic of global English is inherently interdisciplinary, this course creates opportunities for coordination across programs and departments. We describe the materials for this model course as being drawn from a range of social science disciplines, because it would be impossible to say that global English fits into only one space. We can speak of it as a linguistic phenomenon, or define it in anthropological terms, or policy terms, or economic terms, but putting this topic into a single disciplinary space limits our perspective on the issue. In other words, the English language is *global* in nature and its implications are complex and far-reaching. Creating an inclusive and interdisciplinary space for this course allows us to honor its complexity and diversity.

Building a course around a theme that is interdisciplinary in nature makes it much easier to fulfill the cross-disciplinary goals of WAC, and therefore to build more institutional alliances. Though our colleges and universities often operate on a model of disciplinary division, the WAC framework offers one way to enter cross-disciplinary territory by embedding writing instruction across the curriculum. Inviting L2 writing specialists into that space enhances the level of writing support for multilingual writers, and can in turn reduce the isolation of TESOL faculty. This support for interdisciplinary interaction also extends to students' classroom experiences. As a result of this class, students learn to think about global English, and about the act of writing, from multiple disciplinary perspectives: one student who took the WI course at GW said, "I learned the style and form of social science writing (ex. APA) and social science (especially sociological, anthropological, a little linguistic) way of analyzing information." Another said, similarly, "I learned … the fields that social science study, how to read these articles and analyze, how to interact with scholars' ideas." An international student at Middlebury commented in an email, "Now, I can write different type of papers, academic, research and directed to public audience ones. I am not going to say that I have been perfect in writing, but I know that, what I learned in this class was a lot!" This responsiveness to rhetorical situations is a hallmark of WAC writing instruction, and adding the element of global perspectives heightens our students' ability to interact across cultural spaces.

ADDITIONAL CONSIDERATIONS

Our global English courses are one means by which TESOL specialists can contribute to the curricular offerings of WAC programs. In the section below, we offer suggestions for institutions looking to encourage more of these sorts of contributions from TESOL specialists, as well as for instructors looking to incorporate internationalized content, such as the global English theme, into their writing-intensive courses.

First, it is important to tailor the course to each institutional context. Colleges and universities whose mission statements and strategic priorities emphasize global competency may be particularly open to developing globally-oriented curricular options and tapping into TESOL specialists and L2 writers as resources. Schools should also consider their departmental framework and academic culture. In both variations of this course model, there was an infrastructure in place for cross-departmental coordination, as well as a general understanding of the struggles and needs of diverse writers across the campus, which created opportunities for dialogue between writing programs and TESOL programs. Institutions were further willing to approve innovative course offerings that diversified the curriculum and strengthened the level of support for multilingual writers, while at the same time fulfilling requirements. For this sort of coordination to be effective, institutions must recognize that TESOL specialists are often untapped resources in the academic community.

An additional consideration for a course of this kind is deciding who has the interest and expertise to teach it. In both variations of the course model described here, a TESOL specialist designed and taught the course, with input and support from the WAC program. Scholars such as Ruth Spack (1988), however, have warned TESOL specialists about the dangers of building courses around content areas in which they are not proficient. Though such instructors may be highly qualified in teaching the rhetorical principles and skills of writing, they may find that they have "little basis for dealing with the content ... [or] find themselves in the uncomfortable position of being less knowledgeable than their students" (p. 37). For a course like this to be successful, TESOL faculty should be fluent in the methods of inquiry, textual conventions, and scholarly interactions of the field, so that students can be "immerse[d] in the subject matter ... by participating in the field, by doing, by sharing, and by talking about it with those who know more" (Spack, 1988, p. 40). Faculty who have some reservations about teaching global English may wish to pilot a single unit on global English for an existing course, before developing an entirely new course on the topic. It is also important for TESOL specialists to draw on the expertise of colleagues in writing programs, as well as to connect with instructional librarians for support in accessing research materials appropriate to the course content.

The intended mix of students (L2-only or mixed L1/L2) also depends on the institutional setting, as well on the goals of the program offering the course. There are advantages to both options: In an L2-only course, for example, students feel more confident expressing themselves in class. One GW student commented that L2 students "get more active in class when there are only international students," and another offered a remark on the affective environment of the L2-only class: "I think 'international only' is good. This can be contradicted with UW (university writing) because most of my friends don't say anything in that class." However, one of the second language writers in the GW class made the point that it would be valuable to have L1 students in the class as well "because local students can share their views on global status of English." Another reason to consider a mixed classroom is to reduce the stigma of segregation, since many multilingual writers (particularly those who are US-educated) are resistant to "ESL" labels (Ortmeier-Hooper, 2008). Although it can be difficult to address all of the literacy needs present in a mixed class, the diversity of the student population certainly enriches students' understanding of course material, as well as their overall sense of institutional integration.

CONCLUDING THOUGHTS

In this chapter, we have argued that the phenomenon of internationalization presents new pedagogical opportunities within higher education. In order for internationalization to have a transformative impact on students, however, a global orientation must be integrated throughout the curriculum, and must be linked to other institutional goals of diversity and inclusion. WAC and TESOL have a great deal to offer to institutions seeking the integration of internationalization throughout the curriculum, because each has a historical commitment to curricular innovation and inclusive pedagogy. Yet rarely do the two disciplines have the opportunity to partner together in this regard. The writing-intensive global English course is certainly not the only form such a partnership might take, but it offers tremendous potential toward the goal of inclusion—not just for students, but also for TESOL professionals. A course of this kind allows the disciplines to work together as institutional allies, toward a more democratic and globally-competent curriculum for all students.

REFERENCES

Atkinson, D., & Ramanathan, V. (1995). Cultures of writing: An ethnographic comparison of L1 and L2 university writing/language programs. *TESOL Quarterly, 29*, 539-568.

Braine, G. (1996). ESL students in first-year writing courses: ESL versus mainstream classes. *Journal of Second Language Writing, 5*(1), 91-107.

Blumenthal, A. J. (2002). English as a second language at the community college: An exploration of contexts and concerns. *New Directions for Community Colleges, 117*, 45-53.

Canagarajah, A. S. (2006). Toward a writing pedagogy of shuttling between languages: Learning from multilingual writers. *College English, 68*(6), 589-604.

Caruana, V. (2010). The relevance of the internationalised curriculum to graduate capability. In E. Jones (Ed.), *Internationalisation and the student voice: Higher education perspectives* (pp. 30-43). New York/ London: Routledge.

Cox, M. (n.d.). *WAC and second-language writing*. WAC Clearinghouse. Retrieved from http://wac.colostate.edu/slw/

The George Washington University (n.d.). *Writing in the Disciplines*. Retrieved from http://www.gwu.edu/~uwp/wid/wid-about.html

Gray, M. J., Rolph, E. S., & Melamid, E. (1996). *Immigration and higher education: Institutional responses to changing demographics*. Santa Monica, CA: RAND Corporation.

Hall, J. (2009). WAC/WID in the next America: Redefining professional identity in the age of the multilingual majority. *The WAC Journal, 20*, 33-49.

Harklau, L. (1994). ESL and mainstream classes: Contrasting second language learning contexts. *TESOL Quarterly, 28*(2), 241-272.

Hunter, B., White, G., & Godbey, G. (2006). What does it mean to be globally competent? *Journal of Studies in International Education, 10*(3), 267-285.

Ignash, J. M. (1995). Encouraging ESL student persistence: The influence of policy on design. *Community College Review, 23*(3), 17-34.

Jones, E. & Killick, D. (2007). Internationalisation of the curriculum. In E. Jones & S. Brown (Eds.), *Internationalising higher education* (pp. 109-119). New York/ London: Routledge.

Leask, B. (2001). Bridging the gap: Internationalizing university curricula. *Journal of Studies in International Education, 5*(2), 100-115.

Leki, I. (2007). *Undergraduates in a second language: Challenges and complexities of academic literacy development*. Mahwah, NJ: Lawrence Erlbaum.

Matsuda, P. K. (1999). Composition Studies and ESL writing: A disciplinary division of labor. *College Composition and Communication, 50*(4), 699-721.

Matsuda, P. K. (2006). The myth of linguistic homogeneity in US college composition. *College English 68*(6), 637-51.

Matsuda, P. K., & Jablonski, J. (2000). Beyond the L2 metaphor: Towards a mutually transformative model of ESL/WAC collaboration. *Academic. Writing, 1*. Retrieved from http://wac.colostate.edu/aw/articles/matsuda_jablonski2000.htm

Middlebury College (n.d.) *Middlebury's Mission Statement*. Retrieved from http://www.middlebury.edu/about/mission

Olson, C. L., & Kroeger, K. R. (2001). Global competency and intercultural sensitivity. *Journal of Studies in International Education, 5,* 116-137.

Ortmeier-Hooper, C. (2008). English may be my second language, but I'm not ESL. *College Composition and Communication, 59*(3), 389-419.

Roberge, M., Harklau, L., & Siegal, M. (2009). *Generation 1.5 in college composition: Teaching ESL to US-educated learners of ESL.* New York: Routledge.

Shapiro, S. (2012). Stuck in the remedial rut: Confronting resistance to ESL curriculum reform. *Journal of Basic Writing, 30*(2), 24-52.

Shapiro, S. (2012). Citizens vs. aliens: How institutional policies construct linguistic minority students. In Y. Kanno & L. Harklau (Eds). *Linguistic minority students go to college: Preparation, access, and persistence* (pp. 238-254). New York: Routledge.

Shapiro, S. (n.d.). *Curriculum Vitae.* Retrieved from http://shawnashapiro.com

Spack, R. (1988). Initiating ESL students into the academic discourse community: How far should we go? *TESOL Quarterly, 22*(1), 29-51.

Stromquist, N. P. (2007). Internationalization as a response to globalization: Radical shifts in university environments. *Higher Education, 53*(1), 81-105.

Taylor, J. (2004). Toward a strategy for internationalisation: Lessons and practice from four universities. *Journal of Studies In International Education, 8*(2), 149-171.

TESOL (2012). *Position statement on academic and degree-granting credit for ESOL courses in postsecondary education.* Retrieved from http://www.tesol.org/docs/pdf/academic-credit-for-esl-in-postsecondary-institutions.pdf?sfvrsn=0

Van Gyn, G., Schuerholz-Lehr, S., Caws, C., & Preece, A. (2009). Education for world-mindedness: Beyond superficial notions of internationalization. In C. Kreber (Ed.), *Internationalizing the curriculum in higher education* (pp. 25-38). San Francisco: Jossey-Bass.

Van Meter, J. (1990). Academic credit for ESL classes? *Review of Research in Developmental Education, 8*(1), 2-6.

Williams, J. (1995). ESL composition program administration in the United States. *Journal of Second Language Writing 4*(2), 157-179.

Zawacki, T. M., & Cox, M. (2011). Introduction to WAC and second language writing. *Across the Disciplines, 8*(4). Retrieved from http://wac.colostate.edu/atd/ell/zawacki-cox.cfm

CHAPTER 14

GRADUATE WRITING WORKSHOPS: CROSSING LANGUAGES AND DISCIPLINES

Elaine Fredericksen and Kate Mangelsdorf
University of Texas at El Paso

A Graduate Writing Workshop aimed at graduate students from various language backgrounds and disciplines is described. Taught in an English Department by faculty with second-language writing backgrounds, the workshop is structured around a student-created contract that is sufficiently flexible to accommodate a wide range of students' literacies. In the workshop, students work on writing required for their degrees, such as research reports, theses, and dissertations. The results of a survey of former students show that most students thought that working with peers from different language backgrounds and academic fields was beneficial. Because the university is situated on the US-Mexico border, most students are bilingual, which might have made students more receptive to the multilingualism of the course. Suggestions are given for developing a similar Graduate Writing Workshop at other colleges and universities, particularly those in which most students come from various language backgrounds.

In addition to serving the needs of undergraduate students, WAC/WID programs are increasingly playing a role in supporting graduate student writers, who are becoming more diverse every year. The number of international students enrolled in U. S. graduate schools jumped 11% from 2010-2011 (Fischer, 2011), and minority student graduate enrollment is increasing as well (National Center, 2011). To serve these diverse populations effectively, WAC/WID programs require resources, administrative support, and leadership, all of which may be in short supply in under-resourced institutions. Because our own university—the University of Texas at El Paso, or UTEP—has been unable to sustain a WAC program, six years ago one of the authors of this chapter, Mangelsdorf, who directed UTEP's Rhetoric and Composition PhD program, was asked by the dean of the UTEP Graduate School to develop a writing course for graduate students across campus who needed assistance in completing their research reports, theses, and dissertations. The other author of this chapter, Fredericksen, has been the lead instructor for the course that was developed, which is housed in the English department and which has, since it was first offered, attracted English L1, L2, and bilingual students. In this chapter, we describe this course, called the Graduate Writing Workshop, and, using the results of a survey of former students who have taken the workshop, we analyze the benefits and drawbacks of the course, focusing in particular on the effectiveness of the course in offering writing instruction for students from different language backgrounds and disciplines. Finally, we offer suggestions for adapting this type of workshop course to other institutional settings, particularly those with students who have a wide range of language proficiencies and experiences.

GRADUATE WRITING WORKSHOP MODELS

A writing course for graduate students from a variety of language backgrounds and disciplines, with students who might range from new MA students to PhD students writing dissertations, is challenging to develop and teach. Frodesen (1995) has noted that such a course "must not only address writing needs across disciplines; it must adapt to students' various stages of involvement in the larger academic community and in their specific disciplines" (p. 333). Further, the level of student engagement in such a course can be undermined if the students are not given course credit toward their degree. Another challenge of such a course can come from its location within the institution. A course that is housed in the English Department, for instance, can be isolated from students' disciplinary homes, especially if the university lacks a strong WAC/WID program. This isolation can bolster the false notion that form and content are separate: English teachers are responsible for *how* students write while disciplinary faculty take care of *what* students write. Concerning writing in the disciplines, however, Bazerman et al. (2005) argue that "students are aided most by learning how to understand and participate in specific writing situations, including learning and responding to the local criteria and expectations, as well as strategically deploying task-relevant techniques" (p. 89). While we agree that teaching writing within specific disciplinary contexts is preferable, such a program was not on the horizon at our university. In this chapter we argue that in certain contexts and with appropriate curricula, a writing course that crosses disciplines and languages and that is taught by a writing specialist rather than a disciplinary insider, such as the writing workshop that we describe here, can help students develop and improve as writers and raise their awareness of language-related issues.

When Mangelsdorf created and developed this course, she drew on characteristics of successful English L1 and L2 graduate-level writing courses both in the US and abroad. In several of the courses she looked at, students studied genres of writing common to their various disciplines (Belcher, 2009; Cargill, Cadman, & McGowan, 2001; Delyser, 2003; Dudley-Evans, 1995; Swales & Lindemann, 2002), and some involved content-area faculty in the writing course (Barratt, Hanlon, & Rankin, 2011; Dudley-Evans, 1995). Peer review was a valuable component in many of the syllabi she used as models (Belcher, 2009; Delyser, 2003; Dudley-Evans, 1995; Frodesen, 1995; Heinrich, Neese, Rogers, & Farente, 2004; Steinert, McLeon, Liben & Snell, 2008). The course she planned, based on these models, featured peer review groups who were given time to work together at almost every class meeting (thus the name of the course, Graduate Writing Workshop). Because the dean of the Graduate School had emphasized that students needed help with their theses and dissertations, she was also particularly focused on allowing students to work on these projects in the course. She was also aware, however, that the course would attract students just beginning their graduate studies, so, to accommodate the different types of writing that students would be producing, she borrowed an idea from a course described by Frodesen (1995), in which students were given the flexibility of designing their own assignments. Following this model, she decided that most of the course curriculum would originate from contracts that students created at the beginning of the workshop in which they made their own assignments and set their own deadlines (see Phillips [this volume] for a description of a graduate writing course that became more effective when the graduate student was permitted to develop a similar contract.) The flexibility of the contract system would be especially useful for L2 students who needed more time to write. As will be explained later, the contract system became a key feature in the success of the workshop.

UTEP's local context also played a role in the course design. UTEP is a Research 1-aspirational university that draws much of its student body from the El Paso, US/Ciudad Juarez, Mexico region. In fall 2011, 60% of degree-seeking graduate students were Hispanic, 16% were White, 10% were Mexican Internationals, and 7% were "other International" (University of Texas at El Paso, 2012). Thus, the graduate student population is primarily Spanish-English bilingual, though students also come from the Middle East, East Asia, and China. While Mangelsdorf was unable to find a description of a graduate writing course that blended L1 and L2 students, the bilingualism of UTEP's student body made it impractical to offer separate different sections of the workshop for L2 learners, or to separate L1 and L2 learners in the workshop curriculum. This range of language orientations, which is becoming a norm in many US universities (Hall, 2009), posed a challenge, however, because instruction had to be sufficiently differentiated to meet students' various needs. But the blended course also offered opportunities for students to communicate with and learn from students with different language backgrounds. As we've seen, the range and continuum of students' linguistic expertise, combined with the range of disciplines that they represent, has given this writing workshop a complexity and richness that, while challenging, has proven to be successful in our university setting, as we'll explain, and can potentially serve as a model for other institutions with multilingual graduate students with a variety of language backgrounds and proficiencies. (As a model, this course includes many of the pedagogical components of the year-long team-taught writing and language courses offered in the more resource-intensive ACCESS and Bridge programs that Mallett & Zgheib [this volume] describe.)

THE GRADUATE WRITING WORKSHOP CURRICULUM

Our Graduate Writing Workshop (ENGL 5316), a 16-week course that meets three hours a week, was developed in response to requests from the Graduate School, as we noted. Students enroll voluntarily, though they are often strongly encouraged by their faculty advisors, and receive three hours of graduate credit that count toward financial aid but that won't count toward degree credit. A standard grading system is used (A, B, etc.). Students can enroll in the course as many times as they want, and they can take the course at any time during their graduate studies. The course is structured so that students typically complete writing projects in their degree programs, from course assignments to theses and dissertations. Two sections of the course, capped at 15 students, are offered each semester.

The instructors for the course are full-time faculty with PhDs in Rhetoric and Composition and experience teaching second language writers. They teach in UTEP's doctoral program in Rhetoric and Composition, which has intercultural writing as one of its key focuses. At the time of this writing, all but one of the faculty who have taught the course have been English-Spanish bilingual or fluent Spanish speakers, a language background that is helpful but not required. The faculty's disciplinary expertise enables them to ground the course in rhetorical principles and research-based pedagogy, and their status as full-time faculty helps to give them *ethos* when discussing the course with faculty across campus. The course counts as a regular part of the instructor's course load and is subsidized by the English Department as part of its service role in the university. Instructors are asked to follow the course curriculum and assignments (see below), though they might make minor adjustments according to their own preferences.

Because Mangelsdorf wanted to pilot the workshop curricula before handing the Graduate Writing Workshop over to other instructors, she taught the workshop the first two semesters it was offered. Subsequently, Fredericksen became the lead instructor for the workshop and over the years has refined the workshop components based on student feedback, as we'll describe.

Workshop Components

The different parts of the workshop include features frequently mentioned in the published descriptions of similar courses, including an analysis of discipline-specific writing, peer review sessions, mini-lessons, and final presentations and portfolios. The two major innovations are the structure of the peer review workshop and the student-created writing contracts.

Contracts and Evaluation

To make the course structure flexible and individualized and to enable students to communicate regularly with their major professor, the majority of the semester's work is organized according to student-created contracts. In these contracts (written during the first two weeks of the workshop), students specify the writing that they will complete each week. The contracts are created in consultation with students' major professors as well as the workshop instructor; students are encouraged to continue communicating with their major professors about their writing throughout the course. All of the writing comes from the students' required projects in their different degree plans. In their contracts, students explain the type of writing and the number of pages they will produce weekly. Generally, they are encouraged to write at least five pages of original text per week; at the same time, they revise work that has been commented on by peers and the workshop instructor, resulting in a total of up to 20 pages of writing weekly. Many students elect to increase the minimum goal, usually by dividing the finished project (e.g. articles, thesis, dissertation) into relatively equal parts spread out over the available class meetings. Students who are less experienced writing in academic English often need more revision time, so in their contracts they may specify that they will only produce two to four pages early in the semester with the goal of writing more as their skills improve. The student, the student's major professor, and the workshop instructor sign this contract, which becomes the student's syllabus for the rest of the semester and is posted on the course website for everyone to see. For some students who are just beginning their graduate studies, the workshop instructor will act as the major professor and help the student design an appropriate contract; for instance, students might summarize a number of journal articles in their field (for more on the role of summary-writing in L2 learning, see Du [this volume]). (See Appendix A for the contract assignment sheet.)

We'll note here that, because students' linguistic and rhetorical awareness of academic genres and publications is essential to their success (Johns, 2002; Swales & Feak, 2011), the one assignment that all students must complete at the start of the workshop is an analysis of a major journal in their field and an analysis of an article in that journal that can serve as a model for their own writing. The journal and the article are treated as representative artifacts that can reveal how knowledge is created, communicated, and valued in their discipline. Topics covered are both broad (why the journal is important, what kinds of evidence are used, what is assumed about the audience) and specific (the level of style, the citation system, the organizational patterns). This analysis helps to make explicit the discourse conventions in the students' academic disciplines.

Students' course grades are based on successful completion of their self-designed contracts and on the grade they receive for their analysis of scholarly publications. In addition, they must attend class regularly, participate fully in peer-review sessions, make a presentation, and submit a final portfolio, as we explain further below.

Peer Review Workshop

In several of the writing courses described in the literature (i.e., Cargill, Cadman, & McGowan, 2001; Dudley-Evans, 1995; Frodesen, 1995), instructors were concerned that students in multidisciplinary peer review groups would not understand the content of their classmates' papers, and as a result the feedback would be limited to surface-level writing issues. To work around this problem, students in our course participate in two different peer review groups throughout the semester, each of which is mixed linguistically. In "content" peer review groups, three or four students in the same or a similar field focus primarily on the ideas, evidence, format, organization, and coherence in the writing. They are encouraged to consult with their major professors when they disagree with a group member's suggestion or comment. After each content peer review group session, they revise their writing and return the next class period to work with a "proofreading" peer review group, comprising three or four students from different fields. These educated lay readers read these drafts for surface errors, conciseness, parallelism, and other local concerns, consulting with the workshop instructor when necessary. After the workshop, students revise their work for a second time and hand in their drafts to the course instructor, who provides the third reading. Students use the instructor comments to make a final revision that will appear, along with other substantive drafts, in the final portfolio. The portfolio draft is typically the one that goes to the major professor and thesis/dissertation committee.

This separation between "content" and "proofreading" in the peer review groups is necessarily artificial, and students don't always separate their responses in this way. While discussing the appropriateness of a certain feature in a proofreading session, they might begin to discuss more conceptual issues. For instance, a student who corrects the formation of the passive voice in a classmate's paper might initiate a discussion among members of the group about how different disciplines employ the passive voice in research reports. This kind of discussion illustrates how writing workshops can lead students to greater awareness of how discourse is embedded in particular rhetorical contexts.

This three-step workshop structure (content peer review group, proofreading peer review group, instructor review) ensures that each writer has a wide audience. During each step of this process, students can accept the comments they find useful and reject those they do not. Based on our observations of the peer review sessions, we have found that the most productive peer review structure is to require students to share their drafts online before each class session. As a result, students come to class having read and commented on their peers' writing and can thus spend the entire class session discussing, questioning, and expanding on the comments. This hybrid format (online reviewing plus in-class discussion) is especially helpful for students who are slower readers or who want to take their time commenting.

Mini-lessons

Almost every class day, the workshop instructor also conducts a mini-lesson, which lasts anywhere from 10 to 30 minutes and precedes the peer review sessions. The topics of mini-lessons change depending on the type of peer review sessions the students will engage in, and most apply to all of the students in the course, whether L1, L2, or bilingual. The mini-lessons are intended to provide instruction at the point of need and enable students to immediately apply what they have learned to their own (and their classmates') writing. For example, on the days when the students will be in peer review groups that focus on content, the lessons focus on issues related to writing in specific disciplines, such as different types of claims, patterns of organization, forms of evidence, documentation formats, and disciplinary lexicon, register, tone, and stance. On the days when students will be participating in proofreading peer review groups, the focus is typically on punctuation, grammar and usage, vocabulary, and other more local considerations. When discussing parallelism and conciseness, instructors take examples from students' writing. When topics are more specific to L2 students, such as word order, verb tense, articles, and prepositions, native English speakers learn more about the grammar of their own language and gain a greater appreciation of the challenges of writing in an unfamiliar language. When vocabulary is discussed, connections between languages are particularly emphasized as is the reality of world Englishes and how languages change according to particular contexts. (Students read about World Englishes in the handbook used in the course, Raimes and Jerskey's *Universal Keys for Writers*.) Thus while students are improving their ability to use standard written English, they are also becoming more aware that languages are always developing and changing.

Presentations and Portfolios

During the last week or so of the semester, students make oral presentations, supported by slides and handouts, about their class experience. They give a brief synopsis of the completed segments of their projects, present their electronic or paper portfolios for class perusal, and talk about their perceived progress as writers. The presentations are not graded, but do include questions and comments from the audience. These serve as invention material for the self-reflection statements that are included in the end-of-semester portfolios.

The portfolios, not graded but required for successful completion of the course, may be electronic or paper. They include the contract, the journal analysis, and all sections of the project that have been worked on in class, both final drafts and substantive preliminary drafts with peer and instructor comments. Perhaps the most important item in the final portfolio, however, is the self-reflection letter. Here students write about themselves as writers, rather than as scientists, engineers, artists, accountants, and so on. Many students comment that reading papers written by their classmates in a variety of fields made them more conscious of how each field has its own way of creating and communicating knowledge. Students often refer to the frequent discussions about language and culture in the workshop; these discussions appear to help the L2 students in particular become more motivated and write with greater confidence. (The survey results that we give in the next section of this chapter provide a fuller explanation of this point.) This rhetorical awareness of language, audience, purpose, and context is one benefit of a course with a range of languages and disciplines represented; this mix can help give students the rhetorical flexibility and awareness that they will need as they "shuttle" (Canagarajah, 2006) between the languages and discourse communities that they will encounter.

The purpose of these different course components—the students' individual writing contracts, the journal and article analysis, the two types of peer review sessions, the mini-lessons, and the presentation, portfolio, and reflection—is to give students ample writing support and feedback, while at the same time accommodating the students' varied language backgrounds and making language difference an asset. The survey results, explained below, suggest that for the most part this goal has been achieved.

CROSSING LANGUAGES AND DISCIPLINES: A STUDENT SURVEY

Because enrollment was strong in this writing workshop, we believed the course appeared to meet the needs of students. However, every semester a few students missed too many classes. While the most common reasons for absences were either personal (such as illness) or professional (a professional conference to attend), we wanted to make sure that students found the workshop beneficial to attend. Student input would also help us to continue improving the course design, particularly as it pertained to the mixing of language backgrounds and disciplinary specialties within the same class. Using SurveyMonkey, we designed an 18-item survey (see Appendix B) that asked students about the course as well as gathered information about their fields of study and languages. Before distributing the survey, we piloted it by asking several students to take it and make suggestions for revision. Then, we emailed 71 former students to ask them to complete the survey; of these, 27 answered for a response rate of 28%. For the most part, the respondents were students who had taken the course most recently, in the last couple of semesters.

In this section, we focus on the survey results as they pertain to two fundamental characteristics of the workshop, the mixing of languages and disciplines. The 27 students who responded to the survey represented a cross-section of disciplines, with Engineering (6), Health Science (5), and Science (4) being the most common. Seventeen of the students were enrolled in doctoral programs and 10 in master's programs. The students' self-reported language backgrounds reflected UTEP's location on the US-Mexico border to some extent. A slim majority of students (17 or 66%) self-reported as proficient in speaking and writing in English and Spanish. Other languages represented by the students were Nepali, Hindi, Thai, and Telugu. When asked their countries of origin, eleven students indicated Mexico, eight said they were from the US, and the other students listed Nepal (2), India (2), Cuba (1), and Thailand (1). Only one student self-identified as monolingual English.

Survey Results: Crossing Languages

Because the mix of bilingual and monolingual speakers with English L2 speakers in the course is unique, we wanted to know the students' views about how well this mix worked for them. We asked, "Tell us your thoughts about working with students who had different language backgrounds. To what extent, if any, did this benefit you?" Twenty-three students had entirely positive views about working with linguistically diverse writers; three had some positive and some negative perspectives; and two were entirely negative about the experience.

The students who had only positive comments on this question wrote that working with students from a variety of language backgrounds helped them learn aspects of English that they could apply to their own writing, increased their metalinguistic awareness, improved their oral comprehension of English, and enhanced their appreciation of multiculturalism/multilingualism. Here are some sample responses from students who described themselves as Spanish-English bilingual:

> I found myself meeting and talking to people with the same language issues as me, and helping each other in finding the correct words or order.

> I need to hear accented Englishes more (that are different from Spanish).

> It was supportive, enhanced the multicultural setting of UTEP, and my learning experience too.

> This interaction helps in identifying other languages' writing styles.

We speculate that these bilingual English-Spanish students might have been more open about linguistic diversity because at UTEP and in the community at large, bilingualism is the norm. Almost half of UTEP's entering students report that they are equally comfortable speaking Spanish and English.

The two students who expressed problems with working with students from different language backgrounds focused on the time that it took them to read and comment on their fellow students' writing. These students, who spoke neither English nor Spanish as a first language, also expressed a strong preference for working with native English speakers:

> A mix of students helps, but there should be enough English native speakers to help students whose first language is other than English.

> As an ESL student it is better to work with monolingual students because sometimes I doubt other ESL students' corrections.

The assumption in these two comments is that native English speakers are better able to help writers edit their work, an example of what Kubota and Lin (2006), among others, have called "native speakerism." This assumption can occur even though non-native English speakers may have had more preparation and experience writing standard academic English than their native English-speaking counterparts (see Phillips [this volume] for an example of this dynamic in group work assigned at the graduate level). Perhaps these students were not as open to learning from students with different language backgrounds because they were not in the bilingual mainstream at UTEP.

Because so few students had negative responses to this question, we believe that the multilingual course approach is valuable. Throughout the course, instructors emphasize the value of multilingualism, in particular in mini-lessons that focus on correcting surface errors. For instance, when everyone in the workshop recognizes that *in* and *on* both translate to *en* in Spanish, they realize why native Spanish speakers have trouble with these prepositions. When everyone knows that articles seldom appear in Asian languages, they see the need to help native speakers of these languages use articles in English. Awareness of difference not only made the workshop proceed more smoothly, it also strengthened classroom relationships.

Survey Results: Concerns about Standard English Correctness

While students clearly valued the variety of language backgrounds in the workshop, the survey also revealed a persistent concern with writing correct academic English. In a question about the classroom activities that students found most helpful to them, the four most frequent responses were the proofreading peer review groups, the grammar lessons, the vocabulary exercises, and the punctuation practice. Similarly, in a question concerning how students thought their writing had improved, the two most common responses were: "I know more about correcting errors" and "I make fewer errors in my writing." When we asked students "What recommendations do you have for improving English 5316?", the most frequent recommendation was for the course to include more lessons in grammar, vocabulary, and punctuation—this despite the fact that almost all students reported that their proficiency with surface-level correctness had improved as a result of the course.

Pressures to produce error-free writing (from a U.S perspective) are still extremely powerful both in the US in general and in the academy in particular, despite the fact that non-native English speakers outnumber native English speakers at least three to one worldwide (Crystal, 2003). For example, Thaiss and Zawacki's (2006) results from a faculty and student survey found that faculty valued grammatical correctness, some of them emphatically. The students they studied "gave no evidence of resisting this expectation" (p. 132). Grammatical correctness is often associated with positive attributes such as paying attention to detail, a view expressed in a recent article in the *Harvard Business Review* titled "I Won't Hire People Who Use Poor Grammar. Here's Why" (Wiens, 2012). Many studies (i.e., Fredericksen, 2006) indicate that spoken accents and accented writing (such as the misuse of prepositions or omission of articles) create problems for bilingual and L2 speakers when they apply for jobs, present papers at conferences, or teach in the US.

We have found that workshop discussions often function as a release valve for students to express their anxieties about language. Because language insecurities of some kind affect almost all language users whether English L2, bilingual, or English L1, these discussions tended to make the workshop students more supportive of each other. For instance, in one peer review group session, they complained about professors who told them they use too many commas, or not enough commas, or to never use commas at all. Teaching assistants in the course talked about freshmen who say that their accents are too thick. And all shared ideas about how to alleviate nervousness when giving presentations. They often requested mini-lessons on usage topics, such as the difference between *effect* and *affect*, that concern students from all language backgrounds.

Survey Results: Crossing Disciplines

As we noted, students in this Graduate Writing Workshop come from a variety of academic fields, and they spend much of their class time interacting with peers outside of their own disciplines. To discover the usefulness of these interactions, we asked: "What are your thoughts about working with students in different fields? To what extent, if any, did this benefit you?" Twenty-three respondents had positive comments in regard to working with students from various disciplines; three had mixed reactions.

The many students who said that they liked this aspect of the course wrote that working with students in a variety of fields taught them about other disciplines, increased their awareness of different discourse conventions, improved their reading and vocabulary, and helped them write more clearly:

> A multidisciplinary approach not only increased my vocabulary, but also my knowledge of other fields.
>
> It helps students write in a style easy to understand for everyone.
>
> Working with students outside my discipline made me more aware of audience differences and writing style preferences across disciplines. I began to pay more attention to stylistic matters that I had typically shrugged off as being "just my way of writing."

Our students' responses to the mixture of disciplines were similar to the positive reactions by students in the graduate writing courses taught by Dudley-Evans (1995), Frodesen (1995), and Norris & Tardy (2006), who also found that working with peers from other fields can help students understand that there is no single way to conduct research or communicate knowledge.

We do acknowledge, however, that a generalist writing workshop cannot accomplish what writing instruction within a student's discipline can accomplish even when the course instructor seeks assistance from the students' faculty advisors. For instance, the workshop instructor can describe only in a general way the different sections of a research report, while understanding, at the same time, that there is no single research report genre as the genre is shaped by the actions it performs within a particular disciplinary context. So, while working across disciplines can add to students' general rhetorical awareness, they still need instruction and feedback within their own disciplinary communities. We tried to accomplish this instruction in the content peer review groups, in which students from the same or similar disciplines were grouped together. These groups were not entirely successful, however; as one survey student noted, "Content groups often did not catch content errors." Depending on who registered for the workshop, a few of the content groups also lacked disciplinary cohesiveness.

Even in mixed disciplinary groups, however, the feedback could still be helpful. In one class, for example, a group of students from communication, teacher education, and rhetoric and communication engaged in conversations on topics such as the difficulties of conducting qualitative research, the IRB process they each experienced, and the traditional IMRAD (Introduction, Methods, Results and Discussion) report format.

SURVEY IMPLICATIONS

As we've indicated, the survey elicited primarily positive responses from the students regarding the multilingual and multidisciplinary aspects of the course. Overall satisfaction was high as well; when asked if they would recommend the course to another student, all of the students reported that they would. In particular, the overall satisfaction with the multilingual aspect of the course—the wide range of students' language proficiencies and backgrounds—was a pleasant surprise given that a clear demarcation between L1 and L2 students usually exists in higher education (Matsuda, 2006). What facilitated this successful mixture of students from different language backgrounds?

No doubt part of this success was that at UTEP, Spanish-English bilingualism is the norm. As the demographics of our survey indicated, a little over half of the students surveyed self-identified as bilingual, which accords with the UTEP's student body as a whole. A smaller but still sizeable percentage of students self-identify as Spanish dominant, with monolingual English speakers a clear minority. And, as mentioned earlier, all but one of the workshop instructors has been either Spanish-English bilingual or a fluent Spanish speaker. The faculty's personal understanding of the challenges of learning academic English has added to the overall openness about language differences that has permeated the course.

We believe that the structure of the course, in particular the contract system, also has contributed to the workshop's effectiveness regarding the range of student language backgrounds. In the survey, we included a question about the effectiveness of the contracts that students created in which they set their own assignments and deadlines. The responses to the contracts were almost uniformly positive. To the open-ended question, "What did you think of the contract grading system in which you decided on the projects you would complete for the course?" Twenty-four of the 27 students gave entirely positive responses that often focused on how the contracts helped the students with time management. We suggest that a contract system might be particularly helpful for students less experienced with writing in academic English than their peers. Leki's (2007) case studies of L2 writing students, for example, documented the students' struggles to meet deadlines more appropriate for L1 students. The contracts gave all students both flexibility and a sense of control over their writing development. (For further evidence of the importance of allowing multilingual graduate students develop their own plan for graduate writing seminars, see Phillips [this volume]).

ESSENTIAL COMPONENTS OF OUR COURSE AS A MODEL FOR OTHERS

The sustained popularity of the Graduate Writing Workshop, the number of students who choose to repeat it, and the students' positive comments about the course in our survey, albeit based on a relatively small response rate, demonstrate that such a course can be valuable in helping graduate students from a variety of language backgrounds and disciplines develop as writers. In particular, our survey suggests that a flexible and individualized contract system, combined with structured peer review sessions, can give students from different language backgrounds the time and feedback necessary for them to progress. The workshop also addresses students' anxieties about not being able to write "correctly"—an important part of helping students gain the linguistic capital they need to feel confident enough to succeed in their disciplines.

We believe that this workshop model can be adapted for other institutional contexts, in particular institutions with a significant number of bilingual and multilingual graduate students. Based on our own experiences, we suggest the following as essential components of such a course, including the first in this list that we would do were able to revisit the planning phase of our course.

1. **Make systematic connections to disciplinary faculty.** When the Graduate Writing Workshop was in the planning stages, several faculty across campus were contacted informally for their suggestions. However, connections with these faculty were not systematically maintained, and as a result feedback from faculty across campus has been sporadic. In order to maintain faculty input and support, we recommend that early in the planning stages, faculty across the disciplines who have voiced concerns about student writing be invited to join a committee that will assist in gaining institutional buy-in, designing the course curriculum, and assessing the course's effectiveness for graduate writers. These faculty will also likely be the ones to suggest the course to their students, which will help facilitate communication between the workshop instructor, students, and supervising professors.

2. **Ensure that course instructors understand language acquisition and appreciate language differences.** While it is not necessary that course

instructors be L2 or bilingual writers themselves, it is important that they know the challenges of acquiring standard academic English and view multilingualism as an asset to the overall learning in the course.

3. Structure the course around student-created contracts. Organizing the writing course around student-written contracts can ensure that students are producing writing that is part of their degree plans. The contracts also give more time to students who are less experienced writing in English, help to promote time management, and allow students to feel more in control of their writing progress. This individualized course structure can be especially effective for students with a wide range of language backgrounds and proficiencies.

4. Provide students with the linguistic capital that they need to succeed in their graduate programs. Give students the instruction and resources they want to feel competent in producing correct standard language forms. At the same time, allow students to express their anxieties about writing "correctly" and point out that language differences and varieties are strengths rather than weaknesses.

Traditionally, graduate students have not been a major part of WAC and WID programs despite the rising number of graduate students in higher education in the US who need writing support. A multilingual and multidisciplinary graduate writing course, such as the Graduate Writing Workshop that we have described in this chapter, can close this gap by offering writing instruction that can help a variety of students in a setting that affirms and values language diversity.

REFERENCES

Barratt, C., Hanlon, D., & Rankin, M. (2011). Assessing the success of a discipline-based communication skills development and enhancement program in a graduate accounting course. *Higher Education Research & Development 30*, 681-695. doi: 10.1080/07294360.2010.527929

Bazerman, C., Little, J., Bethel, L., Chavkin, T., Fouquette, D., & Garufis, J. (2005). *Reference guide to writing across the curriculum.* West Lafayette, IN: Parlor Press and WAC Clearinghouse. Retrieved from http://wac.colostate.edu/books/bazerman_wac/

Belcher, W. L. (2009). Reflections on ten years of teaching writing for publication to graduate students and junior faculty. *Journal of Scholarly Publishing, 40*, 184-200. doi: 10.3138/jsp.40.2.184

Canagarajah, A. S. (2006). Toward a writing pedagogy of shuttling between languages: Learning from multilingual writers. *College English, 68*, 589-604.

Cargill, M., Cadman, K., & McGowan, U. (2001). Postgraduate writing: Using intersecting genres in a collaborative, content-based program. In I. Leki (Ed.), *Academic writing programs* (pp. 85-96). Alexandria, VA: TESOL.

Crystal, D. (2003). *English as a global language* (2nd ed.). Cambridge: Cambridge University Press.

Delyser, D. (2003). Teaching graduate students to write: A seminar for thesis and dissertation writers. *Journal of Geography in Higher Education, 27*, 169-181. doi: 10.1080/03090260320000107487

Dudley-Evans, T. (1995). Common-core and specific approaches to the teaching of academic writing. In D. Belcher & G. Braine (Eds.), *Academic writing in a second language: Essays on research and pedagogy* (pp. 293-312). Norwood, NJ: Ablex.

Fischer, K. (2011). Admissions offers to foreign students at US graduate schools climb at a faster pace. *Chronicle of Higher Education*. Retrieved from http://chronicle.com/article/Admissions-Offers-to-Foreign/28700

Fredericksen, E. (2006). Educating a multilingual professional workforce: A progressive vision. *Professional studies review: An interdisciplinary journal, 2*(2), 27-35.

Frodesen, J. (1995). Negotiating the syllabus: A learning-centered, interactive approach to ESL graduate writing course design. In D. Belcher & G. Braine (Eds.), *Academic writing in a second language: Essays on research and pedagogy* (pp. 331-350). Norwood, NJ: Albex.

Hall, J. (2009). WAC-WID in the next America: Redefining professional identity in the age of the multilingual majority. *WAC Journal, 20*, 33-49. Retrieved from http://wac.colostate.edu/journal/vol18/index.htm

Heinrich, K. T., Neese, R., Rogers, D., & Facente, A. C. (2004). Turn accusations into affirmations: Transform nurses into published authors. *Nursing Education Perspectives, 25*, 139-145.

Johns, A. M. (2002). Destabilizing and enriching novice students' genre theories. In A. M. Johns (Ed.), *Genre in the classroom: Multiple perspectives* (pp. 237-246). Mahwah, NJ: Erlbaum.

Kubota, R., & Lin, A. (2009). Race, culture, and identities in second language education: Introduction to research and practice. In R. Kubota & A. Lin (Eds.), *Race, culture, and identities in second language education: Exploring critically engaged practice* (pp. 1-23). New York: Routledge.

Leki, I. (2007). *Undergraduates in a second language: Challenges and complexities of academic literacy development*. New York: Erlbaum.

Matsuda, P. K. (2006). The myth of linguistic homogeneity in US college composition. *College English, 68*, 637-651.

National Center for Education Statistics. (2011). *Degrees conferred by sex and race* (Data file). Retrieved from http://nces.ed.gov/fastfacts/display.asp?id=72

Norris, C. & Tardy, C. (2006). Institutional politics in the teaching of advanced academic writing: A teacher-researcher dialogue. In P. K. Matsuda, C. Ortmeier-Hooper, & X. You (Eds.), *The politics of second language writing: In search of the promised land* (pp. 262-279). West Layfayette, IN: Parlor Press.

Raimes, A. & Jerskey, M. (2009). *Universal keys for writers* (2nd ed.). Boston, MA: Wadsworth.

Steinert, Y., McLeod, P., Liben, S., & Snell, L. (2008). Writing for publication in medical education: The benefits of a faculty development workshop and peer writing group. *Medical Teacher, 30,* 280-285. doi: 10.1080/01421590802337120

Swales, J. M. & Feak, C. B. (2011). *Navigating academia: Writing supporting genres.* Ann Arbor: University of Michigan Press.

Swales, J. M. & Lindemann, S. (2002). Teaching the literature review to international graduate students. In A. M. Johns (Ed.), *Genre in the classroom: Multiple perspectives* (pp. 105-199). Mahwah, NJ: Erlbaum.

Thaiss, C. & Zawacki, T. M. (2006). *Engaged writers, dynamic disciplines: Research on the academic writing life.* Portsmouth, NH: Boynton/Cook.

University of Texas at El Paso Center for Evaluation and Institutional Research. (2012). *Enrollment by gender and ethnicity.* Retrieved from http://cierpdata.utep.edu/OnlineFactBook/FAC_Enroll_EthGender.aspx

Wiens, K. (2012). I won't hire people who use poor grammar. Here's why. *Harvard Business Review.* Retrieved from http://blogs.hbr.org/cs/2012/07/i_wont_hire_people_who_use_poo.html

APPENDIX A

Course Contract

For English 5316, you will design most of your writing assignments. You will list these assignments along with due dates in a contract that you will create. In this contract, you will spell out what you are assigning yourself to do each week. **Unless I tell you otherwise, you must produce at least five pages a week.** This is to help you write continuously and without procrastination; substantive revisions count toward that five page count, so you might turn in a five page revision one week of the same content you submitted the week before. Your documents should be word-processed, using 12 point font, and standard 1-1 1/2 inch margins.

You will produce two copies of your contract, with the same assignments but addressed to two different readers.

Contract I: For your major professor to sign. This is an agreement between you and that professor outlining what you hope to accomplish this semester.

Contract II: For your English 5316 writing team members and professor. This contract will be signed by team members and by me and will help us ensure that you stay on track.

You will turn in a copy of both contracts to me **and will upload a copy of your contract to Blackboard by** ____.

Please do not give a copy to your major professor until I have approved it.

Your writing assignments should be based on what you want to accomplish this semester. For example, if your goal is to revise your thesis/dissertation, then you will assign yourself ten or more pages of revision a week. If your goal is to write a journal article for publication, then you'll assign yourself part of the article to draft (or revise) each week. If you are new to your field, you might want to work on summarizing and analyzing journal articles, so your contract assignment could be to summarize several articles a week or write one analysis a week. If you are doing research, you might choose to prepare an annotated bibliography and a literature review.

Your contract should include opportunities for you to write and rewrite (revise, proofread, and edit). Challenge yourself when you design your contract. Know that the harder the work, the more you will gain from the experience. If you need to adjust your contract later in the semester, you may do so by discussing revision with me and then submitting a revised contract to me and your team members. You do not have to resubmit the revision to your major professor.

At the end of the semester, you will compile your finished work into a portfolio and present all or a portion of your portfolio to the class. Your portfolio will include all of your contract assignments plus all of the prewriting, drafting, revising, and editing you do in the course of the semester. You may produce either a paper portfolio or an eportfolio—or some combination of the two. You will have models of each form to use as guidelines, but you are free to innovate as well.

APPENDIX B

Student Survey

Thank you for agreeing to answer these questions about English 5316, Graduate Writing Workshop. Your answers will help us describe this course to other students and faculty around the country. As a result, other universities may begin offering their own Graduate Writing Workshops.

1. What degree are you seeking at UTEP?
2. What is your major field of study at UTEP?
3. How many times have you taken English 5316: Graduate Writing Workshop?

In the following questions, please give us feedback about this course.

4. What did you think of the contract grading system in which you decided on the projects you would complete for the course?
5. What classroom activities were useful to you? Check all that apply.
   - Content peer review groups
   - Proofreading peer review groups
   - Journal analysis
   - Vocabulary exercises
   - Punctuation practice
   - Grammar lessons
   - Readings on style differences in various fields
   - Readings about World Englishes
6. If there were other activities that you found useful that were not mentioned in the previous question, please list them here.
7. What are your thoughts about working with students in different fields? To what extent, if any, did this benefit you?
8. Tell us your thoughts about working with students who had different language backgrounds (some monolingual English, some who learned English as a second language, and so on). To what extent, if any, did this benefit you?
9. What improvements, if any, did you see in your writing as a result of English 5316? Choose all that apply.
   - I have a better understanding of the types of writing done in my field.
   - I know more about what my audience expects from my writing.
   - I improved my ability to understand academic material in English
   - I can organize my writing better.
   - I know more about how to discover and gather ideas.
   - I know more about how to revise my ideas.
   - I can do a better job of giving feedback on my peers' writing.
   - I have a better vocabulary.
   - I make fewer errors in my writing.
   - I know more about how to correct errors in my writing.

10. If there were other improvements in your writing that weren't listed in the previous question, please list them here.
11. What drawbacks, if any, did you find with English 5316?
12. What recommendations do you have for improving English 5316?
13. Would you recommend English 5316 to another student?
    - Yes
    - No
    - Don't know
14. What is your language background? Choose all that apply.
    - I am monolingual English.
    - I can speak in two languages (including English).
    - I can speak in more than two languages (including English).
    - I can write in more than two languages (including English).
15. In addition to English, what other languages do you know?
16. Do you consider yourself totally bilingual in two languages? If so, which languages?
17. What is your country of origin?
18. How long have you been in the US?

Thank you for helping us with this project!

CHAPTER 15

TEACHING WRITING IN A GLOBALLY NETWORKED LEARNING ENVIRONMENT (GNLE): DIVERSE STUDENTS AT A DISTANCE

Jennifer Lynn Craig
Massachusetts Institute of Technology

As institutions of higher education strive for global outreach and innovative distance technologies make that mandate feasible, globally networked learning environments (GNLE) increasingly enroll linguistically and culturally diverse students in university courses in which the ability to write in advanced disciplinary English is necessary for their success. However, this expectation is often difficult for diverse students to meet, especially when their learning takes place in a distance environment. In this case study, data is presented from three cohorts of linguistically and culturally diverse graduate students who participated in seminars held in a distance environment. The seminars were designed to help students to successfully complete their master's theses in engineering manufacturing at the Massachusetts Institute of Technology (MIT) in Cambridge, Massachusetts. A writing-across-the-curriculum (WAC) pedagogical approach was deemed "very useful" although student data revealed students' initial lack of familiarity with WAC strategies as well as their persistent difficulties with grammar, syntax, usage, and organization. This chapter suggests that there is an opportunity for writing specialists to expand writing pedagogy in ways that include the rich linguistic and cultural presence of diverse students, address a full range of L2 writing challenges, and when required, minimize the effects of distance technology on student learning.

The Singapore-MIT Alliance, established in 1998, is a globally networked learning environment (GNLE) enabled by digital technology, and within that environment, several educational collaborations have taken place. The Master of Engineering in Manufacturing degree (M.Eng) was one such collaboration between the Massachusetts Institute of Technology (MIT), the National University of Singapore (NUS), and Nanyang Technical University (NTU).[1] In this one-year graduate program, international students came to MIT for a semester to begin their graduate coursework and then returned to Singapore to continue their coursework over synchronous video while also completing a research internship in a manufacturing company in Singapore. Throughout the M.Eng graduate program, students used synchronous and asynchronous distance technology to interact with their MIT faculty, faculty in Singapore, their internship project advisors, and other groups of students.

The M.Eng (2000-2010) program illustrates a noteworthy characteristic of GNLEs. In contrast to a traditional distance education model in which academic material is packaged and then streamed from a source to a distant classroom or perhaps accessed asynchronously through academic websites, GNLEs are interactive cyberspaces that use technology to initiate and facilitate participation and collaboration between education, research, and industry partners in a globalized context. While *globalization* itself may be a contested term, Starke-Meyerring (2010) provides a useful working definition: "the increasing interdependence and integration of social, political, cultural, and economic processes across local, national, regional, and global levels" (p. 261). In a GNLE, students are linked in meaningful ways to peers, instructors, industry professionals, and to communities from diverse contexts in order to share knowledge making practices across borders (Starke-Meyerring, 2010). Rather than an export model of learning, GNLEs tend to be multi-faceted environments in which "a constellation of social and cultural factors" creates not only opportunities for research, education and collaboration but also opportunities for language and literacy development (Hawisher, Selfe, Guo & Liu, 2006).

In fact, language is central to successful participation in a GNLE precisely because the globalized environment requires such "an unprecedented level of interaction between individuals from diverse language and cultural backgrounds" (Melton, 2008, p. 185). In addition, language (written and oral) in a GNLE is likely to be disciplinary in its content and to include a range of genres, audiences, and contexts as well as a full spectrum of second language (L2) challenges to be addressed. Clearly, a GNLE with its diverse students and their multiple objectives is a learning environment in which writing specialists and English language teachers are essential to student success. But a key question is what writing pedagogy is effective in the GNLE environment? What commonly held assumptions about teaching writing must be examined and modified in order to successfully teach with writing in a distance environment with diverse students?

In this teacher-based research, I describe the challenges encountered in the Singapore-MIT GNLE as I used WAC pedagogy to help students to complete their master's theses in engineering manufacturing. I present data from student surveys that allowed me to understand student responses to the WAC pedagogy used in the GNLE classroom, and that helped me to minimize the combined effects of distance technology and linguistic and cultural diversity. In closing, I reflect on the ways in which my teaching practices were modified as a result of my cumulative experience in the distance classroom and the increased awareness of my previously unexamined assumptions.

WRITING THE M.ENG THESIS IN THE SINGAPORE-MIT GNLE

My work with the students in the M.Eng program began in 2008 at the request of the M.Eng program directors. They and the thesis advisors were dissatisfied by the quality of the theses that the students submitted. According to the engineering faculty's assessment, the documents were characterized by multiple, significant errors that ranged from rhetorical and organizational problems to sentence-level errors. There were semester-long English as a Second Language (ESL) courses offered by MIT's Department of Foreign Languages and Literature in which students could enroll during their semester in Cambridge. However, although these courses focused on writing and oral presentation, the courses were judged by most students to be either too long or not sufficiently focused on thesis preparation to meet their needs. Also, since these courses did not count toward the coursework in their fast-paced degree program, students were reluctant to enroll. (See Fredericksen & Mangelsdorf's [this volume] description of the graduate writing course they developed to address these kinds of challenges.) In addition, M.Eng students usually did not avail themselves of the services of the MIT Writing and Communication Center. When the students returned to Singapore, there were no writing support services available to them at NTU. Thus, each year, many student theses required substantial faculty editing and hasty student revision before the documents were acceptable for submission. Not surprisingly, this process was very stressful both for the students and for their advisors.

The factors contributing to the students' difficulties in writing their theses were multiple. First, some of the contributing factors were systemic. The pace of the one-year degree program and internship was rapid with students completing their research at their internship company in Singapore even as they were attempting to analyze data and also to write about it.

In addition, there was no stable writing process in place that led to thesis preparation; frequently, the advisors were receiving a first draft of the thesis very late in the summer and only days before the document had to be submitted for acceptance. The reasons for this delay varied. Without a structured pace, many students left the writing task until the last minute. From the advisors' perspective, some were preoccupied with their own research and travel while other advisors reportedly did not want to look at the material until the student's research was "complete." Several advisors appeared to track student progress through the oral progress report meetings, a practice that often gave them an illusory sense of how well written the thesis would be. Also, several advisors persisted in the belief that writing the thesis was a simple transcription of reality ("just write down what you did!") rather than perceiving the rhetorical and organizational challenges of this task. Lastly, a few advisors were themselves multicultural and multilingual and thus their guidance on thesis preparation varied, confusing students whose peers were receiving different instructions.

Another factor that complicated the thesis writing task was the composition of the M.Eng cohorts in those years. Most of the students were from Asian countries, and many of them reported that they were non-native speakers of English (in 2008, 80%; in 2009, 100% and in 2010, 82%). They were academically-gifted, high-achieving students, and most of them spoke English at an advanced level. However, they were unfamiliar with the genre of the US-based thesis and particularly with the way the M.Eng thesis was written. Given the high percentage of students writing under pressure in a second or other language, it was not surprising that the results were often poorly organized and full of errors.

Although MIT has a highly successful WAC program at the undergraduate level, there is no similarly comprehensive approach to writing at the graduate level. However, because of my familiarity with L2 writing issues, my experience using WAC pedagogy with engineering students, and my willingness to teach with distance technology, I was asked (independent of my role with the MIT's undergraduate program) to develop resources to help the M.Eng students improve the quality of their theses.

THE M.ENG THESIS WRITING SEMINAR

Writing-across-the-curriculum pedagogy relies on several fundamental practices: a draft and revision process, short and targeted instruction, the use of writing conferences and peer review, and the use of writing-to-learn activities that help students discover ideas, learn material, and strengthen critical thinking. Thus in developing the thesis writing seminar, I incorporated these common WAC strategies, establishing a writing process that helped students write and revise their theses in two stages. Using synchronous video technology in a classroom at MIT, I facilitated three 3-hour seminars in which I gave brief lectures about the thesis genre followed by writing workshop activities and peer review sessions. After the second seminar, each student submitted the first half of his/her thesis that I read and commented upon. With synchronous video, I held writing conferences to discuss my comments and answer their questions. Then after the third seminar, students submitted a revised first half of their thesis along with the second half of their thesis. Again, each student received written comments on the draft, and writing conferences were held over synchronous video. Students then incorporated my comments into a revised draft that went to their advisors for technical review. Based on the advisor's comments, final revisions were made. Subsequently, when I again taught in the M.Eng program in 2009 and 2010, I held team writing conferences because I had discovered that students had many issues in common and also that students who were less confident writers seemed to benefit from the support of their peers. All writing conferences— individual or team—were held either over synchronous video or over Skype™.

Each year, my interaction with the students began with a short face-to-face (F2F) meeting in January before they returned to Singapore. At that meeting, I introduced myself, tried to learn something about each of them, and explained the work that we would do together in the GNLE. Following that initial meeting, I stayed in contact with them via email, and I occasionally attended the cohort meetings that the M.Eng director held via synchronous video. The thesis writing seminars, drafting cycle, and writing conferences began in late April as students entered their full-time internships and concluded in early August as the thesis advisors took over the last stage of the technical review. My interaction with individual students varied depending on their needs. I saw the stronger writers chiefly in the seminar sessions and writing conferences while I spent more time interacting individually with less skillful writers on email and in several cases, in Skype™ conferences.

Facing Challenges in the M.Eng Thesis Seminar

Despite my familiarity with WAC pedagogy, my years of teaching writing to engineering students, and my experience with L2 students, I immediately noticed a different atmosphere as I led the M.Eng seminars and worked with the M.Eng writers. It seemed much more difficult to get to know the students and to establish the rapport that is so fundamental to a writing classroom. As I investigated, I began to examine three of my own assumptions: that "knowing" the culturally and linguistically diverse students was a straightforward task; that "writing" means the same thing and is taught the same way in different global contexts; and that synchronous distance technology is a clear channel that transmits information completely and accurately.

Assumption 1: "Knowing" the M.Eng Students Would be a Straightforward Task

As I began to work with the M.Eng students, I noticed that synchronous video classroom sessions and writing conferences had a distinctly different atmosphere than I had observed when using WAC strategies in F2F classrooms with either L1 or L2 students. The M.Eng students clearly had animated relationships with one another; I could see them —during the break or as the seminar ended— talking or joking with one another on camera (but out of microphone range). However, during class, they took their seats in the classroom silently and for the most part, sat quietly, listening to the short lectures that I gave. When I initiated active learning activities, peer review, or group discussions, they complied hesitantly. It was rare for any student to ask a question or even to respond to my prompting. In writing conferences where I met them on a smaller screen in a smaller room, they were similarly reserved. Students often sat quietly, staring at their individual draft; getting a discussion started was painfully difficult.

When I asked students to write to me about their professional plans or past experiences or their hopes for the seminar, most students easily shared their responses over email. Some writers even became chatty as they shared what it meant to them to write in a second language—stories that they had hesitated to volunteer at first (see, for example, Zawacki, Hajabbasi, Habib, Antram & Das, 2007). But in the classroom, they remained silent and slow to act although basically cooperative. Although we made progress on the thesis drafts, that, too, was slow. Clearly, in that first summer, I did not know how to establish the interactive, student-centered dynamic that is common in most of the WAC-based classrooms in which I have taught. However, other insights into the M.Eng writers' experience in learning and using English helped me understand their reserved classroom presence.

Assumption 2: "Writing" Means the Same Thing in all Contexts

To learn more about the students' experience with writing in a GNLE, I surveyed the first cohort of students at the end of the summer, 2008, and in that survey, I asked if they were native or non-native speakers of English. Yet that way of phrasing the question failed to give a full picture of their English language learning experiences or their language profile. When the question was phrased differently in the surveys of 2009 and 2010, an expanded picture of the M.Eng writers' identities emerged. Rather than describing themselves chiefly as "non-native" speakers of English, most of them detailed their multiple abilities in several other languages other than English and documented their competency in varying roles and relationships as they navigated the global environment, shifting languages as they went (Canagarajah, 2006; Hall & Navarro, 2011).

Although the surveys did not ask for detailed information about the methods by which they had learned English, data in 2009 and 2010 revealed that English was a second language for most of them. Since most of the students were not from Anglophone countries (e.g. India) nor from locales where English was an official language (e.g. Singapore, Bangalore), it seemed probable that most students had been taught English from an English as a Foreign Language (EFL) pedagogical perspective, an approach that is based on language acquisition strategies in all four communication modes with an emphasis on achieving linguistic correctness.

In each of the annual surveys (2008-2010), I asked about the students' familiarity with WAC approaches used in the seminar, and their responses were illuminating. For example, approximately one third of the respondents had *never/rarely* experienced active learning, peer review, or group activities in the classroom. Almost 75% of the respondents had only *rarely/sometimes* been in active, informal discussion with their teacher. More than half of the respondents had *never/rarely* participated in a writing conference. Also, more than half of the respondents had only *rarely/sometimes* received written comments on a written draft.

However another question about their level of *comfort* with WAC strategies revealed that most students had adjusted quickly. Well over 50% of the respondents reported that they had become *very comfortable/comfortable* with informal discussion between student and teacher, with active learning in class, with writing drafts of the thesis, with receiving teacher comments on drafts, and with revising writing based on those comments. (It should be noted that each year one or two students did rate themselves as *uncomfortable* with WAC methods.)

Thus, the reticent classroom behaviors that prompted my inquiry were understandable when illuminated by the data showing students to be largely unfamiliar with the informal give-and-take of a WAC classroom, active learning activities, and writing conferences. What had seemed like their lack of engagement could be better understood as their uncertainty as they tried to figure out what it was that I wanted them to do and how they should do it successfully. As Ferreday, Hodgson, and Jones (2006) note in their work on networked learning environments, participants in a new learning situation often perceive (the new situation) as "alien" and their "actions which could be interpreted as resistance and/or reticence ... are an expected part of learning ... a new way of being in the world" (p. 237). Yet the M.Eng students' responses to the question about *comfort* suggested that despite the "alien" nature of the WAC activities, they were able to actively adapt to new expectations, "strategically realigning themselves and investing in the practices" of the unfamiliar context (Rich, 2005, Para. 10). In fact, their ability to adapt within the short time frame of the thesis seminars was further illustration of their ability as multi-competent users of language.

However, despite the draft and revision cycle, writing conferences, and peer review work and the improved thesis drafts, "writing" for the M.Eng students still meant writing correctly at the sentence level. As I show in Table 1 on the writing difficulties students reported on the survey (see the Appendix), more than 25% of respondents in each year (2008-2010) rated the challenge of writing correctly as *difficult/very difficult*. They also reported difficulty in writing clearly and concisely and in organizing complex information. In writing conferences and as I read drafts, I observed that writers with less control over the language displayed difficulty in developing enough correct prose to convey their thoughts fully. The more skillful writers could write at greater length but still struggled with sentence-level errors as they wrote about progressively more complex material. (See Phillips [this volume] for an account of the same phenomenon in the writing of the graduate student that she followed in her longitudinal case study, which she attributed to the U-shaped learning curve).

Because the thesis document was an official document of record, error-filled prose was not acceptable. Thus my comments to the writers had to address not only the larger features of the genre, rhetorical strategies, and information organization but also to provide direct feedback at the sentence level (Ferris, 2009). Such extensive commenting would be relatively unusual in WAC practice since a teacher would typically rely on more indirect methods to help the writer locate and then address the error in a revision. However, as experienced writing and EFL/ESL teachers know, second language writers who are creating and refining large amounts of disciplinary English are less likely to locate errors easily (even though they usually can address them when they do). In addition, the fast pace of the M.Eng degree program did not allow the time for students to review and revise at a leisurely pace.

In addition, the M.Eng writers tended to lapse into colloquial English. It was one challenge for them to learn the features of the genre and the rhetorical purposes of each section while writing clearly and correctly and another to acquire the appropriate register (Hall & Navarro, 2011). Again, achieving the appropriate style and tone for their thesis required time and experience.

Assumption 3: Distance Technology Transmits Information Completely and Accurately

Entering a new classroom, any teacher must do as I did —begin to know the students and explore the students' backgrounds and expectations—if the teacher is to create a productive learning environment. Yet what proved challenging in the M.Eng GNLE was the way in which a distance environment with a highly technical interface affected my usual WAC teaching approach.

Synchronous distance technology succeeded in that it made our global interaction possible. Still, the 12-hour time difference had a strong influence since the students and I were always at the opposite ends of our day. When I taught in the evening in Cambridge, the GNLE students were barely awake; when I taught in the early hours of my morning, they were tired from a day at their internships and the evening struggle through Singapore rush hour traffic. In addition, we were affected by separate cultural rhythms that were invisible to one another. Even our weather was different, an oddly affecting factor. When there were drastic events (in 2008, earthquakes in China that disrupted some students' villages; in 2009, the suicide of a roommate), it took a measurably longer time for me to "read" the effects on the faces of the distant students, to discover the causes, and to offer support. But aside from major life events, there were also myriad small details of life that affected our moods and behaviors in the classroom: regional holidays, politics, institutional policies and patterns.

Temporal distance also meant that we struggled with what Herrington (2004) calls "real-time dominance" (p. 204). The simplest email exchange had to be timed carefully to account for sleep and internship schedules, and the most basic act of uploading documents for class work had to include an unusually large margin of time. Despite my best intentions (and theirs), it remained a challenge for us to override our actual sense of time (Herrington, 2010). Throughout the seminar schedule, time continued to be the intractable "distance" that had to be actively managed.

On the surveys, most students reported that it was *not difficult* to learn to write a thesis in this distance environment (2008, 82.4%; 2009, 85.7%; 2010, 58.3%).[2] Yet even state-of-the-art technology embodied what Winner (1986) calls the "politics of the artifact," referring to the ways in which "man-made systems ... require or ... (are) compatible with particular kinds of relationships ... and the arrangements of power and authority ..." (p. 20). For example, at times, the sound quality in our exchange was indistinct enough to make it difficult for me to understand a student and, if I asked for clarification, that request was often disconcerting for the student since, in this case, technology made the problem worse. In a F2F setting, I could have made the request quickly, quietly, and with little fuss (Herrington, 2004). However, in the electronic classroom, my voice seemed to boom from a large screen (volume being beyond my control), inadvertently suggesting some lapse on the part of the student.

At times, a camera in Singapore was poorly focused, thus making it difficult for me to see facial expressions of students to gauge their reactions. Also, a time delay (perhaps 30 seconds) sometimes occurred, making our interaction clumsy and slightly asynchronous. Trying to correct these distractions and even to use the classroom interface involved negotiation with technicians who were in the background, manipulating and managing the connection. I appeared to be alone in the "sending" classroom, but in reality, I was team-teaching with invisible facilitators who had their own concept of what was going on and who were not always quick to understand what I needed.

The constraints of technology also had dictated the set up of the Singapore classroom. Rich with computers, keyboards, microphones, and screens, the classroom had been arranged with rigid desks and tautly strung cables. Chairs were bolted down in front of the desks. This physical setup could not easily incorporate active learning or peer review activities. Moreover, when students re-grouped to pursue these activities, they moved away from microphones so I could not monitor their interactions. In addition, the Singapore classroom configuration produced an intimidating effect since when a student clicked a button at his/her desk to ask a question, the camera then zoomed in on him/her, projecting an image on a larger screen. Not surprisingly, questions or comments were infrequent from students, most of whom were strong but perhaps not confident speakers of English.

I observed the ways in which technology cramped what McNair and Paretti (2010) call the "relational space" in which frequent dialogue (teacher-student and student-student) shapes skills and guides practice as student writers establish voice and identity and also a sense of ownership over their work. As noted, student-student dialogue was often constrained by the physical layout of the room while the teacher-student dialogue was also affected by the technical interface. Moreover, technicians opened and closed the screens through which we communicated precisely at the beginning and end of the seminars since the technology channel was expensive to maintain and since other classes often were scheduled. Thus the students and I were deprived of the marginal time that experienced teachers know is valuable in getting to know students and assessing any difficulties occurring in the course. The distance technology could not transmit completely the thousands of smaller cues (e.g. body language, tone and register of voice, eye contact) by which we create our identities and also "read" the identities of others in F2F spaces. In fact, the distance classroom with its mix of virtual and actual realities made it a challenge for students' identities to emerge and also to establish a kind of social presence within the classroom—a presence that practitioners know is particularly valuable in writing-intensive and disciplinary classrooms in which students are learning to use language as emerging professionals (Farrell & Holkner, 2004; Ferreday, Hodgson & Jones; 2006; Grabill, 2007; Järvelä & Häkkinen, 2005; McNair & Paretti, 2010).

ADDRESSING THE CHALLENGES OF TEACHING WRITING IN THE M.ENG GNLE

As I noted earlier, the refinement and expansion of the WAC pedagogy that I used were cumulative as I reflected on my own assumptions and observed my students, trying new strategies and also taking data from each cohort in annual surveys.

First, based on my expanded understanding of the M.Eng students as multi-competent users of English and other languages, I developed and regularly used a specific active learning activity to explore students' language profiles, their language learning histories, and their experiences in using written and oral English. (See the appendix in Zenger et al. [this volume] for an example of one such language questionnaire.) In 2008, students gave me information about their language profiles anonymously, but subsequently, I asked students not only to document all the languages that they used and where and how they used them but also to verbally share their language history with me and with their peers. They did this exercise openly and eagerly. This activity also paired well with student self-assessment (sent to me confidentially) and my greater insight into their needs and also their anxieties about completing the thesis. Even more important, the establishment of student writing identities and language histories also led easily to a discussion of the differences in writing pedagogies experienced in their home countries, in other countries, and at MIT.

Second, understanding that most of the M.Eng students were unfamiliar with WAC strategies, I explained more extensively what we were going to do and why we were going to do it. I talked to them about my expectations, e.g. describing typical student behaviors in writing conferences. I talked more about how to be a useful peer reviewer. I also included explicit explanations of my objectives in written assignments posted on the academic website. I had always introduced classroom activities and written out the assignments, but I had assumed a certain level of student familiarity. Now, I assumed that they were unfamiliar with WAC strategies, and structured more time for questions so that I could check for comprehension. Moreover, instead of merely asking for questions verbally, I invited electronic "muddy cards" sent to me during the break in class. In a F2F classroom, students would hand in the "muddy card" (an index card with a question or a key point that required further explanation) at the end of class. However, in the distance environment, the paper-based technology was replaced by a quick email. Questions continued to be rare, but the invitation was important.

WAC strategies did not address all the problems that the M.Eng writers faced, however. Even these proficient speakers of English struggled to control written language as they grappled with complex thesis material (See Table 1). Therefore, borrowing from EFL strategies, I included gap fill exercises to help the writers choose more appropriate verbs and transitional phrases, more closely approximating the register of the thesis (Swales & Feak, 2004). I developed a style sheet to help the writers consistently use key terms and learn specialized vocabulary, a strategy more common to English for Specific Purposes (ESP) practice than WAC practice. I also developed a strategy for commenting on linguistic features of the writing while still concentrating on content, organization, and coherence, and I shared this strategy with them (Ferris, 2009). Although such intervention would be relatively uncommon in most WAC contexts, it was clear that many of the M.Eng students could not locate the errors in their prose in the time available to them. However, characteristic of many multilingual students, most students could correct those errors once they did notice them. (See Siczek & Shapiro [this volume] for another description of the merging of TESOL and WAC pedagogies).

Students not only welcomed my attention to sentence-level error, they expected it. I had described the differences between the pedagogies of EFL and WAC, but for many of them, the attention to grammatical correctness remained central to their expectations of what writing teachers were supposed to do (a trend also noted by Fredericksen & Mangelsdorf [this volume]). As I helped writers locate sentence-level errors, however, another cultural assumption was revealed. I assumed that my comments on sentence-level error were helpful but not as essential as the development and organization of substantive material. However, some M.Eng writers had a different perspective, assuming that once they had corrected errors and perhaps substituted more formal verbs or inserted some transitions, the revision was complete and the document was improved. Moreover, some M.Eng writers (especially the less skillful ones) assumed that I would correct all the sentence-level errors in their documents. They clung to this idea as the deadline came closer, despite my insistence that they take responsibility for their final drafts. In the end, some less able writers turned to skilled peers for a final proofreading and editing cycle or in one or two instances to their thesis advisors who quietly corrected or revised final drafts of documents, a long-standing but rarely acknowledged practice (Jordan & Kedrowicz, 2011).

Third, realizing that the technical interface affected our interactions, I developed the habit of talking *about* the technology, not just *through* it, so that the slight hindrances were acknowledged between us rather than ignored. For example, my observation that having a camera focus on them when they wanted to ask a question was not always pleasant brought grins and nodding of heads and made it more likely that they might send the muddy card or write to me after class time. Or once in a while, I asked for a volunteer to help me remember to upload specific material at a certain time. This small activity transferred some responsibility to them in addition to proving valuable to me (the volunteers never failed to be diligent with their reminders!).

In addition, to create more social dimension, I began classes with warm-up activities in which I elicited information from each student about weekend activities or internships. In a F2F classroom, I would have done this activity informally and in the few minutes before class, but here I learned to structure it as part of the class. Also I shared a little more personal information about my own activities than I might usually have done. This relatively brief exchange of details was culturally interesting to me and to them, as well. The result was a little more conversation in the classroom; they relaxed a bit and began to show their individual personalities, styles, and senses of humor. I also assigned short pieces of personal writing to help me understand them better as writers and then I responded to that writing.

WHAT THE M.ENG STUDENTS FOUND USEFUL OR DIFFICULT

Curious about the students' assessment of the usefulness of WAC strategies, I asked the M.Eng students to rate the usefulness of various resources.[3] Table 2 (see Appendix) shows the respondents strong preference for interactive WAC strategies (writing conferences, commented drafts) and also shows how valuable they find the involvement of disciplinary faculty in the writing process.

In written comments, students observed:

> I found it very helpful that we constantly had someone reminding us about writing the thesis.

> I learned a lot from the conference with the writing instructor and the draft thesis returned by her and by the MIT advisor.

> I liked the writing conferences.

> I benefited most when the writing teacher talked about the various purpose of each part of the sections.

> ... it was a wonderful and fruitful experience.

The seminar series appeared to help the M.Eng writers improve their theses. Although the usual difficulties of writing about technical material in a second or other language persisted for these writers, the overall organization and focus of the theses were much improved, and the program administrators were enthusiastic. Student responses on surveys and in individual emails showed a strong, positive response to the seminar and indicated their satisfaction with their theses. However, students also reported on what they still found difficult. Table 1 (see the Appendix) gives insight into the linguistic challenges that these strong users of English still encountered as they wrote their theses—the use of correct grammar and punctuation, word choice and vocabulary, writing clearly and concisely, and organizing complex disciplinary material.

REFLECTION ON PAST AND FUTURE WORK

Each year (2008-2010), the M.Eng writers and I worked our way toward a successful thesis for nearly all students. Some aspects of the seminar series were reassuringly familiar to me: young adults developing as professionals by writing about disciplinary material in an authentic and meaningful context. But some aspects remained challenging: the cold eye of the camera focused on distant students who appeared hesitant and reserved; the lack of relational space common in F2F classrooms but cramped in the distance setting; and the stubborn sentence errors persisting even in the improved thesis drafts.

These challenges of fast-paced, high-stakes engineering writing certainly presented learning opportunities for the M.Eng writers. For me, those challenges deepened the ways in which I came to understand diverse students as I became increasingly attuned to their multiple and subtle differences as well as their considerable strengths. Just as importantly, those challenges prompted me to refine the pedagogy I used with the diverse students in a distance setting. While my teaching practice remained grounded in well-tested, successful WAC principles, those familiar approaches became more multi-faceted and more inclusive of L2 writing issues. The challenges that had puzzled me at first turned out to be opportunities for professional development and insight.

The teacher-based research presented here highlights possible opportunities for WAC practitioners and WAC program administrators for teaching with writing in culturally and linguistically diverse distance and F2F classrooms. In addition to representing valuable sites for professional growth and future research, these opportunities also point to contexts in which WAC pedagogies are very much needed. These new contexts, however, demand that we become aware of our implicit assumptions and our—and our students'—cultural biases. To do this, we must identify the strengths that diverse students bring: their rich language histories, multiple competencies, and a wide range of objectives for their use of language (Ferris, 2009; Johns, 2001). And it is essential that we develop sound writing pedagogies—F2F and online—to reach an increasingly diverse student population (Ferris & Thais, 2011). This endeavor means reading the scholarship in ESL and L2 writing and then adding and refining concrete skills that allow us to combine a language acquisition approach with familiar WAC writing pedagogy (Canagarajah & Jerskey, 2009; Cox, 2010; Cox, 2011; Leki, 1992; Matsuda & Jablonski, 2000; Zawacki & Cox, 2011, among others). As WAC practitioners, we must also become more adept at managing various technologies and multiple screens not only in GNLEs but also in a range of distance environments, adjusting WAC approaches to fit the challenges and constraints of those environments. As universities fulfill their mandate for global outreach and for curriculum enhancement through online access, learning to work well with technology and at a distance is becoming a valuable skill for all teachers.

These distance opportunities will require some re-vision of ourselves as practitioners, asking us to be more innovative, receptive to change, and flexible in our approach. Yet WAC practice, itself, has exhibited all these characteristics. Over the years, WAC has come to include not only writing but also oral communication, graphical communication and an increasing range of multimodal literacy. The new opportunities described here—teaching writing to diverse students in globally networked learning environments—represent the next steps in expanding WAC pedagogy to meet the needs of all of our students.

NOTES

1. This collaboration was funded from 2000-2010. Although the M.Eng program continues, it is no longer part of the Singapore-MIT Alliance and no longer taught over distance technology.
2. Data indicates that, in 2010, more students reported that they found it difficult to write a thesis in a distance environment. However, no other information gathered explains their response on the survey and other factors (advisor influence, project success, L2 abilities, team dynamics) may have been influential

3. Other resources were assessed in the survey, but this chapter focuses on several resources common to WAC pedagogy.

REFERENCES

Canagarajah, A. S. (2006). Toward a writing pedagogy of shuttling between languages: Learning from multilingual writers. *College English, 68*(6), 589-604.

Canagarajah, A. S., & Jerskey, M. (2009). Meeting the needs of advanced multilingual writers. In R. Beard, D. Myhill, J. Riley & M. Nystrand (Eds.), *Sage handbook of writing development* (pp. 472-488). London UK: Sage Publications.

Cox, M. (2010). *WAC and second-language writing bibliography.* WAC Clearinghouse. Retrieved from http://wac.colostate.edu/slw/bib.cfm

Cox, M. (2011). WAC: Closing doors or opening doors for second language writers? *Across the Disciplines, 8*(4). Retrieved from http://wac.colostate.edu/atd/ell/cox.cfm

Farrell, L., & Holkner, B. (2004). Points of vulnerability and presence: Knowing and learning in globally networked communities. *Discourse: Studies in the cultural politics of education, 25*(2), 133-144.

Ferreday, D., Hodgson, V., & Jones, C. (2006). Dialog, language and identity: Critical issues for networked management learning. *Studies in Continuing Education, 28*(3), 223-239.

Ferris, D. R. (2002). *Treatment of error in second language student writing.* Ann Arbor, MI: University of Michigan Press.

Ferris, D. R. (2009). *Teaching college writing to diverse student populations.* Ann Arbor, MI: University of Michigan Press.

Ferris, D. R., & Thaiss, C. (2011). Writing at UC Davis: Addressing the needs of second language writers. *Across the Disciplines, 8*(4), Retrieved from http://wac.colostate.edu/atd/ell/ferris-thaiss.cfm

Grabill, J. T. (2007). *Writing community change: Designing technologies for citizen action.* Cresskill, NJ: Hampton Press.

Hall, J. (2009). WAC/WID in the next America: Redefining professional identity in the age of the multilingual majority. *WAC Journal, 20,* 33-49. Retrieved from http://wac.colostate.edu/journal/vol20/hall.pdf

Hall, J., & Navarro, N. (2011). Lessons for WAC/WID from language learning research: Multicompetence, register acquisition, and the college writing student. *Across the Disciplines, 8*(4). Retrieved from http://wac.colostate.edu/atd/ell/hall-navarro.cfm

Hawisher, G. E., Selfe, C. L., Guo, Y., & Liu, L. (2006). Globalization and agency: Designing and redesigning the literacies of cyberspace. *College English, 68*(6), 619-636.

Herrington, T. K. (2004). Where in the world is the global classroom project? In J. R. Di Leo. & W. R. Jacobs (Eds.) *If Classrooms Matter* (pp. 197-210). New York & London: Routledge.

Herrington, T. K. (2010). Crossing global boundaries: Beyond intercultural communication. *Journal of Business and Technical Communication, 24*(5), 516-539.

Järvelä, S., & Häkkinen, P. (2005). How to make collaborative learning more successful with innovative technology. *Educational Technology, 5*, 34-39.

Johns, A. M. (2001). ESL students and WAC programs: Varied populations and diverse needs. In S. H. McCleod, E. Miraglia, M. Soven & C. Thaiss (Eds.), *WAC for the new millenium: Strategies for continuing writing across the curriculum* (pp. 141-164). Urbana, IL: NCTE.

Jordan, J., & Kedrowicz, A. (2011). Attitudes about graduate L2 writing in engineering: Possibilities for more integrated writing instruction. *Across the Disciplines, 8*(4). Retrieved from http://wac.colostate.edu/atd/ell/jordan-kedrowicz.cfm

Leki, I. (1992). *Understanding ESL writers: A guide for teachers.* Portsmouth, NH: Boynton/Cook Heinemann.

Matsuda, P. K., & Jablonski, J. (2000). Beyond the L2 metaphor: Towards a mutually transformative model of ESL/WAC collaboration. *Academic Writing, 1*. Retrieved from http://wac.colostate.edu/aw/articles/matsuda_jablonski2000.htm

McNair, L. D., & Paretti, M. C. (2010). Activity theory, speech acts and the "doctrine of infelicity": Connecting language and technology in globally networked learning environments. *Journal of Business and Technical Communication, 24*(3), 323-357.

Melton, J. (2008). Beyond standard English. In D. Starke-Meyerring, & M. Wilson (Eds.), *Designing globally networked learning environments* (pp. 185-199). Rotterdam: Sense.

Rich, S. (2005). Linguistically and culturally diverse students' perceptions of successful classroom practices in a UK graduate program. *Across the Disciplines, 2*. Retrieved from http://wac.colostate.edu/atd/lds/rich.cfm

Starke-Meyerring, D. (2010). Globally networked learning environments in professional communication: Challenging normalized ways of learning, teaching, and knowing. *Journal of Business and Technical Communication, 24*(3), 259-266.

Swales, J. M. & Feak, C.B. (2004). *Academic writing for graduate students: Essential tasks and skills* (2nd ed.). Ann Arbor, MI: University of Michigan Press.

Winner, L. (1986). *The whale and the reactor: A search for limits in an age of high technology*. Chicago: University of Chicago Press.

Zawacki, T. M., Hajabbasi, E., Habib, A., Antram, A. & Das, A. (2007). *Valuing written accents: Non-native students talk about identity, academic writing, and meeting teachers' expectations*. Fairfax, VA: Diversity Research Group, George Mason University.

Zawacki, T. M. & Cox, M. (2011). Introduction to WAC and second language writing. *Across the Disciplines*, 8(4). Retrieved from http://wac.colostate.edu/atd/ell/zawacki-cox.cfm

APPENDIX

Table 1: What M.Eng students found difficult as they wrote their theses

Element	2008 "difficult/very difficult"	2009 "difficult/very difficult"	2010 "difficult/very difficult"
Using correct grammar, punctuation, and spelling	31%	30%	24%
Choosing right words	46%	45%	41%
Writing clearly and concisely	62%	61%	63%
Organizing complex material	58%	61%	66%

Table 2. What M.Eng students found helpful as they wrote their theses

Activity	2008 (n=15) "helpful/very helpful"	2009 (n=13) "helpful/very helpful"	2010 (n=17) "helpful/very helpful"
Writing conferences with communication instructor	66%	74%	76%
Drafts commented by communication instructor	84%	76%	100%
Verbal suggestions from thesis advisor	73%	58%	83%
Drafts commented by thesis advisor	85%	64%	90%

CHAPTER 16

CAMPUS INTERNATIONALIZATION: A CENTER-BASED MODEL FOR ESL-READY PROGRAMS

Karyn E. Mallett and Ghania Zgheib
George Mason University

Historically in US higher education, the WAC-driven push for institution-wide integration of writing into the curriculum has not been met by substantive language support for L2 writers. In this article, a language-supported approach to campus internationalization is described, contributing to discussions on innovative ways in which the nation-wide WAC agenda might adapt to growing international enrollments. The model presented – the ACCESS program – is an emerging ESL-ready program that has benefitted from the guidance of a well-connected team of writing specialists across the university, including WAC, L2 writing, and ESL/applied linguistics faculty. Research on the ACCESS program is provided, the results of which showcase ways in which faculty and students benefit from a program structure that is comprehensive, realistic, and transferrable to other contexts across the university. The authors conclude by suggesting that the institutional energy that goes into developing language-supported programs for international students should open the door to wider conversations about the language and writing needs of multilingual students across campus, and the faculty who teach them.

In the introductory chapter of *WAC for the New Millennium*, McLeod and Miraglia (2001) present a number of issues and questions related to the staying power and evolutionary potential of WAC programs given multiple nationwide changes affecting higher education throughout the US. Indeed, these questions are addressed with some degree of urgency given that they are presented in response to Walvoord's (1997, p. 70) call for WAC to "dive in or die" and to Haworth's (1997, p. A14) call for public institutions, in general, to become "architects of change." With resolution to endure and adapt, McLeod and Miraglia ask, "How will it grow and change – what new forms will WAC programs take, and how will they adapt some of the present program elements and structures to the changing scene in higher education?" (p. 4). One partial answer to McLeod and Miraglia's question is for WAC, L2 writing, and ESL/applied linguistics faculty to cultivate purposeful, strategic program-building collaborations that clearly support institutional goals for campus internationalization. Specifically, an improved effort to build and showcase intentional alliances with other writing and language specialists on campus could lead to new forms and/or dimensions of WAC programs, fostering greater depth of current WAC structures and a greater range for WAC applications. Further, such strategic program-building collaborations within small, high-profile programs for heavily-recruited multilingual students may lead to the promotion of an integrated network of a team of experts who can advise the university on how best to address a wider scope of need among diverse populations of developing student writers across disciplines, L2 writers included.

While WAC strives to create and sustain a community of writing-pedagogy-minded faculty across the curriculum, formal collaboration with L2 writing and ESL/applied linguistics faculty can add depth and perspective to the WAC agenda with regard to institutional support for a wider range of student writers and the faculty who instruct them. This point resonates among WAC scholars (McLeod, 2008; Zawacki, 2010; Cox, 2011) as well as among L2 writing scholars, including Matsuda (2001). WAC leaders have recently signaled a shift in the profession, moving multilingual-writing-related issues from the periphery toward the center of conversation through reflections on the international and global-oriented WAC agenda. Presenting "The Future of WAC" plenary address at the Ninth International Writing Across the Curriculum Conference (IWAC), McLeod (2008), with regard to the Bologna Process[1] and its potential effects on transnational writers and their teachers, concluded,

> This means that there will be—in fact, already is—a huge increase in the use of English as a lingua franca (if we may call it that) in the world, and an accompanying increase in the teaching of academic English as a second, sometimes a third or fourth language. Of course, students from other countries will bring with them not only linguistic but also cultural differences. What sort of institutional structures will be put in place to support these students and their teachers? How can our WAC experience in North America be helpful, and how can we learn from our international colleagues' experience?

Further signaling a growing concern for a "writing pedagogy of inclusion" among WAC scholars in the field, Zawacki's (2010) plenary address at the IWAC Conference urged greater collaboration among stakeholders and the development of a more complex, global-oriented, ESL-ready framework for WAC programs, suggesting that,

> In comparison to our L2 students, we faculty have quite some distance to travel as we negotiate our expectations for the writing they do in our disciplines. In our negotiations—with student writers, with faculty, and with stakeholders inside and outside of our institutions—the question we need to ask is not "What is good-enough writing?" but rather "What is good writing as it mirrors the professional goals of our students, the work places they want to enter, and the variety of Englishes people are using there?" In the process, we may learn to hear and value the written accents our L2 students bring to our classrooms.

Certainly, given the context of these messages, McLeod's and Zawacki's recent attention to issues of transnationalism, internationalism, multilingualism, and L2 writing gives credence to the goal of locating and fostering sustainable models for a WAC platform that effectively anticipates diverse populations of multilingual writers. But how? What does a "pedagogy of inclusion" entail, pragmatically speaking? Is the emergence and evolution of such a pedagogy affected by the trend to internationalize in higher education? How do internationalization initiatives affect WAC, L2 writing, and ESL/applied linguistics programs (as well as their relationships with one another at the institutional level)? We note in regard to the latter a critique made by Leki (2003) in "A Challenge to Second Language Writing Professionals: Is Writing Overrated?" in which she draws attention to potential adverse outcomes resulting from heightened (and often mandated) institutional focus on student writing across the curriculum (e.g. writing proficiency testing, writing intensive courses). In "WAC: Closing Doors or Opening Doors for Second Language Writers?," Cox (2011) investigated Leki's claim by reviewing scholarship on the intersection of WAC and L2 writing, asking,

> Is it possible that WAC administrators and scholars, like our colleagues in L2 writing studies and first year composition, place the same overemphasis on writing? Have we paid more attention to the potential benefits of integrating writing into curricula than the possible costs to some students? If we are

paying attention, what possible costs for L2 students should we be attending to?

In response, we point to language-supported internationalization initiatives such as the ACCESS program as interesting contexts for WAC, L2 writing, and ESL/applied linguistics faculty to consider as they look for innovative ways to construct a writing pedagogy of inclusion that opens doors for L2 writers.

Presenting an L2 writing perspective with regard to constructing an inclusive WAC approach, Matsuda (2001) concludes,

> In order to provide adequate writing instruction for all students, including second-language writers, all WAC programs must become "ESL ready"; that is, everyone involved in WAC initiatives--including WAC administrators, writing consultants and writing fellows as well as faculty across the disciplines who use writing in their courses--needs to recognize the presence of second-language writers, to understand their characteristics and needs, and to prepare themselves for the challenge of addressing the needs of those students. To practice WAC, then, is to practice ESL. Yet, ultimately, second-language writers are not the only ones who benefit from the efforts to develop more inclusive WAC programs. Such efforts can, in the long run, contribute to the further democratization of US higher education for all kinds of students. (n.p.)

While we fully agree with Matsuda, we note that, even among those WAC, L2 writing, and ESL/applied linguistics faculty most keen to collaboratively construct an ESL-ready program, developing such a comprehensive WAC platform takes time, incentive, and funding. The questions are many (e.g., should collaboration take place at the committee or program level and in what form?), the task is particularly difficult (i.e., preparing faculty across the disciplines to confidently incorporate more meaningful writing in their classes *and* comfortably assume a more linguistically-complex set of students), and the incentive for ESL-ifying WAC may not be obvious to many or even most. Further, one must question the sustainability of collaborative efforts, given faculty/administrator turnover and institutional support (or lack thereof) for the ongoing maintenance, revision, and/or expansion of faculty development trainings, campus outreach, collaborative research projects, resource-development, etc. Still, the goal seems worth the challenge given the potential for making a positive impact across campus. But how and where to get started?

With these goals and questions in mind and in order to examine the conditions for implementing and sustaining a language-supported approach to internationalization and its potential contributions to the evolving notions of "ESL ready," "pedagogy of inclusion," and "the further democratization of US higher education for all kinds of students," we focus in this chapter on one such initiative, the ACCESS program, which is a program for first-year international students as they enter discipline-specific and major courses, administered through the Center for International Student Access (CISA) at George Mason University. Our "ESL-ready" model – ACCESS – has been built with the goal of "opening doors" for the international students we recruit and the faculty from across the curriculum who participate in teaching the courses. While the goal of the research we conducted was primarily to address questions related to program effectiveness, the writing-related data we present are intended to showcase programmatic elements and potential research-guided implications for this writing-rich approach to internationalization in US higher education institutions.

We begin with a description of the ACCESS model focusing in particular on tangible ways in which WAC, L2 writing, and ESL/applied linguistics specialists have collaborated. Then we turn to a description of our research methods and findings, which we have organized according to the benefits of this collaborative approach for students and faculty as well as areas where improvements need to be made. In describing the ACCESS model and our writing-related data, we aim to address two wider questions: 1) What role does/might WAC play in an ESL-ready program model for language-supported campus internationalization? And, echoing Cox (2011), 2) How does a language-supported approach to internationalization open doors for participating faculty and L2 writers that WAC institutionalized practices may have inadvertently closed in the past? Finally, by showcasing features of and research on the ACCESS model – a program for heavily-recruited international students[2] for which much institutional energy has been invested –we argue for the institutional support systems needed in order for these and other populations of multilingual students to succeed.

LANGUAGE-SUPPORTED INTERNATIONALIZATION: A CENTER-BASED MODEL FOR ESL-READY PROGRAMS

While the recent trend in US higher education has been campus internationalization, institutions have differed in their approach: some internationalization initiatives tend to favor a more de-centralized, bottom-up approach whereas others are designed to be more centralized, often implemented from the top down. CISA, formed in 2010, partially in response to George Mason University's own established goals for campus internationalization[3], was formed by and is directed out of the Provost Office. Although CISA is certainly administered as a centralized, top-down program, its reliance on existing faculty and departmental/program structures has fostered an on-the-ground, bottom-up spirit in many ways. CISA is unique in its approach and structure, and such particularities are important to consider in light of their potential effects on language and writing support/development for the international students who participated in this study. Further, such programmatic elements are important for WAC, L2 writing, and ESL/Applied Linguistic specialists to consider if potential implications from this study are to inform collaborations and/or program development at other US universities; for, while the CISA model is built upon the foundation of available resources and collaborations particular to George Mason, it is possible to establish (or begin strategically planning to establish) effective models that are built upon substitutable institution-specific resources elsewhere. To understand our model, such macro-level conditions for successful language-supported internationalization need to be made clear here.

First, rather than partnering with an outside, for-profit company that promised to recruit and provide language and academic content instruction to 700+ new international students per year, CISA is the result of a home-grown initiative (i.e. a "do it yourself" model). At its inception, a new CISA directorship position was created and filled by a candidate with strong prior administrative leadership experience and vision for realistic and thoughtful campus internationalization. In addition, CISA, along with the university's English Language Institute (ELI), an intensive-English program, signed an institutional memorandum of understanding[4] which outlined a joint partnership for administrating and staffing two language-supported programs for two targeted international student populations: the ACCESS program for academically-qualified[5] undergraduate students scoring below the direct admission English language proficiency requirement[6] and the BRIDGE-English Enrichment Track (BRIDGE-EET) program for academically-qualified graduate students scoring below program-determined English language proficiency requirements. The writing-related research reported here is focused exclusively on data collected from faculty and students involved with the ACCESS program in order to more narrowly consider issues particular to undergraduate L2 writing/writers and the faculty who teach them.

Second, on the macro-level, the conditions for effective, collaboratively-constructed internationalization at Mason have been fostered by a process of pooling campus resources and soliciting input from language- and writing-focused specialists across campus. For example, significant contributions with regard to ACCESS program structure and course sequencing were made by the director of the Mason WAC program, the director of the composition program, and the assistant director for language development for the ELI/CISA. Additionally, and of particular significance, these three programs came together to develop a new course design and curriculum outline for a year-long composition course (English 121/122) developed to meet the writing and language needs of incoming ACCESS students, and co-taught by composition and ELI faculty.

A third distinguishing feature of the ACCESS model is the program's novel approach to language-supported internationalization through curricular and instructional innovation. As a program that supports first-year students as they enter discipline-specific courses and courses in their majors, ACCESS students take a full-time academic course load (28 credits) toward a bachelor's degree during the year-long program (for a list of set ACCESS year courses, see Table 16.1). Depending on a variety of factors, one or two of the courses throughout the year are major courses while the others are general education courses or courses considered general electives in which students are enrolled by ACCESS cohort group. As outlined in Tables 16.1 and 16.2, ACCESS students receive varied forms of embedded, curricular language support in addition to full ACCESS to designated writing center tutors.

As is evident in Tables 16.1 and 16.2, from a language-acquisition standpoint, ACCESS students engage in a year-long program wherein they are asked to comprehend (e.g. listening and reading) and produce (e.g. speaking and writing) English in the context of academic study, providing natural content, contexts, and motivation for improved language proficiency and marked growth in content knowledge. For the students, writing is supported in content courses, in language-supported courses, and through significant use of the university writing center ESL-trained tutors. Further, student learning is central to the program, sustained by cross-course and cross-semester sequencing and alignment of language skill development and academic skill reinforcement, a shared responsibility among all involved faculty and undertaken through CISA orientations, monthly faculty meetings, course coordinator meetings, curriculum committee meetings, ongoing materials development project meetings, etc.

Beyond this sensible, strategic linking of academic and linguistic goals for student development, the ACCESS program also supports faculty development, relying on collaboration and input from language and writing specialists across campus. As is outlined in Table 16.3 in Appendix A, language and writing specialists on campus have been utilized as resources to help design, implement, and revise several structural and curricular components of the ACCESS program.

Table 16.1 First Semester – CISA ACCESS Program[7]

Course	Credits[8]	Abbreviated Description of Course and Language Support
ENGH 121: Enhanced English Composition I	3*	General education course. Co-taught, year-long composition course for ACCESS students instructed by a rhetoric/composition faculty and ELI faculty. Course introduces students to the writing process, the conventions of academic writing, writing as a tool for developing critical thinking, and the research process through a specified course theme (e.g. the purpose of the university), focusing heavily on developing reading, writing, grammar, and vocabulary-building strategies throughout the year. Both instructors are present in each class meeting and work closely together to plan assignments and lesson plans, develop materials and grading rubrics, provide feedback on student writing, and assign grades to student work.
UNIV 100: Freshman Transition to College I	1	General elective course. Transitional course for freshmen, focuses on introducing and developing academic skills (e.g. reading strategies, test-taking, study skills, etc.) and student development (e.g. time management, health, relationships, etc.).
COMM 100: Public Speaking	3*	General education course introducing students to various contexts and approaches to public speaking in the US Class sessions are taught by communications faculty and supported by an ELI faculty member who attends each class session, shares in grading/feedback for students' written preparation and oral assignments, and teaches students in a language support course immediately following each communications class meeting.
PROV 103: Academic Language Support for Public Speaking	1	Language support course for ACCESS students which meets for 50 minutes following each COMM 100 class meeting and is taught by ELI faculty member. Course focuses on the development of those linguistic skills pertinent to upcoming assignments/speeches in COMM 100, differentiating instruction according to student ability/need.
PROV 106: American Cultures	3*	General education course. Introduces students to anthropology through observations and analysis of American cultures. Course taught by anthropology faculty.
Math course (per placement exam)	3	General education course, determined by placement exam.

Appendix A provides an overview of some such tangible, collective efforts among CISA, ELI, WAC, and composition program faculty/staff in preparation and throughout the ACCESS pilot year. As is noted in Table 16.3 in Appendix A, several collaboration-focused, sustainable aspects of the ACCESS program have been incorporated into its overall structure, including joint course observations; faculty hiring, staffing, and evaluation tasks; faculty training/orientation; and faculty curriculum and advisory committees. Collectively, such tasks require that those language and writing specialists first involved with the theoretical construction of the ACCESS program stay involved as the program evolves

Table 16.2 Second Semester –CISA ACCESS Program

Course	Credits	Language-supported Aspects
ENGH 122: Enhanced English Composition II	3*	General education course. See description above. Second half of year-long course.
UNIV 100: Freshman Transition to College II	1	General elective course. See description above. Second half of year-long course.
HIST 125: World History	3*	General education course, introducing students to the field of history through the analysis of economic, cultural, and political evolution across various regions of the world. Class sessions are taught by history faculty and supported by an ELI faculty member who attends each class session, shares in grading/feedback for students' written preparation, and teaches students in a language support course immediately following each World History class meeting.
PROV 104: Academic Language Support for World History	1	Language support course for ACCESS student which meets for 50 minutes following each HIST 125 class meeting and is taught by an ELI faculty member. Course focuses on the development of those linguistic skills pertinent to upcoming reading/writing assignments in HIST 125, differentiating instruction according to student ability/need.
Research Methods	3*	General education course. Introduces students to the research process, focusing on question-based inquiry around a course theme (e.g. global hunger).
Major course	3	Major course, determined with advisor approval.

and grows. In addition, as enrollments in CISA programs increase, added or new faculty who teach for the Center are oriented to these sustainable practices in which they are engaged in discussions about language learning, writing instruction, and the multilingual experience. In short, the ACCESS model carries with it many aspects that WAC, ESL/applied linguistics, and L2-writing specialists might consider valuable in the construction of an operationalized ESL-ready program, through which an emerging pedagogy of inclusion is developed and distributed among faculty across the disciplines.

In a variety of ways, then, the ACCESS structure presents itself as a potential ESL-ready model through which academic faculty receive training on and experience with teaching multilingual students while ACCESS students benefit from particular programmatic and curricular innovations that have been tailored to the generalized academic, linguistic, and cultural needs of international students. Further, it should be noted that one significant aspect of the Center-based, centralized approach to language-supported internationalization is its potential for transfer as participating faculty take their pedagogical training and experience teaching multilingual students with them into future classrooms with other student populations. Finally, we note that the program has assumed responsibility for retaining ACCESS students at the university after program completion, therefore spurring conversations about additional and modified support structures that may be needed for these students in the near future. This next phase, we anticipate, will be a clear point at which we can all shift to discussions around writing-intensive courses and writing in the disciplines at the upper division of undergraduate education, with the needs of all L2 writers included.

OUR STUDY

While the ACCESS program model seemed like a promising way to open doors for international students, there was certainly a need to gather quantitative and qualitative data from faculty and students involved in the 2010-2011 pilot year of the program in order to gauge actual student and faculty perspectives on program design and effectiveness in order to inform additional program development and revision. In response to these needs, we began conducting IRB-approved longitudinal research as we sought to answer our driving research question, "How do ACCESS students' perceptions of their academic, linguistic, and cultural experiences compare with ACCESS-affiliated faculty perspectives on teaching multilingual students across the ACCESS-included disciplines?"

While drawing on this larger study, content for this chapter is focused on data that address writing instruction, including surveys, interviews, and analyses of samples of student writing and faculty feedback. Generally-speaking, the purpose of the overall research project was to gather a variety of data from participants in order to help us determine if the structures and resources that we had collaboratively put in place were perceived by both participant groups as helpful and why or why not. We also wanted to know if and how teaching in the ACCESS program was pedagogically challenging and/or rewarding for faculty and why or why not. Finally, in order to explore the potential for a stronger institutional link between the WAC program and language-supported internationalization on campus, we wanted to gather data that would help us address the two main questions we noted at the outset of the chapter regarding the role WAC might play in an ESL-ready program and how the programmatic approach described above might open doors for participating faculty and L2 writers that WAC may have inadvertently closed in the past.

Participants

Participants for the student-focused study included 18 undergraduate students enrolled in the pilot year of the CISA ACCESS program at George Mason University, 91% of whom were classified as international students by the university. Of these, 70% were male, 59% hailed from a Gulf nation, and 70% spoke Arabic as a first language. Forty-eight percent had attended the ELI prior to matriculation into the ACCESS program. Thirty-five percent were interested in studying business, 25% engineering, and 10% global studies. The remaining participants were undeclared majors by the end of the ACCESS year.

Faculty participants included seven faculty members teaching courses in which ACCESS students were enrolled (i.e. courses were either ACCESS-exclusive, sheltered courses or open, lecture-style classes in which the ACCESS students were integrated among other enrolled freshmen). Faculty came from a range of academic disciplines, including history, communications, anthropology, higher education, English, and ESL. Three of the seven participants were English department[9] and ESL faculty; the remaining four faculty had no prior formal training in teaching multilingual writers. Each of the participating faculty members had elected to teach in the ACCESS program, which included faculty orientation and training on teaching L2 writers provided through CISA. Further, each of the participating faculty members had some form of prior cross-cultural experience (e.g. living/traveling overseas, studying abroad in college, participating in the Fulbright program in another country, etc.).

WRITING-RELATED DATA

Surveys and Interviews

The surveys generally had 8 to 12 questions and included multiple choice, ranked, and open-ended question types. The questions directed students to report on their perceptions of language usage, proficiency developments, cultural adjustments, relationships with domestic and other international students, written feedback from faculty, academic challenges, suggestions for program revisions, and engagement with writing and writing assignments. Questions asked of faculty focused on their perceptions of academic, linguistic, and cultural challenges faced by students; experiences teaching in the program generally; perceptions of student progress; reflections on their preparation to teach multilingual students; suggestions for revisions to the program; experiences with providing feedback on student work; etc. Interviews with faculty and students were semi-structured and consistent across all students per initial, mid-year, and final interviews. Faculty were only interviewed once toward the end of the program year. Interviews generally averaged 30-45 minutes each and were audio-recorded. All interviews were transcribed by either one of the co-researchers or our graduate research assistant. Survey data and transcribed interview data were coded by the co-researchers according to emerging, developing themes within a framework of larger questions with branching sub-questions. Some data were coded under multiple themes if relevant to multiple questions/sub-questions. Co-researchers worked together to code data thematically in the beginning stages of data analysis until normed at 93% consistent coding.

Samples of Student Writing and Teacher Feedback on Student Writing

Three samples of student writing with teacher responses were collected from faculty throughout the year. Faculty were also asked to submit course syllabi, descriptions of major assignments, and grading rubrics. The writing samples were varied, including journal entries, essay- and short-answer-format midterm and final exams, reflection papers, language development portfolios, narrative essays, argumentative essays, and more.

Students' Entrance, Midyear, and Exit Language Proficiency Tests

All students in the ACCESS program were required to take the same test—AccuPlacer© ESL—three times during the year. The proficiency test is computer-based with listening, reading, writing, grammar, and vocabulary sections. A separate oral interview was conducted by ELI faculty to gauge oral English proficiency. The test was self-paced and timed, administered by ELI faculty in a computer lab. Students had two hours to complete three sections of the test each time. All sections of the computer-based portions of the test were rated by AccuPlacer©, though ELI faculty also conducted a normed, human rating according to five dimensions for the writing component of the test.

DATA ANALYSIS AND DISCUSSION

As is detailed in the ACCESS program description above, this writing-rich, language-supported approach to campus internationalization does not simply give lip service to the particular needs of L2 writers. Real-time language support is woven into the ACCESS program through curricular, pedagogical, and programmatic support structures in recognition of students' language learning goals. These realistic language-related goals are determined by language and writing specialists, including WAC, L2 writing, and ESL/applied linguistics specialists at the institution. Further, they are jointly communicated to the faculty and to the students. While there may certainly be locally-determined causes to forego real-time, in-class language support for multilingual students (e.g., expense, lack of ESL-trained faculty, lack of willingness among academic faculty to co-teach, etc.), data from this study support our claim that both faculty and students benefit from such an opportunity to address language-related issues as they arise. In short, participating in ACCESS allows all involved the opportunity to explore what it means to administer, teach, and learn in an emerging ESL-ready program. We are confident that the experience will foster the long-term vision for an ESL-ready campus that is supported in strategic ways by a team of writing specialists, including WAC, L2 writing, ESL/applied linguistics experts.

Benefits and Challenges for Faculty Teaching in the ACCESS Program

As is evident in survey responses, interviews, and teacher feedback on student writing, academic faculty who participated in the ACCESS program learned about the value of language-supported internationalization, fostering new teaching practices that more fairly and realistically consider the needs of L2 writers; in short, we found that ACCESS faculty developed more thoughtful pedagogical practices. Our goal is that they will carry the ACCESS experience forward as they teach mixed populations of students across the disciplines in the future.

In an early faculty survey, we asked about the roles writing played in their ACCESS courses. In response, faculty described varied purposes for assigning writing, e.g. writing to engage with content, to critique peers' written/oral work, to reflect on academic and cultural events/experiences, to engage in critical thinking, to develop research questions, to outline lecture/reading content, to develop written English accuracy at the sentence level, and to develop well-structured and supported positions. In response to a question about their expectations for student writing, faculty generally stated that they expected students to make clear, cohesive, and relevant arguments; use evidence to support their claims; and demonstrate marked improvements in both English fluency and accuracy throughout the ACCESS year. Interestingly but not surprisingly, composition and language support faculty responses tended to include additional more general expectations for students as developing writers beyond their ACCESS courses that highlighted their concern that the writing skills they were teaching would transfer beyond the ACCESS year as well as their sense of accountability for such transfer, e.g. "I need to prepare them for writing next year." Asking faculty to articulate the importance and purposes for writing in their courses was a meaningful exercise because it also opened the door to more in-depth reflections on their approaches to writing pedagogy throughout the year.

One important element of that approach, according to our interview data, was the role played by the language-support instructors; namely, academic content faculty noted the relief they felt in being able to defer (at least early on) to the language specialists to address ACCESS students' language development goals/challenges directly. ELI faculty appreciated the opportunity to plan and deliver authentic content-based instruction in coordination with a content-area expert. Because we found that during the pilot year content-area faculty may have marked but not attempted to explain grammar errors, the following year we introduced them to different approaches to corrective written feedback and error treatment with the goal of helping them approach language-related issues with a set of approved, research-backed feedback methods. When asked to report on the most effective forms of collaboration among ACCESS faculty, 83% of faculty said that they communicated regularly with one another outside of class about course-related issues, 33% of academic and language support faculty reported that they co-planned daily lesson plans, and 16% of academic and language support faculty reported that they communicated with one another about specific students/student issues on a weekly basis.

While the option of language-supported content instruction for multilingual students is not available outside of the ACCESS program, we suspect and hope that the varied forms of collaboration among language-support and academic faculty that took place during the ACCESS year may encourage academic faculty to modify their approaches to teaching in the future in order to accommodate their new, heightened awareness of the needs of multilingual students across the curriculum. Although we do not have hard data to support this assumption at this point in our study, participating faculty reflections toward the end of the ACCESS year suggest that revisions to their general pedagogical approach are affected by the ACCESS teaching experience. For example, the participating ACCESS faculty member teaching the world history course reflected on ACCESS student progress and the degree to which his own pedagogical approach and course requirements may have affected student progress:

> Well, again, ultimately the most challenging aspect was that a few kids just didn't improve as much as I would have liked them to. I mean, most of them did, really, so I wasn't despairing, but I had the sense most of them were working pretty hard. I can't prove that about all of them, but I'm sure some of them must be a little frustrated. I mean, I think a history course in the first semester of this program is by definition very challenging because it's a lot of reading and it's a fair amount of writing…I think it's difficult for all concerned. And when a few students just don't quite break the barriers that you could see were there when they first started…you feel sad…you think, "Could I have done better with this?"

Similarly, the composition instructor reflected on collaboration with language-support faculty and her own pedagogical approach throughout the ACCESS program as she considered future applications:

> I realize that I haven't really adapted my pedagogy for a while, like I've been teaching the same kind of people, groups of people…. Anyway, I was just reflecting the other day on my own teaching and I see how I can strengthen it in general, not only for international students…just in general how I can better balance rhetorical skills with language proficiency. I've never ever known how to do that. I've always been sort of

> like ignorant of the language thing and what helped students with that.... But now I realized like "I know how to do that. I've learned how I can merge the two more effectively."

In addition, the ELI language support faculty member, who provided support for the oral communication course, offered this reflection:

> ...I think [teaching in the ACCESS program) is also good for instructors. You have a number of instructors who maybe came from different environments where there wasn't that kind of international mix. So they come in, I think, with certain assumptions about what students will understand and how they will interact with the curriculum. And that gets changed when you bring in different perspectives from different students. So I think it's very healthy for them as well – makes all of us better teachers.

As is evidenced in these quotes from participating pilot-year instructors, one faculty-oriented benefit of the ACCESS program is that it opens doors for faculty to reflect on pedagogical practices in a way that more accurately accounts for the presence of L2 writers in courses across the disciplines. Further, due to the on-scene presence of language-support faculty, the ACCESS model appears to provide a structure by which academic faculty can feel supported themselves as they explore and experience what it takes to teach a more linguistically and culturally diverse set of students.

While more could be said about the curricular and pedagogical adjustments and revisions made by faculty throughout the year, we would like to mention that 100% of participating ACCESS faculty reported that they decided to make significant pedagogical adjustments throughout the year in order to teach the ACCESS students. Specifically, 66.6% of participating faculty reported in surveys that they modified their teaching methods in order to better fit the ACCESS group needs by making one or more of the following adjustments: providing students with more sample work; providing students with more outlines; slowing down the pace of the course; and providing students with more foundational skills in advance of a particular content lesson. In addition, ACCESS faculty reported other forms of pedagogical adjustments during final interviews, such as more thoroughly explaining assignment components and deliverables and introducing students to culture-based knowledge/resources needed to appropriately address assignments/projects. (For more examples of the ways in which faculty across the curriculum make adjustments to writing pedagogy for L2 students, see Hirsh, Nielsen, and Ives et al. (this volume). For advice for creating linguistically and culturally inclusive pedagogy, see Cox (this volume). One hundred percent reported a desire to teach in the program again the following year and described ways they planned to adjust their teaching, even though, as the world history professor said,

> Frankly [teaching in ACCESS] was more work that I'm used to. I don't mind that, but that's the difficult part. I mean, I had more students turning in drafts of papers. I've always had a policy where students could turn in drafts, but frankly, American students turn in maybe 10%. But these kids, some of these kids were turning in three or four drafts each. I was [also] trying to put more into the organizational clarity of the course, and it was work. I think it was good for me to have that, so I'm not complaining, but it was work.

One additional challenge ACCESS faculty encountered with regard to teaching with writing had to do with providing feedback on ACCESS student written work, particularly sentence-level feedback. When asked about the importance of grammatical accuracy for success in their course on the week 8 survey, 66.7% of faculty said that accuracy was "very important," 16.7% said "important" and 16.7% said "somewhat important." (For more on faculty perspectives on sentence-level differences in L2 student writing, see Zawacki & Habib and Ives et al. [this volume].) As we could see in their feedback on student papers, however, they clearly struggled throughout the year with how best to address grammatical accuracy in order to help student writers improve. Some teachers, for example, provided direct correction (i.e. words crossed out and "correct" words written in by the teacher) so that students could see/correct the errors in their writing; some left all sentence-level feedback to the language-support instructors and focused exclusively on the students' ability to engage the course content; some tried different methods throughout the term, sometimes calling attention to grammar errors and other times ignoring them. In interviews, most acknowledged some unease with regard to addressing grammar issues. For example, the freshman transition instructor, who has a background in music and higher education, told us,

> And so when I gave an assignment and the students wrote something, I said [to myself], "Oh, well I need to judge this for their thinking rather than how they're writing it." So that was a big adjustment for me and I found myself, like, getting

> together with grammar books and making sure I was trying to review the correct markings…and I really struggled with this idea of, you know, … that this class is about really just being thoughtful and applying what you're learning and more experiential stuff. So I didn't want to cross their thinking by making lots of edits on their papers, but I felt like they needed that because they're still working on [accuracy].

Notably, however, grammar did not seem to be a focus in teachers' end comments on papers. Nearly all of the end comments we analyzed addressed issues related to the content, organization, development, or support of ideas throughout the students' writing. Even when faculty opted to provide feedback in one form on sentence-level errors in the text, end comments were overwhelmingly positive and encouraging, offering praise, even if mixed, to the student for demonstrating specific signs of good academic writing, e.g. from the world history teacher: "…you have a clear conclusion [although] your evidence points in several directions…" and, for another student, "…not bad. Good data. The main problem is you don't quite take a position on the question as to whether [they are the] same civilization or not."

Although faculty tended to downplay grammar in their feedback on student papers, in the week eight survey, 83.3% requested additional professional development in the form of a workshop on providing effective feedback on student written work. Thus, it may be the case that some participating faculty wanted to provide more thorough sentence-level feedback and hold students accountable for grammatical accuracy as the semester(s) progressed, but felt unsure of their own ability to guide this aspect of student writing, especially given the fact that faculty were also aware of the researchers' interest in L2 writing issues. In response to this request, faculty *and* student orientations were modified the following year to include more information and practice on giving/interpreting sentence-level teacher feedback on student writing.

Benefits to ACCESS Students of a Language-Supported Program

ACCESS students also clearly benefited from and recognized the value of the innovative curricular and pedagogical approaches to language-supported content instruction. As we'll show, they also demonstrated marked language proficiency growth as an outcome. In response to survey and interview questions about their feelings of satisfaction with the ACCESS program, many students noted that they felt particularly satisfied with instruction that was provided through collaborative faculty efforts. When asked for suggestions for program revisions, 26.7% of students recommended adding longer language support class meetings while 33% requested that more team-taught classes be made available for future ACCESS years. Some student comments included:

> It seems very good and I learned a lot from the passing few weeks!! I really can see that the ACCESS program doing good for us.

> What I cherish the most about the [language-support] class is the writing process, not just the grammar part, it's the writing. [The instructor] really helps me develop my writing skills; like, not in a way just how to write, but how to write to think, how to be a good thinker to be a better writer. You know what I mean? Yeah, so I like that we get both.

> I feel that all of our teachers are doing a great job in explaining to us the subjects and taking the time to see if we understand more and if we need any help. I think if the support classes were still on next semester as well it will be much better, though.

These comments were further reflected in the data from the participating students' exit interviews in which they were asked to consider how they might have done had they been directly admitted rather than going through the ACCESS program. Their responses reflect an awareness of how the program structure helped them to be successful as they entered discipline-specific and major courses:

> Education wise, I would've been, I guess I can say, a little bit lost, because I got a lot of support here and I like it. It makes me feel safe, maybe, and I think I am now ready to go, on my own…I guess.

> I'm a whole different person right now …. Something changed me here. I just, I really changed here, this year. I've become, like, I work harder. I just think … more honestly and do things more, not just honestly, but just from the bottom-up. I write what I think is right. At home, I just write things because I have to do it. A lot of things have changed me here, but something has to do with writing.

Further, the positive impact of embedded language support on ACCESS students was evident in the students' overall growth in language proficiency by the end of the year[10]. Put simply, a basic concern for the pilot year group of ACCESS students was whether or not the program structure and language-support elements would "work" in terms of providing an environment in which students' English language proficiency would improve. The results of standardized assessments of student English language proficiency were combined with a Language Acquisition Portfolio project that students constructed during the year-long English composition course[11]. These language-focused data points were added to an overall, individual student profile that included student performance in all ACCESS/major courses and a student-developed portfolio. Taken together, the data show that all students made significant progress, moving from an average "intermediate" level of language proficiency to an average outgoing "low-advanced" level of language proficiency, according to a scale we developed to streamline ELI placements and set entrance scores for CISA[12]. Thus, with regard to student progress, these progress results were in line with our program expectations for general and writing proficiency growth and were deemed realistic goals given the context and time for language learning. Generally, students in the pilot year said they felt satisfied with their overall progress but somewhat frustrated with the pace of such progress, as might be expected. With regard to program design and built-in language policies, these results were significant because they supported our pilot year hypothesis that "low advanced" language proficiency would be an achievable, realistic goal for student language development.

DATA-DRIVEN PROGRAMMATIC REVISIONS

While the ACCESS program structure certainly resulted in many positive outcomes for participating faculty and students, pilot-year data from this study helped to identify several programmatic features in need of further development. Generally-speaking, research data contributed to discussions around the need for program-wide quality control as ACCESS transitioned from pilot-year program creation/launch to later phases of program revision/expansion. Specifically, in order to strengthen and sustain the quality of ACCESS during this transitional time, a three-pronged approach to program sustainability was suggested and established: faculty development, materials development, and curriculum alignment.[13] Further, the program director made the decision to revise the program structure by creating "course coordinator" positions for lead faculty who have taken on the responsibility of ensuring cross-section and cross-course curriculum alignment. In addition, themes that emerged from the data were converted by the researchers into data-driven discussion questions and were presented to all pilot-year ACCESS faculty and consultants (including the WAC director and composition director) at the end-of-the-year program retreat.

The first revision for ACCESS faculty development was to integrate opportunities for faculty to reflect on the importance and purpose of writing in their courses as well as the ways in which they might make their expectations for student writing more transparent to students in their assignments, rubrics[14], and use of models. It was clear from the student-generated and faculty-generated data that both groups would benefit from opportunities to clarify faculty expectations for ACCESS student writing. On the one hand, students repeatedly expressed confusion over academic faculty expectations for student writing. An example of such confusion is evident in one student's interview reflection as she tries to explain her awareness that faculty have different expectations, and that, in some way she still can't quite articulate, these change the way she's supposed to structure her writing:

> Like the writing, Oh my gosh, [the English course] has developed my writing a lot because I knew before that I could deliver an idea, but not in the way that my [other] different teachers had expected. Like, … if you have the river and there are stones you have to put down so the reader could jump across the river, then … my ideas are like the stones and I develop them, but it's like I need to know from my [other] teachers where the river is going. I need to move the stones so that the water can go through smoothly like the teacher expects, and the reader can still jump across my ideas.

When student participants were asked to explain why faculty expectations might differ across the various ACCESS courses (i.e. why rubrics and feedback might differ, depending on the course), they had nearly nothing to say. In fact, they generally laughed when asked in the interview to think aloud about possible reasons for differing faculty expectations of student writing and when asked the same question in a student survey, text boxes were either left blank or filled in with a question mark (e.g. "??"). Such data suggest that students had a developing sense that faculty expectations certainly differed across courses, but that there was no clear sense of how or why such differences existed. This finding aligns with other studies in the fields of WAC (Thaiss & Zawacki, 2006) and L2 writing (Gentil, 2011), supporting the recommendation that faculty can and should purposefully guide students' early awareness of differing purposes and expectations for student writing across disciplines.

In response to these data, the second revision to ACCESS faculty development has been to suggest that faculty expectations for student writing (including an explanation of why/how those expectations are determined by the discipline, the department, or the individual instructor) be made more transparent to students. In short, we want to encourage ACCESS faculty to see that helping students identify and meet these differing expectations is the responsibility of both the disciplinary faculty and the composition/language support faculty, not just the latter. By taking time during the faculty training sessions to have these types of conversations around discipline, department, and/or individual expectations for student writing – those that are different and those that are similar – we hope that faculty will clarify for themselves the particularities of their expectations. Further, we hope that these new understandings will transform participating faculty's approach to teaching with writing both in and beyond the ACCESS program and, as a result, will help students to transfer both writing skills and an awareness of disciplinary differences when they write in and beyond the language-supported ACCESS courses across the disciplines.

Finally, the third revision made to the ACCESS faculty development has been to include a workshop session on providing sentence-level feedback to student writing, primarily through corrective written feedback (Ferris, 2009) and the use of a coded error feedback chart. In short, just as we wanted all faculty across the disciplines to feel that they were responsible for communicating their expectations for student writing, we also wanted faculty to develop some strategies for sentence-level feedback given that they had, in fact, identified grammatical accuracy as an important feature for successful completion of the course.

Together, these three revisions allow the opportunity for participating faculty to explore the realities, complexities, and opportunities of language-supported internationalization and teaching with writing. While our plan is to follow these faculty throughout the coming years to determine if/how they apply what they have learned through the ACCESS teaching experience to other teaching contexts at Mason, we anticipate that this experience and these resources will affect their overall approach to teaching, writing pedagogy included.

CONCLUSION

Based on the ACCESS model programmatic elements described above, we believe that our university is emerging as a leading institution for a center-based, language-supported approach to campus internationalization. While

CISA is in no way a perfect program, we see potential for sensible, realistic program growth and sustainability. Further, for the architects of the ACCESS model, it has been an interesting exercise in the practical application of cross-field theories. Whether we are WAC, L2 writing, ESL/applied linguistics, or other participating academics, we all want to provide a worthy education for these students through a positively-oriented plan for internationalization. We want both faculty and students to feel supported and guided by best practices for the teaching and learning of writing. Yet, no guidebook for collaboratively constructing a successful ESL-ready model that incorporates the best of what we know as WAC, L2 writing, and ESL/applied linguistics professionals exists. As a result, we have had to be creative and patient. We have also had to set aside some disciplinary divisions in order to focus on co-building something new.

In relatively recent years, some have argued that the national WAC-driven push for institution-wide integration of writing into the curriculum has generally cost L2 writers a great deal simply because there have not been enough language-support structures in place to aid in the proficiency development of such writers. If multilingual students are not provided the resources and support needed to improve language proficiency while WAC is encouraging more and more intensive integration of writing throughout the curriculum, the problem for L2 writers is obvious. However, based on the ACCESS model program design and the pilot year ACCESS program data, we believe that language-supported approaches to internationalization can help level the playing field for L2 writers, introducing students to language and writing resources and strategies and preparing them to effectively engage in writing across the curriculum once they leave our program.

In the end, by working together on these smaller programs designed specifically for recruited multilingual students who generally pay high tuitions and for whom the university is strategically invested, there is potential to establish a well-connected team of writing experts and an ESL-ready model program structure that is comprehensive, realistic, and transferrable to other contexts across the university. Further, the institutional energy that goes into developing these programs should open the door to wider conversations about the language and writing needs of multilingual students across campus.

NOTES

1. The Bologna Process is generally known for standards-focused reform among European nations, the results of which have had a major impact on EU higher education systems with regard to university administration, comparability/transferability of credits/degrees, and higher education qualifications.

2. Primarily F1 Visa holders at the undergraduate and graduate levels who do not consider English the primary language of communication. To be clear, the authors purposefully aim to highlight the fact that these students are pursued by university admissions.

3. "The University will develop more fully its leading role as a global university.... [It will] expand the number of international students by at least 20% while improving the integration of international and domestic students in extracurricular as well as academic activities." - *George Mason's 2014 Strategic Plan, Goal 5*

4. This partnership between CISA and the ELI has meant that language instruction has not been outsourced, but rather, it has been built upon the foundation of an IEP that has been part of the university for the past 30 years. This aspect of the program is noteworthy because the local partnership – which carries less of a personnel risk for the university – is considered simple interdepartmental collaboration rather than an internal/external merger of sorts; further, both responsible parties have been able to comfortably assume of each other a fair degree of sensitivity to and familiarity with the institutional culture in general, and with potential complexities tied to campus internationalization in particular.

5. Students are deemed academically-qualified by the Office of Admissions upon review of applicants' high school transcripts (translated and evaluated by outside companies, if needed) and SAT test scores. Admission requirements for Access students are in line with general admission requirements for all applicants to the university.

6. Access students come into the program with an overall score of B1 on the Common European Language Reference (CEFR) scale and Bridge-EET students come into the program with an overall score at the B1 or B1+ level (depending on differing graduate program requirements). A thorough discussion of language assessment measures and scales is beyond the scope of this paper; suffice it to say that Access students generally enter the program with intermediate-level overall language proficiency whereas students who enter the university via direct admission typically demonstrate low-advanced language proficiency at minimum.

7. Access courses that are tied to language support are shaded in order to distinguish them from the Access courses that are part of the program but not directly linked to language support/instruction.

8. Courses for which students receive general education credits are marked in this column with an asterisk(*).

9. Of significance, the participating English faculty member also taught the stretched composition course, English 121/122 , and is the former director of

the university writing center where she had created an "opt-in" program specifically designed for L2 writers. This instructor came to the program having done prior research with the director of the WAC program on multilingual writers' experiences writing across the curriculum and in the disciplines. Finally, she herself is a multilingual writer.

10. Similar growth in overall language proficiency was demonstrated during the second year of the program as well.

11. Additionally, students were provided language reports and consultations with ELI faculty following each language assessment in order to clarify program expectations for language development and to supplement students' strategies for language learning if need be.

12. We aligned the Common European Framework of Reference (CEFR) with commercial language proficiency testing measurements (e.g. TOEFL, IELTS, PTE, etc.) for the purpose of streamlining admissions/placement decisions around English language proficiency at the ELI and CISA. Generally-speaking, students coming into Access needed to demonstrate a B1, intermediate proficiency, on this scale while students successfully completing the program needed to demonstrate a B2, low-advanced, proficiency. Due to length restrictions for this chapter, we are unable to go into detail with regard to these assessments/measures; however, the authors can be contacted for additional information on this topic.

13. Faculty development and materials development were prioritized as year-two areas of focus while curriculum alignment was identified as a year-three priority.

14. Interestingly, we found that even when faculty provided rubrics along with their assignments, students needed help understanding how to use the rubric in to address the assignment effectively.

REFERENCES

Cox, M. (2011, December 21). WAC: Closing doors or opening doors for second language writers? *Across the Disciplines, 8*(4). Retrieved August 17, 2012, from http://wac.colostate.edu/atd/ell/cox.cfm

Ferris, D. R. (2009). *Response to student writing: Implications for second language students.* NY: Routledge.

Gentil, G. (2011). A biliteracy agenda for genre research. *Journal of Second Language Writing, 20,* 6-23.

Haworth, K. (1997, April). Report urges colleges to inspire students and improve teaching. *Chronicle of Higher Education,* A14.

Leki, I. (2003). A challenge to second language writing professionals: Is writing overrated? In Barbara Kroll (Ed.), *Exploring the dynamics of second language writing* (pp. 315-332). Cambridge, England: Cambridge University Press.

Matsuda, P. K. (2001). Opening statement: Academic. Writing forum: Connecting WAC and ESL? *Academic. Writing, 2*. Retrieved August 29, 2012, from http://wac.colostate.edu/aw/forums/fall2001/

McLeod, S., & Miraglia, E. (2001). Writing across the curriculum in a time of change. In S. H. McLeod, E. Miraglia, M. Soven, & C. Thaiss (Eds.), *WAC for the new millennium: Strategies for continuing writing-across-the-curriculum programs* (pp. 1-27). Urbana, IL: NCTE.

McLeod, S. H. (2008). The future of WAC - Plenary Address, Ninth International Writing Across the Curriculum Conference, May 2008 (Austin, Texas). *Across the Disciplines, 5*. Retrieved August 28, 2012, from http://wac.colostate.edu/atd/articles/mcleod2008.cfm

Thaiss, C. & Zawacki, T. M. (2006). *Engaged writers and dynamic disciplines: Research on the academic writing life*. Portsmouth, NH: Heinemann.

Walvoord, B. E. F. (1997). *In the long run: A study of faculty in three writing-across-the-curriculum programs*. Urbana, IL: NCTE.

Zawacki, T. M. (2010). Researching the local/writing the international: Developing culturally inclusive WAC programs and practices. Plenary talk at IWAC 2010, Bloomington, IN. Retrieved from http://www.iub.edu/~wac2010/zawacki.shtml

APPENDIX

Table 16.3: WAC, L2 Writing, and ESL/Applied Linguistics collaborative tasks

Task	CISA Director & Staff	ELI/ CISA[A]	WAC Director	English Composition Program
Providing students with a wide variety of co-curricular, extra-curricular, and complementary programming, including ACCESS-specific student and faculty orientations, Peer Learning Partners, academic advisors, cultural excursions, Living Learning Community activities, etc.	√	√		√

Task	CISA Director & Staff	ELI/CISA[A]	WAC Director	English Composition Program
Development of new content-based English for Academic Purposes (EAP) curricula/materials to support two general education courses (PROV 104 to support World History and PROV 103 to support Public Speaking) specifically for ACCESS students.		√		
Development and revisions of co-taught, stretched, and enhanced English 121-122 specifically for ACCESS students.		√	√	√
Hiring, staffing, and observations of all ACCESS faculty.*	√	√	√	√
Conducting training sessions for CISA faculty across the disciplines on approaches to written feedback on multilingual writers' work.	√	√		√
Assessing and reporting on language proficiency (initial, midyear, and exit) for all enrolled ACCESS students.		√		
CISA Faculty Committees to determine and revise program-wide academic and language policies as well as major curricular and programmatic changes (e.g., Curriculum Committee, Language Acquisition Committee, Advisory Committee, etc.).	√	√	√	√

[A] *Assistant Director for Language Development & ELI Language Support Course Faculty*
[B] *Director & English Faculty Teaching CISA Courses*

CHAPTER 17

RECONSTRUCTING TEACHER ROLES THROUGH A TRANSNATIONAL LENS: LEARNING WITH/IN THE AMERICAN UNIVERSITY OF BEIRUT

Amy Zenger
American University Beirut

Joan Mullin
Illinois State University

Carol Peterson Haviland
University of California, San Bernandino

Drawing on US theories and practices to rethink writing instruction in English at the richly multilingual American University of Beirut (AUB) challenged our assumptions about teaching writing both in Lebanon and in the US. We use this experience to reconsider how existing work in composition, WAC/WID, and L2/multilingual/translingual scholarship should shape the education of students and faculty in each of our universities; how we need to work reciprocally in language-rich sites such as AUB to further develop translingual pedagogies; and how we must rethink objectives and designs of all of our WAC/writing center/writing programs.

Anchored in our own observations and beliefs about teaching English in multicultural settings and buttressed by the work of Canagarajah (2006), Horner et al. (2011), Pederson (2010), and others, this chapter charts Carol and Amy's process for rethinking writing instruction in English at the American

University of Beirut (AUB), both for students and for faculty. However, the process undertaken in the context of Lebanon demonstrates how those of us in other countries, particularly in Anglophone-based systems, might benefit from stretching our own assumptions about writing and writing instruction. This initial work in turn had immediate implications for Joan's ongoing research questions, several of which she and Carol had shared. Thus we began our collaborative work on this project, which has challenged all three of us to think differently about how we teach—and might better teach—writing courses in Lebanon, in the US, and elsewhere.[1]

As Joan and Carol collaborated on their current projects of studying knowledge construction across borders and the role of literacy brokers/gatekeepers in fostering or barring mutual collaboration, links became clear between their work and how writing was being conceptualized with students and faculty at AUB. Likewise, the rich experiences Amy and Carol used to recreate their WAC courses clearly exemplified how Joan and Carol encouraged writing center practices to shift. When Lillis and Curry (2010) published their work on how Anglo-centric expectations had infused international publication and academic performance expectations, all three of us saw the parallel expectations operating in writing programs and writing centers whose supporting theories are built on similar monolingual assumptions. Just as WAC, genre and cultural historic activity theories alerted compositionists to their singular vision of writing, causing a major shift in writing instruction at US universities from the 70s on, so too we saw how the use of multilingual, transnational perspectives must shift—indeed is already shifting—writing within disciplines. In our individual and collaborative work within multilingual settings, we had to consider not only how existing work in composition, WAC/WID, and L2/multilingual/translingual scholarship should shape the education of students and faculty in our own universities, but also how we need to work reciprocally in language rich sites such as AUB to further develop translingual approaches to language difference, to add to our understanding of pedagogies for multilingual writers, and to rethink objectives and designs of all of our WAC/writing programs.

LANGUAGES IN LEBANON AND AT AUB

Due to its complex history, geographical location at the intersection of three continents, and travel-prone population, Lebanon has long been a deeply multicultural and multilingual society. Today, the number of Lebanese citizens who live in a very wide range of locations abroad is reputed to be three times larger than the number of those who live within the boundaries of this small country; dual citizenships are quite common. Arabic is the official language of Lebanon, but family, social, and work connections often must often be maintained across geographic and linguistic boundaries, and Lebanese children may learn more than one language at a very early age. The two most prevalent non-Arabic languages are French and English—French as a legacy of the French mandate that ended in 1943, and English because of its global currency in business and scholarship. Armenian also figures as a strong minority language in the national language landscape, and it is used primarily within the Armenian community, which faithfully preserves the language at home and in school. While English is commonly heard in the capital city, Beirut, it is not spoken everywhere, and often it is used only in very specific places, in very specific ways. Only recently have scholars begun to research attitudes towards these various languages in Lebanon, and to observe how these languages interact and are used for different purposes (Diab, 2006; Shaaban & Ghaith, 1999, 2002).

Language policy in Lebanon reinforces the propensity towards multilingualism by structuring it into the school curriculum. Almost all children are required to learn Arabic, French, and English, although programs vary according to the weight accorded to each of these languages. Any one of the three can be the principal language of instruction, while the other two are relegated to ongoing foreign language courses. Similarly, in the many universities in Lebanon, instruction may take place in English, French, or Arabic. Furthermore, pedagogical approaches tend to gravitate, loosely speaking, towards ways of teaching that may be associated with the language of instruction: for example, a French-educated student not only learns in French, but also tends to write in genres and use textual conventions that are more commonly found in French schools. (For a description of a similarly linguistically rich writing and teaching environment in a graduate program at a Swedish-medium institution, see Lavelle & Shima [this volume].)

One additional twist, which is very relevant to writing instruction, is the fact that Arabic is a diglossic language. The formal written and spoken forms of Arabic that students learn in school are quite different from the spoken dialects that they learn at home in their families. Formal Arabic, which is shared across all Arabic speaking cultures, has a rich literary and linguistic tradition and high prestige; spoken Arabic dialects, however, vary considerably from one country to the next, and tend to be a much more oral phenomenon. The diglossic character of Arabic means that for Lebanese students, all writing may be experienced as somehow already "foreign," even in Arabic. Because of new media, this phenomenon has changed recently: Lebanese Arabic is written using Latin characters and numerals (for text messaging) or Arabic characters, commonly seen, for example, on Facebook, in billboards, or in graffiti.

LANGUAGE INSTRUCTION AT AUB

The impetus for reviewing writing instruction at the American University of Beirut (AUB) has long been underway, first as part of the long rebuilding process that was undertaken after the fighting in the 1975-1990 civil war in Lebanon had stopped, and, later, in response to the urgings of accreditation reports (US accreditation for the university was awarded in 2004 by the Commission on Higher Education of the Middle States Association of Colleges and Schools). Since its inception in 1866, the university has had a highly sensitive relationship to universities in the United States. Its institutional documents anchor it in American liberal arts models of education, and it is bound to address the requirements and concerns of accrediting bodies situated in the United States; at the same time a commitment to serving local needs and communities has been embedded in the institution's purpose from the outset. Thus, the institution has continually negotiated competing and overlapping objectives, values, cultures, and practices as it interprets structures and approaches often generated in the US and performs them in the context of Lebanon and the Middle East-North Africa region.

Unlike the US context, where the assumption of a monolingual English language culture must be countered with strong arguments, in Lebanon, the multilingual character of society is abundantly evident. Teachers at AUB expect students to have complex language identifications and a personal history with two or more written languages, in addition to one or more spoken Arabic dialects. In fact, it is very rare to encounter a student who speaks and writes only in English. The multilingual reality is reflected to some extent in the curriculum: To satisfy general education requirements, students are required to take communication skills courses both in Arabic and in English. (A "foreign" language is not required.) In all courses at AUB, however, except for Arabic and the few foreign language electives, English is the medium of instruction, a status it acquired in 1882. Until then, the primary language of instruction had been Arabic. In the last annual report of his long career, college founder and president Daniel Bliss (1902) reflected on the decision to shift to English, citing three important motivating factors: a desire among students to learn English; the difficulty of enrolling non-Arabic speaking students from other parts of the region, such as Persian or Turkish students; and a lack of Arabic textbooks in technical fields, such as chemistry or modern medicine—a lack that professors of the college had sought to remedy by writing and publishing Arabic textbooks themselves, but which they found too overwhelming to address successfully. According to Jeha (2004), when a debate over Darwinism led to the abrupt departure of several medical school faculty members in 1882, new professors could not be found who were fluent enough to lecture on technical subjects in Arabic. As Jeha explains, the move to hire English-lecturing faculty—driven by practical necessity—sealed the shift to English as the principle language of instruction; however, the historical complexity of the language policy in the university has meant that debates around this issue have always been, and still remain, very alive.

This unique language environment of Lebanon has shaped instruction at AUB in several ways, at least from our perspective as American-educated compositionists. One salient effect is the fact that existing core required courses are framed primarily as instruction in language, rather than in writing or composition. For example, the required communication skills courses are named "Academic English" and "Advanced Academic English"; the courses in Arabic are called "Readings in Arabic Literature" or "Readings in Arabic Heritage." While composition programs in US colleges and universities are broadly conceived as "writing" programs (in English), instruction in writing at AUB derives from English language teaching, and along with listening, speaking, and reading, it has historically been conceived as only one of the several skills important for learning the language. While requiring instruction in two languages acknowledges multilingualism, in one sense, the isolation of the two programs from each other does not reflect the actual language identities of the students, who in everyday practice move freely between the two, as well as French, several local Arabic dialects, and other languages, as the occasion demands.

A third important phenomenon we have noticed is that the tendency to relegate the teaching of writing to English instructors, a familiar attitude in US universities, is magnified at AUB, perhaps because approximately 75% of the faculty learned English as a foreign language. Despite extraordinary fluency and very high levels of proficiency, which allow faculty to teach and publish prolifically in their fields in English, a strong perception remains that commenting and assessing the language of a written document— "the English" —can only be the province of English instructors.

Horner and Trimbur (2004) note that "assumptions about language that were institutionalized around the turn of the century, at a high tide of imperialism, colonial adventure, and overseas missionary societies, have become sedimented in the way we think about writing pedagogy and curriculum" (p. 608), and the same is true at AUB. Here, students are eager to participate in world economies and scholarship, which entails using both spoken and written English, but instruction at AUB, as in most places in Lebanon, remains limited by traditions that focus on conveying rules and conventions for constructing academic texts. Students' lived experience with languages, language acquisition, and cultural rhetorics largely figures as an obstacle to their fluency, as a source of errors and deficiencies: thus students who are "weak in English" are positioned by teachers and policy makers as academic outsiders with problems, rather than as knowledge constructors. Although these practices conveniently maintain traditional and tidy hierarchies and allow status-quo gate keeping, they perpetuate a conservative rather than generative understanding of language, and they silence the contributions that multilingual students can make to language research and to knowledge in their own disciplines. Engaging with the traditional language policy in the AUB allowed us to see in high relief the failure of all of our writing courses to creatively address the needs and abilities of our students. Along with Canagarajah and Jerskey (2009), we wondered, "What kind of pedagogy would accommodate the emerging realizations of literacy, identity, and competence in the context of globalization and postmodern thinking?"(p. 482).

WORKING TOWARDS A MULTILINGUAL WRITING PEDAGOGY IN ENGLISH 300: TRANSLINGUALISM AS DISCIPLINARY WRITING

To explore these questions, Carol and Amy began their initial research within the language rich cultures of AUB in the spring of 2010 with MA/PhD students in two course sections of English 300: Writing in the Disciplines, an academic writing course for graduate students. These English 300 students were beginning graduate programs across the university, in nursing, engineering, computer science, public health, math, agriculture, and many other fields. Graduates primarily of Arabic- or French-language medium universities in Lebanon and the wider Middle East-North Africa region, they had been required to take the course, based on the scores they had received on an English language proficiency exam (88-96 on the internet-based TOEFL or equivalent scores on other tests). This placement at once flagged them as "low proficiency" users of English, yet inducted them into a high-stakes situation, as they would very shortly be expected to present their research, compose theses, and write for publication in English. Many students had very limited experience with academic writing in any language, much less in English. (Almost uniformly, they apologized, particularly to "American" faculty, for their "poor English," in terms that reflected pride, frustration, and embarrassment.)

Before 2007, when English 300 was first added to the curriculum, entering graduate students who were required to take English courses had been placed into the core Communication Skills courses, where they studied side-by-side with undergraduate students. Taking an undergraduate pre-requisite made students ineligible for Graduate Assistantships, however. Moreover, the undergraduate courses were neither tailored to graduate students' academic needs nor amenable to their more mature approaches to learning. The new, 3-credit course was designed to provide students with key academic writing and reading skills that they could situate within their disciplines. John Swales and Christine Feak's text, *Academic Writing for Graduate Students*, provided the guide for exercises and assignments. Students were asked to compose texts that followed common patterns in academic writing (in the language of Swales and Feak, these were identified as: defining; problem/process/solution; critiquing; summarizing; and reporting research). Sessions with information librarians provided an introduction to searching library sources, and the course also stressed learning to document sources appropriately. Informal writing was practiced in the form of journals and reflective essays. The course was offered through the Communication Skills Program, but differed from the other courses (which are almost all taught by Instructors), in that it could only be taught by a faculty member holding a doctoral degree.

As we began to implement the most current version of AUB's English 300 syllabus, we became aware of the mismatch between pedagogies that define students as deficient and that focus on what they can't do and our own observations of how much these English 300 students actually could do with language. As we watched them move across languages, sites, and mediums, we became convinced that we should begin by discovering more of what they did know about written and spoken languages, about cultural conventions, and about disciplinary rhetorics. And so we began to reconsider the traditional roles of these courses and of ourselves as literacy gatekeepers or promoters and instead worked toward Lillis and Curry's description of literacy brokers [2] with both students and faculty. However, as we observed our students' linguistic expertise as well as their "English deficits," we found the term "broker" challenged our own pedagogical inclinations. Although still a position of power, as is a broker, we chose to think of our role as reciprocal: facilitating knowledge construction required all participants to learn as well as teach. Instead of capitalizing on students' image of themselves as inadequate, as needing to be filled with grammatical and syntactic information, we began thinking about where we might shift the usual "professors export information; students import it" ratio; in short, we reversed this ratio and began importing their complex language histories into the work of the course, and into how we think about our own (new) identities as collaborative literacy brokers.

While most key assignments for writing remained essentially unchanged (a literacy narrative, summaries of reading, an annotated bibliography, and a full research proposal), we added new ones; more importantly, we sought to change our role as instructors within the dynamics of the course. We asked students to write and reflect upon their language histories with a language use questionnaire (See Appendix A), which students completed online and then discussed in class. The introduction of the questionnaire and subsequent discussions provided students with a venue to acknowledge and share what they knew about language, explain usages derived from French or Arabic, or articulate the different ways political scientists, nurses, or engineers present data, as well as the perceived need for revised English instruction in this course and in the emerging writing initiative (WAC/WID). The small but significant shift in the course design fostered instruction that views English as an additional rather than replacement language, instruction that positions multilingual students as informants rather than as problems, instruction that changes faculty's gatekeeping function to that of collaborative literacy brokers. (For much the same reasons, a language use questionnaire is also an essential pedagogical element in the graduate writing support courses described by Craig and Lavelle & Shima [this volume]. The latter also describe the ways in which faculty work to foster a view of cultural and linguistic differences as resources not deficits.) Our seeking to be instructed by our students affirmed them as rhetorical agents who are "always doing things that make a difference. Unlike subjects, agents are defined neither by mastery, nor by determination, nor by fragmentation. They are unique embodied, and autonomous individuals in that they are self-organizing, but by virtue of that fact, they, as well as the surround with which they interact, are always changing" (Cooper, p. 425). As instructors, we acted as "observers" and "reflective practitioners," but not as observers of students as subjects who must be corrected. Listening to our students' conversations before and after class showed us the verbal flexibility that allowed them to fit elements of three or more languages into a single coherent conversation. Instead of subjects to be studied for ways in which we as instructors could intervene, students became the linguistic agents with whom we, as literacy brokers, would be working.

Our education began with students' responses to the language questionnaires in which they disclosed how much they knew about language. They detailed rich and complexly layered processes of both simultaneously and sequentially acquiring two, three, four, or five languages. Their descriptions of their current languaging practices showed them selecting and combining from these languages to engage with different audiences and settings. For example, a political science student reported that she and her husband, both Syrian, speak chiefly in English because although they both learned Arabic as their home language, he had had most of his schooling in English and is more comfortable speaking and writing it. She speaks English also with domestic help, but with her parents she speaks Arabic if it is personal—but English for everything else. Several students described home-related differentiations, speaking Arabic with grandparents, French with parents, and English with domestic help (who are usually migrant workers from Sri Lanka, the Philippines, or Ethiopia), as well as campus differentiations, depending upon whether school was conducted in Arabic, French, or English. Several also noted that, in their workplaces, they most often spoke a mix of Arabic and English but wrote most often in English. Their texting practices were a mix of Arabic and English, most often a mystery to both their English and Arabic speaking professors! As observer-teachers in reflective practice, we provided the ground on which we mirrored to students what they already knew about negotiating context-specific expectations, but they in turn continually challenged our own tendency to "teach to" them as "students." They enacted multilingual theories with their linguistic acuity, and in turn they contributed to our own understandings of the ways disciplines and languages interacted.

In class, we watched two electrical and computer engineering students, one Armenian/Syrian and the other Lebanese, both contribute to class discussions and write sophisticated papers in English. They also ably contrasted the ways their ECE journals in different subfields review literature with the ways their Lebanese nursing student counterparts described the same moves in nursing journals. As they described these journal articles, they also observed significant differences in Arabic, French, and English rhetorics. For example, they cited many instances in which Arabic or French logic simply didn't translate into English, and they offered word counts to illustrate what they called the "parsimony" of English and the "elaboration" of Arabic and French. Finally, they noted an important pedagogical implication of these differences as they reflected that assignments written in English seem to invite very open exploration while those in French stipulate both what data mattered and how it should be displayed. These articulations became for us a language of instruction within the class, taken up by us as teachers rather than substituted with a pre-formed rhetorical frame; the more we refrained from naming student reflections, the more our own opportunities as brokers and agents grew—and were exchanged.

Even our seemingly simple responses to interrogate rather than correct produced generative interchanges that more fruitfully pointed to the laminations and subtle meanings that are carried in the grammar and the structure of language/thinking. As a Lebanese public health student described writing a grant proposal for a daycare center for elderly Alzheimer's patients, she showed a thoughtful sensitivity to the Lebanese family constructs. As she watched middle-aged parents struggle to accommodate the shift from women being mostly at home and available to care for aging parents, to men and women working outside of their homes, leaving no one at home to provide that care, she was mindful then that her proposal would need to be sensitive to this cultural shift if elder daycare were to be acceptable. She was equally mindful of her English instruction when she was editing, often carefully telescoping her many elaborated Arabic phrases into more succinct English constructions. Thus, to limit the number of times she repeated "caring for patients who have dementia," she began writing "caring for demented patients." As the writer read her text to the class, Carol was unsure whether this was accurate in Lebanon so asked how they would react if someone said that their grandmother had dementia: the students said "sad." "How about if someone said that she is demented," she asked: they said "mad"—and everyone laughed as the student commented that knowing the English rules doesn't always produce correct usages.

In return, our students' descriptions of how languages "feel" helped us understand and explain some of the ways language embeds cultural habits and shapes assertions. When asked which languages they liked best, many students said that they like Arabic because it "feels good in their ears," because they "don't have to think to use it," and because it is richly elaborated. They like French because it is "elegant and classy," and they like English because "it gets straight to the goal," is compact, easy, and very useful in many workplaces.

Asking about language histories, habits, and feelings allowed the conversations in class and the written comments on papers to focus on understanding how language and texts work and feel and sound, in particular contexts, and to avoid reinforcing teaching that simply conveys rules, conventions and norms that the students must learn to emulate. Talk in the classroom could draw on the knowledge that students brought with them about their languages and previous writing experiences, as well as on the differences among their various disciplines. Just as important, that instructors' acts of asking positioned them as agents/learners along with their students: repositioning ourselves in the classroom, repositions students in as mutually interactive knowledge-builders engaged in a process of mutual negotiated literacy brokerage.

Beyond "interesting," these students' responses helped us think more seriously about that "elaborateness" that Western English conventions undercut, ones that might better be interrogated to avoid losing what might be otherwise lost in the bargain; about the rhythms and music with which different languages and rhetorical styles are infused—the tones that color and convey concepts as well as word choice; about exporting Western notions of argument and conflict, and questioning the act of negatively tagging the "non-linear," or "lack of transitions." A linear, generally deductive, and thesis-driven argument pattern, based on Artistotelian logic, carries with it forms of thinking, ways of questioning and producing knowledge, practices of debate and contestation, expectations of transitions that are not the only ways to build or present knowledge. Yet the very assumptions inherent in how an argument must be made and must proceed, the ones driving this article, may not be the best for approaching issues, raising questions, building knowledge upon which non-western cultural practices are built (Lipson & Binkley, 2009). Challenging the monological mode of constructing communication reframes teaching, learning and communicating as a simultaneously interlingual and interlogical series of inventions that emerge from meshed interactions.

It can be argued that framing the work of this course primarily in terms of collaborative language study and of constructing knowledge in chemistry, nursing, or political science, rather than as "learning English," also afforded the means to alter how students were perceived by others, how they viewed themselves as users of language, and how the work of the literacy classroom could be represented in a different way—focusing on participation in a social discourse, rather than as a display of discrete skills. Drawing on the work of James Gee and Brian Street, Canagarjah and Jersky point out:

> We do not write only to construct a rule-governed text…
> Multilingual writers benefit from a pedagogy that allows
> writing to go beyond narrowly defined processes of
> text construction. Writing becomes instead a rhetorical
> negotiation for achieving social meanings and functions.
> In other words, writing is not just constitutive; it is also
> performative. .…. We write to achieve specific interests,
> represent our preferred values and identities, and fulfill
> diverse needs. (pp. 482-483)

A performative model of writing, and the agency it assumes or allows in the writer, also emerges in the work of Gunther Kress and other members of the New London Group. According to Kress and Jeff Bezemer (2009), "Text making is a semiotic act in which meaning is the issue in every aspect, because it is also a social act with social consequences"(p. 171). The implications of this assertion for writing and writing instruction is that "[c]omposition seen as competent performance is replaced by design, seen as the attempt to make constantly varying rhetorical purposes effective" (p. 171). This definition counters approaches that confine writing to a narrow performance of skills, approaches that inevitably categorize writers according to the skills they lack, while excluding the evident capabilities that they do possess as irrelevant, a consequence that is especially searing for writers like the English 300 students, who have been officially marked as "weak" in English.

A few aspects of the English 300 course worked to undermine the assumption that texts are static, objective, containers of information, and to represent them instead as performative acts of a particular sort. Adding a second required textbook was valuable in this respect because dissonances between the two texts used allowed new perceptions of meaning-making to emerge. We paired *Rewriting: How to do Things with Words*, by Joseph Harris with the Swales and Feak text. At the start of the semester, students analyzed how authors of each of the books represented "academic writing" and compared their two extended definitions.

A model of academic writing that draws on the concept of performativity is at the core of Harris's text. In his "Introduction," Harris describes how his understanding of academic writing, and his desire to provide new terminology for the things writers do when they are composing, is indebted to his powerful encounter with John Austin's book *Doing Things with Words*:

> In this book [Harris writes] ... Austin argues that in thinking about language his fellow philosophers have long been overconcerned with decoding the precise meaning or truth value of various statements—a fixation that has blinded them from considering the routine yet complex ways in which people use words to get things done: to marry, to promise, to bet, to apologize, to persuade, to contract, and the like. Austin calls such uses of language performatives and suggests that it is often more useful to ask what a speaker is trying to do in saying something than what he or she means by it. While I don't try to apply Austin's thinking here in any exact way, I do think of myself as working in his mode. (p. 3)

Harris is intent on describing academic writing in terms of what writers are doing to affect a particular project that interests them. By contrast, Swales and Feak base their representation of academic writing, as well as the textbook's information, tasks, and instructions to student writers, on extensive knowledge of, description, and analysis of, the features of published academic texts. The textbook reveals patterns of organization and language use pertinent to academic writing in any field, and it focuses on supporting writers as they construct similar texts themselves. While Swales and Feak's representation of academic writing tapped into familiar assumptions students brought with them about writing, Harris's discussion challenged these assumptions, and it introduced new ways to think about how texts respond to and shape contexts. Founding our work in the class on an animated analysis of these two approaches helped shift expectations about the course and about writing for all of us.

For example, previous assignments had followed a traditional trajectory of writing summaries, analyses, reports, and critiques, with only tacitly assumed ties to students' majors or professions. One of the new writing projects, an interview with a faculty member in the student's field, contributed significantly to students' understanding of writing as a social act, rather than as a set of discrete skills. Students read an article published by one of their professors and then met with the professor to discuss his or her work as an author. Asking the faculty member about the research itself as well as the process of doing and reporting the research invited students and faculty to think about how writing constructs their fields or professions, about how forms prescribe what may and may not be said, about the implications of having most research activity based in English-only sources. The interview showed students how texts were often composed as an integral part of a broader discourse, and could be viewed not as a "product" but as a medium, often produced collaboratively, for participating in ongoing cycles of research and discussion in their fields. As one student wrote in her end-of-semester reflection, "Research and looking for new inventions and new technologies to help our community is my aim and these projects can't be proven to be true unless they are documented in papers accompanied with experiments and results that show their efficiency and applicability." Her realization echoes the observation made by Canagarajah and Jersky: "Texts are not just context-bound or context-sensitive. They are context transforming" (p. 483). Viewing her work as a writer as integral to her work as a designer of green energy technology allowed this student to perceive the texts she composes as ways to participate in her field, and to weigh the effectiveness of the language and other features of the text according to this purpose.

Finally, course assessment also worked to support a shift from perceiving texts in static ways to seeing them as performative, and to frame conventions, rules and standards as constructions that can be useful or contested. Unlike undergraduate communication skills courses, English 300 was graded on a pass/fail basis. For instructors, assessment meant determining whether work presented and participation could be "Passed"—accorded the equivalent in US terms of a 2.2 grade point average. In one respect, the relatively undemanding requirement made room for the circumstances of this student population, who are often full-time employees, graduate assistants or parents, as well as being students. We found that the pass/fail assessment allowed all of us to focus on commenting and discussion, by removing the effect of this grade on the general grade average. Ironically, by allowing us to encourage more risk-taking, and to keep attention from fixating on texts as objects to be graded, this form of assessment actually supported more sophisticated student writing. Recently, we have also instituted a grading contract, based on the work of Danielewicz and Elbow (2009), to further reinforce the goals for the course. The contract recognizes the agency of students by defining key aspects of the course, such as revising, responding to others, and being present, not as teacher expectations, but as student responsibilities; a passing grade is guaranteed to the student from the outset, as long as the clearly articulated responsibilities are fulfilled.

GOING FORWARD, CHALLENGES AND OPPORTUNITIES: AUB'S CAMPUS-WIDE WRITING INITIATIVE

The lessons learned in the process of rethinking English 300 have continued to inform teaching and program design at AUB, and they have been carried by Joan and Carol to their US institutions. We believe that—from the inception of the program for faculty to the new relationship between student agent-brokers and instructor broker-students—they also provide useful models for us all, and we invite our readers to imagine their own contexts operating similarly and to equally imagine the subtle shifts that might occur as a result.

At AUB, in 2010 and 2011, Carol and Amy began the larger project of designing the university's approach to language instruction across the disciplines, a project that the provost and General Education Committee were enthusiastic about because of recommendations in a recent accreditation report, and because they had been awarded a three-year Andrew W. Mellon Foundation grant to establish a campus-wide writing program. Indeed, the strong endorsement of increased emphasis on writing, mandated in new General Education requirements and widely advocated by the faculty, presented an opportunity for constructive engagement with policies and attitudes represented by "English" and "writing." This approach to constructing a local WAC/WID/CAC program drew on well-established programs in the US. However, it was particularly important to help administrators and faculty assume roles that foster reciprocal knowledge construction and underscore student contributions to learning, to stress social views of literacy that represent writing in performative terms, and to assert the value of situating English not in isolation but in relation with the several other languages that are present in the AUB context and that are used by multilingual writers. (See also Lavelle & Shima [this volume] for a discussion of how faculty conveyed to international graduate students their value as intellectual contributors to knowledge construction, including setting priorities for reading and taking a "let-it-pass" approach to lingua franca surface errors.)

While administrators and faculty initially looked to us as importers of knowledge about WAC/WID programs to AUB, we believed that accepting this role unambiguously would belie all that we claimed to have learned from our work with English 300 students. Thus, in the process of establishing the new writing program, key moments have arisen when this theoretical stance—to construct knowledge about writers collaboratively, to conceive of multilingualism as an asset, and to think transnationally—shaped decisions in critical ways. One important decision arose in relation to how additional General Education writing courses were conceived. Just as English 300 students had been seen as deficient and needing language repair via an "English" course, undergraduate students across the disciplines were seen as deficient writers, particularly in English, and the initial guidelines proposed they take two more "English" courses, delivered in ways that did not participate in or "detract" from the work of their majors. We came to these discussions with the scholarship of our own fields, and we also thought about the commitments to being good brokers we had made to our English 300 students. Thus, we listened carefully to deans' and chairs' descriptions of their students' linguistic failings, but we also urged them to consider the language expertise AUB students and faculty possess and to consider alternate instructional models that might engage students as biologists, nurses, nutritionists, computer engineers, and public health workers. Again, as we took seriously our roles as brokers rather than importers, we were able to learn alongside administrators and faculty as they thought about the writerly moves they made as professionals and then the ways they might create parallel moves for students—with support from the writing center and the teaching-learning center. In this process, they and we discovered ways that intentional and visible work with writing might be part of already existing courses. By the end of this process, the General Education guidelines had been revised to require that each student take two courses within the major that embed explicit disciplinary writing instruction.

The development of ongoing courses to satisfy the General Education guidelines is work that progresses slowly. In individual and small group meetings, Amy and Carol (as well as Joan and Carol in the US and other sites) have thought alongside colleagues in other disciplines about how writing constructs and is constructed by their fields. Only then were they—and we—able to see how, even though it might be untidy and time-consuming, embedding writing in existing courses—using writing for those courses' purposes—was more likely to be "real" for students and sustainable for faculty. To do this work required redefining efficiency, for us, for our colleagues, and for our students. It meant lots of "front-loading": selecting in each major at first just one course that all students would take and that embodied many of the habits and concepts of the major. It meant rethinking that course in terms of language functions, of why, how, and with whom writing typically is done in the field as well as the implications of those habits and features for the discipline and its participants—and then how these moves might be incorporated in students' projects. It meant facing the uncomfortable recognition that sometimes disciplines' traditions conserve unwarranted power or simply no-longer-existing technologies and need to be challenged. It meant trying—and both succeeding and failing. Mutual high points occurred when faculty experienced the "aha" moments of realizing how much writing they already were teaching and saw how making their writerly moves more visible might move students toward more expert roles as biologists or geologists. They then also began to incorporate elements of the base course into their other courses and to watch for the effects of these courses in students' senior projects.

The writing initiative, which reports directly to the provost, has been positioned within the already-existing WAC/WID-oriented Writing Center, a choice that Amy and Carol recommended, for it provides a hospitable and ongoing physical and intellectual location for both students and faculty. To date, 35 faculty members have been directly involved with the development of the courses they teach. In the first three semesters of implementation, 19 pilot courses have been taught at least once, in Agriculture and Food Sciences, Engineering and Architecture, Nursing, and Arts and Sciences, even as more continue to be developed. The courses have enrolled approximately 1,550 students, and have been supported by 2,800 hours of writing center meetings. At the end of three years, we project that faculty will have designed and taught at least one course in each major in which students look seriously at the ways multiple kinds of texts and authors, including themselves, construct both schooling and professional work in their disciplines.

Preserving the important lessons learned in English 300 as this large program continues to unfold calls for strategic approaches that can ensure that pedagogical values remain central to its work. Faculty development is at the heart of the new writing initiative, and thus as writing center staff meet with course instructors, they not only function as literacy "brokers," but they also introduce current scholarship on multilingual/translingual writing into readings and discussions. Also, inspired by the broker role of learning from or with students and faculty, the writing center and English department are collaborating to conduct a four-year longitudinal research project to study writing, writing practices, and representations of writing of students and faculty members.

The education of writing center tutors represents another important area for strategic engagement with writing instruction across the university, an area in which to forward social theories of literacy and multilingual writers and practices that support them. In addition to the formal, intentional discussions of shared readings and tutoring observations in the writing center, meaningful encounters often occur without planning. Recently, for example, a group of electrical engineering students came to the writing center to discuss a report on their project to design a control system for a hard drive. They questioned the value of discussing the report with a writing center tutor, since, "it has hardly any English—it is mostly formulas and figures." When tutors explained that the visit was an occasion to discuss the effectiveness of their whole report, including language and the social context in which it circulates, students engaged in a very lively discussion (in English and Arabic) about revisions.

As we work in AUB's consortium of writing program faculty, writing initiative faculty and administrators, writing center staff, and students (both as tutors and authors), this transnational view of language anchors a pedagogy that asks what students and faculty know about languages and disciplinary structures. As we have studied the answers to these questions, both we and our colleagues have found them to generate thoughtful ways to build on multilingual knowledges. For example, aware that although AUB's language of instruction is English and much professional work takes place in English, neither faculty nor students function in an English-only world. Like the English 300 public health student, most faculty and students work across multiple languages. They interview clients, talk to patients, write grants, read local and global rules of governance, negotiate contracts, and design agricultural reforms in these several languages but also as translinguals or transnationals, using a mix of English, Arabic(s), French, and other languages. With a more nuanced consideration of their own translingualism, they notice how Lebanon's linguistic practices reveal age and class positions as they hear the public performances of the Lebanese Symphony announced in English and the Chamber of Commerce-sponsored performances announced in French—all in the same Catholic church on a French-speaking university campus. They think amid linguistic and cultural conventions and patterns, transforming both local sites and global practices.

Embedding writing within existing courses rather than "adding English courses," is shifting the focus away from English and onto a social, performative view of writing that allows faculty to invest in the project in ways that did not appear to be possible before. Already some faculty teaching the writing-embedded courses have taken the opportunity—and the challenge—of engaging with and arguing about the shift away from "English" and towards constructing meaningful texts. And, in fact, these conversations are occurring with students in classes and with faculty in Teaching and Learning seminars as well as informally in the faculty dining room. Further, to support faculty and students with these projects, administrators have also seen the value of investing in a more broadly conceived writing center that can provide an ongoing home for this richer work with writing.

GOING FORWARD: BEYOND AUB

The three of us are optimistic about these projects and look forward to expanding them at AUB and with other colleagues in other sites. As the AUB program develops the second round of writing-embedded courses, we will continue to study the ways that multilinguals move from using their several languages, yet compartmentalizing each language's words, idioms, and rhetorical patterns, to more cross-fertilized languages, each bearing traces of the other and ultimately being changed by these exchanges. We will look to the work of Berry, Hawisher, and Selfe (2012) to reshape the ways the academy reads

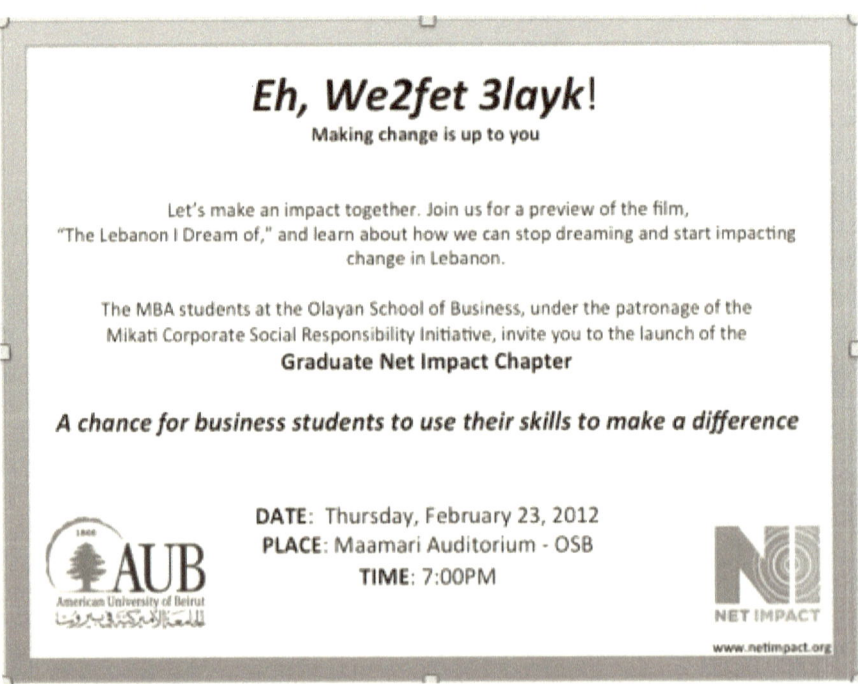

Figure 16.1 Poster produced by graduate business students

multilingual students' writing and likewise the ways that those students' writing enriches the writing of monolingual academics, both faculty and students. We will watch for shifts in the ways instructors' assessments differentiate between errors in meaning and those errors that native speakers might notice but that don't interfere with meaning. We will look to outsider "errors" that indicate different ways of expressing ideas and that make visible the point that language offers many ways of making sense. For example, the three of us adopted one of Carol's English 300 student's "errors" that expanded our use of "discipline" and "field" into "meadow" and began referring to the "meadow" of composition and rhetoric; in doing so, we meant to suggest that we should see our field as capacious, open to different seedlings, participants, and languages.

We conclude with a poster produced by AUB's graduate business students (see Figure 16.1, previous page). Just as they are challenging themselves in the text of the poster to move beyond dreams to reconstruct Lebanon's business practices, we are eager to act more visibly and emphatically upon the implications of transnational language work.

Finally, we want to add to the position statements asserting students' rights to their own languages, the recognition that multilingual students in particular have much to offer monolinguals and monolingual-based writing programs. It is our responsibility to seek out opportunities for dialogue and collaborative inquiry, such as ours, as we construct a richer understanding of translingualism's possibilities for our students and for our programs.

NOTES

1. At AUB, Amy has been a faculty member in the English Department since 2004. Carol, a professor of English at California State University, San Bernardino, received a spring 2010 appointment as AUB Visiting Professor of English and an additional appointment in spring 2011. Her assignment, to embed writing in the majors as part of a revised General Education program, included co-teaching a graduate writing course with Amy. Joan, professor of English at Illinois State University, has been engaged in transnational scholarship through her work with writers and writing instruction in multiple institutions in and outside the US. The authorial "we," thus represents Amy and Carol when they report on AUB, but all three speaking collaboratively out of their engagement with multi/translingual issues.
2. For further use of the term "literacy broker", see Lillis and Curry, 2010; see also Mullin, Haviland, and Zenger, 2012.

REFERENCES

Berry, P. W., Hawisher, G. E., & Selfe, C. L. (2012). *Transnational Literate Lives in Digital Times*. Logan, UT: Computers and Composition Digital Press/ Utah State University Press. Retrieved from http://ccdigitalpress.org/transnational/

Bliss, D. (1902). Thirty-sixth annual report of the Syrian Protestant College to the Board of Managers 1901-1902. Archives and Special Collections, Jafet Library. American University of Beirut.

Canagarajah, A. S. (2006). Toward a writing pedagogy of shuttling between languages: lLarning from multilingual writers. *College English 68*, 589-604.

Canagarajah, A. S. & Jerskey, M. (2009) Meeting the needs of advanced multilingual writers. In R. Beard, D. Myhill, J. Riley, & M. Nystrand, M. (Eds.) *The SAGE Handbook of Writing Development* (pp. 472-488). London: Sage.

Cooper, M. (2011). Rhetorical agency as emergent and enacted. *College Composition and Communication, 62*(3), 420-449.

Danielewicz, J., & Elbow, P. (2009). A unilateral grading contract to improve learning and teaching. *College Composition and Communication, 61*(2), 244-268.

Diab, R. L. (2006). University students' beliefs about learning English and French in Lebanon. *System: An International Journal of Educational Technology and Applied Linguistics, 34*(1), 80-96.

Gee, J. P. (1990). *Social linguistics and literacies: Ideology in discourses. Critical perspectives on literacy and education*. London: Falmer Press.

Harris, J. (2006). *Rewriting: How to do things with texts*. Logan, UT: Utah State University Press.

Horner, B., & Trimbur, J. (2002). English only and U. S. college composition. *College Composition and Communication, 53*, 594-630.

Horner, B., Lu, M-Z., Royster, J. J., & Trimbur, J. (2011). Language difference in writing: Toward a translingual approach. *College English, 73*, 303-321.

Jeha, S. (2004). *Darwin and the crisis of 1882 in the medical department* (S. Kaya, Trans.). Beirut: American University of Beirut Press.

Kress, G., & Bezemer, J. (2009). Writing in a multimodal world of representation. In R. Beard, D. Myhill, J. Riley, & M. Nystrand (Eds.) *The SAGE handbook of writing development* (pp. 167-181). London: SAGE Publications.

Lillis, T. & Curry, M. J. (2010). *Academic writing in a global context: The politics and practices of publishing in English*. London: Routledge.

Lipson C. S. & Binkley, R. A. (Eds.). (2009). *Ancient non-Greek rhetoric*. Anderson, South Carolina: Parlor Press.

Mullin, J., Haviland, C. P., & Zenger, A. (in press). Import/export work? Using cross-cultural theories to rethink Englishes, identities, and genres in writing centers. In B. Horner, & K. Kopelsen. (Eds.), *Reworking English in Rhetoric and Composition: Global Interrogations, Local Interventions.* Louisville, KY: University of Louisville Press.

New London Group. (1996). A pedagogy of multiliteracies: Designing social futures. *Harvard Educational Review, 66,* 60-92.

Pederson, A. M. (2010). Negotiating cultural identities through language: Academic English in Jordan. *College Composition and Communication,* 62(2),283-310.

Shaaban, K. & Ghaith, G. (2002). University students' perceptions of the ethnolinguistic vitality of Arabic, French and English in Lebanon. *Journal of Sociolinguistics, 6,* 557-574.

Shaaban, K. & Ghaith, G. (1999). Lebanon's language-in-education policies: From bilingualism to trilingualism. *Language Problems and Language Planning, 23,* 1-16.

Swales, J., & Feak, C. (2004). *Academic writing for graduate students: Essential tasks and skills* (2nd ed.). Ann Arbor, MI: University of Michigan Press.

APPENDIX A

AUB Language Questionnaire (reformatted for space reasons)

We are interested in learning more about your language experiences as we adapt this and other courses to build on AUB students' multilingual strengths. We will aggregate responses anonymously. Thank you for participating.

I. **Your languages**
    First language:
        Age ____ Teacher ____ Speak? ____ Read? ____ Write? ____
    Second language:
        Age ____ Teacher ____ Speak? ____ Read? ____ Write? ____
    Third language:
        Age ____ Teacher ____ Speak? ____ Read? ____ Write? ____
    Fourth language:
        Age ____ Teacher ____ Speak? ____ Read? ____ Write? ____
    Others?

II. **Speaking**
- What language(s) do you speak at home and with whom? Siblings? Parents? Grandparents? Domestic help?
- What language(s) do you speak with your friends?
- What language(s) do you speak at school and with whom? Classmates? Professors?
- What language(s) do you speak in any work situations and with whom? Peers? Managers?

III. **Reading**
- In which languages do you read for which specific school purposes? For example, you might read engineering reports in English and political science analyses in Arabic?
- In which languages do you read for work or professional purposes?
- In which languages do you read for "everyday" purposes, such as ordering from a menu, installing a printer, learning about the day's news (either online or in print)?
- In which languages do you read for pleasure?

IV. **Writing**
- Do you think that your writing practices are different when you write in the different languages you use?
- For example, when you do exploratory writing (drafting, listing, freewriting), what languages do you use?
- When you talk about your writing with classmates, writing tutors, or professors, what languages do you use?
- When you write in English, do you think in Arabic or French and then translate words or ideas?
- Think about writing specific academic papers in English (summaries, literature reviews, critiques, or proposals): What organizational or rhetorical forms seem "correct" to you? Where did you learn those forms? Does anything surprise/frustrate you when professors ask you to use other forms?
- How does the kind of text you are producing (email, texting, twitter) change your writing?

V. **Thinking:**
- What language(s) do you "think" in?

VI. **Language Attitudes**
- What language(s) do you like best and why?
- How do you think that your language background shapes your language preferences?
- When you say, "We do it this way because we were educated in French" (or Arabic, or any other language), what does that mean to you? How does that experience make you think or speak or write or read differently?
- What else about language practices do you think that your English 300 faculty should know?

CHAPTER 18
WRITING HISTORIES: LINGUA FRANCA ENGLISH IN A SWEDISH GRADUATE PROGRAM

Thomas Lavelle and Alan Shima
Stockholm School of Economics

This chapter presents a case study and analyzes the institutional practices that affect the success or failure of multi-lingual masters students writing theses at a Swedish university in a history program where lingua franca English is the language of instruction. Drawing upon interviews, questionnaires, policy documents and the theses themselves, this analysis of a lingua franca writing environment examines the effects of policy on high-stakes writing, the value of aligning assessment policy and practices, and the function of support, expectations and supervision in a writing/learning community. The central argument is that in many respects this graduate history program succeeds in its educational mission, particularly its engagement with disciplinary writing, but in one key respect it fails. The principal failure is its relatively low and generally slow thesis-completion rate. The successes include reading and assessment strategies that both prioritize disciplinary knowledge making and remain consistent with lingua franca communication strategies, thesis supervision and topic selection that support a difference-as-resource culture and finally proactive support for a multilingual writing environment that includes not only instruction for student writers but also faculty-development initiatives for their teachers.

Roads to Democracy is an English-medium, two-year master's degree program offered by the Department of History at Uppsala University in Sweden. For successful candidates, the program culminates in the completion of a 60-80 page master's thesis. It is these theses and the institutional context in which they are written and assessed that provide the focal points of this study. An overwhelming majority of Roads to Democracy (Roads) students are second-language writers of English, which in this setting functions as an academic lingua franca, not least because relatively few of them speak Swedish, the dominant language of governance, undergraduate teaching and routine administration at Uppsala. In this sociolinguistic context certain structural and curricular features of this program combine with its students' complex mix of backgrounds to foreground several key challenges facing both second-language disciplinary writers, in this case junior scholars of history, and the department committed to educating them. Therefore, in what follows we present the program as a case study in which we describe and analyze institutional practices that, in part, create the conditions under which second-language thesis writers work. As with other case studies, its value for writing scholars and writing-program managers rests upon the degree to which the challenges described and practices analyzed here prove to be relevant and transferable to other settings.

One such challenge revolves around assessment. The roots of this challenge lie ultimately in the decision by the History Department at Uppsala to offer an English-medium master's program. This has obliged the program faculty and leadership to articulate and enact a set of assessment criteria and priorities that, on one hand, maintain the academic standards of the department, the university and the wider disciplinary community and, on the other hand, fairly evaluate a student population that arrives in Sweden, largely from abroad, with many distinct types and levels of disciplinary, linguistic and general academic preparedness.

A second challenge concerns the relevant scope for disciplinary scholarship, simply put, what counts as a suitable thesis topic. Just as their earlier assessment practices had evolved largely in a monolingual and academically homogeneous setting, the selection of thesis topics and research questions in the Uppsala department also traditionally reflected northern European priorities and practices. Under the influence of a new student body and a new curriculum, thesis advisors from the Roads faculty have been obliged to reconsider these practices.

Along with assessing and framing the apprentice scholarship in Roads master's theses, the department faced the challenge of defining and implementing a suitable level of second-language writing support, a practice not widely established in Swedish universities when these efforts began. The relevant choices here involved the precise nature, structure and level of intensity for this support. This was a move into uncharted waters for a department of history and may represent a redefinition of the department's relationship with its students.

AIMS AND METHODS

Given these focal points, the overarching purpose of this chapter is to analyze departmental responses to the challenges outlined above, all of which emerge as a consequence of internationalized graduate studies conducted through lingua franca English, and where possible to trace the affects of those responses on the writing of master theses in English. In describing challenges and analyzing responses, we draw upon data collected over a year-long period during which our engagement with the Uppsala Department of History straddled emic and etic perspectives. With both authors working as visiting instructors in academic writing and one consulting with the department more generally on its transition from a monolingual Swedish to bilingual Swedish-English academic organization, our roles gave us access to students, faculty and program administrators, but it also made us participants in local efforts to improve student writing and to support departmental efforts to enhance student learning.

From this vantage point, we collected data of five types. One was a writing-inventory questionnaire distributed to 20 student writers that asked about their range of languages, their experience with using those languages academically and their academic or professional writing experience in English and in their other languages; 19 of 20 students responded anonymously. A second type consisted of face-to-face interviews with 12 students (eight women and four men), five of whom had not been asked to complete the writing inventory; these interviews were of limited value as the students saw us more immediately as instructors than as researchers and were reticent in expressing judgments about the program. A third was a series of five interviews with faculty members (five men and one woman), four face to face and one via email; all five are tenured at Uppsala University, three in the Department of History, two others belong formally to other departments but teach Roads courses and advise and assess theses; four are native speakers of Swedish and one a native speaker of English. A fourth data type was the set of all 15 theses completed and fully processed by the university (i.e. approved by the thesis advisor, graded by a faculty assessor, examined in a public seminar, and archived in the library); we read graded and archived copies, which proved to be valuable points of departure in interviews with faculty informants. Finally a fifth data source was documentary, the Roads curriculum and a series of departmental and university policy documents.

While our semi-embedded standing in the Uppsala History Department provided opportunities for data collection and dialogue, we chose this particular case study because it illustrates an increasingly important institutional context for second-language disciplinary writing. In the Roads program English is a transnational academic lingua franca, a setting where "English is neither the local language nor that of most of the international students" (Maruanen, 2006, p. 125), and, in Roads, international students outnumber Swedes by far. It is in such settings that we can expect speakers and writers, listeners and readers to employ communicative strategies and exhibit attitudes ascribed to lingua franca users in contact situations, including flexible codes, semantic negotiations, tolerance of temporary unintelligibility and expectation management (Canagarajah & Wurr, 2011). Most generally, "the principle behind all these strategies is alignment. Multilinguals cannot come ready with all the codes they need for an encounter …. What multilinguals aim to achieve therefore is an alignment of the language resources they have with the purposes in question" (p. 5).

This setting, therefore, differs from the writing environments that most often frame studies of either discipline-specific student writing or the writing of second-language academic writers. Typically those studies address North American, Anglophone contexts, for instance the anthologized papers in collections (Belcher & Braine, 1995; Casanave & Li, 2008; Matsuda, Cox, Jordan & Ortmeier-Hooper, 2006; Zawacki & Rogers, 2012), reference guides (Bazerman et al., 2005), and individual studies (e.g. Connor & Mayberry, 1995; Janopolous, 1995; Magno & Amarles, 2011; Seloni, 2012). Some theoretical studies do adopt a more comparative and international perspective, particularly those addressing the role of genre in L2 and WAC (e.g. Hyland, 2003; Johns, 2011). And there are of course valuable case studies of WAC or disciplinary L2 writing drawn from outside North American contexts (Bacha & Bahous, 2008; Emerson, MacKay, Funnell & MacKay 2002; Li, 2010; Pedersen, 2011), but these studies describe and analyze either individuals or broadly homogeneous groups of academic writers. One notable exception is Harbord's study (2010) of L2 English writing programs in central and eastern European universities, but the scale of his study—eight universities in six countries—and its focal points—the evolution of programs and courses and their interplay with writing in the local language—lead to descriptions and findings of a markedly different character from the narrower, localized case presented here. In brief, this analysis of a lingua franca writing environment can add to what is already known from more familiar contexts about the effects of policy on high-stakes writing, the value of aligning assessment policy and practices, and the function of support, expectations and supervision in a writing/learning community. Our central argument is that in many respects the history program under description succeeds in its educational mission, particularly its engagement with disciplinary writing, but in one key respect it fails.

THE PROGRAM AND ITS STUDENTS

At the program-level this educational mission has three dimensions that in some respects dovetail well with its student body and in other respects do not. One is internationalism. A second reflects the objectives of traditional academic history, and a third can be characterized as a critical activist pedagogy applied to the study of democracy and democratic institutions.

The Department of History launched the program at a time when universities across Europe (European Higher Educational Area, 2006) and across Sweden (European Higher Educational Area, 2010) were compelled to internationalize. The internationalist dimensions of Roads' mission are evident in its organizational and curricular structure as well as in its student body. Uppsala developed and operates the program in collaboration with two partner universities, Coimbra in Portugal and Siegen in Germany. Each university grants its own degree for this program; however, free exchange programs, common on-line courses and a commitment across all three institutions to lingua franca English instruction underscore the international nature of Roads. A mandatory exchange underscores it further, requiring at least 15 credits (half a semester's full time study) of the 120 total from one of the partner universities (Uppsala University, 2011b).

The students successfully recruited to the program were even more broadly international. Most cohorts had no Swedes, and students enrolled from Albania, Armenia, Bosnia, Burma, Cameroon, Canada, China, France, Germany, Hungary, Iran, Italy, S. Korea, Malaysia, Mexico, Poland, Portugal, Russia, Turkey, and the United States.[1] With this internationalization came the need for lingua franca English, and Roads students entered the program speaking many different varieties of English and greatly varied kinds of experience with it.

As academic historians, the Uppsala faculty has a mission to train modern comparative historians, specialists in the complex field of democratic development. In Roads they aim to "give [students] insights into the development of democracies in Europe" and help them "develop a broad, comparative understanding of the mechanisms behind democratic transitions, [so they] will be able to assess present-day democratic developments on both the national and the supra-national level" (Uppsala University, 2011a).

The program also acknowledges that an understanding of democracy is multidisciplinary. The partner program in Siegen is run by the political science department and learning objectives for Roads theses explicitly call for interdisciplinary theorizing (Uppsala University, 2011b). This cross of disciplinary and interdisciplinary objectives complicates recruitment—an undergraduate degree in history is not an admission requirement—and almost certainly means that Roads students come differently prepared for the task of writing a master's thesis supervised and assessed by a community of professional academic historians.

Beyond its internationalist and disciplinary mission, there are signs that the program also carries out a critical and activist educational mission. The program description identifies the aim of making students "aware of the fragility of democratic institutions and the importance of citizenship and participation in the democratic process" (Uppsala University, 2011b). Even more directly, one faculty informant explained in his interview that for him extending an historical understanding of democratic institutions to students from countries where democracy was relatively new, emerging, or still to come represented part of the program's raison d'être.

QUALIFIED SUCCESSES

The successes described next are qualified successes to be sure, but the analysis shows that history faculty and program managers in Uppsala largely succeed in creating an environment where diversely prepared students can learn and practice scholarly writing in a lingua franca setting. The principal qualification is that the program has a relatively low and generally slow thesis-completion rate. By spring of 2011, of 32 theses that could have been completed, only 15 had been fully processed by the university (a completion rate of roughly 47%), and it is that set of fifteen that provides the basis for discussing theses and their assessment. With a program launch in 2005, 2007 was the earliest projected completion date, and one thesis was completed that year, tellingly perhaps, by an American Roads graduate and L1 writer of English. Seven more were completed in 2008, three in 2009 and four in 2010.

As the following section on assessment shows, by establishing assessment priorities firmly anchored in disciplinary knowledge making, Roads faculty generally avoid narrow, surface driven ways of reading the students' work and the most damaging kinds of negative expectations associated with these ways of reading (Zamel, 1995; for a counterexample, see Craig's [this volume] discussion about the expectation for error-free English in theses written by Singapore students enrolled in the MIT-Singapore transnational master's in engineering program.) These ways of reading are consistent with lingua franca communicative strategies and also speak directly to the disciplinary mission of training apprentice historians. The section on thesis topics argues that the program uses the required theses to support a difference-as-resource culture of the kind advocated by Canagarajah (2002). This happens largely by encouraging thesis research questions that both engage thesis-writers' national or cultural identity and utilize primary source material written in students' first (or other) language. In addition, by working with source material inaccessible to historians who read only English or Swedish, Roads thesis writers step into roles where they can make relevant contributions to a research community. Moreover, this engagement with primary material that addresses democracy in their own national context speaks directly to the department's critical/activist mission.

The section on lingua-franca-writing support follows the departmental leadership's trajectory of proactive support for their relatively new groups of students. This entails not only some explicit training in disciplinary writing for its graduate students, but also faculty development activities that prepare instructors for work with more diverse international students. The rationale for and limitations of this trajectory are described and discussed below, but irrespective of its limits, training of this kind promotes the kinds of teaching and teaching environments advocated by Zamel (1995) and Kim (2011) or anticipates the kinds of coping strategies described by Leki (1995) and thereby also promotes Road's internationalist mission.

QUALIFIED SUCCESS WITH THESIS ASSESSMENT: VALUES AND PRIORITIES

Fair and educationally relevant assessment transparently aligns intended learning outcomes with student performance (Biggs & Tang, 2007; Elmgren & Henriksson, 2010; Ramsden, 2003). The Uppsala history department articulates learning outcomes for Roads theses that follow straightforwardly from the overarching disciplinary objectives described above and project into a set of explicit grading criteria. Faculty assessors, who by rule cannot have supervised the thesis in question, then apply those criteria. The department's success lies in its having created an approach to thesis assessment—essentially ways of reading—that maintains quality standards, supports disciplinary learning and acknowledges the complexity of this group of writers.

The intended learning outcomes (ILOs) defined for a Roads thesis set a high disciplinary standard. They cover historiographical theories and methods, theoretical input "from other social sciences used in the study of democracy," the framing of research topics and questions, scholarly treatment of both primary and secondary sources, and writing in English "using correctly the various types of writing used in history and the social sciences" (Uppsala University, 2011b). Well aligned with these ILOs are seven published grading parameters: knowledge of historical context; research problem; theories and methods; source criticism;

contextualization of research problem; use of terminology; and textual features (Uppsala University, 2009). Prior to 2011 the department applied a seven-step grading scale, A through F and Fx, a version of Incomplete. Subsequently the university has reverted to the three-step scale long used in Swedish higher education, Pass with Distinction, Pass and Fail. The theses under review were all graded on an A-F scale, and in formulating and publishing descriptors for the seven parameters, the department elected to specify only the levels A, C, E and F. Faculty informants reported widespread confidence that assessors could identify B and D quality work inductively on the basis of the other descriptors. Finally the department applies the same grading criteria to all three of its master's programs, Roads to Democracy, Early Modern Studies, and a history specialization within a humanities program, and therefore in principle makes no distinction between theses written in English or Swedish.

In institutional terms, each thesis approved on the basis of these criteria is a success. They conform to university guidelines set by the Faculty of Arts and meet Department of History requirements. Moreover, their authors have earned their advanced degrees and continued their personal and professional pursuits, in several cases as PhD candidates in well regarded programs in the UK, in the US, in Sweden or in the thesis writer's home country.

Seen purely as textual artifacts, however, nearly all the theses reviewed are flawed. Most show a variously rich and variously dense set of surface errors. Some are repetitive. Some rely heavily on long quotations and summaries of source material. Many fail, at some point or points, to maintain the textual "flow" advocated in graduate writing guides such as Swales & Feak (2004, pp. 26-30). A few even adopt, in key passages, the homiletic stance or voice attributed by David Bartholomae (1985) to inexperienced American academic writers, suggesting that for some apprentice historians, especially those writing history in a second language or relatively new to scholarly writing, it remains difficult to consistently "take on the role—the voice, the persona—of an authority whose authority is rooted in scholarship, analysis, or research" (p. 136), even when their authority *is rooted in scholarship, analysis and research.* (See Lancaster [this volume] for a discussion of the role of stance-taking in creating authority in discipline-specific writing). In other words, these texts hold few surprises for writing specialists accustomed to working with L2 or lingua franca writers of English. What may be surprising is how these flaws are contextualized by academic historians in Uppsala.

In a lingua franca environment seeing theses purely or primarily as textual artifacts would be inappropriate, and readers in the Roads program contextualize them in richer ways, ways that downplay surface-level inaccuracies, coherence gaps and repetitiveness. The history faculty value theses as "evidence of intellectual work," a term that does not appear in departmental documentation, but recurred regularly in faculty interviews. While difficult to define precisely, evidence of intellectual work encompasses writing and thinking that makes discoveries while conforming to disciplinary and linguistic conventions, but not in equal measure. In his interview the Roads program director, for instance, profiled the relative weight of these conventions when he described the role of a thesis advisor: "we help them to write a master's thesis that is recognizable as a master's thesis in English; this includes comments on language, but we can't be English teachers." By framing theses as evidence of intellectual work, Roads readers seem to contextualize them within processes of inquiry and discovery and express priorities that value the process over the product.

Arguably, the departmental grading criteria indirectly provide a partial blueprint for these contextualizations that, again, clearly prioritizes disciplinary learning over the textual artifacts themselves. Six of the seven parameters focus directly on disciplinary performance, and even when descriptors sometimes acknowledge the close relationship between disciplinary knowledge and its expression, the latter serves the former. The parameter for specialist terminology, for example, receives particular attention (Uppsala, 2009). The grading criteria rank writers' application of central terms on the basis of the intellectual work they do. In F-level application, disciplinary terms are "not defined" or "used arbitrarily" and without awareness that their multiple uses had "consequences for the analysis." E-level usage defines all key terms and uses them consistently, yet fails to problematize them. In C-level usage "the choice of definitions is discussed and motivated," and ultimately in A-level usage, a best-practice benchmark, "terms *and concepts* ... are *carefully* discussed, problematized and motivated" and used "stringent[ly] and consistent[ly] ... throughout to make *analytical points*" (2011a, emphases added).

The department's disciplinary and educational priorities also emerge, albeit indirectly, in the descriptors of textual quality, which bundle together an assessment of argumentation, formal conventions and linguistic accuracy. The formulation of these descriptors lacks the precision that applied linguists or writing specialists might give them, especially those addressing accuracy. Failing theses use "language [that] exhibits serious flaws" and "the grammar is poor" (2011a). The language and grammar of bare passes "reveals smaller flaws," and the grammar of solid Cs has "only a few isolated errors" (2011a). In best practice theses, the grammar is "free of errors" (2011a). This imprecision is fitting for a faculty that values theses not primarily as textual artifacts.

Although the Department of History has no explicit policy on how to apply its grading criteria, priorities do exist, and they are traceable in past practice, examples that illustrate which aspects of historical scholarship faculty members value most highly in the writing of junior historians. The first such example is a thesis analyzing the political thought of Mehmed Sabahaddin, a member of the ruling family of the Ottoman dynasty who lived between 1877 and 1948, a period that saw the end of dynastic rule in Turkey. At 55 pages the thesis falls short of the 60-page length requirement, and, according to a faculty informant, it had serious shortcomings along several grading parameters. In his own words:

> ... This thesis was according to my view a little bit tricky. The problem was that it was not living up to the standard of an ordinary thesis. There were problems both with the formulation of the topic, which was actually not really made in a way that we historians like. It was done as a political scientist might do it. There were also problems with the historical context and not least with the timeline. However, I liked the thesis very much. The reason for this was that the author really made a very fascinating analysis. Exceptionally good at this level. That meant that I thought that even if he had made some rather fundamental mistakes, that in an ordinary thesis [would have been] very grave, he had in other areas [done] a fantastic job and therefore I gave him a top grade. Not an ordinary thesis but a very good one.

The priorities emerging here elevate "a fascinating analysis," clear evidence of intellectual work, above all other considerations. The assessor refers to "problems" with two disciplinary grading parameters, the research-problem's formulation and historical contextualization, and mentions his concern with the research question's disciplinary locus, yet he confidently subordinates those problems and concern to the findings that emerge from a strong analysis carried out by an apprentice historian. The thesis was awarded a grade of B, and assessed in terms that valued its intellectual strengths over its academic weaknesses.

A second example is a comparative study of affirmative action in Malaysia and the United States. In this case the faculty informant served as thesis advisor and not therefore the assessor. In discussing the thesis' strengths and weaknesses, he too was greatly impressed by the author's findings and subordinated his other concerns. Those other concerns dealt with the thesis as a written artifact, specifically language accuracy, and its lack of engagement with Malaysian archival source material because the thesis writer's application for access to the national archive was denied when the Malaysian authorities noticed the sensitivity of this study. The advisor's latter concern is particularly salient as the application of archival material to research questions plays a central role in academic history and because another faculty informant, the program director, identified the single greatest challenge for Roads students as work with primary sources: "the problem is with primary studies; they [Roads student from other disciplinary backgrounds and some other history departments] don't know how sources help us answer questions." Like the previous example this thesis too received a grade of B, and like the previous faculty informant, this advisor valued primarily the creation of new knowledge about the history of democracy. In both cases those values seem to govern the assessment and grading of students' disciplinary writing.

These successful aspects of thesis assessment in Roads share two features with well documented lingua franca communication strategies. The first is explicitness (Kaur, 2011; Maruanen, 2006). In lingua franca communication linguistic codes do less meaning-bearing work on their own and are instead complemented with semantic negotiation, moves such as confirmation checks, follow-up questions, counter proposals and interactive repair (Maruanen, 2006). Almost paradoxically then successful lingua franca communication draws more support from explicitness than from tacit communication and conversational implicature (Grice, 1975), because explicit expression quite simply provides more common ground, more material, over which lingua franca interlocutors can negotiate. (Lancaster [this volume] describes a contrasting Anglophone environment where variations in largely tacit, discipline-embedded linguistic codes are identified as error and not as reason for negotiation.) In Roads this explicitness is particularly evident in the published assessment criteria that align learning outcomes and student performances. Published criteria of this kind have become commonplace at Uppsala and other Swedish universities, but that in no way detracts from the communicative function they play in the lingua franca Roads community.

Their reading priorities are a second feature of Roads thesis assessment that is consistent with lingua franca communication strategies. What these reading priorities and those communicative strategies share is that neither is overly concerned with linguistic code per se (Canagarajah & Wurr, 2011), but foreground and prioritize what is most expressive or valuable in a text or communicative act. In Roads thesis assessment, this seems to include the "let it pass" strategy that Firth (1996) established as a cornerstone of lingua franca pragmatics. Importantly, this strategy is not a passive move, but a strategy by which the hearer [or reader] "is actively *though implicitly* engaged in the task of attempting to *make* sense of what is being done and said" (p. 245, emphasis in original). For Roads readers this strategy entails the downgrading of linguistic flaws, rhetorical shortcomings and even some breaches of disciplinary expectation (such as the problem-formulation problem in the Ottoman-political-philosophy thesis and the absence of primary sources in the affirmative-action thesis) in favor of a scholarly understanding of a writer's intentions and discoveries.

These two aspects of successful assessment, explicitness and let-it-pass reading priorities remain however incomplete successes. The Roads program could deploy these operational strengths to address its strategic weakness, its low and slow completion rate. For instance, there are at present no overt guidelines on how assessors should (or do) apply grading criteria. In the absence of such guidelines student writers might quite reasonably interpret the rather unsystematic descriptors on language and expression more literally than faculty members do, leading to an unnecessary focus on form as they work to produce a text that for some of them represents a first significant attempt at scholarly writing. Similarly, writers might complete more often or more quickly knowing that they will be read, interpreted and graded for what they have done most successfully and not dismissed for the weakest sides of their performance. While we recognize the difficulty involved in drafting explicit grading criteria for master's theses that explicate let-it-pass reading strategies, we also recognize that acknowledging a lingua franca approach to linguistic values and textual priorities would further support the multilingual academic writers in Roads.

QUALIFIED SUCCESS WITH TOPIC SELECTION: DIFFERENCE AS RESOURCE

A Roads to Democracy thesis carries 60 credits, half the two-year degree requirement. This curriculum does not however wholly backload this requirement into the program's second year. Instead, students take a thesis-methods course in semester one of year one, and time for thesis work is allocated throughout the program. This longitudinal approach to research writing pays dividends for the writers who complete; again those who do not complete remain a chronic challenge to the program's overall success. One such dividend affects topic selection, where longer-term planning and longer timelines facilitate thesis writers' framing of problems that are personally relevant and that draw upon the linguistic and cultural knowledge they bring to the program. More specifically, longer timelines are relevant to topic selection because if, hypothetically, a Cameroonian student wants to frame a problem addressing, say, the postcolonial unification of Francophone and Anglophone regions drawing on Cameroonian archives or other primary sources, longer timelines support the logistics of finding travel funding, planning the travel, acquiring access to archives and recruiting an expert, either in Cameroon or an Africanist in the Uppsala network, willing to serve as a thesis advisor or co-advisor.

Of the Roads theses defended through 2011, fully two-thirds, 10 of 15, frame and address a research problem of apparent personal relevance: an Italian student examines the inception of the Italian welfare state under fascism, a Chinese student addresses the "New Left" in China, a Swedish student contrasts Swedish and German urban planning and housing policy in the 1930s. In some cases the personal relevance is more than apparent. A Bosnian thesis writer explicitly merges personal and professional engagement by opening her thesis on nation building among Bosnian Muslims with a "personal reflection" on national identity. In a broadly similar vein there are references to personal relevance in a Korean writer's thesis on western perceptions of Korea between 1892 and 1936, a Portuguese writer's study of Portugal's immigration policies after the advent of democracy there and an Albanian writer's analysis of the media's role in Albania's "feeble" democracy. Given the low numbers and what has been said about the program's completion rate, this dividend too remains a qualified success. Nevertheless, at the very least this pattern shows that successful Roads writers emulate senior scholars who, as Hyland (2009) makes clear, often have a personal stake in their disciplinary writing.

Far beyond emulation another dynamic comes into play when thesis topics combine academic relevance and aspects of the writer's native culture, language and identity in a highly internationalized, multilingual setting. That dynamic is a perceptual shift, perhaps ultimately a cultural shift, whereby students move in Canagarajah's terms (2002) from perceptions of "difference as deficit" to perceptions of "difference as resource." As suggested above Roads students in some cases struggle with the program's demands because of their first languages and experience with English, because of their disciplinary backgrounds or because of their earlier educational cultures. Such students, we reason, experience their differences as deficits at times. Supporting that reasoning, in interviews some students reported feeling hamstrung by their English skills or hampered by their limited experience of academic history—particularly archival experience; more report feeling intimidated by the prospect of writing a long academic thesis. We postulate—because the writers of completed theses were not available for interviews or declined requests—that doing archival work on a topic of personal relevance with primary sources in the student's first language changes these self-perceptions. By extension, completing theses based on that archival work and those primary sources changes those perceptions further. By further extension, having those theses read appreciatively by faculty assessors and recognized as scholarly contributions changes those perceptions even further, and difference as deficit has become difference as resource. Finally when a number of thesis writers undergo this transformation, when personally relevant thesis topics researched through L1 primary sources become a norm, a difference-as-resource culture has emerged.

This cultural point is necessarily speculative, but it has received indirect corroboration in four of the five faculty interviews, where informants express clear appreciation for, even professional pride in, the accomplishments of Roads researchers. Parallel to this appreciation is a recognition that this archival work, carried out on Albanian, Bosnian, Mandarin or Turkish sources, for instance, might not have been done or might not have reached international research communities were it not for the efforts of Roads graduates. These conditions and attitudes successfully create a context where multilingualism is an asset, not a deficit.

A balanced understanding of the Roads program's success with difference-as-resource culture may require drawing, however briefly, a conceptual distinction between two variants of difference-as-deficit expectations or experience. While richly international with regard to his multilingual writers, Canagarajah's (2002) initial work on difference-as-deficit attitudes toward academic writing foregrounds dominantly Anglophone settings where English functions as a hegemonic superstrate in academic language contact situations. Subsequent work in writing studies or in broader educational research (Cummins, 2003; Guo & Zenobia, 2007; Mitchell, 2012) also characterizes English as hegemonic in Anglophone settings. In contrast, multilingual Roads students in Uppsala meet a more balanced diglossic context, where Swedish functions as the local/national language and English as an international lingua franca. Neither therefore attains the hegemony that English holds in higher education in Anglophone countries.

Research in American settings has identified some of the roles both instructors and local students play in establishing and maintaining Anglophone hegemony. In a blatant example, a faculty informant described by Zamel (1995) requires that multilingual students employ English grammar accurately and deploy a grammatical metalanguage for talking about errors as an entry condition to substantive feedback and disciplinary engagement. In a study (Kim, 2011) where multilingual graduate students describe their teachers' behavior and its effects, one participant reports that "her name caused her to feel embarrassed because Americans could not say it correctly. Whenever American professors took roll, they mispronounced her name" (p. 289); as a solution one "professor suggested that she use an easier name or an English name" (p. 289), making clear just how completely these students were expected to adapt to Anglophone norms. In the same study, local students are also seen as reinforcing, perhaps unintentionally, the dominant role English plays through their performance in collaborative group work and group discussions, where local students "spoke casual American English at fast speeds" and typically shaped conversations that shifted topics often, which made it difficult for multilingual students to follow the conversation and led to their contributions frequently being off topic (Kim, 2011, p. 287). The reported result of these kinds of interactions is one international student feeling, "I know they did not care about my opinion. They don't try to understand what my opinion is" (p. 287). Kim herself concludes that "professors and native students often did not understand the opinions of international graduate students, *nor did they see the need to include them in the discourse*" (2011, p. 287, emphasis added). (For further examples of English hegemony at work in US classrooms, see chapters by Phillips and Nielsen [this volume].)

Lacking extensive classroom observations, we cannot claim definitively that no such behavior takes place in Roads classrooms. However, there was no mention of it by the students interviewed. Moreover the sociolinguistic context speaks against such linguistic hegemony. Because English is an additional language for almost all the faculty and the vast majority of Roads students, it never attains the full status of a superstrate. Members of the Uppsala history faculty generally acknowledge their own status as L2 English speakers (in interviews and in faculty-development work describe below), and only one instructor (one of two native speaker of English teaching history in the program, but the only one interviewed) complained about accuracy levels in student writing or intelligibility in classroom discourse. Among Roads students themselves, neither the few Swedes nor the few native English speakers enjoy or exercise the same privileged position Kim attributes to the local American students in her study. The Swedish students, like their classmates, must adapt to instruction in English, the program lingua franca, and native English speakers must adapt to life as an international graduate student in a new educational culture.

Briefly then, the Roads program's success in supporting a difference-as-resource culture takes place in an environment relatively amenable to such a culture, a fact that again should not detract from the accomplishment itself. Nor does it color the qualification of that success. The upside of the Roads longitudinal and student-centered approach to thesis research and writing emerges in the program's difference-as-resource culture. The downside rests, according to the program director, in the supervision of these theses, or at least some of them. The Uppsala department cannot house all the expertise necessary to handle the geographic, cultural and linguistic breadth that opens up when Roads students pursue research problems across four continents; few departments could. As mentioned above, the department makes an effort to secure an advisor with expertise relevant to each writer's project. Those efforts however are not always successful, and their limitations show in the thesis contrasting the development of American and Malaysian affirmative action legislation, which was supervised by a Swedish Americanist. That thesis nevertheless was successfully completed.

Even when the department can enlist international experts for Roads students' international projects, the program director explained, those external advisors vary greatly in their depth of commitment, experience with masters-level supervision and adaptability to Uppsala's standards and expectations. These shortcomings lead to predictable outcomes: the most experienced, most talented or most determined students succeed in completing their theses anyway. Those most in need of an advisor's support encounter delays. Concisely, what qualifies the Roads success with the framing of writer-centered, L1-inclusive research problems is that the department lacks the resources to advise on and supervise such a range of theses, and while it encouragingly looks outside the department for relevant expertise, there are no routines, no academic infrastructure, in place to coach those external experts into positions where they can consistently advise Roads writers to completion.

QUALIFIED SUCCESS WITH WRITING SUPPORT: PREPARING WRITERS AND READERS

Since 2003 the Department of History has planned and carried out a series of English-writing support activities, some of which were direct, aiming at student writers and their evolving skill sets, and others which were indirect, aiming at departmental faculty and their preparedness for teaching and reading in lingua franca English environments. Neither type of activity has been subject to systematic follow up or extensive evaluation, which makes it somewhat futile to address certain aspects of success. However both types of activity demonstrate an orientation in the Roads program's host department that is a prerequisite for success with multilingual writers. Essentially this orientation combines an awareness that diverse international students bring with them a new set of educational needs and a willingness to act upon that awareness. However intangible an orientation may seem, successful lingua franca communication rests, as pointed out above, in part on heightened "language awareness" (Canagarajah, 2007, p. 925) and "positive attitudes" (Canagarajah & Wurr, 2011, p. 2). (See Zenger et al. [this volume] for examples of how translingual values were infused into a course providing writing support for graduate students at American University of Beirut and into the revised general education curriculum.)

Direct writing support for the student authors of Roads theses grew out of the Department of History's decision to follow national and university-wide trends towards internationalizing its educational offering, but to do so with an acknowledgement that enrolling international student entailed a commitment to supporting them. That decision unfolded at a time when the department also began internationalizing its mission more generally, particularly its research mission. This relatively broad-based approach to internationalizing the department's missions may help account for what is most successful about the department's L2 writing support, yet it may also be this same generality that also explains the limitations of those interventions in directly supporting Roads thesis writers.

The rationale for this support encompasses the role of English in published research as well as in graduate education. In an op-ed essay directed to Swedish scholars in the humanities, the director of the department's PhD program and a Roads thesis assessor (Ågren, 2005) makes a case for internationalizing Swedish humanities research. The core of Ågren's argument is that Swedish researchers "take as their points of departure internationally grounded theory building or research problems," and in doing so they "see themselves as participating in an international discussion" (p. 2, our translation). They do not however follow through completely in that participation because they "rarely report their results in an international arena" (p. 2, our translation). Ågren goes on to acknowledge that the difficulties of writing well in English represent an obstacle to be overcome if this internationalist turn is to be fully realized, and in a later publication, she extends that argument from an acknowledgment of difficulty to an action plan for addressing that difficulty (Lavelle & Ågren, 2010). The core of that plan consists of improving the English writing of graduate students in history and across the humanities. "PhD students need to be able to present their work in English, and since the PhD programs are too short to allow students to develop [English writing] skills there, it is necessary to start earlier, on the master's level at the latest" (Lavelle & Ågren, 2010, p. 203). On the basis of these rationales, the Department of History organized and in some cases funded three phases of direct English-writing support for its graduate students and a series of three activities for faculty aimed at helping them to teach in an internationalized, lingua franca English pedagogical environment.

The first intervention predated the Roads program and consisted of a modest half-day workshop in 2003 aimed primarily at raising awareness among graduate students, especially doctoral candidates, regarding what writing academic history in English entails and thus making it possible for them to consider writing dissertations in English.

By the time Roads students began arriving in 2005, the department had integrated regular writing-in-English seminars and workshops into the obligatory thesis-methods courses of its fledgling master's programs (eight contact hours per cohort). These workshops were the interventions focused most directly on the needs of Roads students, and they were well received by students, who in traditional course evaluations characterized them as helpful. On the basis of those evaluations the department added in 2007 an elective course to its master's-level curriculum, Academic Writing in English, and discontinued the writing workshops in methods courses. In interviews, both students and faculty members refer to this course as a reason for improved writing outcomes, but there has been no discernible improvement in completion rates. Moreover, for a number of administrative reasons including break-even enrollment calculations, this course has been open at times to graduate students from across the university and at other times to students from across the humanities faculty. Therefore even though the course works with published historical scholarship as well as a range of student writing, the course description suggests that it focuses too little or too indirectly on the work of Roads thesis writing (Uppsala University, 2011b), perhaps because of cross-disciplinary enrollment. After early enthusiasm among Roads students and a peak in the fall semester of 2009 with eleven Roads enrollments across two sections, participation by Roads writers has declined to two Roads students in a single section in the spring semester of 2012, one Uppsala student and one exchange student from Siegen. As a corrective step the department will reintroduce a writing-in-English seminar to the obligatory thesis-methods course for Roads students from the fall of 2012.

These writing-support activities ran or run parallel to traditional in-course writing activities, which are of course also expected to help train student writers, perhaps reasonably expected to provide the bulk of a student's training in disciplinary writing. For the Roads program our interviews found that all master's-level history courses require written deliverables, some on a lesson-by-lesson basis. Some instructors interviewed also report that they employ a range of writing-based pedagogies, including reading logs, peer reviewing and process-driven revision activity.

Paradoxically, while it remains difficult to trace clear links between the Department of History's direct interventions and its greatest success factor, i.e. awareness of variable needs among student writers and a positive attitude towards linguistic differences, we can see a clearer relationship between the indirect writing support and that awareness and those attitudes. The largest of three faculty-development programs aimed at improving the ability of Uppsala's history faculty to work through English with multilingual, international students. It was organized and funded by the department as a voluntary in-service course consisting of 24 contact hours during the fall semester of 2009. Under the title English in the Classroom, its course description identified six ILOs, at least four of which bear directly on the development of awareness

and attitudes needed to create educational practices supportive of students like Roads thesis writers. Those six are:
1. Assess the impact, if any, of lingua franca instruction on a learners' classroom performance.
2. Lecture more fluently in English and adapt lectures for a lingua franca audience.
3. Lead discussions on academic topics in English while recognizing and accommodating participants' diverse communication strategies in discussions.
4. Produce supporting materials (slides, handouts, exercises, exams) in English.
5. Provide feedback for students in English.
6. State and defend a critical position on the question of assessing linguistic form vs. assessing underlying content in student work.

The four learning outcomes directly relevant to supporting lingua franca instruction and reading are 1, 2, 3 and 6. Beyond those a case can certainly be made that the learning of scaffolding strategies inherent in ILO 4 makes it highly relevant to multilingual classrooms as well. From a faculty of roughly 30, 19 teachers initially enrolled in the course and 13 completed it.

The second and third activities, both much shorter, functioned primarily as follow-ups to the course, but because participants included the sitting and pending departmental chairs and all graduate and undergraduate directors of studies, these activities seem to function too as manifestations of the departmental commitments and attitudes. The follow-up dimension focused upon two specific aspects of lingua franca education. One, a simple three-hour workshop, addressed assessment through lingua franca English, and according to the two interviewees who participated, the workshop reiterated and formalized some issues addressed above, including disciplinary reading priorities and let-it-pass approaches to many surface errors. This assessment workshop was attended only by faculty members who had completed the course described above, but the third activity was a two-day retreat for the entire department. The topic of the retreat was the formulation of effective course descriptions and learning outcomes in English with the aim of making these pedagogical documents effectively available to and useful for multilingual students. The content particularly relevant to lingua franca education, again according to the same two interviewees, addressed the identification of embedded (local Swedish) cultural assumptions, the reduction of overly bureaucratic language and the elimination of unintentional ambiguities.

In summary, the principal success of the Department of History's writing-support activities is that there *are* writing-support activities. In a context where no or few such activities were taking place, the simple existence of English writing workshops speaks to a positive approach to multilingual writers. If the direct, student-focused interventions have become too general to help Roads writers optimally, it remains a problem open to correction. The indirect, faculty-focused interventions in many respects reflect and support the internationalist openness expressed in the Roads program's curriculum, reading strategies and handling of research topics. (In this volume, see Fredericksen & Mangelsdorf for an example of a graduate writing course enrolling students across disciplines and Craig for examples of direct writing support for a cohort of international students studying in the same field. Also see Lancaster and Cox for additional examples of faculty interventions.)

CONCLUSIONS AND DIRECTIONS

Our case for the success of the Roads program's approach to writing rests largely on our analyses of three features of institutional context: assessment priorities or strategies that dovetail well with a lingua franca learning environment; the facilitation of thesis research projects that promote a difference-as-resource culture; and the existence (and on-going development) of activities supporting multilingual writers, either directly or indirectly. Our case for qualifying each of these successes begins with the program's low completion rate, but extends into each more positive feature of institutional context. Suitable and successful reading and assessment practices could be codified and through codification become, as we address below, more successful. Success with difference-as-resource research questions would also benefit from codifying or creating routines for recruiting and supporting external (co)advisors. Finally, while efforts to prepare faculty for international, lingua franca pedagogy appear to be succeeding and enjoying departmental support, it seems as though direct interventions for student writers would benefit from a more narrow disciplinary or thesis-directed focus.

Each of these qualifications merits further discussion, discussion that in other discourses might take the form of recommendations to the department under discussion or suggestions for further research. In what follows here we offer brief closing remarks that combine aspects of these two established moves.

In assessing Roads theses, the department has evolved a set of practices describable as lingua franca assessment strategies, yet none of the departmental documentation describes them as such or refers to lingua franca communication at all. Instead, when textual features of theses are mentioned, the vocabulary remains in a traditional and pedestrian domain of *correct, grammar, flaws* and *errors*. While we believe student writers would benefit from a codifying of what we called above let-it-pass reading strategies and assessment priorities grounded in evidence of intellectual work, it is not obvious to us that the Uppsala Department of History should carry out this codification. Instead, we see this, at least in part, as the work of applied linguists and writing specialists, for whom a great deal of work, both theoretical and descriptive, remains to be done on academic lingua francas.

In our analysis above of thesis topics and their role in the promotion of difference as resource, we highlighted the function of external advisors because this is where faculty informants pointed us. Here too, however, a much richer network of practice could and should be explicitly described. This network ranges from the merely logistical arrangement of two-year longitudinal work with theses through the encouragement of internationally grounded projects to a tolerance of primary source material that in many cases faculty assessors cannot read. We interpret these practices as wholly consistent with and supportive of a Roads program mission that is explicitly internationalist, disciplinarily grounded and critically activist. Here the program or department itself is best equipped to re-see the practices that have evolved and articulate them as a part of a research-writing pedagogy for its master's students. However, as this case might illustrate, external actors such as ourselves can help guide the reflection necessary in order to articulate that pedagogy by holding up a mirror to practices that may have developed in silence. Such mirroring of course follows from descriptive or ethnographic research into institutional contexts of multilingual graduate writers and the departments hosting them.

Finally, the active interventions aimed at supporting thesis writers succeed in some respect simply through their existence. This however is too low a standard, and the decisions facing the Uppsala Department of History as it goes forward are familiar ones. Initially, it faces a classic make-or-buy decision (Balakrishnan & Cheng, 2005), where in this case it can either continue to produce its own graduate writing course and occasional workshops or instead buy from other parts of the university services that have come on line since launching its own course in 2007, including a generic course offered by the Department of English and tutorial services from a fledgling writing center wholly new to English writing support. Given that a shortcoming identified in existing support activities is that they have become too general to adequately help Roads writers, then one factor in answering that question is clear. However, even if the department continues on a "make" path, questions will remain regarding program-specific interventions and the internal competition for resources between Roads and other graduate programs. If WID research at some point is able to illuminate the gains and losses associated with each of these decision paths, so much the better.

In closing and on balance, the factors qualifying the success of the Roads program in its work with multilingual writers seem familiar: scarce resources; a disciplinary conservatism that leads to an underselling of successful innovation and praxis; and a shortfall in the follow up and evaluation of departmental initiatives. In contrast the factors most relevant to the successes themselves are refreshingly new: assessment practices aligned with both learning goals and lingua franca communication; a research culture that values individual differences and multilingualism; and an institutional acknowledgement that enrolling international graduate students requires institutional change.

NOTES

1. There is no obvious way to explain why individuals from so many countries choose to study the history of democratic development in Uppsala, but one fact that may be relevant is that when the program was launched and this data collected, Swedish universities charged no tuition. This has subsequently changed and students from outside the EU and EES must now pay fees of 90,000 Swedish Crowns (c. $11,500) per year.

REFERENCES

Ågren, M. (2005). *Svensk humaniora på engelska—en svår men nödvändig kombination* [Swedish humanities in English—a difficult but necessary combination]. *Tvärsnit, 2*, 11-13.

Bacha, N. N., & Bahous, R. (2008). Contrasting views of business students' writing needs in an EFL environment. *English for Specific Purposes, 27*, 79-93.

Balakrishnan, J., & Cheng, C. H. (2005). The theory of constraints and the make-or-buy decision: An update and review. *Journal of Supply Chain Management: A Global Review of Purchasing & Supply, 41*, 40-47.

Bartholomae, D. (1985). Inventing the university. In M. Rose (Ed.), *When a writer can't write,* (pp. 134-165). New York & London: The Guiford Press.

Bazerman, C., Little, J., Bethel, L., Chavkin, T., Fouquette, D., & Garufis, J. (2005). *Reference guide to writing across the curriculum.* West Lafayette, IN: Parlor Press and WAC Clearinghouse. Retrieved from http://wac.colostate.edu/books/bazerman_wac/

Belcher, D., & Braine, G. (Eds.). (1995). *Academic writing in a second language: Essays on research and pedagogy*. Norwood, NJ: Ablex.

Biggs, J., & Tang, C. (2007). *Teaching for quality learning at university* (3rd ed.). Milton Keynes, UK: Open University Press.

Canagarajah, A. S. (2002). *Critical academic writing and multilingual students*. Ann Arbor, MI: University of Michigan Press.

Canagarajah, A. S. (2007). Lingua Franca English, multilingual communities, and language acquisition. *The Modern Language Journal, 91*, 923-939.

Canagarajah, A. S., & Wurr, A. J. (2011). Multilingual communication and language acquisition: New research directions, *The Reading Matrix, 11*, 1-15. Retrieved from http://www.readingmatrix.com/articles/january_2011/canagarajah_wurr.pdf

Casanave, C. P., & Li, X. (Eds.). (2008). *Learning the literacy practices of graduate school: Insiders' reflections on academic acculturation*. Ann Arbor, MI: University of Michigan Press.

Connor, U., & Mayberry, S. (1995). Learning discipline-specific academic writing: A case study of a Finnish graduate student in the United States. In E. Ventola & A. Mauranen (Eds.), *Academic writing: Intercultural and textual issues* (pp. 231-253). Amsterdam: John Benjamins.

Cummins, J. (2003). Challenging the construction of difference as deficit: Where are identity, intellect, imagination and power in the new regime of truth? In P. P. Trifonas (Ed.), *Pedagogies of difference: Rethinking education for social change* (pp. 41-60) New York: Routledge.

Elmgren, E., & Henriksson, A-S. (2010). *Universitetspedagogik*. Stockholm: Norstedts.

Emerson, L., MacKay, B. R., Funnell, K., & MacKay, M. B. (2002). Writing in a New Zealand tertiary context: WAC and action research. *Learning and Languages across the Disciplines, 5*, 110. Retrieved from http://wac.colostate.edu/llad/v5n3/emerson_etal.pdf

European Higher Educational Area. (2010). *Bologna Process*. Retrieved from http://www.ehea.info/article-details.aspx?ArticleId=3

European Higher Educational Area. (2006). Swedish national report for 2005-2007 Retrieved from http://www.ehea.info/Uploads/Documents/National_Report_Sweden2007.pdf

Firth, A. (1996). The discursive accomplishment of normality: On lingua franca English and conversation analysis. *Journal of Pragmatics, 26*, 237-259.

Grice, H. P. (1975). Logic and conversation. In P. Cole & J. Morgan (Eds.), *Syntax and Semantics 3: Speech Acts*, (pp. 41-48). New York: Academic Press.

Guo, S. & Zenobia, J. (2007). Nurturing diversity in higher education: A critical review of selected models. *Canadian Journal of Higher Education, 37*, 29-49.

Harbord, J. (2010). Writing in central and eastern Europe: Stakeholders and directions in initiating change. *Across the Disciplines, 7.* Retrieved from http://wac.colostate.edu/atd/articles/harbord2010.cfm

Hyland, K. (2003). Genre-based pedagogies: A social response to process. *Journal of Second Language Writing, 12,* 17-29.

Hyland, K. (2009). *Academic discourse: English in a global context.* London: Continuum International.

Janopolous, M. (1995). Writing across the curriculum, writing proficiency exams, and the NNE college student. *Journal of Second Language Writing, 4,* 43-50.

Johns, A. (2011). The future of genre in second-language writing: Fundamental, but contested, instructional decisions. *Journal of Second Language Writing, 20,* 56-68.

Kaur, J. (2011). Raising explicitness through self-repair in English as a lingua franca. *Journal of Pragmatics, 43,* 2704-2715.

Kim, H.Y. (2011). The international graduate students' difficulties: Graduate classes as a community of practices. *Teaching in Higher Education, 16,* 281-292.

Lavelle, T. & Ågren, M. (2010). Academic writing in English—pedagogical answers to strategic challenges. In B. Johansson (Ed.), *Att undervisa med vetenskaplig föränkring —i praktiken!* [Teaching with a research foundation—in practice], (pp. 202-218). Uppsala: Uppsala University.

Leki, I. (1995). The coping strategies of ESL students in writing tasks across the curriculum. *TESOL Quarterly, 29,* 235-260.

Magno, C. & Amarles, A. M., (2012). Teachers' feedback practices in second language academic writing classrooms. *The International Journal of Educational and Psychological Assessment, 6,* 21-31.

Matsuda, P. K., Cox, M., Jordan, J., & Ortmeier-Hooper, C. (Eds.) (2006). *Second-language writing in the composition classroom.* Boston & New York: Bedford/St. Martin's.

Maruanen, A. (2006). Signaling and preventing miscommunication in lingua franca communication. *International Journal of the Sociology of Language, 177,* 123-150.

Mitchell, K. (2012). English is not *all* that matters in the education of secondary multilingual learners and their teachers. *International Journal of Multicultural Education, 14,* 1-21.

Pedersen, A.M. (2011). Writing across languages, disciplines, and sources: Second language writers in Jordan. *Across the Disciplines, 8*(1). Retrieved from http://wac.colostate.edu/atd/articles/pedersen2011.cfm

Ramsden, P. (2003) *Learning to teach in higher education* (2nd ed.). London & New York: RoutledgeFalmer.

Seloni, L. (2012). Academic literacy socialization of first-year doctoral students in US: A micro-ethnographic perspective. *English for Specific Purposes, 31*, 47-49.

Swales, J. & Feak, C. (2004). *Academic writing for graduate students: Essential tasks and skills* (2nd ed.). Ann Arbor, MI: University of Michigan Press.

Uppsala University. (2009). *The grading criteria for student research papers required at the advanced level.* Retrieved from http://www.hist.uu.se/LinkClick. aspx?fileticket=cmvG6O we6W8%3d&tabid=2220&mid=5156&language=en-US

Uppsala University. (2011a). *Academic Writing in English.* Retrieved from http://www.uu.se/en/education/master/selma/kursplan/?kKod=5HA707

Uppsala University. (2011b). *Master programme in roads to democracy.* Retrieved from http://www.uu.se/en/education/master/selma/program/?pKod=HVD 2M&lasar=12/13/2011

Uppsala University. (2011c). *Theory and methods in thesis work: Roads to democracy.* Retrieved from http://www.uu.se/en/education/master/selma/kursplan/?kKod=5HA618

Zamel, V. (1995). Strangers in academia: The experiences of faculty and ESL students across the curriculum. *College Composition and Communication, 46*, 506-521.

Zawacki, T. M., & Rogers, P. M. (Eds.). (2012). *Writing across the curriculum: A critical sourcebook.* Boston & New York: Bedford/St. Martin's.

AFTERWORD: WRITING GLOBALLY, RIGHT HERE, RIGHT NOW

Chris Thaiss
University of California, Davis

The rain clouds have moved off east toward the Sierra, but this December's storm is not finished, as new clouds are coming over the Vacas to the west and now rising over my neighbor's persimmon tree, still laden with orange fruit, though the branches are leafless. I'm enjoying the sensations of this place, this time, and thinking how this weather moves the lettuces I just planted, the hibiscus leaves now fluttering in the wind. But I'm also thinking about the message I just emailed to a researcher acquaintance in Greece who sent me a preliminary report of a longitudinal writing assessment in a social sciences course in her university. It hadn't crossed my mind (until I decided to make something of these perceptions) that there might be something clashingly weird about my sitting before a wi-fied computer in a brisk breeze off the Pacific amid the songful chatter of blue rock jays and trying to say/write something helpful and appreciative in English to a Greek internet colleague at a university where her home language is the language of instruction. But of course, until we start thinking about them, there can't be something weird about these clashes of perceptions coming from different places, because this is the world over a billion of us live in here and now.

All of us who have access to the web are continually sending or receiving complex messages via words, sound, and pictures across languages, cultures, and geographies. More and more of us billion inhabit internet locales through websites, blogs, Facebook pages, Pinterest boards, etc., that make us public—readable, interpretable. Such is our desire to build these virtual homes—to get our messages out there—that we spend relatively little worry about how we might be misinterpreted. And we think even less about the fine points of our discourses—nuances of parallel construction, commas, "who or whom?"—because if these delicacies of verbal etiquette really bothered us, we'd be driven so crazy by the unpredictability of individual readers' tastes across this busy world that we'd never have the courage to put our messages out there.

Similarly, why do I explore the web world? Frankly, I'm looking for information about myriad subjects, subjects studied by experts in different parts of the world, who speak a wide range of first languages and whose versions of my first language, English, differ greatly from mine through influences of culture and discipline. Am I looking to see if web writers' prose matches my sense of an appropriate English dialect? Hardly. How much does it matter to me if I see that in order for a writer to reach me as an English speaker, he or she has relied on the still clumsy tool of Google Translate? Not much. I'd be much more disconcerted if the writer used his or her first language perfectly—but unintelligibly to me—rather than trying to reach me imperfectly, but so courteously, in my tongue.

This short reflection on multiple communications within simultaneous contexts in our increasingly global consciousness is pertinent, I believe, to understanding the remarkable collection of articles Michelle Cox and Terry Myers Zawacki have brought together in this anthology, which comes on the heels of the outstanding special issue of *Across the Disciplines* (*ATD*) that they edited in 2011: "WAC and Second Language Writing: Cross-field Research, Theory, and Program Development." Theirs is the first book collection devoted to this important focus, first pointed out by scholars such as Leki (1995), Villanueva (2001), and Johns (2001), and perhaps most emphatically stated by Leki in a series of pieces through 2008. As Cox expressed the problem in her article in the *ATD* issue, "WAC has increased emphasis on writing across undergraduate programs without creating mechanisms that help L2 students succeed as writers and without creating faculty development programs that offer training in working with L2 writers" (Cox, 2011). This collection addresses that problem through chapters that present research on multilingual student writers' strengths, coping strategies, and academic writing experiences; on faculty concerns and expectations for their L2 student writers; and on culturally sensitive WAC pedagogies and practices developed in and for US and international writing contexts.

Among the signal contributions of this collection is how it documents through surveys, interviews, and analysis of teacher responses the values and techniques that faculty bring to their reading and assessment of the writing of L2 students. Some of the news is not encouraging, as it corroborates the concerns of the critics of WAC requirements. It's important that these difficulties be documented through these studies. For example, Zawacki and Habib, in "Negotiating 'Errors' in L2 Writing: Faculty Dispositions and Language Differences," emphasize how even those faculty willing to spend a great deal of time with L2 students on their writing often take a rigidly monolingual view toward what they perceive to be error, using phrases such as "zero tolerance for error" or "blast students on errors" to describe their expectations for *all* student writers with no exceptions.

This focus on student error, however that is perceived, is corroborated in Wu Dan's "'Let's see where your Chinese students come from': A Qualitative Descriptive Study of Writing in the Disciplines in China." Wu reports that the faculty in her study, who teach across disciplines at a number of Chinese universities, and all of whom require student writing in Chinese or English, focus most of their attention on perceived errors in language. She attributes this hyperawareness of students' language deficits to the teachers' lack of training in the basics of WAC pedagogy. As she says, "none of the faculty interviewees mentioned 'writing to learn,' a key concept in WAC in the US. They only focus on grading students' writing or the documents their students are to encounter in future."

The documented tendency of teachers in WAC/WID settings to emphasize the ways that non-native speakers of a language of instruction fall short of native-speaker fluency is represented in the collection by the phrase "difference as deficit." Kathryn Nielsen's essay "On Class, Race, and Dynamics of Privilege: Supporting Generation 1.5 Writers Across the Curriculum," calls this emphasis "discrimination" and describes the ways in which this discrimination is enacted by peers and instructors "in relation to peer review and group work, assessment practices, and in the social dynamics of the classroom." To put the effects of this "difference as deficit" approach bluntly, it has turned what should be an opportunity for learners to use the power of writing as a tool of thought into a trap for students who trustingly take us at our word. Where WAC theory and workshop practice have classically encouraged teachers to avoid linguistic nitpicking of student prose, too often, it seems, teachers across disciplines are allowing their discomfort with the surface of L2 student writing to get in the way of their helpfully responding to these students' explorations of ideas.

But the good news in this collection is that several of the chapters present excellent counterexamples of richer and more helpful responses to student writing by teachers across disciplines. Even more important, individual chapters present programmatic and pedagogical recommendations to modify WAC/WID practices to make programs responsive to the strengths and needs of L2 writers. These plans are founded in traditional strengths and values of WAC/WID pedagogy, but they explicitly recognize the multilinguality of students—and the reinforcing responsibilities of both teachers across disciplines and language support professionals.

In contrast to the "difference as deficit" model, the collection presents the alternative models "difference as accommodation" (Cox) and the more emphatic "difference as resource." These alternatives are embodied in chapters of two kinds in the collection, whether focused on US or international contexts: (1) those that make specific recommendations for changes in response to less than ideal situations for L2 writers and (2) those that describe already enacted teaching practices.

"Difference as resource" recommendations include teaching practices such as those described in many of the chapters:

1. Investigate the ethnic, linguistic, and cultural demographics at one's own institution and students' perceptions of diversity and campus climate (see Cox; Neilsen; Zenger, Mullin, & Haviland).
2. Ask students about their linguistic and educational backgrounds and literacy histories (see Cox; Craig; DePalma & Ringer; Lavelle & Shima; Nielsen; Zenger, Mullin, & Haviland).
3. Develop course curricula, instructional approaches, and teaching-with-writing practices that take these backgrounds and histories into account (see Center & Neistepski; Craig; Dan; Du; Fernandes; Fredericksen & Mangelsdorf; Mallet & Zgheib; Neilsen; Phillips; Siczek & Shapiro; Zenger, Mullin, & Haviland).
4. Acknowledge and find ways to value cultural and linguistic diversity in responses to and assessments of student writers/writing (see Cox; Ives et al.; Lavelle & Shima; Zawacki & Habib).
5. Recognize that differences in L2 students' texts might be purposeful adaptations on the part of the writer to attain his/her rhetorical objectives (see DePalma and Ringer).
6. Allow class time for discussions of global Englishes, valuing "accented" writing, and being inclusive of these in peer review and collaborative projects (see Cox; Fredericksen & Mangelsdorf; Lavelle & Shima; Neilsen; Phillips; Siczek & Shapiro; Zenger, Mullin, & Haviland).

In their chapter "Reconstructing Teacher Roles through a Transnational Lens: Learning with/in the American University of Beirut," Zenger, Mullin, and Haviland delineate "difference as resource" as both a theoretical and pedagogical practice, recognizing that English is just one of many languages by which students in an increasingly multilingual environment negotiate meaning and communication across different languages—*trans*lingually. In that context, they argue, there is a "mismatch" between a pedagogy that focuses on students' language deficiencies and their own observations of how much the students they were teaching "could actually do with language." In redesigning required graduate academic writing and general education writing courses, they began by finding out what students already knew about the languages they speak and write, about the conventions they've been taught, and about disciplinary rhetorics. Their aim, as they write, was to foster "instruction that views English as an additional rather than replacement language, instruction that positions multilingual students as informants rather than as problems, instruction that changes faculty's gatekeeping function to that of collaborative literacy brokers."

Revising curricula and courses to value "difference as resource" requires faculty to invest time and attention, generally in short supply at most institutions. Considering "difference as resource" from the perspective of university financial investment, Zawacki and Habib recommend that attention to student writing across disciplines be funded as part of an institution's overall international mission. Faculty can be "rewarded for engaging in inclusive pedagogies that successfully retain and teach the international populations being targeted" and workloads can be reduced "to accommodate particular curricular and pedagogical work." Moreover, "the affordances such changes also bring to L1 students negotiating an international future" should be recognized.

A chapter that demonstrates the actual embodiment of "difference as resource" pedagogy in the practices of disciplinary faculty is Lavelle and Shima's "Writing Histories: Lingua Franca English in a Swedish Graduate Program." The researchers studied 32 students from more than 20 countries on four continents, all writing history theses at Uppsala University in Sweden—as well as their teachers' responses to their writing. What distinguishes these instructors from most WAC/WID practitioners was their having taken a workshop series specifically devoted to working with multilingual writers working in English. What distinguishes the students from most enrolled in such graduate programs was their taking required coursework on thesis writing in the lingua franca of English as part of a longitudinal emphasis on their thesis-writing abilities. Lavelle and Shima attribute at least part of the students' success in completing their theses to the "difference as resource" approach used by faculty. Rather than focus on the students' still considerable lack of native-speaker fluency in the lingua franca, history instructors emphasized the content of the theses—research methods, evidence, development of ideas—in their comments on and assessment of student drafts. Students were given credit for what they knew and how their backgrounds had contributed to their knowledge. The researchers conclude that the students' success could be attributed to some "refreshingly new" factors: "assessment practices aligned with both learning goals and lingua franca communication; a research culture that values individual differences and multilingualism; and an institutional acknowledgement that enrolling international graduate students requires institutional change."

Similar to the conclusions reached by Lavelle and Shima in Sweden are those by Linda Hirsch in a US multilingual context, Hostos Community College in New York City. In "Writing Intensively: An Examination of the Performance of L2 Writers Across the Curriculum at an Urban Community College," she reports the performance of multilingual writers in writing-intensive (WI) courses across disciplines. Noting that L2 writers earned higher grades in the specially-designed WI sections than in non-WI sections, she attributes this performance contrast both to WAC/WID pedagogies practiced in WI sections and to students "accepting the challenge" that writing-intensive classes pose. When WI classes provide opportunities for students to write to learn and make connections between writing and reading, when assignments are designed to build on one another, when students are given models, instructor feedback, and time to revise, and when faculty address students' language needs, L2 student writers can succeed, as she shows. "The fact that ESL students are choosing to stay in WI classes with their greater demands on writing proficiencies and are passing these classes at a higher rate than their non-WI counterparts," she argues, "indicates that participating in well-designed WI classes ... may be in and of itself an academic benefit."

Yet another overriding message of this collection is that effective WAC/WID programs in our increasingly translingual world require the collaborative efforts of disciplinary teachers and language professionals and research to inform these efforts. Both the Lavelle & Shima and Hirsch examples show the vital role played by WAC/WID leaders in training disciplinary faculty in the "difference as resource" model and the ways in which they used their research findings to support the need for such training. Other chapters in the collection show diverse types of collaboration. For example, Jennifer Craig's chapter analyzing student data from her Globally Networked Learning Environment (GNLE), a collaboration between MIT and engineering master's students in Singapore, emphasizes the multiple roles of the L2 specialist in co-designing the successful program and conducting research to improve its outcomes. In her chapter, language professional Qian Du of Ohio University conducts a comparative study of how a specific genre, the summary, is (1) used and responded to by teachers across disciplines and (2) assigned and responded to by L2 writing teachers. Du's essay recommends ways that the L2 teachers can collaborate with disciplinary faculty to help students understand that the summary is not so much a separate genre to be learned but "an essential literacy skill." In his chapter, Zak Lancaster demonstrates how his findings on stance-taking in texts written by students from two different disciplines, along with interviews with instructors about their responses to the students' authorial stances, can be used by WAC professionals in their faculty development work. In their chapter, DePalma and Ringer suggest that an awareness of "adaptive transfer," that is the choices student writers might be consciously making to achieve their own rhetorical objectives, can be useful to faculty when they question what knowledge and skills these writers may be transferring, or not, from other writing contexts.

ALL ENVIRONMENTS MULTI- AND TRANSLINGUAL

Some teachers may read these examples of "adaptive transfer" and "difference as resource" and wonder, "But aren't I doing my students a disservice if I neglect their syntax errors?" To these teachers, the collection answers with examples of ways that language professionals and subject teachers across fields can include helpful commentary on syntax and other language conventions *without ignoring* larger issues of content and idea development and *without subverting* the power of the "writing to learn" approach. The Craig chapter on the US/Singapore GNLE and the chapter "Campus Internationalization: A Center-based Model for ESL-ready Programs" by Mallett and Zgheib offer successful collaborative examples between disciplinary faculty and language teachers that do just that.

But I would also ask these wondering teachers a question: can we say with utter confidence that we know the syntax that each of our students is and should be striving to achieve? Even in one small section of my course in Writing in Science, for example, I have students from many national and linguistic backgrounds, as well as from a wide array of STEM majors—biochemistry, chemical engineering, psychology, genetic counseling, biotechnology, high energy physics, plant sciences, animal sciences, geology, statistics, to name just a few. All are juniors or seniors; each is preparing for a hoped-for future in research, medicine, veterinary medicine, another type of clinical practice, a career in industry or government. Where? Mostly in the US, but not only there. And even to say "in the US" says little about the transnational and translinguistic mix of scholars and professional colleagues with whom they hope to work, even less about the patients, clients, customers, and communities among whom and for whom they might find their life's work. Even in their relatively short lives thus far, they have encountered a remarkable range of language variations, and they will negotiate many more. If anything, we should be respecting their ability to switch codes; we should teach through our example how they might not only tolerate difference, but in fact develop their ability to read and write bravely amid a sea of different languages, accents, syntaxes, and lexicons. We would not want them to be stopped by unfamiliar sentence structures or vocabulary; so, then, why are we?

Such cross-cultures-and-languages environments that these multilingual students inhabit are the very ones that we all more and more inhabit—even in cultures where the language of instruction matches the dominant language of the people. There are at least three main reasons for this almost ubiquitous translinguality.

First, digital technology has made the diversity of peoples and cultures more familiar and reachable, as I reflected in my opening. This smaller world has facilitated migration of students to universities in other countries. The most dramatic example of this is the Bologna Process in Europe,[1] illustrated in this volume by the Lavelle and Shima chapter. In the US, most colleges and universities are becoming more and more diverse in the cultural and language backgrounds of students and teachers.

Furthermore, even in academic communities that appear comparatively "monolingual," the "language" of "writing" has been redefined by technological affordances to be multi-modal. Writers' choices now include visuals and audio of many kinds, besides words in an amazing array of fonts, effects, and layouts—all of which can affect meaning. Social networks such as Facebook are just the most obvious exemplars of a multi-modal writing that has affected all forms of electronic communication. The "syntax" of contemporary writing involves relationships in the graphical space unknown in previous decades. (For example, what constitutes a "sentence" in a PowerPoint slide with photos or a YouTube link?)

Second, while the lingua franca of most published academic research is English, that "English" has been variegated by its exponentially increasing encounters with the grammars and lexicons of other languages. Yet this form of "code meshing" (Canagarajah's term) is only one type; equally dramatic is the mash-up and remix that has occurred as academic research fields have multiplied and become interwoven through interdisciplinary contacts. So-called "correct English" has been redefined within increasingly esoteric communities. In a single class in "Writing in Science," the students and I attempt to give feedback to drafts written in the distinctive, evolving, and highly challenging languages of high energy physics, genetics, medical diagnoses and treatments, seismology, environmental degradation, bacteriology, statistics science, etc.—all of these fields having emerged from the interactions (collaborations, conflicts, negotiations!) of researchers from different disciplinary backgrounds. We practice the reading of sciences in new forms of publication, such as blogs in a wide array of styles. (One of my Chinese students, a microbiologist, told me that Twitter has become an important tool for her to keep current with colleagues.) Therefore, when an academic specialist in any field judges "error" in student writing, the specialist should recognize how the disciplinary or subdisciplinary context constrains the perception of error. The specialist should not assume that marking an error will be meaningful communication to the student, because the specialist cannot assume that this error will be an error in other contexts in which the writer successfully works.

Third, the digisphere has dramatically increased the variety of readers that any connected writer can reach. This means that what constitutes "correct writing" is being constantly redefined even in a single series of responses to email messages in a given session. The digisphere forces any writer to develop a remarkably versatile "verbal eye" in reading messages, weighing the desires and expectations of readers, and crafting appropriate responses. When a writer is fluent in multiple grammars and lexicons, and communicating with correspondents from these diverse realms, the number of reading and writing decisions made by that writer in, say, an hour on the internet, is truly staggering. Surely such writers—who include the English L2 writers in our universities—deserve respect from other writers, not a label of deficiency in language. Academic specialists across disciplines who judge the work of these students need to learn to respect their versatility as readers and writers, and give them the benefit of the doubt in weighing their linguistic decisions, as DePalma and Ringer argue in the chapter on adaptive transfer. To help faculty shift from seeing linguistic differences as deficits to a "difference-accommodated stance" and "ultimately [to] a difference-as-resource stance," Michelle Cox's chapter provides extensive and detailed information, materials, and suggested activities that can be used in working with faculty on approaches to L2 writers and writing.

MAKING WAC/WID WORK FOR MULTILINGUAL STUDENTS (IN A TRANSLINGUAL WORLD)

Several of the chapters in their critique of US (or Chinese, as in the Wu essay) teachers' approaches to linguistic differences call for more emphasis on writing-to-learn techniques and on larger structural (higher order) criteria in training of teachers to read and respond to student work. The Lancaster chapter for example gives a program based on systemic functional linguistics (SFL) for faculty training in genre. What's remarkable in this call is that these training ideas have been around for many years and have been a staple of WAC workshops, but this volume especially emphasizes the need for such strategies with L2 students in an environment where the L1 of the teachers dominates.

Most basically, as this collection teaches, making WAC/WID work in our translingual world means appreciating the multilinguality of L2 students. Even the most "struggling with English" student in a class taught in English in a US university has achieved technical fluency in the language, even though that person has not reached native-speaker fluency nor a polished academic voice. Since that student is likely to be able to communicate in at least one other spoken language, that student brings to any subject linguistic and cultural depth that a monolingual teacher or student does not possess. Teachers of any subject can ask themselves how that depth can be brought to bear in understanding and illuminating the subject—as well as in communicating its important messages to other linguistic communities. For example, a multilingual (Thai/English) student from a farm background in Thailand, majoring in biochemistry and specializing in plant breeding, brings to my science writing course a cultural/environmental depth that not only enriches her studies and prepares her for varied futures, but that also can illuminate the studies of others in the subject. But she can only be a resource for others if her teachers, including me, provide opportunities for her writing (or talk) to develop connections between environments that she can share with others.

Particularly in a writing class, that depth in multilingual students gives the writer access to audiences, settings, and purposes of writing (the full rhetorical triangle) that can't be accessed by monolingual English speakers, no matter how fluent. That most of our writing classes in US English departments and writing programs have ignored the translingual resources that these students bring to the course shows our fixation on the normative task of "teaching English," rather than encouraging all our students, monolingual and multilingual, to consider how writing, rhetoric, and new communication technologies cross linguo-cultural borders.

In co-editing with an international team the anthology *Writing Programs Worldwide: Profiles of Academic Writing in Many Places* (2012), I've been privileged to meet teachers who exemplify this linguo-cultural border crossing. Essays from 28 countries on six continents present examples of teachers who use multilingual resources in teaching across disciplines. For example, Désirée Motta-Roth of the Federal University of Santa Maria (UFSM) in Brazil, drawing on her research on the writing demands on undergraduate and graduate students in diverse fields, stresses the need for a genre- and rhetorically-based curriculum that can broaden the typically narrow assumption that skilled language use means only perfection of form (Motta-Roth, 2012). Her emphasis on this broader approach is essential, she writes, because students and teachers at UFSM write in both Portuguese and English, with scholarship in Portuguese seen by many as important both toward reaching a Portuguese-speaking readership and as "resistance to [the] 'academic hegemony'" (p. 108) of English publication. Her teaching and research foreground student consciousness of the everyday ways that genre and rhetoric are intrinsic to their working in both languages.

An equally striking but different example comes from Otto Kruse of the Zurich University of Applied Sciences, who profiles the School of Translation at his university (Kruse, 2012). Since Switzerland is a country with four official languages (German, French, Italian, and Romansh) and a fifth, English, as an increasingly important lingua franca, Kruse describes how translation studies have changed from a paradigm of proficiency in separate languages ("'pure' language skills") to "a model of multilingual literacy," where the norm has become the "co-existence" of different languages and practices for individuals (p. 404). As a result, translators can no longer demonstrate proficiency by successfully translating documents from language to language, but must develop "meta-linguistic abilities" that cross languages as well as genres (p. 406).

While these two chapters from my collection as well as exemplar chapters by Zenger, Mullin, and Haviland and Lavelle and Shima in this volume describe programs at institutions outside of the US, they offer model approaches, practices, and perspectives that we in the US can strive to achieve. Which, ultimately, is the goal of this anthology.

THE LAST WORD

WAC/WID has always been about flexibility amid diversity. From its earliest days as a formal "movement" in the 1970s, it has been about respecting the differences among disciplines: appreciating the diverse learning methods of physicists and painters, the distinctive vocabularies and syntaxes of mathematicians and anthropologists, the esoteric genres of chemists and musicologists. More recently, it has been about widening an already wide circle to accept the capabilities of new technologies for learning and communication. The basic motive of "writing across the curriculum" has been to *learn* from all disciplines the most productive ways by which writing can be a tool, a vehicle, a force for increased and more expansive learning and communication, and then to *share* those methods across all fields.

Though WAC/WID has focused on disciplinary differences, its inherent flexibility of approach makes it an ideal construct to appreciate the diversity of language backgrounds of both students and teachers. Because the best-known WAC/WID practices, as espoused in these chapters, give priority to diverse ways and tools of learning, they can be used productively in translinguistic contexts—the new norm in education. What is truly exciting about collections such as this is that by illuminating the confluence of disciplinary diversity and multilingualism, we will never again think of WAC as "only" about the content and methods of academic disciplines. Indeed, we need to reconceive the idea of "the discipline," just as we have reconceived the idea of "writing," as evolving within an ever-richer global mix of languages, technologies, ways of thinking, and desires for expression.

NOTES

1. See the official website of the Bologna Process 2010-2012 (http://www.chea.info/)

REFERENCES

Canagarajah, A. S. (2006). The place of world Englishes in composition: Pluralization continued. *College Composition and Communication, 57*(4), 586-619.

Cox, M. (2011). WAC: Closing doors or opening doors for second language writers? *Across the Disciplines, 8*(4.). Retrieved from http://wac.colostate.edu/atd/ell/cox.cfm

Johns, A. (2001). ESL students and WAC programs: Varied populations and diverse needs." In S. H. McLeod, E. Miraglia, M. Soven, & C. Thaiss (Eds.), *WAC for the new millennium* (pp. 141-164). Urbana, IL: NCTE.

Kruse, O. (2012). The place of writing in translation: From linguistic craftsmanship to multilingual text production. In C. Thaiss, G. Bräuer, P. Carlino, L.Ganobcsik-Williams, & A. Sinha (Eds.), *Writing programs worldwide: Profiles of academic writing in many places* (pp. 401-415). Fort Collins, CO: WAC Clearinghouse and Parlor Press. Retrieved from http://wac.colostate.edu/books/wpww/

Lea, M. (1999). Academic literacies and learning in higher education. In C. Jones, J.Turner, & B. Street (Eds.), *Students writing in the university: Cultural and epistemological issues* (pp. 103-124). (Studies in written language and literacy 8.) Amsterdam/Philadelphia: John Benjamins.

Leki, I. (1995). Coping strategies of ESL students in writing tasks across the curriculum. *TESOL Quarterly 29*(2), 235-260.

Motta-Roth, D. (2012). Academic literacies in the South: Writing practices in a Brazilian university. In C. Thaiss, G. Bräuer, P. Carlino, L. Ganobcsik-Williams& A. Sinha (Eds.), *Writing programs worldwide: Profiles of academic writing in many places* (pp. 105-116). Fort Collins, CO: WAC Clearinghouse and Parlor Press. Retrieved from http://wac.colostate.edu/books/wpww/

Villanueva, V., Jr. (2001). The politics of literacy across the curriculum. In S. H. McLeod, E. Miraglia, M. Soven, & C. Thaiss (Eds.), *WAC for the new millennium* (pp. 165-178) Urbana, IL: NCTE.

NOTES ON EDITORS AND CONTRIBUTORS

EDITORS

Terry Myers Zawacki is associate professor emerita of English and director emerita of George Mason University's nationally ranked Writing Across the Curriculum (WAC) program. Her publications include the co-authored *Engaged Writers and Dynamic Disciplines: Research on the Academic Writing Life,* the co-edited *Writing Across the Curriculum: A Critical Sourcebook,* the co-edited *Across the Disciplines* special issue on "WAC and Second Language Writing," and articles on writing centers and writing fellows, writing in the disciplines, feminism and composition, writing assessment, and WAC and second language writing. The latter was the focus of her keynote addresses at the 2010 International WAC conference and the 2012 Middle East North Africa Writing Center Association conference in Doha, Qatar. She serves on the editorial boards of *Across the Disciplines* and *The WAC Journal,* on the review board for the *Digital Books* series on the WAC Clearinghouse, and is lead editor of the International Perspectives on Writing series, also on the Clearinghouse. She is a member of the Consultants Board of the International WAC Network, the College Composition and Communication Committee on the Globalization of Postsecondary Writing Instruction and Research, and the Scientific Committee of the International Society for the Advancement of Writing Research.

Michelle Cox is Multilingual Specialist in the Institute for Writing and Rhetoric at Dartmouth College, and is the former director of Bridgewater State University's Writing Across the Curriculum (WAC) program, which she launched in 2007. She co-edited *Second Language Writing in the Composition Classroom: A Critical Sourcebook* (Bedford/St. Martin's, 2006), *Reinventing Identities in Second Language Writing* (NCTE, 2010), and a special issue of *Across the Disciplines,* "WAC and Second Language Writing: Cross-Field Research, Theory, and Program Development" (December, 2011), and has published articles on WAC program administration, composition pedagogy, second language writing pedagogy, identity theory, and faculty development. She is a member of the International WAC Network Consultants Board, the WAC Clearinghouse editorial board (where she edits the WAC Clearinghouse pages on WAC and second language writing), the *Across the Disciplines* editorial board, and the College Composition and Communication Committee on Diversity, and is past chair of the Northeast Writing Centers Association (NEWCA) and the Northeast Writing Across the Curriculum Consortium (NEWACC).

CONTRIBUTORS

Carole Center is an associate professor of English and the Writing Program Director at Lasell College. She has published in *Teaching English in the Two-Year College*, *MELUS* (*Multi-Ethnic Literature of the United States*), *Journal of Basic Writing*, *Open Words*, and *Reader*.

Jennifer Lynn Craig is a lecturer in the Program in Writing and Humanistic Studies at the Massachusetts Institute of Technology where she teaches writing, oral presentation and team skills to engineering students. She is the author of *Integrating Writing Strategies in EFL/ESL University Contexts: A Writing-across-the-Curriculum Approach*. She is a co-author of *Learning to Communicate in Science and Engineering: Case Studies from MIT*, the 2012 winner of the CCCC's Advancement of Knowledge award.

Wu Dan received her PhD in Rhetorics, Communication, and Information Design from Clemson University in 2010. She now teaches undergraduate English writing and graduate writing research courses in Xi'an International Studies University (XISU), Xi'an, Shaanxi Province, China. She also works as the Dean of Humboldt College, a joint program by XISU and Humboldt State University, California, US.

Michael-John DePalma is an Assistant Professor of English in the Professional Writing Program at Baylor University. His work has appeared in *College Composition and Communication*, *Rhetoric Society Quarterly*, *Rhetoric Review*, *Reflections: A Journal of Writing, Service Learning, and Community Literacy*, and the *Journal of Second Language Writing*. His co-authored article (with Jeffrey M. Ringer), "Toward a Theory of Adaptive Transfer: Expanding Disciplinary Discussions of 'Transfer' in Second-Language Writing and Composition Studies," received honorable mention for the *Journal of Second Language Writing*'s Best Article of 2011.

Qian Du received her Ph.D. in Foreign, Second and Multilingual Language Education at Ohio State University in 2013. She now works as a Lecturer and Undergraduate Composition Coordinator in the English Language Improvement Program at Ohio University. Her research interests include academic literacy development, reading-writing connections, and intercultural rhetoric.

Marino Fernandes was, at the time of this writing, in the Langauge and Linguistics Master's program at the University of New Hampshire. He is currently a PhD candidate in the UNH Composition Studies program. A version of the essay that appears in this collection was presented at the 2012 Conference on College Composition and Communication in St. Louis Missouri, where he was also named a 2012 Scholar for the Dream.

Elaine Fredericksen has forty years of teaching experience at all levels. She earned a PhD in Rhetoric and Composition from the University of Alabama in 1996 and is Professor Emerita of English at the University of Texas at El Paso. She has authored many scholarly articles and a book, *A New World of Writers: Teaching Writing in a Diverse Society*, published in January 2003 by Peter Lang. She serves on the editorial board for the *Journal of Hispanic Higher Education*. Her 1999 FIPSE grant was instrumental in the establishment of the country's first Bilingual Professional Writing Certificate program.

Anna S. Habib is term assistant professor in the English Department at George Mason University where she teaches the undergraduate and graduate stretched writing courses for Mason's Center for International Student Access. Her collaborative research with Terry Zawacki has been published by NCTE in the edited collection titled *Reinventing Identities in Second Language Writing* and in *Valuing Written Accents*, a George Mason University publication.

Jonathan Hall is an assistant professor of English at York College, City University of New York, where he also serves as Writing Across the Curriculum Coordinator. His work has appeared in *The WAC Journal, Across the Disciplines*, and elsewhere. He's currently working on an investigation of translingual reading and faculty language identity.

Carol Peterson Haviland, emerita professor of English at California State University, San Bernardino, directed CSUSB's writing center and WAC programs for twenty years. She presently teaches in CSUSB's rhetoric and composition program and spent the spring terms of 2010 and 2011 teaching and consulting with the writing faculty at the American University of Beirut. Her co-authored book, *Who Owns This Text? Plagiarism, Authorship and Disciplinary Cultures*, her work at the American University of Beirut, and her current study with first-year-writers challenging the language of remediation represent her interests in the ways writing collaborations within and across borders can challenge often-unexamined "norms."

Linda Hirsch is a professor at Hostos Community College/CUNY where she implemented and co-coordinates the WAC program. Her essays have appeared in journals including *Language and Learning across the Disciplines*, and the *Journal of Basic Writing*, and books including *Making Teaching and Learning Matter: Transformative Spaces in Higher Education*.

Lindsey Ives is a PhD candidate in Rhetoric and Writing at the University of New Mexico, where she serves as assistant director of Core Writing. She is currently completing her dissertation, "Case not Closed: Whiteness and the Rhetorical Genres of Freedom Summer." Her research interests include whiteness studies, L2 writing, WAC, writing program administration, and the intersections between them.

Zak Lancaster is an assistant professor of English at Wake Forest University, where he is working to build a Writing Across the Curriculum program. He is a recent PhD in English and Education from the University of Michigan; to date, his publications and conference presentations have focused on the language of stance and evaluation in academic discourses, for the benefit of informing university-level writing instruction.

Thomas Lavelle directs the Center for Modern Languages at the Stockholm School of Economics, where he also teaches ESP courses and serves as a senior lecturer. He consults widely with Swedish universities on the functions of lingua franca English in higher education. His published articles address such topics as teaching methods for L2 disciplinary writing, communication training in international legal education, Anglophone teaching in international business schools and, in an American context, the 1996-97 Ebonics controversy.

Elizabeth Leahy is currently pursuing a PhD in Rhetoric, Composition, and the Teaching of English at the University of Arizona, where she is co-PI on a study examining an outdated curricular WID requirement. Her research interests include sustainable WAC programs and border rhetorics.

Anni Leming is a reading instructor at Central New Mexico Community College and is pursuing a PhD in Educational Linguistics at the University of New Mexico. She presented at the Conference on College Composition and Communication in 2012. Her current research interests focus on issues in multilingualism, globalisation and e-learning, discourse analysis, and adult education.

Karyn E. Mallet is assistant director of the English Language Institute and assistant director of Language Development for the Center for International Student Access (CISA) at George Mason University, where she constructs, implements, and assesses language-supported programs for undergraduate and graduate international students. Recent publications include a chapter in TESOL's *Effective Second Language Writing* with Jennifer Haan and *Diversity at Mason: The Pursuit of Transformative Education*, a George Mason publication co-edited with Anna Habib.

Kate Mangelsdorf is Professor of Rhetoric and Writing Studies at the University of Texas at El Paso, where she has served as Director of University Writing Programs. She has published a number of articles and book chapters on second-language writing and has co-authored several textbooks for developmental and first-year composition that focus on students with a range of language backgrounds.

Joan Mullin, professor at Illinois State University, has published on, initiated and directed WAC programs/writing centers at the universities of Toledo and Texas at Austin. Her recent co-authored book, *Who Owns This Text? Plagiarism, Authorship and Disciplinary Cultures*, complements her collaborative examinations of international approaches to the teaching of writing. Her current project is *The Research Exchange* with Fishman and Palmquist, a database for the collection, aggregation, and sharing of models of writing research at all levels across borders. She is one of four editors of International Studies of Writing series on the WAC Clearinghouse.

Kathryn Nielsen is an associate director in the Communication Arts and Sciences Department at Merrimack College where she works as the second language writing specialist in the Writing Center and Writing Intensive (WI) program. Her essays have appeared in the *Journal of the Academy of Business Education, Writing in the Center, Teaching in a Writing Center Setting*, and *Adult Education Research Conference Proceedings*. Her research interests include second language writing, transformative learning theory, and critical and liberatory education.

Michelle Niestepski is an assistant professor of English at Lasell College. She has co-directed workshops on archival research at the Conference on College Composition and Communication and has presented at CCCCs and the National Council of Teachers of English conference.

Tom Pierce is Director of Adult Education at Central New Mexico Community College and a PhD candidate at the University of New Mexico. His dissertation focuses on standards of correctness for L2 writers and basic writers in college composition. He has been a frequent presenter at the National Association of Developmental Education, and more recently at the Conference on College Composition and Communication.

Talinn Phillips is an Assistant Professor of English at Ohio University in Athens, Ohio. She co-directs the Ohio University Appalachian Writing Project site and is helping to develop a new Graduate Writing and Research Center.

Jeffrey M. Ringer is an assistant professor of English at the University of Tennessee, Knoxville, where he teaches in the division of Rhetoric, Writing, and Linguistics. His work has appeared in journals such as *College English, Rhetoric Review, JAC*, and the *Journal of Second Language Writing*, among others. He's currently working on a book project that examines how student religious identity shapes and is shaped by academic writing.

Michael Schwartz is an assistant professor at St. Cloud State University, where he is the director of the Intensive English Center and teaches in the MA-TESL program. He has published in *Arizona Working Papers in SLA and Teaching* and has presented at the Conference on College Composition and Communication 2011 and 2012, the High Desert Linguistics Society Conference, and the Ethnography in Education Forum. He is interested in SLA and identity, L2 writing, discourse analysis, and issues in world Englishes.

Shawna Shapiro is a Visiting Assistant Professor at Middlebury College, where she teaches courses in writing and linguistics. Her work has appeared in several volumes of TESOL's Classroom Practice Series, as well as in *TESL Canada Journal, Teaching and Teacher Education,* and the *Journal of English for Academic Purposes.*

Alan Shima is an associate professor at the Stockholm School of Economics where he teaches Business English courses. He also taught academic writing in a master's program at Uppsala University. He has written a book length study on contemporary feminist poetics and published articles on postcolonial fiction. His current research explores the narrative strategies of memoir and the pedagogy of academic writing.

Megan Siczek has been an instructor in English for Academic Purposes (EAP) at the George Washington University since 2004. In addition to teaching academic writing courses to international undergraduates, she works with the writing center and university writing program to meet the needs of second language writers at the university. She is currently pursuing a doctoral degree in Educational Policy Studies, with research interests in transnational migration and internationalization.

Chris Thaiss is Clark Kerr Presidential Chair and Professor in the University Writing Program at UC Davis. Author, co-author, or editor of twelve books and numerous articles and chapters, he coordinates the International Network of Writing-across-the-Curriculum Programs. His most recent book, co-edited with an international team, is *Writing Programs Worldwide: Profiles of Academic Writing in Many Places* (WAC Clearinghouse and Parlor Press, 2012). He teaches undergraduate courses in science writing and graduate courses in writing theory, pedagogy, research, and program administration.

Amy Zenger is an associate professor of English at the American University of Beirut, where she directs the Writing Center and guides a Writing in the Disciplines initiative. With Bronwyn Williams, she has co-authored *Popular Culture and Representations of Literacy* and co-edited *New Media Literacies and Participatory Popular Culture Across Borders.*

Ghania Zgheib is a doctoral student and an instructor at the English Language Institute at George Mason University as well as the language support course coordinator in the ACCESS program. Recent publications include a chapter in *Diversity at Mason: The Pursuit of Transformative Education*, a George Mason publication, co-authored with Karyn E. Mallett.

www.ingramcontent.com/pod-product-compliance
Lightning Source LLC
Chambersburg PA
CBHW051843300426
44117CB00006B/248